A simple guide to Using Your Computer

A simple guide to

Using Your Computer

Manon Cassade, Michel Dreyfus, Gilles Fouchard, Linda Steven and Rob Young

An imprint of PEARSON EDUCATION

Pearson Education Limited

Head Office:
Edinburgh Gate
Harlow
Essex CM20 2JE
Tel: +44 (0)1279 623623
Fax: +44 (0)1279 431059

London Office:
128 Long Acre
London WC2E 9AN
Tel: +44 (0)20 7447 2000
Fax: +44 (0)20 7240 5771
Website: www.it-minds.com

First published in Great Britain 2002

ISBN 0-130-98364-0

British Library Cataloguing in Publication Data
A CIP catalogue record for this book can be obtained from the British Library.

10 9 8 7 6 5 4 3 2 1

Typeset by Pantek Arts Ltd, Maidstone, Kent.
Printed and bound in Great Britain by Ashford Colour Press, Gosport, Hampshire.

The publishers' policy is to use paper manufactured from sustainable forests.

Contents

3 Mice and keyboards .29

4 Printers .39

5 The memory .47

Windows Me

Office 2000

2 Shared commands .277

3 Basic Word functions .289

The Internet

4 Browsing the World Wide Web 441

5 E-mail and mailing lists 457

Building a website

A simple guide to

the PC

Linda Steven

Introduction

A PC that puts you at ease

The aim of this little book is essentially to make you familiar with the hardware environment of the computer. Most people have heard of software programs, whether they are involved directly with computers or not. Many people know roughly how they work and what they are used for. The hardware of the PC, however, is less well understood.

Designed clearly and simply, this book will help you to teach yourself in a day the ABC of the PC. There's no need to follow the lessons in order as each new chapter forms a unit in itself. After reading this book, you will have mastered the common technical terms and will be able to get the most out of your computer, whether at home or at work.

A PC that produces results

Once the technical aspects have been demystified, you are in a position to move on to achievements that are a little more professional. If you equip yourself with peripherals, you can transform your computer into a photographic laboratory and enhance your pictures on-screen. You can transform your computer into a video games base. You can install the latest CD-ROMs or maybe even design one yourself.

A PC that breaks new ground

If you are not already connected to the Internet, after reading this book, you probably will be, because you will have understood its advantages: exchanges with a correspondent from the other side of the world for the price of a local telephone call, and access to instantaneous and exhaustive information. The Internet can also act as a dictionary, an encyclopedia, a records office, a video creation laboratory, a newsroom, and a weather forecasting station.

Icons

This icon introduces handy shortcuts and tips such as keyboard hotkeys, expert options, and quicker ways of getting to the same place.

This icon warns you of any risks associated with a particular action, or any problems you might encounter along the way, and (where possible) shows you how to avoid them.

This icon is used to provide additional information about the topic being covered.

The central unit

1

A better life with your PC

Some history

What is a PC?

Which PC should you choose?

The central unit

A better life with your PC

You will be pleased to know that your PC is going to increase your potential. It will allow you to increase your productivity, reduce the amount of drudgery, and inprove quality in many areas.

If you are artistically-minded, your PC will allow you to create original work very easily. If you write well but make the odd spelling mistake, the spellchecker incorporated in your word processor will correct the faults for you. Finally, if you write illegibly, the handwritten character fonts will allow you to pass as an expert calligrapher.

Your PC is the ideal tool for managing your work more effectively.

Resistance
The hardest part is getting started. It is often non-technical people who need the most persuading. They worry that computers will turn them into cold technicians, unable to think for themselves.

Figure 1.1 Switched-on generation: don't hesitate any longer!

To put your minds at rest, it will be nothing of the kind. Data processing, the Internet and multimedia are in no way incompatible with poetry, drawing, even meditation. Any form of art may find an unsuspected medium in the PC.

Go on, then, switch it on, don't be frightened!

Some history

- **1900:** Samuel Morse's telegraph, Graham Bell's telephone, and Thomas Edison's dictation machine make their appearances.
- **1917:** the company CTR becomes IBM (International Business Machines). IBM produces punched cards and typewriters.
- **1930:** calculating machines are used in offices. A new professional breed makes its appearance: the programmer.
- **1936:** Alan Turing's article on artificial intelligence, *Computing Machinery and Intelligence*, is published.
- **1941:** the Nazi period, alas, contributes towards the development of the computer. The engineer Konrad Zuse creates the Z3.

- **1946:** the ENIAC program, ancestor of the computer, appears. With its 20 000 valves, it performs the calculations necessary for producing the hydrogen bomb.
- **1950–1970:** Robert Noyce creates the company Intel (Integrated Electronics), still number one in the processor market.
- **1975:** the Altair computer is produced by the firm MITS.
- **1976:** Steve Wozniak and Steve Jacobs create Apple I in Silicon Valley.
- **1981:** IBM's personal computer is born.
- **1986:** Bill Gates launches Microsoft Windows™.
- **1989:** Intel presents its new processor, the 80486.
- **1990:** Windows 3.1 is created by Microsoft.
- **1991:** IBM introduces its Multimedia PC.
- **1993:** Microsoft launches Windows NT. Linda Steven is initiated into computing by her professor Jacques de Schryver, whom she thanks.
- **1994–1999:** the Internet and multimedia make their way into our homes.

What is a PC?

Your PC, or *personal computer*, is a friendly assembly of plastic, metal and programs. The plastic and metal is the *hardware* (Figure 1.2). The programs are the *software*. Software includes:

- The operating software: this organises the running of the various hardware aspects of the PC.
- The applications software: word processors, spreadsheets, graphics packages, etc.
- The utilities: software for standard operations such as copying, compression, recovery of lost data, reorganisation of the hard disk, formatting, etc.

Which PC should you choose?

In order to choose a PC wisely, it is necessary to consider all the items that will make up your future installation and what you wish to use them for: case, central unit, screen, CD-ROM drive, keyboard, hard disk, speakers, graphics card, audio card, modem, etc. For more information, see Chapter 11.

Figure 1.2 The hardware.

The central unit

The central unit is the heart of the PC (Figure 1.3). It is composed of the following items:

- case
- power supply
- ports
- floppy disk drive
- motherboard
- microprocessor
- hard disk (see Chapter 6)
- slots
- RAM memory
- cache memory
- bus
- fan.

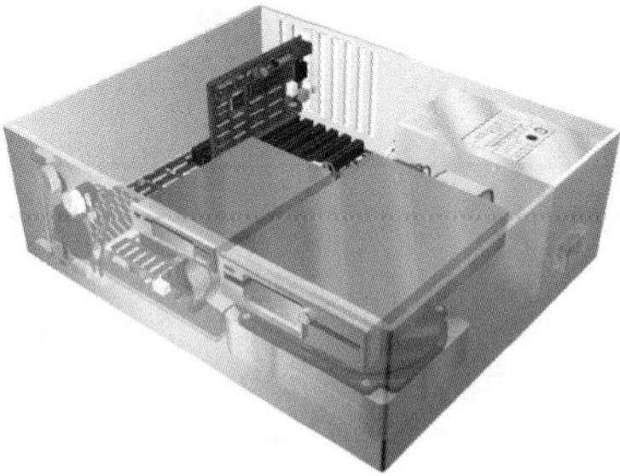

Figure 1.3 The central unit.

The case

Like the screen, keyboard or mouse, the case forms part of what is called the hardware.

The case, which is generally made from metal, protects the components of the computer from interference and shocks. The large format case or tower allows easy access to the expansion cards.

The most practical cases are so-called 'flip-flop' cases, which open under simple pressure, like a car bonnet.

There are vertical or horizontal cases. The choice depends simply on the way in which you intend to organise your desktop.

Desktop or tower?

If you want to share the computer with your family, it is better to choose a case in the form of a desktop. One of its advantages is to support and raise the screen slightly, so it can be viewed more comfortably. However, desktop-style cases have far less capacity than other models and are not, for example, suited to holding large disks (5").

For professional use, you are better to choose a tower. Towers are arranged vertically; this saves space, because they can stand on the floor. There are three categories: miniature, medium and large. A large tower has room for a 3½" drive plus several high-capacity 5¼" disks. Cards can be added or components changed to make it even more accessible.

Power supply

The On/Off switch is situated on the power supply unit.

Wires run from the power supply unit to a socket and to the motherboard (Figure 1.4).

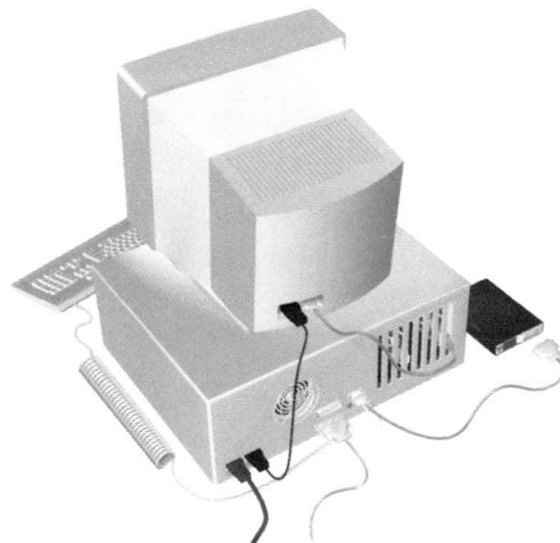

Figure 1.4 The central unit's power supply leads.

The power supply unit (Figure 1.5) converts the power from the 240-volt mains supply to the voltage necessary for the computer, which is between 8 and 12 volts. It must have a power of no less than 200 watts and no more than 230 watts.

Figure 1.5 The central unit's power supply unit.

The PC is sensitive to voltage surges. Power failures can cause you to lose some of your work. You are therefore recommended to protect your PC by using a surge protector or some other form of uninterruptible power supply.

The power supply unit may be multi- or single-socket. The multi-socket unit is more functional.

Advice:

1. Unplug the computer in the event of a thunderstorm.
2. Do not plug your computer directly into an unearthed socket; instead, use an inverter with short-circuit protection.

The ports

The central unit communicates with the outside world using ports: one parallel port (Figure 1.6) and two serial ports (Figure 1.7). Others can be added.

Figure 1.6 Parallel port.

Figure 1.7 Serial port.

For example, the speaker peripheral has ports suited to its use.

- Parallel or LPT (*line printer*) ports: these send the data over eight separate cables (eight channels). They are fragile. The signal is lost after two or three metres. The parallel ports are mainly used to connect printers: the first printer is connected to LPT1, the second to LPT2, and so on.
- Serial ports: these send the data over one cable (one channel). They are slower than parallel ports but more efficient over length.
- SCSI port (pronounced 'scuzzy') (Figure 1.8): this is designed to install several peripherals one behind the other. The SCSI port transmits data at high speed. It becomes useful if you run out of slots.
- Other ports: these are found, among other places, on the expansion cards, which are themselves plugged into the slots. They are destined to be replaced by USB connectors linked to the USB bus (see later).

Figure 1.8 SCSI port.

A port can be 'male' or 'female' (Figure 1.9), and is connected to a cable of the opposite polarity.

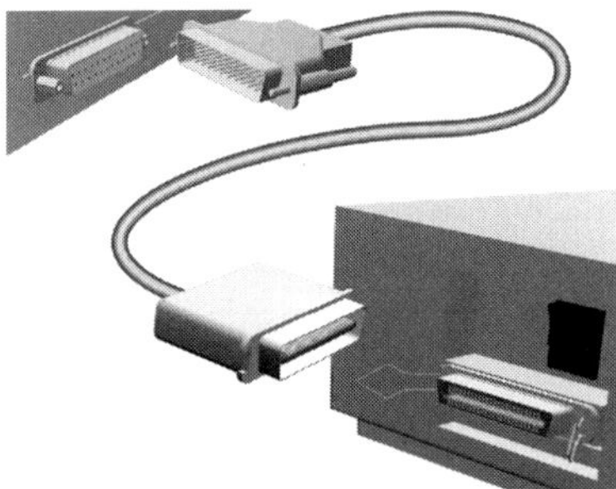

Figure 1.9 Impossible to confuse: male and female connectors.

The floppy disk drive

The floppy disk drive (Figure 1.10) allows information to be read from, written to, or stored on diskettes, or floppy disks. A standard diskette can hold data equivalent to the size of a 700-page book. They cost about 30 pence each.

Figure 1.10 Floppy disk drives.

There are two kinds of diskette: 3½-inch and 5¼-inch (Figures 1.11 and 1.12).

If you want to use the rather outdated 5¼" diskettes, you can add a 5¼" floppy disk drive to your computer (Figure 1.14).

Figure 1.11 5¼" diskette.

Figure 1.12 5¼" and 3½" diskettes.

Most computers sold nowadays are equipped only with 3½" floppy disk drives (Figure 1.13).

The characteristics of the 3½" diskette are as follows:

- The 3½" double density (DD); 135 tpi; capacity: 720 kbyte.
- The 3½" high density (HD); 135 tpi; capacity: 1.44 Mbyte.

tpi = tracks per inch
Mbyte = megabytes = 1024 kilobytes

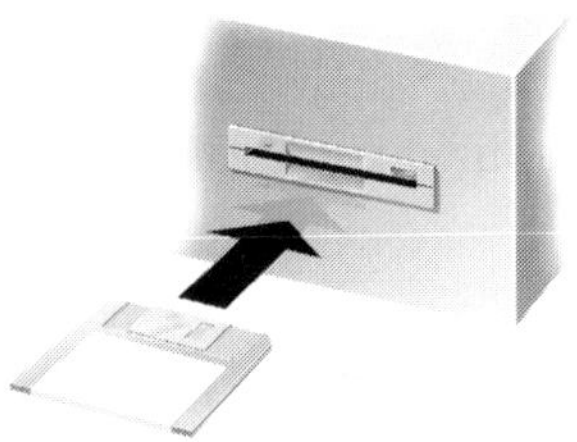

Figure 1.13 3½" floppy disk drive.

Figure 1.14 5¼" floppy disk drive.

A 3½" diskette has the following elements:

- a retractable flap
- a write window
- a write-protect tab (Figure 1.15)
- a filing label.

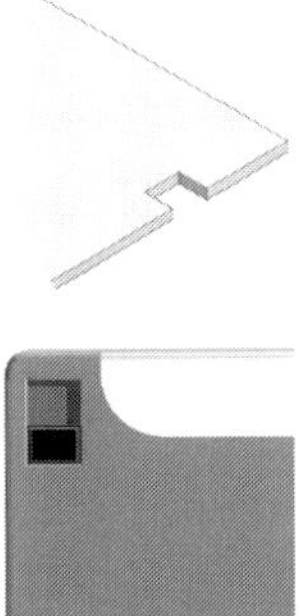

Figure 1.15 Write-protected diskettes.

You must take certain precautions to protect your diskettes:

- Avoid touching the exposed areas of the magnetic disk.
- Store the diskette in a protective case.
- Avoid placing the diskettes close to magnetic fields, such as a television, motor or radio, or near magnetised metal objects.

- File your diskettes vertically, and do not put anything on top of them.
- Fill in the label before sticking it on the diskette. Pressing on the diskette could damage it.

Formatting a diskette

Formatting a diskette means making it capable of being read and of receiving written information. Formatting is the equivalent of drawing horizontal lines on a blank page so you write in a straight line. Formatting divides the diskette into concentric tracks. The tracks are separated from each other, and are sub-divided into small sectors. In this way the information is fragmented into small blocks, each having a precise address. The system has a complete outline of the disk, known as the file allocation table (FAT), so it can find its way around.

To format a diskette:

1. Insert your diskette into the floppy disk drive.
2. Click on **A:** in the Windows File Manager.
3. Press the right button on the mouse.
4. Select the **Format** option from the drop-down menu.

The motherboard

The motherboard (Figure 1.16) is situated at the heart of the central unit. It is the main electronic system. It is composed of the following items:

- The central microprocessor, or CPU. This is the brain of the computer. It manages the information. Since 1998, this has been a Pentium 2 or equivalent, i.e. a very powerful processor capable of multimedia applications.
- The RAM (random access memory). This is arranged on DIMM or SIMM (dual/single in-line memory module) linear arrays, which are plugged into the motherboard (see Chapter 5).
- The expansion slots, or connectors. You can plug additional electronic cards into these. The number of expansion slots depends on the size of your central unit.
- The various preinstalled cards. These include the controller card and the screen card.
- The keyboard connectors.
- The disk connectors.
- The chips. These are integrated circuits that control the computer functions.
- The linear arrays. The RAM comes in the form of components soldered on to linear arrays.

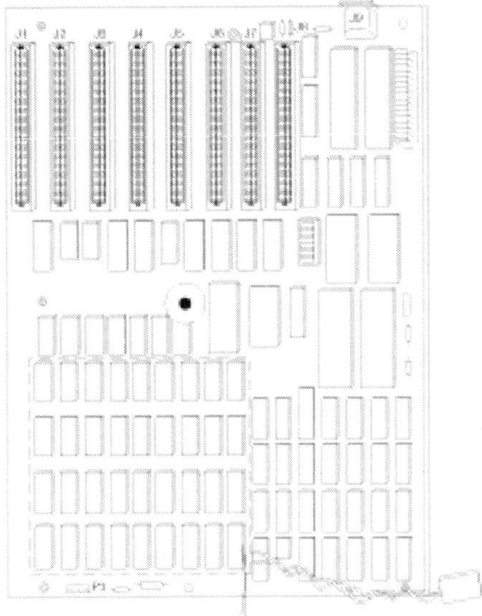

Figure 1.16 The motherboard.

The microprocessor

The Intel 4004 was the very first microprocessor (Figure 1.17), invented by Ted Hoff in 1969–71 for Busicom, a Japanese client of Intel. Since Busicom had financial problems, the order was rejected. The 4004 was then put on sale on 15 November 1971, in the classified advertisements of the magazine *Electronic News*. Its success was immediate. Computing had just entered a new era.

Figure 1.17 A microprocessor.

The microprocessor is the brain of the computer. It is an integrated circuit, a chip specialising in the management of information. It controls the flow of information and performs arithmetic operations, such as additions, or logical operations, such as comparisons. The microprocessor is so much the centre of the computer that the latter is often defined by the former. For example, a 386/33, a 486, a Pentium, Cyrix, AMD and Pentium III are all types of microprecessor.

The standard currently sold in the shops is a 64-bit Pentium III microprocessor. The bits in this case describe the simultaneous inputs of the microprocessor data bus.

A group of 8 bits constitutes a byte, an octet or a character.

The computer uses a binary notation system. Each character, number and symbol is coded into a group of 0s and 1s. Each 0 (off) or 1 (on) is equivalent to a *binary digit*, also called a *bit*.

To summarise:

1 bit = 1 binary position

1 byte = 1 character = 8 bits

1 kilobyte (kbyte) = 1024 bytes

1 megabyte (Mbyte) = 1024 × 1024 bytes

1 gigabyte (Gbyte) = 1024 × 1024 × 1024 bytes

Different kinds of microprocessor

- **Intel 4004:** The first and least powerful microprocessor.
- **86:** an abbreviation of the Intel 8086 chip number. This 16-bit processor can work (like the 8088) only in 64-kbyte sections, and with a total of 640 kbytes.
- **88:** an abbreviation of the Intel 8088 chip number. This microprocessor allowed the use of all the software and peripherals designed for the Intel 8080 and the Zilog Z-80. IBM had chosen it for their first PC but, being able to work only in 64-kbyte sections and with a total of 640 kbytes, it quickly imposed its limits on MS-DOS.
- **286:** an abbreviation of the Intel 80286 chip number. The 286 is the 16-bit successor of the 8088 and 8086. This processor offered new performance for PCs.
- **386/33:** an abbreviation of the Intel 80386 chip number. This microprocessor allows most of the software to be executed but has difficulty restoring the Windows 95 operating system correctly. The programs run slowly.
- **486:** an abbreviation of the Intel 80486 chip number. The PCs manufactured nowadays are almost all Pentiums, but there are still, and always will be, valiant 486s.
- **Pentium 100 to 200:** Pentiums are much more powerful than the old 486s. The MMX versions specialise in the processing of 3D multimedia applications and are ideal for running games.
- **Pentium II (233 to 400 Mhz):** Pentium IIs have been around since the first half of 1998. However, even then it was possible to find versions that ran efficiently at 700 Mhz.

- **Celeron (500 to 766 MHz)**: Intel's budget processor packs a lot of punch and has found its way into many home and small-office PCs.
- **Pentium III (650 MHz to 1 GHz)**: although largely unchanged from the Pentium II, this came along in 1999 with some extra multimedia support and well-timed (if implausible) claims that it could speed up your Internet surfing. More importantly, it broke the 1 GHz barrier during 2000.
- **Pentium 4 (1.4 and 1.5 GHz)**: the latest processor from Intel arrived in late 2000 (although the PIII continues to be sold) offering a huge leap in speed and a move away from the roman-numeral names.

Pentium is the code name of the Intel 80586 component, also called the P5.

The bad news for anyone who has recently bought a computer is that things move very quickly. The good news is that if you continue to wait, prices will continue to fall. A new piece of equipment will lose 40% of its value in its first year.

The most famous microprocessor manufacturers are:

- **Intel Corporation:** besides the microprocessors mentioned above, the creation of many other powerful components is owed to this company. They also market their own supercomputers.
- **Motorola:** the manufacturer of components, including the famous 68000 series, which have equipped the Macintosh, the Atari and the Amiga.
- National Semiconductor.
- AMD.
- CYRIX.

'Coprocessor' means an auxiliary microprocessor. It is the complement of the main microprocessor, which performs the calculations. The coprocessor plays an important role, particularly in graphics applications.

AMD and Cyrix manufacture quality components that are compatible with Intel and less expensive.

Coprocessors assist the processors for operations requiring many calculations. However, old coprocessors have been integrated into the main components for some time now.

Computers have developed so much in the last few years that the main processor is now supported by ultrapowerful cards, particularly the famous 3DFX II graphics card.

The bus

The bus is a system for transporting information. It resembles a motorway with several lanes connecting the microprocessor to the peripherals. The number of channels (bits) determines the quantity of information that can be carried at the same time. This also depends on the speed, i.e. the value in megahertz (MHz).

Buses have evolved in line with technology. The ISA bus appeared at the end of the 1970s. This was an eight-bit (eight-channel) bus with a speed of 8 Mhz. It was followed in the 1980s by the Microchannel bus and EISA (Enhanced ISA) bus, which had 32 channels (32 bits). Their speed has remained the same. The VLB (Vesa Local Bus), characterised by a speed of 40 Mhz and 32 channels, was brought out in 1992, followed two years later by the PCI bus. This had 64 channels (bits) and boasted a record transfer rate of 80 Mb per second. In 1998, the most popular bus was the USB or Universal Serial Bus. This first came out in 1995 and enables up to 127 peripherals to be connected to a PC without the use of multiple types of connector, without IRQ conflicts (i.e. interruptions), address adjustment by means of jumpers, or DMA channel modifications.

New PCs should automatically come with a USB. This replaces Centronics, Mini-DIN and Sub-D parallel ports (ports for games, the printer, keyboard and mouse, modem and network adapter), and will soon replace others that have until now resisted. Thanks to the USB, a peripheral can be connected while the computer is switched on, thus allowing it to be recognised. This technique is known as 'hot swapping' (Figure 1.18).

Finally, there is the AGP (Accelerated Graphics Port) bus. This has cards fitted with the excellent 440LX graphics circuit (or equivalent). Brought out at the end of 1997, the AGP bus is a specialised bus that transports graphics data between the graphics card, the RAM and the processor. It has a transfer rate of 528 Mb per second and is perfectly suited to the processing of 3D graphics.

It should be said that the USB and AGP buses complement each other. They run best under Windows 98, and this operating system is therefore strongly recommended.

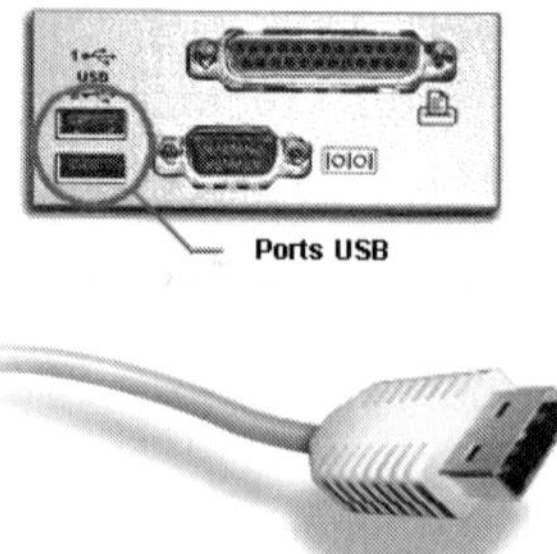

Figure 1.18 USB technology allows you to add a peripheral without switching off your computer.

The monitor

2

The basics

Definition

Resolution

Colour

The graphics card

Configuring the graphics card and display

The monitor is without doubt the most important item of comfort in your computer equipment. It displays all the information you enter, you may look at it for several hours a day, and your well-being can depend on it.

The basics

In order to understand properly how a monitor works, let us see what it comprises.

The monitor (Figure 2.1) can be monochrome or colour:

- Monochrome monitors display two colours: black and white, or black and green, or even black and yellow (amber). They are rare these days.
- Colour monitors display between 16 colours and 16.7 million colours.

Figure 2.1 The monitor.

The monitor is composed of the following elements:

- screen
- on/off switch
- brightness control knob
- contrast control knob
- vertical shift knob
- horizontal shift knob
- vertical size knob
- horizontal size knob
- frequency view knob
- degaus button
- stand.

Most people start off with a 15" colour screen with a definition of 800 × 600. This means that its diagonal measures 35 or 37.5 cm, its height is 600 pixels (dots), and its width is 800 pixels. For a reasonable extra cost, a 17" screen gives much more comfort. Finally, the drop in prices has now made some 19" screens affordable (at around £250), and it is even possible to find 21" screens (diagonal measuring 53 cm), for less than £600.

Screen size

Given that the distance between you and the screen will remain roughly constant once installation is complete, two parameters must be taken into account with regard to readability:

- the distance from the eye to the screen;
- the size of the screen.

On a 14" screen, the most suitable display is 640 × 480.

On a 15" screen, a change to a 600 × 800 display is possible. For those who use a lot of graphics, a 17" screen will allow acceptable conditions of comfort with a 1024 × 768 display.

Screen dot size

Although the screen diagonal is measured in inches (2.54 cm), the accuracy of the screen is measured using *pitch*.

The pitch defines the distance that separates the left extremity of one dot from the left extremity of the next dot.

- A standard pitch corresponds to 0.28 mm.
- A high-quality pitch corresponds to 0.25 or 0.24 mm.
- An exceptional pitch corresponds to 0.21 mm.

The cost difference between good-quality and excellent-quality pitch can be large.

This reference dot, called a *pixel*, is made up of three smaller dots, each corresponding to one of the three components, red, green and blue, which allow colour to be defined.

These dots define the standard dot. They therefore correspond to three photophores, one red, one green, and one blue; that is, inside the screen they correspond to coatings sensitive to one colour only. Each dot of colour is defined by the closeness of these three fundamental dots. When the screen's electron gun selectively scans a precise photophore, this lights up in the colour to which it corresponds.

By means of the electronics, the scanning is performed many times a second. In this way the whole screen is refreshed from 50 to 120 times a second depending on its quality.

Image stability

You may have observed that some screens seem to flicker when looked at from a distance, or that they are crossed by horizontal bands. This phenomenon corresponds to the gap that exists between our perception and reality. An image perceived by the eye benefits from a phenomenon called *remanence*, in which the cells of the eye retain the image for longer than it actually lasts. This explains why we see the cinema and television images as a continuous movement rather than as a series of fixed images.

Animals perceive things differently, often more quickly. That's why cats, for example, are not fascinated by television.

The refresh rate, or the number of times per second that a screen is redisplayed, defines how comfortable it is to use.

In cheaper screens the speed is insufficient and each scan redraws only every other line. This is known as *interlacing*. If you can afford to, you should choose a non-interlaced screen, i.e. a screen in which all the lines are refreshed simultaneously.

To summarise, a good screen must be non-interlaced and must have a refresh rate of at least 75 Hz.

Keep an eye on the capabilities offered for varying the screen definition, that is its number of dots in width and height, during use. The scanning speed is a function of the number of dots to be dealt with. When the definition is increased, for example from 640 × 480 to 600 × 800, the scanning speed is reduced since the system has to deal with a different number of dots.

If your screen remains dark, but you are certain it is on, you have probably inadvertently disturbed the knobs that control the contrast and brightness. Otherwise a screen saver may be on. In this case, all you need to do is lightly touch the mouse to return to the screen.

When the appropriate software is not installed, this abrupt discontinuity in display, which occurs mainly when you change from a Windows application to a game in DOS mode, or vice versa, is accompanied by 'noise' on the screen, which can have serious drawbacks, including damaging the screen because components overheat.

Screen adjustment

The monitor has knobs that allow you to adjust:

- the contrast
- the brightness
- the vertical position
- the horizontal position.

Definition

Definition describes the size of a screen or image as a number of dots. A 600 × 800 screen has 480 000 dots. A 640 × 480 screen has 307 200 dots, i.e. two-thirds less. Therefore an apparently modest change in the definition causes the display of far more information. It is therefore better to avoid scrolling the image too frequently, which you can achieve by choosing a higher definition. For maximum comfort, choose a definition of 1024 × 768.

Resolution

Resolution concerns the density of dots for a given measurement. It is measured in dots per inch; that is, the number of pixels that can be put in line over a length of one inch (2.54 cm).

Whereas definition measures the number of pixels that can be displayed on a screen, resolution measures the quality of the image. This will become greater as each square inch contains more and more dots.

Colour

Some screens claim to display 16.7 million colours. How is such a phenomenon possible? Let us clarify first that very few users are capable of telling the difference between so many colours.

A colour is defined by three characteristics:

- hue
- brightness or intensity
- saturation (the way in which it differs from white).

This last idea requires some knowledge of the eye. The human eye is equipped with three pigments sensitive to red, green and blue, which are known as the *primary colours*. These colours can be combined in different quantities to make all other colours. The system is *additive*.

We use different primary colours. This system is *subtractive*, because it depends on colours not being present:

- **Yellow:** red + green in an additive system, or white – blue in a subtractive system.
- **Cyan:** green + blue in an additive system, or white – red in a subtractive system.
- **Magenta:** red + blue in an additive system, or white – green in a subtractive system.
- **Black:** an absence of colours in an additive system, or magenta + yellow + cyan in a subtractive system, i.e. a total absorption of colours.

The screen works in additive mode, i.e. by superimposing the colours by projecting electrons on to the photophores. The printing system is known as subtractive since the paper absorbs the colours and reflects only those that are able to bounce off. An ink therefore defines the colours through those which it absorbs. For example, a blue ink absorbs all colours except blue. Remember that black is the absence of colour, or is obtained when all the colours are absorbed. White results from the simultaneous presence of all the colours, to the point that none of them in particular can be distinguished any more. A white ink is therefore an ink that does not absorb any colour.

This is why a white page lit by a red light seems red, while a black page under the same conditions remains black. In the first case, the red light bounces off; in the second, the red light is absorbed.

The graphics card

Once you've got these ideas in your head, you can choose a screen and a graphics card. The latter forms an essential addition to a high-quality screen. This is because the 16.7 million colours are obtained by irregular variations caused by the intensity of the electrons.

The more numerous the colours, the more space their coding takes. A 256-colour dot uses one byte, a 65 536-colour dot requires two bytes, and a 16.7 million-colour dot uses three bytes.

The transfer of information is proportional to its size. A high-quality screen with a high definition and a large number of colours will need a graphics card with high-speed components for processing, storing and reconstructing the image.

There are specialised cards available for the display of two- or three-dimensional games.

Other graphics cards allow results close to that of cinema or television. The most developed cards allow the acquisition of images in real time from an external source (camera, camcorder, video recorder, television).

The best type of 3D card for the Pentium III or 4 seems to be the NVIDIA GeForce2. This specialises in processing 3D images (important for playing action games on your PC as well as displaying lifelike 3-dimensional pictures), and it should preferably at least 8 MB of RAM. Numerous manufacturers offer GeForce2 cards. They vary in price about £80 upwards.

Prices

Prices vary from £25 for bottom-of-the-range cards to almost £1000 for video cards. A good graphics card can reasonably cost between 10 and 20% of the total price of the configuration. This is because it constitutes a veritable small processing plant with its own high-speed memory unit for transferring the image directly to the screen.

Today, with powerful operating systems, a memory of 4–12 Mbytes is often needed. The difference will be obvious to people who often switch from one Internet session to another, or from one program to another. With 1 Mbyte of graphics memory, the display may take several seconds. With 4+ Mbytes, it is instantaneous.

Configuring the graphics card and display

To configure the graphics card with Windows 95 or 98, you must follow several steps.

As a rule, the monitor and video card form part of the basic configuration when you purchase your computer.

1. Click on the **Start** menu.
2. Select **Settings**.
3. Click on **Control Panel** (Figure 2.2).

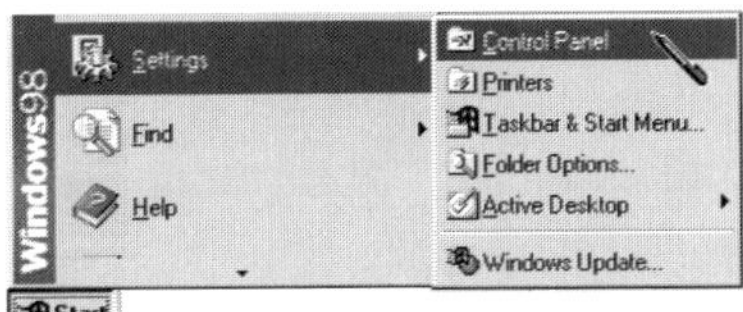

Figure 2.2 Install your graphics card using the Hardware Installation Wizard.

4. Double-click on the **Add New Hardware** icon (Figure 2.3). If you have Plug-and-Play hardware, Windows will probably have already detected it. In this case, the following steps can be skipped. Otherwise, launch the automatic search option. If Windows does not detect your card, you will have to install it manually. If Windows finds nothing new, this may mean that the hardware is already installed. To check and/or modify, click on **Next**.
5. In the ideal case, Windows will recognise your hardware straight away (Figure 2.4). Otherwise, select the type of hardware you want to install (a graphics card in this case).
6. Click on the manufacturer and model of your hardware (Figure 2.5).
7. Click **Next** to have your driver installed from Windows 95 or click **Have Disk** to install your driver from a floppy disk.

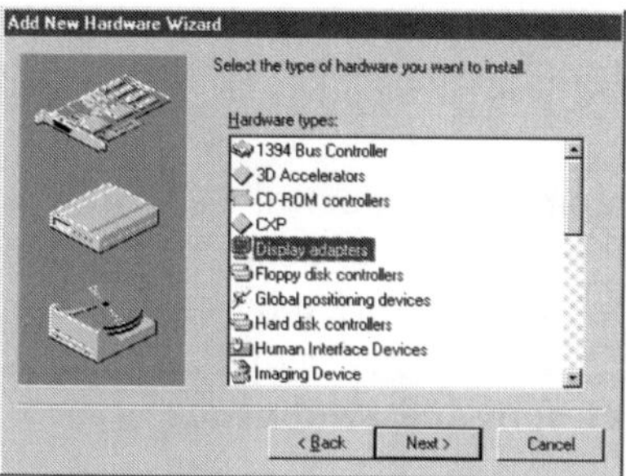

Figure 2.3 Install your graphics card using the Add New Hardware Wizard.

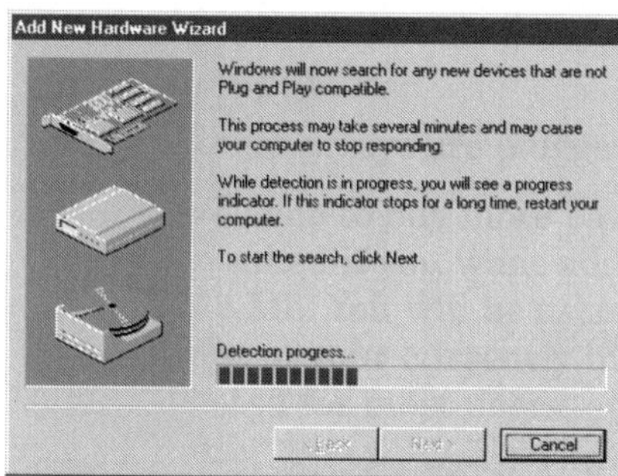

Figure 2.4 Detection of the graphics card.

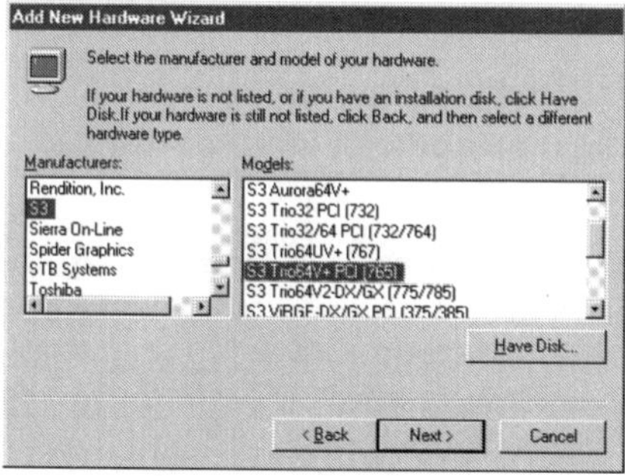

Figure 2.5 Windows 98 has the documentation of the main manufacturers. The chances are your card will be contained in this documentation.

8. Insert the installation disk (or CD-ROM) for your video card (Figure 2.6).

Once your graphics card is installed, you will be able to adjust the display settings for your screen.

1. Click on the **Start** menu.
2. Select **Settings**.
3. Click on **Control Panel**.

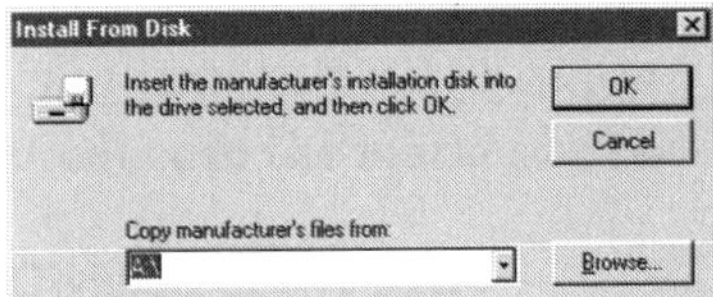

Figure 2.6 The Install From Disk dialog box enables you to install your video card.

4. Double-click on the **Display** icon.
5. Click on the **Settings** tab. Choose your settings (Figure 2.7). For example, 65 536 (16 bits) colours using 1024 × 768.

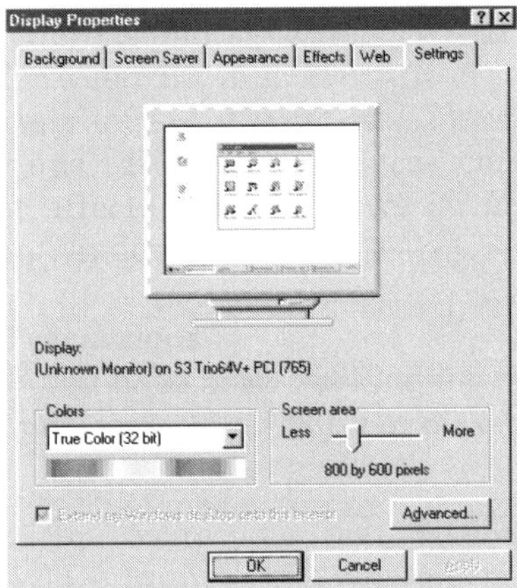

Figure 2.7 The Settings tab of the Display Properties dialog box enables you to set parameters such as the screen definition and the number of colours.

Mice and keyboards

3

The conventional keyboard

The ergonomic keyboard

The mouse

The trackball, trackpoint and trackpad

The joystick

Equipment for disabled people

The keyboard is an input peripheral. A keyboard must have alphabetic keys, numeric keys and function keys. The layout of the keys varies according to country.

The main keyboard type is the QWERTY keyboard (Figure 3.1).

The conventional keyboard

The conventional keyboard is provided with keys with a layout similar to that of old typewriters:

- Alphanumeric or typing keys, which allow you to enter letters and figures.
- The function keys, F1 to F12.
- The cursor movement keys, which allow you to move within the text.
- The numeric keys on the keypad, which allow you to enter figures and move within the text.

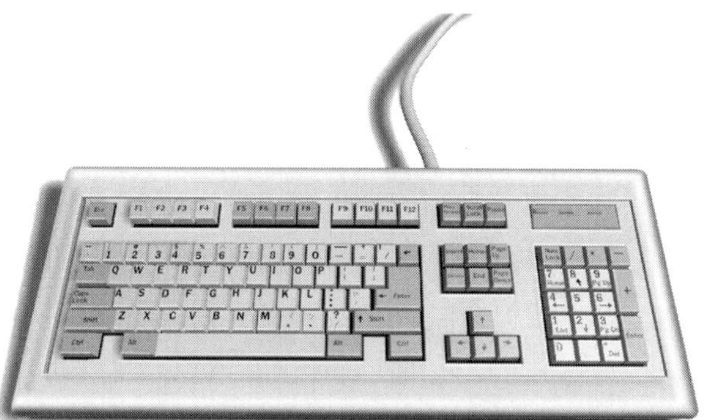

Figure 3.1 Keyboard layout.

The ergonomic keyboard

The ergonomic keyboard (Figure 3.2) has a key spacing different from that of the conventional keyboard: certain keys, in particular Ctrl, Alt, Alt Gr, and sometimes the Enter key, are larger and more practical. The keyboard is divided into three or four blocks by a space, the purpose of which is to space out the keys so that they are more suited to the natural position of the hands.

Some keyboards broaden this principle with extending guides. A keyboard of variable size is then obtained, which can be adapted to the build and posture of the user.

A less common category of keyboards incorporates infrared radiation, which allows communication with the computer without any lead connection. In this way, you really can work with your feet up in complete bliss.

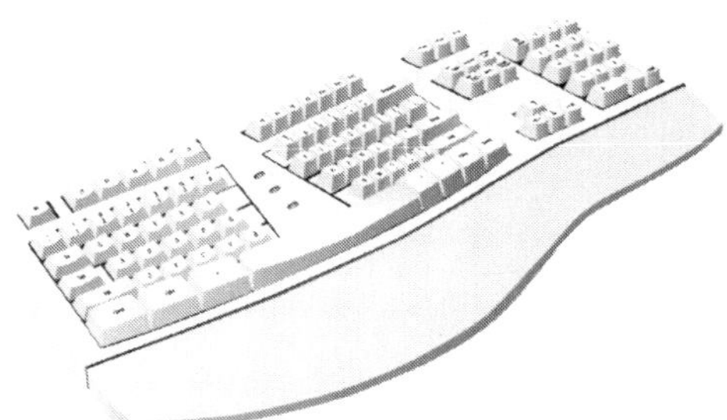

Figure 3.2 The ergonomic keyboard.

Some keyboards have additional keys, for example the Microsoft keyboard has a Windows key between the Ctrl and Alt keys, which gives access to the Start menu.

Configuring the keyboard

To change the configuration of your keyboard:

1. Click on the **Start** menu.
2. Select **Settings**.
3. Click on **Control Panel**.
4. Double-click on the **Keyboard** icon (Figure 3.3).

Figure 3.3 The Keyboard option in the Control Panel.

The Keyboard Properties dialog box will open (Figure 3.4):

- **Speed** lets you change settings such as cursor blink rate or character repetition frequency.
- **Language** lets you add a language from the 50 offered in the drop-down list.

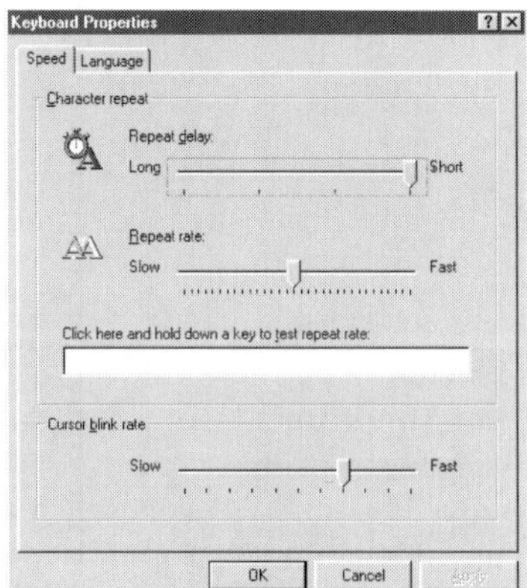

Figure 3.4 The Keyboard Properties dialog box.

To add a language:

To define the shortcut keys for changing from one language to another during typing, go to the Switch Between Languages area positioned under the Language tab.

1. Select the **Language** tab.
2. Click on the **Add** button.
3. Select your chosen language in the Add Language dialog box (Figure 3.5).

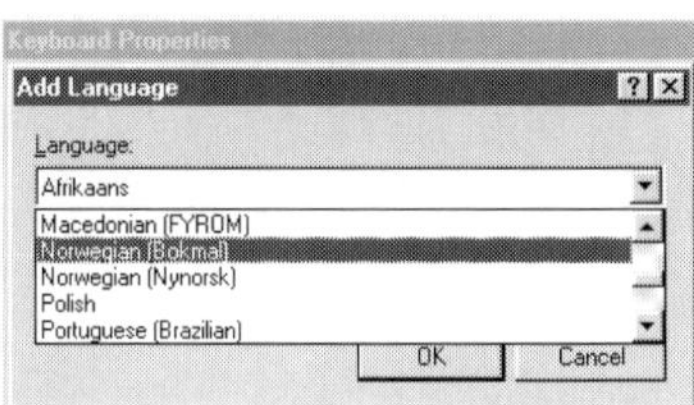

Figure 3.5 The Add Language dialog box.

4. Activate the indicator on the Taskbar once the language has been selected.
5. Once your various languages are installed and the Activate Indicator on Taskbar box has been ticked, an indicator showing the default language appears in the Windows Taskbar. To change from one language to another, click on this indicator, then on the language you want to use.

Keyboard maintenance

Of all the items that make up your computer installation, the keyboard is by far the most exposed to dust. This is all the more true if there are several of you in the family using it. Hair, crumbs, dust, etc. will sooner or later jam the keyboard mechanism unless you clean it from time to time.

Provide yourself with cotton buds, a glass cleaner and tweezers.

1. Lightly spray your keyboard with glass cleaner.
2. Pass the cotton bud between the keys.
3. Using the tweezers, dismantle the keys that are especially dirty.
4. Blow on the keyboard to remove the largest areas of dust.

The mouse

The mouse has become an extension of the hand. It is a fundamental intermediary between you and the computer.

Designed and perfected by Douglas Engelbart (Figure 3.6) and Bill English in 1963, the mouse was improved by Xerox in 1970. It was popularised by Apple at the beginning of the 1980s, but it was the PC that made it universal with the arrival of Windows. When the mouse was designed, it was only as part of an ambitious project aimed at improving human intelligence. As its inventor said during a famous interview: 'At the time, I had been working for 12 years on different ways of helping people increase their capacity for solving complex problems. We had envisaged getting them to work on problem-solving programs on workstations. This assumed that it was possible for them to interact with the displayed information by using an accessory capable of moving the cursor on screen. Several solutions already existed, such as graphic pens and joysticks, etc.'

Figure 3.6 (a) Douglas Engelbart; (b) the first mouse, assembled by Bill English.

In order to carry out his tests, Engelbart managed to secure the support of NASA. While the mouse did better than the trackball and joystick, it lost out by a whisker to another accessory, which was even faster... and knee-operated! The mouse also suffered from another crippling fault: without gravity, it floated in space.

In the end, Engelbart perfected the prototype of the mouse with the help of his collaborator Bill English. It was very simple, with two wheels for drawing straight vertical and horizontal lines. It was not possible to move directly in a diagonal direction.

Since its conception, the mouse has enjoyed three decades of development. Its technology as well as its appearance has been considerably improved. In everyday life, it has replaced the pen, felt-tip and pencil. An extension of the hand, it has become an established feature of the Western world.

There are several different kinds of mouse (Figure 3.7). The quality of a mouse lies in its sensitivity, resolution and movement, and the number of buttons (usually two or three).

Figure 3.7 Three models of mouse.

The standard Microsoft mouse (Figure 3.8) offers two buttons, but some software programs require three.

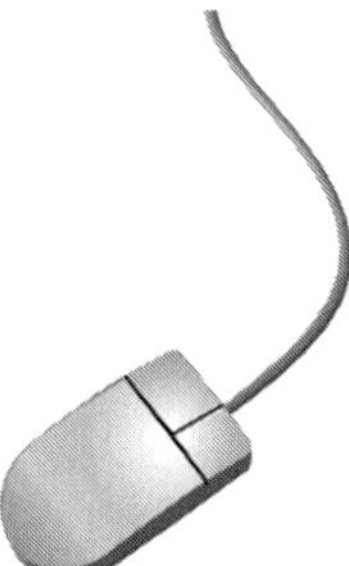

Figure 3.8 The standard mouse.

Configuring the mouse

To modify the double-click speed:

1. Click on the **Start** menu.
2. Select **Settings**.
3. Click on **Control Panel**.
4. Double-click on the **Mouse** icon.
5. Select the **Buttons** tab.
6. Set the speed you require.

There are various tabs in the Mouse Properties dialog box (Figure 3.9).

- **Buttons** enables you to set the button configuration and the double-click speed.
- **Pointers** enables you to change the pointer model.
- **Motion** enables you to set the pointer speed and the pointer trails.

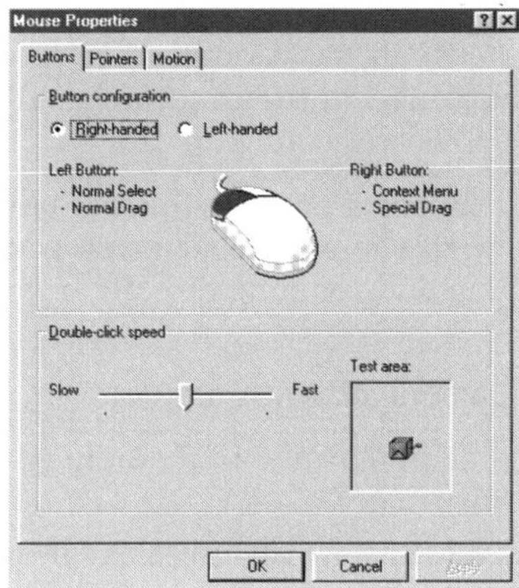

Figure 3.9 The Mouse Properties dialog box.

The mouse has its own language, which you must understand if you are to use your PC properly. You can:

- *Slide* the mouse over the text.
- *Double-click* on a word.
- *Click* on an object.
- *Move* a pointer.
- *Hold* a key down.
- *Release* the button.

Mouse mats

No mouse should be without its mat. The mouse mat cushions the jolts given to the mouse during movements. Without a mat, a mouse will deteriorate quickly. Mouse mats are cheap (some less than £1) and come in a great variety of colours and designs (Figure 3.10) – they are an economical way of making your work space friendlier and more attractive.

Figure 3.10 Mouse mats to make your computer sing.

IntelliMouse

IntelliMouse is the new Microsoft mouse. It has a small wheel situated between the left and right buttons. On turning this small wheel, the document scrolls on the screen very quickly.

The Microsoft IntelliMouse software makes it possible to carry out a greater number of manoeuvres with the mouse. It gives you the capability, for example, of scrolling and zooming directly from the mouse.

The IntelliMouse mouse allows you, among other things, to:

- Scroll a number of lines upward or downward in a single go: turn the wheel forwards or backwards.
- Zoom in or out: hold the **Ctrl** key down while turning the wheel forwards or backwards.
- Enlarge or reduce the titles in Drawing mode: click on a title, then hold down the Shift key while turning the wheel forwards or backwards.

Maintaining the mouse

Like the keyboard, the mouse is particularly exposed to wear and tear and dirt. The slightest clogging of the mouse affects the accuracy of the cursor. To clean your mouse:

1. Undo the cover on the bottom of the mouse.
2. Take out the ball.
3. Wipe the ball with a cloth.
4. Remove the dust from the case by blowing over it.
5. Loosen the dust encrusted on the roller rings with the help of tweezers and a cotton bud.

The trackball, trackpoint and trackpad

The trackball, trackpoint and trackpad are offshoots of the mouse. They are well-known to users of laptops (Figure 3.11).

Figure 3.11 The laptop and its trackball.

The trackball is a ball rolling in a support equipped with sensors and designed to replace the mouse. It can be compared to a mouse placed on its back.

The trackpoint resembles a lozenge; it is situated in the middle of the laptop keyboard between the letters B, H and G. It is equipped with four potentiometers, which enable it to be tilted in different directions depending on the pressure of your finger.

The trackpad is the most delicate of the track cousins. It is a small rectangle marked out in squares with a smooth surface situated in front of the laptop keyboard. It records the movements made by the finger. A simple light touch is sufficient. It combines transmission speed and sensitivity.

The joystick

The joystick (Figure 3.12), or game pad, is used with 3D games; it is connected to a games port on the central unit (Figure 3.13).

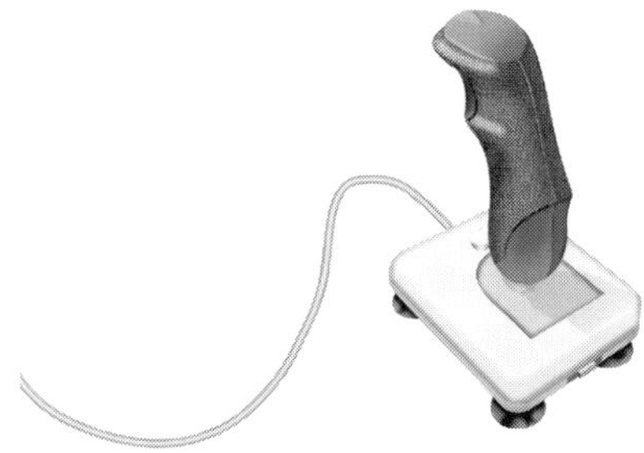

Figure 3.12 An indispensable entertainment accessory.

There are two kinds of joystick:

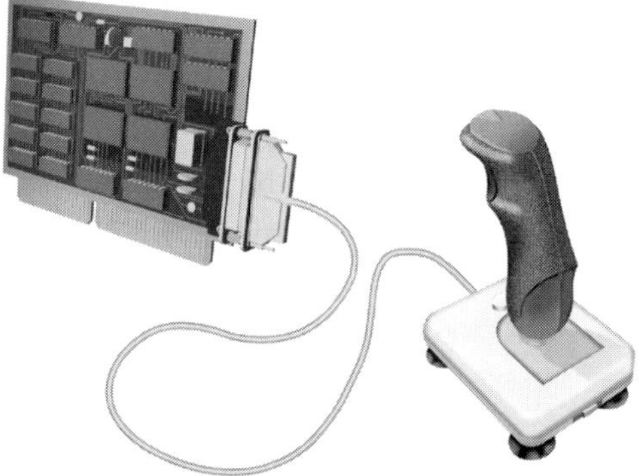

Figure 3.13 The joystick connected to its games port.

- A flat game pad with control buttons.
- A conventional joystick with control buttons.

Configuring the joystick

To install your joystick, you need to carry out the following operations:

1. Click on the **Start** menu.
2. Select **Settings**.
3. Click on **Control Panel**.
4. Double-click on the **Joystick** icon.
5. Select the **Joystick** tab (Figure 3.14) and follow the instructions in the Joystick Properties box.

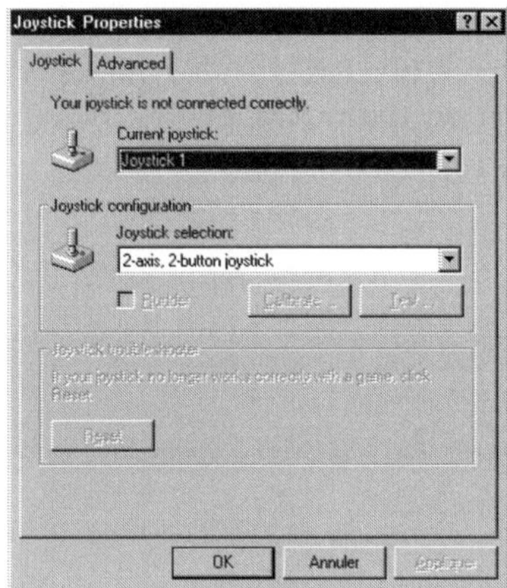

Figure 3.14 The Joystick Properties dialog box.

Equipment for disabled people

As a complement to the conventional keyboard, there are a number of accessories designed for people with disabilities. There are, for example, keyboards with keys that are designed to receive the pressure of a pencil. It is possible to activate this type of keyboard by holding the pencil in your mouth and moving your head. Each key is shaped like a small crater. A helmet fitted with an eye tracker has a system that analyses the movements of the eye and the time the focus of the eye remains fixed on a precise area.

Originally, this helmet was designed for jet aircraft pilots to communicate with their on-board computers without using their hands.

Today it enables paraplegics and tetraplegics to carry out actions that correspond to mouse clicks etc. in an able-bodied person.

Printers

4

Different types of printer

Choosing a printer

Installing a printer under Windows 98 or 95

Configuring a printer

Installing a second printer

Troubleshooting

Different types of printer

The printer is an output peripheral. There are four main categories of printer:

- **Dot matrix printer**. The head of this printer (Figure 4.1) is composed of a matrix of metal pins that strike the paper through a ribbon. The quality of this printer depends on the number of pins that make up the head. There are heads with 9, 18, 24 and 48 pins. Popular in the 1980s, the dot matrix printer is less used today. The print speed varies from 80 to 300 characters per second.

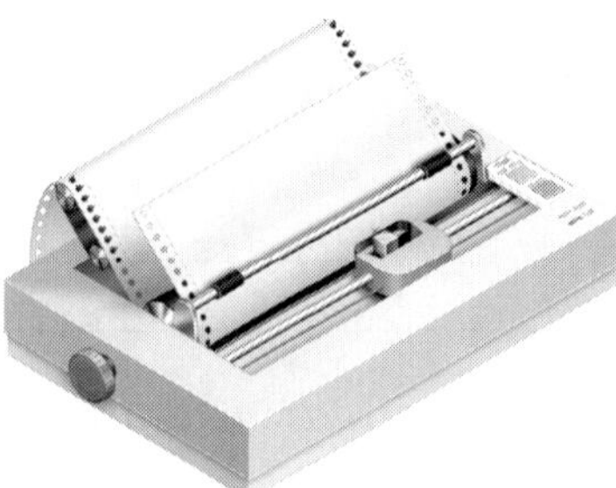

Figure 4.1 A dot matrix printer.

If it were not for marketing decisions, all laser printers could simultaneously be used as photocopiers, fax machines, scanners and modems. They all use the same principle of scanning a document with a laser beam in order to reproduce it.

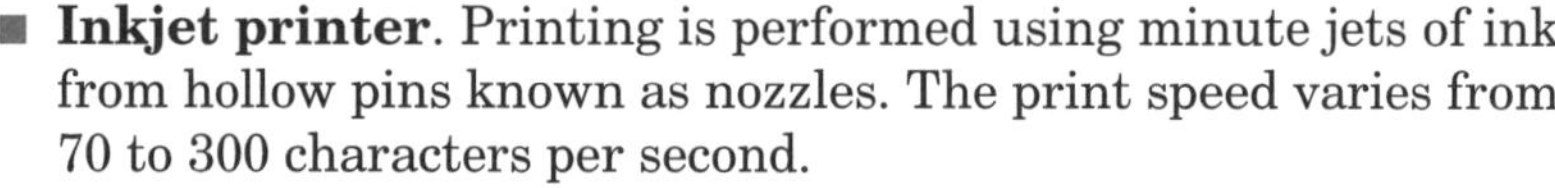

- **Inkjet printer**. Printing is performed using minute jets of ink from hollow pins known as nozzles. The print speed varies from 70 to 300 characters per second.

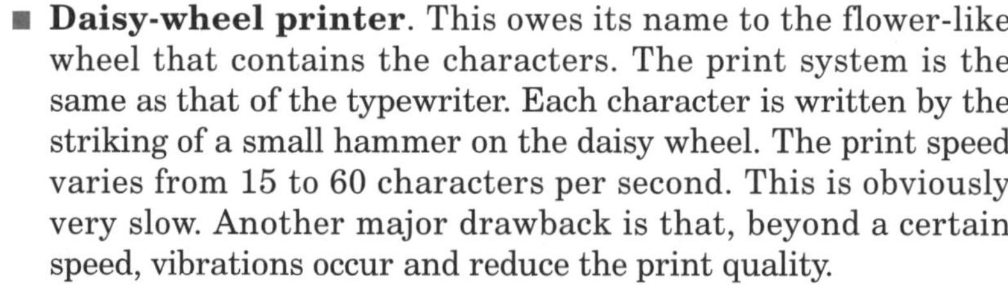

- **Daisy-wheel printer**. This owes its name to the flower-like wheel that contains the characters. The print system is the same as that of the typewriter. Each character is written by the striking of a small hammer on the daisy wheel. The print speed varies from 15 to 60 characters per second. This is obviously very slow. Another major drawback is that, beyond a certain speed, vibrations occur and reduce the print quality.

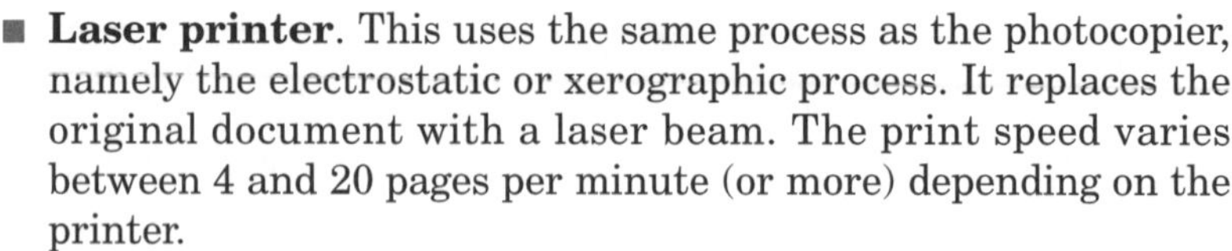

- **Laser printer**. This uses the same process as the photocopier, namely the electrostatic or xerographic process. It replaces the original document with a laser beam. The print speed varies between 4 and 20 pages per minute (or more) depending on the printer.

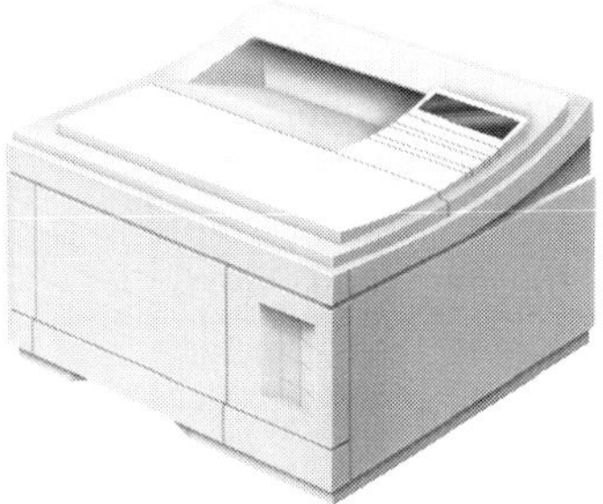

Figure 4.2 A laser printer.

Choosing a printer

Your choice of printer should be determined both by the type of work you wish to carry out and by the quality and speed of the print-out required.

- **Resolution**. The quality of a printer is measured in dots per inch (pdi). Conventional printers print in 300 dpi. Increasingly, manufacturers are offering machines with a resolution of 600 dpi, at reasonable prices.
- **Print speed**. The print speed is measured in number of characters per second (cps) or pages per minute.
- **Strike quality**. Daisy-wheel printers are slower than dot matrix printers but offer a 'letter' strike quality. Laser printers offer the highest quality of characters with the widest variety of fonts.
- **Paper format**. Paper format and type of drive are also important. The pin feed system requires the exclusive use of listing paper. Most other printers are equipped with a single-sheet feed system.
- **Noise nuisance**. Dot matrix and daisy-wheel printers are the noisiest. Inkjet printers and laser printers are quiet.

The laser printer has become the standard for microcomputers.

Advice:

- For printing only black and white text, any printer is acceptable.
- For printing black and white drawings and graphics, laser printers give a more satisfactory rendition than inkjet printers. The line of the drawings is finer.
- For colour printing, the inkjet offers a good quality/price ratio. The colour laser printer is, sadly, still beyond the reach of most personal budgets (around £2000).

600 dpi black and white printers, often very cheap to buy, prove to be quite costly to run. This is because the special ink suitable for this resolution is between 40 and 200% more expensive. Consider asking the salesperson the price of the ink and whether there is any currently in stock. Express surprise at the price difference between this and other ink and you may be told that it is because twice as much ink is necessary, which is not true.

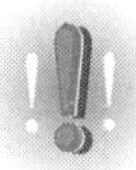

Some printers are delivered with few character fonts. To increase your stock of character fonts, you can buy extra. However, a simpler solution is to use the fonts that come supplied with Windows.

Installing a printer under Windows 98 or 95

To install a printer under Windows 98 or 95, proceed as follows:

1. Click on **Start**.
2. Select **Settings**.
3. Click on **Printers**.
4. Click on **Add Printer** (Figure 4.3).

Figure 4.3 The first step is to click on the **Add Printer** icon.

5. Select the name of the manufacturer of your printer.
6. Click on the name of the printer you want to install.

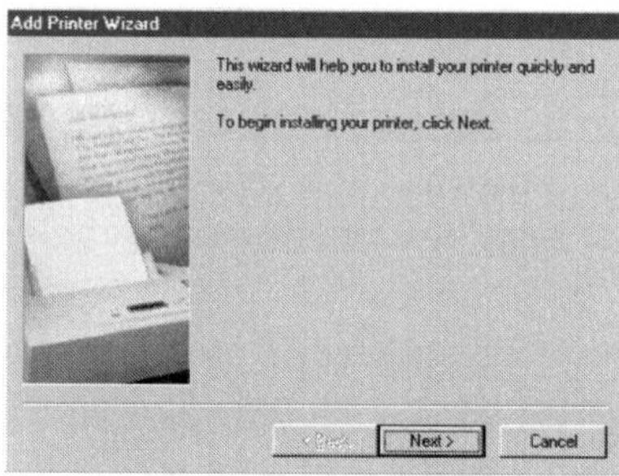

Figure 4.4 Identical under Windows 98 and 95 (with the exception of the image on the left), the Add Printer Wizard guides you throughout the installation of your new printer.

7. Click on the **Have disk** command button if the driver is delivered with the printer (Figure 4.5).
8. Click on **Next** to configure the port.
9. Configure the port. You have two ports. The one assigned to a single printer is LPT1. Tick the **Check port state before printing** box (Figure 4.6).

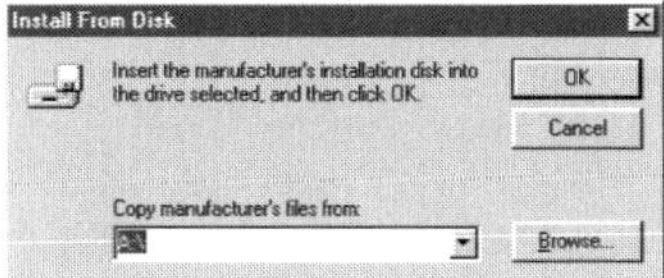

Figure 4.5 The Install from Disk dialog box.

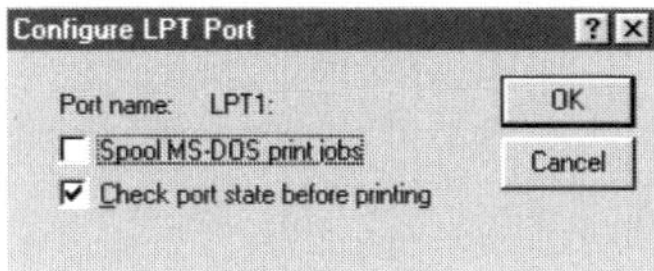

Figure 4.6 Configure LPT Port dialog box.

The port is usually a serial or parallel output, but may be another other type, particularly where telecommunications are concerned. The serial port comes in the form of a plug (connector). As a rule your computer is likely to be equipped with two parallel ports.

Configuring a printer

To print a document under Windows 95, carry out the following operations:

1. Open the document's **File** menu.
2. Click on the **Print** option.
3. Choose the settings you require.
4. Click on the **Properties** command button, which gives you access to the Properties dialog box for your printer. You can choose to print odd or even pages, select the number of copies to be printed, only to include automatic insertions when printing, etc.

Printer properties

In a document:

1. Open the **File** menu.
2. Click on the **Print** option.
3. Select the **Properties** button. The Properties dialog box for your printer appears (Figure 4.7).

The tabs of the Properties dialog box for the printer may include:

- **Paper:** sets the paper size (US letter, A4, executive, US legal, etc.), envelopes, paper orientation (portrait (vertical) or landscape (horizontal)), its source (upper tray, manual feed, manual envelope feed).
- **Graphics:** sets the resolution (75, 150 or 300 dpi), rastering (coarse or fine grain) and intensity (light to dark on a scale of 0–200).
- **Fonts:** allows downloading and printing of TrueType fonts.
- **Device Options:** makes it possible to set the way in which the driver manages the use of the printer's memory.

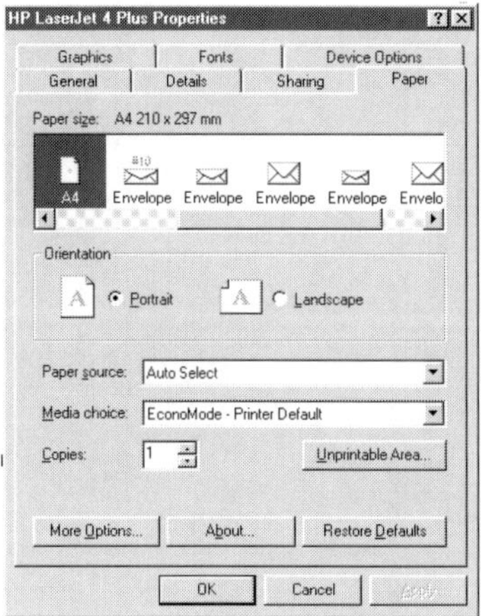

Figure 4.7 The Properties dialog box for the printer

Installing a second printer

Installing a second printer is not difficult, and is becoming increasingly common. People who already own a black and white printer are tempted by colour inkjet printers because they have become cheaper.

First of all, it is important to realise that some printers are installed using a serial port while others use a parallel port. A port is an input/output connection. All you need to do is look at the back of your computer to know which one is available. In the rare event that all the ports are in use, you will have to pay £10–20 to install a Com 3 or 4 port. If this means nothing to you, ask a more experienced friend for help. Otherwise consult a specialist – but be prepared to pay!

Once you have connected your printer, install its software in exactly the same way as you did for your first printer. The different ways in which you use them will depend on what you want to use them for. For example, if you use your computer mainly for word processing, the black and white printer will be defined as the default setting. However, if you decide you want to use your computer to create your own headed paper or logo, you will probably want to use your new colour printer to make the most of your colours.

At this point, rather than clicking on the print icon on the toolbar in order to print, open the **File** menu and click on the **Print** option. In the dialog box, redefine your choice of printer. To do this, proceed as follows:

1. Go to the text field at the top of the Print dialog box.
2. Click on the small arrow to the right of the name of the active printer. A drop-down list appears containing all the installed printers.

3. Click on the printer you want to use. It is easy to switch from one to another.

Now print by specifying the parameters. Colour printers have many different options that need to be properly understood, such as paper category, print quality, adjustment, and many other details. Depending on the options you choose, the printing time can be fast (in draft mode) or rather slow (for high-quality printouts). You therefore should ask yourself whether it is worth having a colour printer if it deprives you of the best quality.

Troubleshooting

You have an urgent document to output and your printer lets you down. Nothing is more annoying. Below is a list of printing difficulties and their solutions.

The toner is an electrostatic ink used for photocopiers and laser printers. Its fineness allows a greater or lesser degree of resolution.

- **Your printer prints several sheets at the same time.** This may be due to the quality of the paper itself. It may be too thin, for example, or packed too tightly. Before filling your printer's feeder, don't forget to fan your paper properly.
- **Your sheets come out crooked.** Make sure that the guides arranged on either side of your paper feed tray grip your sheets properly.
- **The printer indicates 'Paper out' yet the tray is full of paper.** Check that your tray is inserted fully, up to the end stop.

The corona wire is a metal wire mesh that plays a part in the magnetisation of the drum and therefore in the positioning of the ink. Make sure that it does not get clogged up with dust.

- **The sheets are not being inserted automatically.** The paper is driven by rollers. If these get dusty, clean them using a vacuum cleaner with a very fine nozzle. Cotton buds and glass cleaner are also very useful, as is an aerosol ink cleaner. This dissolves traces of ink on any printing hardware, such as paper drive drums, rollers, bearings, rubber characters, etc.
- **The printer doesn't print, there is no power, and the lights are off.** There's probably nothing to worry about. You may have forgotten to plug your printer in. Check that the cable is connected correctly to your computer and that the adaptor is plugged into the mains properly.
- **The colour of the ink is very faint.** The toner cartridge in your laser printer is nearly empty and should be replaced.

5 The memory

The central memory

Read-only memory

Cache memory

The motherboard

The memory contributes to the power and comfort of your computer. A top-of-the-range Pentium III requires a random access memory (RAM) of 64–128 Mb. However, this amount will doubtless soon be exceeded.

If there is one area of this book in which you might well get lost, it is without doubt this section. Many terms are in use to describe different areas of computer memory, and sometimes different manufacturers use different terms to describe the same thing. Without some idea of what each term refers to it is easy to become very confused when making choices over the purchase of memory.

Here are some of the terms you may hear:

A nanosecond is one thousand millionth of a second.

- **Linear array:** a block of computer memory that slots into the motherboard, available in amounts of 16, 32, 64, 128, 256 or 512 MB.
- **Disk cache:** area reserved for dynamic data exchanges.
- **60-nanosecond memory:** normal standard memory that can be found on SIMM EDO linear arrays (Figure 5.1). The default memory is 70–80 ns.

Figure 5.1 SIMM EDO RAM linear arrays.

- **10-nanosecond memory:** rapid standard memory that can be found on DIMM SDRAM linear arrays (Figure 5.2).

Figure 5.2 10-ns DIMM SDRAM linear arrays.

- **Bubble memory:** a once promising technology.
- **Cache memory:** intermediate storage memory.
- **First-level cache memory:** cache located on the processor itself; also known as the main cache memory.

- **Second-level cache memory:** area of memory located in the immediate vicinity of the processor. It stores the most recently requested data and must be fast.
- **Disk cache memory:** part of the disk used to back up the RAM. It often holds up to 40 Mb and enables swapping between the disk and RAM when the latter does not have enough memory to carry out its task.
- **Central memory:** synonymous with RAM.
- **Conventional memory:** first part of the DOS memory from 0 to 640 kb.
- **Main memory:** hard disk.
- **EDO (extended data output) memory:** allows the processor to access information more quickly.
- **Extended memory:** under DOS, memory situated beyond 1 Mb.
- **Flash memory:** memory used in laptops because of its low power consumption.
- **Graphics memory:** 12-ns high-speed memory used on graphics cards.
- **Upper memory:** under DOS, memory between 640 and 1024 kb.
- **Read-only memory (ROM):** fixed, non-volatile memory that stores programs, particularly those for booting up the computer.
- **Buffer memory:** intermediate memory making it possible to increase the speed of a peripheral or, more rarely, a program.
- **Random access memory (RAM):** volatile memory into which you write.
- **Video memory (VRAM):** memory composed of additional memory chips, sometimes integrated directly on the screen card, which supervises the computer's display. This amount of memory determines the display speed, resolution and number of colours of the screen.

The central memory

The central memory, also called random access memory (RAM) or direct access memory, is a volatile memory. It is the memory you use for writing and reading. The information it contains disappears when the central unit is switched off.

RAM can be used directly by the microprocessor. This memory is measured in thousands of characters.

The unit of memory measurement is the byte, also called a character.

1 kb = 1024 characters (bytes)

1 Mb = 1024 × 1024 characters (bytes)

1 Gb = 1024 × 1024 × 1024 characters (bytes)

- To run Windows 3.1, your PC requires a minimum of 2 Mb of RAM.
- To run Windows 95, your PC requires a minimum of 16 Mb of RAM.
- To run Windows 98, your PC requires a minimum of 24 Mb of RAM.

The RAM capacity of a standard PC is between 128 Mb and 512 Mb of RAM.

The RAM linear arrays are plugged into memory expansion slots.

If you go to a shop to buy more basic memory for your PC, you will probably be asked if you want additional linear arrays of 4, 8, 16, 32, 64 or 128 Mb. You will be asked if you want a particular speed to match that of your currently installed memory. This is usually too complicated for most users, even those with some experience of computers.

For some time, the trend has been towards simplification, especially when you are equipped with standard hardware. A reputable dealer should be able to advise you on your purchase.

The minimum amount of memory

How much memory is needed to run the CD-ROM or software that you buy?

As a rule, the minimum amount of memory is shown on the software package. The memory used is kept as low as possible so that owners of older PCs operating under Windows 3.1 are able to buy the products. The only exception to this rule are 3D games, which have a high memory requirement.

This information is usually found under the heading 'System requirements' somewhere on the packaging box. For example, a recent documentary-type software would require:

- a 486 PC or higher;
- Windows 3.1 in extended mode or Windows 95 or 98;
- 8 Mb of RAM;
- 10 Mb of disk space;
- a mouse;
- a colour or black and white printer;
- a CD-ROM drive.

These are minimum figures. Remember that since most users do not have the latest computer, CD-ROM authors will adapt their product to the market by taking older models into account.

Division of the RAM

The RAM is divided into three main categories:

- **Conventional memory:** memory consisting of the first 640 kb.
- **Upper memory:** memory situated between the conventional memory and the first megabyte (from 640 to 1024 kb).
- **Extended or high memory:** memory situated beyond the first megabyte (above 1024 Mb).

There is another category that merits special attention. Memory between 64 and 128 Mb creates problems for certain top-of-the-range configurations. There is a bug that, under certain conditions, drastically reduces computer performance. Fortunately it affects only Windows 95 machines and has been eradicated in Windows 98.

Precautions

If you have been working for any length of time, you should save your work on hard disk or diskette. You are then saving it on what is called the 'main memory'.

If you write your text without saving it, everything that was stored in the RAM, which is a volatile memory, disappears when you switch off the PC.

What memory does my PC have?

If you are working under Windows 98 or 95, to find out how much memory your PC has you should:

1. Click on the **Start** button.
2. Select **Settings**.
3. Choose **Control Panel**.
4. Double-click on the **System** icon.
5. Click on the **Performance** tab of the System Properties dialog box. This tab gives you information concerning the amount of memory available on your computer and shows you, for example, the following items:
   - Memory
   - Virtual memory
   - System resources

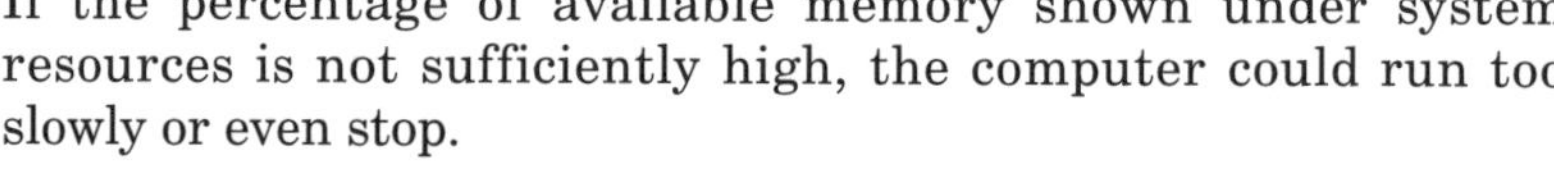

If the percentage of available memory shown under system resources is not sufficiently high, the computer could run too slowly or even stop.

Another way of finding out the amount of memory available on your computer is to look at the screen at start-up. When the PC checks the state of the memory, it displays the number of bytes present.

Read-only memory

Virtual memory is hard disk space used as additional RAM memory.

Read-only memory (ROM) is fixed and non-volatile, even when the computer is switched off. The ROM contains programs that provide:

- start-up
- internal tests
- Operating system search (Boot or Bootstrap).

The information in ROM cannot erased or modified.

The computer permanently contains a program known as a Bootstrap, which is an initial loading program. This program is placed in ROM by the manufacturer and is started automatically when the computer is powered up. This is what loads the operating system.

The amount of ROM is determined by the manufacturer. You cannot add any. However, you should be able to change it for a more recent version.

Cache memory

Electronic engineers have invented various tricks for optimising the operation of today's PCs. These computers are as powerful as the Cray, a giant computer that came out in 1976 and was at the time considered incredibly powerful.

Intermediate storage units, called cache memory, have been inserted between the processor and the RAM to serve as buffer memory. They can be compared to small, temporary warehouses intended to increase the operational flexibility of the main factory.

This cache memory exists at several levels. The first is situated inside the processor itself, which in this way optimises its internal work transparently. Next comes an external cache in the proximity of the processor, the size of which varies between 128 Kb and 1 Mb. This memory is much faster than the normal RAM of the central unit. It is therefore much more expensive. If the RAM has a response speed of 60 ns, that is 60 thousand millionths of a second or a possible 16.7 million responses each second, then the cache memory is five times faster. This is at least the case with first-generation Pentiums. On Pentium IIs, the memory has been improved to such an extent that they have a speed of 10 ns or even less.

Graphics cards have equally powerful memories, in order to take the load off the central processing unit, which often has a good many images to deal with. A good graphics card will easily support 8 Mb but can even go up to 12 Mb.

If there is insufficient memory at one or other of these levels, even the most powerful computer will not live up to its promise.

The motherboard

Inside the central unit is a motherboard (Figure 5.3) on which the microprocessor (see Chapter 1), the memory, the expansion slots and the connectors are arranged (Figure 5.4). The slots make it possible to connect various other cards, such as video cards, controller cards, sound cards, and memory cards for adding more RAM.

Figure 5.3 A motherboard.

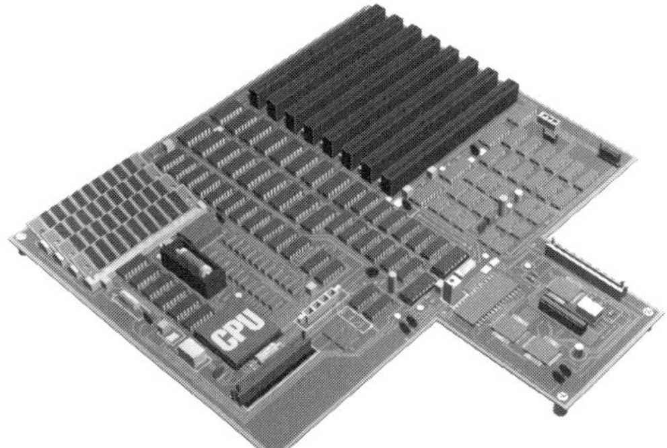

Figure 5.4 The motherboard with microprocessor, memory and expansion slots.

Generally the motherboard contains four small slots making it possible to plug in RAM linear arrays. Because the number of these slots is limited, it is better to choose linear arrays of large capacity, for example, 64, 128, 256 or even 512 Mb, from the start.

Certain computers allow you to combine two linear arrays with different capacities. If the speed that distinguishes them is different, the system, if it is sufficiently advanced, aligns itself to the lowest speed to avoid synchronisation problems.

Layout of the motherboard

- **Microprocessor or CPU (central processing unit):** the computer's brain (see Chapter 1).
- **Arithmetic coprocessor:** installed on old machines up to the 386, this is an electronic circuit that speeds up the processing of mathematical operations (see Chapter 1). Since the 486 generation, these functions have been integrated into the microprocessor.
- **Expansion slots:** connectors, also called sockets, into which you can plug expansion cards, for example modem cards, fax cards, sound cards, SCSI cards, etc.
- **Random access memory slots:** connectors in which the RAM linear arrays are fixed.
- **Keyboard connector:** socket allowing the keyboard cable to be plugged in.
- **Connectors for the serial or parallel ports:** slots into which ribbon cables carrying the information can be plugged.
- **Disk connectors:** these allow connection of the hard disk(s).

Expandability

Expandability (Figure 5.5) is a computer's capacity for receiving additional peripherals and memory.

Figure 5.5 Expandability on the motherboard.

The expandability of your PC depends on three parameters:

1. The memory expansion possible.
2. The free expansion slots present on the motherboard (Figure 5.6).
3. The external expansion ports.

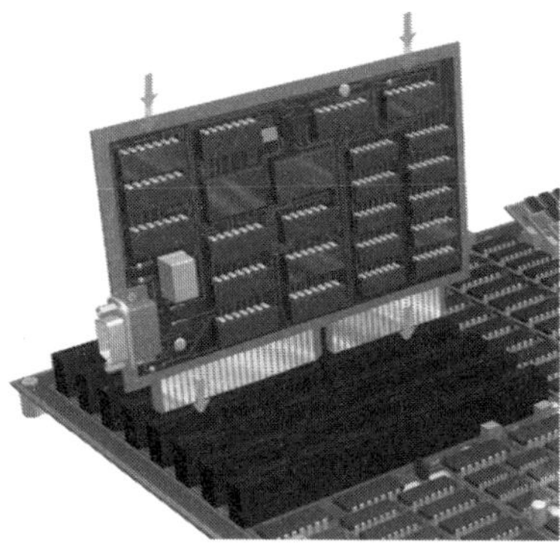

Figure 5.6 The expansion slots on the motherboard.

Figure 5.7 Keyboard and mouse ports.

The hard disk

6

Hard disks (Figure 6.1) make it possible to store and back up large amounts of data, millions (Mb), perhaps even thousands of millions (Gb) of bytes. They are composed of a fixed magnetised disk and a mechanism enabling them to be read.

Figure 6.1 A hard disk.

The current standards are:

- 8.4 Gb
- 10.2 Gb
- 13.6 Gb
- 15.3 Gb
- 20.5 Gb
- 30.7 Gb

The development of multimedia has made it necessary to manufacture disks capable of storing large volumes. Whether it is games, music, video clips or video editing, new formats create new requirements, which is why start-of-the-range disks rarely hold less than 8.4 Gb.

Structure

The structure of the hard disk is the same as that of a diskette: except in the case of large volumes, different disks are stacked one on top of another and enclosed in a case. A disk is characterised by the number of platters (also known as cylinders) it has (Figure 6.2).

Each disk is covered with a thin magnetisable film (brown oxide or pure metal vapour).

The plates turn around an axis, generally at a speed of 3600 revolutions per minute.

A read/write head reads data from or writes data to the magnetised surface.

Figure 6.2 The plates of the hard disk.

The head sends out a magnetic beam. It never touches the surface and is placed at a distance of 0.0005 mm.

The read heads are assembled on a kind of comb.

The hard disk assembly is supervised by the controller card.

Characteristics

- **Capacity:** the memory space capacity, also called storage space, is the volume of data that can be recorded on the hard disk. This is the most important item to be taken into consideration when you purchase a hard disk. Opt for a capacity two or three times greater than you actually expect to use.

  The unit of measurement is the gigabyte (Gb); that is, a capacity of one thousand million bytes.
- **Access time:** the time necessary for the read head to find the exact spot where the data are situated. It is of the order of a few milliseconds.
- **Latency time:** the time for which the computer waits before reading the data. It is a few milliseconds.
- **Data transfer speed:** the number of data items that can be transmitted from the hard disk to the memory during one unit of time. The unit of measurement is millions of bits per second (Mbits/s). The data transfer speed is on average 10 Mbits/s (just over 1.2 Mb per second).
- **Interlacing:** the number of rotations of the hard disk for reading all the sectors on a track.

The FAT (file access table) guides the read heads to the location where the data are arranged in the form of blocks or segments.

A disk-caching program enables you to speed up the mean access time of a hard disk. Windows 98 and 95 have integrated disk-caching programs.

Disk drive nomenclature

The floppy disk drives and the hard disks are represented in Windows Explorer by alphabetic letters followed by a colon.

- **A:** symbolises the first floppy disk drive.
- **B:** symbolises the second floppy disk drive. If you haven't got one, the letter B will remain unused.
- **C:** represents the first hard disk.

- **D:** represents the second hard disk if present. Each new hard disk has an additional letter assigned to it.
- **E:** generally represents the CD-ROM drive.

And so on.

Note: you are strongly recommended to insert your CD-ROM last. Failure to heed this advice may prevent your computer from functioning properly when you install a new hard disk.

Depending on your requirements, it is easy to reach the letters G or H. For example, three hard disks, one of which was partitioned (C:, D:, E: and F:), an external Iomega Zip drive (G:) and a CD drive (H:).

Formatting the hard disk

Formatting segments the hard disk into tracks and tapered sectors (Figure 6.3). The track corresponds to a circle, the sector to a portion of a track. The size of the sector depends on the context. It will not be less than 256 bytes, but it may be much larger.

The Bernoulli involves a technique that consists of making a flexible system rigid by turning it at very high speed. It has a very large storage capacity. Iomega Corporation was the pioneer of this technology, and models were available on the microcomputer market from the 1980s. Daniel Bernoulli (1700–1782) was a Swiss physicist known for a theorem published in 1738, in which he maintained that at any point in a pipe where a fluid under pressure is flowing, the equivalent of the law of conservation of energy is observed.

Figure 6.3 The tracks and sectors of the hard disk.

The address of the file corresponds to a track reference and a sector reference. The location is recorded in a file allocation table (FAT) on the disk.

The hard disk is usually preformatted when you purchase your computer. If you are a novice, it is preferable that you have your hard disk formatted by an expert.

Different types of hard disk

- **External hard disk:** this system is rarely used. The hard disk is physically located on the outside of the case of the computer. It is especially used as a back-up system (streamer or Bernoulli). In the early days, some disks were external because of their size. A single 20 Mb disk could weigh up to 40 kg. Today, there are fewer reasons to justify external disks, unless these have to be shared between several machines. In 1983, a Bull hard disk containing 20 Mb (10 Mb of which were exchangeable) cost £6300. Today, the price has dropped ten thousand fold, with £600 getting you three disks, each with 45 Gb of disk space, i.e. seven thousand times more space for ten times less money!

- **Internal hard disk:** installed inside the computer.
- **Hard disk on a card:** this type of hard disk appeared in 1985. A single electronic card includes the 3½" format hard disk and its controller. The whole thing connects into one or two free slots on the computer.

Well-known makers of hard disks include IBM, Conner, Maxtor, Western Digital, Quantum and Seagate.

The streamer is a tape drive using magnetic tapes for the storage of large amounts of data.

The hard disk controller cards

A controller card is devoted to controlling and driving a peripheral. It performs information switching functions with conversion and error management.

The controller cards indicate how the information is stored on the hard disk; that is, in what order and over what length the digital data have to be converted on the hard disk into magnetic pulses. This operation is known as *encoding*, the reverse operation *decoding*.

ScanDisk

ScanDisk is a software program integrated into Windows 95 and 98. It is responsible for checking the state of the hard disk. It analyses the state of the disks you select, and can carry out a standard or thorough analysis depending on your requirements (Figure 6.4).

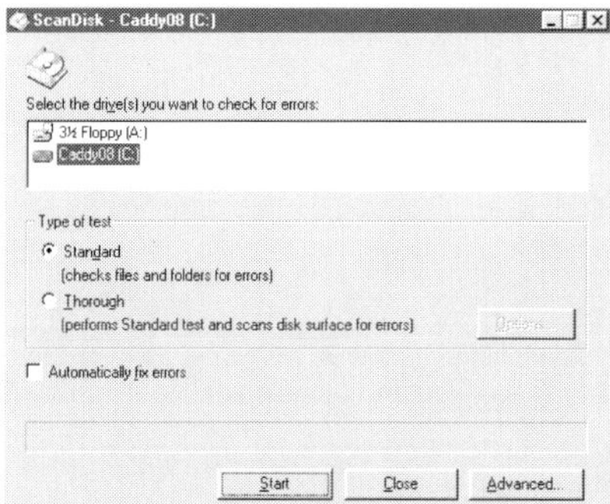

Figure 6.4 The ScanDisk dialog box.

- **Standard analysis:** ScanDisk checks files and folders.
- **Thorough analysis:** ScanDisk performs a standard test and checks the disk surface.
- **Advanced options:** these make it possible, for example, to convert fragments of lost files (Figure 6.5).

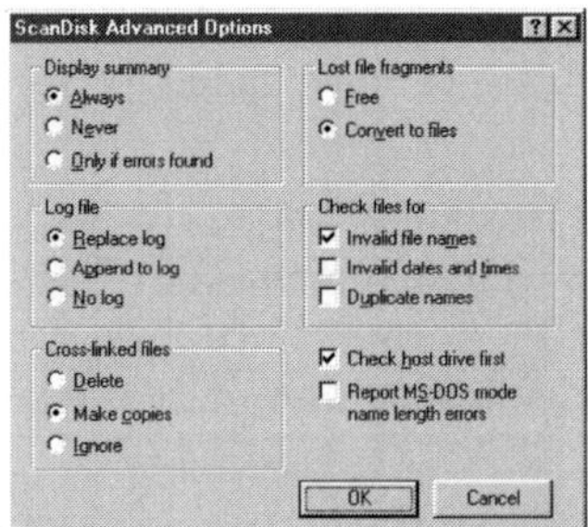

Figure 6.5 The advanced ScanDisk options.

You can also ask ScanDisk to repair errors. ScanDisk can work as a background task, that is, it can run while you are working on another program. This dual task management should, however, be avoided.

At the end of the analysis, ScanDisk draws up a highly accurate report of the errors it detected and the state of the disk it analysed (Figure 6.6).

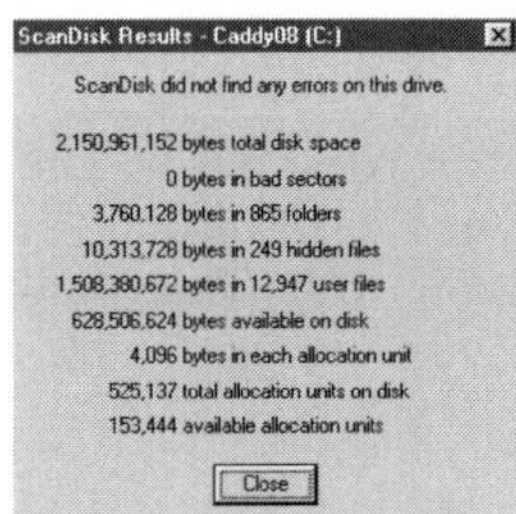

Figure 6.6 The ScanDisk report.

To access ScanDisk:

1. Click on **Start**.
2. Open the **Programs** option.
3. Select **Accessories**.
4. Click on **System Tools**.
5. Select **ScanDisk**.

ScanDisk is useful for repairing errors that occur when you switch off your computer without following the normal shut-down procedure.

Installing a second hard disk

Today's increasingly numerous multimedia applications require a significant amount of space on the computer. The installation of one or more additional 2–6-Gb hard disks can quickly prove essential.

To install another hard disk:

1. Switch off and unplug your computer.
2. Remove the cover.
3. Fix the disk under the first hard disk using the screws provided for that purpose.
4. Insert the free flat connector of the cable from the first hard disk into the second hard disk, known as the 'slave'.
5. Connect a free power supply connector into the plug consisting of four large pins.
6. Replace the cover.
7. Plug in the computer.

As a rule the PC must recognise the characteristics of your new hard disk.

This operation seems easy to carry out; however, it is better to entrust it to an expert if you are a complete novice!

Housekeeping

Your housekeeping will be done all the more quickly and correctly if your hard disk is well organised, with explicit directory names, clear and logical filing, and a well-defined tree structure (Figure 6.7).

Figure 6.7 Your hard disk is your PC's filing cabinet.

1. Your hard disk contains back-up copies that you no longer need as '.bak' extensions. Do not hesitate to delete them.
2. Your hard disk contains originals that are no longer of great use to you but that you are keeping as a precaution. The simplest thing to do is to make a copy of them on diskette and archive them, then destroy the files on your hard disk so that you avoid accumulating useless clutter as the months go by.
3. Programs produce temporary files. They use the hard disk as a working memory, which is not its true function here since that is the purpose of RAM. The extension of these files is .tmp. Most of the time, your computer will do the housekeeping on its own and will delete these files itself once the program is exited, but this is not always the case, particularly if you close down your computer

in an illegal manner by directly switching off the computer without first closing the program. Here are a few solutions for getting rid of these files:

- Check the status of the files. You will see immediately whether or not they are .tmp files.
- If necessary, initiate a **Find** function to search for .tmp. Click on **Explorer**. Once in the File Manager, open the **Tools** menu. Select the **Find** option. Double-click on **Files or Folders**. Initiate a search not only on the C drive but in all other drives. To do this, use the **Find** field in the Find All dialog box. Enter *.tmp in the **Named** field of the Find All dialog box.

A tough customer

Of all the components of your installation, the hard disk is certainly the one that has the longest life expectancy. It contains all the important data, applications, files and the operating system. It runs at 3600 revolutions per minute, several hours a day, every day. It will without doubt outlive your computer.

Nevertheless, if it were to be damaged, by an electrical storm for example, this would be potentially catastrophic for you, given that the hard disk contains all your files, representing a significant amount of work. Never forget to make copies on diskette of the documents that seem the most important to you. Top-of-the-range Zip or Jaz back-up disks can hold 100 Mb, 250 Mb or even 1 Gb.

If the FAT (file allocation table) is destroyed by the action of a virus, for example, complete chaos appears on your hard disk: there is no consistency and nothing is readable. An error message will appear on the screen, 'Sector not found'. There is only one thing to do in this case: switch off the computer and restart with the emergency toolkit. Effective repair softwares include ScanDisk or Disk Doctor. Another solution is the back-up FAT. On a hard disk, you generally find two FATs. Make a copy of the good FAT in order to repair the damaged FAT.

The future

Hard disks have become more compact and less expensive, and benefit from improved transfer rates thanks to interfaces that have become increasingly more powerful. Ultra DMA, Ultra DMA/66, Wide SCSI and Ultra2 SCSI (80 Mb/s flow) hard disks use technologies that are innovative today but will be standard tomorrow.

7 The operating system

What is an operating system?

MS-DOS

Windows 3.1

Windows 95, 98 and NT

The benefits of Windows 98

UNIX and Linux

What is an operating system?

The operating system is responsible for linking the applications and the hardware. It is a set of programs responsible for ensuring the correct vital operation of the computer and for managing the peripherals.

Here are a few of the tasks for which the operating system is responsible:

- formatting diskettes
- copying files
- renaming files
- destroying files
- displaying a list of programs
- displaying a list of folders
- checking the available memory
- launching and running programs
- moving from one application to another
- managing the overall coherence of the system.

MS-DOS

In the beginning, MS-DOS was the most widespread operating system for IBM PC-compatible microcomputers. Created by the American publisher Microsoft, it was supplanted first by Windows 3.1, then by Windows 95, both originating from the same workshop as their predecessor.

Since the success of MS-DOS lasted more than a decade, it merits a few lines of description, especially since it lies at the heart of Windows 98 and 95. Even today you need to use DOS to run these programs. Many high-quality games and applications run only on DOS.

You need to have at least a certain knowledge of DOS, if only because it is required for running a good number of tasks. For example, if you wanted to print the contents of a directory or recover it in a text file, you would have to give the instruction in DOS. To launch a DOS session, select **Start**, **Shut Down**, **Restart in MS-DOS mode**. Once in DOS, type in the relevant instruction. For example:

```
DIR C:\ /S> C:\TEMP\REP01.TXT
```

This instruction allows you to recover the C drive descriptor, sorted by the option `/S`, in a text file called `REP01` located in the `C:\TEMP` directory.

Similarly, if Windows breaks down, the boot disk enables action to be taken in DOS mode. It is therefore a good idea to at least have a basic knowledge of how DOS works or to have someone around you who does.

Single-user and single-task

MS-DOS is a single-user, single-task system, which means that it can be used only by a single user and for a single task at any one time. If several users wish to work together, they must be connected in a network.

Start-up

MS-DOS is installed on the hard disk (mass memory). On power-up, MS-DOS is automatically loaded into the memory and invites you to enter a command as soon as the following prompt appears on the screen: C > or C:\>

The main files

The three main files that make up MS-DOS are:

- **MSDOS.SYS:** a hidden file, i.e. it is not listed or visible by means of the usual commands.
- **IO.SYS:** also a hidden file.
- **COMMAND.COM:** comprises the internal commands loaded automatically when MS-DOS is started. These commands are permanently present in the random access memory (RAM), and can therefore be used at any time.

The main commands

- **DIR:** directory is a request to display the structure of the disk. It makes it possible to find out how the data is organised on the disk or diskette.
- **FORMAT:** formatting is the command for preparing a diskette that is going to be divided into tracks and sectors of fixed size to receive information.
- **COPY:** the command that allows you to copy from one location to another.
- **DEL:** delete is the file destruction command.
- **MD:** make directory creates a directory or subdirectory to be made active.
- **CD:** change directory allows a new directory or subdirectory to be made active.
- **RD:** remove directory makes it possible to remove a directory or sub-directory.
- **CHKDSK:** check disk makes it possible to check the state of the disk.

Operating system may be abbreviated to OS.

Accessing the DOS commands

1. Click on **Start**.
2. Select the **Programs** option
3. Click on **MS-DOS Commands** (Figure 7.1).
4. Enter your command at the prompt.

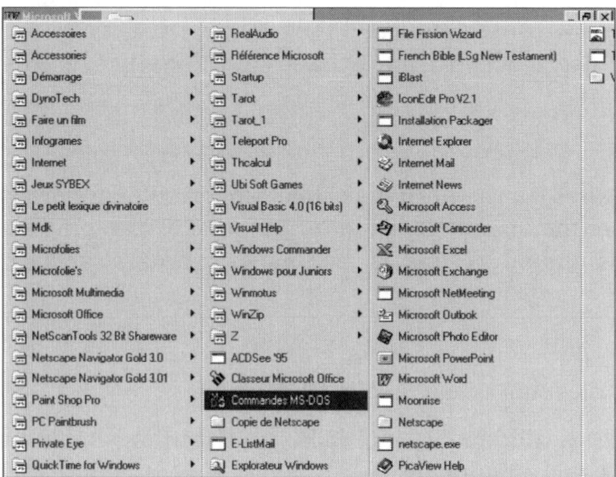

Figure 7.1 The MS-DOS Commands option gives access to a DOS session.

Windows 3.1

Created in 1988, Windows 3.1 constituted an advanced graphical interface that enhanced DOS.

At the time, Windows was not yet an operating system in itself. It would only become so with the 95, 98 and NT versions.

For the first time on PC, the 3.1 version of Windows brought to the screen a quality of presentation to rival that of its competitor, Apple.

It offered multi-windowing, intensive use of the mouse, the simultaneous presence of several programs (only one of which could be active at any one time), and many other features that were to appear with the emergence of different versions, such as Windows 3.11 for Workgroups (Intranet).

At the same time, the leading Microsoft programs, principally Word and Excel, were to benefit from the same development since from now on documents could be shared.

After a slow start due mainly to the relatively low power of the first machines, Windows was to establish itself quickly. Whereas under DOS use of the mouse was limited, it was to become essential under Windows. Drag and move, drag and drop, copy and paste, and cut and paste were to become major features.

The principles brought into play were to sow the seed of the OLE technology, which, under Windows 95, has been progressively adapted to the Internet under the name ActiveX.

All the new features provided by Windows from Version 3 onwards have been characterised by a flexibility and fluidity that lead to an intuitive user interface. At the same time, certain simple manoeuvres, such as mouse movements, have been enhanced and made more sophisticated. For example, Microsoft has introduced the Intellisense technology, making the mouse 'intelligent.'

Use of the right mouse button has grown, allowing access to advanced functions, such as the activation of context-sensitive menus, which hang near the spot that is clicked on. In this way, using a number of optimised movements, you can access menus, commands and options without going through the menu bar situated at the top of the screen. Better still, the mouse has become programmable and even context-programmable, which means that the same action will be different depending on the program in use. Overall, you can think of your PC as being as simple to use as the Macintosh but costing less and offering more power. Although in the beginning it was difficult to run Version 3.0 because of numerous and sometimes disheartening bugs, Version 3.1 remedied these drawbacks and won over the public.

Windows 95, 98 and NT

Windows 95 (Figure 7.2), Windows 98 and Windows NT use the same principles but with different aims and power. Windows 95 and 98 are directed at the PC whereas NT aims to become the operating system of future machines and platforms.

Although Version 3 of Windows could multi-task, it could only do so to a limited extent. The applications were active only in turn, even though certain background printing jobs could run at the same time, showing what was to come. Each application present could be accessed simultaneously by using the key combination Alt + Tab. However, if you exited an Excel application during a long task recalculating a folder, and switched to Word or File Manager, the previously exited application ceased to function even if it was still present. Windows 95 really does multi-task. The term is known as pre-emptive multi-tasking, which means that the operating system devotes a fixed and constant time to each application. A master system manages time sharing, making sure that no program forgets to hand back control, which was often the case in the previous version.

At the same time, Windows 95 and 98 provide access to the Internet: first with the Microsoft Plus! accessory software for Windows 95, and since with much-improved versions of the software built into Windows itself.

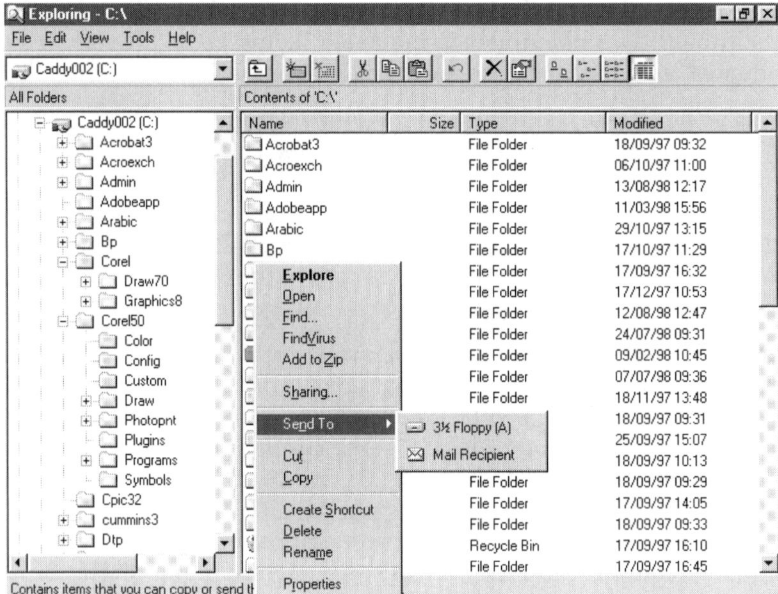

Figure 7.2 The user-friendly Windows 95 interface.

New facilities are characterised by progressive adaptation to the principles of the Internet, opening up the system to more extensive sharing of data with the outside world. The set of connection tools included in the new versions facilitate connection and make extensive use of electronic mail and standardised data exchange in all its forms, to the point that the graphical interface of Windows 98 looks just like that of the Internet, sometimes making it difficult for users looking at their screen to establish the difference between what belongs to their hard disk and what belongs to the outside world.

The numerous improvements that are appearing require more and more power. The latest operating systems work much better on Pentium IIIs and Fast Pentium IIs, and need at least 64 Mb of RAM and a 2 Gb hard disk. As for the systems being comfortable to use, this is improving substantially. The peripherals are benefiting from the same progress. The screens, in particular, deliver the advertised performance only if they are accompanied by powerful graphics cards with 16 + 1 Mb of high-speed graphics memory. Otherwise, displaying becomes excessively slow and it is irritating to navigate between two Internet sessions in order to display graphics. It could be said that Windows and its hardware are evolving as functions of each other, each pulling the other upwards and creating new markets with every move.

Windows NT, and its successor Windows 2000, differ from Windows 98 and Me in that they need more powerful computers and are aimed at business users with networks of PCs. Programs used with NT and 2000 are not always compatible with 98 and Me, and vice versa. In late 2001, these two separate collections of operating systems will merge into one, named Windows XP.

The benefits of Windows 98

Windows 98 is a not a new concept but rather a collection of small improvements providing a range of services and paving the way for Windows NT, which is destined to rule in the near future.

The new Windows 98 interface, which is oriented towards the use of 'pages', makes it easier to access files and the Control Panel and to customise the Start menu. Once everything is installed, there is the advantage that upgrades are available from the Internet, which gives users more autonomy. If you get a computer bug, or a version is improved, all you need to do is download the changes and install them.

Another major advance is the FAT 32, which has increased the available disk space by replacing the basic 32 kb blocks with smaller 4 kb ones. This reduces the space that was previously lost and thus optimises the read/write speed. It has been confirmed that on a 2 Gb disk containing 16 000 files, including a large number of small images, a FAT 32 provides 20–25% more memory (more than 400 Mb). Using the FAT 32 does not result in a loss of data. The system carries out the conversion transparently, provided that the disks have enough free space (approximately one-quarter of the surface of the disk) for the work to be carried out.

Eight screens at the same time

A major innovation, which brings Windows 98 closer to UNIX systems, has been the ability to have several screens open at the same time in order to monitor an application. Developers can have one screen for coding, one for developing windows and another for testing programs. Games fanatics can have, for example, an overall screen and a screen showing an enlarged section of their game. It is also possible to have several applications running at once in order to monitor the progress of tasks.

Other improvements

Other benefits of Windows 98 include:

- Register bases can be handled better.
- Disk drives function faster because the software that drives them has been improved.
- Windows 98 incorporates hundreds of new modem, screen, printer, network card and other drivers.

- It is now much easier to install and manage the USB.
- In the case of what is known as a fatal error, the Doctor Watson program will detect the error in a more user-friendly manner by providing the necessary details to understand the error.

For the experts

To be on the safe side, Windows 98 must be able to be reinstalled using a boot disk that manages the high memory. Note that if the Windows 98 boot disk does not do so, you must prepare it yourself. Here are the steps and code that must be followed in order to obtain the 445 kb or so that are required under DOS.

1. Use a standard Windows 95 (not Windows 98) boot disk
2. In the Config.sys program, add the following lines using a text editor:

```
device=c:\windows\himem.sys
device=c:\windows\emm386.exe noems
dos=high, umb
```

3. Replace all the 'device' instructions with 'devicehigh'
4. In the Autoexec.bat program, load the resident programs into the high memory using the Load High (LH) instruction. For example, to load the driver required to use the Windows 98 installation CD-ROM, type in:

```
lh a:\MSCDEX.EXE /D:MTMIDE01 /L:G
```

5. Resave the Autoexec.bat and Config.sys programs.
6. Install Windows 98 using the install program in the \codefr\ directory of the Windows 98 CD-ROM.

This will stop the system repeatedly refusing to install itself because of insufficient memory. If in doubt, contact somebody with some computing knowledge.

UNIX and Linux

Invented in 1970 in the Bell Laboratories by Ken Thompson and Kernigan Richtie, UNIX and the C Language put a stamp on their era by spreading computer knowledge both in American universities and in companies. The first to be created was the C Language, which was used to write the UNIX operating system. This progressively established itself as the language of computing in an age when even the idea of microcomputing had not been conceived. Because UNIX and C were the dominant languages taught at university, they became the most commonly used by computer engineers.

For this reason, as soon as the power of PCs allowed it, a number of users preferred to install UNIX on their PCs. At the same time, a strand of thought from the USA, extolling free of charge software programs and operating systems, progressively established itself and gave rise to a family of products that were free, high-performing and evolutionary. Among these were GNU and Linux.

The free part of UNIX, GNU, represents a recursive acronym for 'GNUs not UNIX'.

Linux, which is also free, is very similar and has become increasingly more widespread on PCs, with more and more books being written on the subject.

Today, you are recommended to use Windows 98 or Windows 95 in order to take advantage of the numerous multimedia possibilities of the software available. Although many users remain faithful to Windows 3.1 or enjoy using Linux, the future is likely to belong to Windows 98 and NT.

Figure 7.3 Icons contribute towards making an operating system user-friendly.

8 Multimedia

The features of multimedia

The sound card

The graphics card

The CD-ROM

The DVD-ROM

The scanner

The digital camera

The features of multimedia

Multimedia is the combination of sound, words and pictures to create stunning aesthetic effects, allowing you to explore and develop your creative talent.

Combining the senses

In his book *The Doors of Perception*, Aldous Huxley explains the phenomenon of synaesthesia, making one sense correspond to another sense. Today, thanks to multimedia, you can buy CD-ROMs that allow you to do just that. For example, there are ground-breaking CD-ROMs that allow you to listen to a musical piece by Debussy, read a text by Verlaine and admire a watercolour painting by Monet on your computer screen all at the same time.

Creativity and play

A computer equipped with a CD-ROM drive and sound card is a computer that allows you to learn and play. The play dimension of multimedia no longer needs to be proved. Just look at the figures and you'll get an idea: of CD-ROM sales in 1995, games represented 57% of the market, art and culture 22%, education 16%, and erotica 5%.

A multimedia computer

To support a multimedia installation, your computer must have the following minimum characteristics (Figure 8.1):

- a 486 or Pentium processor with 256 kb of cache memory
- at least 16 Mb of RAM
- SVGA graphics screen card
- 16-bit sound card
- external speakers
- 1.5 Gb hard disk.

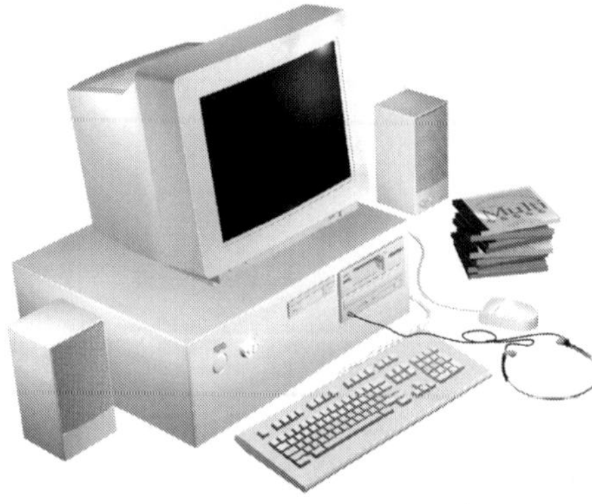

Figure 8.1 Your multimedia PC.

This means that you don't necessarily need the latest model of computer to support multimedia.

The sound card

The sound card (Figure 8.2) plugs into an expansion slot on the motherboard. This is what converts analogue data (sound) into digital data (the sound file). All sound cards have connectors for the microphone inputs, and outputs to the enclosures. The SoundBlaster is an established make.

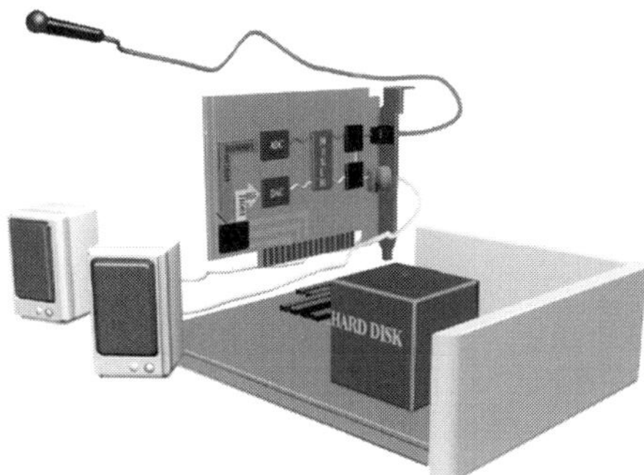

Figure 8.2 Layout of the sound cards in the central unit.

You also use the sound card for connecting your computer to speakers, microphones and musical instruments compatible with the MIDI standard.

Sound files

The WAV format is the standard for Windows sound files on PCs. However, the MP3 format, which is compressed ten times without a loss in quality, is much better. 1 Mb of MP3 corresponds to approximately one minute of sound. This means you can get approximately 12 hours of music or speech, on a single CD. A rival format to MP3 is Microsoft's WMA (Windows Media Audio), which offers better sound quality and slightly smaller file sizes.

There are other standards on the market, particularly the ASJ, AU or Real Audio (.ra) formats, which allow access to some radio stations via the Internet. However, there is little chance that these will displace MP3 as the standard format.

Music files

A MIDI file is like the old-fashioned piano roll: it uses the sounds stored in your sound card to play the notes in the file, so the quality of the result will depend to some degree on the quality of your card's sounds.

More and more PCs have a MIDI connector as a result of the increasing success of multimedia.

The graphics card

The graphics card makes it possible to work creatively (receiving/ sending), and manages your screen. This card translates the signals handled by the monitor into a format that the monitor can display.

In general, this screen card is integrated into the motherboard. Sometimes, it is an expansion card that is plugged into one of the expansion slots.

The image processing speed determines the number of colours that can be displayed.

The memory capacity of screen cards is on average 1 Mb or more, supporting up to 16.7 million colours with a resolution of 640 × 480 pixels.

The SVGA card

SVGA cards represent the current standard. They add the 800 × 600 and 1024 × 768 graphics modes to the VGA card capabilities. With a suitable card driver, you can display up to 1600 × 1200.

There are various graphics cards that specialise in either 2D or 3D. There is no point in purchasing a 3D card, such as a 3DFX II, if you do not use your computer to play games or create computer-generated images.

A good card has a graphics memory of at least 16 Mb. This comfortably allows you to properly run graphics programs, which always require a large amount of memory.

The CD-ROM

CD-ROM (Figure 8.3) means compact disc read only memory. ROM, or read only memory, cannot be erased or rewritten, and allows reading only. The CD-ROM stores any type of digitised information, that is information translated into binary (0s and 1s), the language that the computer understands.

Storage

The CD-ROM has a storage capacity of 650 Mb of data, which corresponds to around one hundred books on a single disk.

Installation

Once you have slid your CD-ROM into the CD-ROM drive, how do you install it?

- **The Device Manager:** the components of the computer, whether CD-ROM drives or graphics cards, for example, are managed by a software program called the device manager. This must be configured to fetch the data from the peripherals.

- **Install.exe:** there are two types of CD-ROM: those that run as soon as they are put into the drive, and those that require information to be installed on the computer first.
- **The importance of Quicktime:** in order to display video sequences, the majority of CD-ROMs use the Quicktime software program.
- **Copy as little as possible:** the fewer CD-ROMs you install, the less you will clutter up your hard disk. Complete installation, which copies the application itself and other files as well, may occupy several megabytes.
- **Uninstall:** the best way of deleting everything after use is to run the Uninstaller program. You can also select **Add/Remove Programs** in the Windows 95 Control Panel.

Your version of Quicktime may conflict with the version loaded by the CD-ROM. For this reason, install the most recent version only.

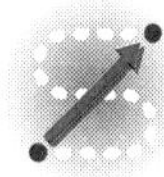

CD-ROMs wear out in the course of being used and should be cleaned from time to time. Grease spots or finger marks prevent the disk from being read correctly. CD-ROMs are covered with a very thin plastic film. To clean your CD-ROM wipe it with a clean, lint-free cloth in a straight line from centre to edge.

The production cycle

Several people are involved in producing a CD-ROM:

- The author is the creative inspiration behind the product. The author conceives the need for the CD-ROM, designs its features, sketches out a draft and submits it to the publisher. If there is agreement, a contract is signed with the author and production of the CD-ROM will begin. In three months, the CD-ROM may be finished.
- The associate designer helps the author in handling any aspects of content in which the latter is less of an expert. The associate designer will share any profits that are made.
- The programmer works together with the author to sort out aspects relating to programming and creating the CD-ROM interface and is responsible for implementing, point by point, the specification. The programmer is mentioned in the tripartite contract signed with the publishing house.
- The technicians supervise the work of the programmer and check, amongst other things, the effectiveness of the installation program.
- The marketing person, using the catalogue in which the future appearance of the CD-ROM is announced, canvases retail outlets, supermarkets and specialist shops, presents the product, outlines its area of interest, and sometimes performs demonstrations.
- The publisher, given the results of the first quarter's sales, for example, takes the decision to proceed with a second run of 1000 or 2000 copies, and to have it translated and marketed in other countries.

Manufacture

CD-ROMs are manufactured as follows:

- **Digitisation:** the elements that make up the data on the CD-ROM (sound, video, image, text) are translated into digital data.
- **Creation of the glass master:** the digitised data is sent for laser recording. The beam engraves the glass disc (glass master) with a pattern of hollows and bumps corresponding to the 0 and 1 binary data.
- **The nickel original:** from the glass disc, a nickel original called the 'father' is produced. This will be used as a mould.
- **Pressing:** plastic is injected into the mould, pressed and then cooled. The operation lasts four seconds. The digital data is engraved on the plastic disc.
- **Metallisation:** the plastic disc is covered with a thin layer of metal (aluminium) to allow it to be read with a laser beam.
- **Varnishing:** the aluminium layer is covered with a film of varnish.
- **Silk-screen printing:** this makes it possible to illustrate the CD-ROM with a colour image.

Figure 8.3 The CD-ROM.

The CD-ROM drive

CD-ROM drives may be installed internally inside the case, which makes it possible to save space on your desk, or externally, with the drive connected to a port located on the central unit.

The CD-ROM drive can be connected in two different ways:

- **IDE ATAPI:** the drive is connected to the IDE controller.
- **SCSI:** the drive forms part of a SCSI chain.

Setting the parameters

To set the multimedia parameters for your installations, carry out the following operations:

1. Click on **Start**.
2. Select **Settings**.
3. Select **Control Panel**.
4. Click on the **Multimedia** icon.

The Multimedia Properties dialog box opens on the screen (Figure 8.4). This contains five tabs: Audio, Video, MIDI, CD Music and Advanced.

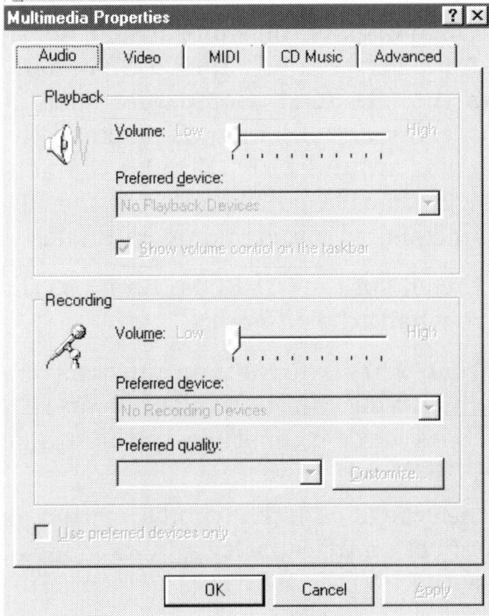

Figure 8.4 The Multimedia Properties dialog box allows you to set the sound, image and all the multimedia peripherals.

Speed of rotation

CD-ROM drives differ by their speeds of rotation. The oldest models run at a speed of 200–535 revolutions/minute, the most recent models run at 1680–4320 revolutions/minute. During these rotations, the CD-ROM transfers the digitised data in the form of kilobytes per second (kb/s). The first models had a transmission rate of 150 kb/s, that is they transmitted 150 000 characters per second to the computer. This transmission rate is four to five times greater than that of the hard disk. As it was insufficient for videos, it was necessary to increase the speeds.

- Dual-speed: 2 × 150, i.e. 300 kb/s CD-ROM
- Quad-speed: 4 × 150, i.e. 600 kb/s CD-ROM
- 8-speed: 8 × 150, i.e. 1200 kb/s CD-ROM
- And so on up to 24 and 32 or 4.8 Mb/s

In 1998, the 24X CD constituted the new standard. However, it should be emphasised that the four-speed CD suffices for the majority of applications.

Reading

The data are read from the CD-ROM using a laser beam. This scans the surface of the disc in order to interpret the differences in relief corresponding to the binary data: 0 = hollow, 1 = filled.

The DVD-ROM

The DVD-ROM, or digital video disc, is the same size as a CD-ROM (12 cm diameter). It stores between 4.7 and 8.5 Gb of data, almost 13 times more than the CD-ROM. Companies such as Panasonic, Pioneer, Philips, Sony and Toshiba all make DVD-ROMs. DVD-ROM drives sell at around £100. Besides the data storage capacities that are eight times larger than that of the CD-ROM, the DVD-ROM offers unequalled sound and image quality.

DVD-ROM does not herald the end of the CD-ROM. Both use the same format and interface. So what's the difference?

- **The drive:** in order to read a DVD-ROM, you must have a DVD-ROM drive, into which you can also insert your CD-ROMs. The DVD-ROM is backwards-compatible, so there is no need to throw out your CD-ROM collection.
- **The storage capacity:** the type of data that can be written on this new medium has an effect on its capacity and its mode of operation. This is because the DVD-ROM can store computer data and video films, which occupy much more memory and space.
- The laser for the DVD is 10 times more accurate than that used by current CD-ROM drives.

The transition between CD-ROM and DVD-ROM will not take place overnight. Publishers and manufacturers are progressively preparing for this new technological change by devising not only new drives but also computers specially dedicated to the DVD-ROM.

Pixel is a contraction of 'picture element.' The dot is the smallest level of the image. Sixteen grey levels require a pixel of four minipixels each side. Grey is therefore much more difficult to produce than colour.

The scanner

The scanner breaks down documents (photographs, graphs, text, etc.) into the form of a series of dots, or pixels, which can be used by the computer. Depending on the amount of light each square contains, the scanner chooses a shade of white or black. The most advanced scanners take grey levels into consideration.

Once the document is digitised and stored on the hard disk, you can work on it. If you have scanned an image, you can rework it using graphics software.

Digitising the image results in a loss of definition. The greater the increase in number of pixels, the greater the improvement in definition.

There are different types of scanner.

- **The flatbed scanner:** this works on the photocopier principle, except that it sends its results to a file instead of printing them on a sheet of paper (Figure 3.5).

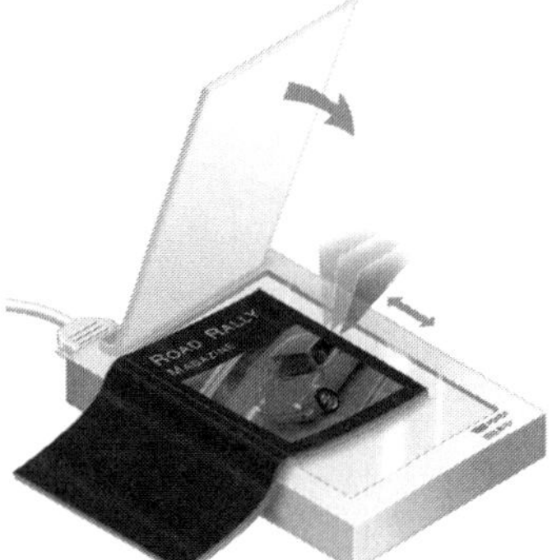

Figure 8.5 A flatbed scanner.

- **The hand-held scanner:** inexpensive, this is sufficient for scanning small documents, but is unsatisfactory for larger formats, even complete pages (Figure 3.6).

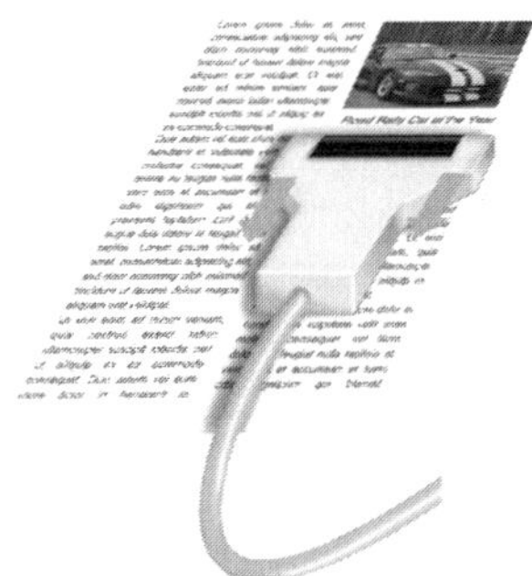

Figure 8.6 A hand-held scanner.

- **The platen type scanner:** this was the first-generation scanner. Not very practical, it accepts only detached sheets, so you cannot, for example, scan a sheet in a book without cutting it out first. The platen type scanner, also called a drum scanner, has become almost obsolete, and should be avoided for home use.

It is pointless spending a fortune on a scanner for general use; perfectly satisfactory models may be bought for as little as £90.

The digital camera

Digital cameras are becoming more and more popular. Standard consumer models will cost between £80 and £2000. The fact that you can buy one for as little as £80 shows how fast the technology is advancing.

If you already have a scanner, what are the advantages of having a digital camera?

- The film is free.
- There is no need to use a scanner to transfer photos.
- You can load your photos directly on to your laptop.

And the disadvantages?

- They cost more than conventional cameras.
- The resolution is not as good as with a conventional camera.
- You can take a limited number of photos before you have to unload the memory card.

A digital camera replaces the film with pixel matrices, each one of which senses light and transmits the results to the memory in the form of a card. The sensors use a technique called CCD (charge-coupled device), which converts the light into digital data.

Your photos are stored on flash cards (CompactFlash) or Smartmedia. Some Sony models even have a built-in disk drive. The number of photos you can store depends on the definition (the size of the photo in pixels) and the compression mode (JPEG) used, which strikes a balance between quality and storage volume.

Bottom-of-the-range models create photos with a definition of 240 × 320, 480 × 320, or 640 × 480 pixels. However, certain models have a definition of 1280 × 960 or even 1600 × 1200 pixels, such as the Sony DSC-F505. To obtain high-quality printed photos, it is better to choose a higher definition (1024 × 768 pixels or more). High-quality models, which often have a built-in flash and zoom, can cost less than £500. For a little more, you can get models with more than a million pixels plus 8 Mb memory cards and macro-photography functions. The best-known makes are Canon, Epson, Casio, Agfa, Kodak and Sony.

Once you have copied your digital or scanned-in photos on to your computer, you can use one of the many retouching programs available on the market. By acting on the colour components, these allow you to improve or 'save' defective documents. For example, you can improve the appearance of old, poor-quality photographs and lessen the effect of over- or underexposure and colour shift. Scanners and digital cameras often come with these software programs included.

9 The Internet

The computer

The modem

The subscription

Access providers

The connection

The Internet, which allows you to make contact with people and access information from anywhere in the world, has revolutionised the art of communication, making it simpler, more direct and far more suited to the needs of today. Thanks to its amazing speed, the Internet is able to provide you with almost instant answers to your questions and allows you to converse with people whose geographical distance from you means you would never have met under normal circumstances. What is more, it is so simple that anybody, not just computer programmers, can use it. By simply clicking on the mouse, you can obtain information on whatever subject you want, from the latest news to a favourite recipe. More and more people are coming to realise the importance of the Internet as an indispensable information and communication tool. So much so that in many homes it is now considered as natural to be online as it is to have a phone, television or car.

The computer

You can access the Internet with just about any type of computer, whether it is a Mac or a PC. To access the Internet, it is recommended that you have a minimum of:

- A PC with a 75 or Pentium processor.
- A hard disk with a minimum capacity of 1 Gb. While you only need a few tens of Mb for installing the programs needed to gain access to the Internet, you can very quickly download several hundred of them.
- A 16 Mb random access memory, which will allow you to open several Internet applications simultaneously (electronic mail, Web, file transfer).
- A SoundBlaster-compatible sound card and speakers if you want to download recordings. The speakers may be integrated or external, with or without bass enclosures. Audio cards are essential for games and CD-ROMs.
- A graphics card.
- A CD-ROM drive: this is essential if you opt for an IAP (Internet access provider) that offers you the connection kit only on CD-ROM.
- A 15" or 17" screen. These sizes will allow for more comfortable viewing.

The modem

The modem (short for 'modulator/demodulator') is one of your PC's peripherals, increasingly being incorporated into the computer. Using it, your PC can communicate with the rest of the network via a telephone line (Figure 9.1).

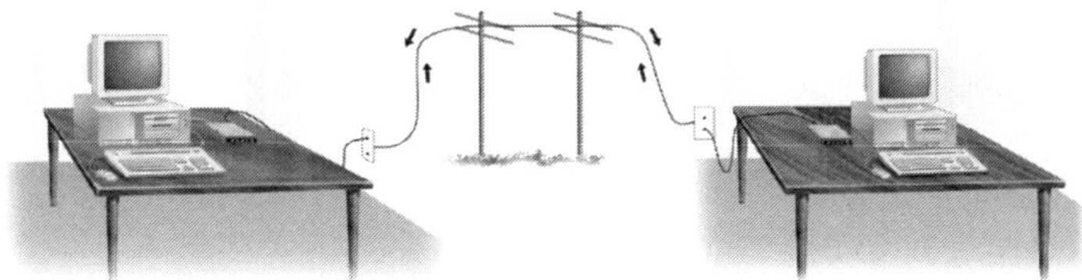

Figure 9.1 The PC communicates with the rest of the network via a telephone line, cable or satellite.

At a speed of 36,000 bps, a page of text containing 5000 characters will take about one second to reach its destination. At a speed of 56,000 bps, the transmission time falls to five eighths of a second.

Files sent to or received from the Internet pass through your modem. Its quality and price vary according to its data transmission speed, expressed in bits per second (bps). If possible, choose a powerful 56 000-bps modem. The average price of a modem is around £50.

External and internal modems

The modem may be external or internal.

- **Internal:** the modem comes in the form of a card that can be plugged into a slot (Figure 9.2).

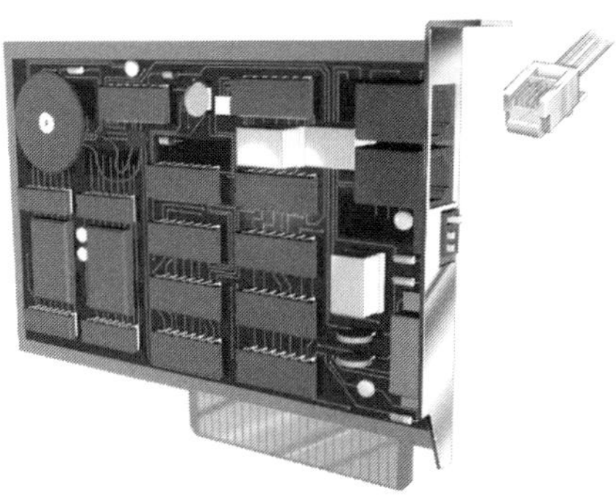

Figure 9.2 An internal modem.

- **External:** the equivalent of the modem card is incorporated in an external case and connected to the computer by means of a cable fastened to one of the communication ports (Figure 9.3).

You can install your modem on the same line as your telephone.

You can make or receive telephone calls when you are not using the Internet, and use the Internet when you are not on the telephone. You won't be able to use the Internet and make a call at the same time if you use the same line.

Figure 9.3 An external modem.

The subscription

Nowadays, all access providers offer a similar type of subscription. You can connect to the Internet whenever you want, and you'll pay the provider a fixed monthly or annual subscription fee rather than paying for the time you spend online. You will also have to pay the cost of local calls when you connect, which will be added to your telephone bill. Many access providers actually charge no subscription fee at all, taking a small percentage of the cost of the connection phone call from your telephone company instead.

Most services offer a mailbox and space for creating your own Web pages.

Online services

The simple subscription costs from £5 to £10 per month. For this price, you receive a credit of connection hours to one of the main online servers, such as Compuserve or AOL, or to a small, often excellent local server.

The large commercial services are electronic publishing services that offer the conventional Internet services, such as e-mail and newsgroups, as well as a fairly extensive range of diverse information designed and produced by the service itself. You will find among other things:

- daily newspapers
- tourist information
- mail-order catalogues
- games.

One advantage of these commercial services is that they offer you access to their own banks of information, which is inaccessible to other Web users.

The main drawback of such commercial services is that they invoice you for everything, from the time of use to the amount of information requested. Each unit of mail is invoiced, as is each unit of connection time.

It is better to start by carefully analysing your needs and taking into account that they might change. You can then choose a suitable solution.

Access providers

Internet access provider (IAPs) give you the following services for a subscription of between zero and £15 a month:

- no restrictions or charges for the time you spend online;
- a connection kit;
- a hotline service, i.e. a telephone support service intended to help you out if you have difficulties.

At the moment there are several hundred providers in the UK. Some are specific to a particular area of the country and others offer UK-wide coverage.

All offer email, World Wide Web, FTP, Telnet, Gopher, IRC and newsgroup access. Some offer ISDN and other extras.

The majority of access providers will offer you local telephone access, which will allow you to contact family and friends the other side of the world for the price of a local call.

Be aware that certain hotline services, or services claiming to be such, can be always busy or impossible to contact. They also cost a premium.

If in doubt, ask for advice from members of Internet discussion groups or mailing lists. You will find them to be very well informed and often fiercely opposed to service providers who do not keep their promises. Strangely enough, you will find that some access providers are excellent in some areas (if you live close to an Internet service provider) and much less so in others (if you live in an area that is not very well served).

The connection

Before connecting your modem, you must first configure it.

Configuring your modem

If you have not yet bought your modem, choose an external model if you can, since this leaves a slot free for other extensions (scanners, sound or graphics cards, SCSI cards).

1. Connect your modem to the serial port (COM port) and to a telephone line. If your computer is equipped with an internal modem, you just need to connect it to the telephone socket.

2. Check that the serial port supports the UART 16550 AF standard provided for high-speed transmission rates (this should be in the instruction booklet that came with your PC).

The following operations are far from straightforward. To carry them out, use the documentation supplied by your access provider, but do not hesitate to enlist the help of a computer specialist ... if necessary.

If you are working with Windows 3.1:

1. Install the modem driver manager using the diskette supplied.
2. Open the **Program Manager**.
3. Select the **Accessories** group.
4. Double-click on the **Terminal** icon.
5. Select the **Communications** command in the dialog box.
6. Define the settings for your modem in the Settings menu: transmission speed, data bits, stop bits, parity and flow control.

If you are working with Windows 95 or 98:

1. Click on **Start**.
2. Select the **Settings** menu.
3. Open the **Control Panel** submenu.
4. Click on the **Add New Hardware** icon (Figure 9.4).

Figure 9.4 The Windows 98 Add New Hardware icon.

5. The Add New Hardware Wizard opens on the screen (Figure 9.5).
6. Click on **Next**. Answer the questions that appear. If your hardware is plug-and-play (which would be logical), Windows 98 will detect it. If not, you will be asked to choose between

automatic detection and selecting from a list. Do not worry about which one you choose; either one will do. Let's say you decide to select from a list.

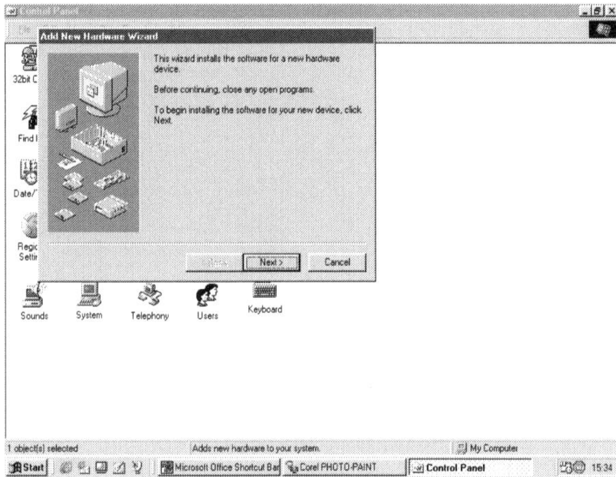

Figure 9.5 The Add New Hardware Wizard guides you step by step.

7. Select the Modem option (Figure 9.6).

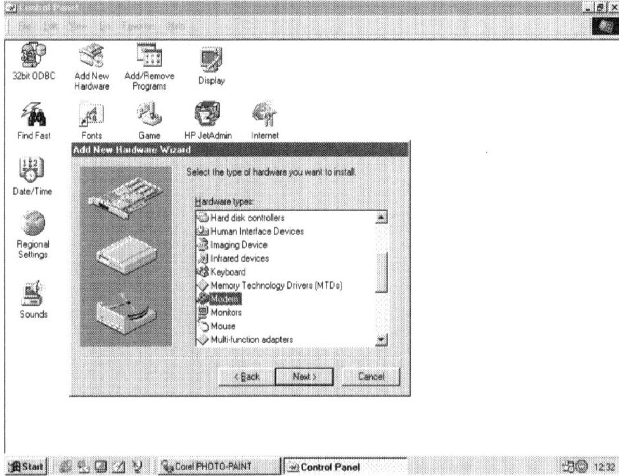

Figure 9.6 Select the Modem option.

8. The Install New Modem dialog box informs you that Windows is preparing to detect your modem (Figure 9.7).
9. Select the name of your modem manufacturer.
10. Click on **Next**.
11. Windows copies the data on to your hard disk.

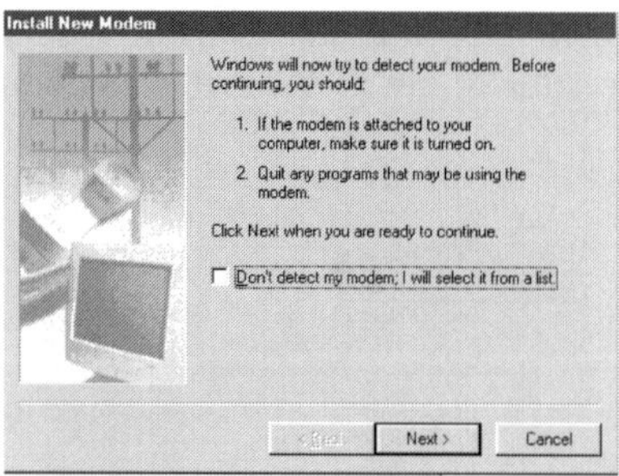

Figure 9.7 If your modem is not recognised as plug-and-play, either choose automatic detection or select one from a list.

12. You should now indicate which communication port is to be used by the modem. In the majority of cases it is COM2. Select COM2.
13. Click on **Next**.
14. The Location Information dialog box opens on the screen. You must provide information on your current location so that your calls are dialled correctly. You must specify which country you live in and in which telephone area you are situated.
15. Return to the **Control Panel**.
16. Click on the **Modem** icon. The Modems Properties dialog box opens on the screen (Figure 9.8).

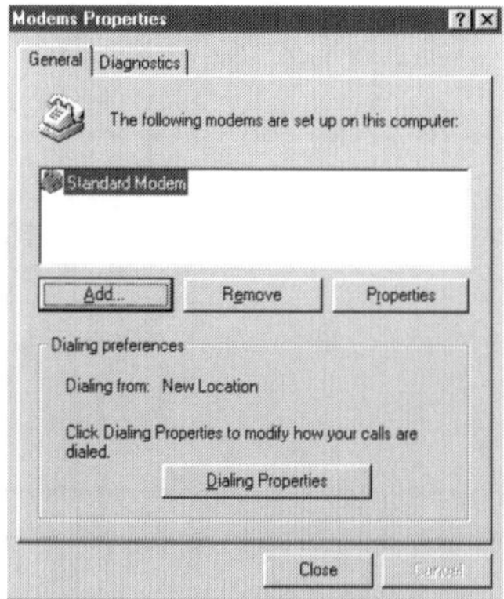

Figure 9.8 The Modem Properties dialog box.

17. Click on the **Properties** tab to configure your hardware.

    – . . . .The General tab concerns the settings for the speaker volume and the speed chosen for making the connections.

    – .The Connection tab concerns the connection parameters and call parameters.

For the time being, use the default call parameters.

18. Select the **Connection** tab, then click on the **Port Settings** command button. This new dialog box enables you to set the size of the buffers (Figure 9.9).

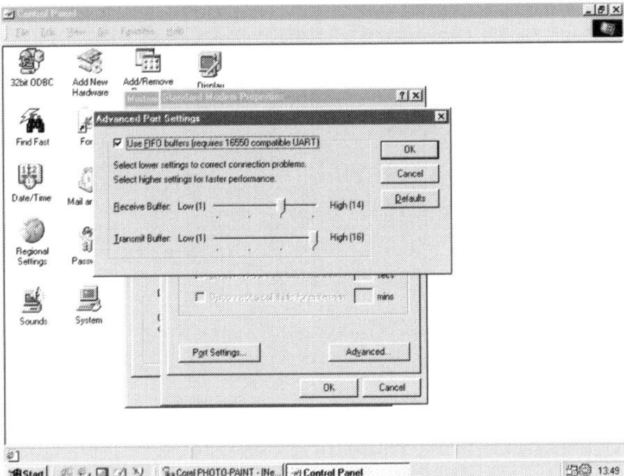

Figure 9.9 The Advanced Port Settings dialog box allows you to adjust the buffer size.

Configuring your connection

Once your connection kit diskettes are installed, the only thing that remains for you to do is to enter the data supplied by your access provider.

What does connecting your computer to the Internet mean? It is quite simply giving it the capability of making contact with other computers on the network. The two keystones of this computer-to-computer dialog are:

- Internet Protocol (IP)
- Transmission Control Protocol (TCP)

Current terminology speaks of TCP/IP. These two protocols take care of breaking down the information into data packets, transferring them, and then unloading them in the correct order. Here is how to proceed.

With Windows 3.1:

The first operation consists of installing a TCP/IP program suite. With Windows 3.1, the most common is Trumpet Winsock, which you should as a rule find in your connection kit.

1. Start **Trumpet Winsock**.
2. From the **File** menu, select **Setup**.
3. Define the transmission protocol in the dialog box that appears on the screen. In the majority of cases, this is Internal PPP.

4. Specify the port used by your modem in the SLIP Port section.
5. Indicate the transmission speed in the Baud Rate section.
6. Specify the ID of your access provider.
7. Specify the gateway used in the Name Server and Default Gateway sections.
8. Click on **OK** to return to the main menu.
9. Open the **Dialler** menu.
10. Start the program SETUP.CMD.
11. Enter the telephone number of your access provider in the dialog box that appears on the screen.
12. Confirm by clicking on **OK**.
13. Enter your user name or login.
14. Confirm by clicking on **OK**.
15. Enter your password.
16. Close Trumpet Winsock.
17. Restart Trumpet Winsock.
18. Choose the **Dialler** menu.
19. Select the **Login** command to activate your connection.

With Windows 95 or 98:

1. Open the **Control Panel**.
2. Select the **Network** icon.
3. Click on the **Add** button of the Network dialog box.
4. Select **Protocol** in the list then, click on Add in the Select Network Component Type dialog box (Figure 9.10).

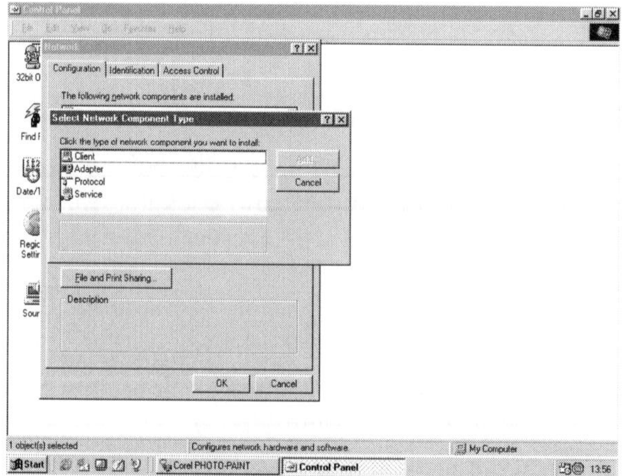

Figure 9.10 Click on the Add option in the Select Network Component Type dialog box. This example allows you to install a modem cable connected to an Ethernet card

5. Choose **Microsoft** in the Manufacturers section of the dialog box.
6. Choose TCP/IP in the Network Protocols scrolling list.
7. Confirm by clicking on **OK**. You return to the Network dialog box.
8. Select the protocol you have just added.
9. Click on **Properties**.
10. Select the IP Address tab.
11. Tick the box **Obtain an IP Address automatically** (Figure 9.11).

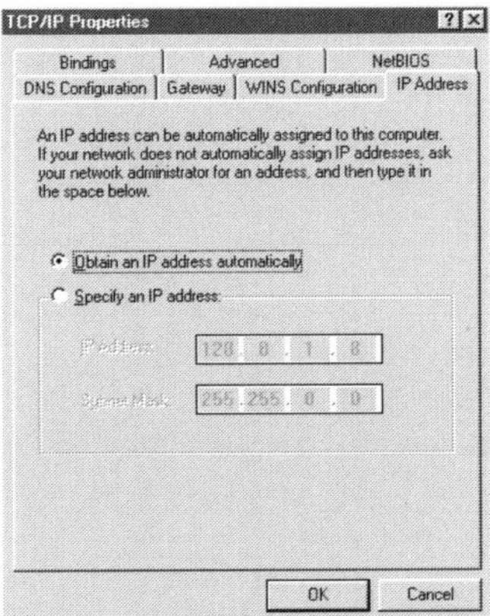

Figure 9.11 Tick the box Obtain an IP Address automatically in the TCP/IP Properties dialog box on the IP Address tab.

12. Select the **WINS Configuration** tab.
13. Select the **Disable WINS Resolution** option.
14. Select the **Gateway** tab.
15. Enter the address of your access provider.
16. Click on **Add**.
17. Select the **DNS Configuration** tab.
18. In the Domain text field, enter the name of your access provider.
19. In the Host text field, enter your name.
20. In the DNS Server Search Order field, enter the numbers that have been sent to you by your access provider.
21. Confirm by clicking on **OK**.
22. Close again.
23. Click on **Start**.
24. Select the **Programs** menu.

25. Select the **Accessories** submenu.
26. Click on the **Dial-Up Network Access** option.
27. Double-click on the **New Connection** icon.
28. Assign a name to this connection (Figure 9.12).

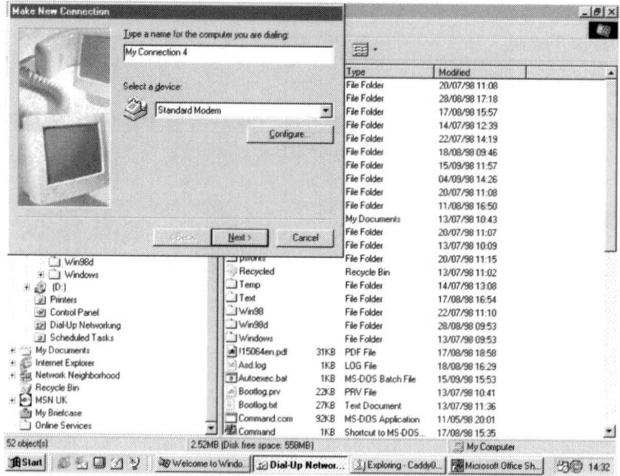

Figure 9.12 The New Connection dialog box enables you to assign a name to your connection.

29. Enter the number of the server of your access provider.
30. Click on **Finish**.
31. Select the **Connection** icon.
32. Click on **Configure**.
33. Select the **Options** tab.
34. Tick the box **Bring up terminal window after dialing**, then tick the box **Display modem status** (Figure 9.13).

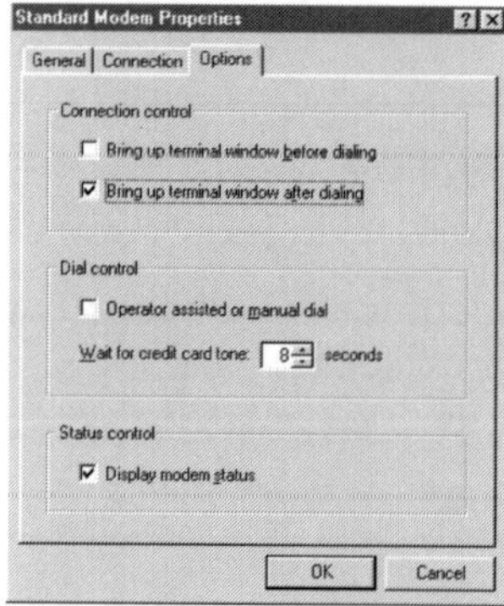

Figure 9.13 Tick the box Bring up terminal window after dialing, then tick the box Display modem status.

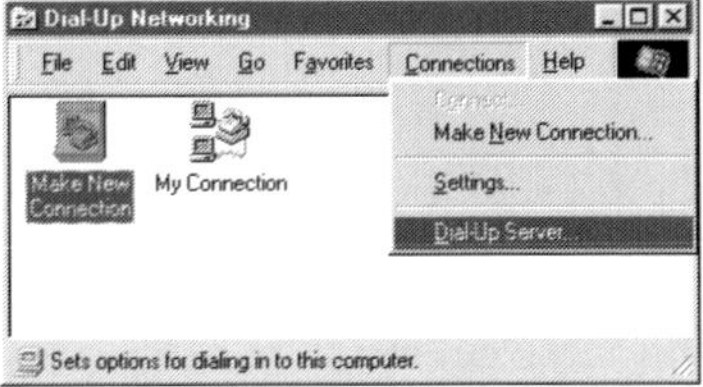

Figure 9.14 Open the Connections menu of the Dial-Up Networking dialog box, then click on the Dial-Up Server option

35. Open the **Connections** menu of the Dial-Up Networking dialog box.
36. Select **Dial-Up Server**.
37. Click on the **Server Type** command button.
38. Select the TCP/IP protocol.
39. Request the TCP/IP settings.
40. Select the options IP address assigned by server and addresses of the named server assigned by server, Use IP header compression, and finally Use Default Gateway for the Dial-Up Network.
41. Activate your connection by double-clicking on the **My Connection** icon.
42. The Connect to dialog box asks you for your password and user name (Figure 9.15).

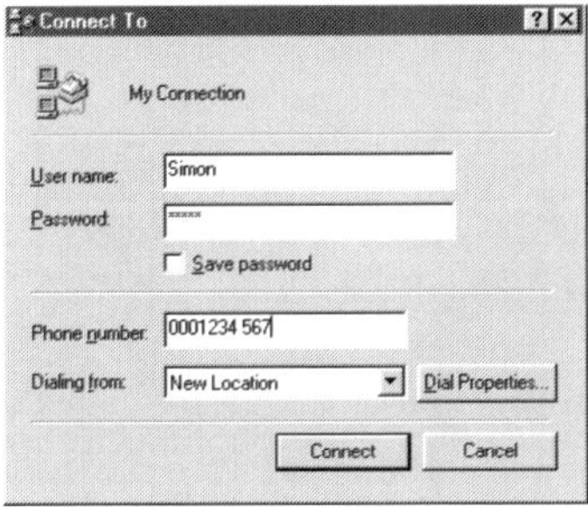

Figure 9.15 The dialog box that allows the connection to be initiated.

43. Click on the **Connect** button.
44. You will hear the modem dialing. The icon at the bottom left of the dialog box will flicker.
45. You should now be connected to the Internet.

The work corner

10

Workstation ergonomics

Sharing a computer

Visual comfort

Comfortable surroundings

The work station

Teleworking

Workstation ergonomics

Ergonomics is the study and research of the methodical organisation of work and the development of equipment adapted to workers' needs. Over time, the term 'ergonomics' has also come to cover the quality of life and the comfort of the user. Workstation ergonomics means feeling good when you are working.

Sharing a computer

The first factor you must take into consideration when choosing an area in which to install your PC is the number of users. Is it a PC that you alone are going to use, or will you share it with other members of the family, your children for example? If this is the case, it is better to organise a place with easy access.

For young users, a sturdy and adjustable chair is essential, as is a solid and resistant keyboard. Do not allow your children to eat or drink while using the keyboard, and teach them to leave the computer and accessories such as diskettes and printouts as they found them.

Visual comfort

Many computer users think that working on a computer damages the eyes, but studies carried out so far do not indicate conclusively that working on a screen harms your eyesight. On the other hand, if you unknowingly suffer from poor eyesight, it is possible that a series of sessions on a computer will reveal it.

Eye strain

When you use a screen, your eye muscles are forced to work repetitively and intensely. This is why the majority of eye problems caused by the use of computers are related to eye strain. If you feel this type of fatigue coming on, the simplest thing to do is give yourself 15 or 20 minutes' break.

The most common sight problems are redness, watering, blurred vision, double vision and headaches.

The cause of your problems could be one or more of the following:

- **Length of time working facing the screen:** two hours continuously facing the screen is inadvisable. It is difficult to draw up valid rules for everybody, so listen to your personal warning signals and take breaks accordingly. Health and safety guidelines recommend taking a break every 20 minutes.
- **Lighting environment:** optimum comfort depends on the contrast and intensity of the light that reflects off the visual fields and surfaces you are using. Indirect lighting (e.g. a halogen lamp pointed towards the ceiling or the wall) is often more pleasant to work in than direct light.

- **Quality of the documents to be input:** the presentation and legibility of documents are not always as good as they could be. Be particular: refuse to type documents if you consider them difficult to read; likewise, remember to produce legible and neat documents yourself.

Comfortable surroundings

Here are a few suggestions for obtaining the best possible comfort.

Lighting

For optimum comfort, try to observe the following conditions:

- A satisfactorily bright overall visual field, with no reflections on the screen.
- Sufficient contrast between the brightness of the screen background and the brightness of the characters.
- A ratio of brightness between the screen, the document and the peripheral visual field.

As a general rule, make sure that the background of your screen is not too dark so that it does not contrast too much with light-coloured work surfaces.

Sources of glare should be excluded entirely:

- Do not face a window.
- Do not have your back to a window.
- Use indirect lighting, together with an antiglare screen over the monitor.
- Arrange individual lights around the work surface.

The work surface lighting must be able to be positioned according to your requirements.

It is advisable to have some sort of movable protection against the sun in the work room, for example:

- venetian blinds with slats that can be angled
- mesh fabric blinds
- net curtains.

There are three types of artificial lighting:

- direct: 90% of radiation downwards
- semidirect: 50% of radiation downwards
- indirect: 90% of radiation upwards.

In your work room, do not use:

- vivid colours
- shiny surfaces
- accentuated geometric shapes.

Sound

The presence of sources of sound that differ from those generated by the workstation itself can be a disturbing factor.

The consequences of these annoying factors immediately make themselves felt, and therefore impinge on the quality of your work, leading to, for example:

- headaches
- tension
- loss of concentration
- decrease in the ability to think
- decrease in productivity.

The decibel tolerance thresholds for sounds are:

- 30–40 decibels: quiet
- 50–60 decibels: noisy
- 60–70 decibels: difficulty hearing over the phone
- 80+ decibels: very noisy

The noisiest things in a work room are the telephone, the printer and the fax machine. There are different ways of reducing the sound intensity of a room and the noisiest work tools:

To work comfortably for a long time, avoid a sound environment above 50 decibels.

- use a sound-proofing device
- decrease the telephone ringing volume
- use sound-absorbent telephone booth panels
- use sound-absorbent ceilings
- insulate the walls

The workstation

The workstation must be as comfortable and attractive as possible. Given that you may spend several hours a day there over a number of years, it is essential that you feel good about it. It is inevitable that it will have an effect on your morale, your enthusiasm for work, and your creativity.

Do not hesitate to give it a personal touch. If you telework, you have complete room to manoeuvre. If you work for an employer, you will inevitably be dependent on an existing work plan and budget.

Do not be afraid to brighten up your work space. Be innovative, and improve depressing working conditions for you and your colleagues.

Here are a few suggestions:

- Repaint the walls.
- Change the type of lamp (choose halogen lamps rather than neon ones).

- Buy some plants.
- Install some brightly coloured venetian blinds.
- Decorate your office with paintings or familiar objects.
- Add a few (colourful) personal touches.

Posture

The posture chosen for working is fundamental. Sustained stress on the vertebral column in a poor position may cause fatigue and, in the long term, painful and sometimes permanent backaches. The first rule is therefore to find a table/seat/body/hand relationship that allows you to comfortably work for a long time (Figure 10.1).

Symptoms such as aches in the back, neck, shoulders, arms and wrists may entail curvature of the vertebral column, muscular pains, varicose veins, chronic fatigue and headaches. The symptoms are warning signals: do not take them lightly!

Figure 10.1 The ideal working position.

The work surface

The work surface must be functional, practical and uncluttered.

- The height of the surface on which the screen and computer rest must be 65–75 cm. For short people, a footrest is essential.
- The horizontal area of the work surface must be at least 80 × 120 cm.
- The depth for the knees and legs should usually be 90 cm so that they do not hit the uprights of the work surface.

The screen

- The position of the display screen in terms of the distance from your eyes must be 50–70 cm.
- The slope of the front of the screen must be 15–20°.
- You must be able to pivot and rotate in several directions.

The seat

The seat must be chosen with regard to your:

- back shape
- blood circulation
- body shape and size.

Figure 10.2 Your day-to-day work corner.

It must be fitted with castors if you have cause to pivot frequently. It may be fitted with armrests, but these should not hinder the mobility of your arms and hands.

The keyboard

The ergonomic keyboard reduces the curvature of the wrist during typing to a minimum (see Chapter 3).

The ten commandments

- The level of the eyes should be about 1.15 m from the ground, with a standard seat height of 40–45 cm.
- The keyboard must be 70–80 cm above the ground.
- The seat back must be adjustable to match the back shape for each person who will be using the PC.
- The height of the seat must be adjustable.
- The seat must pivot and be fitted with castors if movements and rotations are frequent and necessary.
- The seat must not have armrests that hinder the mobility of the arms.
- There must be a footrest for short people.
- The height between the seat and the table must be 20–30 cm so that there is sufficient room for the knees.
- The screen must be at right angles to the plane of vision.
- Use a copyholder, located 70 cm from the screen, if inputting is the main activity of your job.

Workstation ergonomics should be taken very seriously. It has an effect on both the quality of your work and your psychological well-being. Do not add stress to stress! Professional life is often quite difficult enough. Make sure that your working environment is as pleasant as possible in order to spare you unnecessary pain and upset, anxiety, chronic fatigue, appetite problems and, of course, aggressiveness.

Conquering the working environment is very often the result of conquering yourself. Create a pleasant and comfortable environment and you will find that you become more motivated in your work.

Teleworking

Your computer need not only be for leisure and games – you can also use it to earn a living. Along with a printer, fax machine, telephone, modem and Internet connection, you can use your PC to conduct business at local, regional or even global levels from the comfort of your own home.

Advantages

- **Freedom:** teleworking allows you to be your own boss, with no more duties to perform other than your own. You no longer need work in difficult surroundings and circumstances. Instead, you are free to do whatever you want.
- **No more travelling:** in recent years, the time spent commuting to and from the workplace has increased greatly in urban areas. Not only does travelling waste a lot of our time, it also generates significant fatigue and stress.
- **Savings:** teleworking allows you to save money on travelling expenses and clothes.
- **A tailor-made job:** because you have chosen to work for yourself, there is no conflict between what you consider should be done and what you actually do.
- **Job creation:** in developing your own work situation, you are bound to have opened one or more markets. These opportunities are beneficial not only to you but may also benefit others. In the course of time, you may – if your business goes well – become an employer yourself.

Disadvantages

- **Freedom:** some people attracted by the prospect of teleworking quickly become disillusioned. Remember that teleworking is not for everyone. Some people feel reassured by the presence of an employer, a structured organisation, and the regularity of pay slips. Confronted with complete freedom, they may very well slip into bad habits and laziness.
- **Lack of stress:** many of us function on surges of adrenaline and stress. But when you are working on your own at home, how do you generate this atmosphere of stress and competition? Stress is an essential regulator of tension. How do you

recover from tension when you are alone, facing your computer screen?

- **The psychological aspect:** some people are terrified of solitude. They have a vital need for conversation and contact, and adapt very badly to working on their own. Before starting to work from home, you must make sure that you have the right temperament.
- **Working 24 hours a day:** when you start up, it is tempting to work 24 hours a day, sacrificing quality of life, well-being and contact with your family. Remember that nobody is safe from depression related to tedious and unenjoyable excess work. Take regular breaks, exercise or even go on holiday. You might even consider taking a nap in the middle of the day – it is better to work efficiently for two or three hours than to work unproductively for seven or eight hours without a break.

Figure 10.3 To telework or not to telework?

Teleworking occupations

- **Writer:** the main quality required of an author is relative independence of mind and a certain creativity in order to be in a position to design and submit projects. You also need to be tenacious, good at forming relationships, persuasive and patient.
- **Freelance journalist:** if you are looking to earn lots of money, it is better to forget freelance journalism. Few freelance journalists manage to earn a fortune. Those who do are usually involved in other activities. Only choose freelance journalism if you are prepared to work hard initially to establish a reputation.
- **Computer consultant:** this may work out well quite quickly. Computer service companies use the services of independent consultants, which spares them from having to pay employees. Depending on your abilities, you can easily ask for between £150 and £200 per day.

- **Graphic designer or illustrator:** publicity and communication agencies may call upon your talents as a graphic designer for publicity or commercial brochures. With a little luck, you may even get into newspaper publishing and become a cartoonist. This would of course require you to have expertise in Quark XPress, Adobe Illustrator and Photoshop, plus access to a colour laser printer.
- **Secretary:** the time devoted to canvassing is one of the keys to business success. In addition to mastering current electronic office tools, a secretary must therefore be excellent at marketing. Secretaries carry out tasks such as book-keeping and administrative work for small companies, but tend not to be involved in inputting work. If you want to become a secretary, remember that the market has a tendency to be overcrowded.
- **Trainer:** trainers provide instruction in the Internet and office software programs. They also act as on-call computer consultants, sometimes working from home and sometimes working at the premises of the training organisation.

Other teleworking occupations include engineers, remote maintenance technicians, draughtsmen, translators, proofreaders, marketing people ...

The status of the teleworker

Labour regulations specify clearly that someone who works from home is an employee. Nevertheless, nine out of ten people who carry out an activity from home are self-employed, or have created their own company.

To enjoy employee status, you must first of all work for one or more employers who provide you with regular or intermittent work.

Figure 10.4 What type of teleworker are you?

As evidence of your employee status, you will get either a signed contract specifying the collective agreement to which your employer is bound, or pay slips.

You, of course, enjoy all the advantages of employee status, including paid holidays, Social Security and unemployment benefit.

You may be paid by the hour, by the day, or by the task.

- **Self-employed person:** the self-employed person has no hierarchical connection with an employer. You are your own boss. You can practise a profession, be a craftsperson, a tradesperson or a sales representative, for example.

  If you sell a product, you are a tradesperson. If you produce, repair or convert, you are a craftsperson. If you practise an intellectual activity, you practise a profession (e.g. author, freelance journalist, computer consultant, etc.). Half the people practising a professional activity choose the form of **sole trader**, since this requires no initial capital. You need to fill in a self-employed business declaration. You will also need to keep your own accounts and fill in your own tax returns. However, you can reclaim tax on expenses connected with your business, for example purchasing your computer, business phone calls and travel expenses. For more detailed information you should contact your local tax office.

Many people, particularly the under-40s, would like to try teleworking, since it offers them the chance to better manage their time.

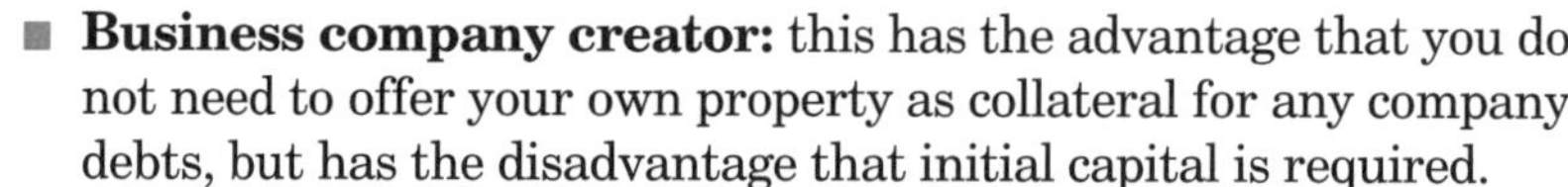

- **Business company creator:** this has the advantage that you do not need to offer your own property as collateral for any company debts, but has the disadvantage that initial capital is required.
- **Limited liability company:** requires a start-up capital of £5000, with a minimum of two partners. If you are a minority partner, you benefit from the tax system for employees. If you are a majority partner, the profits from your company will be integrated with your tax on the income.
- **Private limited company under sole ownership:** requires a start-up capital of £5000 and a minimum of one person.

Different forms of teleworking

There are different forms of teleworking, according to the individual, the socio-economic context and the catchment area:

- **Working from home.**
- **Mobile teleworking:** mainly used by sales representatives equipped with a mobile phone, and by sales engineers who have a fixed base.
- **Part-time teleworking and telecommuting:** an employee carries out certain tasks at home using remote data transmission in order to reduce the time wasted due to travelling.
- **Teleworking from a tele-office:** making appointments for a doctor's surgery, canvassing for a business firm, etc.

- **Teleworking away from the office:** employees stay in contact with the parent company by means of remote data transmission tools.

One of the major ingredients for making teleworking profitable is the Internet, which allows you to draw on sources of information for hours on end – hours that you would otherwise use for travelling, thus making you more productive. A normal employee may spend 5–6% of his or her working time on learning, whereas you have three hours every day – from the comfort of your own home.

11

Making the right purchase

Breaking even

Well-known brands

Buying over the Internet

Buying from supermarkets

Assembling your PC

Promotions

Knowing what and when to buy is an art in itself. It is better to wait for the right moment rather than to rush out and buy the latest product as soon as it is released. You will find the wait is worth it when the product is upgraded. If a product is well marketed, its price invariably drops; if the number of models sold increases tenfold, the price is reduced by approximately half. For example, a CD writer cost approximately £1600 in 1995; in 2000 it cost less than £130.

Breaking even

In order to make the right purchase, you have to take into consideration what the equipment offers. Between 1995 and 1997, it was possible to rent CD writers for £25 per weekend, while CDs cost between £5 and £8. Obviously, as rewritable CDs now cost no more than £1 and machines no more than £200, it is better for you to buy rather than rent.

You can buy your equipment from:

- your nearest retailer, who should stock individual parts as well;
- a dealer specialising in well-known makes;
- a supermarket;
- a mail-order company or via the Internet;
- a second-hand market.

Well-known brands

It is tempting to buy a well-known make, especially if you want to resell your hardware for a reasonable price. However, be aware that major suppliers have for some time now operated proprietary systems. This means that you often have to continue buying the same make. What happens is that particular features are artificially integrated that make the hardware incompatible with other systems and sometimes prevent the supplier's hardware from functioning properly on other configurations. In some cases, you can get round these difficulties using patches and drivers that you can find on the Internet.

Having said that, buying from a well-known supplier gives you security, as it is in the interest of the supplier to provide you with high-quality products in order to retain your custom.

Buying over the Internet

Buying over the Internet is tempting and offers numerous advantages, not least the fact that products are up to 20% cheaper. Compared to shopping from catalogues, you can save up to 20% on high-quality software. If you are content to download a product (only paying the licence and not receiving the full package), you will obviously pay considerably less. You will not get an instruction manual or CD-ROM, but the help files are often enough.

Figure 11.1 Mail-ordering – the LDLC site.

Figure 11.2 The Soft Gallery logo.

Buying from supermarkets

It is important to pay attention to what you buy. At first sight, the prices may appear excellent, but in the end you usually get what you pay for. Promotions on specific items of hardware may look attractive, but complete configurations do not always contain parts that are standard across the board. You may not get as high-quality a model as you would if you bought from a local dealer.

Assembling your PC

The best way of purchasing a PC is to specify or construct it yourself, which allows you to carefully choose each individual component you install and therefore to customise the computer to your needs.

If you choose to assemble your PC yourself, you will probably want one that includes the following applications:

- graphics
- word processor
- games.

For each of these applications, you can choose from various options.

Using your PC for graphics applications

Choosing a Pentium III motherboard with an Ultra-Wide SCSI controller in order to use a hard disk of this type allows you to work faster when using Windows to run software programs such as Adobe Photoshop, Painter, 3D Studio MAX and other memory-intensive software applications. The speed of the hard disk will enable you to work faster. You will also find it easier to add numerous peripherals. These will need 64 Mb or more of SDRAM.

Pentium III motherboards have an in-built AGP video bus. An AGP video card can also be used if you have cable television. In all cases, it is best to go for a digital format if you want to rapidly switch from your TV to your computer.

Finally, a 20" or 21" 1200 × 1600 screen is the ultimate in luxury. You can buy one for less than £700 with an on-site three-year guarantee. Having said that, a 17" screen is just as good once the settings have been changed to 1024 × 768.

Using your PC for word processing applications

Word processing applications do not place major requirements on the configuration. A Pentium with 32 Mb of RAM will do fine. To comfortably handle most tasks, you will need a 4 Mb graphics card and a 17" screen.

Using your PC for playing games

Today's games require power, memory and preferably a 3D graphics card. This takes the strain off the processor and cuts down on the time you have to wait. If you can, choose a Pentium II motherboard, a minimum 650 Mhz Pentium II Intel processor, and 64 Mb of SDRAM.

Promotions

These never last long and are intended to attract and keep customers. They concern all kinds of equipment: screens, memory peripherals etc. Although computer magazines are a good source of up-to-date information, many dealers advertise their promotions in fliers that you can only obtain from their store. Prices change so quickly that updates sometimes appear every week.

Remember that promotions only run while stocks last. You will also find promotions on various Internet sites.

Obtaining information from the Internet

A good way of keeping informed is to consult lists available on the Internet. These deal mostly with configuration problems or questions regarding what equipment to buy. These issues are well discussed and will help you solve your problem or make your decision. For example, if you want to buy a CD writer, consulting these lists may help you avoid making the wrong purchase.

Some lists also offer links related to a particular subject. For example, if you want to buy a 3DFX graphics card, people who have the same card may be able to point you in the direction of other sites exclusively dedicated to this card. You may, for example, have problems installing a new hard disk or AGP card. If you do, just connect to the mailing list address, describe your problem, and you may be lucky enough to get a reply from someone who has experienced exactly the same problem and can offer a solution.

You may have to wait a few hours for a reply, or you may get one in a matter of minutes. It is this almost instantaneousness of information that is the main advantage of the Internet. All you need to do is to be able to navigate around it properly.

Receiving the latest software on free trial

You can also subscribe to mailing lists from which you can obtain advice on downloading the latest software on free trial. Each day, you will find 20 or so new products accompanied by a description and their file size.

12 The future

Becoming an advanced user

No time to read the instructions?

Forums and lists

Courses

Learning to program

Becoming an advanced user

Approximately 80% of users use less than 20% of the features of their programs. This is especially true of Excel, but it is also true of word processing programs, such as Word. There are at least two reasons for this:

- the instructions are dense and often difficult to understand;
- different people have different needs and it is not necessary to know everything.

There are three ways of becoming an advanced user:

- read a little bit of the instruction manual every day;
- register with Internet forums or mailing lists;
- go on a course.

No time to read the instructions?

You will probably have to buy one or two dedicated instruction manuals in order to use your software. Some of them are small and practical, while others are so large that although you might want to have them as a reference, you are rarely likely to consult them. If you feel you just do not have the time at work, try reading small sections while in the bath, on the bus or train, or in a waiting room.

Forums and lists

The Internet and its forums can provide you with a wealth of information. All you need is some knowledge of online communication and you can obtain information on almost anything you want – sometimes without knowing it.

Courses

A good way of learning is to go on a course. Some companies will contribute a certain amount of money towards having their employees trained in IT, since it is the company that ultimately benefits. However, even if yours does not, it is always worth attending a course, as your newly acquired skills could help you in your career (particularly if you wish to train as a software or hardware engineer, for which there is always a demand). Courses may last from one to three days right up to three to nine months. There are also 'universities' on the Internet that provide distance learning courses. You can even get a diploma – usually by paying a certain amount of money. There will always be a way for anyone who wants to learn IT to do so.

Learning to program

Few activities offer as many options as programming. Not only is there the satisfaction of creating your own software program, there is also the challenge of mastering the difficult syntax and logic of the computer. However, you will find that the hard work pays off. Learning to program is probably one of the best investments you can make as the owner of a PC. All you have to do is choose a language.

Visual Basic

For fans of Microsoft, Visual Basic constitutes the best choice, even if the language was initially a bit heavy and limited. It is probably still a bit too heavy, particularly because you have to add a few error management lines to each module and cannot add them globally to the application that is running. However, Visual Basic has improved with each new version. It is not as object-oriented as one might wish and, until Version 5 at least, you had to use another language to create objects to put in the library with a view to using them later.

Nevertheless, Visual Basic has made good progress, with each new version containing a large chunk of what the previous version lacked. The visual and graphic aspect of the language makes it easy to work with, while the Internet and most dealers have large libraries full of additions in the form of OCX or ActiveX objects.

Delphi and Pascal

Pascal is a language, whereas Delphi is a language that also offers a complete environment that is almost an operating system (one level up from an application system, at any rate).

Delphi and Pascal are structured languages that derive their popularity from the power that their structures offer. Although they have devoted fans, their syntax is a little heavy, with the systematic use of conventional symbols restricting the modules somewhat. A major advantage of Delphi is that it allows you to create objects directly and put them in the library for later use.

You can download a trial version of Delphi from the following address: **www.inprise.com/download.html**

Other languages

You can also choose from the following languages:

- C
- C + +
- Assembler

- SmallTalk
- Eiffel.

These languages are all used in the workplace. They may initially be more difficult to learn than those previously mentioned, and they are not always particularly powerful. They are usually taught at university or college and are not well suited to self-instruction.

Glossary

@ The @ sign is one of the constituent elements of the electronic address. Since a person always has an address at an access provider, the name of the latter always appears after the @ sign. For example, **Lulu@sdv.co.uk**. In plain language, Lulu has an address at the access provider 'sdv' located in the UK; 'co' indicates a company.

Access provider The service provider that offers an Internet connection to its subscribers.

Access time The time that a disk drive, floppy disk drive or CD-ROM drive requires to find information.

Address Location of data on the hard disk or on the diskette.

Alta Vista One of the most efficient search engines on the Net.

Application Synonym for a software program whose aim is to implement certain specific computing tasks, such as word processing or mathematical operations. The word processor and the spreadsheet are examples of applications.

Back-up Make a copy of a document on a diskette.

Bandwidth Maximum amount of data measured in bits per second (bps). The bandwidth can be compared to the width of a motorway. Depending on the number of lanes available on each side, the amount of traffic allowed under good conditions will vary enormously. The bandwidth defines the number of users and amount of traffic that a server can reasonably handle. There is a conflict of interest between the desire of the access provider to acquire the maximum number of clients while investing as little as possible, and that of the client who hopes to pay a minimum amount for a quality service. In order to make the most of the bandwidth, modems should be as fast as possible.

BIOS Abbreviation of Basic Input Output System. The BIOS adapts an operating system to its hardware environment.

Bit Contraction of binary digit. Information element with a value of zero or one. 1 byte = 8 bits.

BPS Bits per second; unit of measurement for the data transmission speed.

Browser Navigator that makes it possible to gain access to information on the Web, e.g. Internet Explorer.

Buffer Buffer memory used as a temporary storage area. Printers have their own buffer.

Bug Error in a software program.

Bus Set of cables and communication channels that transfer the information inside the computer.

Byte 8 bits.

Cache Intermediate memory intended to store the most recently used information.

CAD Computer-aided design. Used for production and wherever there is industrial design.

Capacity Amount of data that can be stored on a disk. The unit of measurement is the byte, divided into kilobytes, megabytes or gigabytes.

CD-ROM Compact disc read-only memory. This collects together text, images and sound, which may be read from a CD-ROM drive installed on a computer.

Chip Integrated circuit.

Client A computer that requests data from the server computer.

Client/server architecture Combination of a server computer, client computer, and network.

Clip-art Drawings on a computer supplied in library form and classified by subject.

Compatibility Ability of a computer to run software produced for another computer.

Computer Machine that automates the processing of information. The first computer was the ENIAC; the most user-friendly is the Macintosh; the most widespread is the IBM PC. The PC has a strong position in the market and has become indispensable to many people.

Computer language Code made up of a syntax and a grammar making it possible to program. The efficiency of a language stems from its simplicity, the richness of its vocabulary, and the way in which it is structured. Some of the best known languages are Cobol, C++, Fortran, Java, Pascal and Visual Basic.

CPU Central microprocessor.

Cracker Computer specialist who resolves problems, as opposed to a hacker, who creates them.

Cyber The cyber culture is made up of everything to do with the new communication technologies and the modes of thought they generate. Comes from the Greek *cyber*, which means to steer.

Cybercafé Café in which it is possible to access the Internet. The cost of access is around £3 for half an hour.

Dedicated A software program dedicated entirely to a specific function, e.g. graphic design.

Density Amount of data that a diskette may contain. There are double density diskettes (360 kb–720 kb) and high density diskettes (1.44 Mb–2.8 Mb).

Digital The opposite of analogue. A system used by computers to analyse data, whereby 0 signifies off and 1 signifies on.

Dongle Electronic key that plugs into a port and makes it possible to protect a software program against piracy.

DOS Disk operating system. DOS is one of the most widespread operating systems.

Dpi Dots per inch; the unit for measuring resolution.

Driver Small program that enables the transfer of data between two items of hardware that are not compatible. For example, a printer is delivered with a driver that translates its compatibilities.

DVD-ROM Digital versatile disc read-only memory. The successor of the CD-ROM, with a data storage of 4–16 Gbytes.

Electronic address Personal address for receiving electronic mail (e-mail) on the Internet. Not to be confused with the URL, the Internet address for a site.

Electronic mail Mail exchanged between two computers. Popularly known as e-mail.

E-mail Electronic mail.

Ergonomics Study of methodical organisation of work, and the development of equipment adapted to workers needs.

Eudora Software that manages electronic mail.

FAQ Short for 'frequently asked questions'. On the Internet, each newsgroup contains a FAQ column, which is intended to reply to the most common questions asked by users.

FAT Short for 'file allocation table'. Table created by disks to pinpoint the location of files.

File Transfer Protocol (FTP) Protocol for transferring files on the Internet.

Formatting Technique that prepares the disk or diskette for receiving computer data.

Four-colour printing Cyan, magenta, yellow and black make up the set of subtractive colours.

Freeware System for distributing free software, written for glory alone and often excellent. Spreadsheets, word processors and management programs flourish in this form. Not to be confused with shareware.

GIF Graphic image file format. The most widespread compressed graphics format of the Internet.

Graphics accelerator Screen card that makes it possible to accelerate the processing speed of information to be displayed.

Hard disk System composed of a mechanism and a rigid disk situated inside the central unit. The hard disk is used to store millions, perhaps even thousands of millions, of bytes.

Hardware Computer hardware: case, keyboard, screen, central unit and peripherals. The opposite of software.

Home page On the Internet, the welcome page or first page of a site.

Hotline Telephone assistance concerning the software and hardware of the computer.

Hypertext Technique that allows you to create links between documents of different types. Multimedia and its CD-ROM applications promote the creation of hypertext links and make navigation from term to term and from concept to concept much richer and much faster.

Hypertext link Link between information from document to document. Allows information to be accessed extremely quickly.

Infoway Information highway. International transfer of information by cable.

Infopoor/inforich Expression designating the gulf that is widening between the companies and countries with access to computing, the information highways, communication in general, and those that do not. Is the Internet going to increase the difference or promote equality of opportunity?

Integrated An intergrated software package contains all of the following: a spreadsheet, word processor, database, and perhaps even a graphics program.

Interface Connects the user to the software and hardware environment of the computer. It should be user-friendly and pleasant to use. Windows is considered to be a user-friendly interface since graphics with icons is a highly intuitive method of access.

Internet Also called the World Wide Web. The system that makes it possible to connect several million users who exchange electronic mail and information, and participate in discussion groups. Often abbreviated to the Net.

Internet Explorer The Microsoft browser program for navigating the Net. Competes with Netscape Navigator created by the company Netscape.

Intranet A local network, as opposed to the Internet, which is a worldwide network. An intranet is often set up so all employees of a firm can access all information.

Java Language developed by Sun Microsystems, used for programming on the Net. Created by James Gosling.

Joystick Lever connected to the computer allowing very quick movements on the screen. Used for games software.

JPEG Joint Photographic Expert Group. The data compression standard for fixed images. Graphics file format widely used on the Internet.

Laser Light amplification by stimulated emission of radiation. Technique using a beam of light to perform various tasks.

Local network Group of computers connected by cable in the same office or the same company.

Macintosh Created in 1984, the Macintosh succeeded the Apple II.

Maintenance Function that makes it possible to keep both the software and hardware of the computer in good working order.

Megabyte 1 048 576 bytes.

Modem Short for modulator/demodulator. A microprocessor peripheral enabling the PC to communicate with other computers via a telephone line and to connect to the Internet network.

Multimedia Simultaneous use of text, sound, image and video within the same application.

Multitasking Quality of the operating system allowing it to run several applications at the same time. Windows is a multitasking operating system.

Nano Prefix signifying one thousand millionth.

Netscape Navigator The Netscape browser program for navigating on the Net. Competes with Microsoft's Internet Explorer.

Network System for communicating between computers connected to one another by cable. The aim is to facilitate the exchange of data and to promote co-operation in work and skills.

Notebook Small lightweight portable computer (3–6 kg).

Notepad Diary provided with software, which allows you to manage appointments.

Novell Company that specialises in network management.

Offline Used to describe a peripheral that is disconnected or put on standby. Also an electronic product such as a diskette or CD-ROM that does not require any connection.

Online Used to describe a computer when it is switched on. Also characterises the exchange of data from computer to computer.

Optical fibre Cable made of a transparent material that allows information to flow in the form of light. At the start, it is coded by a laser. On arrival, it is decoded by a diode. It is instantaneous and totally reliable.

OS/2 Operating system created by IBM for PCs.

Package Group of several software programs in the same sales promotion. By extension, the packaging of the software or CD-ROM.

Parallel port Port situated on the central unit, used for connecting printers.

Path Path for accessing data on the hard disk.

PC Personal computer.

Pentium Name of the Intel 80586 microprocessor.

Pitch Distance that separates two pixels on a screen.

Port Connector situated on the external face of the computer, which makes it possible to connect the motherboard situated in the central unit to the peripherals. The majority of computers are equipped with at least one serial port and one parallel port.

Portable Small travelling computer that works on batteries. From the heavy transportable to the lightweight notebook, a wide range is available.

Program Manager Part of the Windows 3 graphical interface that allows programs to be run.

QWERTY Name given to the standard keyboard, which derives from the first line of keys.

Rack Case that packages software or CD-ROMs, provided with a hole that allows it to be threaded on a metal rod.

RAM Random access memory. Computer memory that can be read and written.

Reverse video Reversal of the writing and the background.

Root Initial directory of the hard disk or diskette.

Scanner Device that allows you to 'scan' photographic or text documents into a computer. It operates in the same way as a photocopier.

Search engine Program for searching on the Internet according to keywords entered by the user. It may be compared to the index of a book: the Internet is a giant book of several thousand million pages and keywords make it possible to quickly access relevant specialised information. The main search engines are offered as free services. They periodically run through the whole Internet: the sites, newsgroups and FTPs. In this way, outdated or modified links are removed from the database or updated.

Serial port Port situated on the central unit, used for connecting serial peripherals (modems, printers, etc.).

Server Central computer offering its services on a network.

Shareware Software protected by copyright, part of which you can try out and pay for if satisfied with it.

Silicon Valley An area near San Francisco, USA, where many companies responsible for the development of computing have been established.

Site Location on the Internet consisting of a welcome page and various other pages, the aim of which is to present a work, an idea, or simply act as an introduction using multimedia tools such as sound, text and images. There are millions of sites on the Internet.

Site extractor A program that copies a complete site from the server to the user's hard disk. The importance of this is to allow offline perusal. For example, you can download when telephone charges are cheaper, then look at the site at your leisure.

Snail mail Name given to the normal mail service because of its slowness compared with electronic mail.

Software Program.

Splash window Waiting window intended to help the computer user to be patient when an application takes a long time to start up. The splash window indicates the origin of the program, the name of the designer, etc.

Spreadsheet Software used to perform operations with figures and tables. The most famous spreadsheet is Microsoft Excel.

Station-to-station network Group of computers, each of which can act as both client and server.

Surfer An Internet user who goes from site to site.

SuperVGA (SVGA) High-quality screen card.

Switch Device that makes it possible to change from one printer to another.

System diskette Diskette whose function is to start up the computer.

TCP/IP Transmission Control Protocol/ Internet Protocol. Protocol for transmitting files on the Internet, co-invented by Vinton Cerf.

Teleworking Working from home using a computer and the Internet. This solution grants you freedom of action to go beyond the constraints of your work catchment area. Teleworking can be very efficient if the status of the teleworker is clearly established at the beginning.

Tree structure Structure of the directories on your disk.

Uninterruptible power supply Device that protects computers from power failures.

UNIX Operating system written in the C language.

URL Uniform resource locator The address of a site on the Internet.

Usenet Newsgroup network on the Internet.

VGA The PC display standard. Its definition is 640 × 480.

Virtual In the computing field, the term 'virtual universe' is used to describe a structure in which all the parameters can be offered in a variety of forms and updated. In today's language, this term is the opposite of real.

Virus Program devised by a hacker to destroy other programs or files.

Warm start Starting up the computer without turning off the power.

Webmaster On the Internet, this person is responsible for managing a server or a discussion forum. Also used to describe a company's Web site manager.

Wide area network Group of computers geographically very far apart and connected by cable.

Windows User-friendly graphical interface created by Microsoft.

Winsock Set of standards intended for programs running on the Internet.

Word processor Software used to process text and written documents. The most famous is Microsoft Word.

Worldwide network The Internet.

World Wide Wait Nickname given to the Internet when data transfers take too long.

World Wide Web The interface for navigation on the Internet. Abbreviated to WWW and Web.

XLS File extension for Excel spreadsheet files.

XPress Desktop publishing software designed for the Macintosh and published by Quark Corporation.

Yahoo! American Internet search engine.

Zip File compression format. The expression 'zipping a file' is used.

Zoom Function allowing the magnification of an image represented under Windows.

A simple guide to

Windows Me

Gilles Fouchard

Introduction

Windows Me (Millennium edition) is the latest version of Microsoft's world-beating operating system. Windows Me is strongly biased towards the Internet. In fact Windows Me comes complete with all the navigation and communication tools required for the most effective use of the World Wide Web. But this system does not mark such a significant distinction as that between Windows 3.1 and Windows 95. The Windows 98 working platform is retained for users who wish to continue using it, but the Web style of operating will be seized upon by those who wish to combine their PC operating methods with those of the Web facilities on offer.

Absolute beginners, or those who have just bought their first PC, do not need to know about the history of the software. They will be able to catch up with the Internet and enjoy the full benefits of all the new system features.

In fact, Windows Me has all the winning cards in terms of meeting consumer expectations; it contains all the features that made Windows 98 such a success. With Windows Me, computing is a real pleasure.

This book is:

- a **complete guide** to discovering the Windows Me working platform and its tools and features, as well as the special features of individual software products, including Internet Explorer 5.5 and the e-mail manager Outlook Express;
- a **teaching method**, setting out the system features in 12 easy to handle sections.

Who is this book for?

This very versatile book addresses a wide range of readers:

- **first-time users**, who have just bought their first PC, will enjoy the best of the technology available and will benefit from significant strides forward in the day-to-day use of a PC. Newcomers to the PC have an advantage over their predecessors who had to tolerate systems that were far less user-friendly.
- **Windows 3.1 users** will appreciate the simplified interface, the plug-and-play features and the virtual disappearance of DOS.
- **Windows 95 and 98 users** will discover how Windows Me is now integrated with the Web, and will find an array of software for the Internet plus more advanced system tools.

The book will provide an essential aid to:

- discovering Windows Me features
- working or playing in Windows Me
- linking you to the Internet
- learning to surf the Web
- using e-mail
- improving the performance of your PC and preventing faults
- using the latest multimedia innovations.

Adopted conventions

All commands are displayed in bold. Throughout the text, a number of symbols alert you to terminology issues and technological details, and indicate shortcuts or advice to the user:

This icon introduces handy shortcuts and tips such as keyboard hotkeys, expert options, and quicker ways of getting to the same place.

This icon warns you of any risks associated with a particular action, or any problems you might encounter along the way, and (where possible) shows you how to avoid them.

This icon is used to provide additional information about the topic being covered.

The Windows Me philosophy

1

A more user-friendly system

A system plugged in to the world

A version that can be used by anyone

An intuitive graphics interface

Plug-and-play technology

Since Windows 95, Microsoft has been simplifying the use of the PC on a day-to-day basis to win over new users and promote the system to all consumers. The major concepts developed for Windows 95 were reproduced in Windows 98 and have been taken a step further with Windows Me. We will go into these in more detail later on.

A more user-friendly system

It is no longer necessary for new computer users to learn about DOS (the *disk operating system*): personal computing has moved on. However, applications operating in DOS can still be run, so you will be able to make the most of your old programs and especially all your favourite games.

Figure 1.1 The MS-DOS Prompt window.

The DOS prompt

*If you need to run a program in DOS, find the **MS-DOS Prompt** on the **Start** menu (it should be in the **Accessories**).*

Compatibility with existing systems also includes recognition of the peripheral drivers and the network software. It was important that the system was able to accept the installation of a new item of equipment or peripheral (such as a printer or modem) quickly and easily. This new feature was based on a product strategy known as *Plug-and-Play*, implemented jointly by Microsoft and the leading players in the computer industry.

Although Windows Me is compatible with the existing system with regard to certain matters, this is not the case in terms of performance. The idea of running Windows Me on a 486 PC or even an entry-level Pentium processor is out of the question. In addition, memory (RAM) of 32 Mb is essential in order to run the system. For many existing users, the transition from Windows 3.1 to Windows Me will call for a change of PC.

The 32-bit architecture

The major technical advances, beginning with Windows 95, have been 32-bit architecture and better system resource management, which have created a more powerful, stable system. Windows Me reproduces the 32-bit print manager and graphics manager technology that came with Windows 95 and the 32-bit model (the 32-bit Windows Driver Model – WDM 32) for peripheral drivers and the new file system in 32-bit mode which was introduced with Windows 98.

Windows 3.1 users will also appreciate the multitasking mode of Windows Me, also a feature of Windows 95 and 98 which enables several applications to be run simultaneously. In Windows Me, 32-bit and 16-bit applications can run independently of each other. Each application is executed using its own disk space and does not affect any other applications.

The 32-bit file system

When installing Windows Me (see Chapter 2) on a Windows 95 PC, you can request that your existing Windows and DOS files be retained in order to reinstall them at a later date. You can uninstall Windows Me, provided you kept the default file management mode. Windows Me is supplied with a system utility (FAT 32 converter), which allows you to change the file manager to 32-bit mode. If you make use of this facility you will not then be able to change back to Windows 95.

The Windows Me Registry

All technical information is stored centrally in a database known as the Registry. This database continually updates the PC configuration, thereby ensuring that Windows Me operates at its best. It also has a role in the Plug-and-Play technology by establishing, each time an item of equipment is installed, which resources are unassigned (IRQ, 1/0 addresses, DMA channels, etc.) and allocating them elsewhere. Another advantage of the Registry is that it bypasses the notorious DOS configuration files AUTOEXEC.BAT and CONFIG.SYS, as well as the Windows 3.1 .INI files. Windows 95 and 98 users have already benefited from this new feature. The Registry can be looked up and modified from a remote location via a network, which is important for business users and DP managers.

A system plugged in to the world

Under Windows 95, access to remote information servers was greatly enhanced. Access is gained in point-to-point mode or with specialized connection systems. As well as these connections, Windows 95 incorporated a centralized information send-and-receive system called Microsoft Exchange. This system, which supports the MAPI standard, provided a single location from which to retrieve fax messages or e-mail. Although Microsoft Exchange still exists in Windows Me, it is somewhat redundant since e-mail traffic can now be handled by the Internet message system, Outlook Express.

The facility designed for Windows 95 no longer meets the needs generated by the phenomenal development of Internet communications. Windows 95 anticipated this development by adapting its basic architecture: it already incorporated a 32-bit version of the TCP/IP protocol (the communication and interchange protocol used on the World Wide Web). But making a successful Internet connection was a feat in itself. Since then, all possible resources have been deployed to integrate the connection process more effectively; the Internet Connection Wizard, supplied with the Internet Explorer 5.5 software package, now performs that function.

A version that can be used by anyone

For novices, Windows Me brings its own clutch of new features and clears up a number of problems encountered in earlier versions of Windows. These significant changes bring the PC within range of a vast number of people, and encourage its adoption by the home user. Here we should note that use of the PC differs greatly between business and domestic environments. Home users can now enjoy the benefits of the new generation of multimedia games, which rely increasingly on sophisticated synthesized animations. To this end, the new graphics display standards (*Accelerated Graphics Port* – AGP) are recognized by Windows Me. There is also the opportunity to enjoy easy, rapid Internet access and to use the Internet Explorer 5.5 navigation software to surf the Web, or to join in the discussion forums (*newsgroups*), not to mention the Outlook Express message system to send and receive e-mail. Naturally, the PC running Windows Me, together with its electronic office software, remains an outstanding work tool. With the growth of part-time employment, teleworking and distance learning, the domestic PC bridges the traditional business–home gap.

Windows Me incorporates all the key features that meet the requirements of the general public. It continues to use the features that made Windows 95 and 98 such a success and now incorporates the extra Intemet dimension. With Windows Me, computing becomes a genuine pleasure. Here are a few aspects of the system to illustrate this point.

An intuitive graphics interface

The Windows Me graphics interface is the same as that in Windows 95 and 98; it may take some time to get used to if you have previously remained faithful to Windows 3.1. The Windows Me interface offers a number of working methods – including the Web (see Chapter 7) – and enables you to customize your own environment. There is more than one way to execute most commands in Windows Me, for example, there are four ways of starting an application or opening a document:

- **Method 1.** Click on the **Start** button, then choose your program or document (Figure 1.2).
- **Method 2.** Find the program icon on the Desktop, click the right mouse button, and select **Open** from the pop-up menu (Figure 1.3).
- **Method 3.** Drag the program icon to the Start button; the application will then be entered on the main list under that button and you simply click on it to execute the program (Figure 1.4).

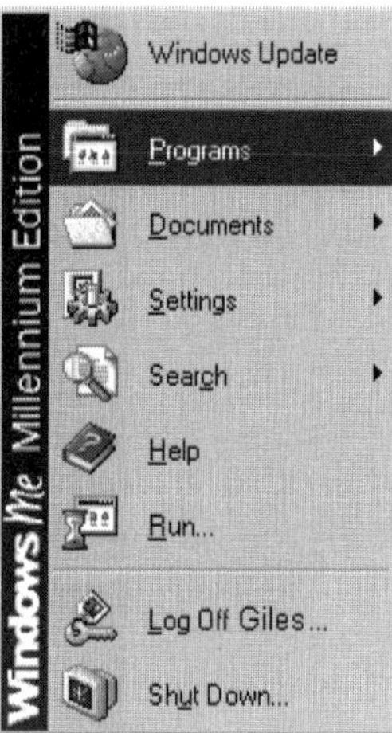

Figure 1.2 Clicking on the **Start** button brings up a list of programs, documents and submenus.

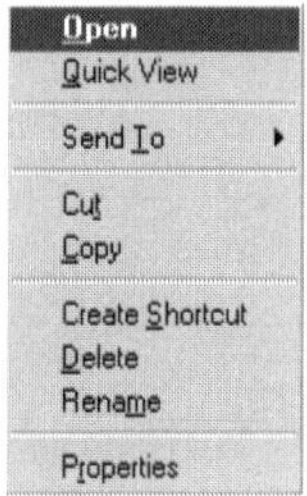

Figure 1.3 Opening a program from the Desktop.

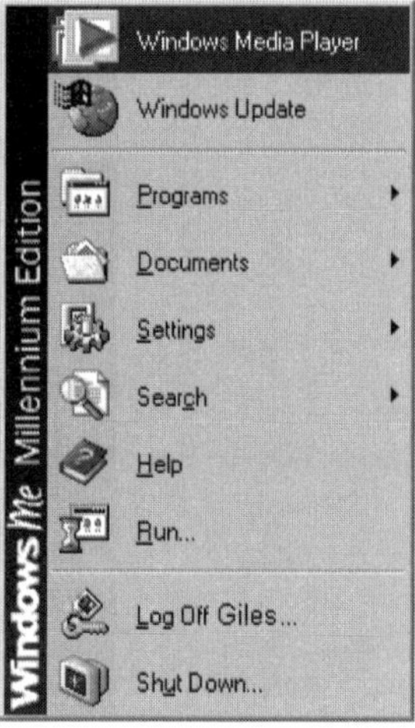

Figure 1.4 Windows Media Player has been added to the Start menu by a drag-and-drop action.

- **Method 4.** Create a shortcut that can be accessed on the Windows Me Desktop. A shortcut is a quick link to an object (i.e. a program or a document) stored in the PC or accessible via the Internet. A shortcut is recognized by the little folding arrow that appears on the icon. To create a program shortcut, right-click on the program icon in question and select the **Create Shortcut** option (Figure 1.5).

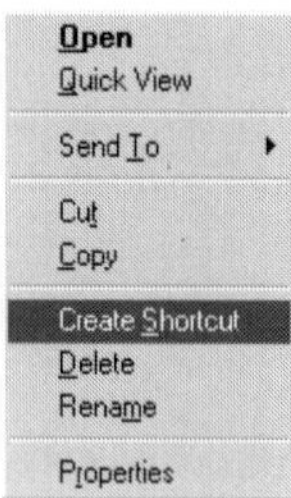

Figure 1.5 The Create Shortcut command.

The Windows Me Desktop

The Desktop provides the main work screen. On starting up Windows Me, it includes the following items: the Start button, the Taskbar, a number of icons on the Desktop, and an access area to Web channels. The Taskbar is at the bottom of the screen to the right of the Start button. The Desktop icons represent objects or shortcuts to objects. We will discuss these in greater detail later.

You can change the Windows Me environment to suit your own needs. This is ideal for use in a family context, since the PC can be adapted to children's tastes. You can add background images, change the shape of icons, or even use sound to give a games arcade effect. Windows Me provides a set of desktop user profiles, Microsoft Plus, which previously formed part of the Windows 95 add-on package. To choose a profile, click on **Start**, **Settings**, **Control Panel**. Then select **Desktop Themes**. Now choose the theme and click **OK** (Figure 1.6).

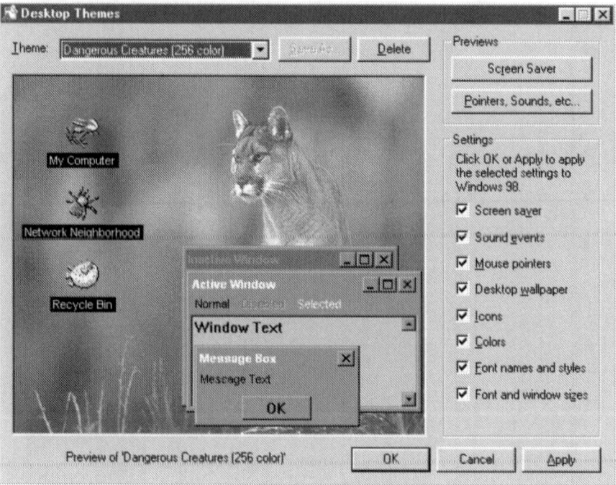

Figure 1.6 Changing the Desktop Theme in Windows Me.

Plug-and-play technology

Whilst the success of the PC is due mainly to its open-ended flexibility, this is a setback for users who are nervous of installing new equipment. With its new plug-and-play technology, Microsoft has imposed certain specifications on PC and peripherals equipment manufacturers. The aim of this has been to ensure total compatibility with the Windows operating system and to simplify, or even automate, the installation of memory and any add-on equipment. For this reason, Windows Me is supplied with more than 1000 drivers responsible for recognizing over 1000 different devices.

The Control Panel (**Start**, **Settings**, **Control Panel**) window contains an Add New Hardware icon, which guides you through installing new internal (e.g. a graphics board) or external equipment (e.g. a printer or modem) (Figure 1.7).

Why plug-and-play?

The purpose of plug-and-play is to avoid conflicts such as interrupt handling (IRQ) or memory access management (DMA) by making the installation of equipment much simpler for the user: plug-and-play technology is based on three PC components: the BIOS on the motherboard, the controllers (ISA, EISA, PCI, PCMCIA, SCSI, etc.) and the operating system itself. The BIOS is a manufacturer's program that determines the hardware configuration of the PC. Each manufacturer must therefore make their BIOS compatible with Microsoft specifications. A plug-and-play BIOS sends Windows Me all the information that might assist the end user.

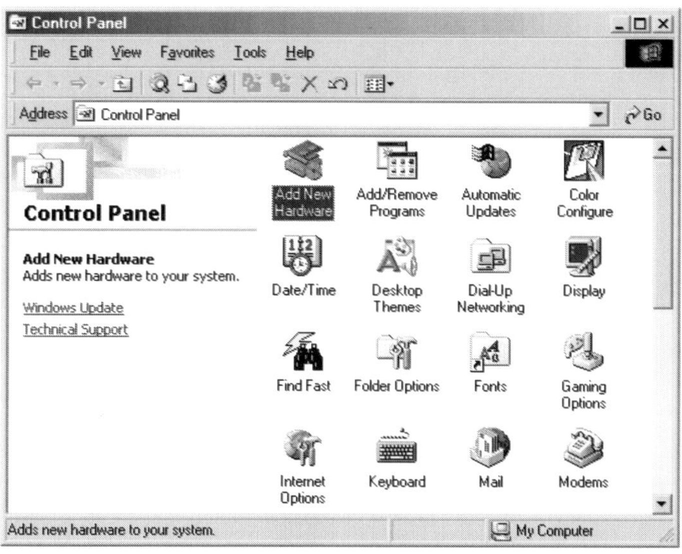

Figure 1.7 Using the Control Panel to add new hardware.

The Add New Hardware Wizard (Figure 1.8) automatically recognizes the new Plug-and-Play peripherals. If it fails to do so, select a hardware family and use a diskette to install the necessary driver. You can also download the driver from the manufacturer's Internet site.

Plug-and-play technology
Plug-and-play technology must satisfy a wide range of constraints. It is of vital importance that the hardware to be installed on a PC can be connected to the majority of known buses and connector types. These includes ISA, EISA, VESA Local Bus, PCI and USB buses, and PCMCIA, SCSI and IDE connections, as well as the monitor connections and the serial or parallel ports. This technology must guarantee automatic installation, loading into RAM and the unloading of drivers. It must also enable dynamic (hot) configuration changes that do not require Windows Me to be shutdown; this feature allows, for example, a PCMCIA board to be inserted without shutting down the machine. Finally, individual applications must be able to respond to these dynamic configuration changes.

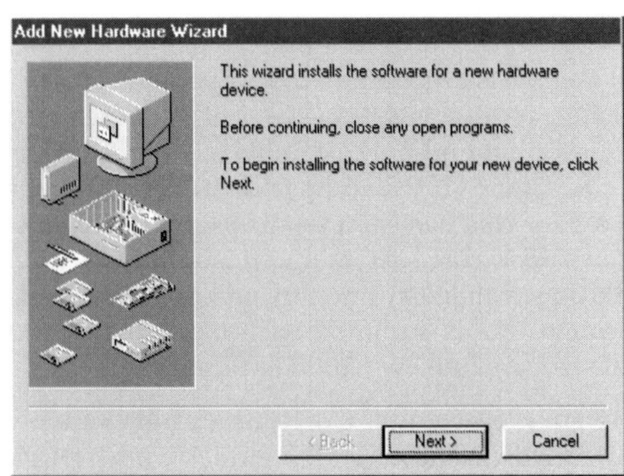

Figure 1.8 Using a wizard to install new hardware.

Setting up Windows Me

2

Installing Windows Me

Help and Support

This section is for the benefit of those readers who are upgrading from earlier versions of Windows. If your PC came with Windows Me, move straight on to Help and Support (page 143).

Windows Me can be installed directly on a PC running Windows 95 or 98.

Insert your Windows Me CD-ROM. In Windows 95 or 98, Autorun mode automatically starts up the Windows Me CD-ROM, without the user needing to know the name of the start-up file.

The dialog box shown in Figure 2.1 asks whether you wish to upgrade your computer to Windows Me. Click **Yes** to start the Windows Me Setup procedure.

32 Mb for Windows Me

First of all, check that you have at least 32Mb of RAM – this is a prerequisite for installing Windows Me.

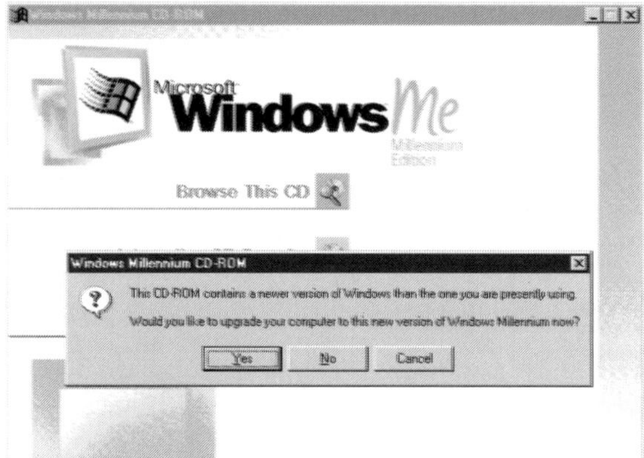

Figure 2.1 The Windows Me welcome screen.

The set-up procedure will now check your system and then prepare the Windows Me Setup Wizard (Figure 2.2) to guide you through the rest of the process.

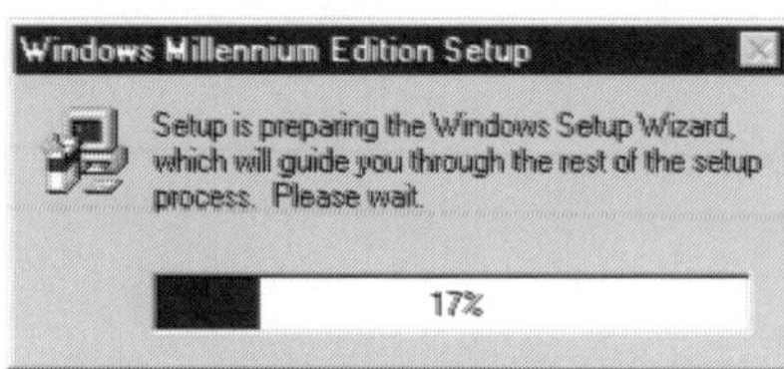

Figure 2.2 Preparing the Setup Wizard.

You may be given a warning that you should close down all Windows programs before continuing. When you have done this, click **Next** to continue the set-up (Figure 2.3).

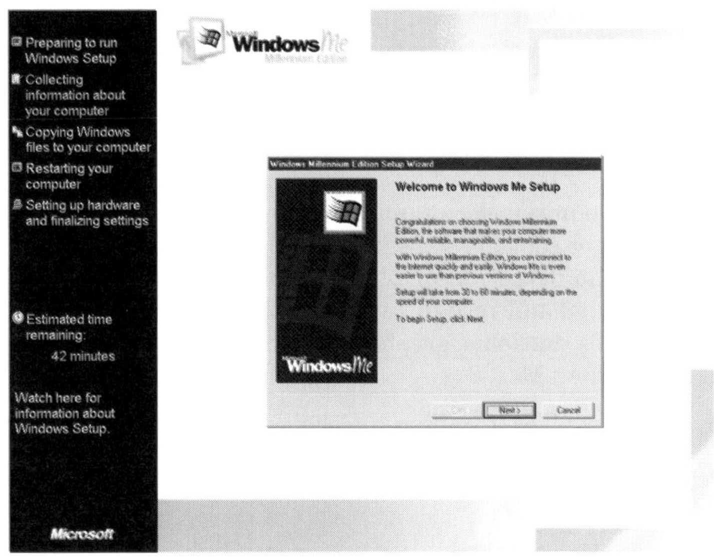

Figure 2.3 Ready to begin the Setup.

Installing Windows Me

The installation phases are as follows:

- preparing for installation;
- collecting information;
- copying files on the computer;
- rebooting the PC;
- hardware installation and final parameter set-up.

The procedure tells you what the average installation time will be (about 45 minutes in our case). This time is updated at each stage.

The Windows Me Installation Wizard starts by checking the Registry database and preparing the Windows directory from the beginning.

Installation involves the following steps:

- **Acceptance of the licence agreement**. Click on **Next** to accept the terms.
- **Save system files**. Click on **Yes** to allow you to uninstall Windows Me and revert to your original environment.
- **Creating a start-up diskette**. This enables you to restart your PC if a problem occurs or to run certain diagnostic routines.

As you might expect, Windows Me facilitates Web connections and recognizes the various types of network you can use, especially the high bit rate links such as ISDN. It includes numerous features,

Uninstalling Windows Me

At the start of the installation phase, you can ask to save existing Windows and DOS files in order to reinstall them later. You can then uninstall Windows Me. To do this you will need 120 Mb of hard disk space. Click ***Yes*** *at the prompt.*

which will be described in detail throughout this book; it contains more multimedia and more games than Windows 95 or 98, and is also more user-friendly.

On completion of file copying, the Installation Wizard will reboot your computer.

Preparing for the initial execution of Windows Me may take a further 10 minutes or so. This stage includes building the peripheral database and the detection of plug-and-play components. The latter are installed and recognized correctly by the new system. Over 1000 devices (modems, graphics boards, printer, etc.) are recognized by Windows Me.

The next stage involves installing the elements required for:

- the Control Panel
- Start menu programs
- the Windows Help facility
- DOS program settings
- setting the application start-up routine
- system configuration.

The system then reboots automatically, assembling the driver files required for machine operation.

On completion of the installation process, you will be offered the opportunity to register with Microsoft.

- Register Now
- Connect to the Internet
- Discover Windows Me
- Maintain Your Computer.

Register Now

Click on **Register Now** to access the online Registration wizard (Figure 2.4). After registering you will be notified of new products and updates, and you will be able to obtain the best possible technical support. You will also be able to access the Windows Update program, the Web extension of Windows Me. This program will keep you up to date by:

- keeping your system updated, by downloading the latest drivers and system files;
- finding quick answers to technical questions you might like to ask.

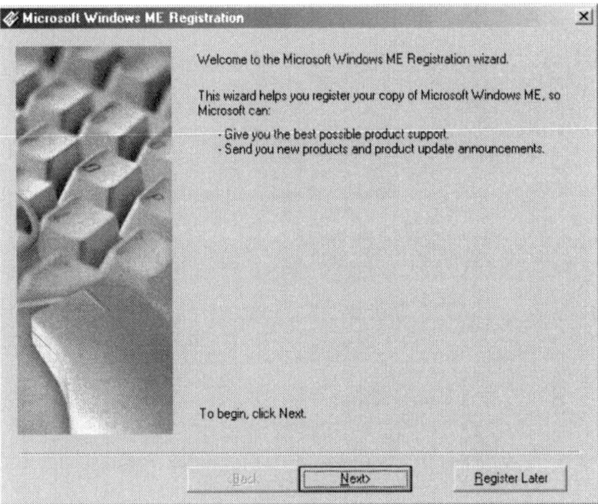

Figure 2.4 The online Registration wizard.

The Registration wizard will detect your modem and the communications port to which it is connected, unless you provide this information yourself.

The online Registration wizard then lists details of your configuration. You can send this list with your registration particulars. Click **Yes** and then click **Next**. Record the identification number of your product, because you will be asked for this whenever you contact Microsoft.

Help and Support

Windows Me has a comprehensive Help system, that covers all the features of the system and provides help at a range of levels, from beginners to experts. In fact, you can use the Help system to turn yourself from a beginner into an expert!

When first started, Help and Support opens at its Home section (Figure 2.5). This works like a contents list. Here, as everywhere in this sytem, any underlined item acts as a link to another part of the system. Browse through it to see what is available. Click one of the links on the left to get a list of links under that heading. Some of these links will lead on to other lists of links, others will lead directly to a Help page, which will be displayed on the right.

If you know what you want help on, you can find it faster in the Index section. Type in a keyword to find, and you will see the Index entries. Click on one and you will either be shown the related page, or given a small list of pages to choose from.

Before you go much further with Windows Me, you should visit the Tours and Tutorials area (Figure 2.6). Take some of the Tours that introduce Windows Me and its key features, and use the tutorials to learn how to get the best out of the system.

Web-style Help

The Windows Me Help system is different from the Help systems that you will meet in applications. This is based on Web pages, which makes it as easy to use as a browser, but it is significantly slower than other systems. Be patient, the Help is worth the wait.

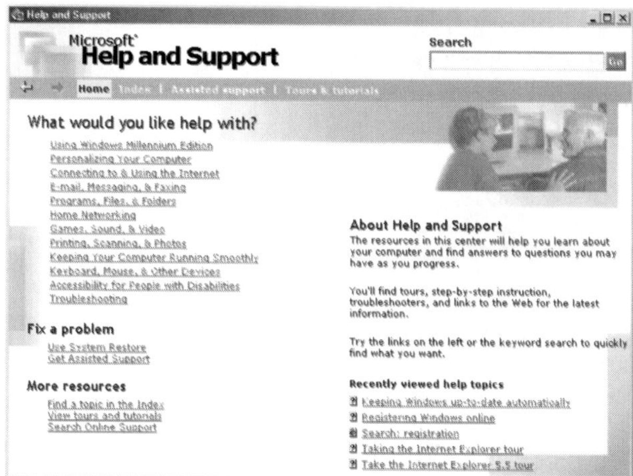

Figure 2.5 Windows Me Help and Support open at the Home page.

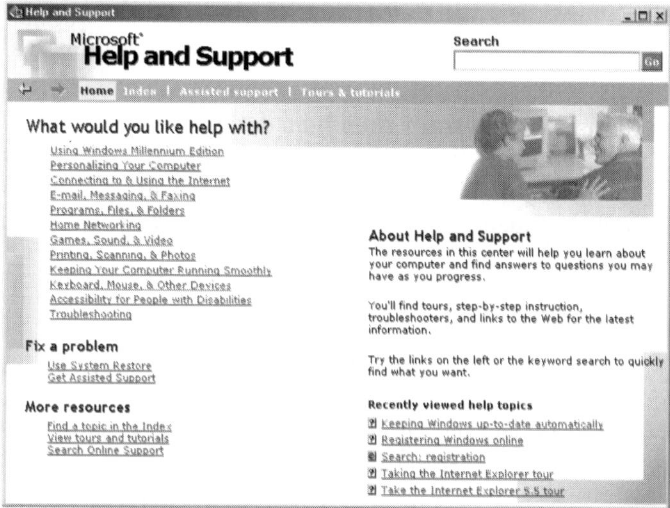

Figure 2.6 Use the Tours and Tutorials to learn more about Windows Me.

Search for Help

An alternative way to get Help on a topic is to type a keyword into the Search slot and click Go.

Maintain your computer

You can set up your PC so that Windows Me carries out certain maintenance procedures on a regular basis. The Maintenance Wizard offers you two options (Figure 2.7):

- Express – Use the most common maintenance settings
- Custom – Select each maintenance setting myself.

When using the Express option, you first define the time band for the Windows Me automated settings. Choose from the three time bands offered – night, day or evening. Click **Next** and tick the 'When I click Finish, perform each scheduled task for the first time' box to carry out these tasks immediately.

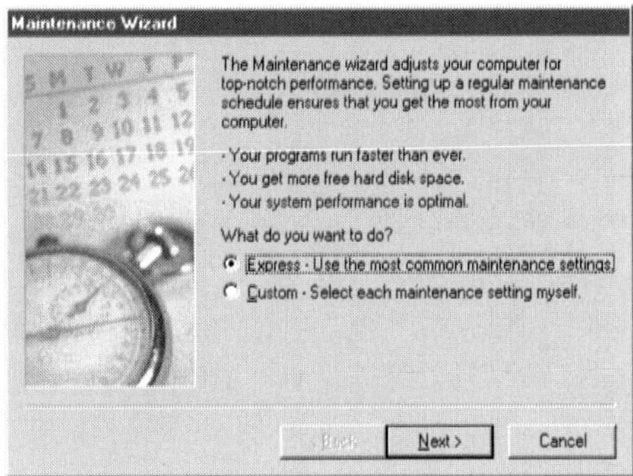

Figure 2.7 The Windows Me Maintenance Wizard.

If you want to alter the default settings of any of the scheduled tasks, open the **Control Panel** from the **Start** menu and click **Scheduled Tasks**.

Defragment programs

Select Defragment programs by double-clicking its icon (Figure 2.8). Under the Schedule tab you can define the interval between running the program, the date (e.g. every Friday at 9 p.m.), and select the disk drive that you want to defragment.

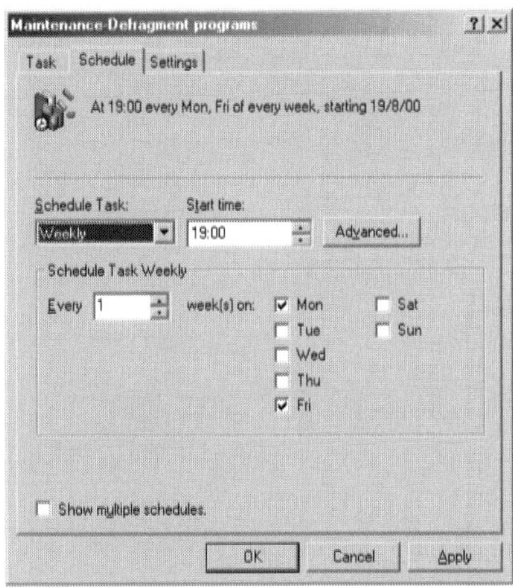

Figure 2.8 Scheduling disk defragmentation.

ScanDisk

ScanDisk detects and corrects any errors in a disk drive (Figure 2.9). Select it by double-clicking its icon. The system will also ask you to run Scandisk if any problems arise. You can now schedule this task and opt for a standard scan (checking files and folders) or a more thorough analysis. The latter includes a test of the disk surface. This takes quite a long time.

Defragmenting a hard disk

This consists of retrieving vacant spaces and reorganizing data files on your hard disk so that the data in a particular file is contiguous rather than scattered around. The various additions, deletions and modifications you make in the course of your work cause the data in a file to be stored in areas that are not necessarily physically adjacent. As a result, reading a fragmented file becomes a much longer task. Defragmentation involves reorganizing the disk space more rationally, thereby speeding up access.

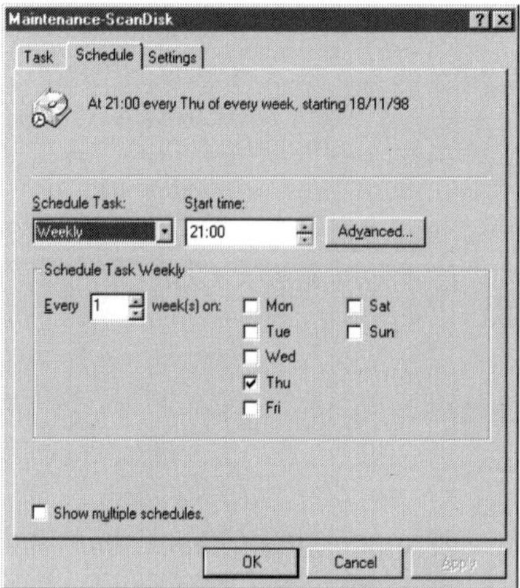

Figure 2.9 Scheduling disk checking with ScanDisk.

Disk cleanup

Disk cleanup (Figure 2.10) clears out unwanted files, such as:

- temporary Internet files
- downloaded files
- old ScanDisk files stored in the root directory
- temporary files
- temporary installation files
- the contents of the Recycle Bin
- Windows Me uninstall information.

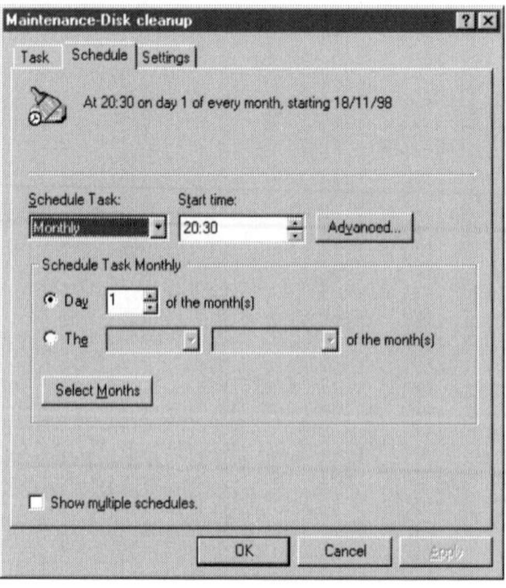

Figure 2.10 Dumping unwanted files.

Select it by double-clicking its icon.

On completion of the set-up procedure, the wizard provides a summary of the programmed sequences. Simply click on the **Close** button to confirm the selected options.

The Microsoft Windows Me Web site

To learn more about Windows Me, you can find the Microsoft Web site at the following address: ***http://www.microsoft.com/windows/windowsme***.

Connect to the Internet

Chapter 8 is dedicated to connecting to the Internet. For now you should note that, on completion of the Windows Me installation routine, a number of Internet programs will have been added to the Internet Explorer folder, which can be accessed from the Programs menu in the Start procedure. These programs are:

- the Internet Explorer 5.5 navigator (see Chapter 9);
- the mail and Outlook Express manager and the Address Book manager (see Chapter 7);
- the NetMeeting communications software;
- the Internet Connection Wizard (see Chapter 8);
- the Web page creation software, Frontpage Express;
- the Web page publication tool, Personal Web Server.

Discovering the interface

3

Your workbench: the Windows Me Desktop

My Computer properties

The Taskbar

The Start button

Smart menus

Microsoft wanted not only to meet the needs of new PC users, but also to offer solutions to problems encountered by more experienced users. The Program Manager, File Manager and Print Manager in Windows 3.1 were poorly designed; they have now been replaced by more consistent concepts and tools. Similarly, the Control Panel has been revised and improved. New concepts and a new working philosophy were good reasons for introducing a radically different presentation and operational procedure. Join our guided tour of the Windows Me interface.

Your workbench: the Windows Me Desktop

Once you have completed the PC start-up procedure in Windows Me, the workbench, or Desktop, is displayed. The system starts with the default presentation (or display) mode, which you can change later (see Chapter 7) to Web mode. Various icons, distributed about the Desktop, give access to:

- programs (the Internet Explorer navigator, and the Outlook Express message system);
- folders (the online services offered on completion of the installation sequence);
- shortcuts to documents;
- resources (My Computer);
- dedicated tools, such as Recycle Bin.

This highly organized Desktop facility conceals all the Windows Me features and the application programs that might have been installed beforehand by the PC manufacturer, and all documents. Do not worry if you have just installed Windows Me on top of Windows 95 or 98: all your tools, programs, texts, images and multimedia files will still be there.

Taskbar and Switch To function

The Taskbar replaces the Switch To function of Windows 3.1. The new method is infinitely more practical. However, the Switch To facility can still be accessed by pressing the key combination ***Alt + Tab***.

You will see three types of object (Figure 3.1) the *icons*, the *Start* button (at the bottom left of your screen) and the *Taskbar* (along the bottom of your screen). One of the items shown on our bar is the Paint Shop Pro button, which is the program that was used to create the screenshots for this book. The bar in our example also features the My Computer and Media buttons, which represent the windows open on the Desktop.

The Taskbar allows you to:

- use the Start button and run a program;
- open the window of a program waiting in the background (e.g. Paint Shop Pro);
- swap from one task to another (i.e. from one program to another, or from one window to another).

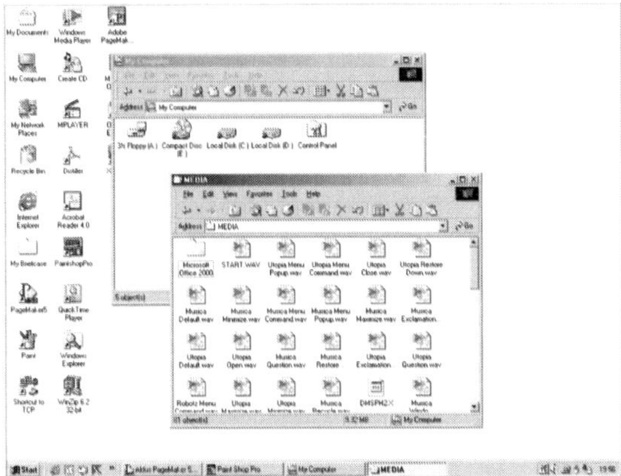

Figure 3.1 The Windows Me Desktop, with two windows open.

The My Computer icon provides an overview of your PC. It is more logical and easier to take on board than in earlier versions of Windows. Double-click on the My Computer icon on the Desktop to open it.

The My Computer window displays the hard disk drive and CD-ROM drive and the Control Panel folder (Figure 3.2).

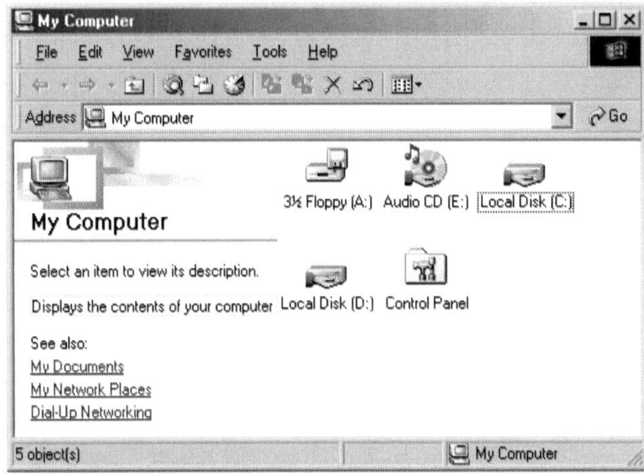

Figure 3.2 My Computer, a logical and global view of the PC.

By double-clicking on [C:], you can open the contents of the hard disk (Figure 3.3). Each directory is represented by a folder and any files entered in the hard disk drive are shown.

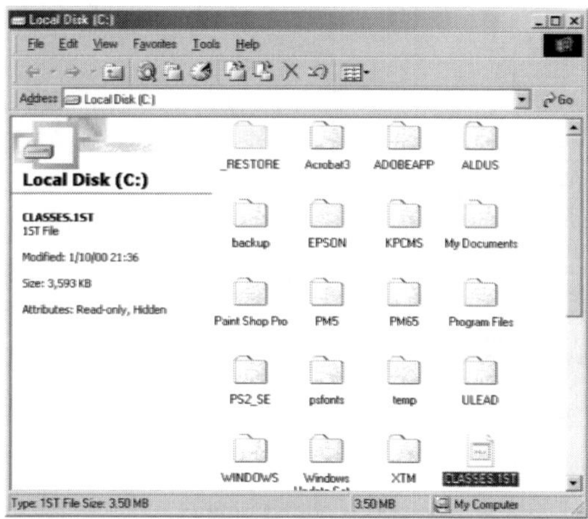

Figure 3.3 A logical view of the hard disk with its files and folders.

My Computer properties

In Windows Me, each object shown on the Desktop has properties that can easily be looked up or modified. Right-click on the My Computer icon. This brings up a 'context-sensitive menu' that allows you to open My Computer or activate its properties. Click on **Properties** to open the System Properties dialog box (Figure 3.4). Click on the relevant tab to display the properties you are interested in: General, Device Manager, Hardware Profiles, and Performance.

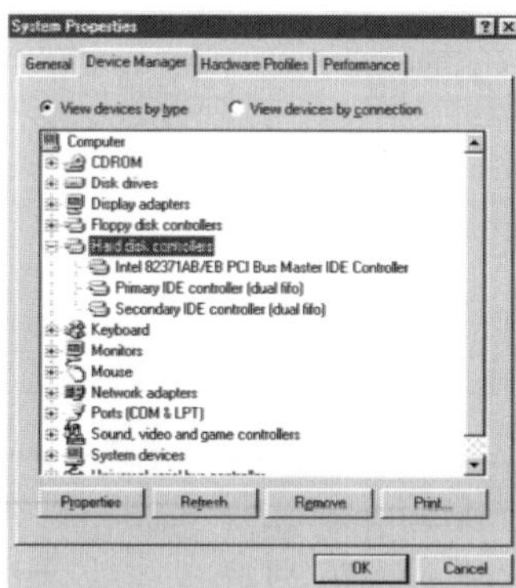

Figure 3.4 The System Properties dialog box.

The Device Manager dialog box is used to examine the hardware configuration in precise detail. It is structured hierarchically: level one, or the root, represents the PC itself, whilst the second level brings together the major device families, shown according to hardware type.

The + sign to the left of each device means that the equipment in question may be detailed and comprises subsets. Click on the + sign to open out the tree structure. In Figure 3.5 you can see a drop-down list of the system devices. The list shows individual components, such as the PCI bus, the motherboard, and the memory access (DMA) controller.

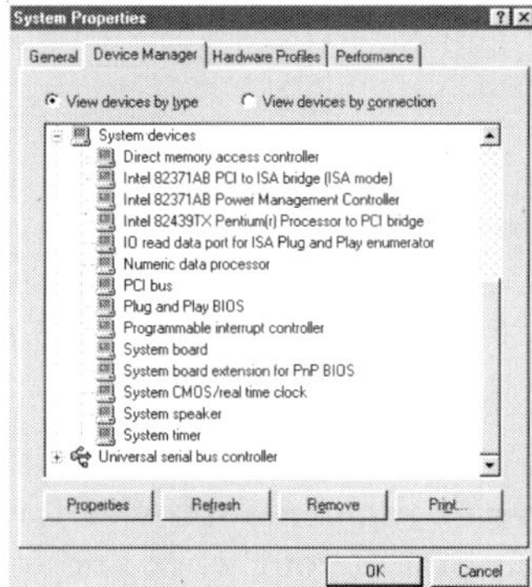

Figure 3.5 Scrolling through the hardware tree structure, showing the list of system components.

Inexperienced users need not concern themselves with all this technical information. It is mainly to enable advanced users to examine their PCs in meticulous detail and to make any necessary changes. Double-clicking on any hardware component in the tree structure brings up a display of the technical characteristics of that component. The Properties button provides information on equipment operation, parameter assignments (settings), the resources deployed (in this case, the driver) and any hardware conflicts detected.

The Performance tab of the System Properties dialog box (Figure 3.6) provides information on the performance of your computer. From the basic information supplied, you can see the percentage of system resources used. Other advanced parameters relating to disk optimization (File System button), Virtual Memory management or display optimization (Graphics button) may be used by experienced users or corporate system administrators.

We will discuss object properties in more detail later. The example chosen here, although somewhat technical, shows how easy it is to obtain information on your working environment (in this case, the computer). At this stage, we shall confine ourselves to pointing out that the object properties procedure applies to all object families: an object can be the PC hard disk, a local network, a program or a document.

The hardware profile

The PC or computer you are working with is described by a hardware profile. Once you have installed Windows Me, a default hardware profile is created, which collates all the technical characteristics of your machine. You can also create other profiles that can be activated at will when you start Windows. Whilst this facility is of limited use to the beginner, it can be implemented at corporate level when the same PC is used under different conditions, i.e. by more than one user.

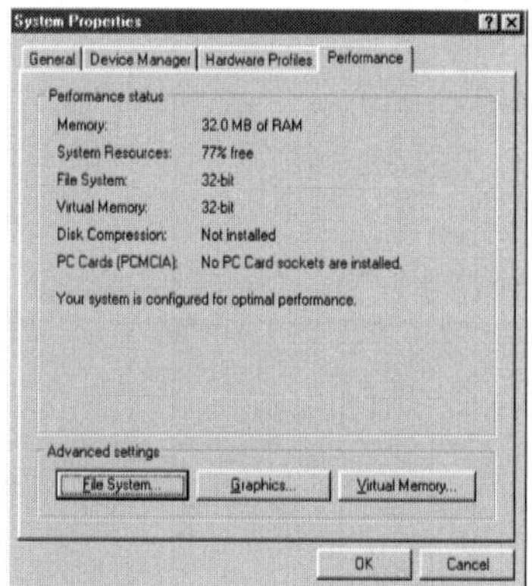

Figure 3.6 The Performance tab.

The Taskbar

The Taskbar is very important. It serves as the control tower for your workbench. Its chief aims are to help you in your work and to speed up the transition from one program to another or, to be more accurate, from one task to another.

The Taskbar was designed to meet day-to-day requirements, i.e. starting applications, finding documents, moving from one task to the next, and so on. The Taskbar is split into parts (from left to right) (Figure 3.7):

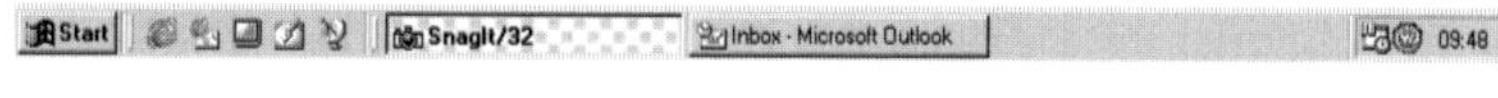

Figure 3.7 The Taskbar.

- the Start button
- the Quick Launch bar (see Chapter 7)
- a list of active tasks
- a series of system settings icons.

The right-hand side of the Taskbar contains icons that give access to volume control, display parameters, scheduled tasks (see Chapter 11), and the date and time properties.

The Start button

The Start button is your real contact point in Windows Me. Simply click on the button to display a menu giving access to programs and documents using Windows, or major commands such as shutting down the operating system (Figure 3.8).

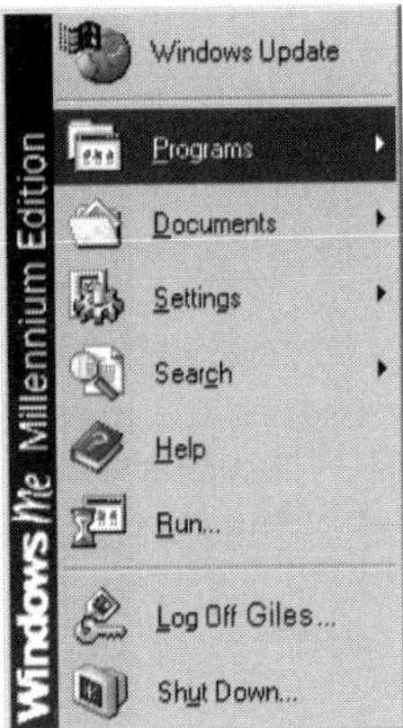

Figure 3.8 The Start menu.

Opening the Start menu from the keyboard

For convenience, when you are busy typing text at the keyboard and you do not want to use the mouse, you can activate the Start button by pressing the Windows key (the one with the flying window) or the ***Ctrl + Esc*** *key combination. Hit* ***Esc*** *to Close the Start menu.*

The small arrow to the right of certain parts of the menu means that there is a sub-menu for that option. Simply point to the selected menu with the mouse to display details. In Figure 3.9 we have scrolled through the Programs, Accessories and Communications menus in turn.

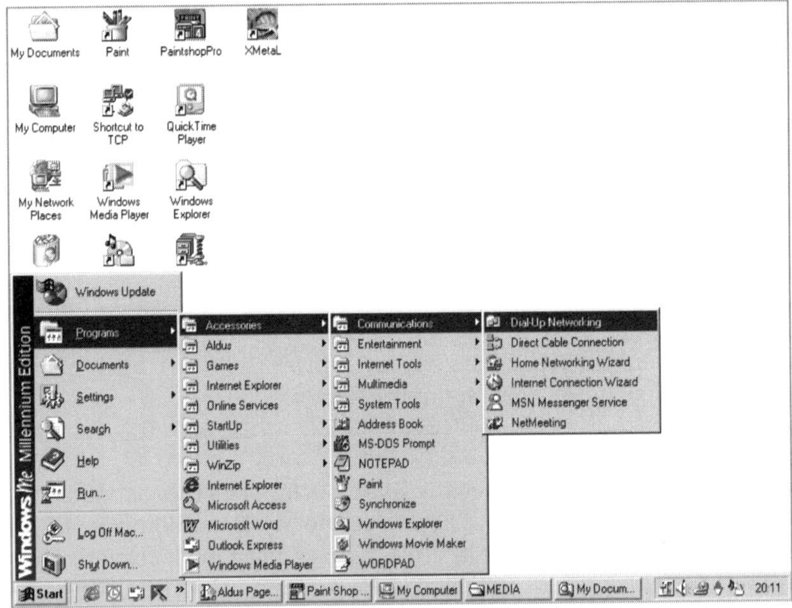

Figure 3.9 Direct access to a program using tree-structure lists: simply click on an object to open or execute it.

Windows Update *will link you to Microsoft's Website to update your copy of Windows Me with the latest developments.*

With the Start button you no longer need to conduct time-consuming searches amongst different groups of programs. Nor is there any need to double-click on the icon of the program you wish to run (as you have to in Windows 3.1). The Start button gives you faster access to a program or document. It also does away with the 'program' aspect of the Windows 3.1 interface since, from the Start button, the Documents menu gives direct access to the last documents used.

Smart menus

The Windows Me Start menu is a smart menu! It is designed to respond to the way you work, displaying at first only the core items and those that you use regularly – once it knows which they are. The rest are tucked out of sight, but can be revealed either by waiting a few moments or by clicking on the double-arrow bar at the bottom of the menu. If you use a program, it will be added to the menu, and become part of the displayed set in future. If you don't use a program for several days, it will be dropped from the menu. As smart menus are normally much shorter, it makes selection simpler and faster.

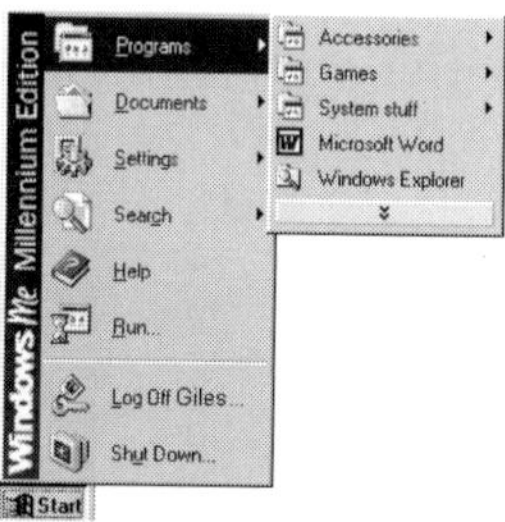

Figure 3.10 The Windows Me start menu will respond to the way you work. For example, the programs shown automatically will be the one you use the most.

The Programs menu

The Programs menu contains the most frequently used applications. To run a program, simply select it and click. This list of programs, and all other lists accessed from the Start button, can be customized, as we shall soon discover.

The Documents menu

The Documents menu under the Start button lists the last 15 documents used and gives direct access to the My Documents (and My Pictures) folders. A simple click brings back a document you recently worked on, irrespective of the program in which it was created. Remember that a document can be text, a spreadsheet, a graphics image, a photograph, a sound file or even a video clip.

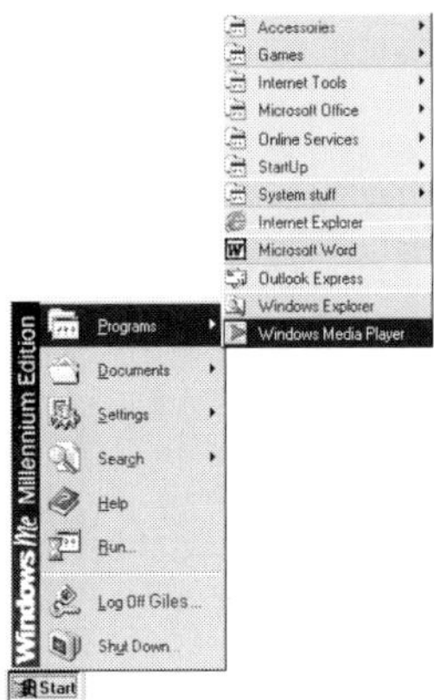

Figure 3.11 Collect a program from the Programs menu in order to run it.

The Search menu

The Search menu (Figure 3.12) under the Start button is used to find a program or a file; to find a PC in a local area network, or a document or service on the Web; or even to find individuals on the Net. The features offered here are considerably more powerful than those offered by the old File Manager, whilst their extension to the Internet greatly increases their usefulness.

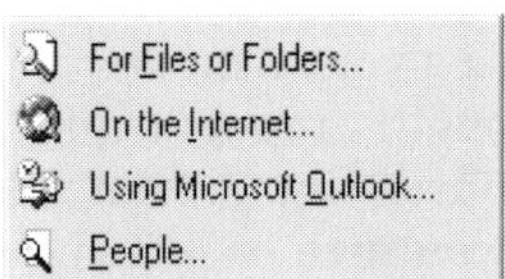

Figure 3.12 The Search menu.

To find a file or folder, click **Files or Folders.** The **Search Results** window will open (Figure 3.13). This is actually My Computer (see Chapter 4) with the Explorer Bar set to Search mode.

A simple search can be by all or part of the filename or for some text within a file – or a combination of the two. Suppose, for example, you were trying to find a letter to Mr Ree but could not remember what you called it or where you stored it. You at least know that it contained his name and that it was a **Word** document – and so would have the .doc extension. You could simply give 'Mr Ree' as the Containing text, and the search would find it, but if you gave 'doc' in the filename slot it would speed up as the search would then only have to read through document files (plus any others that happened to have 'doc' somewhere in their names) and could ignore all the rest.

Manipulating windows

When you run a program, it opens an application window that you can close again by clicking on the X symbol at the top right corner of the window; you can expand (maximize) or contact (minimize) it by clicking on the underscore symbol (_). When the window is minimized, its icon can be seen on the Taskbar – restart it by clicking on it. This operating mode applies to any type of window.

Find by contents

*The **Containing text** box enables you to conduct a search based on specific contents. Hence, in a set of signed documents, you can carry out your search based on the signature or key words of your choice. You can also find on your PC all the files that contain certain groups of words.*

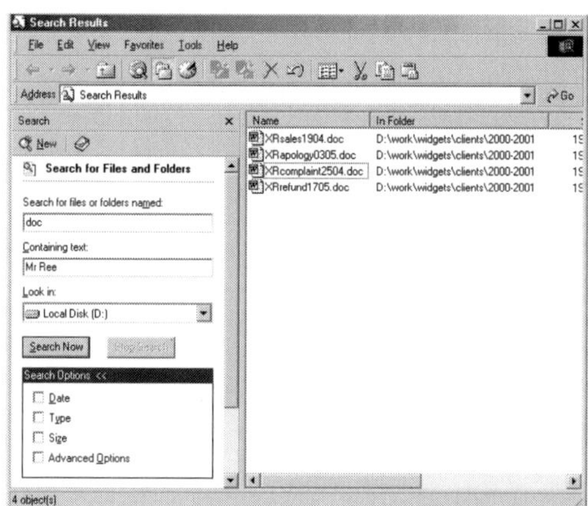

Figure 3.13 Search by name and by containing text.

You can speed the seach up further by specifying which drives or folders to start looking in. Note that the search will normally look into all the subfolders below the start point.

Click **Search Now** to start the search. It may take a few moments.

In the **Search Options** area you can define a search by specifying Date, Type, Size or other Advanced options. If you know when a file was created, modified or last accessed, you can set the date limits. The little drop-down calendar provides a very neat way to set dates! The Type can be picked from the (long!!) drop-down list. Specifying the size might be useful sometimes. The Advanced options are rarely much use. They simply let you turn off the sub-folder search or turn on case sensitivity.

This file search by name facility uses a character string that may contain the wildcard characters '?' and '*'. Here are a few examples:

- **Mode**: find all objects containing the letters 'mode'.
- **M?de**: the '?' can replace any character.
- **Mo*e**: the '*' character can replace any string of characters between 'Mo' and 'e'.

Figure 3.14 shows a typical search pattern, displaying details of the files found. The result may be displayed in one of five ways: Large Icons, Small Icons, List, Details or Thumbnails. These options are available by clicking on the **View** tab.

Click on the File tab for a range of options, that change according to the nature of the object selected. Thus, in the case of a text file, the menu offers alternatives such as Print or Send To (Figure 3.15). In the case of a folder, an Explore option or a fresh search (Find) within the same folder are offered (Figure 3.16).

Figure 3.14 Using the options to define a search.

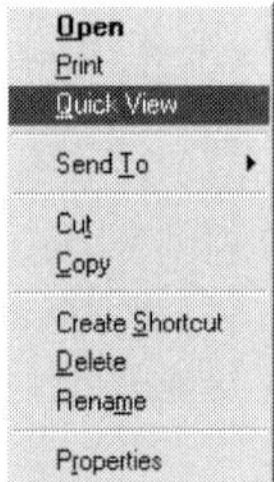

Figure 3.15 For a text file, the File tab reveals this menu ...

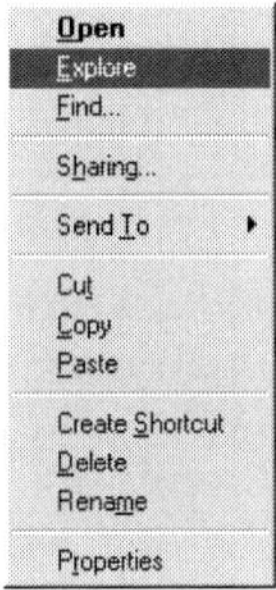

Figure 3.16 ... for a folder, the File tab reveals this menu.

Windows Me deploys the principles of dynamic processing, depending on the properties of the objects you wish to find. In the file tab, some options are common to all objects, whilst others are dependent on the type of object:

- **Open**. Opens a document or starts the selected program or, if the object is a folder, opens a My Computer window to display its contents. We will deal with this utility in the next chapter.

Stopping a search

*The **Stop** button allows you to suspend processing at any time. This is useful if the processing seems to be taking too much time, especially if the file sought has just been added to the results list.*

- **Open with**. When the nature of the selected object is not identified, Windows Me sets out a list of programs that might be able to open the selected file.
- **Print**. Prints a text file directly.
- **Play**. Plays a sound file immediately. To do this, Windows Me uses the Media Player, which is supplied as standard. At the same time, a video clip will be displayed in an independent play window.
- **Explorer**. Uses a folder file to start up Windows Me Explorer. We will deal with this utility at a later stage.
- **Find**. If the selected object in the resulting list is a folder, this option opens a new search window.
- **Send To**. This is a particularly powerful communications option, which we will also discuss in detail at a later stage. Three despatch options are offered: a fax addressee, a message addressee, and a diskette. If your PC is equipped with a fax/modem facility, mail can be sent directly in this way. Instructions are given by the Compose New Fax Wizard.
- **Delete** and **Rename**. Delete sends the object to the Recycle Bin, which we will describe later. Rename lets you do just that.
- **Properties**. Looks up the object's properties.
- **Create Shortcut**. Provides a quick method for accessing the object at another time.

The Help menu

The Help menu under the Start button opens the Windows Me Help facility. Online Help operates like hypertext language used on the Web: one click and you obtain links to another explanation, other programs or wizards.

Change of user on a PC

The Log off submenu, which can be accessed from the Start menu, closes down all active applications and opens a new working session. If you choose this option, Windows Me invites you to enter a new user name and password, so connection is re-established under a different working environment.

The Run menu

The Run menu is used to run a program directly when you know its name. If you cannot remember its name, press the **Browse** button to search the Desktop or work from My Computer.

You will find that this command also allows you to open an Internet site or Web page address.

The Shut Down menu

You know how to start Windows Me, but you also need to know how to shut it down. To access the Shut Down menu, click **Start**, **Shut Down**. The Shut Down menu offers you a number of options (Figure 3.17):

- total system shut down
- shut down with immediate restart.

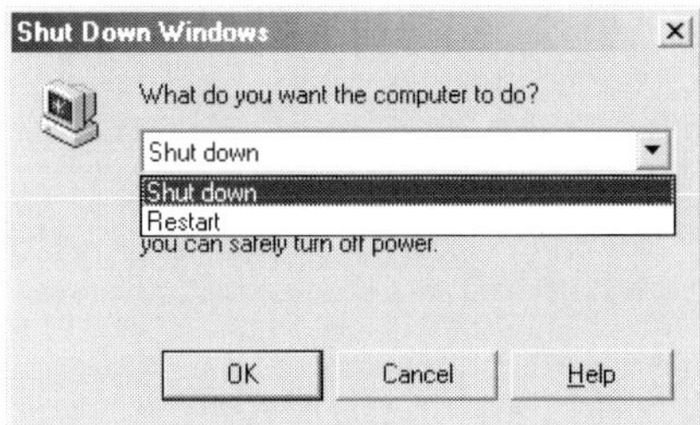

Figure 3.17 Shutting down Windows Me.

The Settings menu

The Settings menu comprises the following:

- Access To Taskbar and Start menu settings (Figure 3.18).

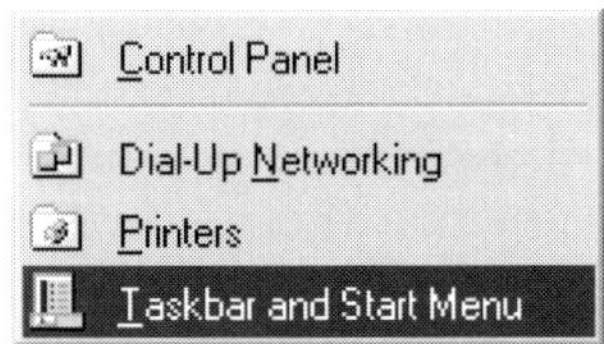

Figure 3.18 Windows Me settings.

- Control Panel activation (see Chapter 4).
- Access to the Printers folder (see Chapter 4).

The Control Panel, which will be described later, gives access to all the settings features (Display, Modem, Joystick, etc.), and also allows you to add components (programs or peripherals). The printers folder, described later, lets you change the settings for a printer (either local, or accessed via a local area network), and to manage the transmission and reception of fax messages (by Microsoft Fax).

Stopping a task without shutting down Windows Me

*Pressing the **Ctrl+Alt+Del** keys simultaneously in Windows 3.1 was irrevocable and forced you to restart the PC. In Windows Me, you can use this key combination to halt a current task and carry out the necessary back-up procedures; these are displayed in a dialog box.*

Taskbar settings

Finally, we shall look at the Taskbar settings. In the **Settings** menu, click on **Taskbar & Start Menu**. This brings up a dialog box with five options, which you have to tick or un-tick (Figure 3.19).

If the Always on top option is deactivated, the Taskbar may disappear or be partly obscured by a working window.

If the Auto hide option is activated, the Taskbar disappears from the Windows Me Desktop. It remains active, however: simply drag the mouse pointer to the bottom of the screen to slowly bring it back into view. If you put the cursor back on to the Desktop, the Taskbar will drop down again and disappear.

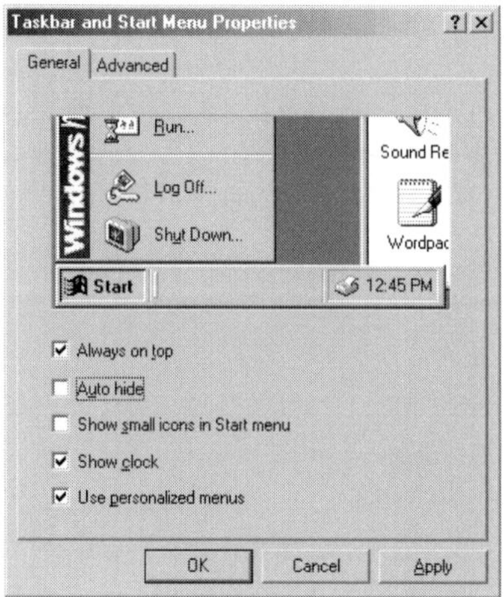

Figure 3.19 Taskbar settings options.

If Use personalized menus is activated, this turns on the 'smart' menus. Note that it takes several days before these start to take effect.

You can also decide to display smaller icons under the Start button, and to show the time on the right-hand side of the Taskbar.

Start menu settings

Now let's customize the Start menu. In the Taskbar Properties dialog box (**Start**, **Settings**, **Taskbar & Start Menu**), click on the **Advanced** tab (Figure 3.20).

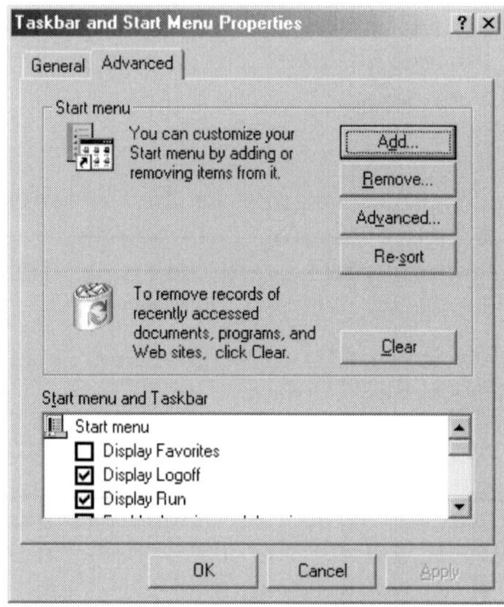

Figure 3.20 Customizing the Start menu.

In the **Start menu** area there are four buttons which you can use to customize the start menu: **Add**, **Remove**, **Advanced** and **Resort**. In the next chapter we will come back to these options. By clicking the **Clear** button, you can erase the list of the last documents from the Documents menu, which can be accessed from the Start menu.

In the **Start menu and Taskbar** pane are a set of options. Click on these to turn them on or off to suit your way of working.

4

Working in Windows Me

Changing from one task to another

The Recycle Bin

Starting a program

Managing objects with Explorer

Properties of objects

Shortcuts: the fast way to fetch an object

Customizing the Start menu

Handling diskettes

Working on a daily basis in Windows Me requires familiarity with a certain number of operations (shortcuts) and tools (the Explorer).

Changing from one task to another

The Taskbar enables you to change easily from one task to another, from one program to another or from one document to another. The Windows Me user is a true 'screen hopper' with the ability to keep several jobs (windows) active simultaneously. The role of the Taskbar is to ensure a smooth transition.

This bar, conventionally positioned at the bottom of the screen, can actually be relocated to any part of the screen. As various applications are activated, it shows all the buttons for the relevant active programs. These buttons are scaled down so that they can all fit on the Taskbar (Figure 4.1).

Figure 4.1 The Taskbar.

In our example in Figure 4.2, Paint Shop Pro has been started first, followed by Windows Explorer, Miscrosoft Word, WordPad and Media Player. WordPad Media Player are open and Media Player is active. A CD is playing.

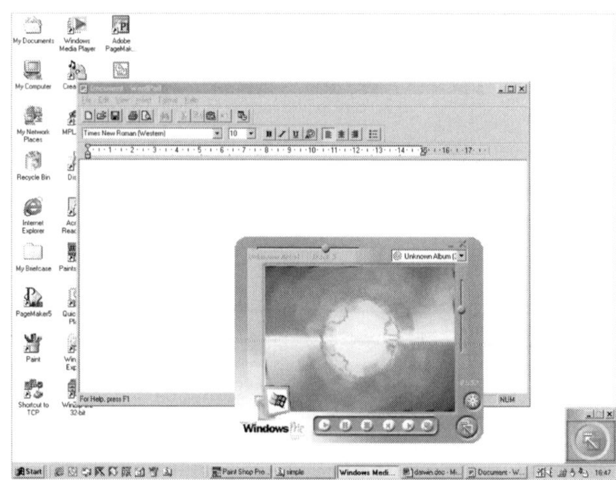

Figure 4.2 The Desktop with two applications open, one of which is active.

Finding out the properties of objects on the Taskbar

By clicking the right-hand button of the mouse on free areas of the Taskbar, you can call up the properties of objects and adjust them accordingly.

In Figure 4.3, the Media Player window has been minimized by clicking on the _ symbol at the top right corner of the window. The task remains active and you can listen to music at the same time as running the Windows Me WordPad program.

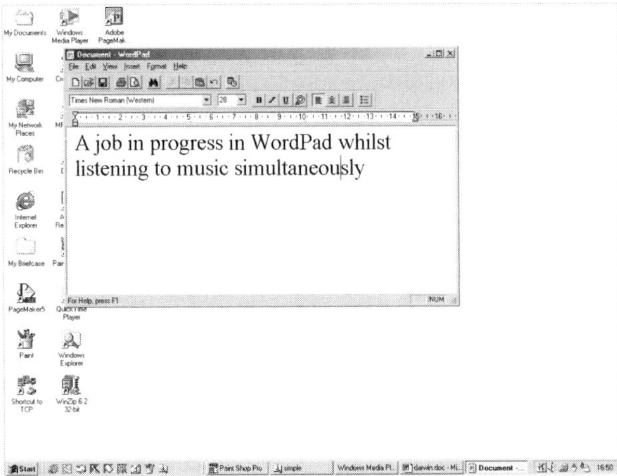

Figure 4.3 The Desktop with a job in progress in WordPad whilst simultaneously listening to music.

Next, all the windows have been minimized again by clicking on _ at the top right of the window (Figure 4.4). To activate them again, click the relevant program button on the Taskbar. When you minimize a task by clicking on _, a fast, animated image shows the window being reduced until it takes the form of a Taskbar button.

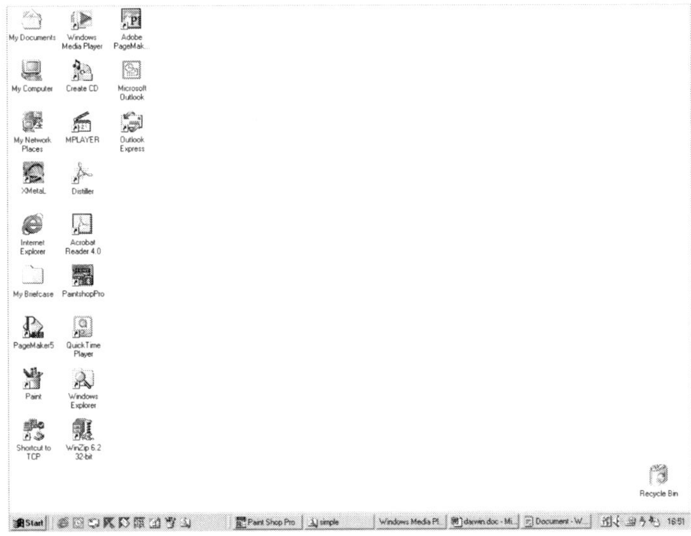

Figure 4.4 You can activate the program of your choice from the Taskbar.

Conversely, reactivating a task restores the size of the button to the initial size of the working window.

The number of buttons on the Taskbar is the same as the number of active tasks. Buttons are automatically resized so that they all fit on the bar. For improved legibility, you can increase the size of the Taskbar by dragging its upper edge with the mouse.

The Recycle Bin

Windows Me Recycle Bin is used to get rid of objects (folders, programs, text documents, images, etc.). In Figure 4.4, the Recycle Bin is visible at the bottom right of the Desktop. To dump a file, simply click and drag the object in question to the Recycle Bin icon. Alternatively, right-click on the object you want to send to the Recycle Bin, then click on **Delete**. To delete several objects at a time, hold down **Ctrl**, select all the objects to be deleted, right-click, then click on **Delete**.

If you make a mistake, you can open the Recycle Bin by double-clicking on its icon (Figure 4.5). Point the mouse to the items you wish to retrieve and then press the right button: click **Restore** to correct the mistake. The Delete option in this menu is irreversible, unless you have a dedicated retrieval utility (undelete or unerase) on the disk. If you want to retrieve the entire contents of the Recycle Bin, you can activate the Restore option in the **File** tab. To empty the bin, use the Empty Recycle Bin option (Figure 4.6). If a confirm option has been set (it exists as a default), you will receive a final message asking you whether you really do want to empty the Recycle Bin.

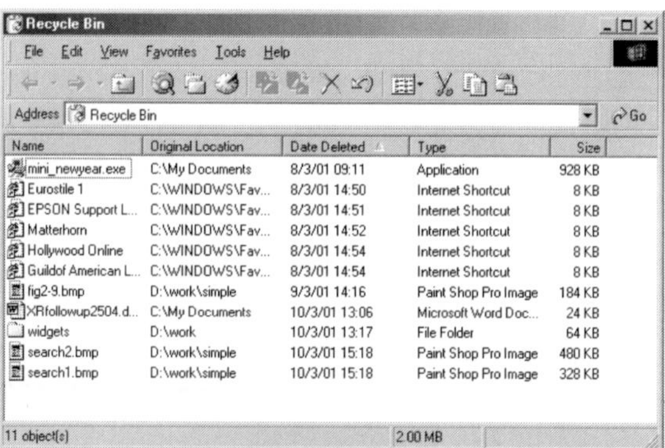

Figure 4.5 The Recycle Bin.

Starting a program

Several methods are available for starting a program that is not currently active. These methods show the versatility of Windows Me:

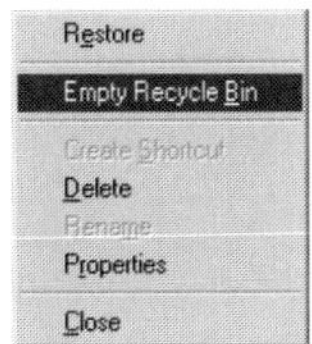

Figure 4.6 **Empty Recycle Bin** irrevocably deletes the files from your hard disk.

- Click on **Start**, **Run**.
- Click on **Start**, Programs, then click on the program of your choice.
- Double-click the **My Computer** icon, and scroll through the hard disk contents [C:]. Position the cursor over the name of the program you want to open, then double-click. Alternatively, right-click on the name of the program and click **Open**.
- Use the Search option in the Start menu to locate the program.
- Open Explorer, find the application then double-click on its name.
- If you have a shortcut to the program on the Desktop, double-click on the shortcut icon.

We can see from this example how the Desktop, My Computer and Start button provide resources for organizing your work to suit your personal needs.

My Computer

In the My Computer menu (accessed from the Windows Me Desktop), a disk or folder can be opened by double-clicking on it or, after selecting it with the right-hand button of the mouse, by activating the Open command. This calls up a window that displays the relevant files and folders as large, easily readable default icons.

Experienced users can reconfigure the display mode if they wish. Open My Computer, then click on the **View** tab. Choose one of the five display modes from the menu (Figure 4.7):

- Large Icons
- Small Icons
- List
- Details (size of file, update time, etc.).

Thumbnails shows a miniature image of the document, if possible. This option is not always available.

We shall learn how to use the Explorer Bar command in Chapter 7.

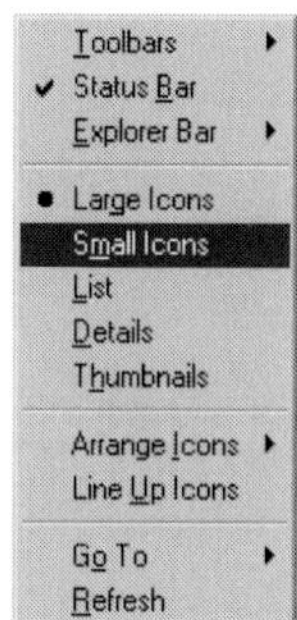

Figure 4.7 My Computer View options.

File names

The limit on the size of file names in Windows 3.1 (eight characters, plus a three-character extension) was a legacy of DOS. With Windows Me, as with Windows 95 and 98, you can use extended file names (up to 255 characters). You do not need to type in an extension, as the relevant extension for the file type is handled automatically by the program in which the file has been created.

The default display mode uses icons that are easier to read and easier to control than lists of files. This display method is also used in Windows 95 and 98. Lists will be appreciated by more advanced users, whilst icons are likely to appeal to new users. An icon might, for example, represent a folder that can be opened by double-clicking on it, or by clicking the right-hand mouse button and selecting Open.

The View menu also lets you activate the toolbars. In the View menu, click on **Toolbars**:

- **Standard Buttons**. This bar gives access to basic functions (parent buttons to go up the tree structure, cut-and-paste functions, deleting an object, etc.).
- **Address Bar**. This bar allows you to type in a file location on the hard disk or, as we shall see later, a Web address.
- **Links**. This option allows you to display a bar of links to Internet addresses.
- **Radio**. Use this to listen to radio on the Internet when you are online.
- **Customize**. This option lets you add buttons to and remove them from the toolbar. You can also turn text labels for the button on or off here.

Handling files and folders

Files and folders can be handled very easily and moved around using the mouse. Right-clicking on a file brings up a menu (Figure 4.8) that allows you to cut, copy, paste, rename or delete the file.

Managing objects with Explorer

Windows Me Explorer is the program you use to navigate folders and files. Explorer provides an overall view of the PC's environment. All local disk resources (My Computer), as well as the disks that can be accessed via a network (My Network Places), are displayed on the same level. Explorer can also find documents on the Internet. This unique presentation simplifies life for the user.

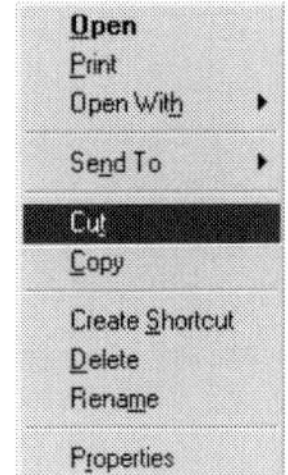

Figure 4.8 File operations.

Windows Me Explorer can be called up in a number of ways:

- Click on **Start**, **Programs**, **Windows Explorer**.
- Right-click on the My Computer icon, then click **Explore** (Figure 4.9).

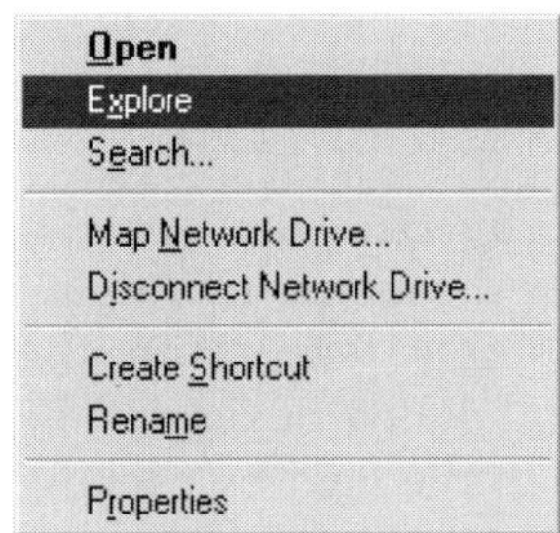

Figure 4.9 Using the right-hand button, you can activate the Explorer option.

Windows Me Explorer enables you to determine the contents of an object, whether it is My Computer, a hard disk or a folder (Figure 4.10). The left-hand pane of the window shows all the objects in the environment (this is the Explorer pane), whilst the right-hand pane shows the contents of the object being explored.

Generally speaking, a folder contains files and other folders. To sort your folders and files, click on **View**, **Details**. You will see four columns: Name, Size, Type and Modified (Figure 4.10). Decide how you want to sort your objects, then click on the relevant column heading. Clicking on the same heading reverses the sort direction.

To create a new object (e.g. a folder, shortcut, text file, WordPad document, image or sound), point the mouse at a free area to the right of the contents, click the right-hand button, and click on **New**. Select the type of object you want. A new icon appears in the window; you then simply give it a name.

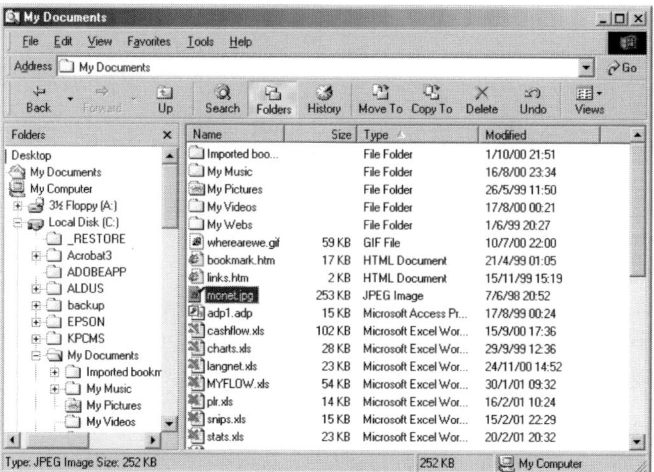

Figure 4.10 The contents of a folder in Explorer.

Properties of objects

All objects handled in Windows Me have properties that you can look up at any time, simply by right-clicking the mouse to activate the Properties command. You can find this feature in the Properties screen of My Computer. Several dialog boxes will be offered and you can change from one page to the next by clicking the relevant tabs.

The information supplied in the hard disk Properties box will, of course, be quite different. The space available on the disk is displayed in the General dialog box as a graphic (Figure 4.11). The Tools menu offers two options:

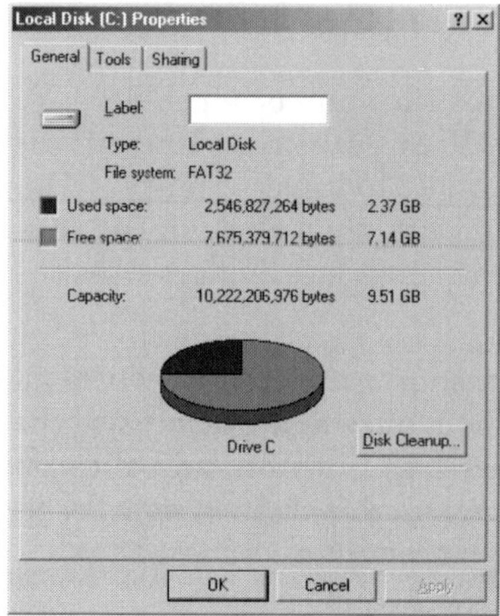

Figure 4.11 Displaying the properties requested for the hard disk.

- ScanDisk, for checking for disk errors
- a disk defragmenter.

These two programs are part of the System Tools facility that can be found from the Start menu (see Chapter 11).

Shortcuts: the fast way to fetch an object

Shortcuts are powerful links that will enhance your productivity in Windows Me. You can create a shortcut to any type of object – a file, program, folder or even the hard disk. Even better, you can put the shortcut where you want on the PC, even in a document. When you open a shortcut, the object it is pointing to is automatically activated. Shortcuts are displayed in the same way as any icon: they represent the image of the object they are pointing to. They are distinguished by a little folded arrow at the bottom left of the icon.

For our example, we will create a shortcut to the program Paint Shop Pro. This can be called up from the Start menu but, as we have several screenshots to do, we would like to access it from the Desktop. A search (Find) will enable us to find this program on the disk: the program, named PSP, is in the Paint Shop Pro folder, which is stored in the Program Files folder of Windows Me. From Explorer, right-click on this object. The drop-down menu that appears offers the Create Shortcut command (Figure 4.12). In the drop-down menu, click on **Create Shortcut**. A second icon for the object will appear. Now either drag the icon on to the Desktop, or right-click on the icon, click **Send To**, and click **Desktop (Create Shortcut)**.

Organizing your shortcuts

The shortcut concept allows you to place an application, document or object in several files without the need to copy them. For instance, when running a multimedia application you need to delve into a number of folders. Each time you want to open a document, you have to change directory. If you create shortcuts, you can put all the shortcuts in the same folder, whilst leaving the original items where they were. Since the shortcut is merely a pointer to data, it occupies only a tiny piece of memory (255 bytes).

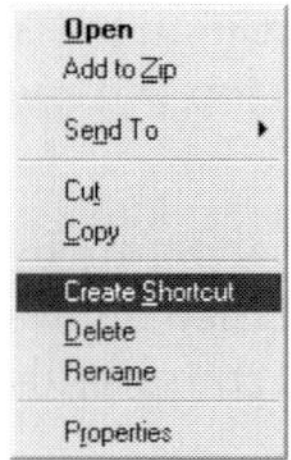

Figure 4.12 Creating a shortcut.

Shortcuts can be moved to any location: to the Desktop, the Start menu, and the My Computer icon. It's up to you! The most frequently used programs could be placed under the Start button along with key documents, whilst you could position the disk drives or shared network resources with, for example, current business on the Desktop.

Customizing the Start menu

From the Start menu, click on **Settings**, **Taskbar and Start Menu**. The Taskbar and Start Menu Properties dialog box allows you to add or delete a shortcut (Figure 4.13). The Advanced dialog box button opens the Start menu in Explorer. At this stage, you are able to completely reorganize this menu by means of cut-and-paste or add operations. You can also drag a Desktop object to the Start menu.

Placing a shortcut in the Start menu

To do this, drag the shortcut icon to the Start button. The shortcut will then automatically position itself in the main menu under this button, from where you can then run the programs you use most often without having to worry about where to find them. To place the shortcut in a submenu of the Start button, simply drag it to the Start button and release the mouse button. Now drag it from this position to another, e.g. in the Programs menu.

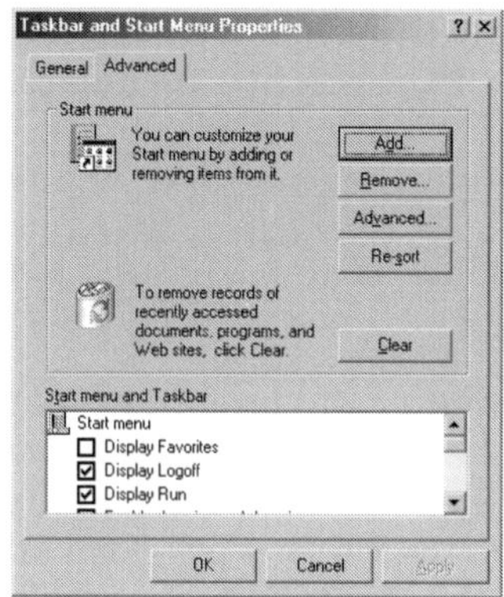

Figure 4.13 Selecting programs in the Start menu.

New shortcuts can be created directly by clicking on **File**, **Create Shortcut**. Existing shortcuts can be moved, copied or deleted in the Explorer window, or even placed in this window from the Desktop (drag and drop with the mouse).

Handling diskettes

The disk drive can be accessed from My Computer. If the drive is used frequently, you can create a shortcut on the Desktop to read a diskette quickly.

The diskette is opened by double-clicking on the [A:] icon, or by right-clicking the icon, then clicking **Open**. This menu also allows you access to the diskette formatting and copying commands (Figure 4.14).

Copying files

To copy a PC file to diskette, simply drag and drop it with the mouse. Alternatively, right-click on the file's icon, click on ***Send To****, then click* ***3 1/2 Floppy [A]****. Similarly, you can drag and drop one or more files from the diskette to a folder in the PC.*

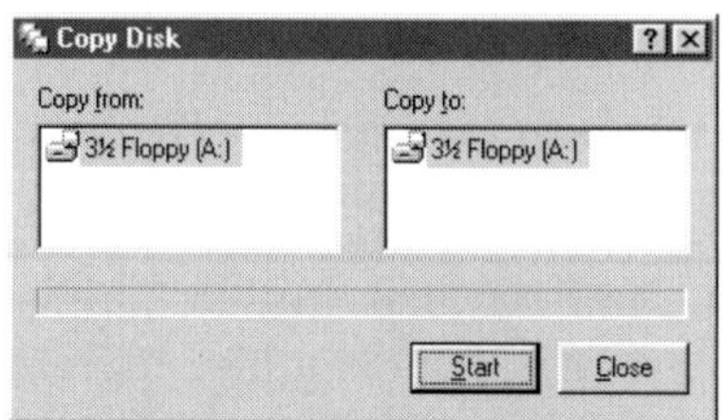

Figure 4.14 Copying a diskette.

The Control Panel

5

The Control Panel

Accessibility set-up

Monitor display settings

Mouse set-up

Joystick set-up

Modem settings

Date and time management

Sound management

Multimedia set-up

Printer management

Font management

Mail management

Connecting to the Internet

Creating a password

Adding applications

The Add New Hardware Wizard

The Control Panel

At installation, Windows Me will have optimized your system and set parameters for the individual components. You can use the Control Panel to look up settings, improve them and adapt them as your environment changes. Thus, you can change your password, modify your monitor display settings or even install a new modem. The Control Panel (Figure 5.1) can be accessed from the Settings menu under the Start button.

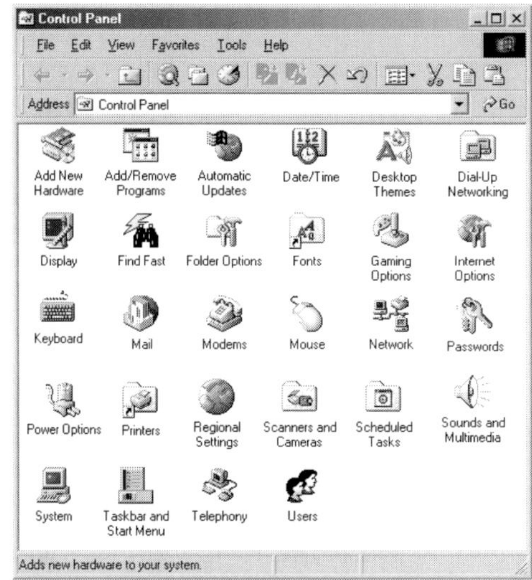

Figure 5.1 The Windows Me Control Panel.

Most configuration options are accompanied by wizards to assist you. Wizards take the hard work out of installing new peripherals, thanks to plug-and- play technology.

Accessibility set-up

The accessibility settings enable you to tailor Windows to your own particular working environment. This is especially useful for new users, and also for users with physical disabilities, as special settings have been created to suit special needs.

In the Control Panel, click on **Accessibility**, **Options**. The Accessibility Properties window (Figure 5.2) comprises five boxes which you select by clicking on the appropriate tabs. For all the settings proposed, click **Apply** to try out the individual setting; click **OK** if you are happy with the setting and want to validate it.

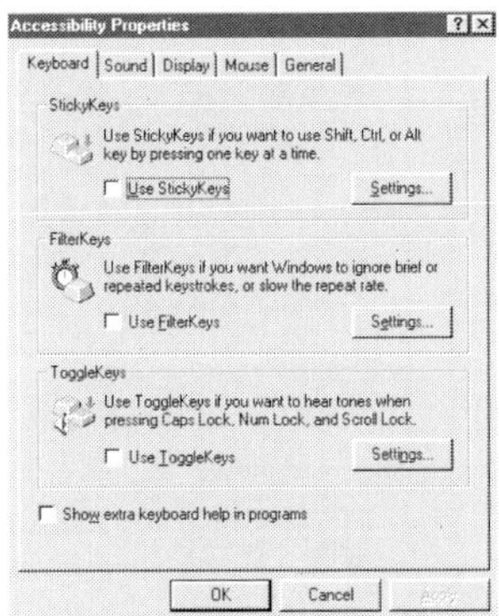

Figure 5.2 Accessibility Properties.

Keyboard set-up

The keyboard tab enables you to set up the keyboard. It offers three setting modes:

- StickyKeys
- FilterKeys
- ToggleKeys.

To activate one of these modes, tick the appropriate **Use ...** box, then click on the **Settings** button to specify the key settings.

The FilterKeys setting overrides accidental or repeated keystrokes.

The ToggleKeys function instructs the PC to generate a high-pitched sound when you press Caps Lock, Scroll Lock or Num Lock, or a low-pitched sound when you deactivate one of those keys.

Sound and picture settings

The Sound tab in the Accessibility Properties dialog box (Figure 5.3) is used to link an image or text to a sound message in Windows Me. People who are hard of hearing appreciate this option. Two features are offered. You can use SoundSentry to show a flashing sign on the screen for each sound generated by the PC. The area that flashes can be designated by clicking on the **Settings** button. Alternatively, use ShowSounds to display written captions instead of sounds.

You can also adjust the monitor display and select colours or fonts that are easier to read. To do this, click the **Display** tab, the **Use High Contrast** box, and click the **Settings** button.

Monitor display settings

In the Control Panel, click on **Display**. The Display Properties dialog box lets you change the appearance of your screen. The Background tab lets you set the background for the Desktop

StickyKeys

StickyKeys is ideal for people who find it difficult to press two keys at the same time. With this setting, you can apply the Shift, Ctrl or Alt key simply by hitting the key once followed by the next key – you don't have to keep your finger on the Shift, Ctrl or Alt key when you hit the next key. For example, to type a capital letter, you would hit Shift and then the relevant character key, rather than hitting them both at the same time.

Mouse set-up

*The mouse settings tab enables you to use the four arrow keys on the numerical keypad to move the cursor, to click and double-click, and even to drag objects. The **settings** screen allows you to define a shortcut key to switch this function off and to adjust the pointer speed.*

Testing screen saver mode

The selected screen saver can be viewed on the full screen by clicking on the **Preview** *button. You can also protect your PC by means of a password. When your system is on standby, the animated screen saver starts, but your PC can only be used again by entering the password. To activate a password, tick the* **Password Protected** *box, click on* **Change**, *then enter your password in the* **New Password** *box. Click* **OK**. *The Wait counter indicates the desired period of inactivity before the screen saver becomes active.*

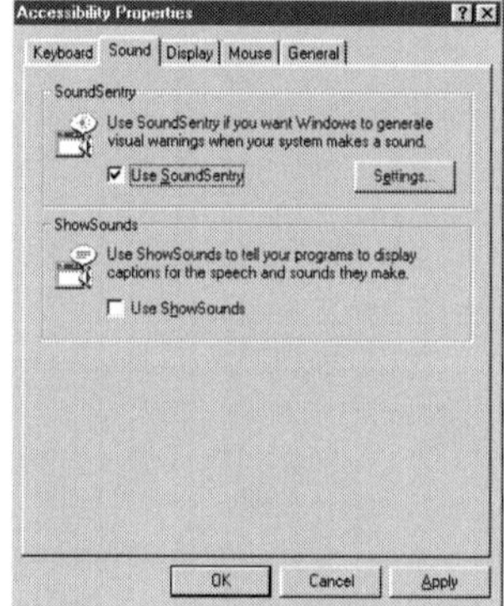

Figure 5.3 Linking an image or text to a sound message.

(Figure 5.4). You can pick a wallpaper in bitmap format (BMP), which is then applied to the Desktop. By clicking on the **Browse** button, you can find a BMP file on the hard disk and assign it to the Windows Me screen background.

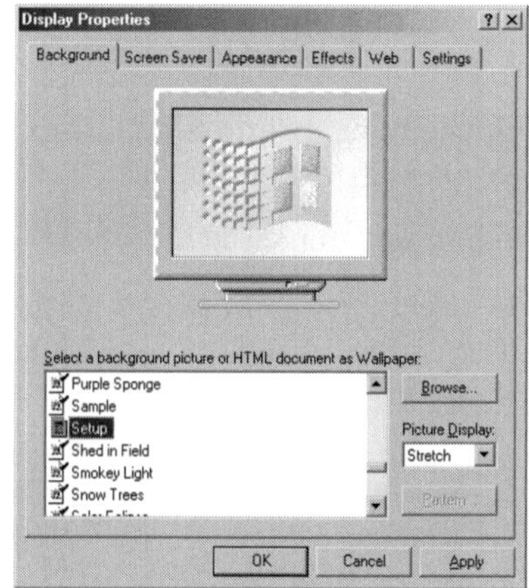

Figure 5.4 Changing the wallpaper.

The Screen Saver tab is used to set up a screen saver.

The Appearance tab (Figure 5.5) enables you to set interface colours (screen background, window title bar, control button, etc.) based on a given specimen.

The Settings tab is used to adjust screen resolution and the colour box, provided the graphics board connected to the monitor accepts the selected values. The colour box can be set to 32-bit 'true colour' mode (16.7 million colours), a mode used for processing photographs and bitmap images.

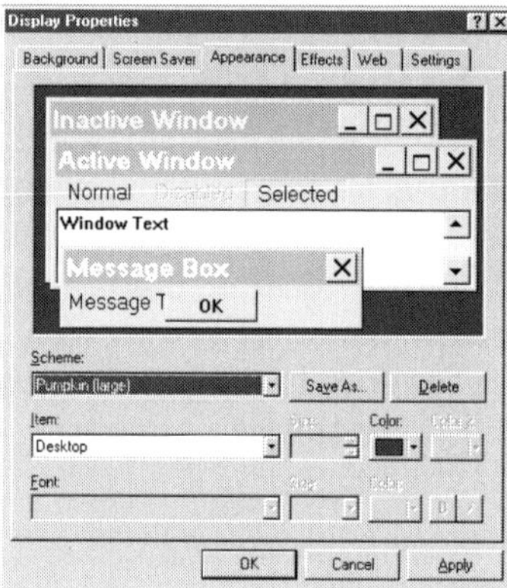

Figure 5.5 Desktop appearance settings.

The Web tab is used to set the positioning of Web content (see Chapter 8) on the Desktop.

Mouse set-up

The mouse is so familiar to most users that it seems unnecessary to talk about it. Yet it does deserve some attention, particularly since once the mouse is set correctly, it can help you work more efficiently in Windows Me.

In the Control Panel, click on **Mouse**. The dialog box you see will depend on what sort of mouse you have. Somewhere, you will find a box entitled 'Buttons' (Figure 5.6). This is of interest to left-handed users. Until now, left-handed users have battled away, using the left button of the mouse for selecting options and the right button to obtain the context-sensitive menu (which allows you to access the properties of objects); now you can change the rules of the game. Simply click the left-handed option in the Button configuration menu.

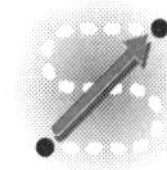

From double- to single-clicking

The double-click action enables you to run a program or open any type of object. You can bypass this by using the right-hand button to display a context-sensitive menu, from which you can open the object.

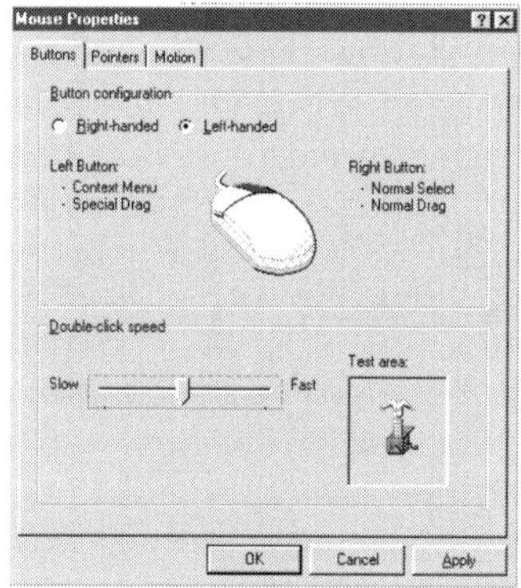

Figure 5.6 Left-handed use of the mouse.

Joystick set-up

A few years ago, joysticks were not very sophisticated; today, there are a number of models adapted to a range of games software: flying a fighter plane, driving an F1 racing car, etc. Broomstick, multi-axis spinners, multibutton controllers, rudders – there are many variants of games devices. The Gaming options dialog box, accessed from the Control Panel (Figure 5.7), enables you to select your equipment and set it up properly. It is simply not possible to indulge in aerial stunts without the correct broomstick settings.

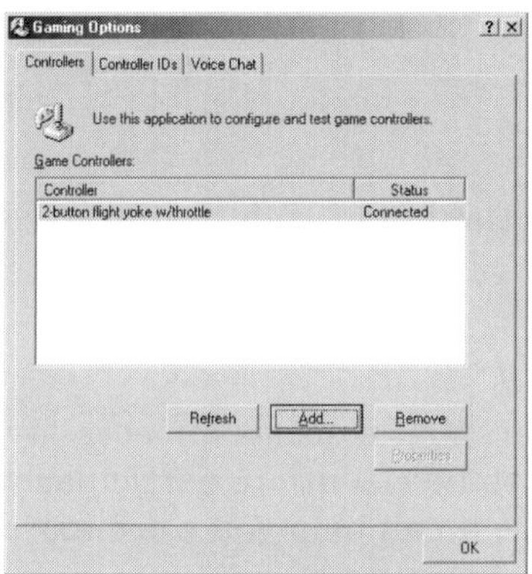

Figure 5.7 Joystick set-up.

Modem settings

In Windows Me, everything has been done to help you communicate with the outside world. With a PC, all types of communication are possible, provided you have installed the modem correctly. If your modem was present when Windows Me was installed, it will in most cases have been recognized and configured automatically. But you may need to enter new settings or switch from one device to another. The Modems Properties dialog box (Figure 5.8) allows you to look up the properties of the modem installed. The Diagnostics window indicates the connection port used; the More Info button (not seen in the figure) is used to confirm that the equipment is working satisfactorily.

The Properties tab of the General dialog box provides more technical information on connection and dialling settings. Further clicking on **Connection** provides buttons that show the communications port settings and the advanced connection set-ups.

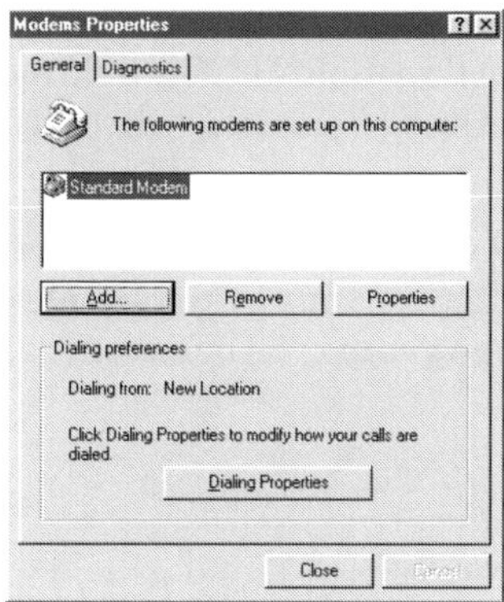

Figure 5.8 Properties of the modem installed.

Setting the time

You can display the date and time properties by clicking directly on the time displayed on the right-hand side of the Taskbar. Use the Date/Time Properties dialog box to modify the date and time.

Date and time management

It is important that the date and time in your PC are set correctly. This enables you to program events (downloading on the Internet, PC monitoring) and to store your documents with the correct details (such as the date of last modification). You should also set the time zone by clicking directly on the map displayed, or selecting a region in the world from the drop-down list.

Sound management

It is possible to link a sound to a Windows Me event. Nearly 30 events (Windows start-up, Program error, Opening a window, Receiving new mail, etc.) can be set in this way for amusement or operational reasons. For example, you might link a sound to create battery run-down alerts for portable PCs (Figure 5.9).

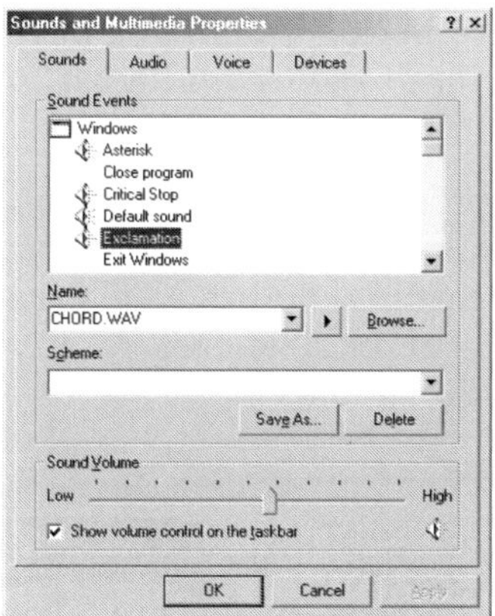

Figure 5.9 Sounds settings.

When Windows Me is installed, the sound board is automatically detected and is referenced as a peripheral by default. By ticking the show volume control box, you can alter the setting directly from the Taskbar.

These sounds or audible messages are .WAV format files. If you have a sound board and a microphone, you can record your own messages with the Sound Recorder (**Start**, **Programs**, **Accessories**, **Entertainment**, **Sound Recorder**).

Multimedia set-up

The Sounds and Multimedia folder in the Control Panel provides you with all the sound, music and video settings required. The Audio tab (Figure 5.10) controls the sound board volume.

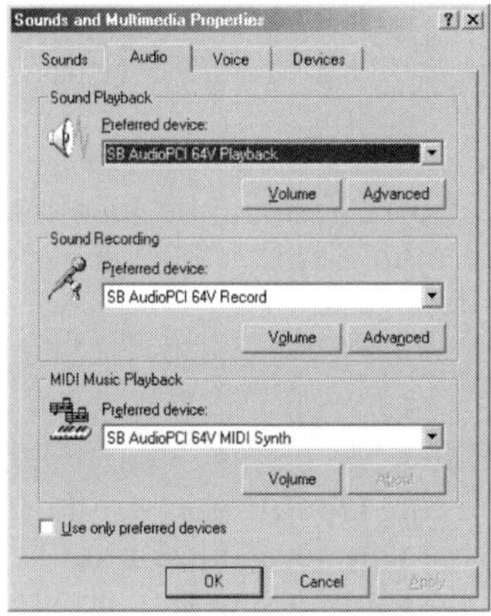

Figure 5.10 PC Audio settings.

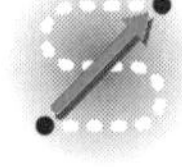

Listening to audio CDs on your PC

If your CD-ROM drive incorporates a headphone socket, you will be able, via the software, to set the volume level for listening to audio CDs.

The same screen allows you to set the recording level if you have a microphone or other type of audio input device and wish to record files in WAV format.

In the Advanced Properties box, a drop-down menu enables you to select the required quality: the higher the quality, the larger the sound file will be. A number of recording quality levels are offered and can be adjusted using the cursor. The best quality offered is equivalent to that provided by an audio CD.

Printer management

The Printers folder (Figure 5.11) in the Control Panel is a shortcut that allows you to call up printer and fax settings, provided you have installed a fax board or module in your PC. The folder can also be reached from My Computer.

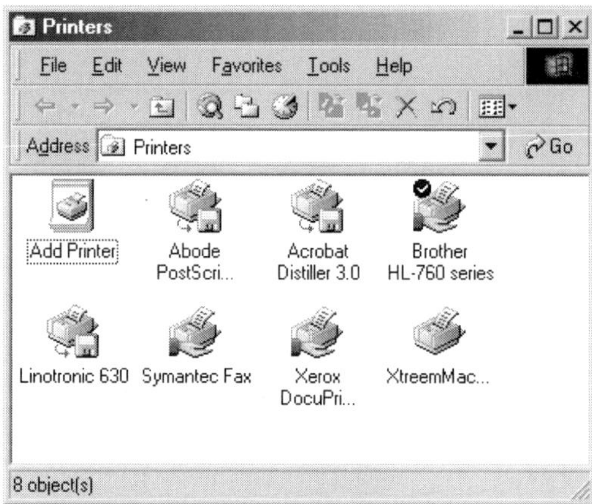

Figure 5.11 The Printers folder.

From here you can set up a printer or install a new one. By clicking **Add Printer**, you activate the Add Printer Wizard. You can choose the make and model and specify the connection port. You can decide whether this printer is to be the software default printer. On completion of the installation process, the wizard invites you to run a print test. This enables you to check that the printer is working properly.

Opening the Printers folder

*The folder can also be opened directly from the **Start, Settings** menu.*

Font management

The Fonts folder in the Control Panel gives access to all the typographical styles stored in the PC.

When you open a Fonts file, it gives you information on the font in question and you can display the characters in different modes and sizes. The Print button gives you a hard-copy sample of all the possible variants based on that font (list of characters, character size, etc.). To add a font, click **File**, **Install New Font**. Select the font to be added, then click **OK** (Figure 5.12).

Mail management

The Mail settings can be used to create new Internet mail accounts, if these are not created as part of the installation routines when you set up your connection to your Internet Service Provider. Click the Add button to start the Wizard, then respond to its prompts to supply the details of your mail service.

Unlike Window 95 and 98, Windows Me has no fax software of its own, though you may well have some that came with your modem.

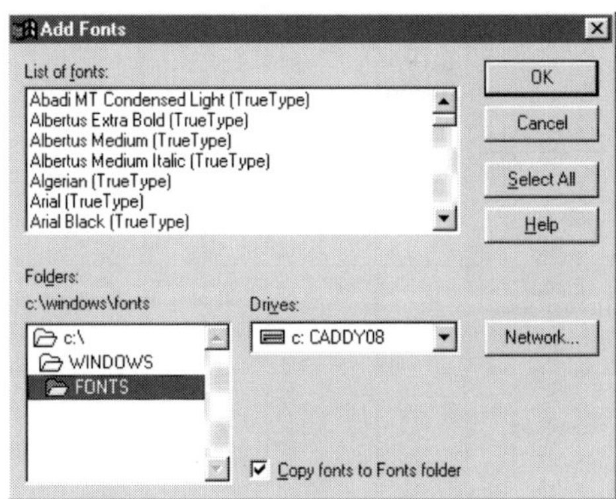

Figure 5.12 Adding one or more fonts.

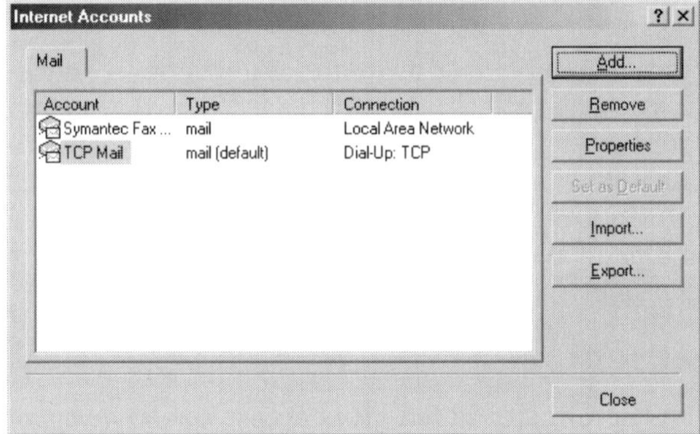

Figure 5.13 The Internet Accounts dialog box called up by the Mail icon.

Connecting to the Internet

The Internet Properties dialog box in the Control Panel allows you to check your Internet connection and, if necessary, to modify its settings. You use the Internet Connection Wizard to specify an initial (or new) connection to an access provider. The Wizard can be accessed from **Start**, **Programs**, **Accessories**, **Internet Tools**, **Internet Connection Wizard**, or from the **Connections** tab (Figure 5.14) in the Internet Properties dialog box.

For information on the other dialog boxes, see Chapter 8.

Changing a password

*To change a password simply click on **Change Windows Password** or enter the old password, followed by the new one, and confirm the new password.*

Creating a password

Windows Me and its various related services can provide protected access by means of a password (Figure 5.15). You can change your passwords by entering the Passwords Properties dialog box from the Control Panel. Use a little imagination if you really want to protect access to the system, and make sure you remember your new password!

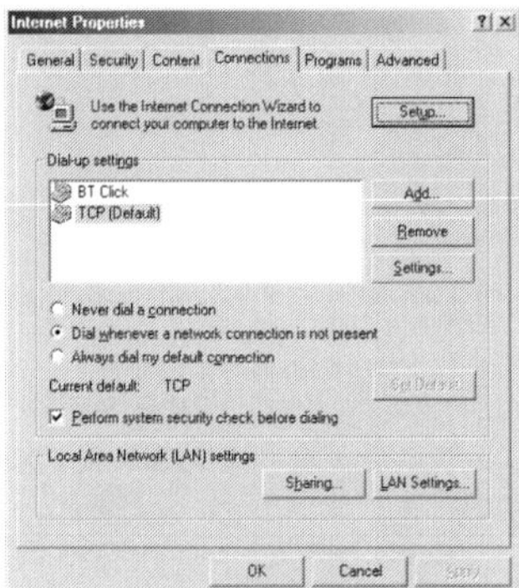

Figure 5.14 The Internet Properties dialog box.

Figure 5.15 Changing passwords.

Adding applications

From the Control Panel, select the Add/Remove Programs icon. From this dialog box, you can install (or uninstall) programs from the floppy disk on CD-ROM drives. Click on the **Install/Uninstall** tab, then click **Install** (Figure 5.16).

As well as installing applications, you can fine-tune Windows Me by adding or removing a component. To do this, click on the **Windows Setup** tab. The program scans the PC to detect the resident programs. In the working window, you can select new components, or uninstall others.

The Add New Hardware Wizard

Windows Me also offers a guided procedure for installing any type of peripheral: CD-ROM drive, additional hard disk, display board, keyboard, modem, mouse, monitor, multifunction board, network adapter, PCMIA device, printer, SCSI controller, sound board, digitizing board or joystick. This wizard can be called up from the Control Panel: click on **Add New Hardware** (Figure 5.17).

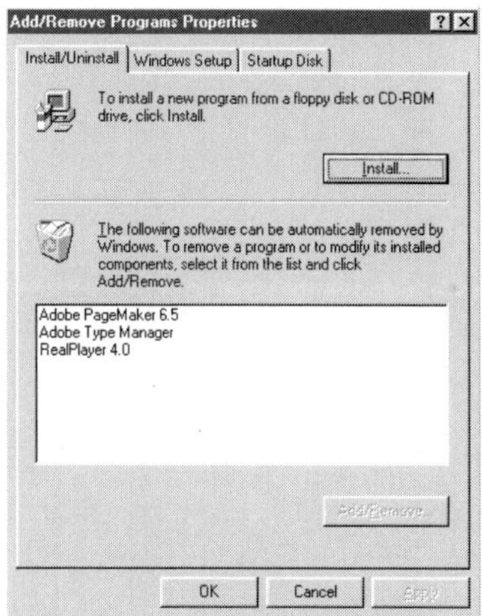

Figure 5.16 Installing a new program from a diskette or CD-ROM.

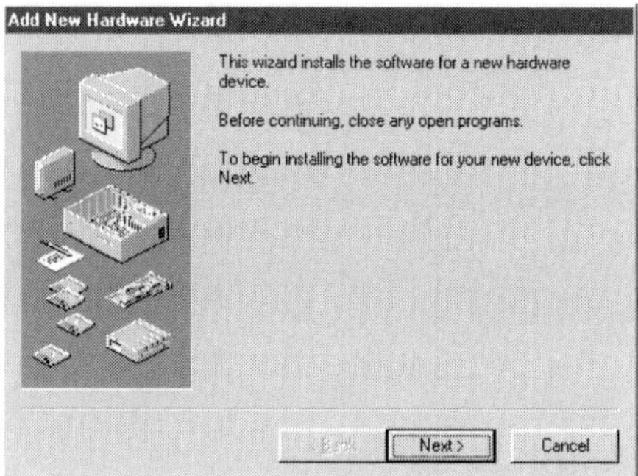

Figure 5.17 Installing hardware on your PC.

Windows Me tools

6

Windows Me contains all the accessories that were included with Windows 98. These can be called up from the Start button by selecting **Programs** and then **Accessories**.

The Calculator

The Windows Me calculator can operate in standard or scientific mode. To toggle from one to the other, simply select the type of calculator required in the View menu.

Notepad

Notepad provides a highly practical way of displaying a text file (Figure 6.1) or entering text quickly.

Date your activities in Notepad

You can create a dated log using Notepad. To do this, simply enter the command '.LOG' on the first line of the document, in the left-hand margin. Then save the file. When you call it up at a later stage, it opens with the current date and time at the end of the text. This enables you to keep a list of activity dates on a particular topic.

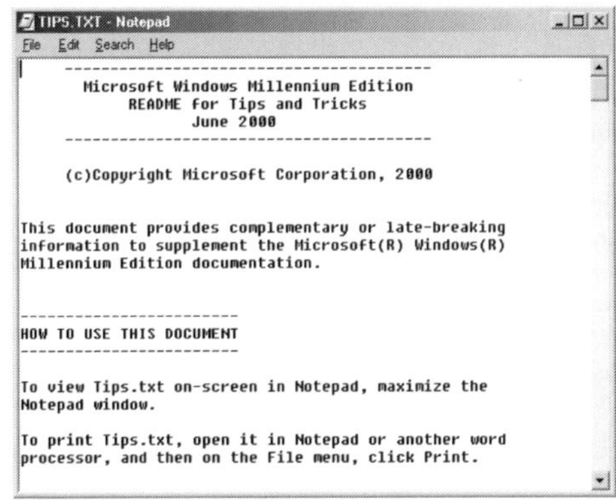

Figure 6.1 The Windows Tips and Tricks file opened with Notepad.

Word-processing in WordPad

If the Notepad facility does not meet your needs for inputting and editing text documents, you can use WordPad, a 32-bit word-processing program supplied as standard with Windows Me.

WordPad (Figure 6.2) is an extremely powerful word-processing package, with a highly functional interface. Texts entered or retrieved in WordPad can be saved in the following formats (using the **Save** command in the File menu):

- text only (.txt)
- RTF format, useful for exchanges with Macintosh computers (.rtf)
- Word 6 for Windows format (.doc).

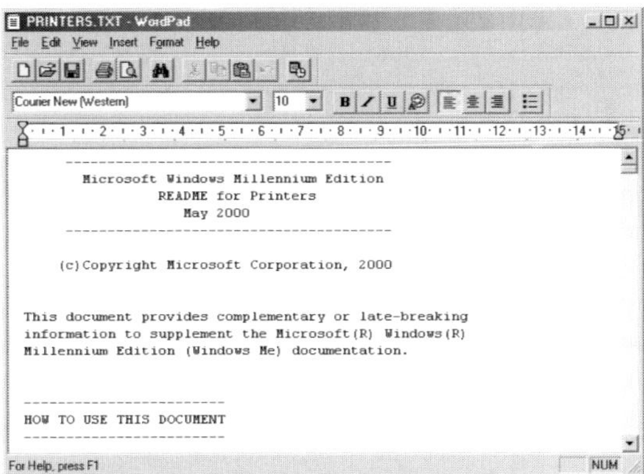

Figure 6.2 Word-processing in WordPad.

Inserting multimedia objects in WordPad

The Insert menu allows you to insert objects in a document. WordPad supports OLE 2.0 technology (object linking and embedding) for incorporating objects. This enables you to use the functions of another application in WordPad and to create genuine multimedia documents.

The Paint program

Windows Me is supplied with Paint, a bitmap drawing software package that enables you to create customized background pictures for the Windows Desktop, or to prepare images to be inserted in WordPad documents.

From the File menu, you can ask for the image to be applied as wallpaper for the Windows Me Desktop, either tiled or centred (Figure 6.3).

Figure 6.3 Customizing the Desktop wallpaper using the Paint program.

Special effects

The Image menu allows you to work on the selected portion of the image. For example, with Flip/Rotate you can rotate the selected zone horizontally or vertically, or you can choose a particular angle. You can also invert colours: this gives you a negative of the image.

The Paint software incorporates a toolbox, a colour box and a status bar. These areas may be closed down from the View menu. The toolbox offers all the conventional drawing functions.

The Colors menu (Figure 6.4) brings up the colour-handling functions. The menu enables you to define a set of customized colours. The palette you create can be saved and then used again later.

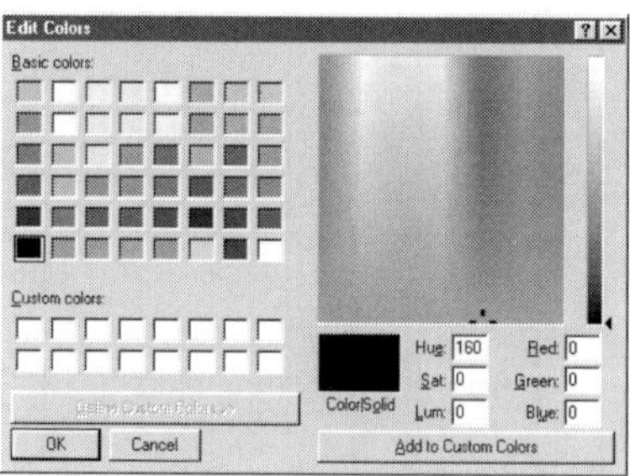

Figure 6.4 Defining customized colours.

The Phone Dialer

The Phone Dialer facility (**Accessories**, **Communications**) is used to set up telephone calls from your PC via the modem or any other telephone peripheral. The advantage of this lies in the ability to easily establish voice calls from your PC. To set up a call, you lift your handset and click **Talk** in the dialog box. To simplify your connections, the Phone Dialer facility incorporates eight memory locations (Speed dial) for your most frequently used numbers. Simply click on each field to store details. A dialog box allows you to enter the names of correspondents and their telephone numbers.

Dial-Up Networking

The Dial-Up Networking function (**Accessories**, **Communications**) enables you to set up a connection to a computer or remote server. Once the call has been set up, you can access the network resources in the usual way. The only restrictions are those that might be imposed by the network manager.

A call is easily set up with the Make New Connection Wizard (Figure 6.5). First, you must give a name to the computer you want to call and select the calling modem. Then you fill in the ringing settings, including the line number of the remote server. When the settings have been confirmed, the Dial-Up Networking folder will contain a new icon that provides the connection reference. This icon is used to establish the connection.

Dial-Up Networking is also used to set up an Internet connection. For this, you use the Connection Wizard (see Chapter 8).

Direct connection by cable

The Direct Cable Connection (**Accessories, Communications**) transfers data between two PCs over a single serial or parallel cable. If you need to transfer data between a portable and a desktop machine, or between two PCs, this utility will be useful to you.

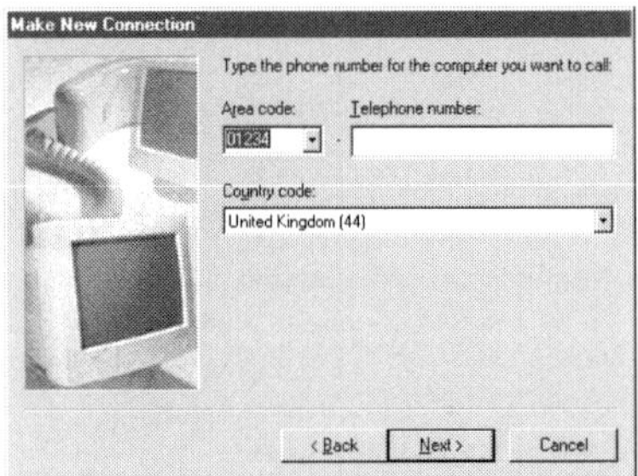

Figure 6.5 The remote server telephone number.

The HyperTerminal utility

The HyperTerminal application (**Accessories, Communications**) connects you to remote sites or PCs by emulating a PC in terminal mode. In this way, your PC can be used as a terminal for a UNIX machine, for example.

You need to define the connection step by step (for the initial connection), including the name of server or PC to be called and the related icon, plus the server telephone number. You start the connection process and a dialog is set up in the text window of the HyperTerminal utility. At this stage, you are recognized by the server and you must enter the login information (server name, user identifier, etc.). You can then send and receive files (using the Transfer menu).

7 Windows Me and the Internet

The Start button

The Taskbar

Windows Explorer

The Windows Me Desktop in Web style

Folder settings

Windows 95 made it easier to use Windows 3.1 programs and introduced a document-oriented design philosophy. This philosophy has been continued in Windows 98 and Me. Windows 95 or 98 users can therefore switch to the new operating system without difficulty. Nevertheless, we shall spend the next chapter describing the enhancements and extra features introduced in Windows Me, especially the integration of the Internet environment.

The Start button

Everything begins here in Windows Me. When you click on the Start button, you immediately find the user Log Off function (Figure 7.1). This is a useful feature for use in offices when a PC is shared among a number of people. At the end of a working session, you can log off without shutting down Windows. The next user can start the system using his or her own custom settings.

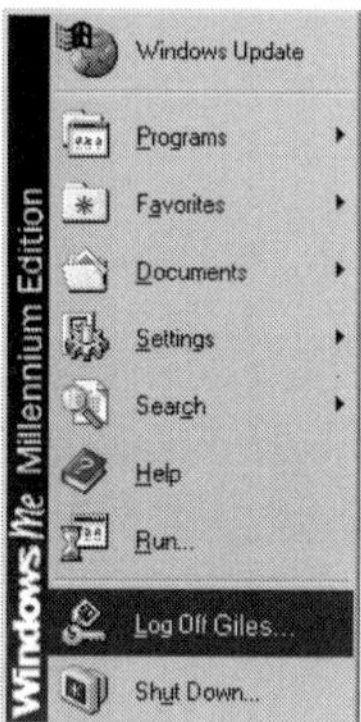

Figure 7.1 The user Log Off function.

Calling up favourite Websites

From the Start button, you can access your favourite Websites. Click **Favorites** to call up your personal list of Websites (Figure 7.2). The contents of this menu will soon change as you start to add your own favourites. Initially it will contain some links set up for you. These will include:

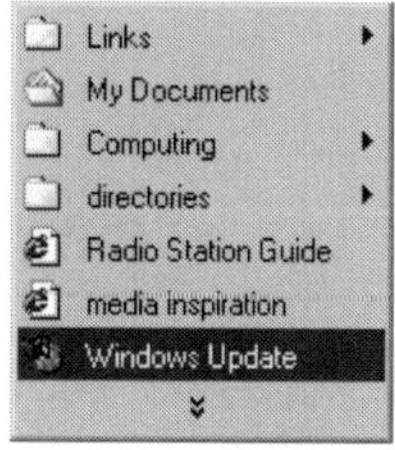

Figure 7.2 Calling up Favourites.

- Recommended sites, generally determined in collaboration with your PC manufacturer.
- Technical links to the Microsoft site.
- Connection to the Microsoft site to update your Windows software.

No point, then, in starting up the browser first. It is quite normal to select a Web resource (URL address) first of all; the Internet Explorer browser will then start up automatically.

Improve your search skills

The Web offers hundreds of search engines, directories, metasearchers and search tools. Each has its particular advantages and individual features. You would not, for example, use the same tool to look for a virtual travel agency, access a Web shop or call up a software product.

Finding documents on the Web

If you click on the **Search** option in the Start menu, you will see that it includes these two commands (Figure 7.3):

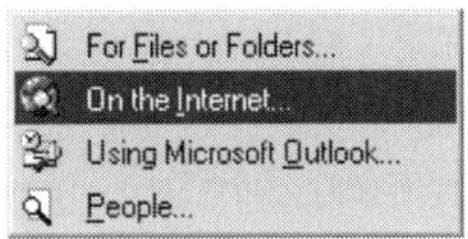

Figure 7.3 The search functions on the Internet.

- On the Internet
- People.

Once you have logged on by clicking **On The Internet**, **Connect**, the navigator opens with the Search facility in the Explorer Bar, and connects to Excite (www.excite.co.uk) where it will run the search. Enter one or more words to define what you are looking for, and click **Search** (Figure 7.4).

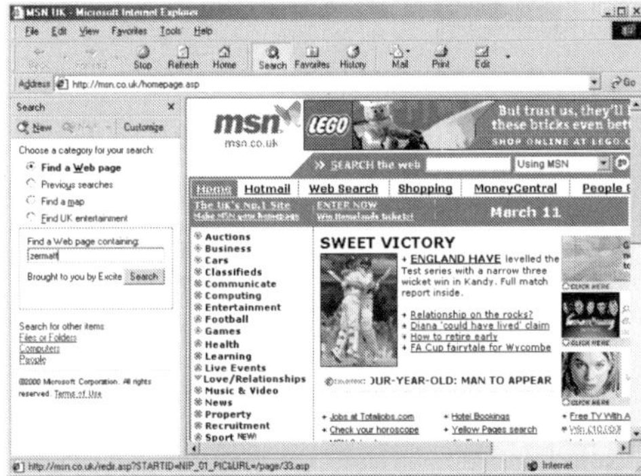

Figure 7.4 Starting a search in the Explorer Bar.

When the results come in, click on a link in the Explorer Bar to load the page into the main area (Figure 7.5). Your search results remain accessible in the Explorer Bar, so that you can browse through the found pages without having to go back to the search site.

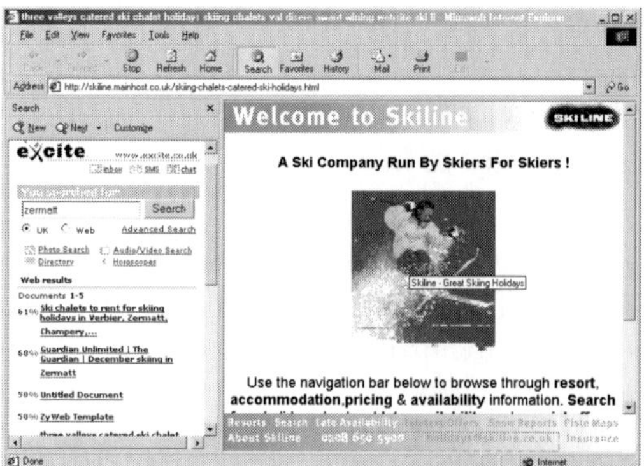

Figure 7.5 The search results stay visible in the Explorer Bar so that you can browse them conveniently.

Paging

Paging (searching for individuals) can be conducted offline or online. You can look up a person's particulars in your Address Book (the one offered in the messaging software Outlook Express) or on the Web using the extensive search engines offered.

Searches in the Address Book are based on name, address, e-mail address or telephone number.

In the Find option, click on **People**. Then click the **Advanced** tab, and select your choice in the **Look In** box (Figure 7.6).

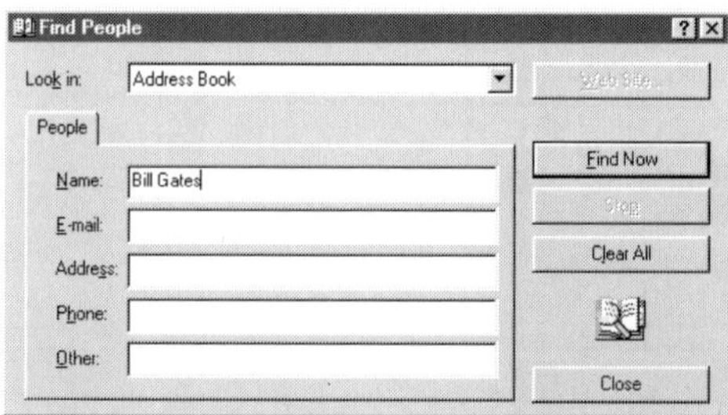

Figure 7.6 The paging window in the Address Book.

There are paging directories and search engines on the Web, such as FourII, Bigfoot, InfoSpace, WhoWhere, Switchboard and VeriSign. If you are looking for the e-mail address of someone whose surname you know, these search engines can be really useful. Select a directory, enter the information you have and click the **Web site** button to start the search.

Executing a command

The Run option in the Start menu has a new feature in Windows Me. You can still fill in the name and path to a program you wish to run, but now you can enter a Web address (URL) directly (Figure 7.7).

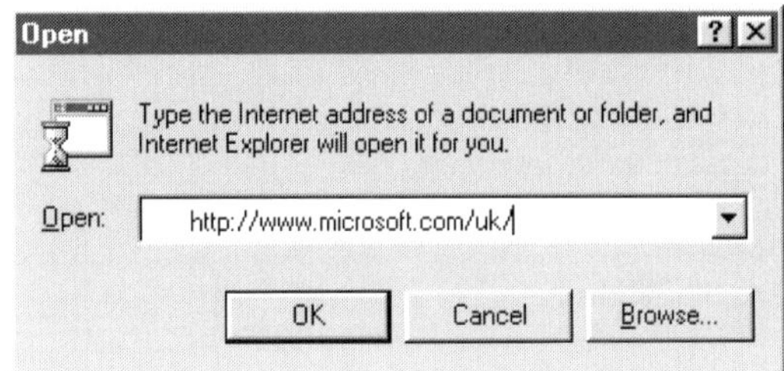

Figure 7.7 Entering a Web address and logging on directly.

The Taskbar

Another new development for Windows 95 users concerns the Taskbar, which shows three new icons to the right of the Start button.

The Quick Launch bar

These icons perform the following functions (from left to right in Figure 7.8):

- Quick return to the Windows Me Desktop: one click on this icon minimizes the windows of active applications. Those applications can still be called up from the Taskbar. Just click on the icon again to go back to your original applications.
- Start Internet Explorer 5.5.
- Start Outlook Express.

Figure 7.8 The four new icons on the Taskbar.

Adding new toolbars

Three other pre-programmed toolbars can be activated from the Taskbar:

- The **Address** toolbar is used to enter a Web address without the need to run the browser.
- The **Links** toolbar enables you access important Websites without the need to open the browser.
- The **Desktop** toolbar arranges the shortcuts on your Desktop in a single location.

Creating a customized toolbar

You will be able to enhance the Taskbar yourself by adding the tools that are most convenient for you. To do this, right-click on a free area of the Taskbar, select ***Toolbar*** *and then click on* ***New Toolbar****. Enter a Web address or select a folder. The Web site or the contents of the folder can now be called up directly from the Taskbar.*

Adjusting a customized toolbar

The settings for this customized toolbar can be altered to suit your needs. You can easily adjust its size by increasing or decreasing its width. Move the cursor on the edge, when it changes to a two-headed arrow, drag it left or right as you wish. You can also move the bar away from the edge of the screen. To do this, click on the top part of the bar; when the cursor changes appearance, bring the toolbar to the middle of the screen. Position it and adjust its size as you wish.

To display and use these toolbars (Figure 7.9):

1. Right-click on a free area of the Taskbar.
2. Select **Toolbars**.
3. Click on **Address**, **Links** or **Desktop**, as you wish.

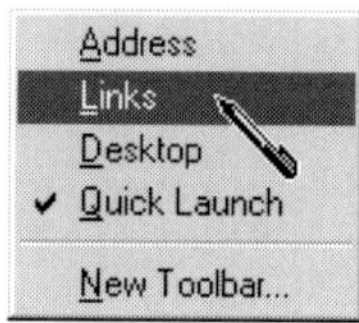

Figure 7.9 Adding a toolbar to the Taskbar.

Creating a toolbar on the Desktop

If the toolbar is a bit crowded, you can create a toolbar on the Desktop from any folder. That folder may contain other folders, documents or Web addresses.

This procedure is straightforward. Click a folder, then keeping the mouse button pressed, drag it to the edge of the screen, as in Figure 7.10. Release the mouse button and the folder contents can then be accessed directly from a vertical bar.

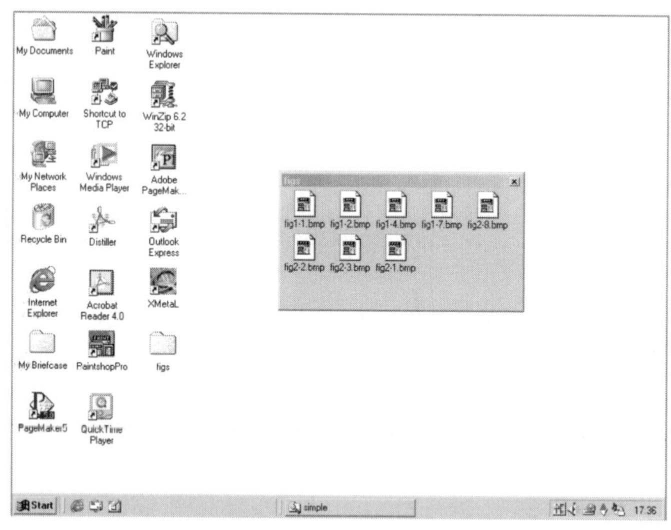

Figure 7.10 The toolbar has been moved from the edge of the screen and placed on the Windows Me Desktop.

By right-clicking on a free area of the customized toolbar, you can open the context-sensitive menu. This presents you with a number of settings:

- Display objects as large (the default setting) or reduced size (**View**, **Large** or **Small**).
- Hide the toolbar automatically (**Auto-Hide**). When the cursor drops below the edge of the screen, the toolbar pops up; as soon as the cursor moves away, the toolbar disappears. Only a vertical line (or a horizontal line, if the toolbar is positioned at the top or bottom of the screen) is visible when the bar is not open.

Hiding a toolbar

You can only hide a toolbar positioned at the edge of the screen; this feature does not work if the toolbar is positioned in the middle of the Desktop.

Windows Explorer

We will now look at some of the new features offered by Explorer. Due to the increasing popularity of the Internet, we now need to be able to work on objects stored on the hard disk and resident on Internet servers. Microsoft has thus adapted the Windows Explorer accordingly.

Explorer runs the folder contents display windows: as the folders are scanned, you can call up the results pages using the Back and Forward buttons on the toolbar. With the Search, Favorites, History and Channels buttons, the Explorer acts like a browser.

To start Windows Explorer, click on **Start**, **Programs**, **Windows Explorer** (Figure 7.11).

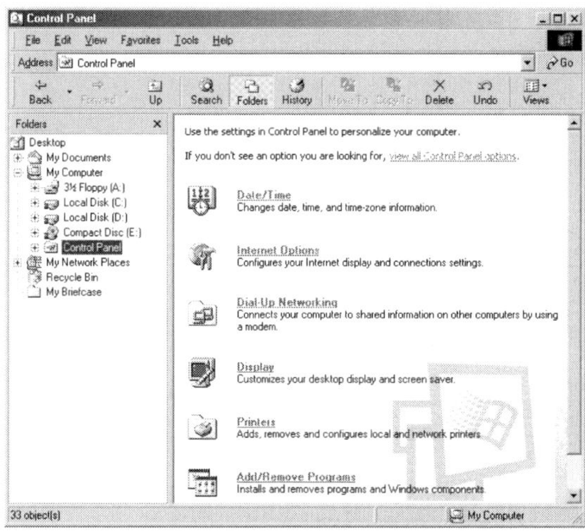

Figure 7.11 Windows Explorer.

The Windows Explorer components are as follows:

- **Toolbar**. The new buttons, Back and Forward, are used to scan pages. Use the Up folder to go back through the tree structure.
- **Address bar**. To input a path on the hard disk or even an Internet address.

- **Left-hand pane**. Shows the tree structure of the disk being explored. The + sign means a folder contains subfolders.
- **Right-hand pane**. Shows the results of the exploration.

Windows Explorer handles the folder contents display windows: as you browse, you can call up the results pages using the Back and Forward buttons. The toolbar also has a Properties button, which gives you immediate access to the Properties window for the object selected. Click on the View button to select the display mode (large icons, small icons, list and details). A Thumbnails option will also be offered for most folders.

The various browsing methods offered can be called up from the View menu by selecting **Explorer Bar**:

- **Search**. Activates a search engine on the Web.
- **Favorites**. Opens a list of folders containing your Internet Favorites.
- **History**. Opens a history file of past searches.
- **Folders**. This is the conventional system-wide exploring mode.
- **None**. This command shuts down the Explorer bar.

Displaying a Web site in optimum conditions

Once you have found the site you want, you will find it easier to view the page in full-screen mode. Click on the ***Full screen*** *icon on the Explorer toolbar. The Explorer pane vanishes and the page occupies the entire screen (Figure 7.12). You can even hide the small toolbar temporarily: right-click on a free area of the bar and select* ***Auto-Hide****.*

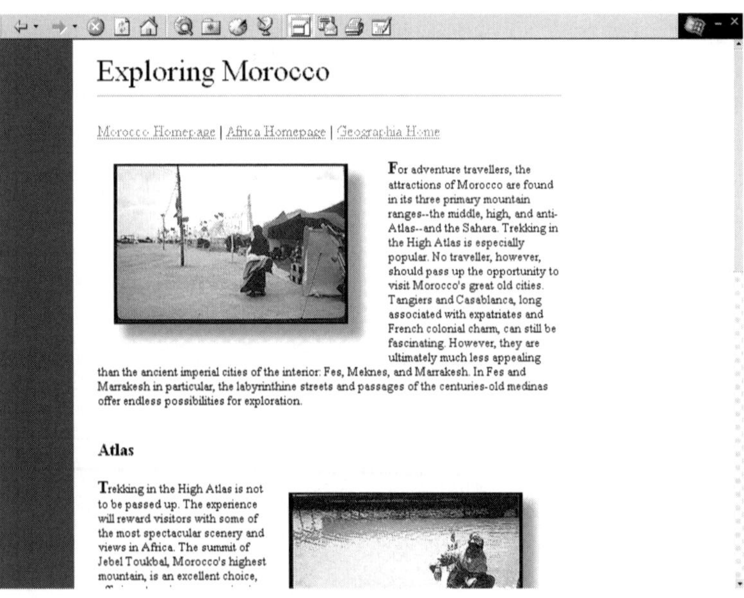

Figure 7.12 Switching to full-screen mode.

Surfing the Web with Explorer

To surf the Web, click on **View**, **Explorer Bar**, **Search**. You are presented with a simple form where you can set up a search that will be run at Excite.

The search result is first posted in the Explorer Bar (to the left). When you click on the addresses, the Web page shifts into the right-hand frame of Explorer. Just point to an address to display the site on offer in the right-hand part of the screen.

Adding a page to Favorites

You can easily add Web pages to your Favorites list. Right-click on the page, then select **Add To Favorites** from the menu that appears (Figure 7.13).

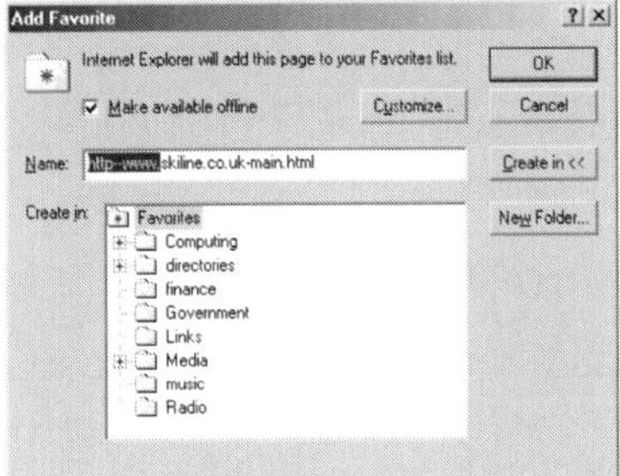

Figure 7.13 The Add Favorite dialog box.

If you tick **Make available offline**, Explorer will download and store pages so that you can read them later. The **Customize** button runs a wizard where you can define which pages to download and when to do it. The **Name** may need editing to make it more meaningful. If desired, you can choose which Favorites folder to **Create** the new link in.

Similar features are also offered in the Internet Explorer browser facility (see Chapter 9). These are the original features of the Internet Explorer browser, which, for practical reasons, have been duplicated in Windows Explorer. These two tools may well be merged in future. In this way, Microsoft could realize its ambition to standardize the way in which we work with documents, whether they are stored locally in a PC or are resident on an intranet or Internet server.

Arranging your favourite sites

When you add sites to the Favorites menu, you can choose which folder to place it in, or let it be added to the main list. If need be you can rearrange your favourites: in Explorer, click on ***Favorites, Organize Favorites****.*

Alternatively, click on ***Favorites****, click on the Web site to be moved, then keeping the mouse button pressed, drag it to the chosen folder.*

Sending a Web page by e-mail

You have probably noticed that the enhanced Explorer toolbar contains a Mail icon (Figure 7.14). Apart from the proposed link to Outlook Express, this button allows you to send the site link (or the page itself) to another party. This is a very practical way of sharing your Internet discoveries with fellow Net users.

Figure 7.14 Sending a page by e-mail.

You can send pages:

- **As attachments**. The addressee can open the page directly or store it on their PC hard disk.
- **In read-only mode**. The page will be contained in the body of the message.

The Windows Me Desktop in Web style

With Windows Me, you will discover new ways of working with the Windows Desktop. Web style enables you to browse through the folders on your PC in the same way as you look up Web pages.

To switch to Web style:

1. Double-click the My Computer icon which is displayed on the Desktop.
2. Select **Tools**, **Folder Options** (Figure 7.15).

Classic operating style

*If you want to go back to classic operating style, you can cancel Web style. To do this, bring up the Folder Options menu and select the **Classic style** options on the General tab.*

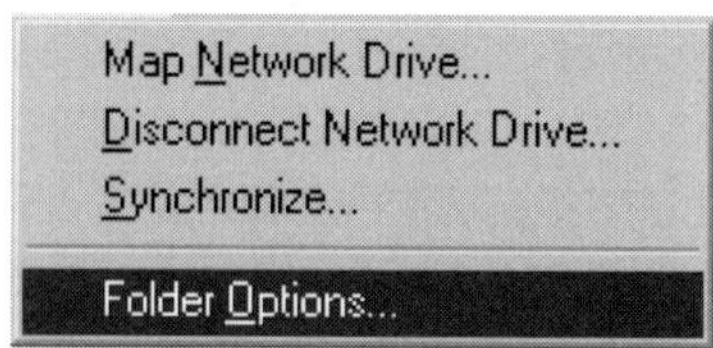

Figure 7.15 The Folder Options command.

3. Tick the Enable Web content on my desktop and Enable Web content in folders options in the General tab (Figure 7.16).

Folder settings

By using Windows Me Web style, you can display and handle files in a totally different way. When you open a folder, it is displayed in a new way (Figure 7.17). The folder name is clearly shown in the look-up window. Two buttons indicate the option to switch from one window to another (Back and Forward).

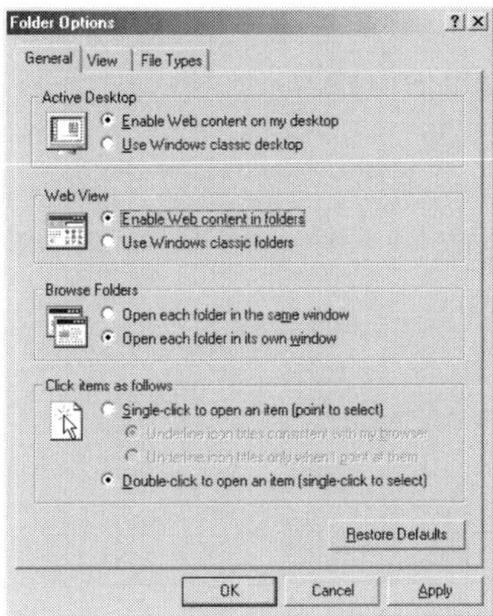

Figure 7.16 Select the Enable Web content options to adapt your PC to Internet working methods.

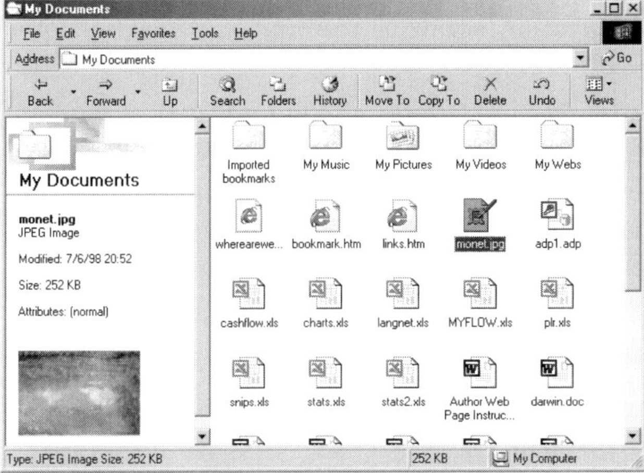

Figure 7.17 The contents of a folder.

Folder display settings

You may have noticed that the contents of folders are displayed as Web pages. Each constituent object (whether it is a file or a folder) is a link that you can open with a single click. You can do all sorts of things with these Web pages; the Folder Display Wizard in particular will help you in your task.

You may customize folders as follows:

1. Select the folder by pointing the cursor at it. You will see that information about the folder appears on the left-hand side of the window (name, file size, date of last modification, etc.).

2. Click on **View**.
3. Select **Customize this Folder** (Figure 7.18).
4. The Customization wizard starts up.

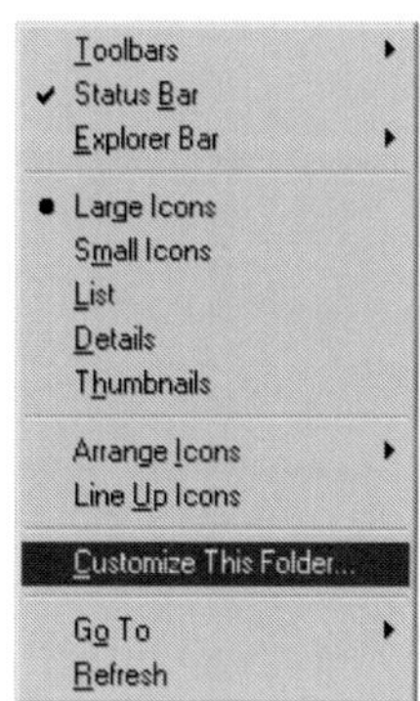

Figure 7.18 The Customize this Folder command.

Once the Customization wizard is running, you are presented with three options:

- The first option is to create or modify an HTML document, which will allow you to alter the display of the selected folder.
- The second option displays a background graphic of the icons (objects belonging to the folder) that are contained in the folder.
- The third option add a comment to describe the folder.

Choose the second settings option and click the **Next** button. Find a graphic in .BMP, .GIF or .JPG format on the hard disk and select it as a folder background.

Display settings for all files

We have just discussed folder presentation and customization methods. There is also a group of settings that governs the display and the way in which we work with all the files resident in the PC. From the Tools menu, select **Folder Options**, **View** (Figure 7.19).

Now choose the files and folders options that suit your needs; you can also decide to display the file attributes in detailed mode, display hidden files, or use layout settings such as font scaling. Use these options as you wish, but remember that the default settings are adequate most of the time.

Image file management

A major new feature in the image file management facility allows you to view the contents of an image file in thumbnail form before you open it in a software package. Use the **Thumbnails**

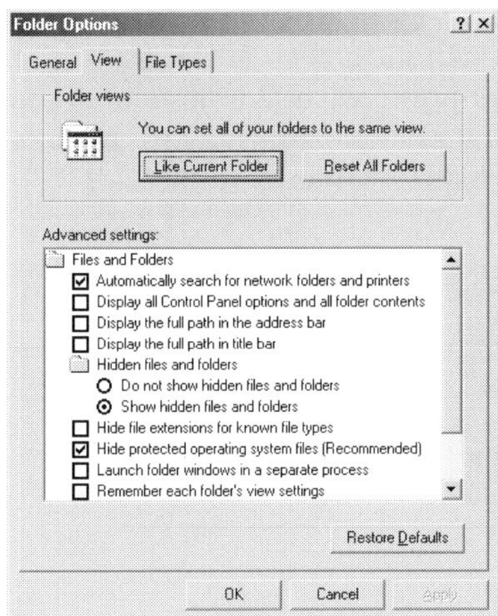

Figure 7.19 Folder display options.

View to see all the files in the folder in this way. If you have enabled Web content, you can see a thumbnail of a selected file in any view mode. Just click on the icon of the file to see an image in the left-hand panel (Figure 7.20).

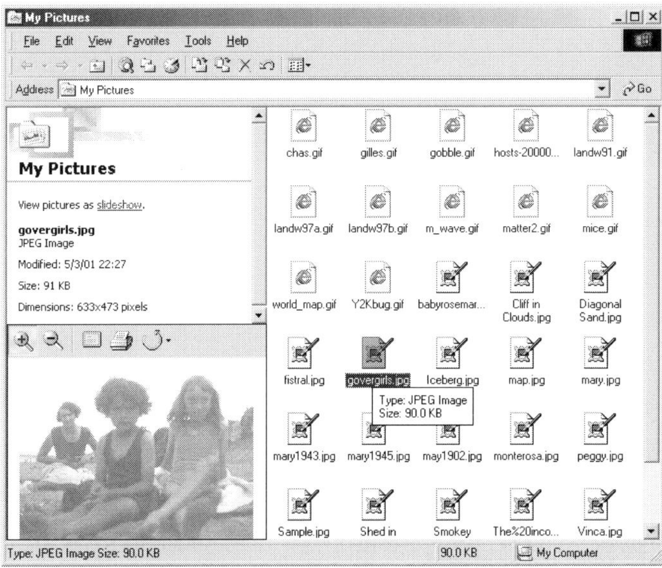

Figure 7.20 Displaying the selected file in reduced size.

The My Computer folder

To obtain details about hardware when in Web style, go to the Desktop, click **My Computer** and point with the mouse at the disk drive [C:] The total disk space and the space available are shown on the left-hand side of the display window (Figure 7.21).

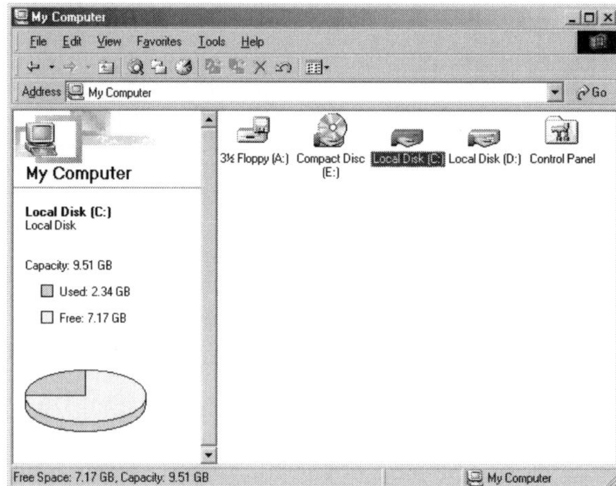

Figure 7.21 My Computer: by pointing to the hard disk, you can obtain a graphic display of the total disk space and the free space.

8

Internet connection and Home Networking

To log on to the Internet, your PC must incorporate a program that can handle interchanges with the network. Do not forget that so-called 'personal' computers are designed to work independently and any connection to a network is based on the assumption that there is an interface. These add-ons may be supplied with the operating system, in which case you just need to install them. This is the case with Windows Me.

When you access the Internet, the connection (log-on) program performs the following tasks:

- It sets up the link to the site of your Internet access provider (IAP).
- It handles the data interchange protocol used on the Internet.

The Internet connection

Your first attempt to access the Internet can be a tricky operation because you may be required to set up a string of parameters. However, the data to be entered is too technical for most users. Remember also that what works on your mate's machine does not necessarily work on yours. Your Internet access provider should supply you with all the necessary information. Most also provide you with installation programs that handle the bulk of the work for you. Once you have set the Internet parameters, you do not have to reset them.

There are several ways to set up the log-on parameters:

- Use the automated installation script supplied by your access provider.
- Register a dial-up connection.
- Use the Windows Me Connection Wizard.

To a certain extent, the first method automates your dial-up networking. The second can be difficult, but is worth knowing. The third is more user-friendly. We shall now look at the last two options in detail.

Setting up a dial-up connection

From the Start button, click on Settings then select Dial-Up Networking. When its window opens (Figure 8.1) click **Make New Connection**. Make sure that you have first noted down all the relevant information you need to supply to your Internet access provider (you will need at least the telephone number of the Internet server you wish to call).

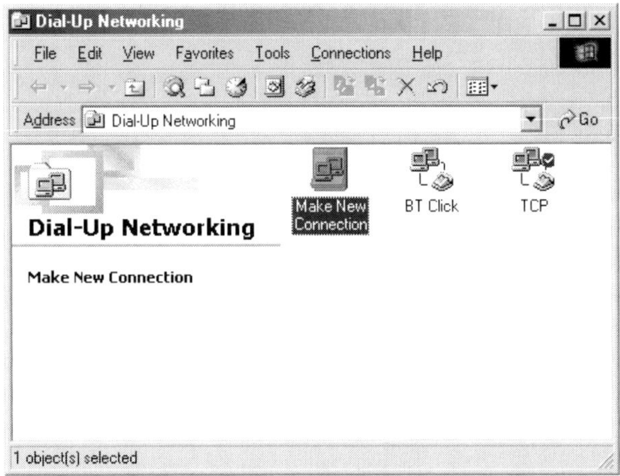

Figure 8.1 The Dial-up Networking folder.

As you will see later, you can register several connections. Working in the Outlook Express messaging software, you can handle a number of mail and discussion forum accounts. In the Make New Connection dialog box, enter a name for your connection and give details of your modem. Now alter the settings by clicking **Configure**, if necessary. Enter the telephone number of the server for your access provider and confirm the information entered (Figure 8.2).

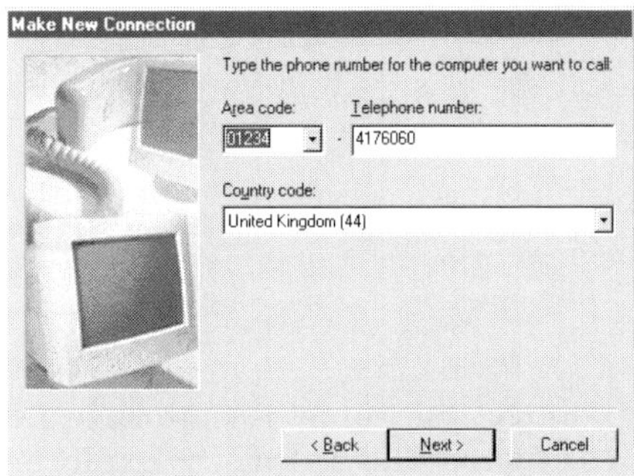

Figure 8.2 Entering the server telephone number for your access provider.

The connection is marked by a new icon in the Dial-up Networking folder. Right-click this icon and select **Properties**. Next, click **Networking**. Here you can change or define the dial-up server type (usually PPP for Windows) and check the communication protocols to be used (Figure 8.3). For the Internet, you must select TCP/IP.

Next, click **TCP/IP Settings** to enter (where applicable) the server IP (Internet Protocol) addresses and the Internet address of the server (Figure 8.4). These addresses, in the form xxx.xxx.xxx.xxx (where x is a digit between 0 and 9), are forwarded by the access provider.

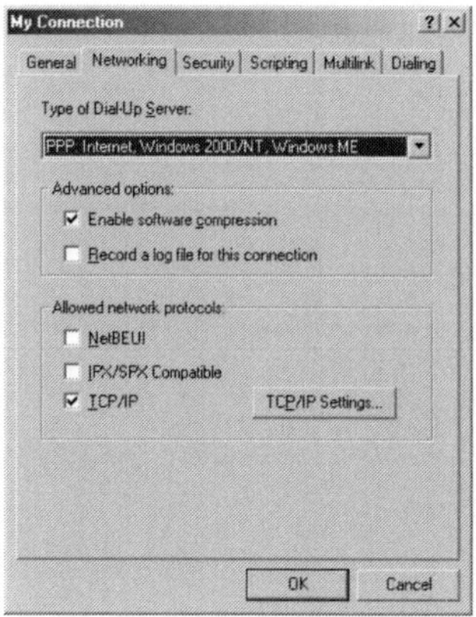

Figure 8.3 The type of dial-up server called.

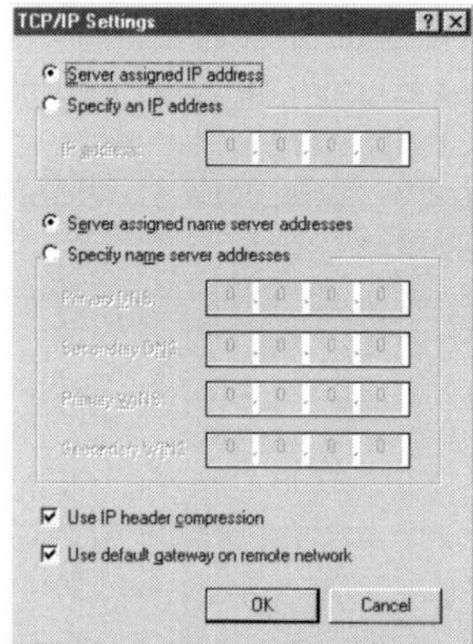

Figure 8.4 TCP/IP settings.

At this stage, an Internet type connection can be set up with the server. But you should still configure the Internet Explorer browser and the Outlook Express messaging software to conduct interactive communications with the server resources (access to the Web, mail server access, etc.).

If the connection you have does not work, check your PC network settings based on the following.

The basic protocol

In the Control Panel, click the Network icon. Check that you have at least the following two lines:

- Dial-up Adapter

- TCP/IP.

The first option simulates a dial-up networking board, while TCP/IP is the general purpose Internet exchange protocol.

TCP/IP settings

Now you need to check the server settings before you can access the Internet. To do this, select the TCP/IP line in the Network dialog box and click **Properties**.

The values you need to tick (or enter) are under the DNS (domain name server) Configuration tab. Most connections now are designed to work with DNS disabled. If your Internet access provider needs you to enable this, they will supply you with the necessary values. You should then select **Enable DNS** and enter your address (or log-in) in the Host field, then enter the server name in the Domain box. Enter the identification of the name server in the DNS box. You should receive this information from your access provider. The name server translates an address like **aol.com** or **compuserve.com** into a physical address on the Internet network of the type xxx.xxx.xxx.xxx. The name server also has a physical address that you should communicate to the log-on software.

Check your Internet access provider options

Generally, the access provider procedure is designed for a specific browser. Get all the necessary details beforehand and make it clear that you will be using Windows Me and Internet Explorer 5.5. If the set-up procedure has been designed for Netscape, it may not work.

This procedure is not easy, and it is preferable to fall back on the access provider installation procedure or, even better, to call up the Connection Wizard provided by Windows Me.

The Internet Connection Wizard

The Internet Connection Wizard can be run from the Start menu. Click **Programs**, **Accessories**, **Internet Tools**, **Internet Connection Wizard** (Figure 8.5).

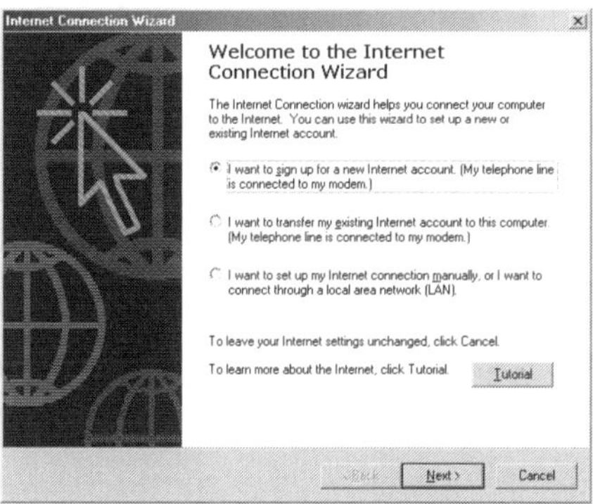

Figure 8.5 Running the Internet Connection Wizard.

The Wizard offers three types of installation:

- Opening a new Internet account. During this procedure, you will have to choose an access provider.
- Transfer an existing account, where the PC is connected directly to the modem.
- Transfer an account manually, or connect through a LAN.

Choosing a provider and opening an account

If you are not sure which access provider to choose, go for the first option mentioned above. Follow the procedure step-by-step. Set up your modem if you have not done so already. Tell the software where you are. It will then display a list of telephone numbers indicating the servers you can call. Choose a server near to you so that you will be charged local telephone call charges.

The Connection Wizard will log on to the Microsoft Internet reference server and download a list of access providers near to you. The choice is then yours.

Adding a log-on account

Whether this is your first account or a new one, use the second option if you have already selected an Internet access provider. Then follow the procedure step-by-step.

First of all, state the nature of your connection:

- direct by modem, using a telephone line
- through a local area network.

Then select your modem. Enter the telephone number of your Internet access provider server. Next, enter your Internet user name and your password. Check beforehand with your provider whether you need to enter advanced settings: click **Yes** or **No**, as applicable.

Enter a name for your connection. This name will appear in the Dial-Up Networking folder. You are then asked if you want to configure your messaging account. Click **Yes** and confirm by pressing the **Next** button. After that, enter your full name to send mail. Then, enter your future e-mail address (**name@server.domain**), which is the name allocated by your access provider.

Enter the mail server name (Figure 8.6); usually, this is the same as the **mail.server.domain** name supplied by your provider.

Enter your name and password to log on to the server (these should be the same as you use to log on to the access provider). Then enter a name for your mail account, which will be used by the Outlook Express software.

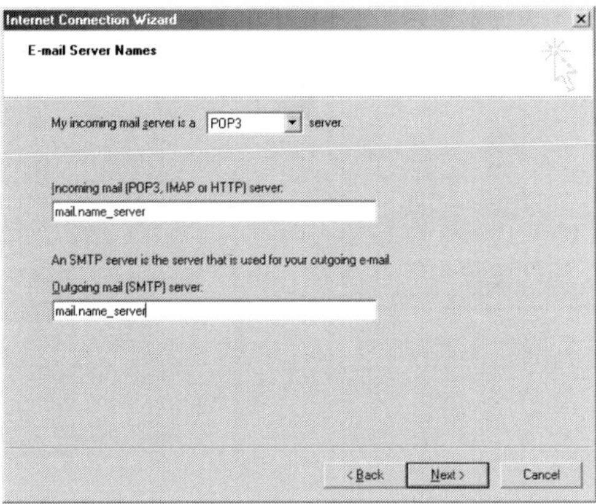

Figure 8.6 Entering the mail server name.

By doing this, you also usually install the news server (discussion groups) offered by your provider (of the **news.server.domain** type). Next, state whether you wish to have an entry in an Internet directory (or your corporate intranet).

You are now ready to log on to the Internet with your Web browser or your communications software: Outlook Express (for mail and forums) or NetMeeting or Microsoft Chat. Happy surfing!

Home Networking

Setting up even a small network used to be a real chore. Windows 95 introduced some tools which simplified it, but it was still not a job for the faint-hearted or the non-technical. But the Home Networking Wizard transforms the business. It is so easy to use – with two provisos.

- Networking is quite straightforward as long as you are just connecting Windows Me PCs together. You can also connect to older Windows 95 or 98 PCs, but you won't get quite the full range of facilities through the link. If you want to share an Internet connection, the PC with the modem must be a Me PC.
- You still have to open the PCs' boxes and install the network cards, and their software, then cable them together.

ISPs and connection sharing

Internet connection sharing may not work with some ISPs. If you have problems, check that they can handle it.

The Home Networking Wizard takes care of setting up the Windows' networking software. All you need to do is tell the Wizard a few things about your system, and decide what to call your machines and which folders and printers to share – and that is it!

Once the network is in place, you can then run the Internet Connection Wizard on the PC that does not have the modem. Tell it you want to set up the connection manually and through a LAN (Local Area Network).

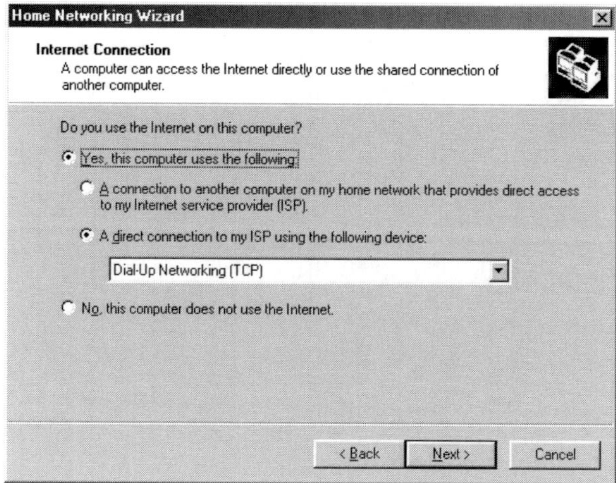

Figure 8.7 Starting to work through the Home Networking Wizard. If the PC has an Internet connection, the Wizard will ask for details.

This is the crucial stage. The PC with the modem is acting as a 'proxy server' - one that makes the connection for another. Don't try to configure it yourself - that option is there for special situations and keen techies. Select Automatic discovery of proxy server and let the Wizard sort it out for you. It may take a minute or so. The rest of the Wizard collects details of your e-mail account.

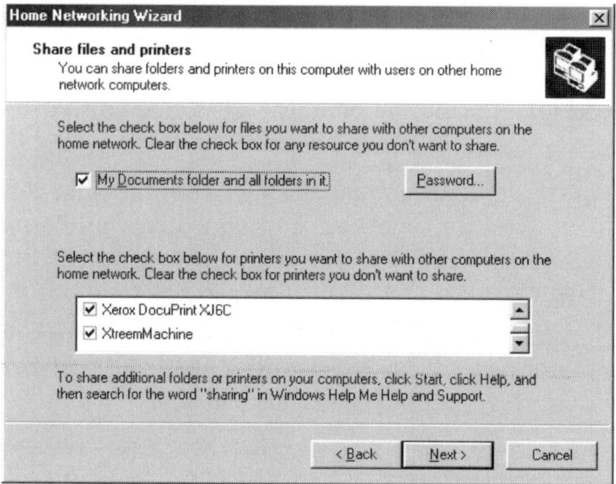

Figure 8.8 Setting sharing options in the Wizard. You can adjust how you share folders and printers at any time.

- The connection is fully shared. Not only can all the networked machines use the connection, they can use it at the same time.

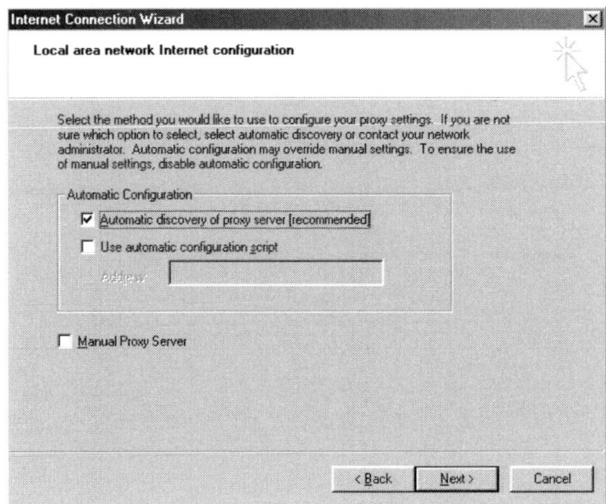

Figure 8.9 The most technical bit of setting up a shared Internet Connection - tick the Automatic option!

9

The Internet Explorer browser

Running the browser

Browsing principles

Web surfing

Managing your favourite Websites

Internet Radio

Internet Explorer 5.5, a software package distributed free by Microsoft, is already installed with the Windows Me operating system.

In this version, Microsoft has made a number of small but significant improvements in the functionality and ease of use of their browser. The most visible changes are:

An improved Search facility
The ability to sort the History list in different ways, making it simpler to revisit sites.

Easier routines for organizing Favorites
The replacement of the 'channel' concept with a more useable method for storing pages and reading them offline.

An Autocomplete facility which offers to complete URLs for you when you start to type them into the Address bar.

Support for multiple connections
The MSN Messenger Service, that informs you when your friends are online.

Once your Internet connection has been set up you can surf the Web using all the resources your browser offers.

Your home page

By default, the browser is configured to display a Microsoft site. To display a different site of your choice, click on ***Tools, Internet Options****. In the General dialog box, enter the URL (address) of your home page and confirm your choice by clicking* ***OK****. When you next run the browser, this is the page that will be displayed by default. A good idea is to use your favourite search engine as the home page. If you run a company, you could use your intranet welcome page as the default.*

Running the browser

Internet Explorer 5.5 can be called up from **Start, Programs, Internet Explorer**. You can also use the shortcut displayed on the Desktop or you can use the Quick Launch bar (to the right of the Start button) on the Taskbar.

When the browser opens, start the Internet log-on procedure by clicking **Connect**. The default home page will then be displayed (Figure 9.1).

If you want to browse a Web page that you have stored locally or recorded using the History facility, you can work offline (saving on your telephone bill). The Work Offline box will be ticked in the File menu. If you try to open a page that you have not stored, a dialog box will invite you to log on. To log on, either untick the Work Offline box, or click **Connect** in the dialog box (Figure 9.3).

If you click Cancel while the PC is connecting, the connection attempt is interrupted and the browser opens the Dial-up Connection window. You can alter the log-on settings (**Settings** button) if you wish, or choose to stay offline, or resume the connection procedure. If several users share the PC, it is at this point that you enter your log-on password (Figure 9.3).

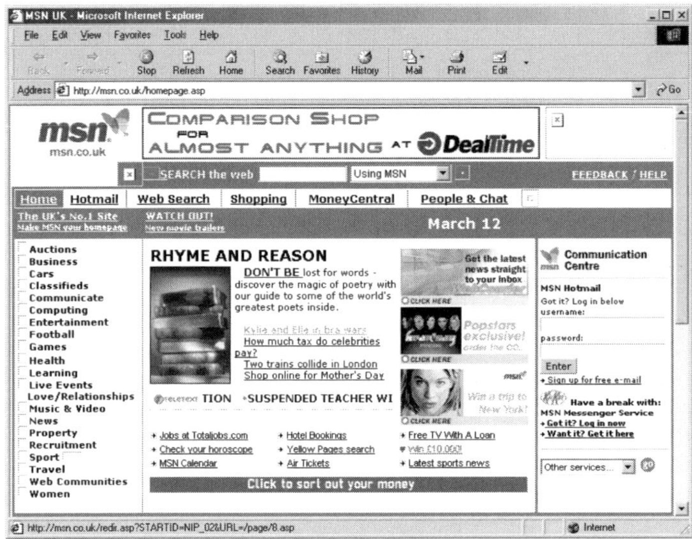

Figure 9.1 Opening the browser by displaying the default page; in this case, the MSN homepage.

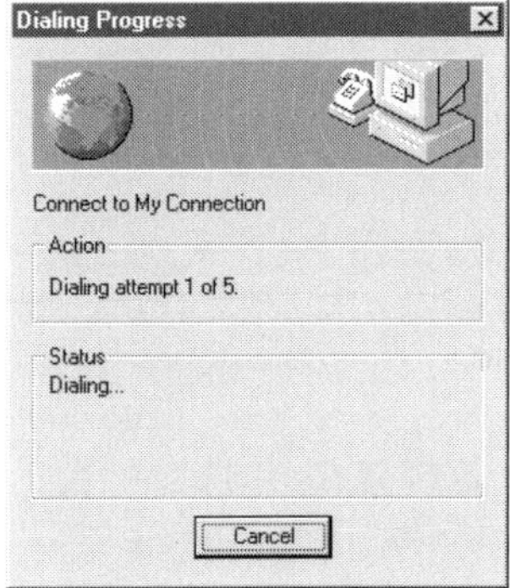

Figure 9.2 Starting up an Internet connection.

Figure 9.3 Entering your password.

Are you ready to Connect to the Internet?

If your Internet log-on settings have not yet been configured, call up Internet Options from the Tools menu. Click on the ***Connections*** *tab, then click* ***Settings*** *to start the Connection Wizard (Figure 9.4). You can use this as a reference for your first Internet account (to call up an access provider), or to establish a new access account, or to gain access via a local area network. For further details, refer to Chapter 8.*

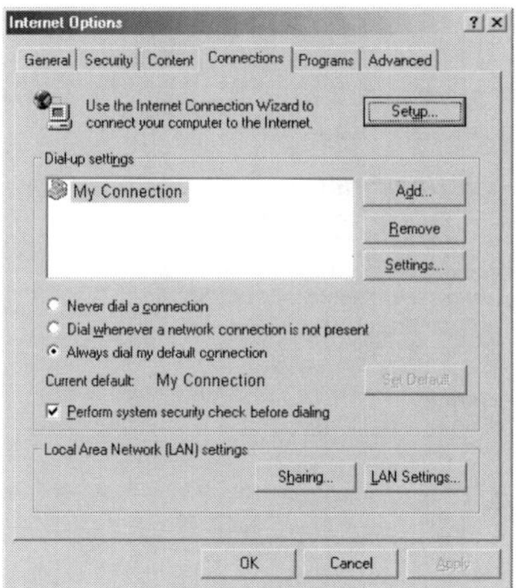

Figure 9.4 Internet log-on options.

Register your password by ticking the **Save password** box – then you will not have to enter the password again.

Establishing your connection before running the browser

*You can establish your Internet connection routine before you run the browser. Just open My Computer, then select **Dial-Up Networking** (Figure 9.5). Start the log-on sequence by clicking the icon representing your Internet access provider. Then click **Connect** in the Connect To dialog box (Figure 9.6). You can also select the Connection icon (one click) and press **Dial** in the toolbar.*

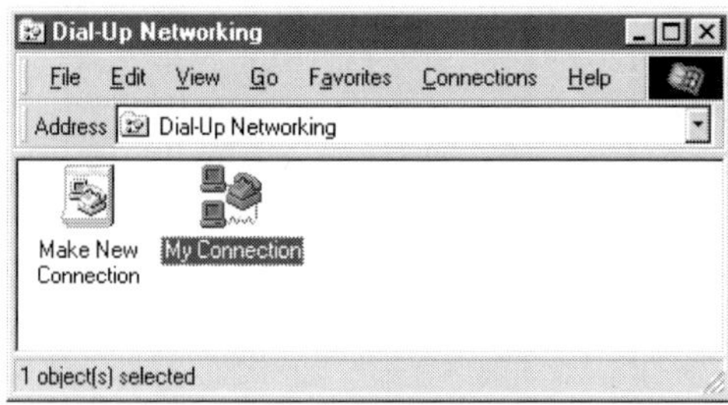

Figure 9.5 The Dial-up Networking folder and the specified connections.

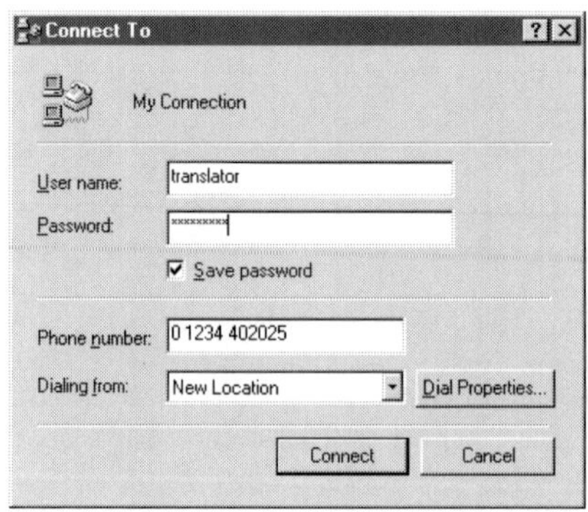

Figure 9.6 Starting the Internet connection routine without the browser.

Establishing or terminating your Internet connection

Most of the time, the log-on start-up routine is automated. Entering a Web address in the entry box or asking for a page update is sufficient for the browser to invite you to accept the connection.

Once you have established your connection, you can run your browser and surf the Web. A connection indicator is visible on the Taskbar (to the right).

To log off, right-click on the active connection icon and select **Disconnect** (Figure 9.7).

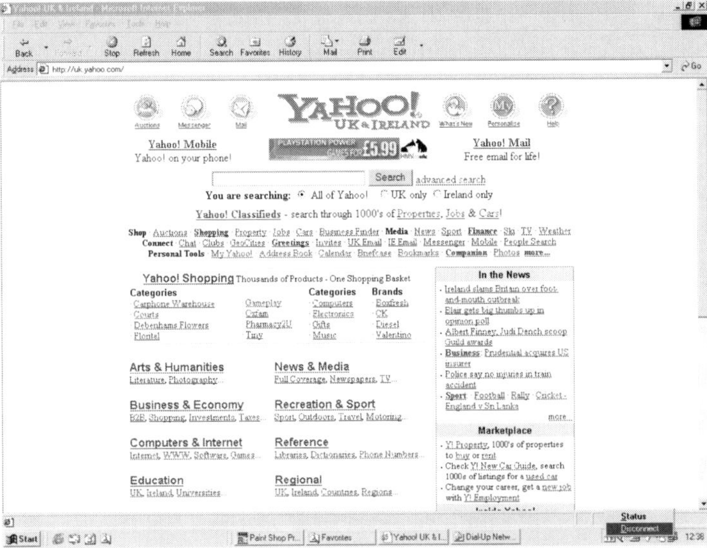

Figure 9.7 The connection has been established; click **Status** to display the log-on status, or **Disconnect.**

Click **Status** to check the speed of the log-on process, the quantity of data interchanged between the server and your PC, and the time elapsed.

Browsing principles

Since everything begins with an address, enter one in the address bar (just under the toolbar). The address of your company, for instance, might be **http://www.enterprise.com.** If you enter the address incorrectly, you will be alerted. The error message 'nffl 404' means that the URL is not known.

The navigation buttons

If you have entered the address correctly, the page requested will then be displayed. You can then browse from that first page by clicking on the active links offered. The browser stores the pages displayed previously. To go back to the previous page, click **Back** on the toolbar. After you have gone back, you can display the following pages again by clicking **Forward**.

When loading a page, the browser icon, which is shown in reduced size at the top right of your browser screen, moves. At the same time, the information and the objects being loaded are shown on the status bar, at the bottom of the browser. When the page has been loaded, the icon stops moving.

You progress from one page to the next, from one site to another, or one service to another (and, sometimes, from one country to another) by clicking on the links offered. These links can assume all sorts of different shapes on a Web page. They are active areas and your browser shows them clearly by changing the appearance of the cursor: the arrow becomes a hand, meaning that you can access another page.

To return to a particular page, you can click several times on **Back** to return. Alternatively, click on the small down arrow to the right of the Back button to show a list of pages with their names (Figure 9.8). Click on the page you want to revisit. This is a practical way of quickly accessing a specific page.

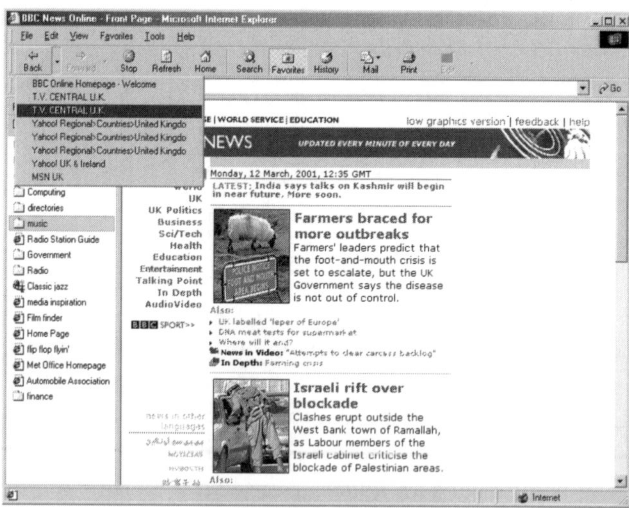

Figure 9.8 A list of pages displayed previously.

The History file

The History file stores details of your browsing over several log-on sessions. To display the History file, click on **History** on the toolbar. The History pane opens to the left of the browser. You can pick a specific date or display all the visits you have made earlier in the day.

If you click on a particular site, the pages of that site are then also listed. If you change sites, the previous list is closed and the list of pages at the new site is shown.

Displaying links

When a list is offered in the conventional way (in underlined text), you can check whether it has been used previously. This allows you, on a page with a number of links, to determine which links you might want to explore. The link colour changes the moment you use it. The colours of links that have and have not been activated can be programmed. Just go to the Internet Options feature in the Tools menu, click on the **General** tab, then select **Colors** at the bottom of the box.

Here, you can define the colours for:

- links not used or visited
- links used or visited
- highlighting a link when the mouse pointer passes over it: simply tick the **Use hover color** box.

By clicking on a colour box, you bring up a display of the palette: just select the colour you want.

Full-screen surfing

Internet Explorer 5.5 allows you to browse in full-screen mode. Apart from a small icon bar at the top of the screen, the entire visible surface of your monitor can be used to display Web pages. In this way, you can make the most of the sites you have visited.

To switch to full-screen mode, click **View, Full Screen**. The vertical and horizontal risers only appear if the Web page is longer or wider than your display. Not only has the browser environment been reduced, the Taskbar (at the bottom of the screen) has also disappeared from the screen at the same time.

To return to classic style, press F11 or click on the Restore icon at the top right of the screen.

In full-screen mode, you can go back to the previous page or display the next by opening the context-sensitive menu: right-click on a non-active area of the current Web page, then click **Back** or **Forward**.

Total full screen

*To obtain a total full screen, you need to hide the reduced size full-screen bar. To do this, right-click a free area on the toolbar and select **Auto-Hide**. The bar then disappears: it will not be displayed again until you point the cursor to the top of the screen. To get the bar back, point the cursor at the top of the screen, right-click in the bar, then untick **Auto-Hide**.*

Opening Web pages in a new window

It is possible to alter the way in which the results of all your Web requests are opened in the browser window, and to switch from one page to the next by pressing the Forward and Back buttons.

All sorts of links

Usually, a link is shown as underlined text. But Web programming also allows a link to be assigned to an action button, a graphic or a map. A graphic can even comprise several links, depending on the place in which you click the mouse button. A drop-down list might also offer a series of access links. On certain Web pages, you can find specific icons representing the next or previous pages, inviting the user to browse a series of screens.

This enables you to open pages in a new browser window. From the **File** menu, select **New**, **Window**: a new browser window opens. You can then switch between browsing operations in several windows without mixing up the Web pages you have received by using the tabs in the Taskbar.

Another option is to open a link, chosen from a Web page, in a new window. To do this, right-click on the link, and select **Open in New Window** (Figure 9.9).

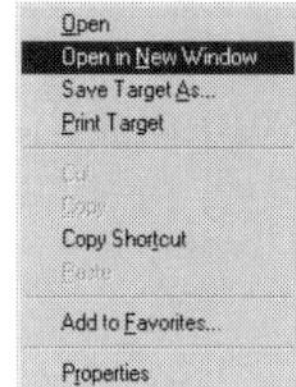

Figure 9.9 Opening a link in a new window.

The explorer bar

The explorer bar opens to the left of the browser and allows you to view Web pages on the right-hand side of the screen, whilst you carry out searches and select options in the left-hand list. Of the lists offered, you will find History, Favorites, Channels and search results. You can access all these lists by clicking on the relevant buttons on the toolbar.

You can close the explorer bar by clicking on the cross at the top right of the frame. If the list is long, you can use the down arrow to display the rest of the links on offer and the up arrow to go back up the list.

A list contains objects, i.e. folders and addresses. When you click on a folder, you open a submenu, which is a list of the addresses entered in the folder. In your Favorites, a document is a subject (Hobbies, Finance, etc.) that you have defined in order to classify your Websites to suit your particular tastes. In History, there are three organizational levels: the enquiry day (or week), the site visited, and the pages you looked up at a given site.

Web surfing

To start a search, click on **Search**. The explorer bar opens and, if you are offline, the Internet connection procedure begins. The operating mode is the same as that described for the new features of Windows Explorer. The search module links to the Excite search engine.

The Back and Forward buttons do not operate in the explorer pane, only in the main part of the browser. To conduct a new search, type the new keyword(s) in the search area and click **Search**. If the search does not find what you want, try going to a search engine site and search there. Three of the best are:

- Google at http://www.google.com, which has indexed over 1 billion pages.
- Jeeves at http://www.askjeeves.com, a very friendly place to start.
- Yahoo at http://www.yahoo.com, which has millions of selected links to pages.

Managing your favourite Websites

You should make your favourite site your home site. You have seen how it is possible to enter Web areas on the Desktop, and you can even choose an HTML page that would point to one of your favourite sites. To keep a record of your other favourite pages, store them in your Favorites folder. Favorites is a collection of folders and links that you can activate at any time.

Using the Favorites search tools

You can continue searching using the tools selected on the Web. Beforehand, you should have specified the search engines that you find the most useful in a Favorites folder. If you have done this, click on ***Favorites****, select the relevant folder and click on one of the search engines. In this case, the search results will be displayed not in the explorer bar but on the overall page sent back by the search engine server.*

Storing Favorites

To record a Website in your Favorites list, select the Favorites menu and click **Add to Favorites**. You are now presented with a number of options (Figure 9.10):

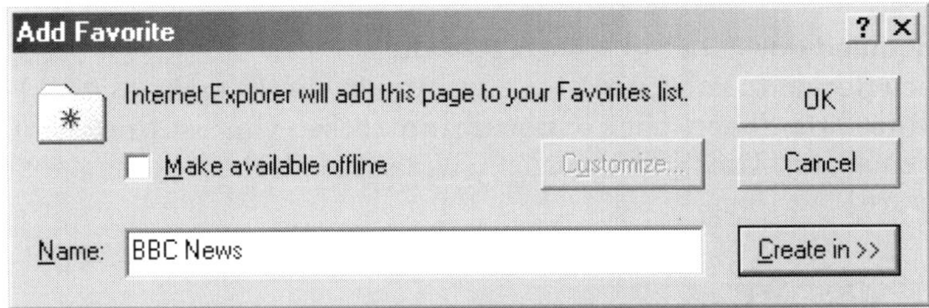

Figure 9.10 Adding a Favorite.

- storing the page directly (or the link to the page) in the Favorites root directory;
- storing the page in an existing folder;
- creating a new folder for a new Web page subject.

A new name to the Web page you want to record in your Favorites will appear automatically. If the title is not self-explanatory, or if it is in another language, you can change its title. Click **OK** and the page will be stored in the root directory. In the list of Favorites, it will be visible at the end of the list after any folders. A good method is to store the pages systematically in folders and to define in advance (or when needed) the folder types.

Rearranging your Favorites

As time goes by, you might need to tidy your Favorites or rearrange them. You can delete a site, a complete folder or even transfer one folder to another. To do this, select the Favorites menu and click ***Organize Favorites****. Click the folder you want to organize: you can now delete it, rename it, open it to fetch specific links, or move it to another location.*

To store a page in a folder, click **Create**. Two options are presented (Figure 9.11):

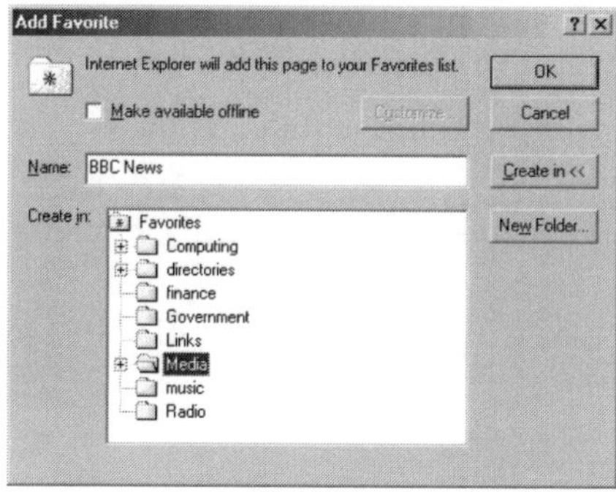

Figure 9.11 Storing a Web page in a Favorites folder.

- If the folder exists, locate it in the list (but be careful, the list is a tree structure; a folder may contain other folders), select it, then click **OK** to confirm.
- If the folder does not exist, go to the place where you want to create it (in the Favorites root directory or another folder), click **New**, enter the filename, and confirm.

You can go even further when arranging your Favorites and set up a programmed subscription to a site (for downloading and offline reading). If you want to do this, tick the make available offline option.

Scheduled downloading from a Website

If you decide to subscribe to a site, simply check 'make available offline' box. Then click **Customize** to set your subscription parameters. The Subscriptions Wizard will then do the rest (Figure 9.12).

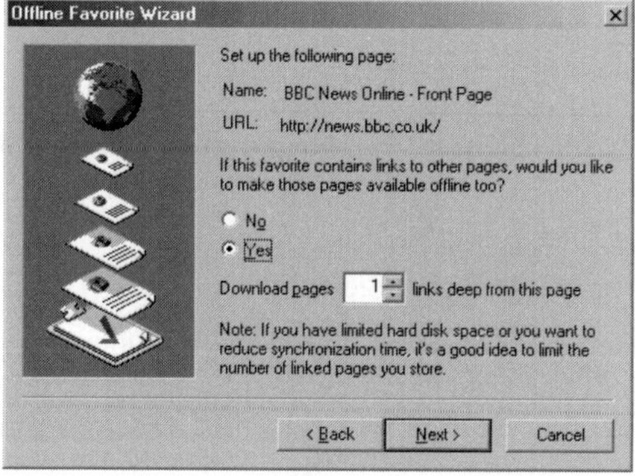

Figure 9.12 The wizard for subscribing to a Web site.

You can opt to download a Web page or part of the site (the page itself and any linked pages). To do this, tick one of the two options offered. Click **Next** to confirm.

You can now select when and how to synchronize with the site (i.e. download the latest pages). Your choices are (Figure 9.13):

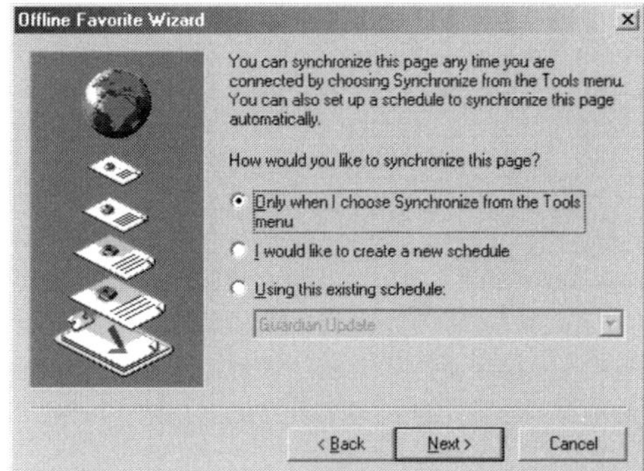

Figure 9.13 Choose when to download pages from the Web site.

- Download at any time that suits you by selecting Synchronize from the Tools menu.
- Create a new schedule.
- Use an existing schedule, so that you download from this site at the same time as from other synchronized sites.

If you choose to create a schedule, you will be asked to set the frequency and the time of day, and give a name for the schedule. If you find that you need to change the time later, you can redefine the schedule through the favourite's properties in the Synchronize dialog box (Figure 9.14).

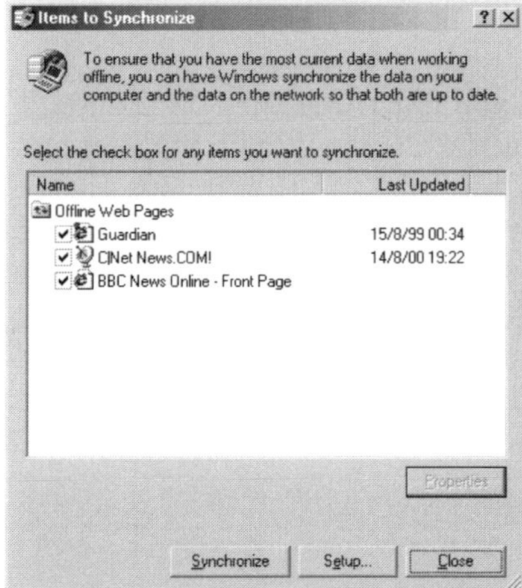

Figure 9.14 Managing the synchronized Web sites.

If you choose to use an existing schedule, you should then select one from the drop-down list.

At the next stage, you will be asked if the site required a username and password. If it does, they should be entered into the dialog box.

Once that is done, click Finish to end the wizard and return to the Add Favorites dialog box. Click OK to save the settings and close the box.

You can handle all your offline sites through the Synchronize dialog box. To open this, select the Tools menu and click Synchronize.

At the Synchronize dialog box, you can synchronize selected sites, or edit their properties. If you need to change their schedules, you can access the schedule for a selected site through the Properties button, or access all the schedules through the Setup dialog box.

Internet Radio

With Internet Explorer you can now listen to radio broadcasts from all over the world through your PC. The radio reception is good, but not perfect. The problem is not in the quality of the sound, which is almost as good as a CD, but in its continuity. Modern compression techniques have greatly reduced the size of sound files, but they still take a lot of bandwidth, and there's not much to spare. If you get online through an ISDN line, you should have few problems. If you link through a dial-up connection, you will find that data comes in from the Web at rarely more than 2Kb per second. That should be enough to cope with a broadcast, but if you are also surfing elsewhere, that will add to the overall quanitity of data trying to come in. Expect occasional breaks in transmission of a second or so, and expect other sites to download slower.

If you want to listen to the radio, you must first turn on the Radio toolbar, from the View, Toolbars menu. Click on Radio Stations and select Radio Station Guide. This will take you to WindowsMedia, where they have links to radio stations all over the world. There are hundreds of radio stations – far too many to show as a single list. Select a format, language, call sign or other feature to get a list of matching stations, then select from that. The station will be added to your own Radio Stations list, and can be selected from there next time you want to listen to it.

You do not have to be at the station's site to listen to a broadcast. You can start it playing then surf on elsewhere.

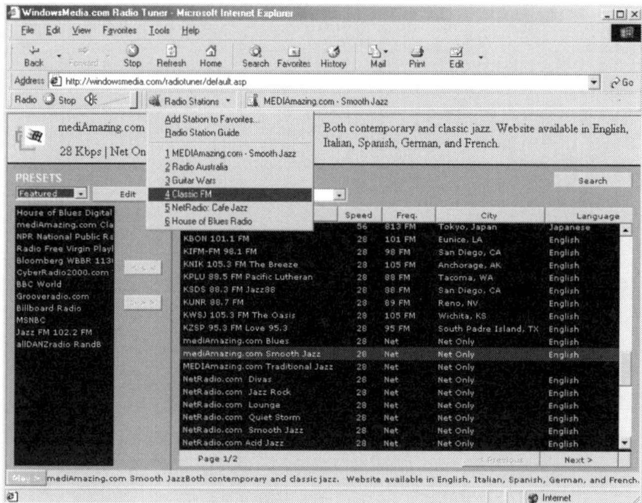

Figure 9.15 Setting up a new radio station. Once the link is created, you can change stations by picking from the Radio Stations menu.

Electronic mail

10

Handling your messages effectively

The Address Book

Filtering messages

Reading your mail from more than one computer

Windows Me is supplied and installed complete with an electronic mail software package known as Outlook Express. Electronic mail, or e-mail as it is more widely known, is the most frequently used Internet tool.

Whether you use this facility in a private or business capacity, e-mail has become an indispensable tool.

Users of Internet Explorer 5.5 (in Windows 95 and 98) may already have tried out Outlook Express. The software operates as a communications centre, managing, sending and receiving e-mail and messages from discussion groups. It incorporates an address book, and offers a wide range of features. Outlook Express replaced the communications centre offered in Windows 95,which was known as Microsoft Exchange. It is a program for sending messages and joining discussion groups using Internet standards. It represents a merger between Internet Mail and Internet News, which is a considerable step forward. Outlook Express allows you to configure your connection settings and manage mail efficiently, also enabling you to handle several Internet accounts. This is of value when you link a business account and a personal account; it is also practical in terms of sharing software at home.

As with any browser, the mail software can be called up from the Start menu, on the Desktop, or from the Quick Launch bar on the Taskbar.

The main software screen (Figure 10.1) shows the following components:

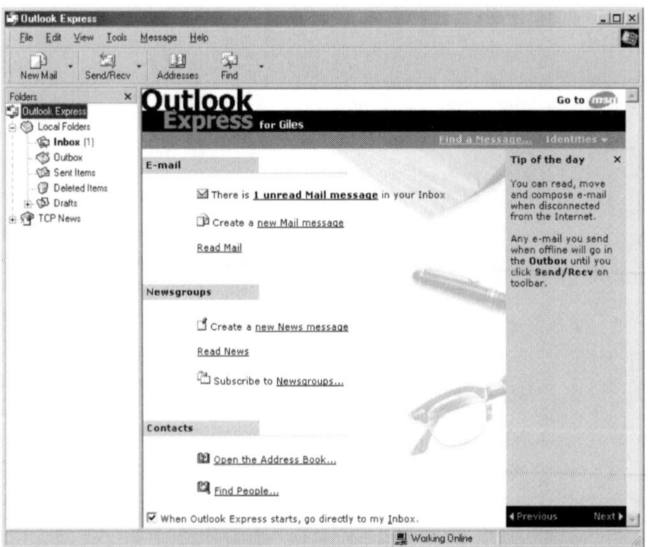

Figure 10.1 Outlook Express mail software.

- the toolbar
- the mail document folders in the left-hand column (the display pane)
- access to major software features in the main frame.

When using the software for the first time, five default folders are available:

- **Inbox**. Contains the mail messages sent to you.
- **Outbox**. This contains all the mail written offline or to be sent later.
- **Sent Items folder**. This keeps a record of messages sent.
- **Deleted Items folder**. When a file is deleted, it is sent temporarily to this folder, unless you have configured the software settings differently. Remember to regularly clear out messages in this folder or request that the data be deleted when you quit the software.
- **Drafts folder**. This is a holding folder in which mail you are currently working on can be kept temporarily.

There may be an additional folder for the discussion forums suggested by the Internet access provider.

Handling your messages effectively

The Inbox may be less practical when you are dealing with a large number of messages. If you communicate with a large number of people, or if your e-mail address is published on Websites or other media, or if you subscribe to information services supplied by e-mail, you will soon find out just how restrictive your single mailbox is. You therefore need to create new folders to store messages received (or, at least, those you wish to keep).

Creating document folders

Outlook Express enables you to handle a folder tree structure easily and to despatch your messages by subject. In this way, you can create an initial personal folder and another for business if you have a multipurpose account.

To create a new document folder, right-click on the Outlook Express root directory on the software explorer bar. From the context-sensitive menu select the **New Folder** command. Give the folder a name and then place it amongst the tree structure of existing folders. By doing this, you can create a new folder in an existing folder (Figure 10.2).

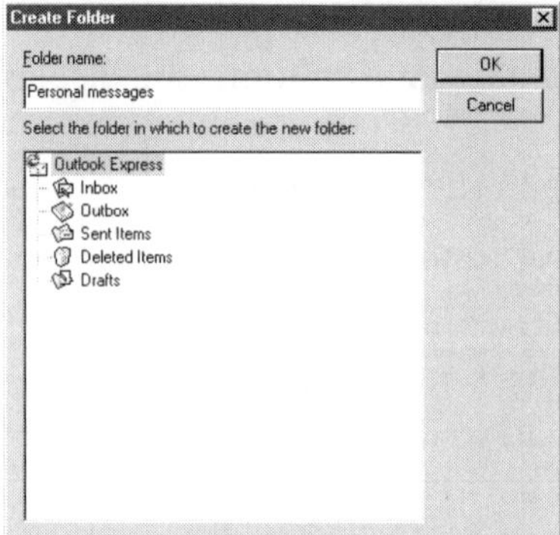

Figure 10.2 Creating a document folder.

Handling the arrival of new messages

By this stage, your Internet connection settings have been configured and your access provider server should be correctly identified. When starting up Outlook Express, the connection may be set up automatically, or you can log on at your request. You can also specify a start-up without logging on. This allows you, for example, to prepare mail offline, place it in the Outbox, and initiate a bulk despatch once you are online. In this way, you save on the cost of your calls. But you might also decide to start up the Internet connection every time you open the program in order to retrieve any new messages. To do this, go to the **Tools** menu and click **Options**. Select the **Connection** tab and tick the chosen option.

You can configure other settings from the **General** tab in the **Options** window. For instance, you can check the arrival of new messages every hour. Irrespective of the automatic procedures you may have instituted to read your e-mail, you can also open your e-mail box at any time by clicking on **Send and Receive** on the Outlook Express toolbar.

When you click **Send and Receive**, the Send function is initiated first. All the messages that may be stored in the Outbox are then sent, so make sure you have drafted them properly (the right spelling, attachments present, etc.). If some messages are incomplete, you should store them in the Drafts folder before moving them to the Outbox.

Once the connection has been established, a window shows the progress of messages being sent and received (Figure 10.3).

The **Details** button in Figure 10.3 provides information on the tasks performed and any problems arising. If you tick **Hang up when finished** button in the Details dialog box, your line will be disconnected automatically when the sending tasks have been finished and you have received any messages waiting.

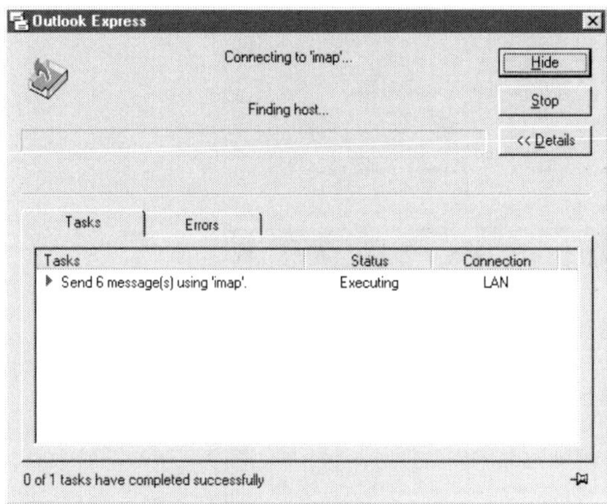

Figure 10.3 The progress of message transfer (messages sent and received).

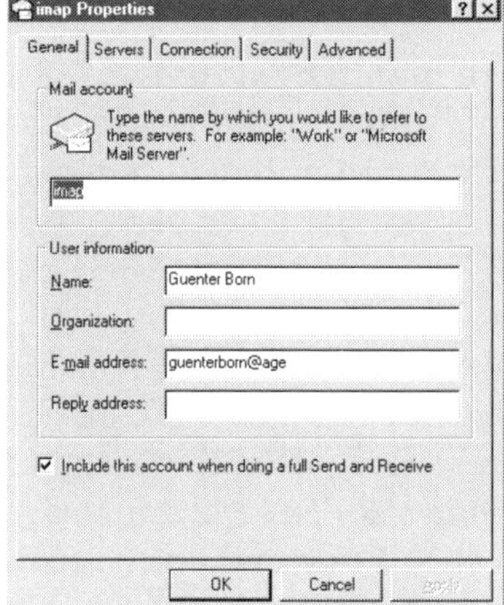

Figure 10.4 Mail account properties.

Check your connection

From the Tools menu, click ***Accounts, Mail****. Your access provider's mail server references are shown here. The Properties button enables you to fine-tune your settings (Figure 10.4).*

Looking up your messages

To check the messages you have received, click on **Inbox**. A list of the messages received is shown in the right-hand frame; at the bottom of the window, you will see the contents of the message selected in the list (Figure 10.5).

The Inbox has five components:

- the degree of urgency of the message (a red exclamation mark (!) means an important message is waiting)
- attached items (if the 'paperclip' icon is showing in this column)
- the name of the sender
- the subject of the message
- the date and time of receipt.

Displaying an attached document

*The software tells you when a document has been attached to an e-mail by displaying the paperclip icon. Click on the message in question and then, in the reading area, click on the paperclip. The list of attachments is displayed. Click one of them and, depending on the document format, the appropriate software will start to run. Alternatively, click on the paperclip, then click **Save Attachments**. Choose where you want to save the attachment, then click **Save**.*

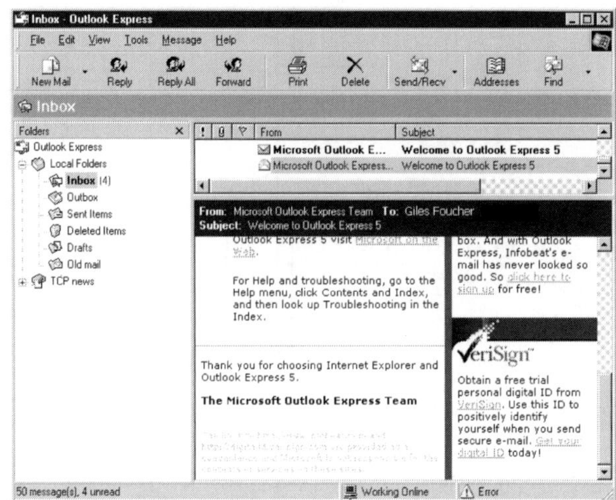

Figure 10.5 Looking up messages received.

Messages that have not been read are highlighted in bold. The number of unread messages is also indicated in the Inbox. The contents of the selected message are displayed in the bottom portion of the screen.

Transferring a message

You can transfer a message from the Inbox to a storage file using the drag-and-drop facility. Similarly, you can right-click on the message and ask to move it. The same menu also allows you to send the message in question to someone else. To send a message you have received to another person, click **Forward** on the toolbar. A Send window opens, and you then specify the addressee.

Deleting a message

To delete a message, right-click, then click **Delete**, or click **Delete** on the toolbar. Items deleted are sent to the Deleted Items folder. To delete items permanently, click on the Deleted Items folder, then click **Edit**, **Empty 'Deleted items' Folder**.

Sorting messages

You may find it useful to sort the messages in your folders. By default, messages are stacked in date order: the one with the most recent date is at the top of the stack. To sort the messages, click the bar in the From/Subject/Received field. When you click **From**, you sort the messages by name in ascending order. When you click a second time, you reverse the order of the sort to descending order. You can revert to the initial dated sort by clicking **Received**.

You can also sort messages and put them into 'urgent' (red!) groupings, or group those with attachments (these are the first two fields on the field bar above the list). The sort functions can be called up from **View**, **Sort By**.

Drafting a message

To compose a message, click **New Mail** on the Outlook Express toolbar. Complete the To, Cc, and Subject fields, then type the message (Figure 10.6).

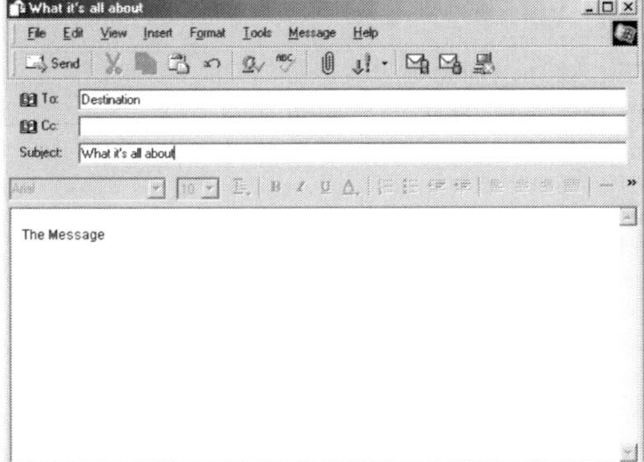

Figure 10.6 The message drafting window.

Using existing text

*You can prepare a message using the Windows Notepad or your usual word processor. Select the text, copy it (**Ctrl** + **C**) and, when you get back to the message drafting window, paste it in (**Ctrl** + **V**).*

To enter the addressee's details, type the first few letters of his or her name. If there is a reference to the addressee in the Address Book, the Input Wizard suggests a complete name. Alternatively, click the book icon to the left of the input line to open the Address Book, and select your addressee (Figure 10.7). In the same way, you can specify those whom you wish to receive a copy (Cc; carbon copy). Their names will be seen by the other addressees. To hide the recipients of copies, use the line Bcc (blind carbon copy).

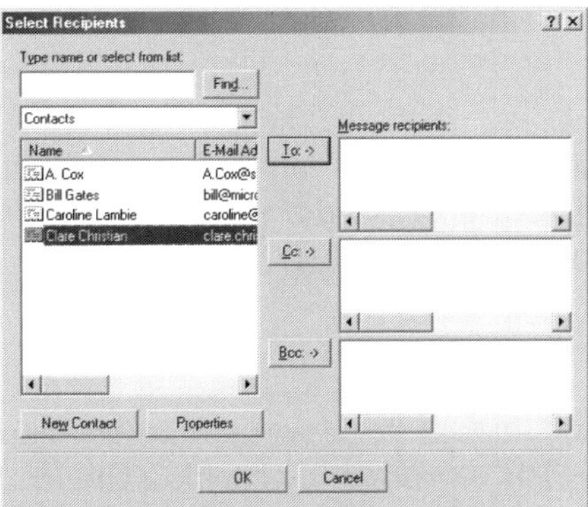

Figure 10.7 Choosing a message recipient in the Address Book.

Inserting a link in a mail message

*To insert a link, select the text to be converted to a link e.g. **http://www.company.uk,** then click **Insert**, **Hyperlink**. Enter the name of the link. This will be displayed with the usual hypertext link attributes (colours, underlining, etc.). To display an e-mail address, use the **Mail To** command, followed by the address of the person to contact. Your addressee can then click on the link to contact that address.*

Inserting a picture in a mail message

To insert a picture, click the icon at the far right of the message drafting toolbar. In the window that then opens, enter the path to the picture file or browse the hard disk to locate it, then confirm. The picture appears in the message drafting window. You can select it, move it and resize it as you wish (Figure 10.8).

Once you have composed your message, click **Send**. Or, click **File, Send Later**. A message to be sent later is kept on hold in the Outbox. It will be sent, along with any others, the next time you activate **Send and Receive** on the software toolbar.

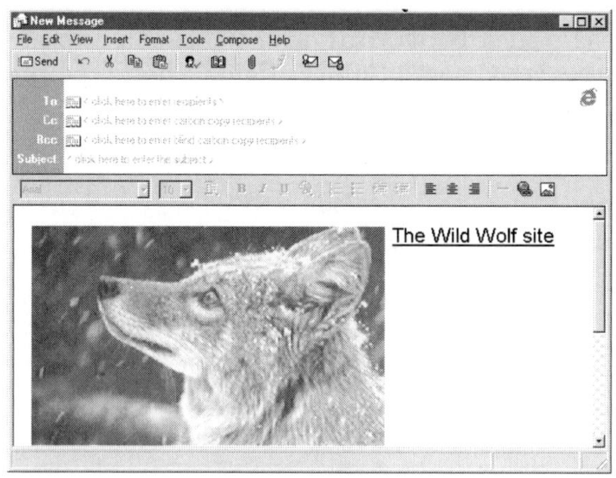

Figure 10.8 A message containing a picture and a hypertext link.

Inserting an attachment

One of the best features of e-mail is the ability to insert an attached document. You can append as many files as you wish to your outgoing mail; you can send a text written in Word, a photograph or an Excel spreadsheet.

To insert a file, click **Insert File Attachment**, then browse the hard disk to find the file you want. Repeat the operation as many times as you need.

The attached files are summarized at the bottom of the message drafting window (Figure 10.9). Do not overload the message if there is no need to do so as very bulky files can take a long time to be sent and received.

The right format

If the person you are e-mailing cannot handle HTML format, send your message as an attachment, otherwise the enhancements may be lost. To get the most out of the enhancements, make sure the settings are configured correctly: ***Tools, Options, Send, Reply to messages using the format in which they were sent.***

The Address Book

Entering the electronic address of a person you wish to contact can be carried out by the Outlook Express Address Book (Figure 10.10). This feature supplies you with the Internet addresses of your contacts.

Handling the Address Book

Click on **Address Book** in the Outlook Express toolbar. You can also do this via the message drafting window, by clicking the icon next to To.

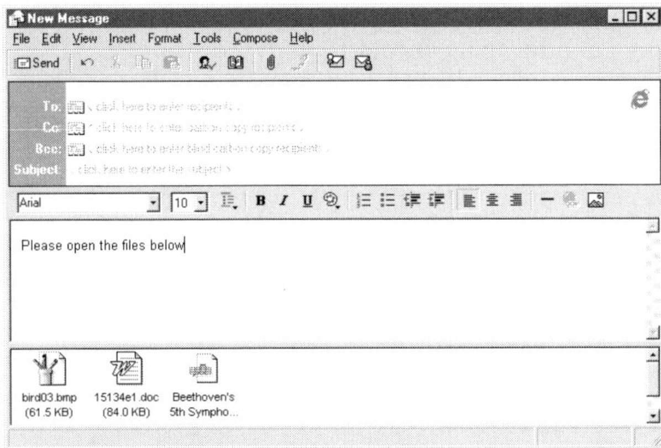

Figure 10.9 Attached documents are displayed at the bottom of the message drafting window. In this case, three files (text, a picture and music) are attached.

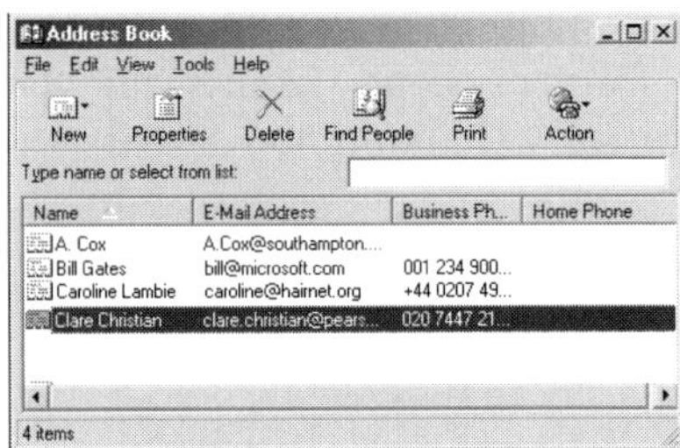

Figure 10.10 The Address Book.

Adding a new contact

You can add a contact manually by clicking **New, New Contact** on the toolbar. Enter the name and electronic address in the Name tab; you can also enter details of other contact information (Figure 10.11).

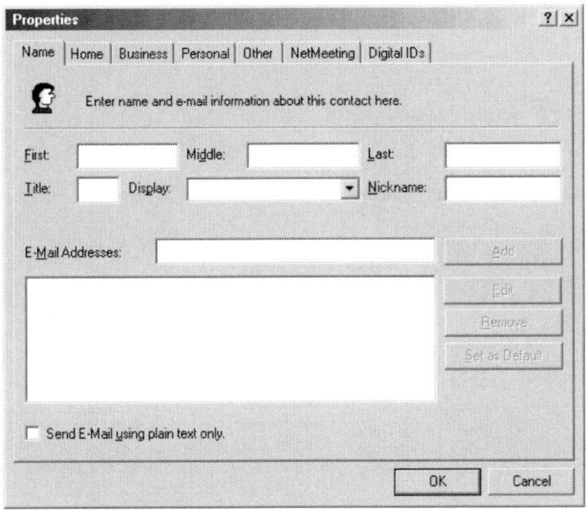

Figure 10.11 Entering details of a new contact.

Adding a contact automatically

*You can also automate the add new contacts function as follows: select **Tools**, **Options**, **Send**, and tick **Automatically put people I reply to in my Address Book**.*

Filling in the Address Book automatically

There are two ways of adding a contact to your Address Book:

- manually, when you receive a message from a new contact
- semi-automatically for each new contact you reply to.

To add an address semi-automatically:

1. Position the mouse cursor on the message title.
2. Right-click, then click **Open** to activate it, or just double-click.
3. Point the mouse to the name of the sender.
4. Click the right button to display the context-sensitive menu.
5. Select **Add to Address Book**.
6. The Address Book window opens: make the necessary adjustments and confirm.

Setting up an electronic mailshot

You can group certain contacts under a single entry. This enables you to send the same message to a group of people. In this way, you can define work groups or communities with a common activity.

Filtering messages

You can process messages received and, depending on their contents and source, you can automate particular tasks. To do this, click **Tools**, **Message Rules, Mail Rules** (Figure 10.12).

Handling your subscriptions effectively

*If you subscribe to an online information service, you might find it useful to file the messages automatically in the same document folder. Use the **'from'** option for the sender as a condition and ask for the message to be moved to the folder. In this way, your Inbox will not be filled by subscriptions that you can read at your leisure from your customized folder.*

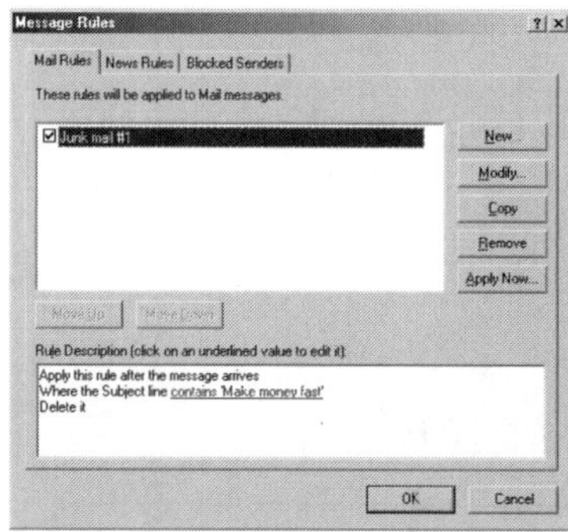

Figure 10.12 Setting up mail management rules.

In the Message Rules window, click **New** to create a new mail management rule. At this point, you can define conditions relating to the incoming message such as:

- the destination (To)
- the people who are to receive copies
- the source (From)
- the subject.

If one or more of these areas contains the information specified, you can initiate certain actions automatically, such as:

- transferring the message to a document folder;
- copying the message to a folder;
- transferring the message to another contact;
- preventing the message from being downloaded from the server;
- overriding the server.

Reading your mail from more than one computer

To manage your mail most efficiently from a portable or desktop PC, you must retain it on the server when you look it up from the portable and copy it to the desktop PC for centralized reception. By default, the messages are copied from the server to the PC it is connected to. With these settings, the mail will be distributed amongst the various machines, depending on the connections set up, and you cannot get a central view of your messages. To block deletion of the message at the server end on one of the PCs, this is how you need to configure your software:

1. Activate the Tools menu.
2. Select **Accounts**.
3. Click the **Mail** tab.
4. Select your mail server.
5. Click **Properties**.
6. Select the **Advanced** tab.
7. In the Delivery area, tick the **Leave a copy of messages on server** box (Figure 10.13).

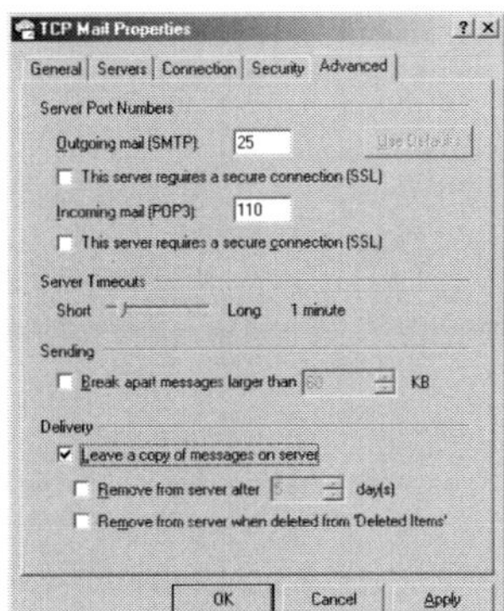

Figure 10.13 The mail remains stored in the server.

System tools

11

Windows Me is considered to be both more powerful and easier to use than its predecessors. With more high-performance settings and a faster shut-down, the day-to-day operations of Windows have been greatly improved. As we saw in the installation procedure, these operations include technical monitoring of the PC to enhance performance and prevent problems.

Scheduled tasks

Tasks scheduled at installation time can be altered later. To do this, open the **Scheduled Tasks** folder from **My Computer**. These tasks can also be called up from the Start menu, by selecting **Programs**, **Accessories**, **System Tools** (Figure 11.1).

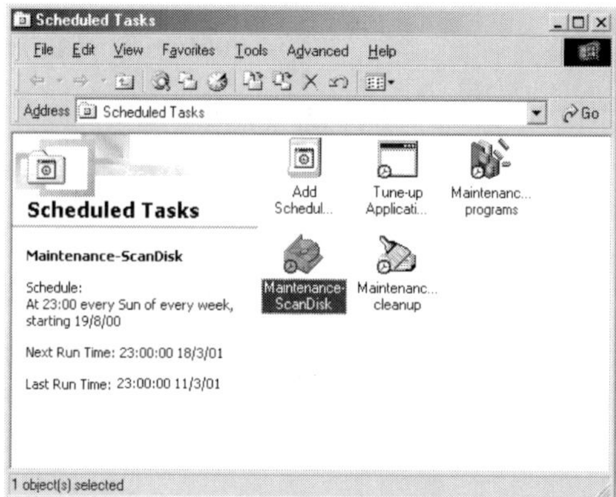

Figure 11.1 The scheduled system tasks folder.

To check a task, right-click on the relevant icon and click **Properties**. Three tabs are displayed:

- a task general description box
- the programming schedule (Figure 11.2)
- additional settings.

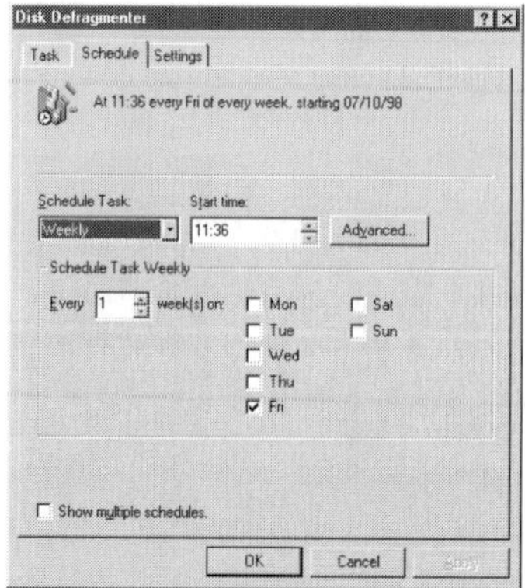

Figure 11.2 The task schedule for Disk Defragmenter.

In Settings, you can ask for a task to be deleted as soon as it has finished running. You can also halt the task at the end of a specified time limit.

You can also set the following rules:

- task start-up can only begin if the machine has been idle for *x* minutes;
- do not run the task if the PC is currently in use.

Finally, you can also optimize the power supply resources (in the case of portables) so that:

- the task will not start if the PC is running on a battery;
- the task shuts down as soon as the PC switches to battery mode.

In this way, you can modify or delete existing tasks. Back in the Scheduled dialog box Tasks, click on **Add Scheduled Task**. This brings up the Scheduled Task Wizard (Figure 11.3).

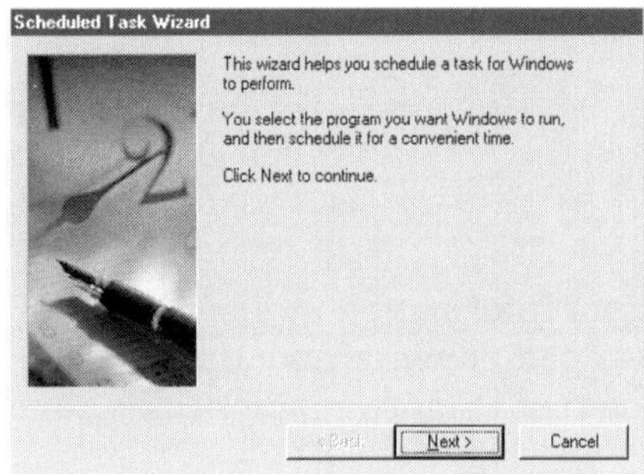

Figure 11.3 The Scheduled Task Wizard.

Once the wizard is up and running, click the programs you wish to run in Windows Me, e.g. select Outlook Express to schedule your mail reading routine. You indicate the frequency with which you want to run the program, every day for example.

Once you have configured the settings, check the **Open advanced properties for this task when I click Finish** box. You are then able to limit the task execution time. On completion of the settings, the task is added to the Scheduled Tasks folder. Windows Me now stays on continuous alert, ready to run the tasks you requested.

The system software

This can be accessed from the Start menu, through **Programs**, **Accessories**, **System Tools** (Figure 11.4). Some of these tools will only be of interest to the more technically minded, but there are others that all users should know about.

Figure 11.4 Windows Me system tools.

System Information

Windows Me incorporates a System Information utility, which provides an overview of resources, components and the software environment (Figure 11.5). This tool is more sophisticated than

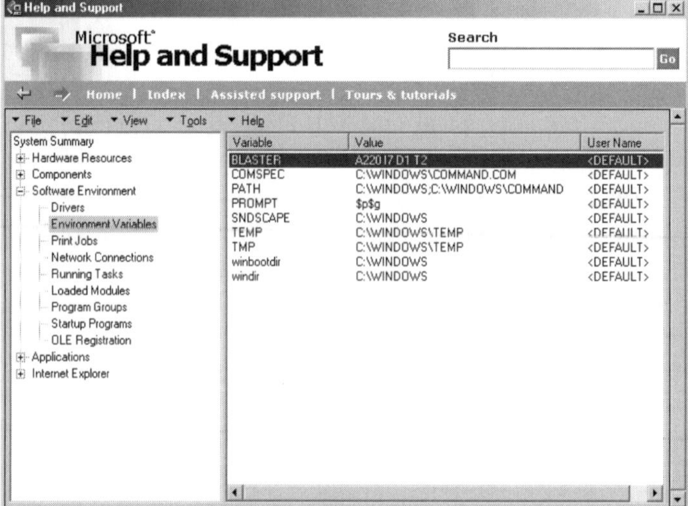

Figure 11.5 The software environment data, in this case the environment variables.

that accessed from the Control Panel. It provides far more information, though as it works through the Help and Support system it takes its time.

The pane on the left allows you to access the information headings, whilst the pane on the right displays the system data.

This utility contains a series of ActiveX checks, which collect the information requested and display it in the software.

The System Information tool is very powerful and enables you to carry out quick technical checks. If there is an operating problem with the PC, it can be used to detect any fault or a pilot version problem.

System Restore

With any luck you'll never need this, but it's good to know that it is there. Windows Me stores system restore points – backup copies of your important system files – at regular intervals. If these files become corrupted for any reason, whether it is user error, new software installation problems or hardware failure, System Restore will get your system running again.

To resore your system, go to the **System Tools** menu and select **System Restore**. At the first stage, select **Restore my computer ...** At the next panel, pick the most recent checkpoint when you know that the system was running properly.

Creating a restore point

A Windows Me computer is robust; modern software and hardware is normally reliable and thoroughly tested, but things do go wrong. Before you do anything which might upset the system, such as installing new hardware or software or making any other major changes, create a restore point. It takes only a few minutes and could save you endless hours of pain!

Start **System Restore** and select **Create a restore point**. Type in a description to help you identify it – the point will have the date and time added, so it is not too crucial to put that information in your description. Click **Next** to start the process.

Tidying up the hard disk

On start-up, this disk cleaning tool determines the spaces it can purge and therefore release on the hard disk. The Disk Cleanup window opens and indicates the volume (in megabytes) that can be released for each type of file. The evaluations are divided into file types (Figure 11.6):

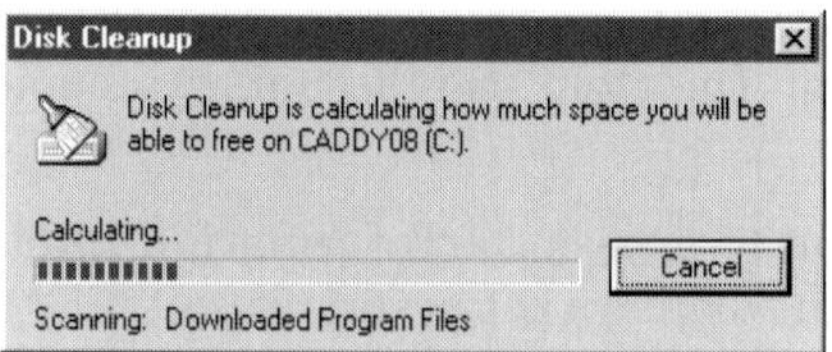

Figure 11.6 Determining the disk space that can be released.

Uninstalling Windows Me

If you upgraded an older PC to Windows Me, do not delete the Windows Me uninstall files if you think you might want to revert to your old operating system at a later stage.

- temporary Internet files
- files downloaded from the network
- files sent to the Recycle Bin
- temporary files
- Windows Me uninstall information files.

The More Options tab in the purging window is used either to delete unused Windows Me files, or to erase programs that are no longer used or to change the amount of disk space used by System Restore.

If you are removing a program, the software starts up the program uninstall window.

An irreversible conversion

If you choose to change to the 32-bit FAT mode, you will not be able to change back to 16-bit mode. Another consequence is that you will not be able to uninstall Windows Me from this point forward and revert to Windows 95. Progress is forward; you cannot go backward.

The FAT 32 converter

This is only of interest to people who have installed Windows Me over an earlier version of Windows.

This program is designed to convert the File Allocation Tables (FAT) to 32-bit format, thus bringing Windows Me into line with the Windows NT business family. This is a basic Windows 95 module, since it helps you manage hard disks of more than 2 Gb capacity more efficiently and improve the overall performance of your PC.

However, the decision to switch to the FAT 32 format is not an easy one and you are advised to read the online help on this subject before you start the procedure. You should be aware that some system utilities that work well with a FAT 16 facility may no longer operate.

Defragmenting the hard disk

By defragmenting your hard disk, you speed up subsequent processing. The aim is to store the data belonging to a particular file in a contiguous pattern. Any additions, modifications or deletions performed on all sorts of files (text, spreadsheet, database, etc.) generate pointers that provide a logical link between the data locations allocated to a given file. In effect, a particular file may have been created originally in an area of a given size and in the meantime that area may have been found to be too small to accommodate later additions. The additional data are stored in a vacant location away from the original file. So, defragmentation consists of reallocating adjacent spaces to various files.

The new defragmentation software keeps a record of the most frequently used files and keeps a close eye on the files generated by the program. It actually positions those files close to their respective programs, thereby improving performance and speed. Figure 11.7 shows the defragmenter in progress.

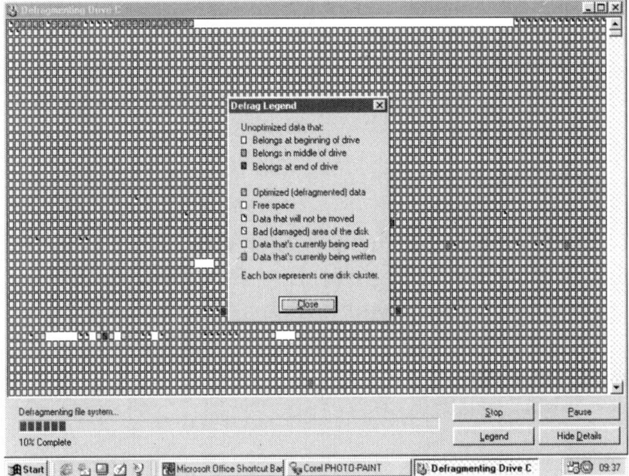

Figure 11.7 The defragmentation process, showing the types of sector in different colours and patterns.

Checking the disk with ScanDisk

ScanDisk is one of the most frequently used system tools. It checks the files (file allocation tables, or FAT) and the surface of the hard disk. If your PC responds oddly, run ScanDisk straight away. There are two checking methods:

- a standard check of files and folders;
- a more exacting check, which consists of analysing the disk surface (this can be quite a lengthy process, so you should run it when you do not need to use the PC).

You can ask ScanDisk to correct errors automatically. The Advanced button allows you to configure individual settings (Figure 11.8):

- display a summary of the operations performed;
- use an overall log, keeping a record of all ScanDisk actions (i.e. a bill of health for your PC);
- handle files with cross-links;

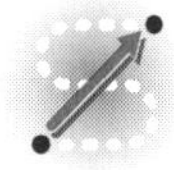

Troubleshooting system files

Do not check System file repair until you have run the System file Troubleshooter. This should provide you with all the information you need if a major problem arises, and will attempt to carry out repairs by restoring any damaged files from the Windows Me CD-ROM.

- convert fragments of lost files;
- check file names.

The Compression Agent

The Compression Agent utility is used on a drive that has already been compressed to configure settings at file level. In this way, you adopt higher compression ratios for the least-used files.

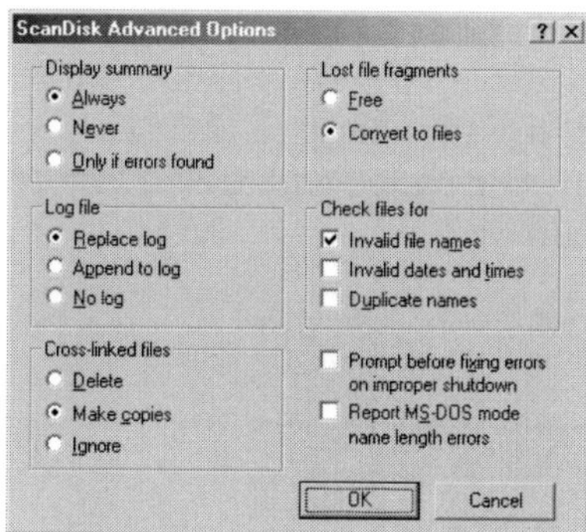

Figure 11.8 The ScanDisk settings.

Calling up the host drive

The host drive is shown in My Computer if it has a free capacity of at least 2 Mb. Drive C, the source disk, is always accessible, as well as the files it contains: however, it offers more free space.

If you choose to analyse the disk surface, click **Options** to tell the software which areas to check (Figure 11.9). ScanDisk can repair defective system or hidden files if you tick this option.

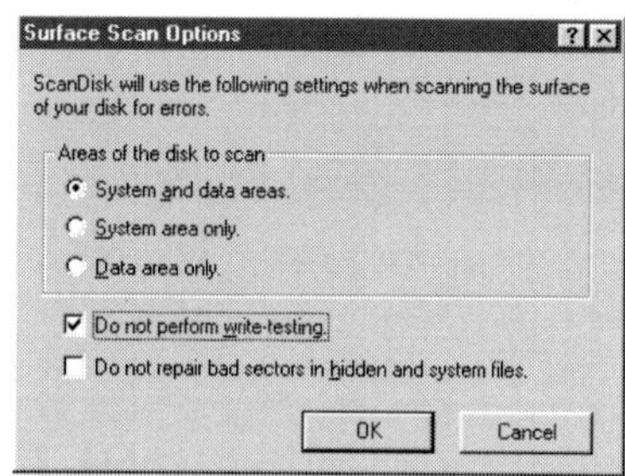

Figure 11.9 Analysing the surface of the hard disk.

DriveSpace

This program was originally designed to pack more data on hard disks. With modem, large hard disks and the FAT 32 storage system, it can no longer be used on hard disks. However, you can still use it to increase the capacity of floppy disks, if required.

Activity monitoring tools

There are two activity-monitoring tools:

- **System Monitor.** This monitors processor activity and resource usage.
- **Resource Meter.** This works in the background, calculating usage of the system, user resources, and graphic display resources.

Windows Me and multimedia applications

12

AutoPlay mode for CD-ROMs

Multimedia utilities

Media player

Plug-ins and players

Audio and video

Movie Maker

Playing DVDs

Image processing

Audio compression

Sound, like video, gobbles up disk space. For example, one second of CD-quality music requires about 170 kilobytes of storage space. To prevent your hard disk becoming full, you need to use sound compression algorithms. Windows Me offers different compression tools. To this, you should add support for the MIDI (musical instrument digital interface) standard.

The MIDI standard for music

The MIDI standard is important for music files. Music scores enable us to describe a Beethoven sonata in just a few pages. But to play it, you need a quality piano and a talented interpreter. MIDI files resemble scores: they are control files that enable us to 'describe' music concisely. Windows Me incorporates MIDI Polymessage, which handles MIDI files.

Compression is the multimedia spearhead on a PC. Without compression, just wave goodbye to the whole notion. For example, by compressing music files, you can quarter file sizes whilst keeping a sound quality close to that of an audio CD. The process known as PCMCIA is most common, but Windows Me can also accept most other compression techniques. The compression methods employed do not result in any appreciable loss of quality. Only experienced music-lovers will detect the difference between two recordings.

Some audio compression tools are designed to process voice. This applies, in particular, to TrueSpeech, a process that allows you to compress voice signals and record them on the hard disk in real time. The TrueSpeech compression ratio is significant, because the frequency range used to reproduce faithfully the human voice is very narrow.

Whether for music or voice, compression opens up new horizons. Space-saving on the hard disk is not the only objective – far from it, because multimedia transmissions and networks have to be taken into account.

Windows Me also incorporates all the resources needed to handle video in digital format (AVI – audiovideo interleave). Different compression methods (codecs) are available, including MPEG-oriented methods. This latter technology, which consumes vast decompression resources, normally requires the installation of a dedicated compression board.

In Windows Me, everything has been done to improve multimedia facilities and to assist their use. The AutoPlay mode (which appeared originally in Windows 95) is a typical example.

AutoPlay mode for CD-ROMs

When you insert an audio compact disk in your hi-fi, the system automatically goes to the first track and plays the piece. So, why do we need to install a CD-ROM? And when it has been used once, why do we have to go back to the control to run it again?

With AutoPlay mode, when you insert a CD-ROM in your drive, Windows Me checks whether an Autorun.inf file exists; if so, the file is executed. Otherwise, Windows Me carries out an automated installation procedure, creates the start-up file and runs it, without the need for you to do anything. Simply inserting the disk means that you want to 'play' it. So, Windows Me takes over all the tasks which, until now, you had to carry out yourself.

Multimedia utilities

Windows Me is supplied with a number of multimedia utilities, which you can call up from **Start**, **Programs**, **Accessories**, **Entertainment**.

Media Player

Media Player is the new Windows Me multi-purpose audio/video player. It can handle sound files in MIDI and in the native Windows format, WAVE – as well as audio CDs – or video in the standard Video for Windows (AVI), Media Audio/Video (WMA and ASF) or the many ActiveMovie formats.

CD Audio

If Media Player is not running, it will start up and play an audio CD when you insert it into the drive. If it is already running, then to play a CD, click the CD Audio button, insert the CD and wait for a moment for Media Player to read the track information.

The CD will play in the tracks in their playlist sequence – initially this will be the standard order. To change the order of tracks, click on one to select it, then drag up or down. To skip over tracks, select them, then right-click and choose Disable from the shortcut menu (Figure 12.1).

Figure 12.1 Media Player playing an audio CD.

Any choices or other information that you enter here are recorded by Windows Me in a file (on the hard disk) and will be reused next time the same CD is loaded.

Once the playlist is set up and the CD is playing, you can switch into compact mode. This doesn't just occupy less screen space, it also has some great 'skins' (window designs). Select a skin from the View, Taskbar, Skin Chooser display.

When a CD is playing, a 'visualization' is shown. If you don't like the default there are plenty of alternatives. Open the View menu, point to Visualization, select a set then pick from there. The names are not terribly helpful – you'll have to watch them to make a proper choice.

Radio

This offers another way to get radio over the Internet (see Chapter 10). There are a dozen pre-set stations, catering to a range of tastes, or you can use the Station Finder facility to pick from the hundreds of stations that are now broadcasting. You will find, when choosing a station, that Internet Explorer will normally open to show you the station's Website. This can be closed down, if not wanted, to save screen space and speed up download of the broadcast.

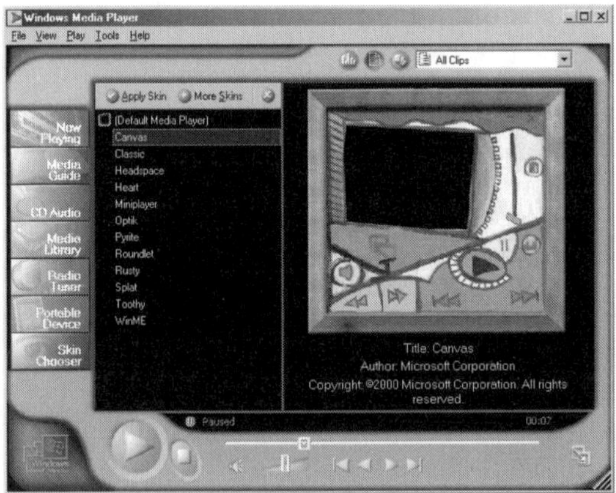

Figure 12.2 There are a dozen Media Player skins to choose from, and you can find more at Microsoft's Web site.

Obviously, if you are paying for your phone time when you are online, this is not an efficient way to listen to the radio!

Video

Newer, faster hardware and more efficient software has significantly improved the quality of videos on PC, but they are still small and jerky – or run them in full-screen mode and they are large and blocky and jerky!

The main sources of videos are multimedia packages, where Media Player can be called up automatically to play the clips, demos and samples on CDs, and – most of all – the Internet.

There are three main ways in which you will get video from the Internet:

- Clips for downloading – the new high-compression formats have brought a better balance between download time and playing time. 1Mb of video gives you around 90 seconds of playing time, and will take up to 10 minutes to download – and you must have the whole file on your disk before you can start to play it.
- Streaming video in TV and webcam broadcasts and, increasingly, in movie and pop video clips. Here the videos are played as they download. The images are jerkier, but at least you don't have to wait to see whether they are worth watching at all.
- Home movies e-mailed to you by relatives, who also have Windows Me and have been playing with its Movie Maker (see below).

Portable Device

CD audio tracks and files, from the Internet or elsewhere, in MP3, WAV, WMA or ASF formats can be copied through Media Player onto your MP3 player or other portable device.

The Sound Recorder

The Windows Me Sound Recorder reproduces the conventional interface of a real sound recorder, with the addition of a screen to display a graphic curve of the sound emitted (Figure 12.3).

Figure 12.3 The Windows Me Sound Recorder.

To record music or speech, you should first connect an audio source or a microphone to the sound board line input. Adjust the sound quality settings as required. To do this, click on **Edit, Audio Properties**. You can then set the recording conditions.

Then follow these steps:

1. From the File menu, click **New** to open a blank file.
2. Then click the record button (the red circle).
3. Finally, click on the black square to stop recording.

You can then check the recording by playing it back (the single, black triangle).

In the File menu, click **Save As** to save the sound file on the PC hard disk.

From the Effects menu, you can increase or decrease the volume, adjust the echo, or even invert sounds. These few features allow you to create all sorts of special sound effects.

You can only add an echo and invert the sound signal on an uncompressed file. The same applies to adjusting the volume level. You can modify the initial quality of a sound with the converter incorporated in the sound recorder. To do this, click **File**, **Properties**.

The sound recorder is a genuine mixing panel that also enables you to record a sound in a sound file. To do so, open a sound file and go to the position you want using the cursor and pressing Pause on play. Then start your recording. In this way, you can insert a sound file in another sound file or mix the sounds.

Overall volume adjustment

The volume control can be called up directly or from a multimedia accessory. It can also be accessed via the icon at the right-hand side of the Taskbar. It allows you to adjust the volume for all the audio devices in your PC (Figure 12.4). To alter the volume, slide the vertical bar. The horizontal cursor is used to set the balance between the loudspeakers.

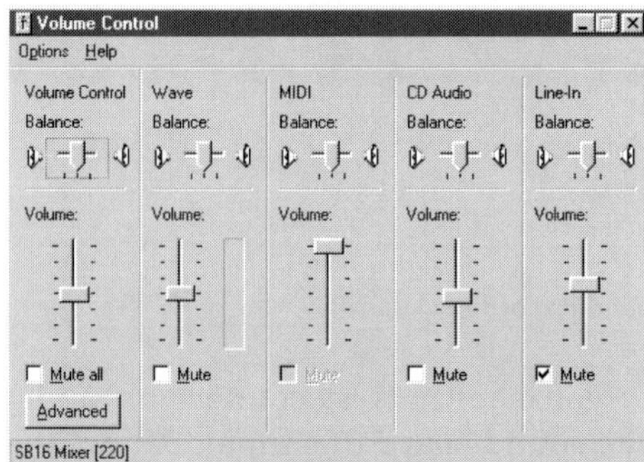

Figure 12.4 Adjusting the volume of audio devices.

The volume and balance controls affect WAV files, MIDI files, the audio CD, the line input and even your microphone or loudspeakers. In **Options**, **Properties** you can tick the devices to be displayed and call up the volume control for playback, recording or voice commands.

Plug-ins and players

With the help of software search and compression techniques, the multimedia phenomenon has surfaced on the Web to the point where we now talk of Web channels, rather than Websites. Of course, marketing accounts for much of this, but we should not ignore the facts: computer animation, audio and video have had a profound effect on the Web.

Even with our good old telephone line on the Public Switched Telephone Network (PSTN), we can benefit from the wealth of multimedia facilities offered by the Web. To do this, you need two sorts of tools:

- plug-ins
- players.

These names conceal very simple concepts. A plug-in is a small program that is placed in the browser in order to run certain features, such as executing a computer animation. This is what is done by Real Audio and Real Video from Progressive Networks (Figure 12.5).

Figure 12.5 Listening to Real Audio files on the Web.

A player is a stand-alone software package responsible for meeting requirements that the browser cannot offer as standard, such as playing audio or video files available on the Web. Media Player can cope with many formats, but you may find it worthwhile to get a copy of Quicktime from Apple (www.apple.com) as many video clips are in Quicktime formats.

Of course, other technologies are available and, to make the most of them, you should from time to time load the plug-ins that have been incorporated in the Internet Explorer 5.5 browser.

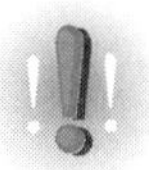

Listening to the radio on the Web

For this you need a quality modem connection: at least 28.8 kbps and a PC with a good configuration. Needless to say, microwave radio stations have seized upon this technology. Today, hundreds of radio stations throughout the world offer 'live' listening from their transmitters. Whilst direct hi-fi broadcasting has not yet arrived, it is still possible to download audio programmes using high fidelity technology.

Audio and video

Audio and video are new features on the Web. The bandwidth of the telephone network currently does not allow you to display video in real time in optimum conditions, with the result that playing video is slow and image quality is poor. You have to settle for smaller documents with image refresh once a second at best.

Consequently, on the Web, audio is overtaking video because it requires fewer resources. We should distinguish between two sorts of audio-video application:

- **Offline.** The files are downloaded to the PC and then played locally.
- **Real time, or 'live'**. The sources are played back directly from the Web, without storing them in the PC.

Whilst real-time video at present is something of a misnomer, real-time audio – radio, in effect – works perfectly well.

Movie Maker

This software is new with Windows Me. You can use Movie Maker to edit digital video, taking images in directly from your camera. The software can sense the change of scenes and will split the video into clips for you. The clips can then be split further or trimmed and set into a new sequence. You can merge in other video clips, or add still pictures, for titles and credits, or a voice-over or background music. Movie Maker has all the essential editing suite facilities to allow you to produce good movies, if you have the time and the skill.

The Movie Maker format takes around 10Kb for each second of playing time. This means that while video files are not small, they are very much more compact than the ones produced by older formats. Sharing videos with distant friends and relatives via the Internet is now quite feasible. There are two ways to do it:

- Send the movie by e-mail. Files are increased in size by 50% when attached to a message (because of the way that data is transferred through the mail system), but you can normally download e-mail at 3Kb or more per second.
- Upload the file to your home page, and send the URL to people. This allows people the choice of whether they want to spend time getting your video, but download times from the Web are typically less than 2Kb per second through dial-up lines. Of course, you have to have at least a basic grasp of making Web pages to be able to do this.

Figure 12.6 Movie Maker being used to edit file.

What it boils down to is that it is going to take your distant friends and relatives around one minute to download 100Kb of video, which will play for 10 seconds. That 10 minute video of the little one's birthday party will take over an hour to get, and as for the school's Christmas panto...

Playing DVDs

Windows Me comes ready to cater for the new generation of very high capacity disks, in this case the DVD (*digital versatile disk*). This allows you to show sophisticated films and multimedia programmes on your PC.

DVD drives use USB or IEEE 1394 type connections. Once the drive has been fitted in your PC, you should configure the settings or make Windows Me recognize it automatically (use the **Add New Hardware** icon in the Control Panel).

Finally, you need to install the DVD player supplied with Windows Me. To do this, go to the Control Panel again, click **Add/Remove Programs**, then select the **Windows** setup tab. In the Multimedia window, check the DVD Player box and start the installation process from the Windows Me CD-ROM.

Hi-fi on your PC

The tools required to play a CD-ROM (or audio CD), or video clip, or adjust the volume control, can be called up in the Entertainment menu in the Accessories folder (through ***Start*** *and* ***Programs****). This is also where you access the DVD player software.*

Image processing

You may already be familiar with the Microsoft Paint software, which evolved slowly through the various versions of Windows. It is still available in Windows Me, but it is now challenged by Imaging for Windows, a program designed by Kodak.

Being comprehensive and more powerful, this incorporates a colour management module, document digitizing settings (Tools menu), the ability to store documents in a format adapted for sending images by fax, and quick annotation functions (Annotation menu) (Figure 12.7).

Figure 12.7 Image processing with Imaging.

A simple guide to

Office 2000

Manon Cassade

Introduction

Office 2000 comes to you with many enhancements and improvements, including improved stability, a better response to users' needs (the environment responds to your actions) and increased integration with the Internet – with new functionalities to publish on the Web, navigate, and so on.

This book will help you to become acquainted with Office 2000 and to discover all the new features that have been introduced. Whether you are a beginner or an expert user, this book is meant for you, because it explains all the procedures proposed by Microsoft for you to be able to work quickly and easily. It also suggests expert tips and tricks to improve your performance.

How do I use this book?

Since the chapters are independent of each other, you can read them in the order you choose. To find a command quickly, consult the index at the end of the book. The book is structured as follows:

- Chapters 1 and 2 are a quick introduction to Office 2000. You will discover the various interface features as well as the commands which are shared by all the applications: opening a file, saving, and so on.
- Chapters 3 and 4 teach you how to use basic and more advanced Word functions.
- Chapters 5 and 6 explain how to use Excel.
- Chapters 7 and 8 are dedicated to creating presentations with PowerPoint.
- Chapters 9 and 10 deal with Outlook.
- Chapters 11 and 12 will make a perfect typesetter out of you, thanks to Publisher.

Adopted conventions

All commands are displayed in bold. Throughout the text, a number of symbols alert you to terminology issues and technical details, and indicate shortcuts or advice to the user:

This icon introduces handy shortcuts and tips such as keyboard hotkeys, expert options, and quicker ways of getting to the same place.

This icon warns you of any risks associated with a particular action, or any problems you might encounter along the way, and (where possible) shows you how to avoid them.

This icon is used to provide additional information about the topic being covered.

This icon indicates features new to Office 2000.

Help, checks and Web tools

1

Office Assistant

Help

Wizards and templates

Spelling and grammar

Find and Replace

Office 2000 and the Web

The functions you are going to discover in this chapter are shared by all Office applications.

In this chapter, we will look at the various procedures you can follow to get help. We will also look at the tools you need to speed up your work, check spelling and grammar, and so on.

Office Assistant

Introduced with Office 97, the Office Assistant takes you through all operations. If you are not familiar with version 97, the Office Assistant is a little paper clip that works very hard to provide advice when you need it. A faithful, effective and competent assistant, it never fails you.

When you launch an Office application, the Office Assistant is activated by default (Figure 1.1).

If the Office Assistant does not come up when you launch the application click on the ***Help*** *button in the Standard toolbar in the active application.*

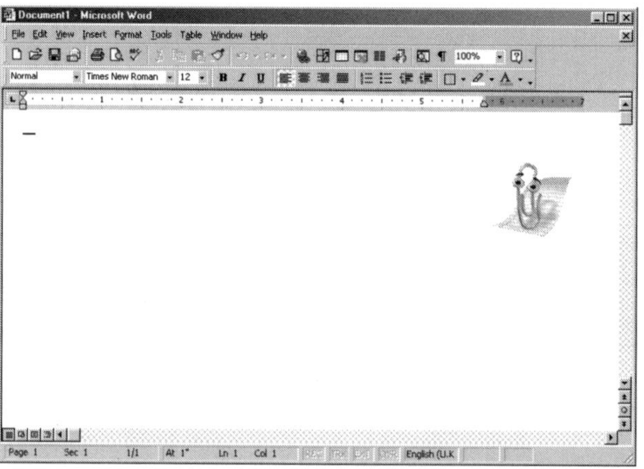

Figure 1.1 As soon as you start an application, the Office Assistant is displayed.

To ask the Office Assistant a question, click on it. Type the question in the text area (Figure 1.2), then click on **Search**. A list of icons is displayed; click on the one that corresponds to your search. If the list of icons is not relevant, click on **Next** to display the follow-up.

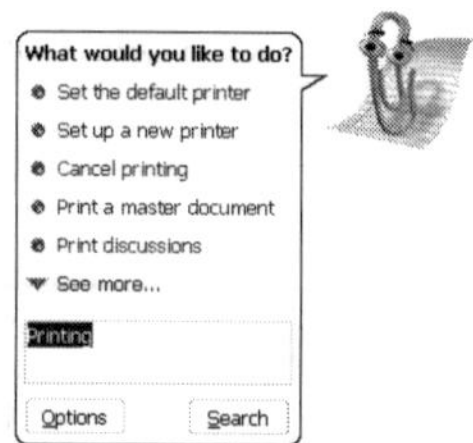

Figure 1.2 Ask the Office Assistant a question.

To hide the Office Assistant, click on **?** in the Menu bar, then select **Hide Office Assistant**.

For some tasks, the Office Assistant may offer help of its own accord. In this case it displays a text balloon. Click on the assistant to view its advice.

Office Assistant options

You can modify the Office Assistant default options. For example, you can choose a different look:

1. Click with the right mouse button (right-click) on the assistant, then select **Choose Assistant**.
2. Click on the **Gallery** tab. Scroll through the various types of assistants by clicking on the **Next** button or the **Back** button. The display area shows the 'face' of the selected assistant.
3. Once you have specified your choice, click on **OK** to confirm.

To modify the Office Assistant options, click on the **Options** tab in the Office Assistant dialog box (Figure 1.3). Activate/deactivate the options you require or do not require. Click **OK** to confirm.

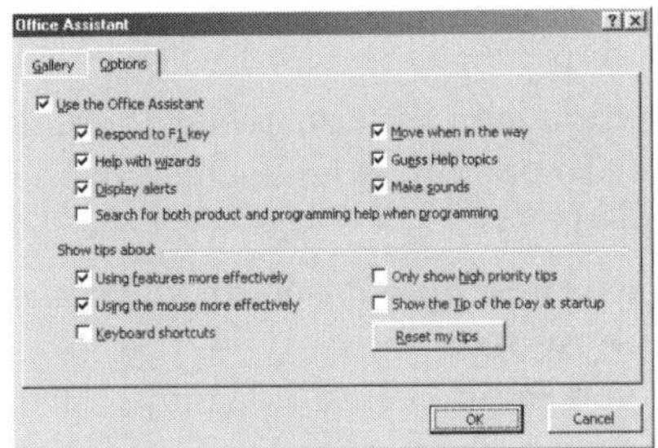

Figure 1.3 The Options tab in the Office Assistant dialog box allows you to set options for this function.

The options and the look you specify for the Office Assistant will apply to all Office applications.

Help

If you have chosen to deactivate the Office Assistant, you must use the Help and/or Context Help icons to obtain help.

Context help

Context help is a help option that matches the context in which you are working; you can also get help for a command, a button, and so on.

To obtain Context help, click on the **?** in the Help Menu bar and select **What's This?** The pointer becomes a question mark. Click on the button or the command for which you require help. A ScreenTip is displayed, which describes the command or button (Figure 1.4).

To obtain Context help in a dialog box, click on the ? in the box, then on the button or the command for which you require help.

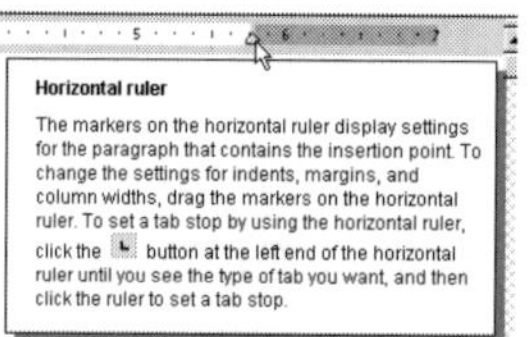

Figure 1.4 The ScreenTip describes the item you have just selected.

Help icons

To open the Help summary, click on the **?** in the Menu bar, then select **Help**. A window opens on the right-hand side of the screen.

- The **Contents** tab displays a list of topics. Double-click on a topic to display it.
  - A closed book next to a topic indicates that it contains a list of detailed icons. Double-click on it to open the list.
  - An open book next to a topic indicates that it is selected. Double-click on it to close the topic.
  - A question mark next to a section icon indicates that there is detailed text about this topic. To open it, double-click on the question mark or the topic label.
- The **Index** tab allows you to search a topic based on the command name. In the **Type keywords** box, type the text corresponding to the command you require. Box 3 displays a list of icons concerning the entered text. To display the topic that corresponds to your search, click on it in box 3: the topic is displayed on the right-hand side of the window.
- The **Answer Wizard** tab allows you to refine your search for Help. Type a word corresponding to the topic you are looking for in the **What would you like to do?** box. The outcome of the search is displayed in the **Select topic to display** area. Double-click on the topic of your choice in the second box.

*To print a Help topic, display it, then click on **Print** in the toolbar.*

Wizards and templates

Office 2000 contains a number of wizards and templates that you can use to speed up your work.

Templates

A template (with the .dot extension) is a default document into which you simply insert your text.

To select a template, click on **File, New** (Figure 1.5). The various tabs in the **New** dialog box offer several templates.

Click on the tab that corresponds to your requirements, then double-click on the template you wish to use.

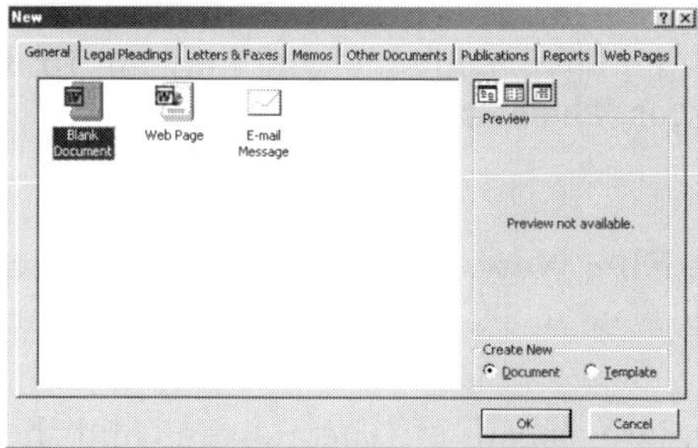

Figure 1.5 The tabs in the New dialog box allow you to select a template.

To work with a template (Figure 1.6), you usually just need to modify the various text boxes. For example, in the **Click here and type name** text box of the Letter template, click on the text and type the required name. Before printing the template, just follow all the instructions. The boxes containing instructions will not be printed.

You can also access the choice of templates by clicking on the ***New Office document*** *button in the Office Manager Shortcut bar.*

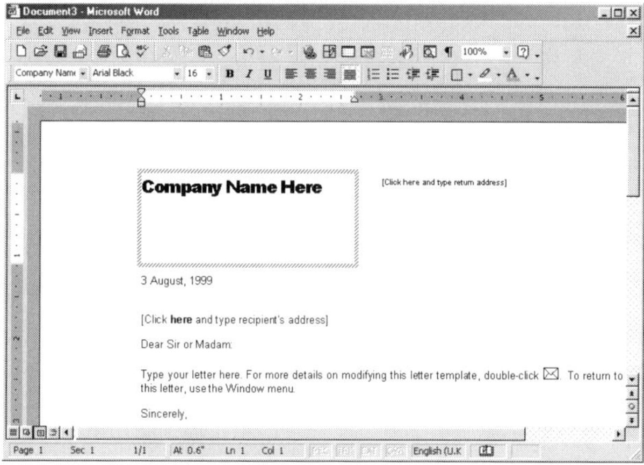

Figure 1.6 The letter template.

Wizards

A wizard is a sequence of dialog boxes where you specify your choice corresponding to the processing of a personal document.

To select a wizard, click on **File, New**. The tabs in the New dialog box offer several wizards. Click on the tab that corresponds to your requirements, then double-click on the wizard you wish to use. After completing each stage, click on the **Next** button to move to the next stage. If you make a mistake, or you wish to modify one of your choices, don't panic: click on the **Back** button. Once you have finished the procedures, click on the **Finish** button and the document will be displayed on the screen. You can implement customised formats by following the procedures included in the first chapters for each program.

When, in a wizard, you have clicked on the ***Finish*** *button, you will not be able to go back.*

Creating a template

Although there are several templates available, you may not find exactly what you are looking for. The solution? Create one!

To create a template:

1. In the application, click on **File, New**. In the **Create New** area (underneath the **Preview** area), click on the **Template** option and then on **OK**.
2. Create the document template, specifying the margins and the styles you require. When you have finished, click on **File, Save As**. You can also click on the **Save** icon in the Standard toolbar.
3. In the dialog box, type the name of your template in the **Name** box, then click on **Save** (Figure 1.7).

*When you save a template in the **Save As** dialog box, check that the **Save As type** box displays Document Template. If this is not the case, click on the **Up One Level** button (the icon of a folder with an upwards pointing arrow), then select Document Template.*

Figure 1.7 Enter the name of your template.

The application adds the template you have created to the existing ones. Whenever you wish to use it, simply select it in the **New** dialog box.

Spelling and grammar

Office 2000 allows you to check spelling and grammar for documents, presentations, worksheets, and so on.

Automatic spellchecking

You can ask the application in which you are working to flag possible spelling errors. Click on **Tools, Options**, then click on the **Spelling & Grammar** tab and then the **Check spelling as you type** option (Figure 1.8). Click on **OK** to confirm.

Once this option has been activated, everything the software thinks is an error will be underlined with a wavy red line (Figure 1.9).

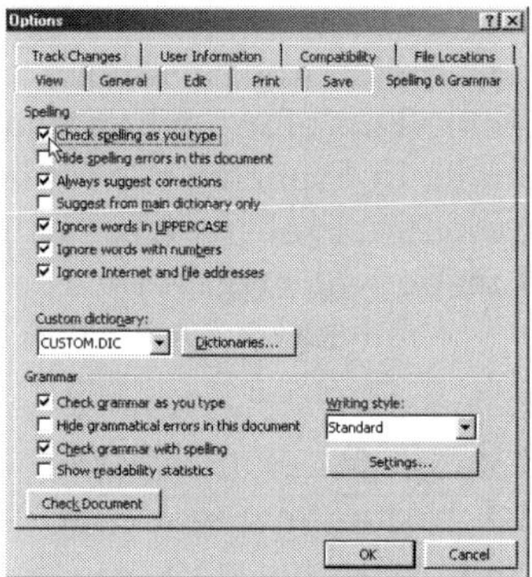

Figure 1.8 Activate the spellchecker as you type.

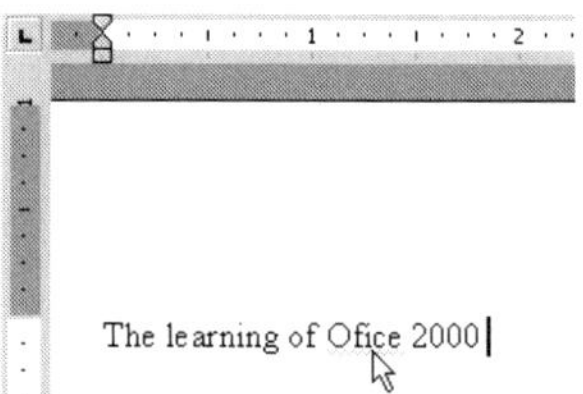

Figure 1.9 Spelling mistakes are underlined with a wavy red line.

To correct spelling errors, right–click on the underlined word, then select an option in the context menu.

- To select a word for correction, click on it.
- To add this word to the Office dictionary, click on **Add**.
- To ignore the error and to make sure that it is no longer shown as an error in the document, click on **Ignore All**.
- To choose another language, select **Tools, Language, Set Language**.

If you have chosen not to activate automatic spelling and grammar checking, you can still check your documents with the ***Spelling & Grammar*** *option in the* ***Tools*** *menu. Spelling errors will be highlighted for you to correct.*

Automatic grammar check
You can ask the application in which you are working to flag possible grammatical errors. Click on **Tools, Options**, then click on the **Spelling & Grammar** tab and click on the **Check grammar as you type** option. Click on **OK** to confirm.

Once this option has been activated, everything the software thinks is a grammatical error will be underlined with a wavy green line.

To correct grammar errors, follow the same procedure as for spelling.

Activating a language

In Office 2000, French, English, German, Italian and Spanish are recognised by default by the spellchecker. Therefore, when you need to correct a text written, for example, in French, the words will not all be underlined as errors. Only actual French errors will be identified and the correction context menu will suggest the correct spelling. The available languages are marked with an ABC icon next to them in the list.

You can also activate other languages. In any of the Office applications, click on **Tools, Language, Set Language** (Figure 1.10). Select the language you wish to add from the list and click on **OK**.

Figure 1.10 Activate other languages.

If this option is not active, click on ***Tools, AutoCorrect****. In the AutoCorrect tab, tick/clear the required options, then click on* ***OK****.*

AutoCorrect

When you start working in an application, you will notice that when you enter text, some misspelt words are corrected immediately. For example, if you have typed the word 'accomodate', this is automatically replaced with 'accommodate'. Furthermore, if you forget to start a sentence with a capital letter, the software replaces your lower-case letter with a capital. This is the AutoCorrect function. A list of words has been created in all office applications which tells the application how these should be spelt.

The list of misspelt words with their corresponding correct versions is not static: you can easily add your own corrections to it.

To widen the scope of the AutoCorrect function:

1. Click on **Tools, AutoCorrect** (Figure 1.11).
2. Type the misspelt word in the **Replace** box. Press the **Tab** key to move to the **With** box, then type the correct word. Click on **Add** to confirm this creation.
3. Click on **OK** to close the dialog box. You can create as many automatic corrections as you want.

The ***Exceptions*** *button in the AutoCorrect dialog box allows you to specify exceptions for some corrections.*

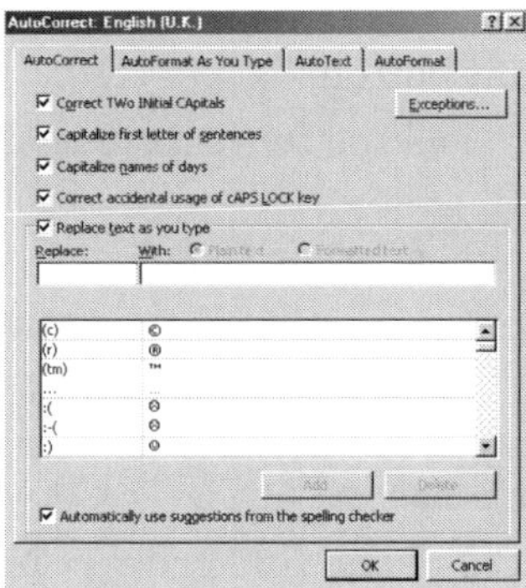

Figure 1.11 The AutoCorrect dialog box allows you to specify your correction parameters.

To delete an automatic correction, open the AutoCorrect dialog box. Select the word to be deleted in the list, then click on the **Delete** button. Then click on **OK**.

Find and Replace

So what happens if you have used a wrong word throughout a document? This is not difficult to correct manually if the document is only a few lines long, but if the document runs over several pages, Office suggests a better solution: the **Find** and **Replace** functions. Find allows you to search the whole document for the required word; Replace replaces the required word with a different one.

To find and replace a word or a group of words:

1. Go to the beginning of the document by pressing the **Ctrl+ Home** keys.
2. Click on **Edit, Find**, then click on the **Replace** tab (Figure 1.12).

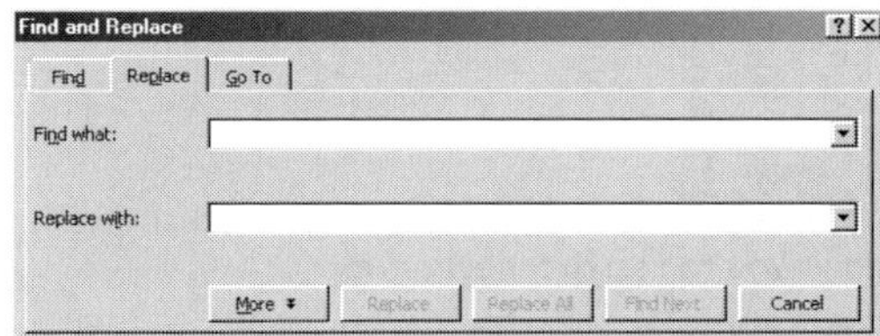

Figure 1.12 You can replace text quickly and easily with Find and Replace.

3. Type the word or group of words you wish to replace in the **Find what** text box. Type the word or group of words to replace this text within the **Replace with** text box. You can

refine your replacement by clicking on the **More** button. To start the search, click on the **Find Next** button.

The first instance of the word you are looking for is displayed and highlighted.

4. Click on one of the proposed buttons remembering that:
   (a) **Find Next** goes to the next instance and ignores the selected one.
   (b) **Replace** replaces the selected instance of the find criteria, finds the next occurrence and then stops.
   (c) **Replace All** replaces all instances of the find criteria in your document.
   (d) **Cancel** closes the dialog box without saving any changes you have made.
   (e) **Close** closes the dialog box and retains the changes you have made.

Finding synonyms

When you proofread your document, you may well find that the same word has been used too frequently. It would be better to find a synonym.

To find a synonym for a word, select the word, then click on **Tools, Language**. In the drop-down menu, select **Thesaurus** (Figure 1.13). (You can also press the **Shift+F7** keys to do this). In the **Replace with Synonym** box there will be a list of words or expressions suggested as synonyms. In the **Meanings** box you can see the various dictionary meanings of the selected word. Choose a synonym and click on the **Replace** button.

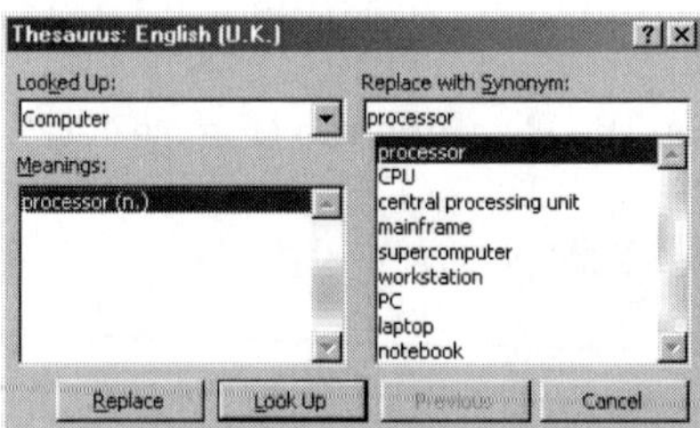

Figure 1.13 The Thesaurus allows you to search for synonyms.

Office 2000 and the Web

We will not launch into a long-winded explanation of how to use the Web and how useful it is, as there are several other books dealing specifically with this subject (e.g. *Internet* and *Internet Explorer 5* also available from Prentice Hall).

Office 2000 comes with Internet Explorer 5, a Web browser. When you installed Office, this navigator was also installed. If you have a modem and an Internet connection, you can connect directly to the Web from Office.

See p.281 to learn more about how to save a document to HTML format.

Browsing the Web from Office

If you have a connection to an Internet Service Provider (ISP) and are using Microsoft Internet Explorer as your browser, you can open Web pages directly from the Office applications with the Web toolbar. To display this toolbar, right-click on one of the active toolbars, then click on **Web** (Figure 1.14). Then use the various buttons to carry out the operation you wish to execute.

Figure 1.14 The Web toolbar.

To access a discussion group from one of the Office applications, click on **Tools, On-line Collaboration, Web Discussions**. Select the news server of your choice and get on-line.

Opening documents in Internet Explorer

The compatibility of Office functions with Internet Explorer 5 allows all data in the browser to be retrieved once a document has been translated to HTML format. This means that the complexity of PivotTables will be no problem for the browser: it will retain the original formatting of the document!

To open a document in Internet Explorer once it has been saved in HTML format, click on **File, Open**. Select a file, then click on **Open**.

Web preview

Once a document or a presentation has been saved in HTML format, you can view it in a Web preview so that you can see exactly what your document will look like when it is published on the Web.

To display a Web preview for a document or a presentation, click on **File, Web Page Preview**.

On-line collaboration

To implement an on-line collaboration from one of the Office applications, simply connect to the Internet. Then, click on **Tools, On-line Collaboration, Meet Now**. Select the server name in the relevant option box. Netmeeting is launched and you can start to chat.

E-mailing from an application

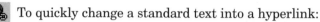

You can now send a document by e-mail from any Office application. Use the **E-mail** button, accessible from the Standard toolbar in all the applications. Once this command is active, the editing window for the message is displayed (see Chapters 7 and 8). Get information on the various options, then send your message.

Creating hyperlinks

A Web page is not complete unless it has hyperlinks. A hyperlink allows you to direct the visitor, with a simple click, to another part of the page or to another site. All Office 2000 applications have an icon that allows you to insert hyperlinks to other documents, files or pages.

To quickly change a standard text into a hyperlink:

1. Select the text, then click on the **Insert Hyperlink** button in the Standard toolbar (Figure 1.15).

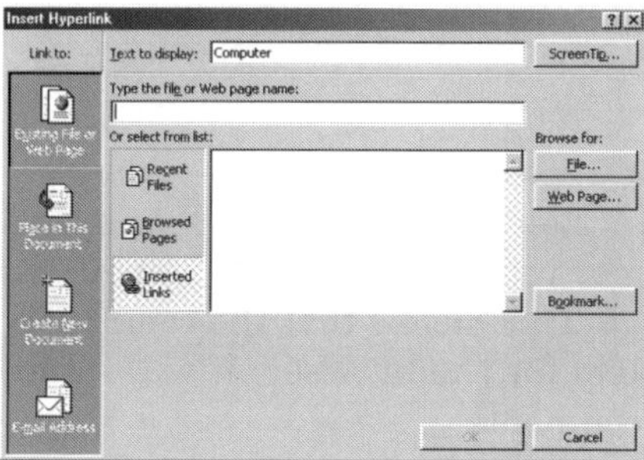

Figure 1.15 The Inset Hyperlink dialog box.

2. Specify the URL (Web address) of the page to which the link goes. Type the hyperlink name in the **Type the file or Web page name** option, or select the address in the list, or click on the **File** button, then select the file to which the hyperlink is directed. Click on **OK**.

Top marks for PowerPoint. Its 2000 version allows you to automatically create a resume to the left of the site. Once you have displayed the presentation in the navigator, simply click on one of the points you wish to be included in the resume to display its contents directly in the window on the right (see Chapters 7 and 8).

Shared commands

2

Starting and quitting applications

Undoing and redoing actions

Interface elements

Saving data

File management

Printing

Cut, copy, paste and move

Clipboard Intelligent

Inserting text styles

Copying a format

Inserting pictures

In this chapter we will look at the functions and commands shared by all Office applications.

Starting and quitting applications

When you have installed Office, the names of the various applications are placed in the **Start** menu in **Programs**.

Launching an application

To launch an application, click on **Start, Programs**, and then the relevant application (Figure 2.1). You can also open an application by clicking on the corresponding button in the Office Manager.

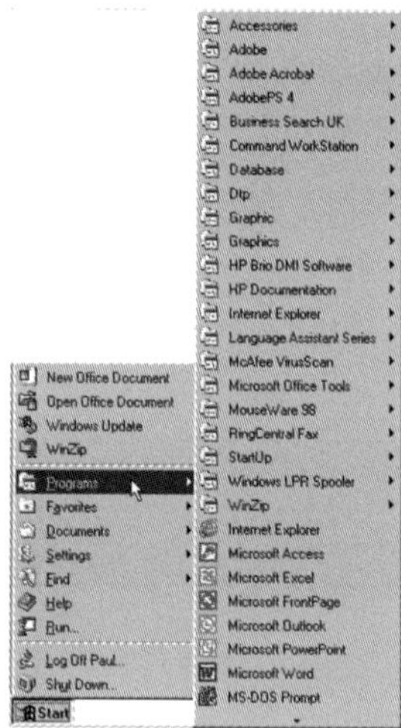

Figure 2.1 Start the application of your choice with **Start, Programs**.

The other solution is to place shortcut icons on your Windows Desktop. This function is useful for common applications: you simply double-click on the icon to quickly launch the program.

To create a program shortcut icon, click on **Start, Programs**. Click with the right mouse button on the program of your choice then, keeping the button pressed, drag it on to the Desktop. In the context menu, select **Create Shortcut**.

Quitting an application

To close a program, several solutions are offered:

- Click on **File, Close**. If a file is open, you will be asked whether you wish to save it. Click on **Yes** or **No**.
- Click on the **system** box, at the top left of the screen, which displays the program icon, then click on the **X** (Close).
- Press the **Alt+F4** keys.

Undoing and redoing actions

The Undo and Redo functions allow you to undo or redo the action or the command you have just executed.

*If you wish to repeat your last action, press **F4**.*

Clicking on this button undoes the last action. If you wish to undo several actions, click on the small arrow and select all that you wish to undo. You can also click on **Edit, Undo [name of action]**.

Click on this button to redo the last action you have just undone. If you wish to redo several actions, click on the small arrow and select all that you wish to redo. You can also click on **Edit, Redo [name of action]**.

Interface elements

All the elements in this section are shared by all the applications running under Windows 95 and 98. It is not our intention here to show you the procedures for using your system, but you should be acquainted with some basic principles.

Menu bar

The Menu bar is positioned underneath the Title bar. Each menu (File, View, and so on) opens a drop-down list that offers several commands (Figure 2.2). Menus follow a number of parameters:

Figure 2.2 The Menu bar in Word.

- Greyed commands are not available; commands in black are available.
- An arrowhead next to a command indicates that the command has a drop-down sub-menu.
- An ellipsis (...) after a command indicate that the command opens a dialog box that allows you to select options, specify choices, and so on.
- A button positioned in front of a command indicates that the command can also be found as a shortcut in one of the toolbars.
- A key combination, such as **Ctrl** or **Alt** followed by a letter, displayed next to a command confirms that this command also has a keyboard shortcut. By pressing these keys, you will automatically open the command or its dialog box (for example, with the **Ctrl+P** keys, you open the Print dialog box).

Dialog boxes

*In addition to the **Open** and **Save** dialog boxes, there is the **Position** bar, which looks the same as that in Outlook. This allows quick access to the most used folders and documents. Dialog boxes are now larger for better viewing. Finally, some dialog boxes include a button that allows you to return quickly to recently used folders or files. This button is easily recognised: it is an arrow pointing to the left.*

*The **Back** button is the same as the one used in Internet browsers.*

To make your tasks easier, the 2000 version allows automatic menu customisation. Therefore, while you work, menus are adapted to your choice and display only what you are using. To view a complete menu, simply click on the two arrowheads (<<) at the bottom of the menu, or double-click on the menu name (for example, double-click on **File** to view the default menu).

Toolbars

Positioned underneath the Menu bar, toolbars allow quick access to some of the most commonly used commands. By default, programs display two toolbars: **Standard** and **Format**. However, you can display several others.

To display a toolbar, click with the right mouse button on a toolbar and select the required toolbar from the menu.

To hide a toolbar, right-click on a toolbar and click on the one you wish to hide.

The toolbar customisation options are very simple. To customise a toolbar once you have it on the screen:

1. Click with the right mouse button on any toolbar and, at the bottom of the drop-down toolbar menu, select **Customize**.
2. In the Customize dialog box, the **Options** tab allows you to specify the display (large icons, list of fonts, ScreenTips, and so on). The **Toolbars** tab allows a toolbar to be activated and new ones to be created, while the **Commands** tab lists the various categories of buttons as well as their icons.
3. To add an icon to a toolbar, select the category, click on the button to be added in the list on the right and drag it into the relevant toolbar. Click on **Close** to confirm.

To delete a button, click on the arrowheads in the relevant toolbar, select **Add/Remove** buttons (Figure 2.3), then click on the option check box against the command to be removed.

Saving data

To save a document, worksheet or slide, simply click on the **Save** button in the Standard toolbar or click on **File, Save**. The procedure is very different depending on whether you are saving the file for the first or the *n*th time.

To save a file for the first time:

1. Click on the **Save As** command in the File menu (Figure 2.4).
2. Select the folder in the **Save in** area or use the Views bar by clicking on the folder (for example **My Documents**).

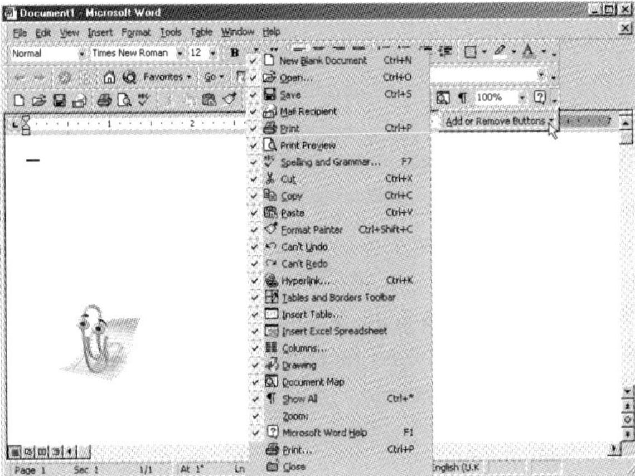

Figure 2.3 You can easily turn off a toolbar button.

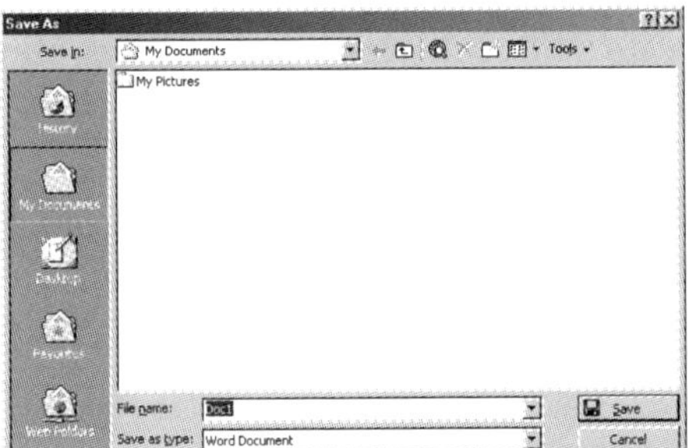

Figure 2.4 The Save As dialog box.

Previously static and unattractive, toolbars are now more functional: they take up little space because they are displayed next to each other and they change according to the user's needs. To view the whole of a toolbar, simply click on the two right-pointing arrowheads on its right edge.

3. Type the name of the file to be saved in the **File name** box (do not type the extension; this is generated automatically by the application from which you are saving). Click on the **Save** button.

When you save the document the next time, simply click on the **Save** button in the Standard toolbar.

Saving documents in HTML format

The HTML format is the format used on the Web. Regardless of the document you wish to publish (text, presentation, worksheet, and so on), you must change it to an HTML document before publishing it. Without this transformation, it will not be readable on the Web.

To save a document or a presentation to HTML format:

1. Click on **File, Save as Web Page**.
2. Name the file in the **Name** box. You can edit its title by clicking on the **Change Title** button. Click on **OK** in the **Set Page Title** box (Figure 2.5), then on **Save**.

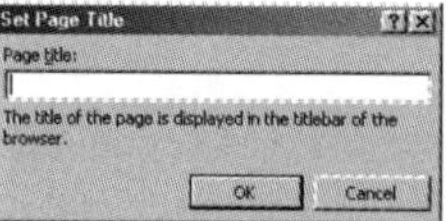

Figure 2.5 Changing the name of your Web page.

You can now save a document directly on to a server, for example on your company's intranet.

Saving on a server

To save a document on a Web server, click on **File, Save as Web Page**. In the Views bar, click on **Web Folders**, which contain possible shortcuts to the Web server(s). Select the server of your choice. Name the document and click on **Save**.

File management

The concept of file management will be familiar to you if you have some experience in using computers. If you are a beginner, here are some explanations. In Windows, when you create a document, table, presentation, and so on, you create a file. Files are kept in folders. You can see all the files in your computer in Explorer.

Opening files

To open a file, click on the **Open** button in the Standard toolbar or on **File, Open** (Figure 2.6). Select the folder that contains the required file in the **Look in** box, or use the Views bar. Then simply double-click on the file.

*To open a recently opened file, click on **File**: the file is displayed at the bottom of the menu; simply click on it to open it. If the program is not open, you can also click on **Start, Documents**. A list of the last 15 files used is displayed. Select the one you wish to open.*

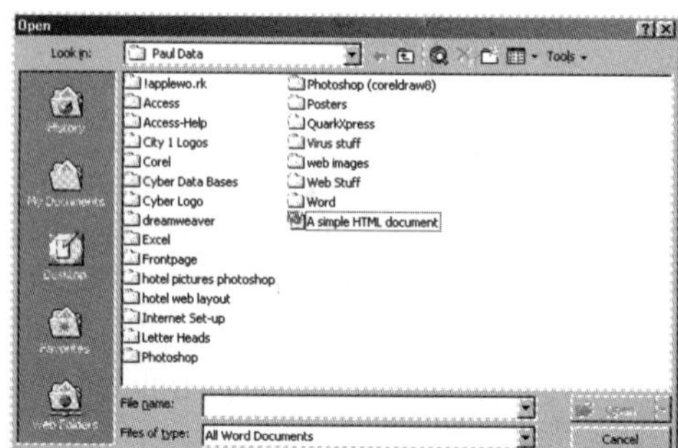

Figure 2.6 Opening a file in the Open dialog box.

Closing files

To close a file, either click on the **Close** window button (shown by an X), or click on **File, Close**.

Deleting and renaming files

To delete a file, click on the **Open** button. In the dialog box, click with the right mouse button on the relevant file and select **Delete**. Click on **Yes** to confirm the deletion.

To rename a file, click on the **Open** button. In the dialog box, click with the right mouse button on the relevant file and select **Rename**. Type the new name and press **Enter** to confirm.

Printing

First, switch on your printer, then click on the **Print** button. Or, if you wish to specify the printer to be used, the number of copies to be made, and so on, click on **File, Print**, then specify your choice in the Print dialog box (Figure 2.7). Click on **OK** to confirm your choice and start printing.

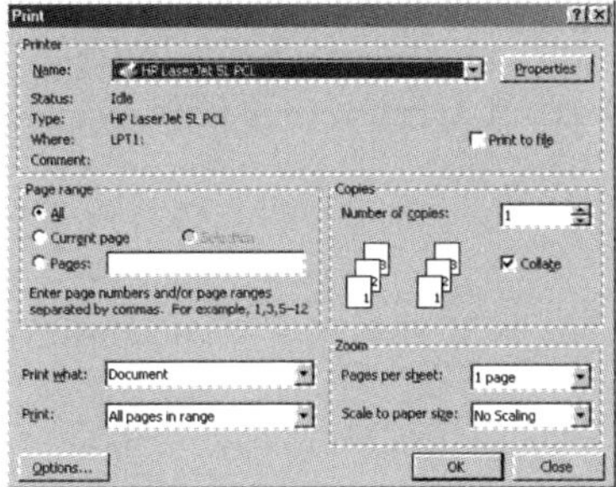

Figure 2.7 The Print dialog box in Word.

Cut, copy, paste and move

When creating documents, you may need to move, cut or copy a word, sentence or object. These procedures are very simple.

To copy, select the element you want, then press the **Ctrl+C** keys. You can also click on **Edit, Copy**.

To cut, select the relevant element, then press the **Ctrl+X** keys. You can also click on **Edit, Cut**.

To paste an item, press the **Ctrl+V** keys. You can also click on **Edit, Paste**.

To move, select the item on your document, then click on the selection. Keeping the mouse button pressed, drag it to where you wish to move it to. Release the mouse button.

You can also use the **Copy, Cut** or **Paste** buttons. Their procedures are identical to those we have just seen.

*When you copy or cut a piece of text or an object with the **Edit**, **Copy** or **Edit**, **Cut** commands, the element is stored in the **Clipboard**, which is a sort of waiting room. You can then paste the contents of this Clipboard into another document or page.*

Clipboard Intelligent

In previous versions of Office, when you copied or cut an item, the action automatically deleted the previous Clipboard contents. This is no longer the case. Now, you can store up to 12 items in the Clipboard. When you wish to paste an element, simply select it in the Clipboard.

When you cut and/or copy several items, the Clipboard toolbar is displayed automatically (Figure 2.8). Position your cursor where you wish to insert one of these items. Click on the item of your choice in the Clipboard toolbar: the item will be inserted in the document.

Figure 2.8 The Clipboard toolbar.

Inserting text styles

If the Clipboard toolbar is not displayed, right-click button on a toolbar and select ***Clipboard****.*

With WordArt, you can produce texts that stretch or curve, create angles or even display characters in 3D.

To insert a WordArt text object:

1. Click on where you wish to place the text then click on **Insert, Picture, WordArt** (Figure 2.9).

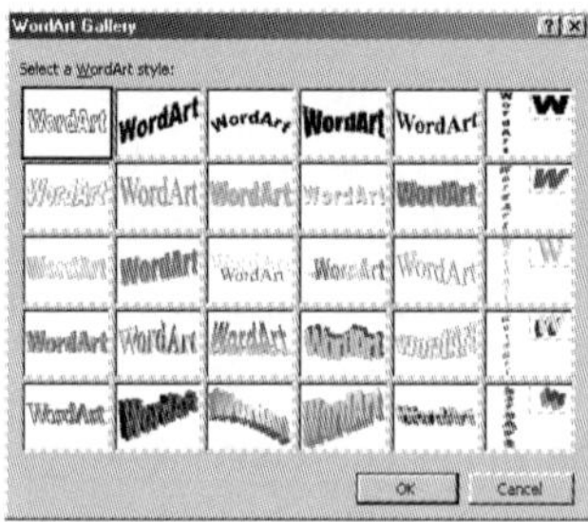

Figure 2.9 The WordArt sub-application allows you to create titles.

2. Click on the style, then confirm by clicking on OK.
3. A new dialog box is displayed. Enter the text to which the selected style will be applied; make your formatting choices, such as font, size, attributes, and so on, then click on **OK**.

The text is inserted in the document (Figure 2.10).

Text Styles

Figure 2.10 Place WordArt text to add the finishing touches to a document.

Moving, resizing, copying and deleting a WordArt object
A text created with WordArt corresponds to a graphic object: when you select it, it becomes surrounded by small squares known as 'handles', which allow the object to be moved, resized, and so on.

To move a WordArt object, click on it. Then, keeping the button pressed, drag it to where you wish it to go and release the button.

To cut, copy or paste a WordArt object, use the Cut, Copy or Paste commands in the Edit menu, or use the corresponding buttons.

To resize the WordArt object, click on one of its handles and drag it in the required direction.

To delete a WordArt object, click on it to select it, then press the delete key.

WordArt toolbar

The WordArt toolbar, which is displayed when you select the text object, allows you to modify and format the object. Table 2.1 shows the various buttons and their functions.

Table 2.1 WordArt toolbar buttons

Button	Action
	Inserts a new WordArt object into the page.
Edit Text...	Modifies the text of the WordArt object.
	Selects another style for the WordArt object.
	Modifies size, position and colour for the object, and places the text around it.
Abc	Selects another shape for the WordArt object.
	Displays the round handles around the object to make it rotate.
2000	Defines text wrapping.
Aa	Sets all the object characters at the same height.
Ab	Displays characters vertically.
	Modifies text alignment.
AV	Modifies character spacing in the WordArt object.

Copying a format

Not only is formatting characters quick and easy in Office; it is also possible to copy the various formatting choices.

To reproduce a format, select the word or the sentence, then click on the **Format Painter** button on the Standard toolbar. The pointer becomes a paintbrush. Drag the paintbrush on to the word or the sentence in which you wish to copy the format. Release the button. To copy the formatting to more than one item, double-click and then click on each item you want to format. When you are finished, press **Esc** or click again to turn off the Format Painter.

Inserting pictures

Office allows you to insert pictures into any document. Pictures come ready-made in the ClipArt Office 2000 gallery, which also contains sound files and animated clips.

Inserting a personal picture

When you insert pictures into a document, you will make the document easier to understand and, above all, more original. You can insert a picture that you have scanned, or even one you have found on the Web.

To insert a picture that you have saved:

1. Click on **Insert, Picture, From File**.
2. Select the type of graphic file you wish to insert. Select the folder that contains the file. For the picture to be inserted into your page, double-click on the file that contains it.

Inserting a ClipArt picture

ClipArt offers a vast number of pictures that you can insert into a document as you wish.

To insert a ClipArt picture:

1. Click on **Insert, Picture, ClipArt** (Figure 2.11).
2. Pictures are accessible from the **Pictures** tab. They are classified by category. To view the contents of a category, simply click on it. Once you have made your choice, click on the picture to be inserted; then, keeping the button pressed, drag it into the document and release the button.

If you need to insert several pictures into your document, you can leave ClipArt open to be able to return to it quickly. To display it again, click on the button in the taskbar.

If you do not have much time and you want to find a picture quickly, open the ClipArt dialog box, type the term that describes the picture in the **Search for clips** box, then press the **Enter** key.

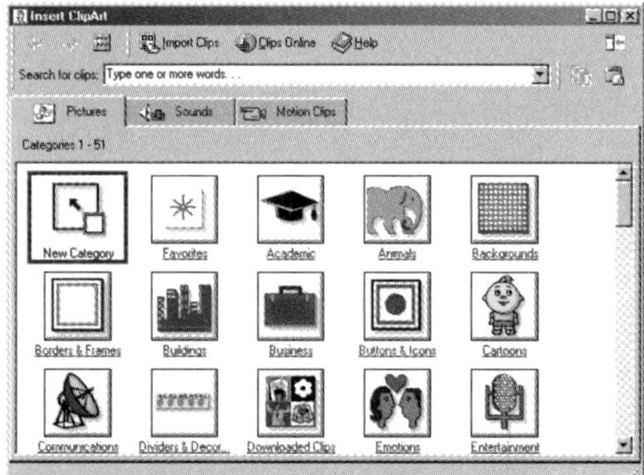

Figure 2.11 Choose an image from the ClipArt library.

See Chapters 7 and 8 for further information on how to edit a picture.

Pictures downloaded from a site that is not in the public domain cannot be used for commercial purposes.

The Web is a gold mine for those who need pictures. In fact, there are thousands of sites where you can retrieve pictures to use in a document.

To find a picture on the Web:

1. Open ClipArt. Click on the **Clips On-line** button in the toolbar. Obviously, you must first be connected to the Internet.
2. In the dialog box click on **OK**: the navigator is launched. Surf the Web. In the site that contains the picture you like, select the picture: this is then inserted automatically into ClipArt.

Basic Word functions

3

Creating a new document

Entering text

Moving within the text

Selecting text

Correcting text

Views

Formatting text and paragraphs

Formatting pages

In this chapter, you will learn about basic Word functions, including entering text, formatting it, and modifying the page view.

Creating a new document

By default, when you launch Word, a blank document and the Office Assistant are displayed.

To open a blank document, click on the **New** button. You can also click on **File, New**. If required, click on the **General** tab (Figure 3.1), then double-click on **Blank Document**.

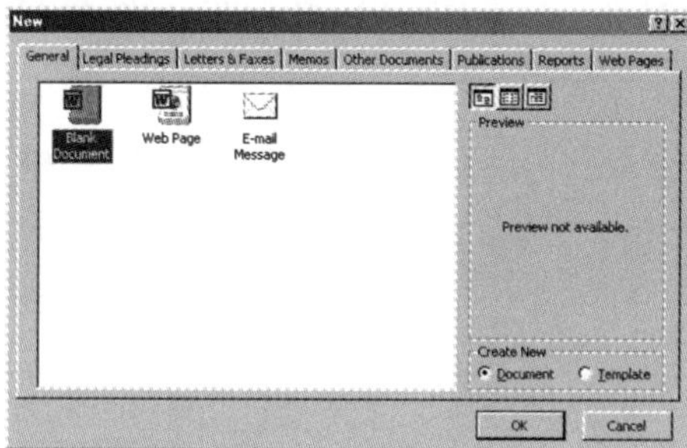

Figure 3.1 Opening a new document.

The Word screen

Before going any further, let us examine the Word screen and its various items (Figure 3.2). From the Menu bar you can access all the Word functions; the various toolbars offer shortcut buttons for more frequently used commands or functions. The flashing cursor is the default insertion point for your text. Scroll the vertical or horizontal scroll bar to move within the page.

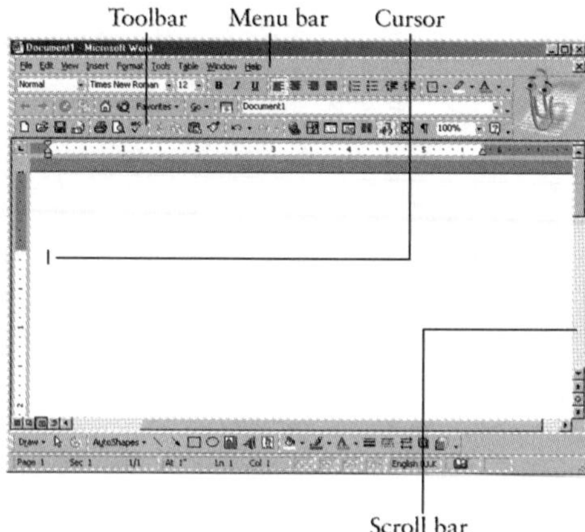

Figure 3.2 The Word screen.

Entering text

Here are some rules and tips you should know when entering text:

- By default, the flashing cursor, or insertion point, shows where the text will be entered.
- Word automatically goes on to a new line when you reach the right margin.
- To create a new paragraph, press the **Enter** key. Also use this procedure to insert a blank line.
- To go to a new line without creating a new paragraph, press the **Shift+Enter** keys.
- At the bottom of the page, the horizontal line marks where the page ends. If you wish to insert text beyond this line, Word automatically creates another page. To insert a forced page break, press **Ctrl+Enter**.
- Avoid using the Tab key to create indents in the text. It is better to do this with the **Indent** keys.

When you move the cursor on the page, it displays some small dashes to its right. If you wish to enter text somewhere other than at the beginning of the page, simply double-click where you want to be, then start typing: Word will look after the formatting.

When you create paragraphs or insert blank lines, Word generates characters known as 'non-printing characters'. To view them, click on the button that displays the **Show/Hide formatting marks** symbol in the Standard toolbar. You can also click on **Tools, Options**. In the **View** tab, click on the icon in the **Formatting marks area**, then click on **OK** to confirm your choice.

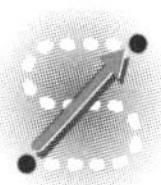

*If this option does not work, click on **Tools**, **Options**, then on the **Edit** tab. Tick the **Enable click and type** option, then click on **OK**.*

Non-breaking hyphens, non-breaking spaces and accented upper case

When typing, Word automatically wraps text over on to new lines. If a word should not be split over two lines, you must create a non-breaking space or a nonbreaking hyphen.

To create a non-breaking space, type the first word, then press **Ctrl+ Shift+Spacebar**. Type the second word and again press **Ctrl+ Shift+Spacebar**.

To create a non-breaking hyphen, type the first word, press **Ctrl+Shift+the hyphen key**, then type the second word.

When you type titles or any other text in upper case, Word does not display accents. For more sophisticated entry, you can create titles with accented upper-case characters.

To insert accented upper-case characters:

1. Click on **Insert, Symbol** (Figure 3.3).
2. Click on the character you wish to insert. Click on the **Insert** button, then on the **Close** button.

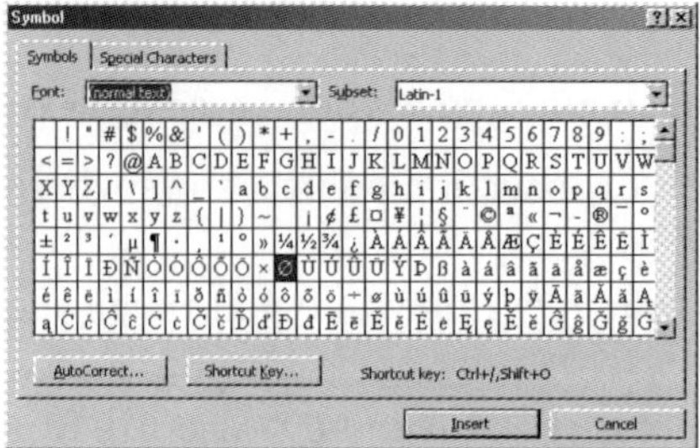

Figure 3.3 Use Symbols for accented capital letters.

Moving within the text

To move within the text:

- Point to where you want to be, then click.
- Scroll the vertical or horizontal scroll bar in the direction of your choice (up, down, left or right). A little box will appear: this shows the number of the page that will be displayed if you release the mouse.
- Click on the **Previous Page** or the **Next Page** arrows to display the previous or the following page. These arrows are positioned at the bottom of the vertical scroll bar.
- Click on one of the arrows at the bottom of the vertical scroll bar to scroll the text up or down. Release the mouse button when the text is displayed.

Going to a specific page

To go to a specific page, click on **Edit, Go To** (Figure 3.4). Type the page number, then click on the **Go To** button. To go to a specific item in your document, in the **Go to what** list, click on the item, then enter the item number, and click on the **Go To** button. Click on the **Close** button.

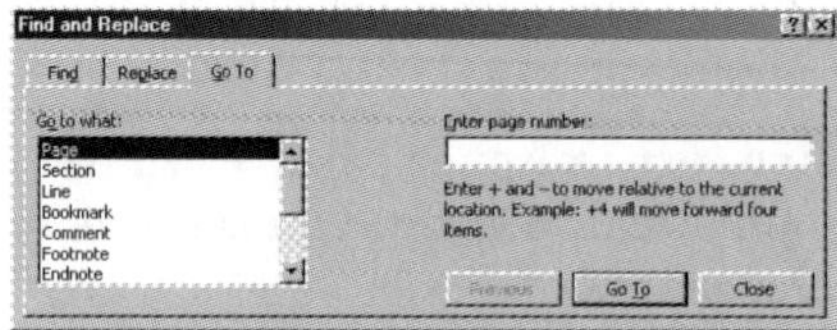

Figure 3.4 Use the **Go To** tab to display a page or specific element.

Selecting text

For all text manipulations (moving, copying, deleting, formatting, and so on) you must first select your text. Selecting consists of marking the text on which you want to act. Selected text is shown as highlighted.

To select a word, click on the beginning of the word, then drag the mouse over it keeping the button pressed.

To select a group of words, click in front of the first word to be selected, press the **Shift** key then, keeping the mouse button pressed, use the arrow keys to reach the end of the group you want to select.

To undo a selection, click outside the selected item.

Correcting text

Once your text has been entered, you may want to insert, replace, or delete one or more words or characters:

- To insert a word or character into existing text, click where you want to insert it, then type the new word or character.
- To replace a word with another one, double-click on the word, then type the replacement word.
- To delete text, select it, then press the delete key.
- To clear text positioned before the insertion point, press the backspace key.
- To clear text positioned after the insertion point, press the delete key.

Views

When you launch Word, a new document is displayed. It corresponds to a page, but you can see only half of it. You are in Page Layout view, which is the default display view. When creating a document, you might want to modify the display of pages. Word has several options for viewing pages on the screen.

Display views

Each view allows the execution of a specific task. You can access these views by opening the **View** menu, then selecting the view to be activated. You can also use the views buttons in the bottom left corner of the document.

The display views buttons are:

- **Normal View**. Displays pages as a long text divided into pages by automatic page breaks (dotted lines). This mode is easy to use because it requires very little memory.

- **Web Layout View**. Shows the document as it would look when published on the Web.

- **Print Layout View**. Displays the document as it will appear when printed. This view, which takes up a lot of memory, slows down the scrolling of the document.

- **Outline View**. Allows you to display the structure of your document, giving you the chance to modify it (Figure 3.5).

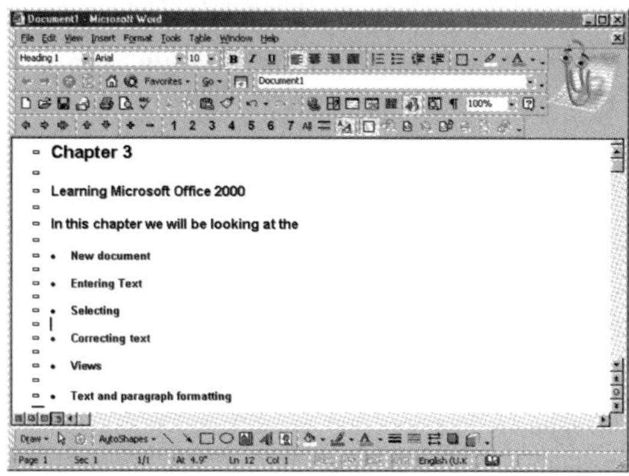

Figure 3.5 A document in Outline View.

Zoom

The Zoom option allows you to modify the size of the page on the screen. To modify the amount of the zoom, click on the arrow in the **Zoom** drop-down list, then select the display percentage. You can also double-click on the text box, enter the percentage and press **Enter** to confirm.

Switching between several documents

It is possible to work simultaneously on several different documents.

To switch between various documents, click on **Window**. At the bottom of the menu, the list of open documents is displayed. Click on the document you wish to display.

To display several documents on the screen, click on **Window, Arrange All** (Figure 3.6).

Formatting text and paragraphs

The Word default font is Times New Roman, 10 points, without attributes; paragraphs are left-aligned and have no indent.

Formatting procedures

You can define the format for characters and paragraphs before or after entry:

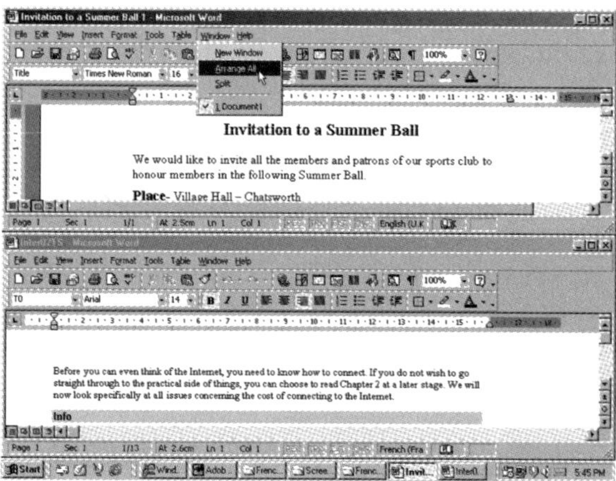

Figure 3.6 You can display several documents on screen at the same time.

*A paragraph is a set of characters that finishes with a carriage return executed with the **Enter** key.*

- **Format before entry**. Select the various formats as explained in this chapter, then type the text.
- **Format after entry**. Select the text, then choose the various formats required.

To format a single word, there is no need to select it: simply click on it, then choose the various formatting options.

Quick character formatting

The simplest and quickest method to format characters is to use the Format toolbar. Table 3.1 shows the various formats. Some of the buttons displayed on the Format toolbar are not included in this table: see p.297 to learn about them.

To delete a format, select the relevant text, then click on the attribute to deactivate it.

Table 3.1 Buttons for formatting characters in the Format toolbar

Button	Action
	Modifies font.
	Modifies text size.
	Makes text bold.
	Makes text italic.
	Underlines text.
	Selects highlight colour.
	Selects font colour.

Sophisticated character formatting

The Font dialog box allows you to select all the character format options.

To use the Font dialog box (Figure 3.7), click with the right mouse button on the text to be formatted and choose **Font**. Carry out your format choice, then click on **OK**.

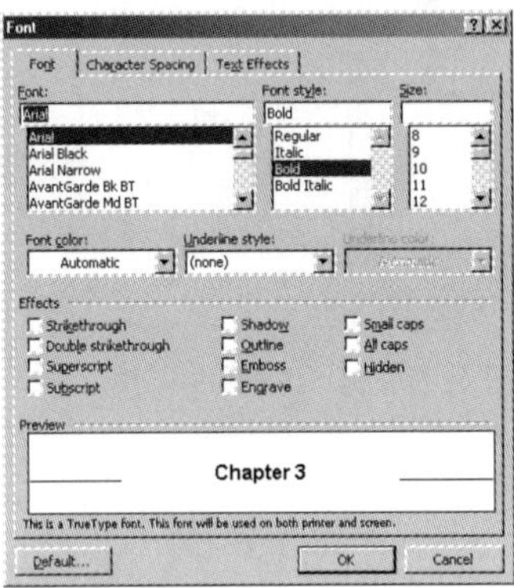

Figure 3.7 The Font dialog box allows you to select all the options for character formatting.

This is what can be done in the other tabs in the Font dialog box:

- **Character Spacing**. Allows you to modify spaces between characters.
- **Text Effects**. Allows you to animate the text, for example, by adding flashing lights round it. This function is important only if you are transferring your document as a file rather than as hard copy.

*The **tOGGLE cASE** option allows you to display in upper case text that was in lower case, and vice versa.*

To modify the character case, click on **Format, Change Case** (Figure 3.8). Select the required option, then click on **OK**.

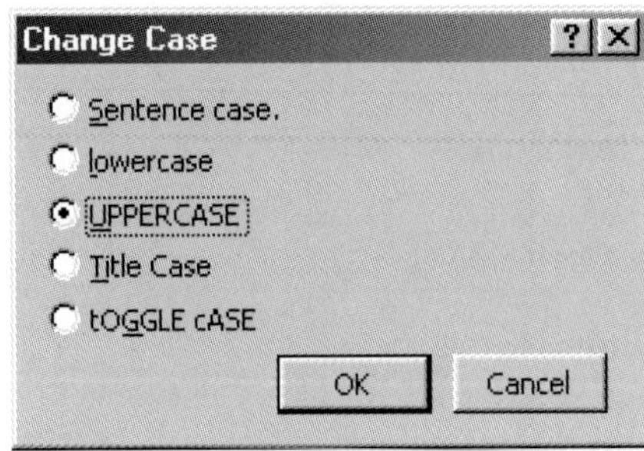

Figure 3.8 The Change Case dialog box offers several options.

Quick paragraph formatting

The simplest and quickest method to format paragraphs is to use the Format toolbar. Table 3.2 shows the various formats.

Table 3.2 Buttons for formatting paragraphs in the Format toolbar

Button	Action
	Aligns the paragraph flush with the left margin.
	Centres the paragraph between left and right margins.
	Aligns the paragraph flush with the right margin.
	Spreads the text in the paragraph over the whole width of the page, between left and right margins.
	Creates a numbered list.
	Creates a bulleted list.
	Decreases the value of the paragraph indent in relation to the left margin.
	Increases the value of the paragraph indent in relation to the left margin.
	Frames a paragraph.

Sophisticated paragraph formatting

The Paragraph dialog box allows you to select all the paragraph format options.

To use the Paragraph dialog box (Figure 3.9), click with the right mouse button on the text selected for formatting and choose **Paragraph**. Execute your formatting choices, then click on **OK**.

To delete a paragraph format, select the paragraph, then click on the relevant button to deactivate it in the Format toolbar.

This is what the Paragraph dialog box allows you to do:

- **Indents and Spacing**. Allows you to modify paragraph alignment, indents and spacing. Alignment allows you to define the position of paragraphs in relation to the margins (Figure 3.10). Indents apply either to the whole of the paragraph, or to its first line (Figure 3.11); they allow you to indent the text in relation to the left margin. You can also modify indents with the ruler (Figure 3.12).

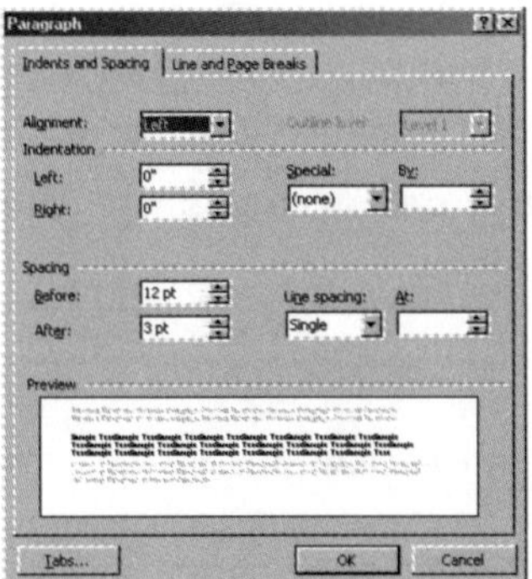

Figure 3.9 The Paragraph dialog box allows you to select paragraph formatting options.

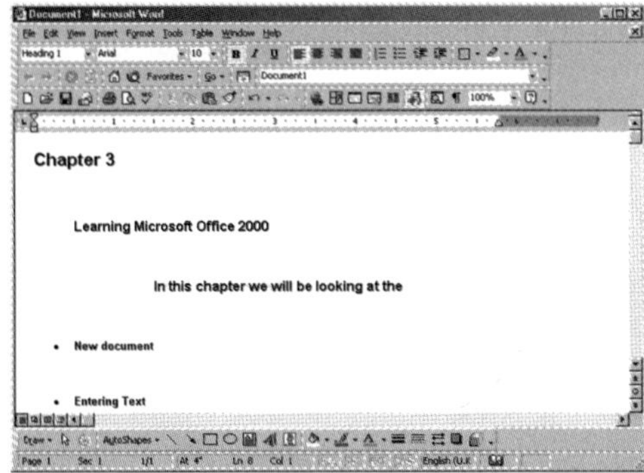

Figure 3.10 The various ways of aligning text.

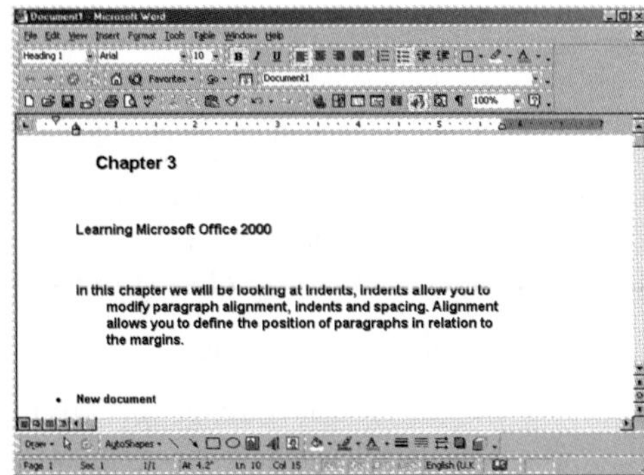

Figure 3.11 Examples of indents.

- **Line and Page Breaks**. Allows you to define the position of the paragraph in relation to other paragraphs. For example, you can request that the paragraph is not split at the end of the page.

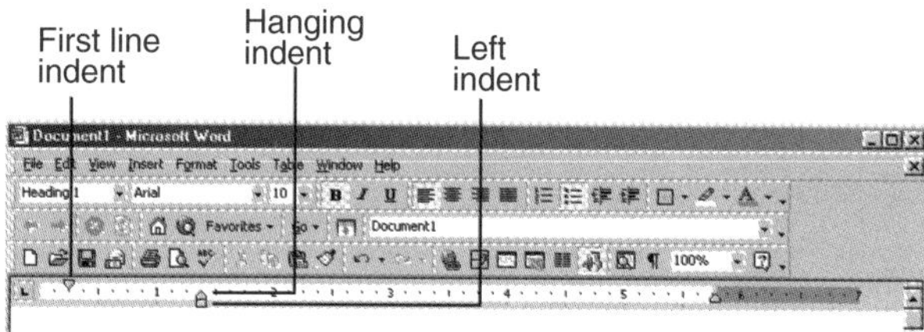

Figure 3.12 Using indents on the ruler.

Bulleted lists

To quickly create a bulleted list, use the **Numbering** or **Bullets** buttons in the Formatting toolbar (Table 3.2). When you click on one of these buttons, Word inserts a number or a bullet. Each time you enter an item in the list, simply click on **Enter** and the next number or a new bullet will appear. When you have finished entering the bullet list, press the backspace key or click on the relevant button in the Formatting toolbar to deactivate it.

To undo paragraph formats and go back to the default options, select the relevant paragraph then press ***Ctrl+Q****.*

You can modify the bullet or the type of number displayed in the bullet list.

To modify bullets or numbers:

1. Click with the right mouse button on the bullet list and select **Bullets and Numbering** (Figure 3.13).

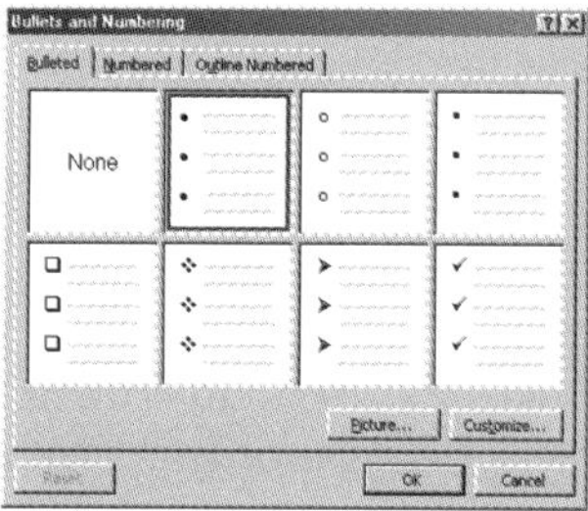

Figure 3.13 The Bullets and Numbering dialog box allows you to modify numbered and bullet lists.

2. Click on the tab corresponding to your choice (**Bulleted** or **Numbered**). Click on the type of bullet or number you want. The **Customize** button allows you to select other types of bullets. Click **OK** to confirm your choice.

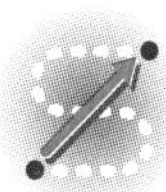

To delete a border, click on ***Format, Borders and Shading****. Click on the* ***Borders*** *tab, then select* ***None*** *in the border style. Click on* ***OK*** *to confirm your choice.*

Borders and shading

The Borders and Shading functions allow you to frame a paragraph and to display it in varying shades of grey.

To create the border and the shading for a paragraph:

1. Select the paragraph, then click on **Format, Borders and Shading**. Click on the **Borders** tab (Figure 3.14).

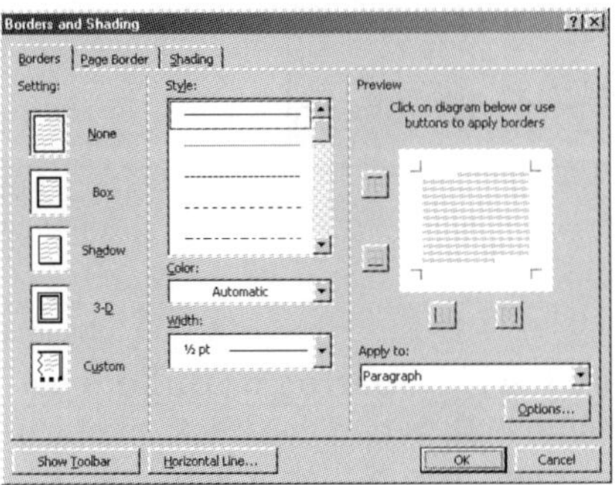

Figure 3.14 The Borders tab of the Borders and Shading dialog box.

2. Select the style for the border, then choose the settings. You can modify the colour and the width of the border. If you wish to colour the background of the paragraph, click on the **Shading** tab. Choose the fill colour and the shading pattern, then click on **OK**.

Formatting pages

Word includes commands to enhance your page: you can frame the whole of a page, assign a coloured background or a picture background, and so on.

Framing a page

To frame your page, use the **Borders and Shading** function (see p. 299).

Background

You can assign a background to your page or to the whole document. The background will not print: it will be seen only in Web view. This function is therefore useful when you publish your document on your company's intranet or on the Web, or if you are going to send the document to someone on diskette or e-mail it.

*To delete a background, click on **Format, Background**. In the pop-down menu, click on **No Fill**.*

To choose a background, click on **Format, Background**. In the drop-down menu, click on the colour you want. The **More Colors** option opens a dialog box with two tabs: the **Standard** tab allows you to select another colour, and the **Custom** tab allows you to define the required colour by specifying the percentage for each component colour. If a simple background colour is not enough, click on the **Fill Effects** option. In the **Fill Effects** dialog box and its various tabs, you can choose gradient, texture (droplets, mosaic, and so on) and pattern. Click on **OK** to confirm your choices.

You can also opt for a picture as a background. This will appear as a watermark on the whole page. You have two possibilities: either use a picture from one of your files, or a ClipArt picture (see Chapter 2).

To choose a background picture:

1. Open the **Fill Effects** dialog box. Click on the **Picture** tab, then on the **Select Picture** button.
2. Select the file that contains the picture you wish to display as background. Click on **OK**.

Inserting a header and a footer

To insert a header or a footer, click on **View, Header and Footer**. A specific toolbar is displayed. The header will be shown framed by dots. Simply enter your wording, then use the various header and footer buttons in the toolbar to position it, for example, in the centre of the page.

Formatting

This is the last stage to complete before sending your document to print.

To execute formatting:

1. Click on **File, Page Setup** (Figure 3.15):

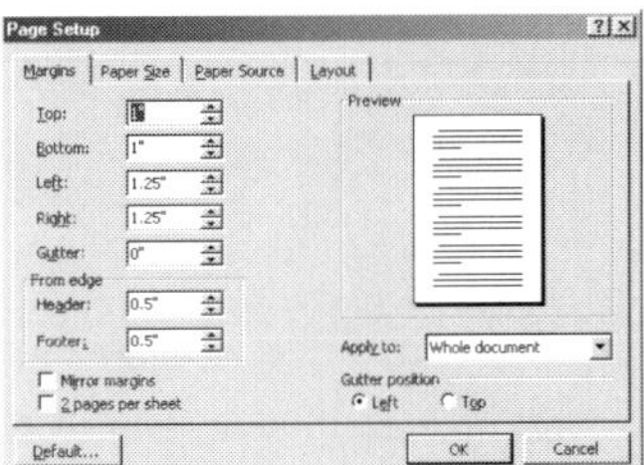

Figure 3.15 The Page Setup dialog box.

   (a) The **Margins** tab allows you to modify the margins for your document and to define gutters. The **Mirror margins** option is for recto–verso printing. The **Preview** area displays the defined choice. The **Apply to** option, by clicking on its arrow, opens a drop-down list in which you select the part of the document to which formatting applies.
   (b) The **Paper Size** tab allows you to choose the orientation of your document (Portrait (vertical) or Landscape (horizontal)).

(c) The **Paper Source** tab allows you to define the printer feed for this print job.

(d) The **Layout** tab allows you to define the position of the text in your document (vertical or horizontal alignment). You can also choose to number lines in your document.

2. Click on the required tabs, then execute your choices.
3. Click on **OK** to confirm.

Advanced Word functions

4

Creating a table

Creating columns

Mailshots

Automatic format with styles

We have now reached the stage where we are able to look at more sophisticated functions in Word, such as creating tables, using mail merge, and so on.

To customise rows and columns, use the ***Tables and Borders*** *toolbar before drawing them.*

Creating a table

Whenever you have difficulties in aligning two text blocks or any other elements, you can use the Table function. A table is made up of rows and columns. Their intersections create cells.

Drawing a table

The Draw Table option allows you to create the general outline for your table. Once this is done, you split it into several parts by tracing lines and columns.

Use the eraser to clear incorrect rows or columns. The ***Eraser*** *button is available in the Tables and Borders toolbar.*

To draw a table:

1. Click on **Table, Draw Table**. The pointer becomes a pencil.
2. Click on the page where you wish to insert the table. Drag to draw a rectangle, which will form the frame for your table (Figure 4.1). Draw rows and columns to complete the table.

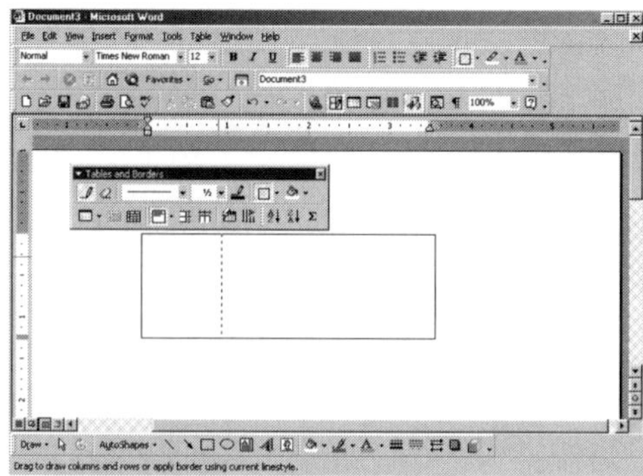

Figure 4.1 The Draw Table function allows you to create the outline for your table.

3. Once you have finished the 'drawing', click on **Table, Draw Table** so that the pointer goes back to its original shape.

Inserting a table

To quickly create a table, simply click on the **Insert Table** button: a little frame is displayed, which shows rows and columns for a table (Figure 4.2). Simply drag the mouse over it to select the number of rows and columns you require for the table. The textual description of the number of rows and columns selected is displayed at the bottom of this frame. Once you have finished, release the mouse. Word then inserts the table you have specified into the page.

Figure 4.2 With the Insert Table button you can quickly create a table.

Table dialog box

The Table dialog box allows you to specify the number of rows and columns you want. You can assign up to 63 columns to a table.

To use the Table dialog box:

1. Click where you wish to insert the table, then click on **Table, Insert Table** (Figure 4.3).

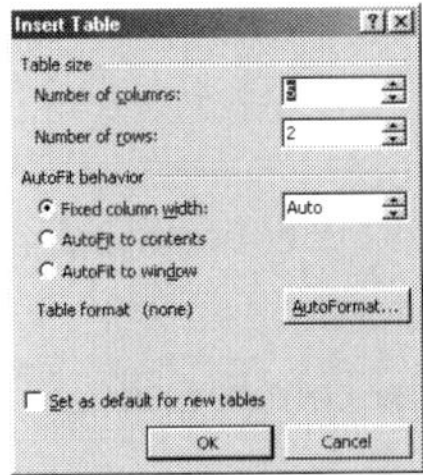

Figure 4.3 You can specify the number of columns and rows in your table in the Insert Table dialog box.

2. Type the number of columns in the **Number of columns** box. Type the number of rows in the **Number of rows** box. In the **AutoFit behavior** area, select your choices. The **Auto** choice inserts columns of equal size between the document margins. The **AutoFormat** button automatically applies predefined formats to your table, including borders and shading.
3. Click on **OK** to confirm your choices.

The table defined in the dialog box will be shown in your document.

Moving within a table

Before entering data into the table, you must be able to move quickly within it. See Table 4.1 to see how you can achieve this.

Table 4.1 Moving within a table

To	Press
Go to the next cell	**Tab**
Go to the previous cell	**Shift+Tab**
Go to the first cell in the line	**Alt+Home**
Go to the first cell in the column	**Alt+PageUp**
Go to the last cell in the line	**Alt+End**
Go to the last cell in the column	**Alt+PageDown**

Table 4.2 The various selections in a table

To select	Procedure
A cell	Point towards the bottom left corner of the cell, then click.
A column	Point to the top border of the column, then click.
A row	Point to the left border of the row, then click.
The whole table	**Table, Select Table**.
The text of a following or previous cell	**Tab** or **Shift+Tab**.

Selecting within a table

Once your table has been created, you will be able to format it, add rows and columns, assign a border, and so on. To execute this formatting, you must know how to select the various items. Table 4.2 shows the selection procedures.

Inserting and deleting cells and rows

Once the table has been produced, you can edit it by deleting cells, adding rows, and so on.

To delete a cell, select it and press the delete key.

To draw a table within a table, insert a table with the procedure shown above, then click on a cell and repeat the procedure – **Table, Insert Table** (Figure 4.4).

To insert a cell, select a cell, then click on **Table, Insert Cells** (Figure 4.5). Click on the option, then on OK.

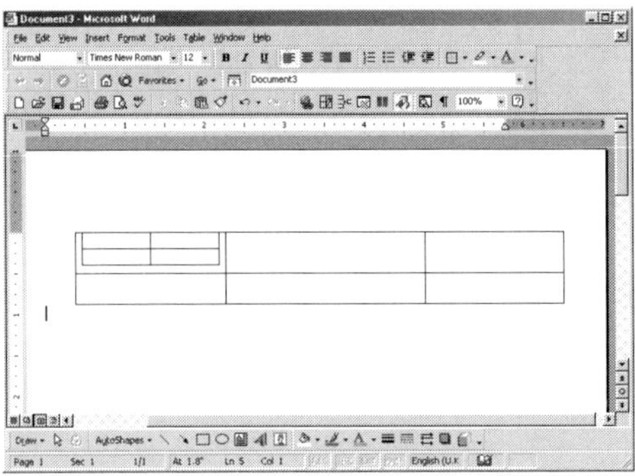

Figure 4.4 You can insert a table into a table.

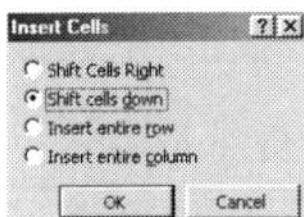

Figure 4.5 You can insert a cell into a table.

To insert, for example, four rows, select four rows in the table, then click on the ***Insert Rows*** *button. Word automatically inserts four empty rows into the table.*

To insert a row, click on **Table, Insert Row**, then select the option. There is also a quicker method: click on the row below where you wish to insert the new row, then click on the **Insert Rows** button in the Tables and Borders toolbar.

To insert a column, select the column before the insertion, and click on the **Insert Columns** button in the Tables and Borders toolbar. You can also click on **Table, Insert Columns**.

Orientation and display of the title row

You can change the orientation of text in cells. Click on the relevant cell, then on the **Change Text direction** button in the Tables and Borders toolbar.

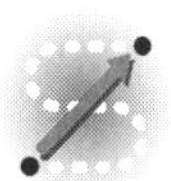

To delete a row or a column, select it and press the delete key.

When you create a table with several rows, not all the table will be visible on the screen. It is then difficult to enter text in the table: pretty soon, you start to get mixed up because you can't see the column headers. The best solution is to leave the title for all columns permanently displayed at the top of the page by selecting the title row then clicking on **Table, Titles**.

Formatting tables

To format a table – not the characters in the various cells – you can choose one of these methods:

- **AutoFormat**. Select the table, and click on **Table, Table AutoFormat**. Select the template, then click on **OK**.

- **Borders and Shading**. Select the table, and click on **Format, Borders and Shading**. Click on the **Borders** tab, then choose the border in the **Style** area (Figure 4.6). Click on the **Shading** tab if you wish to assign shading to the table. Define your choices, then click on **OK**.

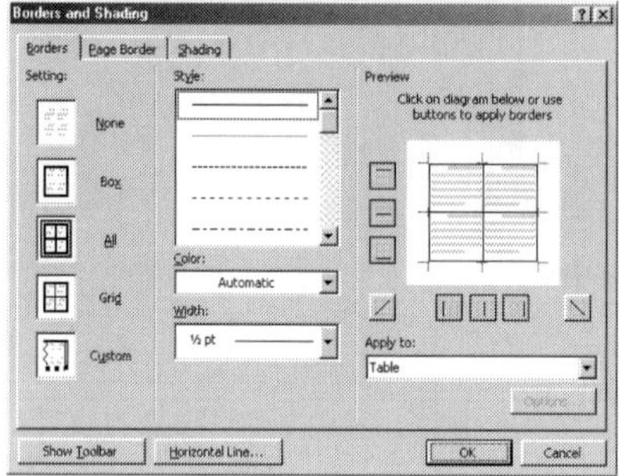

Figure 4.6 The Borders and Shading dialog box.

Creating columns

There are two methods of creating columns. Click on the **Columns** button in the Standard toolbar, then select the number of columns you wish to apply. The second method consists of clicking on **Format, Columns** (Figure 4.7), selecting the appropriate **Presets** option, and then clicking on **OK**.

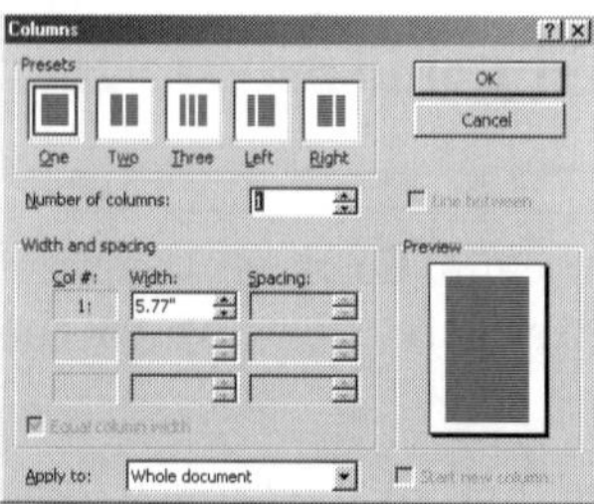

Figure 4.7 Choose the number of columns in the Columns dialog box.

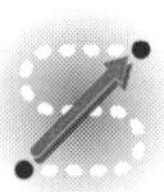

Have you inserted a column break and now the columns are not balanced? To balance columns, insert a Continuous break.

Once you have created columns, simply insert your text with the following procedures:

- Just type away: Word automatically 'wraps' to the next line when you reach the end of the column.
- To go to the following column, click on **Insert, Break**, then select the type of break in the **Break** dialog box. The page break goes to the next page; the section break goes to the next column.

Mailshots

When you need to send an identical letter several people, use the Mail Merge function and its various elements:

- **Main document**. This is the basic document to which your variable data will be added when doing a mail merge. These data are placed in the relevant fields according to various criteria. This document contains the text that is common to all the letters you need to print, as well as the fields where the variables go when merging takes place.
- **Data source**. This is the document that contains all the variable data. The variable data are inserted into the relevant fields when merging takes place. It is the database to which the main document refers when printing the letters.
- **Merge fields**. These are areas in your main document where the data from the data source will go.
- **Merge**. This command allows you to create letters, and merges the main letter with the contents of the variable data source. Once this merge is executed, you can print your letters directly or display them on screen.

Main document

The first thing to do is to create the main mail merge document, i.e. the letter you are going to send to all the people included in your mailshot.

*If you wish to create the main document from an existing document, open the relevant file and click on **Tools, Mail Merge**. Click on the **Create** button in the Mail Merge Helper dialog box, select the **Form Letters** option, then click on the **Active Window** button.*

To create the main document:

1. Open a blank document. Then click on **Tools, Mail Merge** (Figure 4.8).

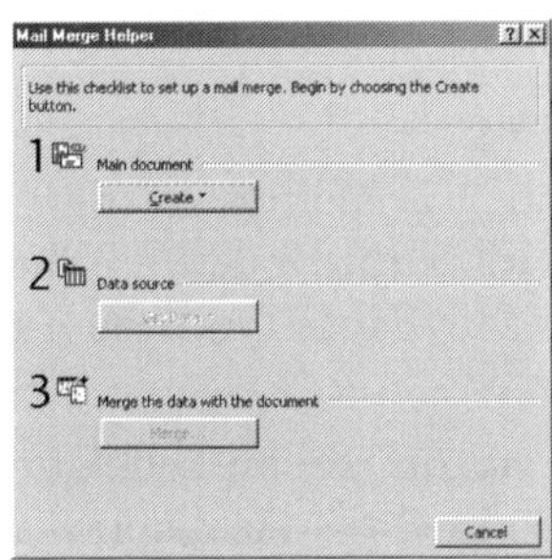

Figure 4.8 The Mail Merge Helper makes it easy for you to choose and merge all the different elements.

2. Click on the **Create** button, then select **Form Letters**. A new dialog box is displayed, which asks if you wish to create your letter from your active document or if you wish to display a new

document. If you have followed the procedure, click on **Active Window**. Otherwise, click on **New main document** and type the text for your form letter as you usually would.

Data source

Once your main document has been created, you must enter the various data you wish to be inserted. This is the step when you actually create the database. Since you have just created the main document, the Mail Merge Helper dialog box is still displayed.

To create the database:

1. In the Mail Merge Helper dialog box, click on the **Get Data** button in the **Data source** area. Click on **Create Data Source**. The **Use Address Book** option allows you to use one of your address books as a database (see the chapters on Outlook).

   The **Create Data Source** dialog box is displayed. Here you are going to select the fields you need to insert into the form letter (name, surname, address, town, and so on). The **Field names in header row** list is displayed with all the available fields (Figure 4.9).

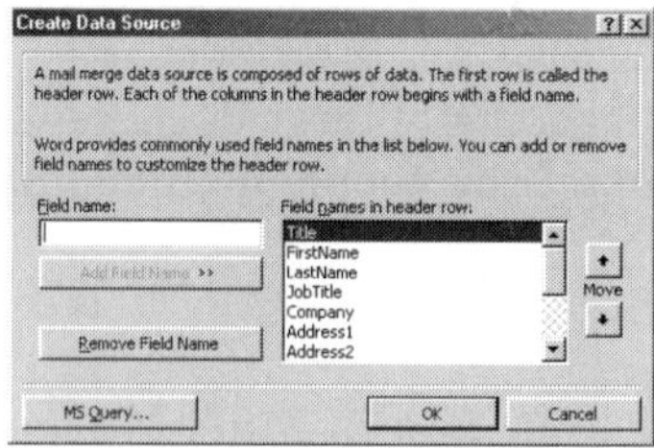

Figure 4.9 You can define various field names in the Create Data Source dialog box.

2. Format the set of fields in the following way:

   (a) Delete the fields that are not relevant by clicking on them, then clicking on the **Remove Field Name** button. The deleted field will disappear from the **Field names in header row** list.

   (b) To add a field, enter it in the **Field name** box and click on the **Add Field Name** button. The defined field is displayed in the **Field names in header row** list.

   (c) To move one of the fields in the **Field names in header row** list up or down, select the relevant field, then click on the arrow pointing to the direction you want (on the right of the list).

*If you have already created a database, open the Mail Merge Helper dialogue box, click on the **Get Data** button and select **Open Data Source**. Now simply select the database you wish to use.*

3. When you are satisfied with the fields and their positions, click **OK**.
4. Save the database as prompted by Word.
5. Click on **Edit Data Source** to start entering the data to be used for the merge.

Entering data

When you have chosen the **Edit Data Source** command, the Data Form dialog box is displayed. This is made up of the fields you have already defined in Create Data Source. Type your merge data (the list of your mail merge addressees) and use the **Tab** key to move from field to field. When you have finished entering a record, click on **OK** to confirm and exit from the database or click on the **Add** button to display a new record to enter.

*To edit a data record, click on the **Edit Data Source** button in the Mail Merge toolbar. Now carry out your modifications.*

Merging

Before starting the merge, you must tell Word where you wish to insert the data on the page.

To insert merge fields:

1. If necessary, right-click in a toolbar, then select **Mail Merge** to display it. Click where you wish to position the first merge field (usually surname or name).
2. Click on **Insert Merge Field** in the Mail Merge toolbar. Select the first field to insert into the list which opens (Figure 4.10).
3. Repeat these procedures for all the fields you wish to insert.

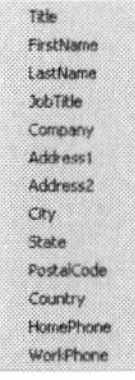

Figure 4.10 The Insert Merge Field drop-down menu.

You should achieve the type of document that is shown in Figure 4.11.

Before starting the merge, check your work. Click on the **Check for Errors** button in the Mail Merge toolbar. In the **Checking and Reporting Errors** dialog box, click on your choice, then on **OK**. If everything is as it should be, Word displays a dialog box to confirm that no errors were found. Click on **OK**.

You are now ready to start the merge. Click on the **Merge** button in the Mail Merge toolbar. Several options are proposed for the merge in the **Merge To** area:

Figure 4.11 The main document with merged fields.

- **Merge To**. Allows you to merge directly to a new document on to your e-mail program, or to print the letters.
- **Records to be merged**. Allows you to print the letters for the addressees selected in the data source only (see later in this chapter).
- **When merging records**. Specifies to Word whether it must print blank lines when data fields are empty.
- **Query Options**. Displays a dialog box from which you can sort the merged letters or filter your data so that your letters are printed only for a specific type of addressee, selected from among all the data.

Once you have defined your choices, click on the **Merge** button. If you have started the merge to the printer, Word prints the letters. If you have chosen to save the merge in a new file, the letters are displayed in a new document.

To create a query when merging occurs – that is, to sort the data and print or only create letters corresponding to this criterion (for example, you have decided to create letters addressed only to people living in London) – open the Mail Merge dialog box and click on the **Query Options** button. Type the query items, then click on **OK**. Then repeat the procedures shown above to start the merge.

Automatic format with styles

A style is a set of formatting characteristics (size, alignment, attributes, and so on) that can be applied to a paragraph or character. This function means you do not have to repeat formatting instructions when the document contains several pages.

Some styles apply only to paragraphs, others only to characters.

Choosing a style

Word 2000 offers a certain number of styles that you can apply to paragraphs or to characters.

To choose a style:

1. Click in the relevant paragraph or select the required words. Click on the little arrow in the **Style** button (Figure 4.12).

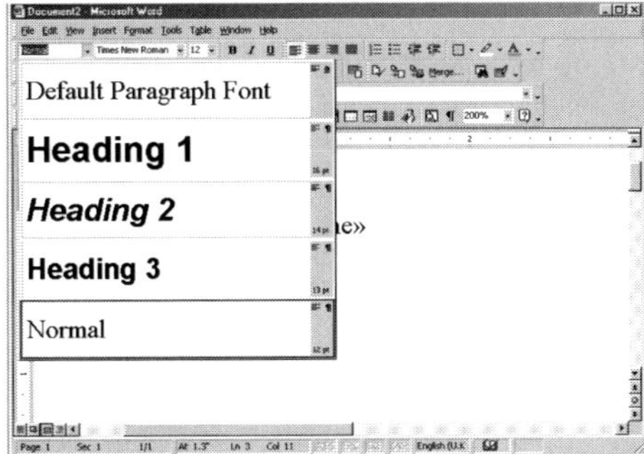

Figure 4.12 You can quickly choose a style with the Style button.

2. Select the style.

   The paragraph is now displayed with the selected style attributes, and the Style button displays the active style in its text box.

Creating a style

Word offers a large variety of styles, but it is possible that none of them is suitable for one of your documents. In this case, you can create a personal style that you can then apply to all your documents.

To create a style, specify all the formatting (size, font, attributes, alignment, indent and so on) and click on the arrow in the **Style** button. Type the name of your new style and press **Enter**. The style that you have just specified is now an integral part of the styles for this document. To apply it to another paragraph, simply click on the relevant paragraph, then select the style of your choice in the drop-down list from the **Style** button.

5 Basic Excel functions

The first step

Worksheet management

Data

Managing cells, rows and columns

Help with your entry

Formatting

We will now look at the basic functions of Excel, including how to enter data, how to manage a workbook and its worksheets, the functions that help with entering data, and the various formatting procedures.

The first step

By default, when you launch Excel, a blank workbook is displayed. We have already seen how to open an existing workbook. To open a new workbook, simply click on the **New** button.

Screen

Before going any further, let us examine the screen and its various items (Figure 5.1). From the Menu bar you can access all the functionalities of Excel; the various toolbars offer shortcut buttons to the most frequently used commands or functions. The A1 cell (see below) is surrounded by a black frame, which indicates that it is selected.

2000

Microsoft has really caught up with the euro. When you launch Excel, a toolbar called EuroValue is displayed. This allows you to select functions that use the euro. If this is of no use to you, click on the **Close** (X) button in the Title bar.

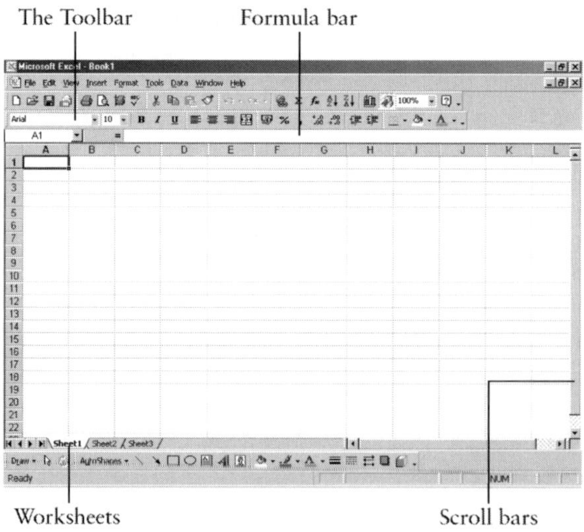

Figure 5.1 The Excel screen.

Workbooks and worksheets

A workbook is made up of worksheets. By default, the workbook has three worksheets. Worksheets can be opened with the tabs positioned at the bottom of the workbook. Each worksheet is made up of little boxes known as cells. These are arranged to a maximum of

256 columns, named A to IV, and on 65 336 rows, named 1 to 65 336. Each cell has the name of the intersection between the row and the column where it is placed. For example, the A5 cell is at the intersection of the first column and the fifth row.

Worksheet management

Worksheets are the basic working tools. You should know how to move within them, how to add, delete, and so on.

Moving between worksheets

To move between worksheets or to select a specific one, use the tabs positioned at the bottom left of the screen. Here are some tips to speed up your work:

- To move between worksheets, use the scroll buttons positioned to the left of the tabs. The two middle buttons allow you to go back or forward by one tab; the left button goes back to the first tab; and the right button goes to the last one.
- Click with the right mouse button on one of the scroll buttons, then select the worksheet to be displayed (Figure 5.2).

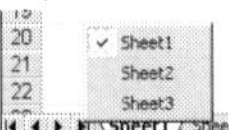

Figure 5.2 Choose which worksheet to view in the context menu.

- To select several worksheets, press the **Ctrl** key. Keeping it pressed, click on the tab of each worksheet to be selected.

Adding, deleting, copying and moving worksheets

By default, a workbook offers three worksheets. Let us now see how to add, delete and move worksheets.

To add a worksheet, click on one of the tabs, then click on **Insert, Sheet**.

To delete a worksheet, click with the right mouse button on its tab, then select **Delete**. Confirm its deletion (Figure 5.3).

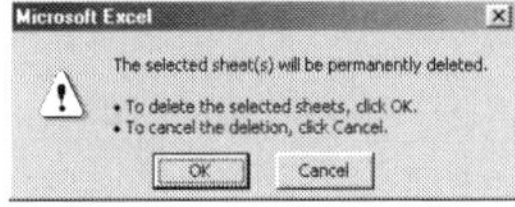

Figure 5.3 Confirm the deletion of the worksheet.

To move a worksheet within the workbook, click on its tab then, keeping the button pressed, drag it to the position of your choice.

To copy a worksheet in its workbook, click on its tab, then keep the **Ctrl** key pressed and drag it to where you wish to place the copy.

To copy or move a worksheet to another workbook:

1. Open the two workbooks. Right-click on the tab of the worksheet you wish to move or copy. Select the **Move or Copy** option (Figure 5.4).

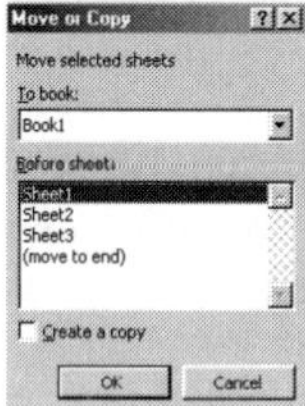

Figure 5.4 The Move or Copy dialog box allows you to specify the workbook into which you want to copy your worksheet.

2. Click on the arrow in the **To book** box. Select the workbook into which you wish to copy or move the selected worksheet.
3. In the **Before sheet** list, click on the worksheet in front of which you wish to position the new sheet tab. Click on **OK** to confirm your choice.

Hiding and showing a worksheet

You may wish to hide one of the sheets in a workbook; for example, if your PC is connected to your company's intranet, you may need to hide some data.

To hide a worksheet, select it and click on **Format, Sheet, Hide**.

To view a hidden worksheet, click on **Format, Sheet, Unhide**. In the dialog box (Figure 5.5), click on the worksheet you wish to display and click on **OK**.

Your worksheets' names can be up to 31 characters long. However, it is better not to make names too long, as the name tab will take up too much space.

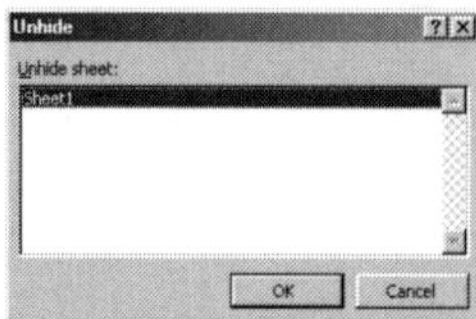

Figure 5.5 View a hidden worksheet.

Naming, grouping and ungrouping worksheets

To name a worksheet, right-click on its tab, then select **Rename** (Figure 5.6). Type the new name and press **Enter**.

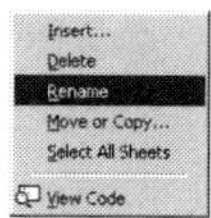

Figure 5.6 Renaming a worksheet.

You can group worksheets together to speed up your work. This is the equivalent of inserting carbon paper between worksheets: everything you enter and format on the first worksheet is reproduced on the other worksheets in the group.

To group together several worksheets, click on the first tab of the group, keep the **Ctrl** key pressed, then click on the other tabs you wish to group.

To ungroup worksheets, click on one of the tabs that is not grouped.

Data

Before starting your calculations, you must enter data. Data for a worksheet can be numbers, legends or formulas.

Types of data

Excel allows the insertion of several types of data (Figure 5.7):

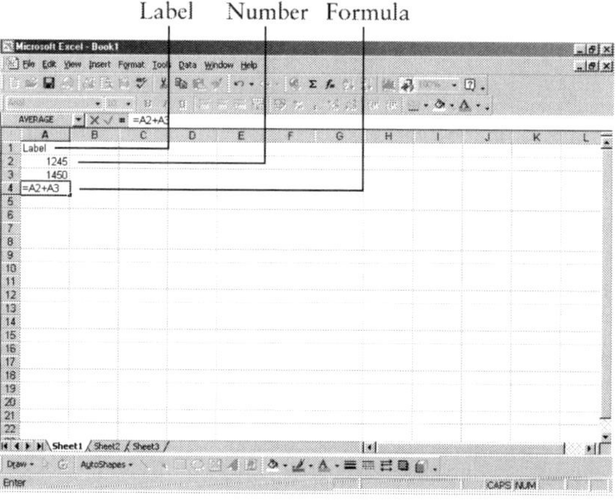

Figure 5.7 Excel allows you to enter several types of data.

- **Numbers**. Raw data. These numbers are entered in cells.
- **Legends**. Text typed at the top of a column or the start of a row to specify its contents.

- **Formulas**. Entries that tell Excel which calculations to carry out. For example, the formula =A2-A5+B8 indicates to Excel that it must add cell A2 and B8, then subtract cell A5.
- **Functions**. Predefined formulas that execute more complex calculations with a single operator. For example, the **Average** function calculates the average for a set of values.

Excel applies a different alignment to cells according to the nature of the inserted data. Text is left-aligned, while numbers, functions, dates and formulas are right-aligned.

Entering data

To enter data, click on the relevant cell. A black frame will be shown around the cell to indicate that it is selected. As soon as you start entering data, it is displayed in the active cell and in the Formula bar (Figure 5.8). Click on the green box in the Formula bar to confirm the entry and insert it in the cell (you can also press **Enter**). Click on the red X to undo your entry (you can also press **Esc**).

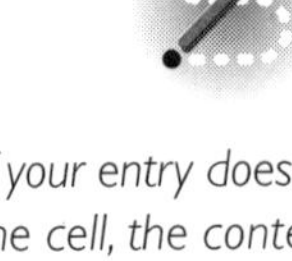

*If your entry does not fit into the cell, the content is cut if it is text, or displayed as asterisks if it is a number when you confirm the entry. To fit the column automatically to its contents, click on **Format, Column** and select **AutoFit Selection**.*

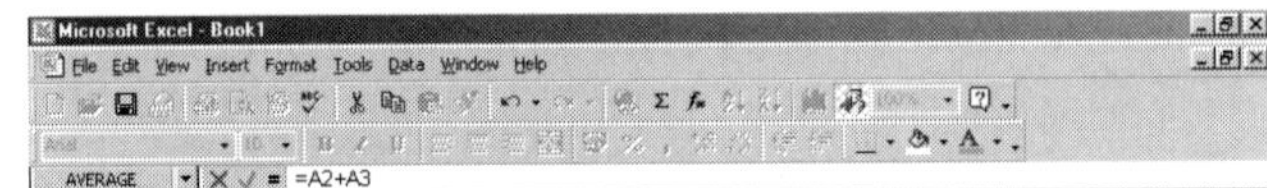

Figure 5.8 You can insert, confirm and delete data in the Formula bar.

To edit the contents of the cell in which you are entering your data, use the backspace or delete keys, then type your correction. To edit the confirmed entry, double-click on the cell, then implement your correction. You can also click on the cell and edit its contents in the Formula bar.

Special data

As we have already said, text is left-aligned and values are right-aligned. However, in some cases you may wish to insert numbers as text (for example, a postcode). In such cases, you must tell Excel that this is text by left-aligning it. Before starting your text entry, press the **apostrophe** (') key.

On the other hand, a date or a time, although it is text, must be considered as a value because it may be used for calculation purposes. To insert date or time values in a worksheet, enter them in the format you wish to be displayed (Table 5.1).

Table 5.1 Date formats

Entry	Outcome
DD/MM	1/1 or 01/01
DD/MM/YY	1/1/99 or 01/01/99
MMM-YY	Jan-99 or January-99
DD-MMM-YY	1-Jan-99
DD-MMM	1 January
DD Month YYYY	1 January 1999
HH:MM	17:15
HH:MM:SS	10:25:59
DD/MM/YY HH:MM	25/12/99 13:15

Selecting

These are the various selection procedures:

- To select a cell, click on it.
- To select a row, click on its number in the row header.
- To select a column, click on its letter in the column header.
- To select the whole worksheet, click on the greyed button at the intersection of a row header with a column header.

Cell range

You may need to select the same group of cells several times. To speed up the task, you can create a cell range:

- For a range with adjacent cells, click on the first cell, then drag the mouse to the last cell in the range.
- For a range with non-adjacent cells, click on the first cell, keep the **Ctrl** key pressed, click on the second cell, and so on.

To name a range:

1. After selecting a range, click on the reference, which is on the left-hand side of the Formula bar (Figure 5.9). Type the name following these rules:
   (**a**) The range name must start with a letter or an underscore.
   (**b**) The range name must not be the reference for any cell.
   (**c**) Do not use spaces between characters or digits.
   (**d**) Use the underscore to separate two words.
   (**e**) Type a maximum of 255 characters.
2. Press the **Enter** key.

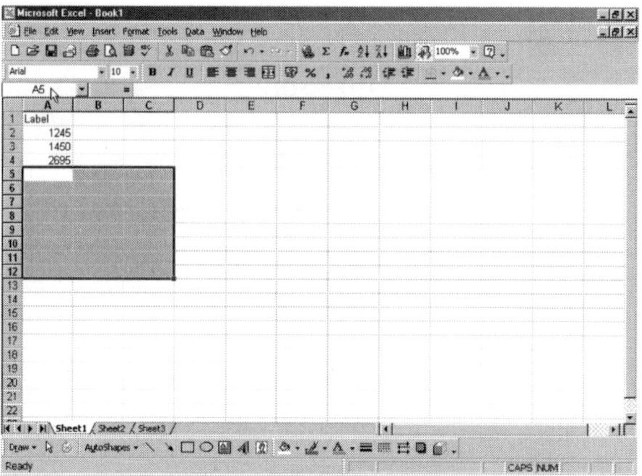

Figure 5.9 Naming a cell range in the reference box.

Once you have named your range, to select it you simply click on **Edit, Go To** and specify the range you want (Figure 5.10).

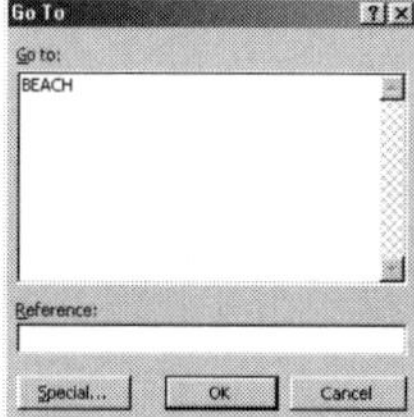

Figure 5.10 Selecting a range in the Go To dialog box.

Managing cells, rows and columns

Sometimes you need to insert or delete cells, rows or columns.

To insert a cell, row or column, right-click on the cell before or after the place you wish to insert the new element, then select **Insert, Cells** (Figure 5.11). Click the choice you require, then click **OK**.

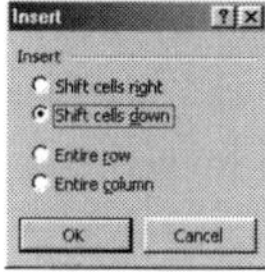

Figure 5.11 You can insert cells, rows and columns using the Insert dialog box.

To delete one or more blank cells, rows or columns, after having selected them, right-click on the selection, then select **Delete**. You can also click on **Edit, Delete** (Figure 5.12). Select your choice from the list, then click on **OK**.

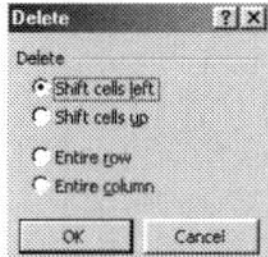

Figure 5.12 With the Delete dialog box, you can delete cells, rows and columns.

To delete only the text or the values from one or more cells, select the relevant cells, and press the delete key. The cells are kept, but their contents are deleted. On the other hand, if you wish to delete the contents of a formula, but not the format or the comments, select the formula, click on **Edit, Clear**, then select the appropriate option in the drop-down menu.

Remember that:

- **Contents** clears text from the cell.
- **Format** clears the format, but keeps the existing text.
- **Comments** clears the comments.
- **All** clears the set of choices defined above.

Help with your entry

Excel offers several functions to help you with entering data, which allow you to work faster.

Fill

To insert the same label value or date into several cells, use the **Fill** function.

To fill a value, date or label in the same worksheet:

1. Drag your mouse onto the cell that contains the entry for the fill, then onto those to which you wish to apply the fill. Click on **Edit, Fill**.
2. Select the direction for the fill – **Down, Right, Up, Left** (Figure 5.13).

   Excel fills the selected cells with the contents of the first cell.

To copy one or more cells, you can also use the ***Copy, Paste*** *or* ***Cut*** *buttons in the Standard toolbar.*

Fill handles

To fill a cell, you can also use the fill handle (Figure 5.14). Before using this handle, make sure you are aware of all its different uses.

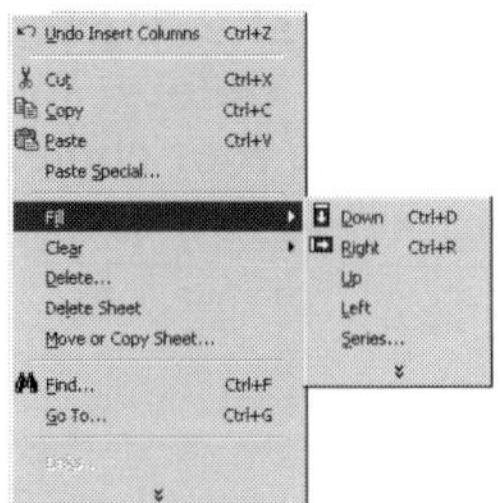

Figure 5.13 The Fill command.

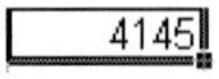

4145

Figure 5.14 A fill handle.

- A fill handle will be shown in a row header when you select it. Drag it to fill the contents of the row. Repeat this procedure in a column header to fill the whole column.
- To insert blank columns, rows or cells, press the **Shift** key, then drag the fill handle.
- Drag the fill handle with the right button to display its context menu.

To use a cell fill handle, click on the relevant cell. A little square is displayed on the bottom right corner: this is the fill handle. Click on it, then drag it on the cells to be filled.

According to the contents of the cell, Excel executes different types of fill:

- If the cell contains a numerical value, Excel fills this value.
- If the cell contains, for example, a month, Excel inserts the following month in sequence.

This function corresponds to inserting a series. Excel offers several integrated series in AutoFill. You can create your own fill series.

To create an automatic fill series:

1. Click on **Tools, Options**, then on the **Custom List** tab. If required, click on **NEWLIST** in the list on the left. Type the new list and click on the **Add** button.
2. Click on **OK** to confirm your automatic series.

Formatting

Excel offers several possibilities for formatting a table. You have the same choice of attributes (font, bold, italic, and so on) offered in Word. See Chapter 3 for details. Here are some formats that are specific to Excel.

AutoFormat

To use **AutoFormat**:

1. Select the table. Click on **Format, AutoFormat** (Figure 5.15).
2. Select the desired format.

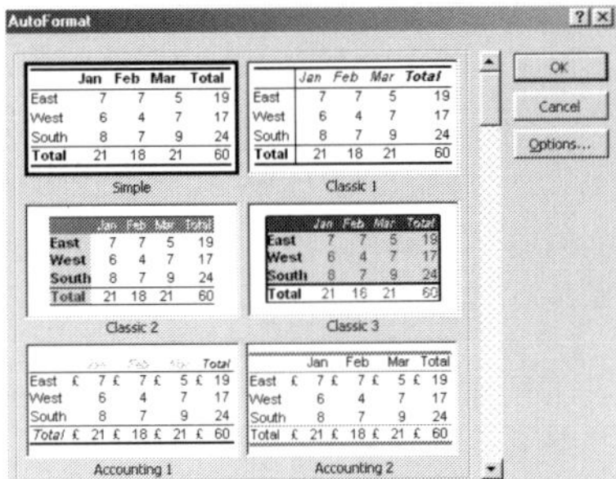

Figure 5.15 Choose AutoFormat.

3. If you wish to modify one of the default format attributes, tick the relevant check box in the **Options** box, then carry out your changes and click on **OK**. Again, click on **OK** to confirm the format you have selected.

Conditional formatting

Conditional formatting allows you to apply a format according to specific criteria. For example, you may wish the cell containing the profit to be displayed in a different colour if it is a negative amount, allowing you to spot immediately the size of the trouble.

To apply **conditional formatting**:

1. Select the relevant cell. Click on **Format, Conditional Formatting**.
2. In the second option of the **Condition 1** box, select the parameter to be applied.
3. In the third option of the **Condition 1** box, type the value. Click on the **Format** button.
4. In the **Color** option, select the colour to be used, then click on **OK** (Figure 5.16). Click on **OK** again.

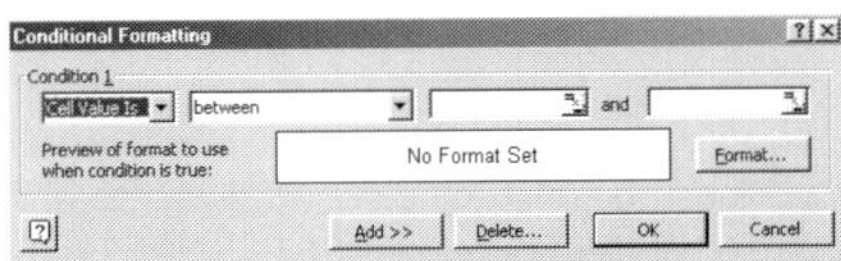

Figure 5.16 The Conditional Formatting dialog box allows you to define a conditional format for certain cells.

6 Advanced Excel functions

Formulas

Functions

Scenarios

Sorting and filtering data

Auditing

Creating a chart

In this chapter we will use advanced Excel functions, such as creating formulas, using functions, sorting data, and so on.

Formulas

A formula allows simple arithmetical operations, such as addition or subtraction, to be carried out using the data in the worksheet.

Before you start, get to know the various mathematical operators used and their order of priority in terms of their application:

1. operations in brackets;
2. raising numbers to *n* power;
3. multiplication and division;
4. addition and subtraction.

Remember this order of priority and always bear it in mind when creating calculation formulas, otherwise you could end up with the wrong results.

Creating formulas

To create a formula:

- The formula is inserted into the cell that will contain the results.
- A formula always starts with the equals sign (=).
- A formula uses the reference of each cell included in the calculation. For example: =A1_B5.
- A formula may use numbers. For example: =4*5.
- A formula uses one or all of the following symbols: + to add, – to subtract, * to multiply, / to divide, and an exponent to indicate an *n* power.

To create a formula with numbers:

1. Select the cell that will display the results of the formula. Press the = key, then type the formula.
2. Press **Enter** to confirm the formula or click on the green box in the Formula bar. Excel calculates the result and displays it in the originally selected cell.

To enter a formula with cell references:

1. Select the cell that will display the results of the formula. Press the = key.
2. Click on the first reference cell for the formula and press the arithmetical operator. Click on the second reference cell, and so on. Repeat this procedure for each cell in the formula.

3. When you have finished, press **Enter** to confirm the formula (Figure 6.1) or click on the green box in the Formula bar.

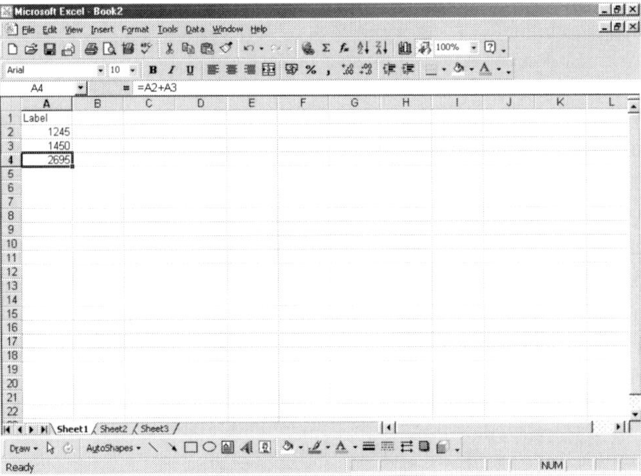

Figure 6.1 A formula in Excel.

With the created formulas, Excel executes calculations and enters the outcome in the appropriate cells.

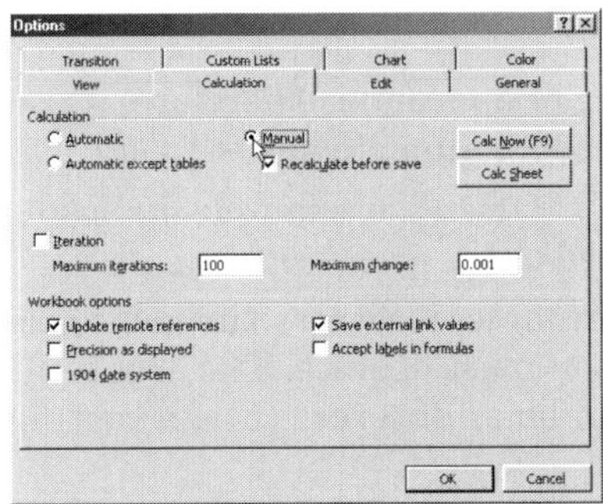

Figure 6.2 You can deactivate automatic calculation.

Automatic calculation, in the context of formula creation, slows down the processing of the worksheet. If you wish to deactivate it, click on ***Tools, Options****, then on the* ***Calculation*** *tab and finally on the* ***Manual*** *option (Figure 6.2). Confirm with* ***OK****.*

Converting into euros

With an eye on the difficulties Europeans will encounter when they switch to the euro, the programmers of Office 2000 have developed a tool that allows you to convert currencies into euros quickly and easily.

To use the EuroConverter, in the relevant cell click on **Tools, EuroConverter** (Figure 6.3). Confirm the conversion and click on **OK**.

Figure 6.3 Click on the euro currency symbol on the toolbar to convert to and from the euro.

Copying and moving formulas

When you copy a formula from one point in the worksheet to another, Excel adjusts the references to the new position. For example, when you copy cell C11, which contains the formula =SUM(C4:C10), and you insert it in D11, this displays =SUM(D4:D10). If you do not want Excel to adapt references and want instead to keep the initial cell references, you must give the instruction that the referenced cells are fixed and should not be modified. You must therefore mark up each reference cell as an absolute reference. Press **F4** immediately after having typed the reference. A dollar icon is displayed in front of the letter and number of the reference (for example D11).

*If you do not wish to use the F4 function key, type the **$** sign in front of each reference letter or number.*

Functions

Excel offers a number of predefined functions. They are available to carry out a series of operations on several values or on a range of values. For example, to calculate the average quarterly turnover, you can use the @AVERAGE function (A6:D6).

Each function contains three distinct items:

- The @ sign marks the beginning of a formula. Therefore, if you type the = sign, Excel will replace it automatically with @.
- The name of the function, AVERAGE in our example, indicates the type of operation to be carried out.
- The argument, A6:D6 in our example, indicates the reference cells on whose values the function must operate. The argument is often a cell range. This could be an interest rate, a sorting order, and so on.

There are three types of arguments: database, criteria and field arguments. The first two refer to cell ranges and the last to a column label.

Wizard function

To make the task of entering functions and arguments easier, the wizard function will assist you.

To use the wizard function:

1. Click on the cell in which you want to insert the function. Click on **Insert, Function**.
2. Select the function category of your choice in the **Function category** list. Select a function in the **Function name** list. A description of the function selected is displayed in the lower part of the box (Figure 6.4). Click on **OK** to confirm your function. A dialog box is displayed for the selected function.

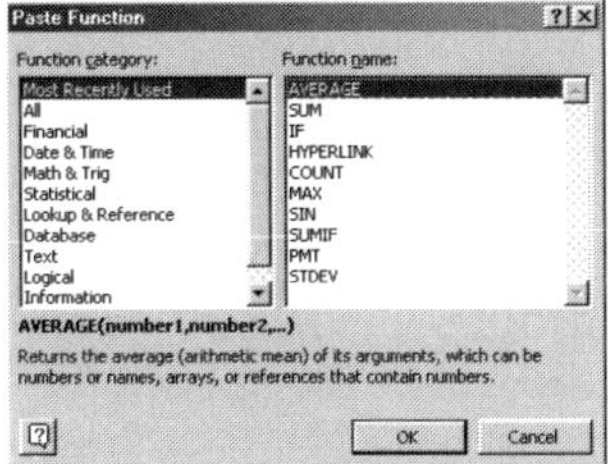

Figure 6.4 Use the Insert Function wizard to create your functions quickly.

3. Work through the options, bearing in mind the instructions displayed in the lower part of the box. Click on **OK** or press the **Enter** key. Excel inserts the function as well as its argument in the selected cell and displays the results.

Automatic entry

When processing a worksheet, the most frequently used function is working out a total.

To obtain the total of a row or a column, click on the cell at the edge of the row or the column. Click on the **AutoSum** button. In the cell, the range of the column or the row is displayed. Press **Enter** or click on the green box to confirm (Figure 6.5).

*When you use the **AutoSum** function, the cell range you wish to add must not contain blank cells.*

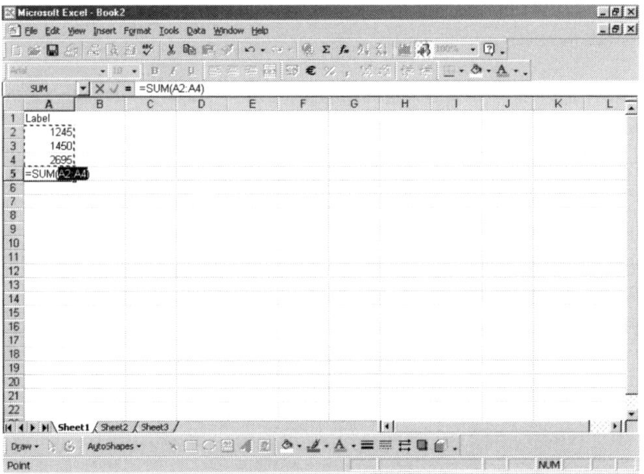

Figure 6.5 Clicking the Sum button allows you to add the contents of a column or row.

Scenarios

Scenarios allows you to create calculations based on theoretical values and to determine their effects on the results. Let us take a simple example: you are a writer and you wish to work out your potential royalties if you sell 500, 5000 or 10 000 copies of your book.

You can create a scenario with a few clicks:

1. In your worksheet, click on **Tools, Scenarios**. The Scenarios manager is displayed and indicates that the worksheet does not contain a scenario. Click on the **Add** button.
2. Name the scenario in the appropriate area. Click on the **Changing cells** option (Figure 6.6).

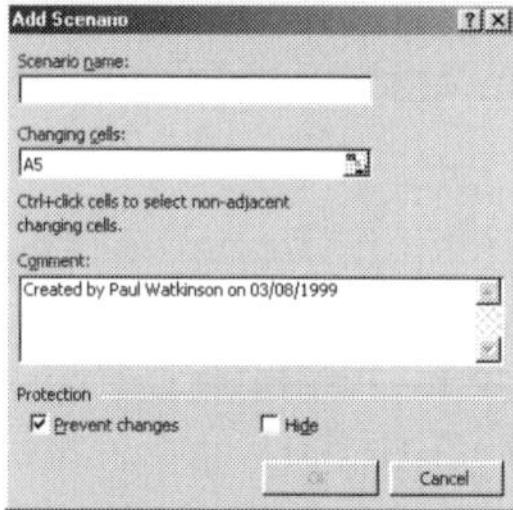

Figure 6.6 The Add Scenario dialog box allows you to specify the cell you want to create the scenario in.

3. In the worksheet, click on the cell in front of the one that will contain the scenario (in our example, the cell that contains the total sales). If you wish to modify several cells for the scenario, select each one by separating them with a semi-colon. Click on **OK** to confirm your cells. The **Scenario Values** dialog box displays the values shown in the cells to be edited.
4. Type the values to be used for the scenario, then click on **OK**. For our example, you should enter 500 and 5000. The Scenarios Manager displays the name of the scenario you have just created.
5. To display the results of a scenario, click on its name, then on the **Show** button.

Sorting and filtering data

Once you have finished inserting functions and formulas, you can use some Excel tools that allow you to manage, sort and filter data.

Sorting data

When you type data, it is rare that you follow specific criteria. You must therefore sort your data as follows.

1. Select the cells range you wish to sort. Click on **Data, Sort** (Figure 6.7). Select the sort criterion in the **Sort by** box.

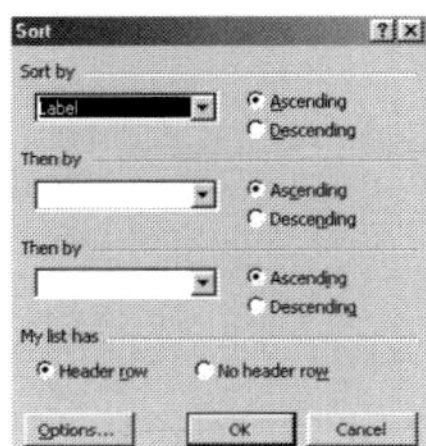

Figure 6.7 You can specify how you want your data sorted in the Sort dialog box.

2. If required, select a second sorting criterion in the **Then by** box. Click on the option corresponding to your choice for each criterion (**Ascending** or **Descending**).
3. Specify whether the table contains a header in the **Header row** box. Click on **OK**.

*To sort a column quickly, you can use the **Ascending** or **Descending** buttons in the Standard toolbar.*

Filtering data

When the worksheet contains several rows or columns, you can view only those on the screen. To access specific data, you can use the **Find** function (Chapter 1): the **Filtering** function allows access to any data within a few seconds.

To create automatic filtering:

1. Click on one of the cells, then on **Data, Filter, AutoFilter**. Each column header displays an arrow (Figure 6.8).

You cannot use the Filtering function if the table does not contain a column header.

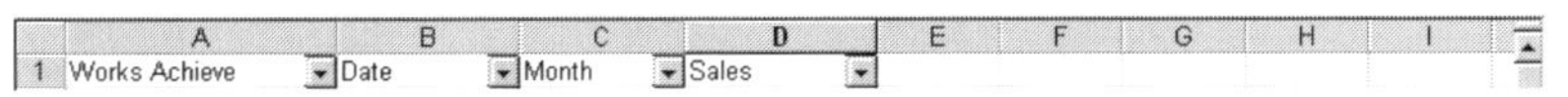

Figure 6.8 By clicking on the arrow in one of the headers, you can select the filtering criteria to be used.

2. To implement a sort, click on the arrow in one of the headers, then select the filtering criteria to be used. Excel displays row numbers and the arrows of the headers of filtered data in blue.

To customise the filter:

1. Click on the arrow of the header for which you wish to customise sorting, then select **Custom**.

*To delete a filter, click on the arrow in the relevant header, then on **All**.*

2. Define the first filtering criterion in the area with the name of the column, then specify the second filtering criterion, if you need to, after having ticked the appropriate option (**And, Or**). Type the cell, the date, the town, the client, and so on, then click on **OK** (Figure 6.9).

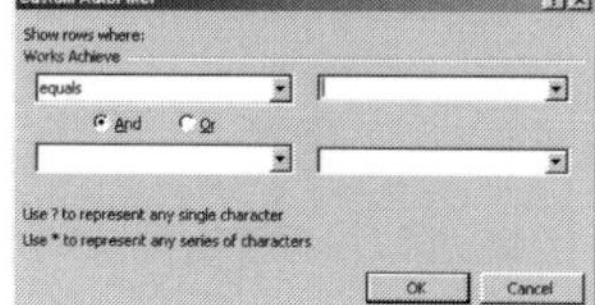

Figure 6.9 You can also create custom filters.

To deactivate AutoFilter, click on ***Data, Filter, AutoFilter****.*

Auditing

Excel offers several auditing tools that allow you to check dependencies between cells. Once you have used the various auditing buttons, it is guaranteed that the results are correct.

To implement an audit:

1. Click on **Tools, Auditing** (Figure 6.10).

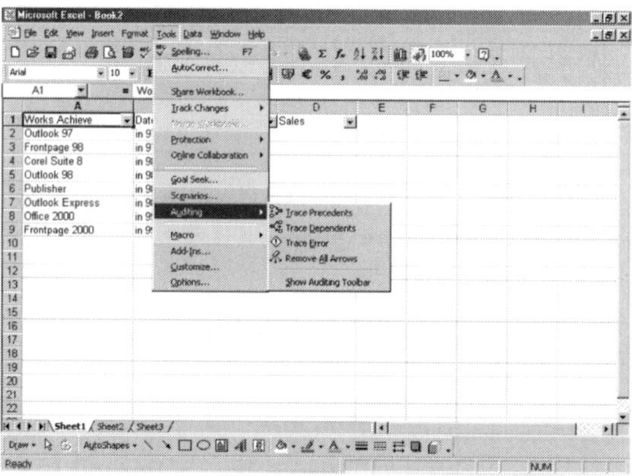

Figure 6.10 Select the type of auditing to implement.

2. Select the type of auditing to implement.

To implement the various checks, click on the cell whose interdependencies you wish to check, then click on the button corresponding to the verification you wish to carry out in the Auditing toolbar.

Creating a chart

To simplify the task of creating a chart, Excel puts a wizard at your disposal.

To start the Chart Wizard:

1. Select the data you wish to use for your chart, then click on the **Chart Wizard** button.
   (a) **Chart type**. Lists the various charts that you can implement.
   (b) **Chart sub-type**. Displays the sub-types available for the type of chart selected. The description of the selected sub-type is displayed underneath this list.
2. Click on the type of chart to be applied. Click on the chart sub-type. The **Press and Hold to View Sample** button allows you, by clicking on it and keeping it pressed, to view the chart you are creating (Figure 6.11). Click on the **Next** button.

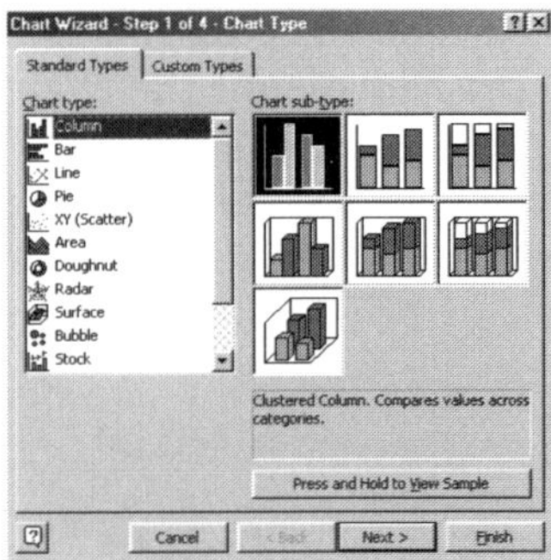

Figure 6.11 Select the type and sub-type of the chart you want.

   (a) **Data Range**. Allows you to modify the range previously selected and to specify the position of the data (Figure 6.12).
   (b) **Series**. Allows you to edit, add or delete a series.

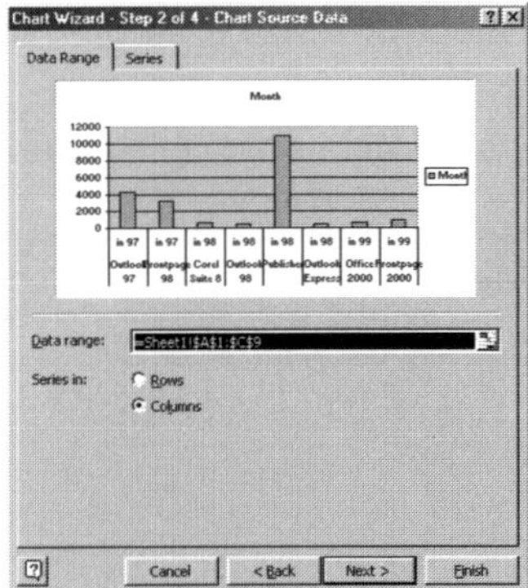

Figure 6.12 The second step of the Chart Wizard is to select the source data.

3. When you have finished your modifications, click on the **Next** button. This step allows you to create settings for one or more items in the chart. The dialog box has several buttons you can use for your editing: Titles, Data Table, Axes, Legend, Data Labels and Gridlines (Figure 6.13).

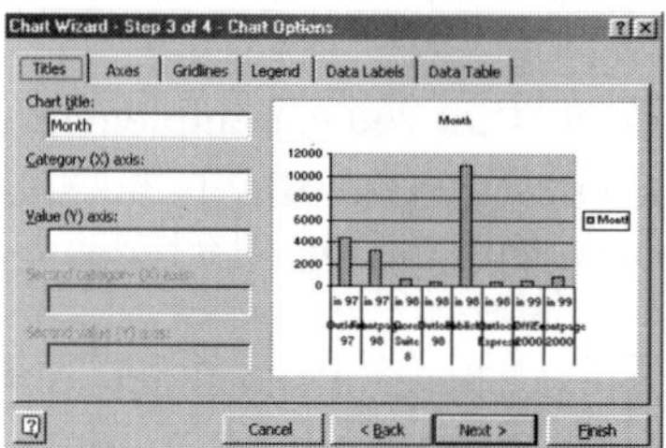

Figure 6.13 The third step of the Chart Wizard is to chose the options you want for Titles, Data Tables, Axes, Legend, Data Labels and Gridlines.

4. When you have chosen your options, click on the **Next** button. This final step allows you to specify the address for the chart (Figure 6.14).

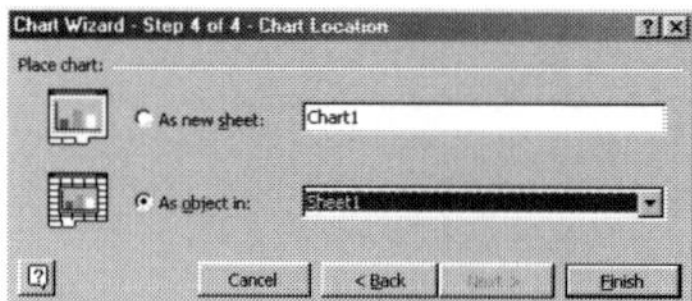

Figure 6.14 The fourth and final step of the Chart Wizard is to choose the location of the chart.

   (a) **As new sheet**. Allows you to add a worksheet chart to your workbook. If you choose this option, remember to enter the name of the new worksheet.
   (b) **As object in**. Allows you to insert the chart in the worksheet where you have selected the data. This is an embedded, but independent object. You can easily move or resize it because it is not linked to the cells in the worksheets.

5. Once you have defined these options, click on the **Finish** button.

According to the options in the fourth step, the chart is inserted into a chart worksheet or into the active worksheet.

To select a chart, click on it. Around the chart, Excel displays small squares known as 'handles'.

To move the chart, click on the chart. Then, keeping the button pressed, drag it to where you want to place it and release the mouse button.

To reduce or enlarge a chart, click on one of the handles, then drag to achieve the size you want.

Editing a chart

Excel offers several options for controlling the appearance and functioning of a chart. There are several tools available for editing charts:

- **Chart menu**. Available when the chart is selected. Offers options that allow you to edit the type, to select other data, to add data and so on.
- **Context menu**. Available with a click of the right mouse button on any object in the chart.
- **Chart toolbar**. Allows you to edit format, objects, type, legend, to display the data table, and so on (Table 6.1).

Table 6.1 Buttons in the Chart toolbar

Button	Action
Chart Area	Displays the list of the items in the chart. By clicking on the item of your choice in this list, you select it.
	Opens a dialog box that lets you apply formats to the selected item.
	Chooses another type of chart.
	Displays or hides a legend.
	Activates or deactivates the data table which displays the data in the chart.
	Shows the data selected by row.
	Shows the data selected by column.
	Angles text downward, from left to right.
	Angles text upward, from left to right.

7 Basic PowerPoint functions

The first step

Display views

New presentations

Text

Harmonisation

Formatting slides

Pictures

Charts

In this chapter, we will study the basic functions of PowerPoint, such as opening a new presentation, formatting and so on.

The first step

When you start the program, the PowerPoint dialog box is displayed (Figure 7.1). From this dialog box, you can choose a number of options:

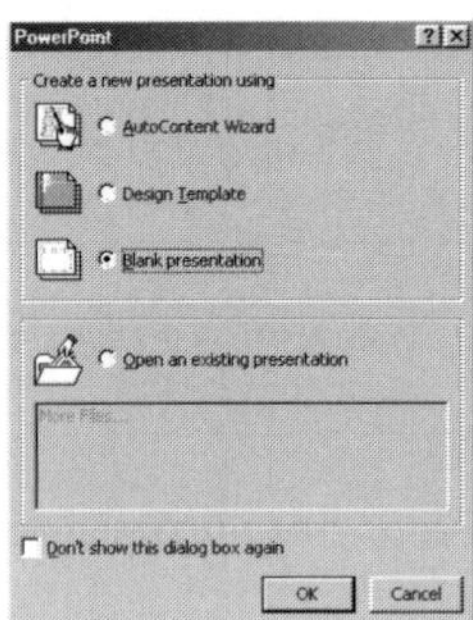

Figure 7.1 The PowerPoint dialog box allows you to choose how you will create a new presentation.

- **AutoContent Wizard**. Allows you to launch a wizard that helps you to quickly create a presentation.
- **Design Template**. Allows you to select themes, backgrounds, predefined presentations, animation and so on.
- **Blank presentation**. Allows you to open a blank presentation.
- **Open an existing presentation**. Allows you to display a previously created presentation.

Converting a presentation

You can also open a presentation created in another program. Click on the **Open** button in the Standard toolbar. In the **Files of type** box, select the application in which the required document was created. Double-click on it in the list that is displayed. PowerPoint automatically converts the presentation so that it can be modified.

*If the PowerPoint dialog box is not displayed, click on **Tools, Options**. Click on the **View** tab. Tick the **Startup** dialog option, then click on **OK** to confirm.*

Applying a template

You can change a format by changing it to a predefined template. To apply a template to an already created presentation:

1. Click on **Format, Apply Design Template** (Figure 7.2).
2. Select a template, then click on **Apply**.

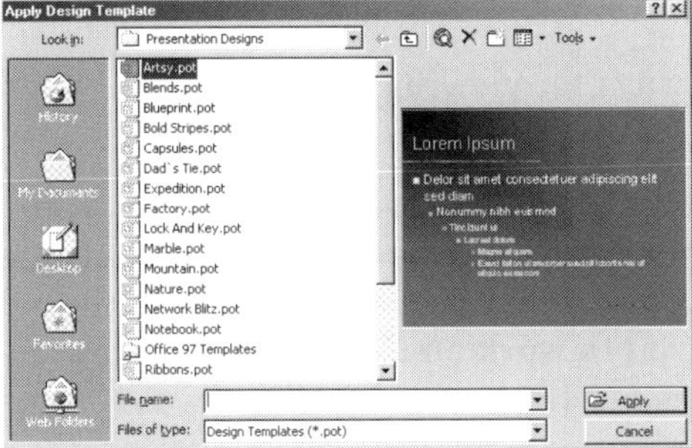

Figure 7.2 You can apply a template to a presentation that has already been created.

AutoContent Wizard

When you require a presentation quickly, use the AutoContent Wizard:

1. Click on **AutoContent Wizard** in the PowerPoint dialog box. If this dialog box is not active, click on **File, New**. Click on the **General** tab. Double-click on the **AutoContent Wizard** icon. Click on **Next**.
2. Now choose the presentation type (Figure 7.3). PowerPoint offers a number of themes to cater for most business needs. Press a category button (list on the left) for the type of presentation you are going to give and then select the presentation that best fits your needs (list on the right). You can add one of your own presentations by choosing a category and then pressing **Add**. Click on **Next**.

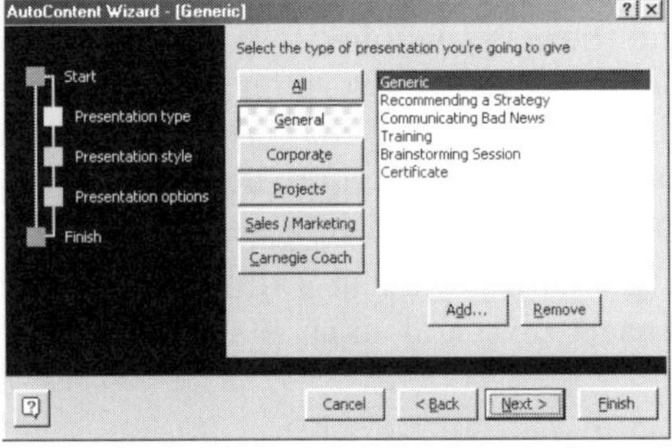

Figure 7.3 Choosing the presentation type.

3. You must now select the type of output for your presentation. Click on **Next**.
4. You can specify the presentation title, the contents of the footer, the slide number and so on. Click on **Next**, then on **Finish**.

Display views

PowerPoint offers several ways for viewing a presentation. Each view allows a different type of intervention:

- **Normal**. A new feature in the 2000 version, this gives you a three-sided view: on the left, an Outline view, in the centre, a Slide view, and at the bottom, a view that corresponds to the old Notes view. This allows you to work on the presentation structure, contents and notes all at the same time (Figure 7.4). This is the default display view.

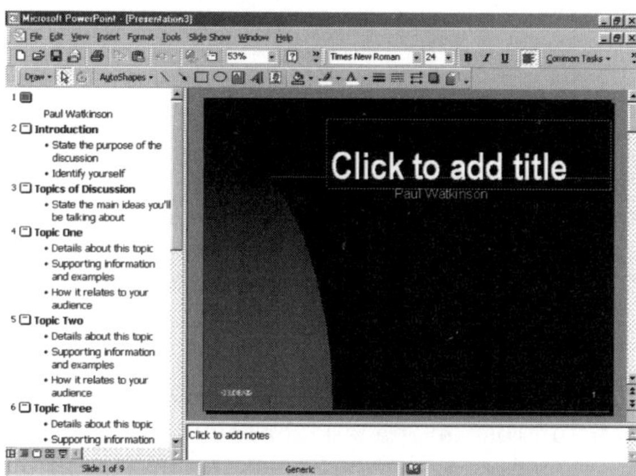

Figure 7.4 Slide view in Normal viewing mode.

- **Outline**. Allows you to view the slides by title level: the text of the various slides is on the left, a small preview of the slide is in the right-hand corner, and there is a window in which to insert notes (Figure 7.5). In this view, you can work on the presentation contents and organise the flow chart that creates a logical sequencing for the various slides. To navigate between slides, double-click on the title of the slide you wish to display.
- **Slide view**. Allows you to view one slide at a time. This is the view that allows you to insert text, add objects (sound, charts, pictures) and so on.
- **Slide Sorter view**. Allows you to view all the slides in your presentation. This is the ideal view to sort, move and copy slides.
- **Slide Show**. Allows you to view the set of slides in sequence. In this view, the slide takes up the whole screen. You can test the actual show and any animation effects you have created.

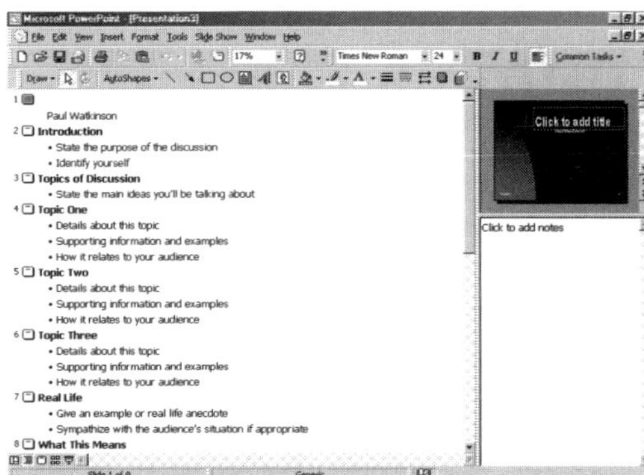

Figure 7.5 Slide view in Outline viewing mode.

To change the view, click on the appropriate display button in the bottom left corner of the window (Figure 7.6). You can also click on **View**, then make your choice.

Figure 7.6 Viewing mode buttons.

If you wish to enlarge or reduce any part of a slide, click on **View, Zoom**. Choose the zoom percentage (Figure 7.7).

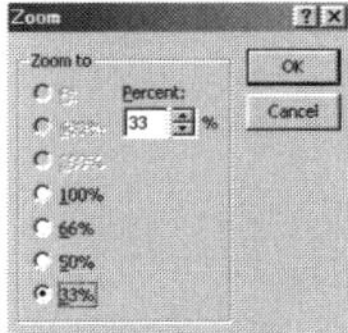

Figure 7.7 You can use the Zoom dialog box to change the view on screen.

New presentations

Let us now see how to create a new presentation.

1. Click on **Blank presentation** in the PowerPoint dialog box, or on **File, New**. Click on the **General** tab, then double-click on the **Blank presentation** icon.
2. In the New Slide dialog box, choose the type of slide to be created by clicking on the relevant icon (Figure 7.8). The right-hand side of the box displays a textual description of the selected type. Click on **OK**. The number of the slide is displayed in the status bar (slide *x* of *y*).

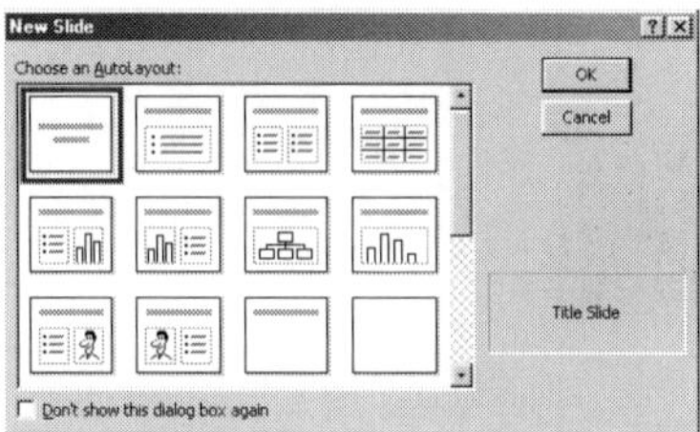

Figure 7.8 You can choose between AutoLayouts in the New Slide dialog box.

Inserting, deleting and formatting slides

- To delete a slide, display it in Outline or Slide Sorter view, then click on it and press the delete key.
- Insert slides by clicking on the **New Slide** button. Select the type ofslide as explained above and click on **OK**. PowerPoint inserts the new slide and assigns the previous format to it.
  You can also click on **Insert, New Slide**, or on the **New Slide** icon in the Format toolbar. Repeat the above procedures to choose the type of slide.
- If you are not happy with your choice of slide, you can change it. Click on the **Common Tasks** button and select **Slide Layout** (Figure 7.9). Select the new type, then click on **Apply**.

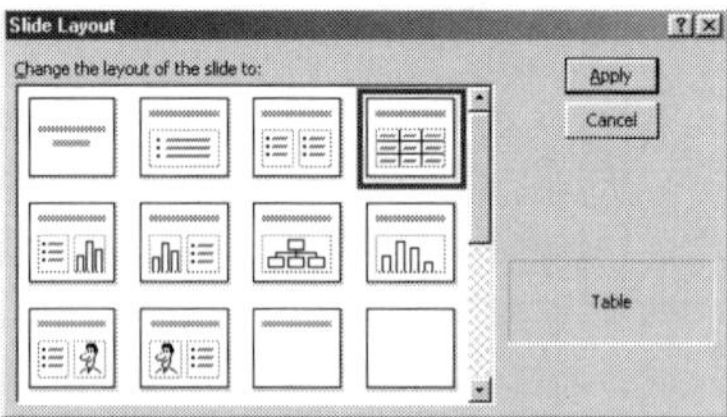

Figure 7.9 You can change the layout of your slide in the Slide Layout dialog box.

Moving between slides

- To navigate between slides in Normal or Slide view, click on the up or down double arrow in the vertical scroll bar. You can also drag the scroll bar. A balloon displays the number of pages while you are scrolling. Release when you get to the slide you wish to display.
- To navigate between slides in Outline or Slide Sorter view, click on the slide to be selected (Figure 7.10).

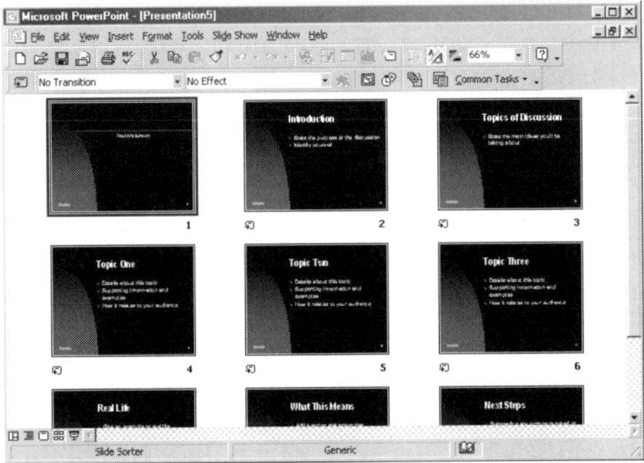

Figure 7.10 Move quickly between slides in the Slide Sorter.

Text

Once you have selected the type of slide you wish to create, you can start inserting text. Whatever the type of slide you have chosen, you follow the same procedures:

- To insert text, click on one of the text boxes that reads **Click to add**. The frame around the text box becomes greyed and the pointer flashes. Type your text. To exit from the text box, click outside it. You can write whatever you want as you would do in a text processing program; the line feed is automatic.

In PowerPoint 2000, the text automatically fits the frame.

To activate Auto-fit text:

1. Click on **Tools, Options**, then on the **Edit** tab (Figure 7.11).

The function that allows the text to fit automatically to the text frame is not active for titles.

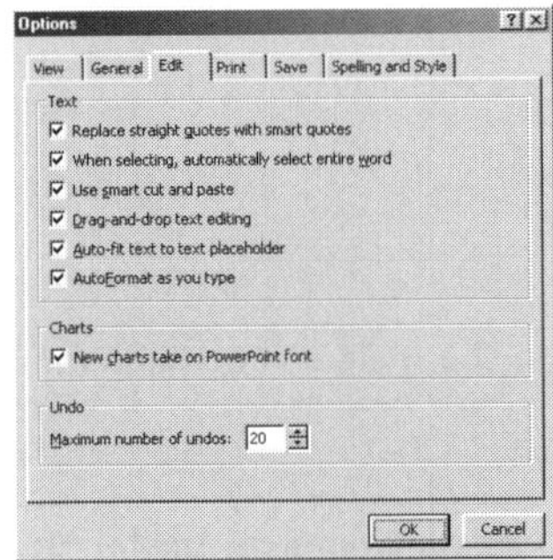

Figure 7.11 Activating the Auto-fit text.

2. Tick the **Auto-fit text to text placeholder** option to activate it. Click on **OK**.

*To insert a text box, click on the **Text Box** button in the Drawing toolbar and draw the frame in the slide.*

Selecting text

For any editing or deleting operation, you must know how to select the text on which to act. These procedures are explained later in this book.

Bulleted lists

A bulleted list presentation is extremely practical because it allows each topic to be displayed point by point. To display a slide of this type, click on the **Bulleted list** template in the New Slide dialog box.

*To change a bulleted list to normal text, select the list, then click on the **Bullets** button to deactivate it.*

The 'bullet' is the icon displayed to the left of each topic. Type the text in the area that contains the bulleted list, then press the **Enter** key each time you wish to display a new bullet. By default, PowerPoint displays small round black bullets.

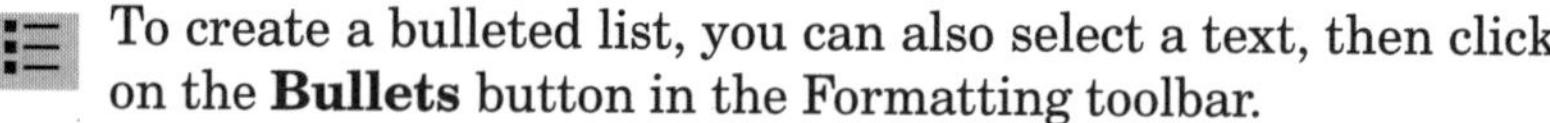

To create a bulleted list, you can also select a text, then click on the **Bullets** button in the Formatting toolbar.

You can change the type of bullets used:

1. In the bulleted list, press **Ctrl+A** to select the entire list.
2. Click with the right mouse button on the selection, then select **Bullets and Numbering** (Figure 7.12). Click on the type of bullet you want. You can modify the colour and size of the bullets in the **Color** and **Size** options. The **Character** button allows you to select a letter or any other icon as a bullet. Click on **OK**.

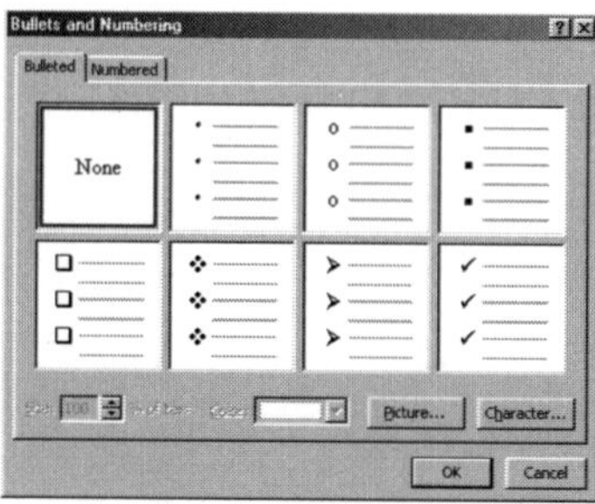

Figure 7.12 Selecting a different bullet style in the Bullets and Numbering dialog box.

PowerPoint also allows you to use a ClipArt picture as a bullet. In the **Bullets and Numbering** dialog box, click on the **Bulleted** tab, then on the **Picture** button. In ClipArt, click on the bullet of your choice, then on OK.

Harmonisation

PowerPoint allows you to harmonise presentations thanks to its masters and colour schemes.

Slide Master

The Slide Master controls font, size of characters for all titles, bullet lists, sub-titles and so on, and contains the charts shared by all the slides. It also allows you to insert date, slide number and any other information you may wish to include.

To display the Slide Master for a slide, click on **View, Master**. In the drop-down menu, select **Slide Master**. Then follow the instructions below to use or edit the Slide Master:

- To edit titles, select the master title, then use the **Font** and **Size** drop-down list. For more complex modifications, use the Font dialog box; to open it, click on **Format, Font**.
- To edit the text in bulleted lists, select the bulleted list in the master, then use the **Font** and **Size** drop-down list. You can use other buttons in the Formatting toolbar such as the **Font Size** arrow.

Slide Master controls all aspects of slides. When you edit an area in the master, the modifications apply to all the slides in the presentation. If you do not wish to use this format for all of the slides, display the slide to be unformatted in Slide view, then click on **Format, Background**. In the dialog box, tick the **Omit background graphics from master** option to activate it, then click on **Apply**.

Colour schemes

Each predefined template offers a different colour for each of the items in slides: titles, bulleted lists, numbered lists, fill and so on. You can easily modify the colour for each category of items as follows:

1. Click on **Format, Slide Color Scheme** (Figure 7.13).

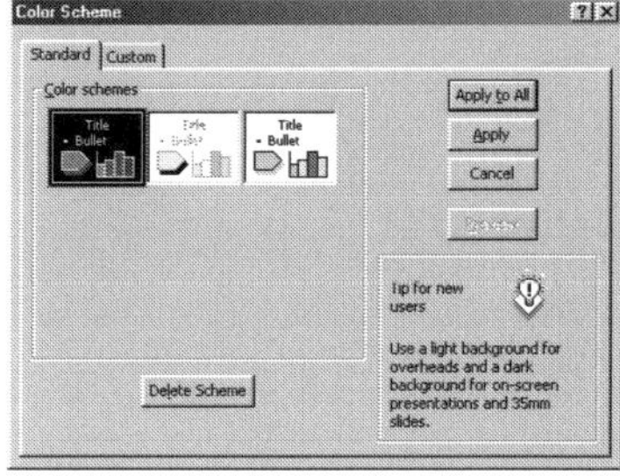

Figure 7.13 Colour schemes allow you to harmonise your presentation.

2. In the dialog box, you can choose a standard scheme or customise your own scheme. It is better, however, to use a standard scheme to avoid problems (clashing colours and so on). If you do not like any of the standard schemes, click on the **Custom** tab, then select a colour for each element of the slides. Once you have completed your choice, click on **Apply to All** so that the colour scheme applies to the whole presentation or click on **Apply** so that it applies only to the selected slide.

Formatting slides

Just as in Word, you can create a custom format.

Tips for formatting text

To format text, you must first select it as explained earlier in this chapter. To select all the text in a slide in Outline view, click on its icon. In Slide view, simply press **Ctrl+A**.

If you have added text boxes to some slides, the master cannot control them.

For text, formatting options are the same as in Word (see Chapter 3). Here we provide some hints and tips:

- **Slide Master view**. Allows you to modify the appearance of text for all slides. To give coherence to the format, carry out the modifications in the master.
- **Slide view**. Displays the various slides of the presentation one by one. To format the text of one slide differently from the master, use this view because it allows you to see the text exactly as it will appear in the slide show.
- **Outline view**. Displays only the text. This view allows you to display the text effect of each slide and compare it to the others. It is ideal if you wish to modify the font or the character size for the whole text in all the slides of the presentation. Click on **Edit, Select All**, then select the required font. You can also use the various buttons in the Format toolbar.

Background

Each slide has a background, which may or may not be coloured depending on how you created the slide.

To modify the background:

1. Click on **Format, Background** (Figure 7.14).

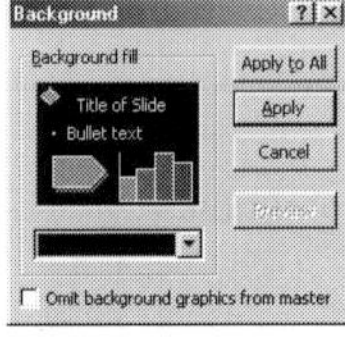

Figure 7.14 Choosing a background colour.

2. To choose a background colour, click on the arrow in the **Background fill** drop-down list, then choose the colour. To choose another colour, click on the **More Colors** button, then choose a colour or specify it yourself. The **Motifs** option in **Fill Effects** allows you to select a gradient, texture, pattern or picture for the background. Click on **OK**.

Pictures

Pictures are great to use in a slide show because they support the presentation and explain visually – and therefore more immediately – the contents of the slides.

PowerPoint allows you to insert several types of pictures:

- Digital pictures, produced with a scanner or a digital camera.
- Vector pictures produced with image-creation programs, such as Illustrator. These are created from mathematical shapes and are made up of basic elements: lines, regular areas and so on.
- Pictures from the Office ClipArt Gallery.

Remember that a digital picture may be in black and white, greyscale or colour.

To insert a picture, follow the procedures given in Chapter 2.

Picture toolbar

The Picture toolbar allows you to retouch a picture. This is displayed automatically when you select a picture (by clicking on it) and offers buttons for editing contrast, brightness, cropping, display in colour or black and white, and so on. Refer to Table 7.1 to see how to use these buttons.

Table 7.1 The buttons in the Picture toolbar

Button	Action
	Insert Picture from File. Inserts an existing picture in the active file at the insertion point.
	Image Control. Changes a picture colour to greyscale, black and white or as a watermark (a transparent image that appears under the text without hiding it).
	More Contrast. Increases the picture contrast.
	Less Contrast. Decreases the picture contrast.

Button	Action
	More Brightness. Increases the picture brightness.
	Less Brightness. Decreases the picture brightness.
	Crop. Trims or restores portions of a picture. Click on this icon, then drag a sizing handle on the picture.
	Line Style. Modifies the lines framing the picture.
	Recolor Picture. To enable this command, select a single picture or OLE object.
	Format Object. Defines formatting options for the picture.
	Set Transparent Color. Makes one of the colours in the picture transparent.
	Reset Picture. Restores the picture to its original status.

Charts

When giving presentations, you often need to present series of figures. In such a situation, the audience does not have a great deal of time to understand and analyse figures. To help overcome this problem, add a chart to simplify the figures and to make your point clearly and forcefully.

Refer to Chapter 6 for further information on creating and modifying charts.

If you have created your slides with AutoContent Wizard or you have selected a slide predefined for charts, simply double-click on the **Double-click to add chart** message. If you have chosen a blank slide, or if you wish to insert a chart in a text slide, you must click on the **Insert, Chart** button in the Standard toolbar.

Whichever procedure you use, the PresentationNumber – Datasheet window is displayed with data as examples.

OLE is a special interprogram technology that allows you to share information between programs. All Office programs support the OLE technology.

To enter the data you wish to format, click on the cell you want, type the data, then press **Enter** to confirm. You must use the direction keys to move within the table cells. By default, data are arranged by rows. Column titles are displayed on the horizontal axis (x) in the chart. If you want to arrange your data by columns, with row titles on the x axis, click on the **By Column** button in the Standard toolbar.

Advanced PowerPoint functions

8

Placing objects

Drawing

Style coherence

Sorting, structuring and adapting slides

Animation

Starting a slide show

Slide shows on paper, slides or other media

Speaker notes

Transferring a slide show

In this chapter, we will examine advanced PowerPoint functions, such as drawing, placing objects, organising a slide show and so on.

Placing objects

You have several methods available for placing your items exactly.

Ruler and guides

To place an object exactly, the ruler and the guides are indispensable.

To activate the ruler, click on **View, Ruler**. When you drag the object, a dotted line will appear in the ruler, showing the exact position of the object edge. Release when you are exactly where you want to be (Figure 8.1).

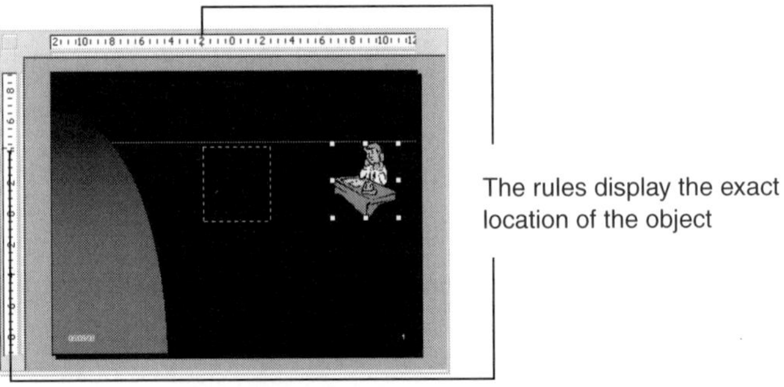
The rules display the exact
location of the object

Figure 8.1 You can place objects exactly with the ruler.

To activate the guides, click on **View, Guides**. On the screen you will see a dotted cross. When you drag an object on to a guide, the object sticks to it. To move a guide, click on it, then drag it to where you want to be. This allows you to align objects on the slide with absolute perfection (Figure 8.2).

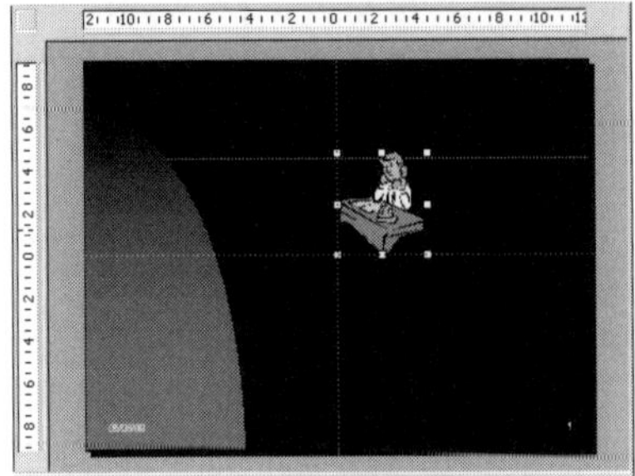

Figure 8.2 The guides help you to position two objects exactly.

Arranging objects

While you are creating your slide, you pile up objects until you can no longer see the objects in the background. If you wish to modify one of the hidden objects, you must bring it back to the foreground. If the object is still visible, click on it; otherwise, click with the right mouse button on one of the objects of the pile, then select **Order**. In the sub-menu (Figure 8.3), click on the choice you want:

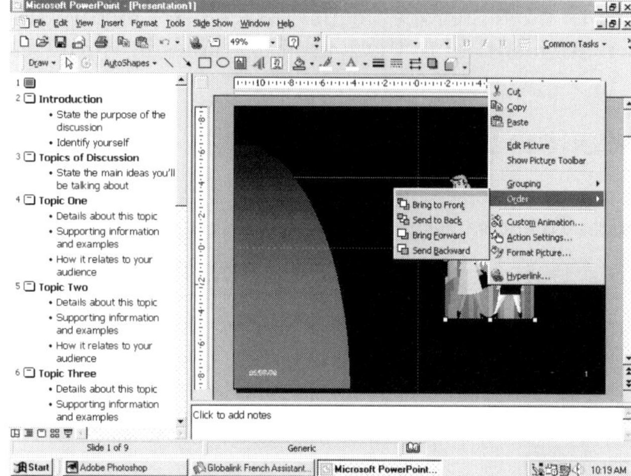

Figure 8.3 The options available for organising your objects.

- **Bring to Front**. Places the selected object on top of the pile.
- **Send to Back**. Places the selected object at the bottom of the pile.
- **Bring Forward**. Brings the selected object forward by one place.
- **Send Backward**. Sends the selected object backward by one place.

Drawing

With PowerPoint, you can insert shapes and arrows and draw and create tables for your presentations.

Drawing toolbar

The various drawing tools are available in the Drawing toolbar at the bottom of the screen. You can draw lines, shapes and arrows, or even select AutoShapes. Simply click on the tool, then insert it into the slide. Use the various buttons to add colour, modify the line style and so on.

Creating tables

To create a table for a presentation, click on **Insert, Table** (Figure 8.4). Define the number of columns and rows for the table, then click on **OK**.

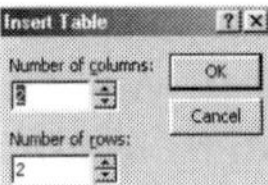

Figure 8.4 Inserting a table into a presentation.

To insert new rows or columns, use the pointer, which has now become a pencil, and draw.

The procedures to move between cells, insert text, modify the colour and so on are identical to those used for tables in Word (see Chapter 4).

Style coherence

PowerPoint offers a tool for checking the style of the presentation and its coherence. To activate the checking of the style:

1. Click on **Tools, Options**, then on the **Spelling and Style** tab.
2. In the Style area, tick the **Check style** option box (Figure 8.5). Click on **OK**.

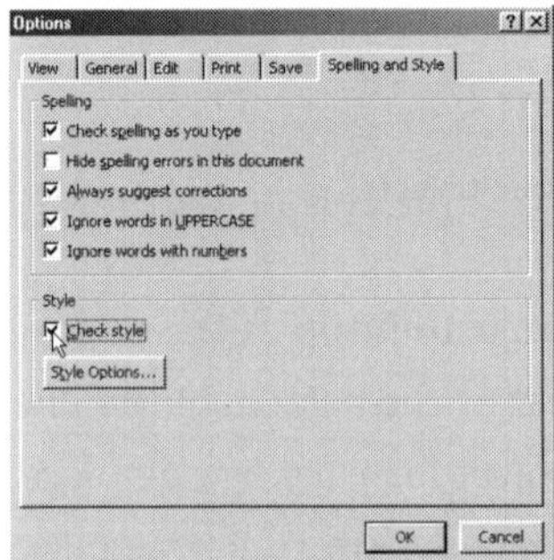

Figure 8.5 Activating the style checker.

To define the style to be used:

1. In the **Spelling and Style** tab, click on the **Style Options** button (Figure 8.6). The two tabs, **Case and End Punctuation** and **Visual Clarity**, give you all the options you need for your checks.
2. Specify the options required, the title text size, the title case, the sentence case and so on. Click on **OK** to confirm.

If your presentation has any style discrepancies, PowerPoint warns you with a dialog box.

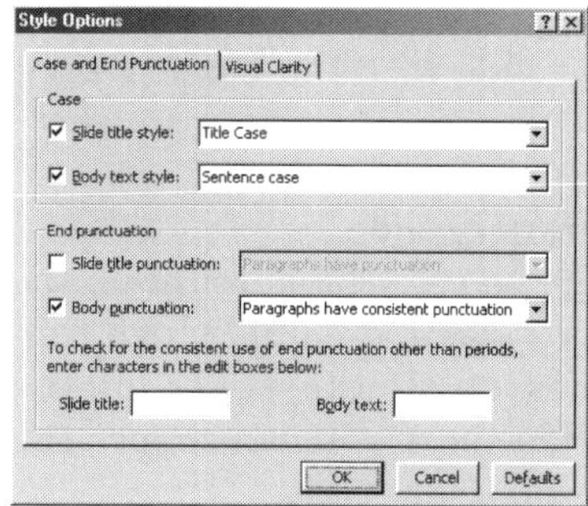

Figure 8.6 Setting the style options to achieve the desired style coherence.

Sorting, structuring and adapting slides

To make your slide show perfect, you must sort the slides. The best way to do this is by using the Slide Sorter view. Click on the **Slide Sorter View** button at the bottom left of the screen (Figure 8.7).

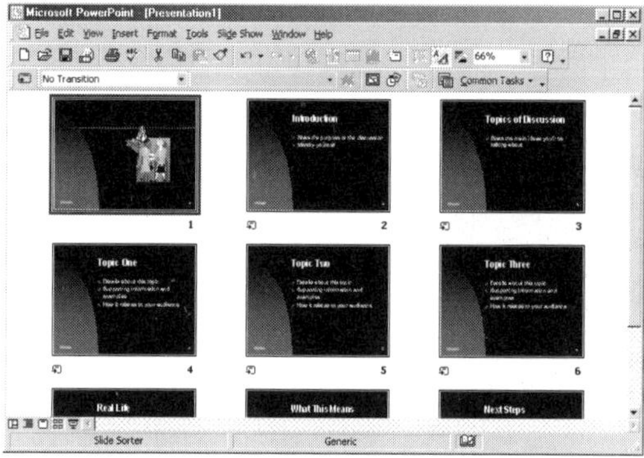

Figure 8.7 Slide Sorter.

To copy a slide:

1. Click on the slide and press the **Ctrl** key.
2. Keeping this key pressed, drag the slides. A vertical line follows the drag, showing you where the copy is going to be inserted when you release the key.

To move a slide, repeat the above procedure without pressing the **Ctrl** key.

To delete a slide, click on it, then press the delete key.

To move slides, you can also use the Outline view. In this view, all slides are reduced to their title levels. You can then move them by dragging their icons up or down. A horizontal line moves as you move, showing where the slide will be placed when you release the mouse button. You can also move the slide with the **Up** or **Down** buttons in the Outlining toolbar.

Organizing a slide show with the summary slide

When you create a slide show to be shown on a computer or on the Web, you can use a summary slide as a starting point, which contains a bulleted list with the titles of all the slides in the presentation. When you start the slide show, you can choose the direction you wish to follow from the summary slide.

 To create a summary slide:

1. In Slide Sorter view, click on the first slide to be included in the summary slide.
2. Press the **Shift** key, then click on the second slide, and so on, keeping the key pressed.
3. Click on the **Summary Slide** button in the Slide Sorter view or Outlining toolbar (Figure 8.8).

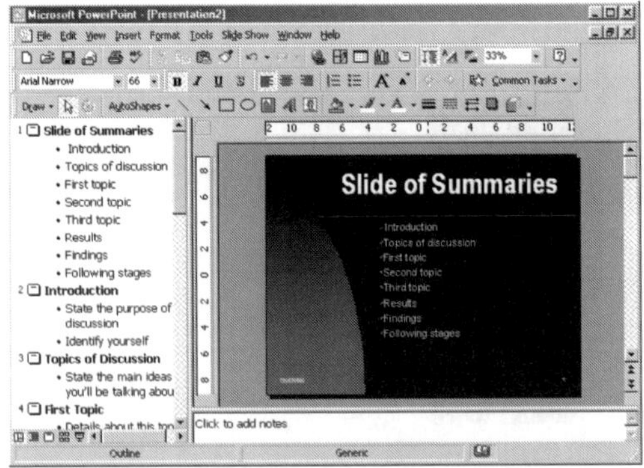

Figure 8.8 The summary slide allows you to see the structure of the presentation.

Creating bookmarks

To navigate more quickly through the presentation, you can create bookmarks that allow direct access to the required place when you click on them.

To create a bookmark:

1. In the slide, select the relevant text.
2. Click on the **Insert Hyperlink** button (Figure 8.9).
3. Click on the **Bookmark** button (Figure 8.10). Click on the name of the slide you want. Click on **OK** in the two dialog boxes.

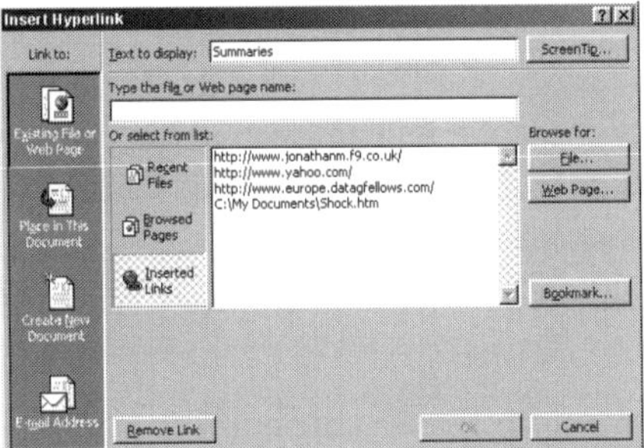

Figure 8.9 Inserting a hyperlink with the Insert Hyperlink dialog box.

Refer to Chapter 1 to discover the new PowerPoint Web functions. These allow you to create a frame sequence at the left of the window, so Web surfers can access the slides of interest by clicking on that frame.

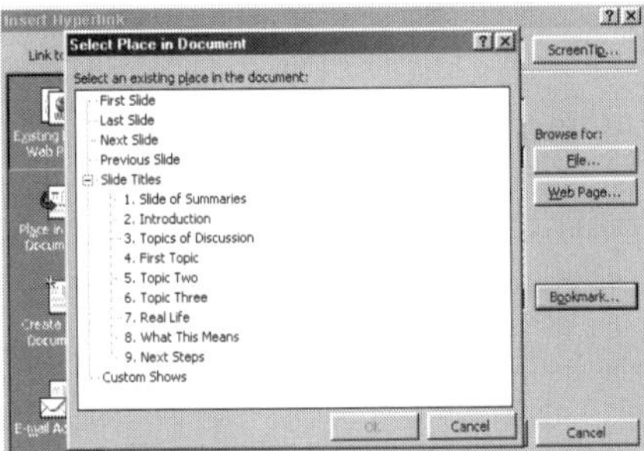

Figure 8.10 Creating bookmarks in a slide.

Narration

PowerPoint allows you to add a sound commentary to your slide show. Before recording your narration, look at the various buttons and what they do:

- To pause during the slide show, right-click anywhere in the active slide, then click on **Pause Narration**.
- To start recording again, click with the right button, then click on **Resume Narration**.

To record a narration:

1. Switch on your computer and check the connection. Click on **Slide Show, Record Narration** (Figure 8.11). Click **OK**.

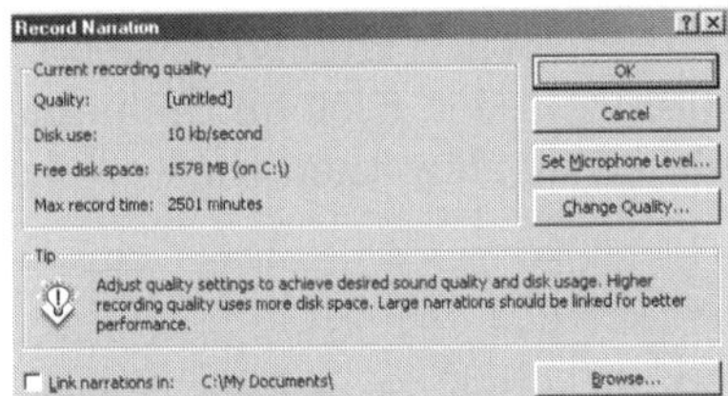

Figure 8.11 Starting the Record Narration function.

2. Click on the next slide to move it without interrupting the commentary.

   At the end of the slide show, a message is displayed asking if you wish to save the slide timings as well as the narrations that have been saved for each slide.

3. To accept, click on **Yes**. To save only the commentary without timings, click on **No**.

When you scroll through the slide show, the commentary is started automatically so that the audience can follow your presentation better.

If you do not want the commentary to start with the slide show:

1. Click on **Slide Sorter view**.
2. Right-click on one of the images and select **Set Up Show** (Figure 8.12).
3. Click on **Show without narration**, then on **OK**.

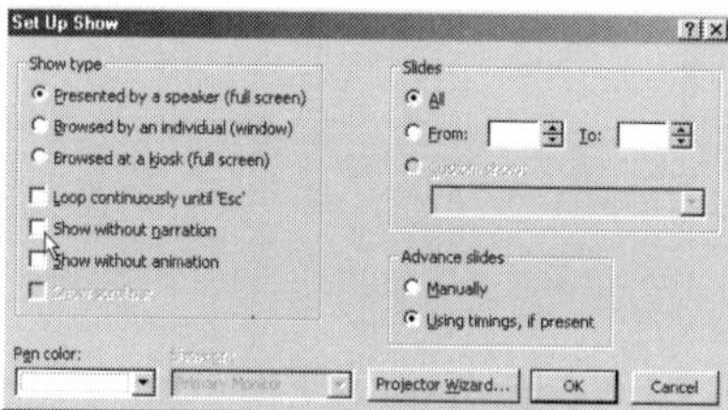

Figure 8.12 Deactivating the Record Narration function.

Adapting the slide show to the audience

PowerPoint allows you to adapt the slide show according to your audience, for example, excluding some information from certain audiences. To control a slide show:

1. Click on **Slide Show, Custom Shows**. Click on the **New** button.
2. In the **Define Custom Show** dialog box (Figure 8.13), name the slide show in the **Slide show name** option. In the list on the left, click on the first slide to be inserted, then click on the **Add** button. Repeat this procedure for each slide you wish to insert. To put your slides in a different order, click on the name of the relevant slide in the right-hand window, then click on the up or down arrow buttons.
3. Click on **OK** to save the custom slide show.

To launch the controlled slide show, click on **Slide Show, Custom Show**. Select the show you want, then click on the **Show** button to start it.

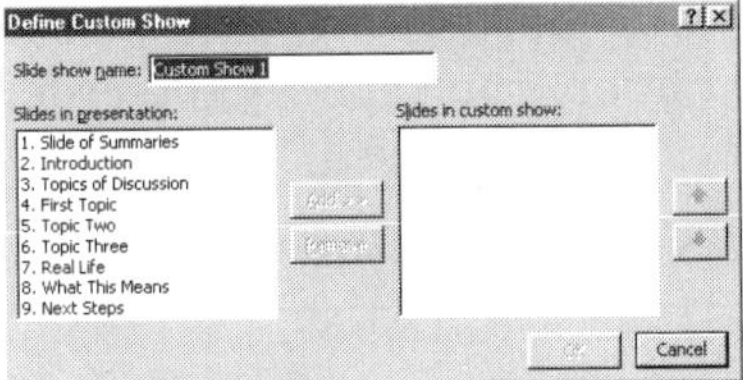

Figure 8.13 Customising your slide show to suit your audience.

Animation

We will now look at creating animation effects.

Animating transitions between slides

In a standard slide show, the speaker must press a button or click on an icon to move to the next slide. This technique can be inefficient because there is usually a lack of synchronisation between the speaker's voice and what you see on screen. With PowerPoint, you can time transitions between each slide and create animations.

To manage transitions between slides:

1. Click on the slide to be animated, then on the **Transition** button in the **Slide Show** menu.
2. Click on the arrow in the **Effect** area, then choose an option. The display area shows the effect of the selected transition.
3. Click on the required option underneath the drop-down list (**Slow**, **Medium** or **Fast**) to define the speed of the transition. In the **Advance** area, click on **On mouse click** to control the slides' progression manually, or click on **Automatically after** for PowerPoint to automatically display the following slide after the specified number of seconds.
4. To assign sound to the transition, click on the arrow in the **Sound** drop-down list, then select the sound you want. For the sound to last until the next slide comes on, click on **Loop until next sound**. Click on **Apply** when you have finished. If you click on **Apply to All**, the specified effects will apply to all the slides.

Animating slides

You can also animate images, text, bulleted lists, and so on in the slides. These animations are available from the Animation Preview icon in the Animation Effects toolbar displayed in Slide Show:

1. Display the relevant slide with the Slide Show view, then click on the **Animation** button (yellow star) in the Formatting toolbar (Table 8.1).

2. Select the effects you want according to Table 8.1, click on the arrow of the **Animation order** option, then specify the order in which the objects should appear on the screen.

Table 8.1 The Animation Effects toolbar buttons

Button	Action
	**Animate Title**. Activates the animation effects for the title of the slide.
	Animate Slide Text. Activates the animation effects for other texts in the slide.
	**Drive-In**. Car noise.
	**Flying**. Makes the object fly.
	Camera. Makes the click of a camera.
	**Flash Once**. Flashes once on the object.
	**Laser Text**. Displays the text with a laser effect and sound.
	Typewriter Text. Displays the text as if you have been typing on a typewriter.
	**Reverse Text Order**. Writes the text from bottom up.
	**Drop-In Text**. Drops the words one by one from the top of the slide.
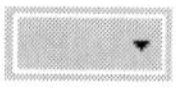	**Animation Order**. Calculates the animation order of items in the slide.
	**Custom Animation**. Customises animation.
	**Animation Preview**. Shows in a small window the selected animation effects.

To create an animation effect, you can also click on the object, then on **Slide Show, Preset Animation**. In the list of effects, select the one you want. When going through the slide show, the chosen effects will appear on the screen with a simple click.

Customizing animation effects

PowerPoint allows you to create more targeted animation effects:

1. Click on **Slide Show, Custom Animation** (Figure 8.14).

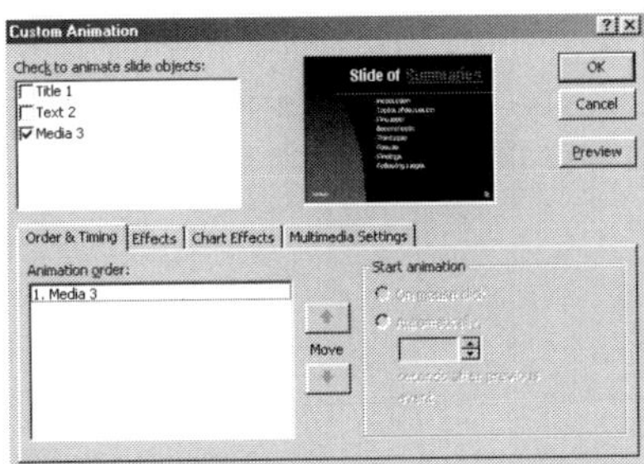

Figure 8.14 Customising the animation of a slide show.

2. In the **Check to animate slide objects** area, the various objects of the slide are listed. To select an object, click on it in this area: it will be shown in the Animation order list in the **Order & Timing** tab. In the area to the right of this tab, you can define the **Start animation** options for the selected object. The **Effects** tab allows you to define the effects to be applied to the object. The **Chart Effects** tab allows the slide chart to be animated, and the **Multimedia Settings** tab allows you to define sound effects, animated clips, and so on.

Starting a slide show

Let us now see what the slide show is like and check that it works.

To start the slide show, display the first slide, then click on the **Slide Show** button at the bottom of the screen. You can also click on **View, Slide Show**. The slide is displayed on the whole of the screen. To scroll the slide show, follow the procedures shown below:

- To scroll the slide show slide after slide, click anywhere in the screen or press the arrow keys at the bottom of your keyboard.
- The slide show scrolls automatically if you have defined a specific transition time.
- Press the **Esc** key to exit from the slide show.
- To display the slide show control menu, right-click on the greyed button in the bottom left corner of the slide.
- Double-click on the audio or video clips icon to open them.

Slide shows on paper, slides or other media

So far, we have seen a slide show only on screen. However, you can transfer slides on to transparencies, 35 mm slides or paper.

To specify the medium for your presentation, click on **File, Page Setup** (Figure 8.15). To adapt your slides to the medium you are going to use, click on the arrow in the **Slides sized for** drop-down list and select the option corresponding to your medium:

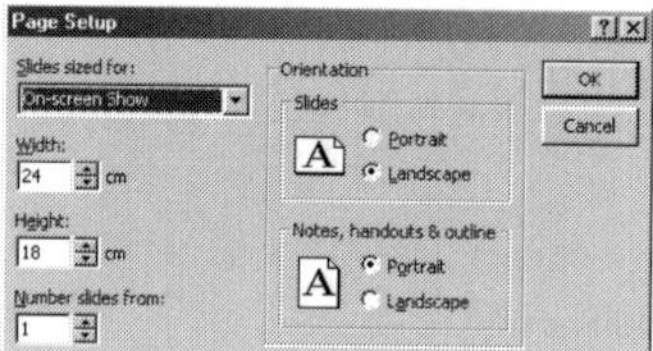

Figure 8.15 The Page Setup dialogue box allows you to specify the medium you are going to use for your slide show.

- **Letter Paper**. 8.5" × 11" format.
- **A4 Paper**. Corresponds to the traditional 210 × 297 mm size.
- **35 mm slides**. Corresponds to the photo slides format.
- **Overhead**. For overhead projectors.
- **Banner**. For printing on continuous paper.
- **Custom**. Allows you to fit the size of your slides to the printer's print area.

You can also change the orientation of your slides (Landscape or Portrait).

Speaker notes

Inserted notes are not visible to the audience.

To avoid memory lapses during your slide show, you may want to create some notes. These notes can be entered in the bottom right area in the Normal view.

Transferring a slide show

You may need to transfer your slide show, for example if you are doing presentations at several locations. PowerPoint offers a wizard that helps you put the whole of your presentation on a disk.

To start this wizard:

1. Click on **File, Pack and Go**. The Pack and Go Wizard is displayed. Click on the **Next** button to display the second window for this wizard.

2. Select the presentation you wish to export. Click on the **Next** button to continue. Specify the type of computer you wish to use for your presentation. Click on the **Next** button.
3. You must now include linked files or include TrueType fonts in your presentation. Once you have finished your choice, click on the **Next** button. The wizard offers to load PowerPoint Viewer in case the computer on which you are planning to install your presentation does not run PowerPoint. Click on the **Next** button, then click on the **Finish** button.

   The wizard loads your data on to the disk in your floppy disk drive. Have several disks at the ready, just in case.

Basic Outlook functions

9

In this chapter, we will study the basic functions of Outlook, its main folders, what you can do with them, and so on.

Discovering Outlook 2000

With Outlook, you can exchange e-mail, share information with other Office applications, and manage a variety of information concerning your activities (appointments, meetings, clients, tasks, and so on).

When you first start Outlook, you may need to configure the installation of Outlook as well as the Internet connection. Follow the steps indicated by the wizard.

The Outlook bar

The Outlook bar, positioned to the left of the screen, allows you to navigate between the program folders (you will find a description of this later on). If this is not displayed, click on **View, Outlook bar**. To display the folder of your choice, click on its shortcut in the Outlook bar: it is displayed in the central window (Figure 9.1).

Figure 9.1 The Outlook bar.

Underneath the Outlook bar there are two buttons that allow access to other group bars. To open one of these groups, click on the corresponding button.

- **My Shortcuts** offers folders that help manage, organise and sort your e-mail messages.
- **Other Shortcuts** offer quick access to folders or files in another application.

Outlook Today

This folder lists today's activities and allows access to Messages folders (Figure 9.2). It is a reminder of your activities and daily work.

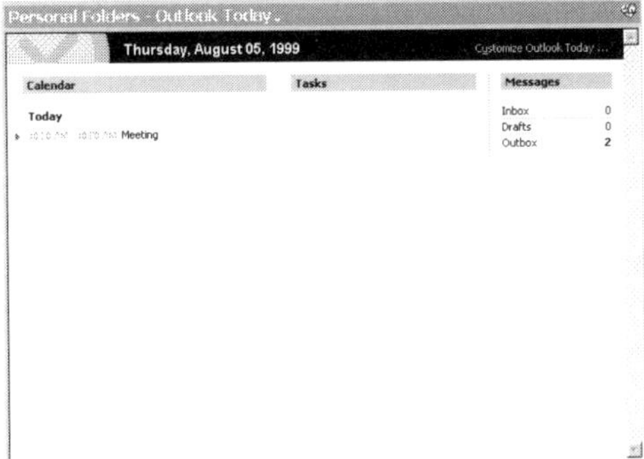

Figure 9.2 The Outlook Today folder.

Customizing Outlook Today

By default, the Outlook Today folder displays all the tasks to be carried out as well as the contents of your Inbox dialog box. You can customise options for this folder and ask, for example, for it to be displayed automatically when you open the program.

To customise Outlook Today:

1. In the Outlook Today folder, click on the **Customize Outlook Today** option.
2. In the customisation options (Figure 9.3), specify your choices. When you have finished, click on **Save Changes**.

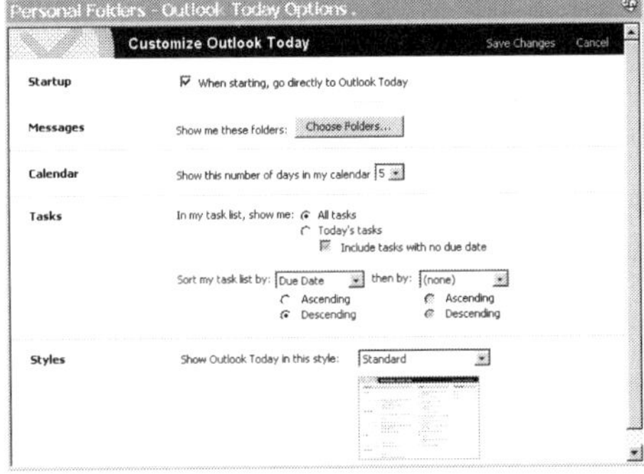

Figure 9.3 You can customize the Outlook Today folder.

Calendar

This folder plans your activities. It allows you to manage your time, note your appointments, plan your meetings, establish a list of your daily tasks, and so on. To display it, click on **Calendar** in the Outlook bar. Calendar offers three main items: Appointments, Dates and TaskPad (Figure 9.4).

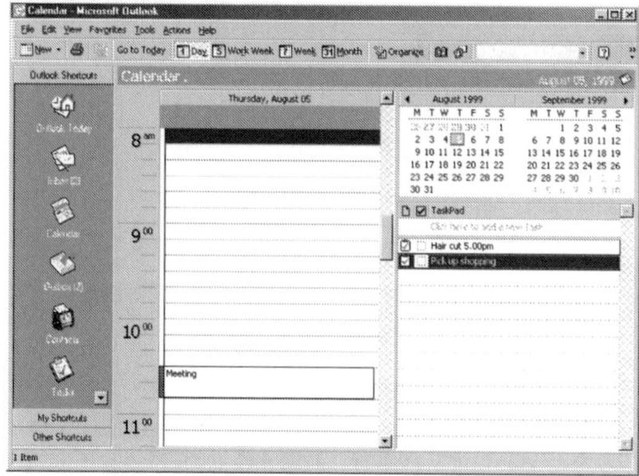

Figure 9.4 Outlook's Calendar folder.

Contacts

This is your address book. To display it, click on the **Contacts** icon in the Outlook bar (Figure 9.5).

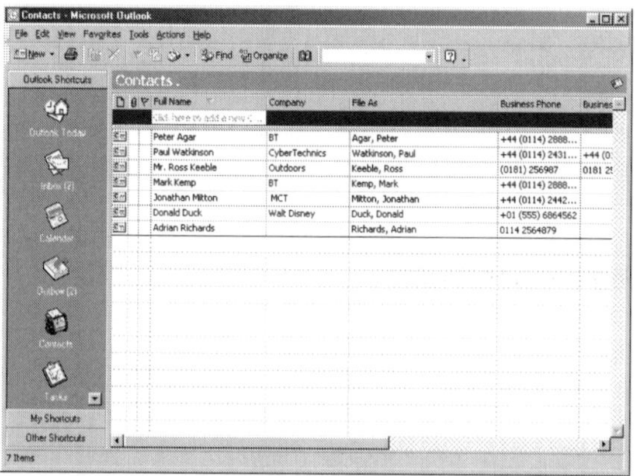

Figure 9.5 The Contacts folder.

The Contacts folder is your address book. It is available to all Office applications to send messages, make telephone calls, and so on.

If you have a modem, you can quickly dial a telephone number in this folder, send an e-mail message and even go to one of your correspondents' Web pages. To learn how to create or phone a contact, see Chapter 10.

Tasks

A task is a professional or personal mission you need to carry out to its completion (reports, investigations, and so on). The Tasks folder allows you to create various tasks, to follow their status, to assign them to another person, and so on. To display this folder, click on the **Tasks** icon in the Outlook bar (Figure 9.6).

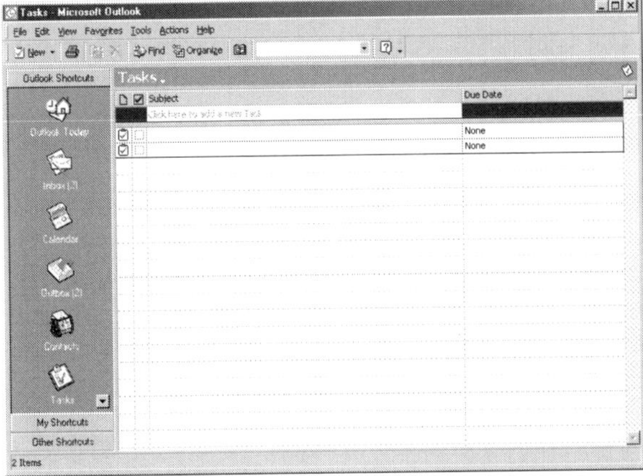

Figure 9.6 The Tasks folder.

Managing tasks

To create a task, click on the **Tasks** folder icon in the Outlook bar. Click on the **New** button in the Standard toolbar. If it is not already displayed, click on the **Task** tab (Figure 9.7). In the **Subject** box, type the subject or the definition of your task. In the **Due date** box, choose the date you wish to set as the deadline for your task, either by entering a date or by clicking on the appropriate date in the drop-down calendar. If you do not wish to set a deadline, click on the **None** check box. Give the start date in the **Start date** box. The **Status** option allows you to assign a holiday period during the implementation of the task. You can also indicate a priority level, a completion percentage, a reminder signal – with sound, if you want – defined by date and time, a category, and so on. Once you have defined your choices, click on the **Save and Close** button. The task you have created is displayed in the tasks list in the Tasks folder as well as in Calendar.

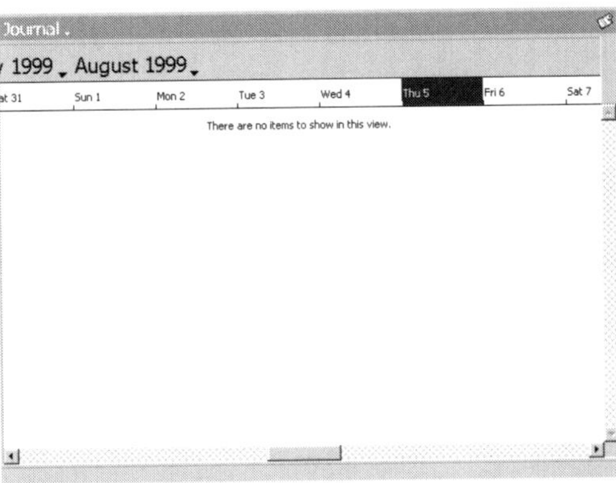

Figure 9.7 Creating a task.

When a task is completed, click on the check box in front of the completed task in the tasks list. A tick appears in the check box and Outlook crosses it out to indicate that it is complete. If you wish to delete it, select it, then click on the **Delete** button in the Standard toolbar.

Journal

This folder is your diary. You can record meetings with clients, and store items, messages, and so on. You can also create a journal entry without reference to an item. To display this folder, click on **Shortcuts** in the Outlook bar, then on **Journal** (Figure 9.8).

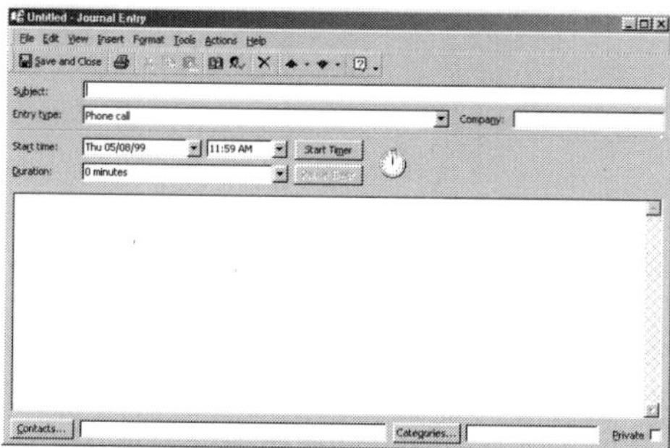

Figure 9.8 The Journal folder.

Creating journal entries

You can create two types of records or entries for your journal: automatic records and manual records.

To create a manual journal entry without links to any item:

1. Click on the **New** button in the Standard toolbar (Figure 9.9).

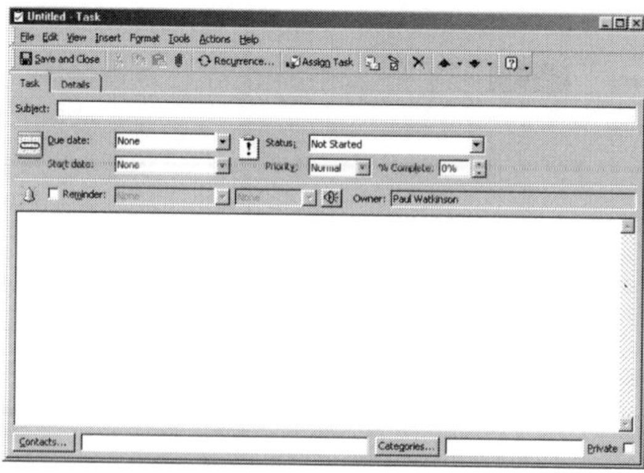

Figure 9.9 Creating a journal entry.

2. In the **Subject** box, type the wording for your entry. Click on the arrow of the **Entry type** option and select the type you want. In the **Company** box, type the name of the relevant company. In the **Start time** box, specify the required date. Click on the **Categories** button if you wish to indicate a category. Type your comments in the text box. Click on the **Save and Close** button when you have finished.

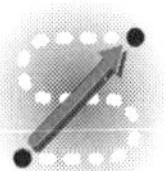

*To delete automatic recording of activities or contacts click **Tools, Options**, then **Journal Options**. Point to the entry to be deleted, then click on the right button. Select **Delete** in the context menu. Click on **OK** to confirm your deletion.*

In the Journal folder, click on the + icon next to the entry type of your choice to display the list of entries of this type.

To create a manual entry linked to an item:

1. Select the item (contact, task, message, and so on), click on **Tools, Save to journal**.
2. Carry out your modifications as required in the dialog box. Click on the **Save and Close** button.

To delete a journal entry, click on it in the list, then on the **Delete** button in the toolbar.

To create automatic journal entries:

1. In the Journal folder, click on **Tools, Options**.
2. In the dialog box, click on the **Journal Options** button. Tick the check boxes of the items you wish to record in the journal. Click on the contacts for which you wish to record elements. If you wish to record all the elements of an application, click on the check box in the **Also record files from** box. Click **OK**.

   All the activities will scroll in the programs, and the contacts or the tasks that you have selected will be recorded in the Journal folder.

Notes

Outlook offers an electronic version of Post-it notes. Use Notes to jot down ideas or reminders.

To create a note, click on **Notes** in the Outlook bar. Click on the **New** button, then type the text of the note (Figure 9.10). When you have finished, click on the **Close** button.

Figure 9.10 A note.

To customise a note, click on the note icon in the top left corner of the Note window, point to **Color**, then choose a colour.

To open a note, double-click on it. It will be displayed on top of all the other Desktop windows. If you change to another window, the note will go into the background. To find the note again, simply click on its button in the taskbar.

Inbox

The Inbox allows you to organise your e-mail and display received messages (Figure 9.11). This is the folder that is displayed by default when you start Outlook. It shows the list of messages you have received. To read a message, double-click on it in the list. You can learn more about this folder in Chapter 10.

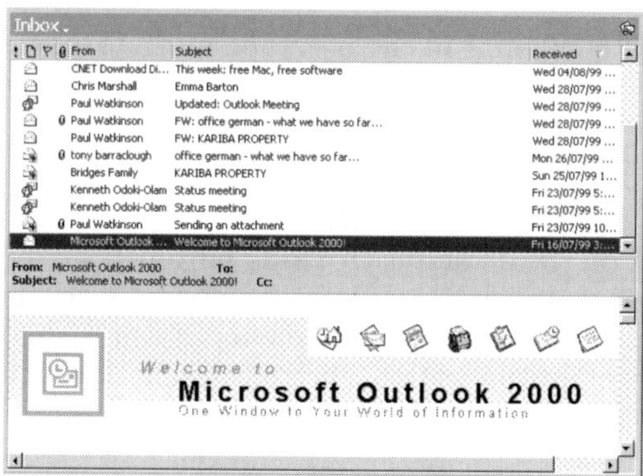

Figure 9.11 The Inbox displays your e-mail messages, both sent and received.

Creating contacts

In this folder, you can list all your contacts with their addresses, telephone numbers, e-mail addresses, and so on. You can use this record whenever you want to e-mail or telephone a contact.

To create a business card, click on the **New** button in the toolbar (Figure 9.12). Click on the **Contact** button, type the title, name and surname of the relevant person, then click on **OK**. Type in all the other required options. Once you have finished, click on the **Save and New** button to save your business card and open a new blank card, or the **Save and Close** button if you do not wish to enter another business card.

Once you have entered your business cards, they will appear in the Contacts folder in alphabetical order. When you want to access one, click on the first letter of the contact name in the **Alphabet** tab.

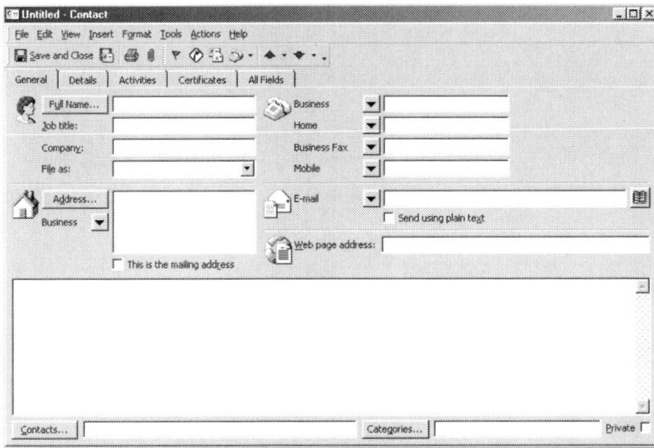

Figure 9.12 Creating a business card in the Contact dialog box.

To select a business card, click on it. To display all the information it contains, double-click on the card.

Making a telephone call from a business card

If you have a modem connected to your computer and your telephone line, and your telephone is connected to your modem, Outlook lets you make calls directly from your computer.

To make a telephone call, click on the business card of the person you wish to call, then click the **Dial** button in the Standard toolbar. Click on the number you wish to call. The **New Call** dialog box is displayed (Figure 9.13). Click on the **Start Call** button. Outlook dials the number and displays a dialog box that prompts you to lift the receiver. Click on the **Speak** button when you get through to your correspondent. Click on **End Call** when the conversation is over.

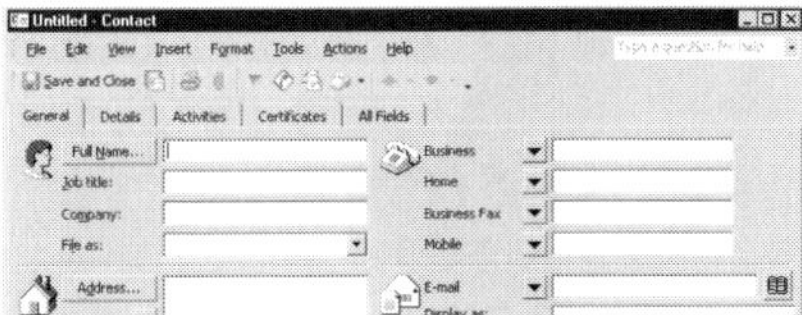

Figure 9.13 Making a telephone call through Outlook.

Sending e-mail messages

If your contact has an e-mail address, you can send a message from the Contacts folder.

To send an e-mail message, click on the person's business card, then on the **New Call** button in the Standard toolbar. A dialog box is displayed containing the address of the person you have selected. Type a title in the **Object** text box, type the complete message in the large message area positioned in the bottom part of the dialog box, then click on the **Send** button.

10

Advanced Outlook functions

Using Calendar

Sending and receiving e-mail messages

In this chapter, we will study the advanced functions of Outlook, such as creating appointments, organising meetings, sending messages, and so on.

Using Calendar

Outlook puts a calendar at your disposal to record your appointments, plan your meetings and organise your holidays. You can also use this function to remind you about meetings and appointments.

Before we look at the procedures you need to follow in order to record and plan your time, you should get to know the terminology used in Outlook:

- An *appointment* impacts on your working time but affects only your personal time.
- A *meeting* impacts on your working time but it also affects the time of people participating in the meeting.
- An *event* is an activity spanning a whole day but not affecting your own time. A yearly event is periodical.

Customise your working week on the basis of your various activities. For example, if you do not work on Wednesdays, or you play golf every Friday afternoon. Obviously, you are well aware of these portions of free time and do not need reminding of them, but if one of your colleagues wants to arrange a meeting, he or she might not know that you are not available on Fridays after 4 pm.

To customise your working week:

1. Click on **Tools**, **Options**.
2. Click on the **Calendar Options** button. Define your choices – work day, first day of week, start and end time (Figure 10.1).

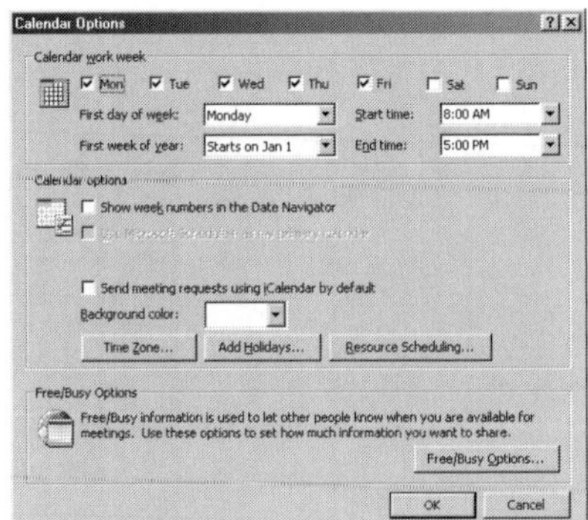

Figure 10.1 Customising your working week with the Calendar Options dialog box.

Views

Outlook allows you to modify the Calendar view: click on **View, Current View**. In the sub-menu, select a view.

By default, a single day is displayed in Calendar. If you wish to modify this setting, click on one of the buttons in the toolbar – Day, Work Week, and so on (Figure 10.2).

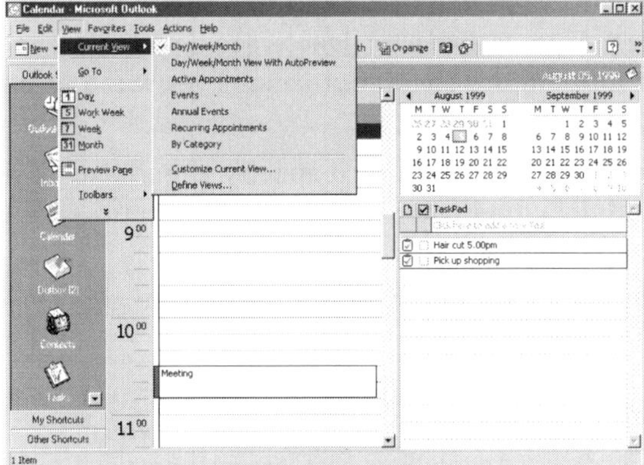

Figure 10.2 The main types of view

Recording an appointment

To record an appointment, you have a choice of two procedures: one is quick and simple, the other is slightly longer but more accurate.

To create an appointment quickly, click on the date you want on the dates panel. The selected date is displayed in the work time. Click on the required time box. Type a brief description of your appointments, then press **Enter** to confirm.

To create a more detailed appointment, click on the **New** button in the Standard toolbar. The Untitled – Appointment dialog box is displayed (Figure 10.3). If necessary, click on the **Appointment** tab. Specify the following options:

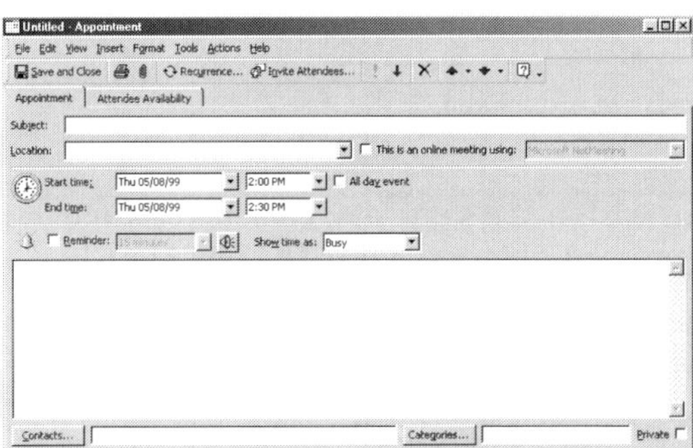

Figure 10.3 The Appointment dialog box.

- **Subject**. Allows you to enter a description of the appointment.
- **Location**. Allows you to specify the appointment address.
- **Start time**. Opens a drop-down list of dates and times. If the appointment is likely to last for the whole day, tick the **All day event** check box.
- **End time**. Opens a drop-down list that allows you to specify the estimated end date and time for the appointments.
- **Reminder**. Allows you to activate or deactivate a sound signal and to specify how long before the appointment you wish to be reminded.
- **Attendee Availability**. Allows you to specify the status of a time block. For example, when you are on a training course, you will mark such a day with the 'Out of Office' option.
- **Text box**. Allows you to enter additional information concerning the appointment.

Once you have finished specifying options, click on the **Save and Close** button. Your appointment will be displayed in your work time window (Figure 10.4). According to the options you have chosen, a number of symbols are displayed to allow you to see the appointments options at a glance.

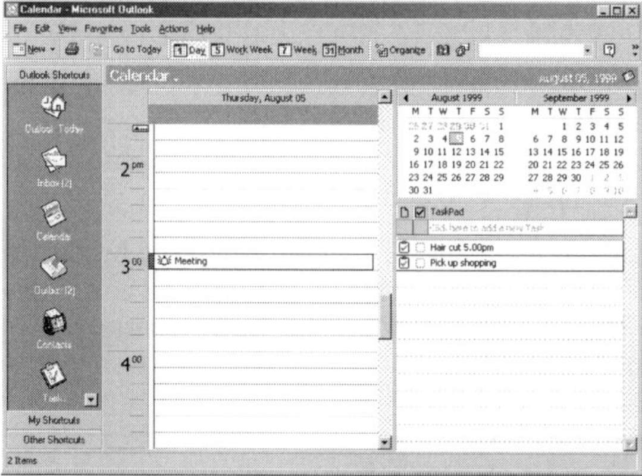

Figure 10.4 The new appointment is displayed.

To move an appointment within the same day, click on its time box with the mouse button pressed, then drag into the new time box.

To delete an appointment, click with the right mouse button on the appointment time box, then select **Clear**.

To change the length of an appointment, drag the upper or lower border of the appointment time box.

Regular appointments

If an appointment occurs on a regular basis, you can enter the appointment once only, specifying that it is regular.

To create a regular appointment:

1. Double-click on the regular appointment time box or click on the **New** button. Click on the **Recurrence** button in the dialog box toolbar (Figure 10.5).

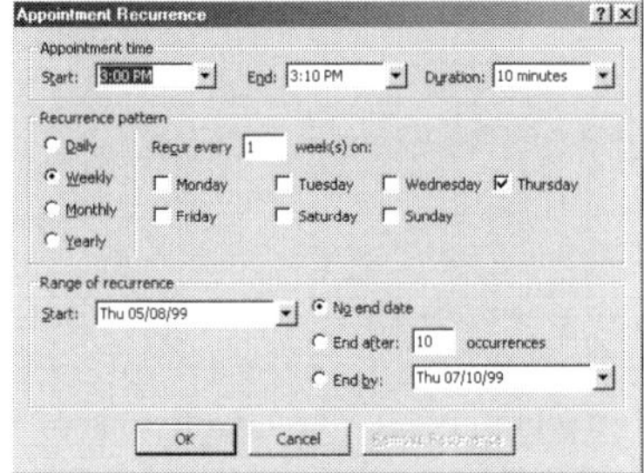

Figure 10.5 The Appointment Recurrence dialog box.

2. Specify the recurrence pattern, duration, range of recurrence, and so on. Click on **OK** to confirm your choice in the Recurrence dialog box. Click on the **Save and Close** button in the **Appointment** dialog box.

Planning a meeting

When you are planning your next business meeting, you no longer need to make all those telephone calls to find out which days people are available. Outlook puts the Appointment Manager at your disposal, allowing you to specify the time range that is likely to suit everybody. Note that this can work only if all your colleagues also use Outlook, and their work time schedules are correct and up to date.

To organise a meeting:

1. Click on **New, New Appointment**. Provide all the specifications for the meeting (date, time, and so on). Click on the **Attendee Availability** tab, then on the **Invite others** button. The **Select Attendees and Resources** dialog box is displayed: this lists the various contacts created in the address book (Figure 10.6).
2. If required, click on the arrow of the **Name** drop-down list, then click on the address book you wish to use to choose the names of the participants: **Contacts, Outlook Address book** or **Personal Address book**. To invite somebody to the meeting, click on their name in the list, then on one of the buttons on the right (**Required, Optional** and **Resources**). Click on **OK** when all the participants have been included.

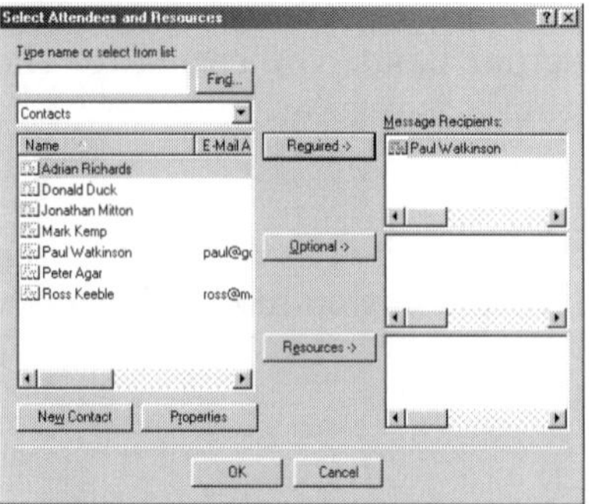

Figure 10.6 Selecting participants in the Select Attendees and Resources dialog box.

3. To check the availability of each participant, click on their name, then use the scroll bar in the planning area to select a time when everybody is available (Figure 10.7). Alternatively, click on the **AutoPick** button to show the next available time block suitable to all participants. When you have found a time that suits everybody, drag the vertical bars that mark the start and the end of the meeting. Click with the right mouse button on the icon in front of each participant and select **Send meeting to this attendee**. Click on **Send** and close the dialog box.

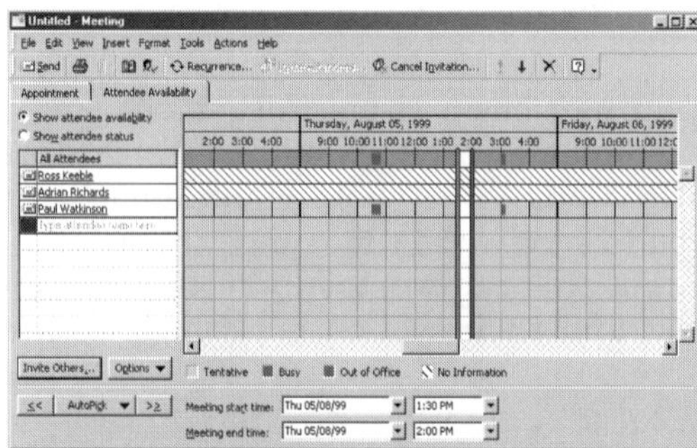

Figure 10.7 Verifying the availability of participants at your meeting.

Outlook sends the invitation to all listed people. Their replies will arrive in your Inbox folder.

Recording an event

Events allows you to remember important dates.

To record an event, click on **Actions, New All Day event** (Figure 10.8). Specify the event subject. Type the event place in the **Location** option. Click on the arrow of the **Start time** option, then select a date. Click on the arrow of the **End time** option, then select the date. If necessary, tick the **All day event** option. If you want to, tick the **Reminder** check box, then click on the arrow and select how long before the event you wish Outlook to send out the sound signal. You can also specify your availability, put down some comments, and select a category. Once you have finished, click on the **Save and Close** button.

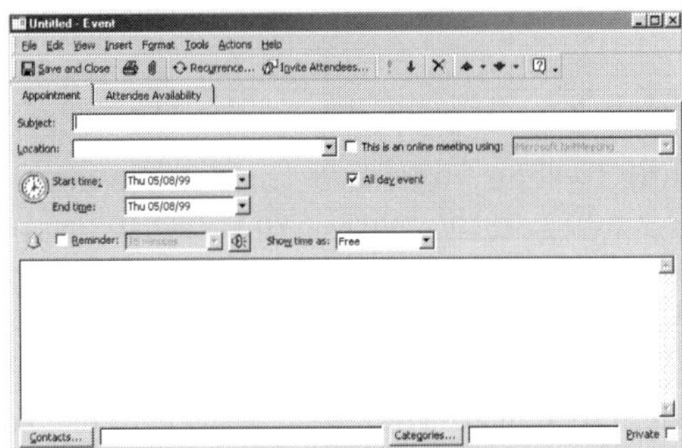

Figure 10.8 Creating an event is quick and easy.

The event is displayed, greyed out, in the work time of the relevant day.

To delete an event, click on it in the work time, then click on the **Clear** button in the Standard toolbar.

Sending and receiving e-mail messages

When you start Outlook for the first time, the Inbox contains a welcome message from Microsoft. Afterwards, all messages will be displayed in this folder. The Inbox folder is displayed by default when you start Outlook.

To modify an event, double-click on the event in the work time. Carry out your modifications in the dialog box, then click on the ***Save and Close*** *button.*

To have better control of your messages, check the markers displayed as column headers at the top of the receive area (Figure 10.9):

Figure 10.9 The Inbox displays all the e-mail messages you have received.

- **Importance**. The presence of this icon indicates that the sender has given the message priority.
- **Icon**. Shows a sealed envelope. When you double-click on a message to read it, the envelope opens.
- **Flag status**. Displays a flag if you have chosen to mark the message to read it again later or to reply to it.

- **Attachment**. Specifies that the sender has attached a file to the message. You can either view the attached file, or you can save it on disk.
- **From**. Displays the sender's name.
- **Subject**. Displays a brief description of the contents of the message.
- **Received**. Displays the date and time the message was received.

To read a message, double-click on it in the list.

To sort messages according to their subject or their importance, click on the header corresponding to the marker you wish to use to sort your messages. For example, if you wish to sort your messages by importance, click on **Importance**.

If you wish the markers to be displayed in a different order, click on the header to be moved, then drag it to where you want it to be. To delete one of the headers, click on it, then drag it outside the bar.

The **My Shortcuts** button at the bottom of the Outlook bar offers other e-mail folders. This group allows you to sort sent messages, messages to be sent later, and deleted items.

E-mail configuration

For Outlook to display your mail, you must tell it which e-mail service you are working with.

Once you have installed the directory service program, add it to the list of services that Outlook can use:

1. Click on **Tools, Accounts**: the directory services that Outlook can currently use are listed.
2. Click on the **Add** button, then on the name of the service in the list, and then on **OK**.
3. The wizard may ask for additional information depending on the directory service you wish to install. For example, it may ask for your name and fax number, or to select the fax/modem you are going to use. When you have finished, click on **OK**.

Now, you can use Outlook to manage your messages.

Sending messages

To create a message, click on the **New** button in the Standard toolbar (Figure 10.10). In the **To** text box, type the e-mail address of the person to whom you are sending the message. If you have this stored in the Contacts folder, you do not need to type it all over again. Simply click on the **To** button, then select the name of the person from the list in the dialog box. If you wish to send a copy of this message to another person, click on the **Cc** button, then select the person to whom you wish to send the copy from the list or type their e-mail address in the text box. When you want to enter several addresses, separate them with a semi-colon (;).

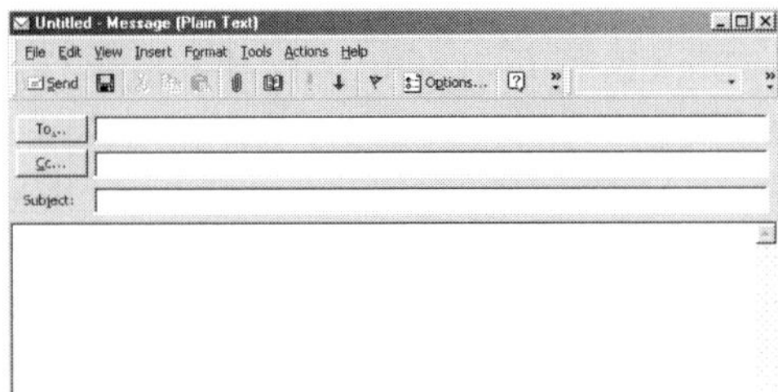

Figure 10.10 Creating an e-mail message.

Once you have filled the addressee boxes, fill in the **Subject** box. Then, in the bottom part of the window, type your message. If you are sending only text, click on the **Send** button. If you wish to attach a file to your message or indicate an option in terms of importance, choose one of the following procedures:

- To format the text, drag your pointer on to the relevant text, then choose font, size and attributes in the toolbar.
- To attach a file to your message, click on the **Insert File** button, then select the file you wish to attach.
- To flag the message, click on the **Flag for Follow Up** button. In the dialog box, specify the options (**Flag to, Clear Flag, Due by,** and so on).
- To indicate the degree of importance for the message, click on the **Importance: High** or **Importance: Low** buttons.
- The **Options** button offers other choices to create buttons for tracking, accepting and refusing messages (Figure 10.11).

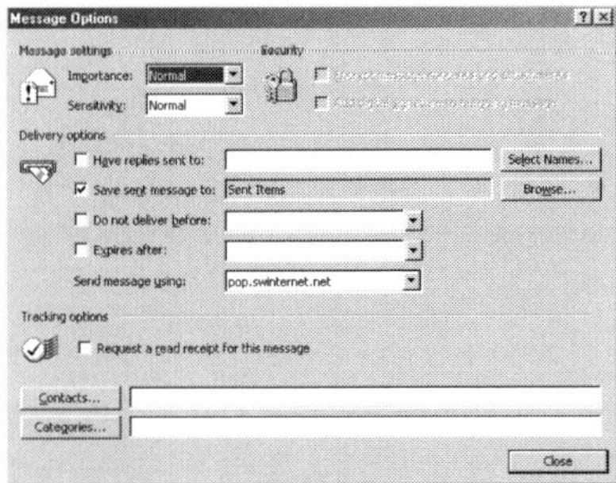

Figure 10.11 E-mail message options.

Receiving messages

When you are working in Outlook and you want to know whether you have received any new messages, click on **Tools, Check New Mail** or press **F5**. Outlook then connects to the installed server, retrieves your messages, and displays them in your Inbox.

To read your message, double-click on it. Outlook displays the message in the window. This window offers various buttons:

- **Reply**. Allows you to send a reply message to the sender. Click on this button to open a message window with the sender's address (the person who has sent you the original message to which you are now replying). The text of the original message is also displayed in the text box. You can clear it or keep it. Type your reply, then click on the **Send** button.
- **Reply All**. Allows you to send a reply to all the people on the **To** or **Cc** lists.
- **Transfer**. Allows you to send the message directly to another person.
- **Back** or **Next**. Allows you to scroll through all your messages.

Basic Publisher functions

11

Discovering Publisher

Creating a publication

Managing pages

Moving within a publication

Views

Frames

Entering text

Page background

In this chapter, we will study the basic functions of Publisher, including frames, views and inserting text.

Discovering Publisher

To start Publisher, click on **Start, Programs, Microsoft Publisher**.

The Catalog dialog box

When Publisher starts, the Catalog dialog box is displayed (Figure 11.1). This allows you to choose a wizard, open an existing publication or choose a style. You need to know that:

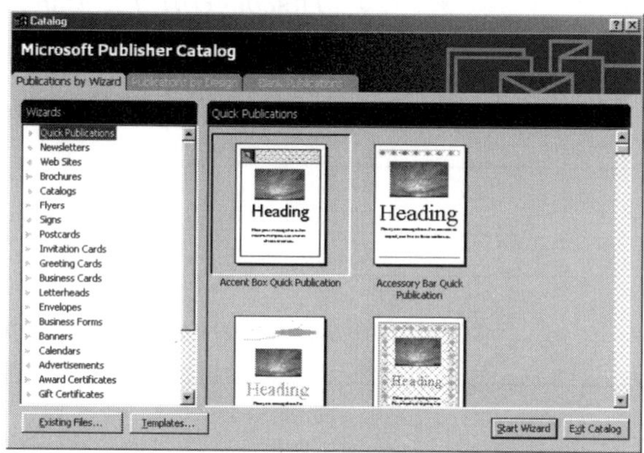

Figure 11.1 The Catalog dialog box allows you to choose a wizard, open an existing publication or choose a style.

- The **Publications by Wizard** tab allows you to use a wizard that will guide you through the creation process.
- The **Publications by Design** tab allows you to preview different publications created with a variety of designs, such as geometrical shapes, a series of pictures, and so on.
- The **Blank Publications** tab allows you to choose a preset type of publication according to its use (Web page, postcard, etc.).
- The **Existing Files** button allows you to open an already created publication.
- The **Templates** button allows you to select an Office template to create the publication.

*To display the Catalog dialog box, click on **File, New**.*

To open an existing publication in the Catalog dialog box, click on the **Existing Files** button (Figure 11.2), then double-click on the publication to be opened.

Assistance

Publisher offers a number of wizards, templates and styles to speed up the publication process.

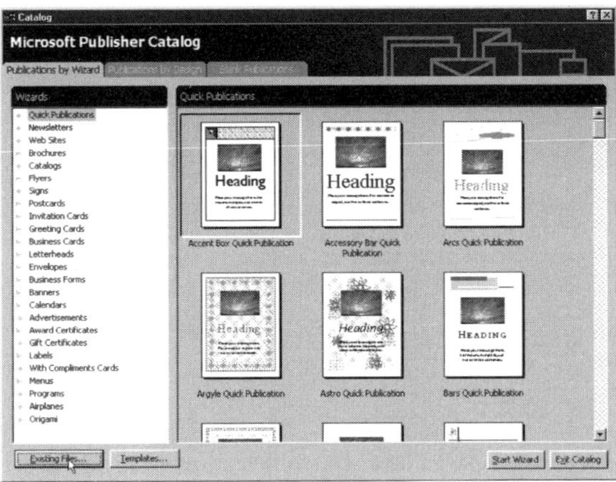

Figure 11.2 Opening an existing file.

Creating a publication

The Catalog dialog box is the central point for managing publications. From here, you can open a blank publication:

1. In the Catalog dialog box, click on the **Blank Publications** tab (Figure 11.3). Click on the category in the left pane, then on the type in the right pane.
2. Click on the **Create** button.

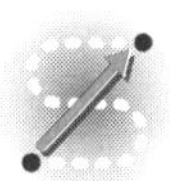

Use wizards or templates when you need to create an effective, attractive and well-structured publication quickly.

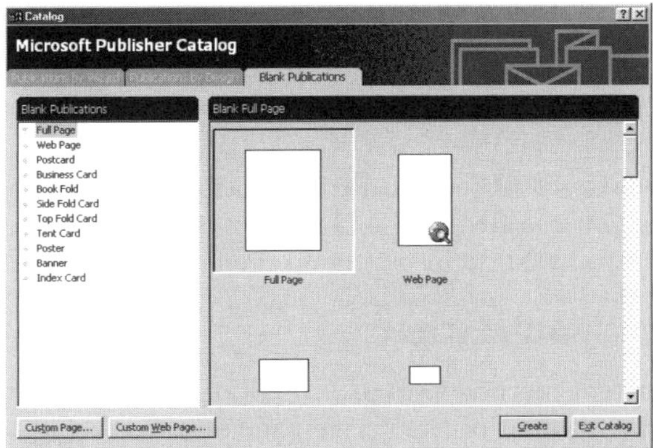

Figure 11.3 Choosing the style of a new publication in the Blank Publications tab.

To choose a new publication, you can either click on its textual description in the left pane or on its graphic description in the right pane.

Managing pages

By default, a blank publication contains a single page in the chosen format. You can add, delete, move or copy pages in a publication.

Inserting pages

To insert pages:

1. Click on **Insert, Page** (Figure 11.4).

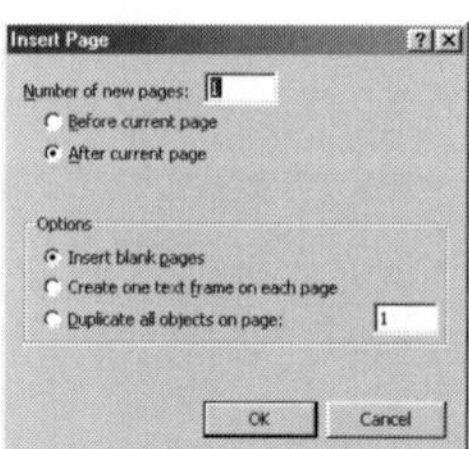

Figure 11.4 You can quickly insert pages into your publication with the Insert Page dialog box.

2. Specify the number of pages you want to insert in the **Number of new pages** box. Then specify where you wish to insert the new pages (before or after the existing page). Click on **OK**.

   The new publication is displayed, with page numbers, in the Status bar.

Deleting pages

To delete a blank page, simply click on **Edit, Delete Page**. Confirm the deletion by clicking on **OK**.

Copying pages

If you wish to create several similar pages, it is simpler just to copy your page:

1. Position the cursor on the page to be duplicated. Click on **Insert, Page**.
2. Select the **Duplicate all objects on page** option. Specify the number of copies you require in the **Number of new pages** box. Specify where you wish to insert them, then click on **OK**.

Moving within a publication

The simplest and fastest method is to use the Status bar (Figure 11.5). In this bar, the number of the active page on the screen is displayed in the Page box. To move between pages, click on the symbol of the page to be displayed.

To move within the page, use the scroll bar; drag the bar in the direction you wish to move.

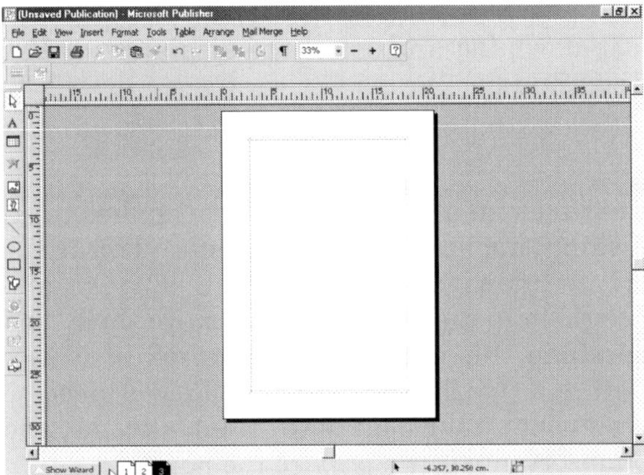

Figure 11.5 The Status bar allows you to move quickly from one page to another.

Views

There are many view options in Publisher. The Page view corresponds to the way you will view the page on screen and, eventually, display certain special characters. The default page view in a publication is a single page with a 33% zoom.

When you create a publication that contains several pages, you can choose to display two pages next to each other. Click on **View, Two-Page Spread** (Figure 11.6). To navigate between two pages in the double-page spread, simply click on the page in which you wish to work. To go back to single-page view, click on **View, Two-Page Spread** to deactivate it.

*The **Whole Page** option in the Zoom command displays the whole of the page on screen with a 33% zoom.*

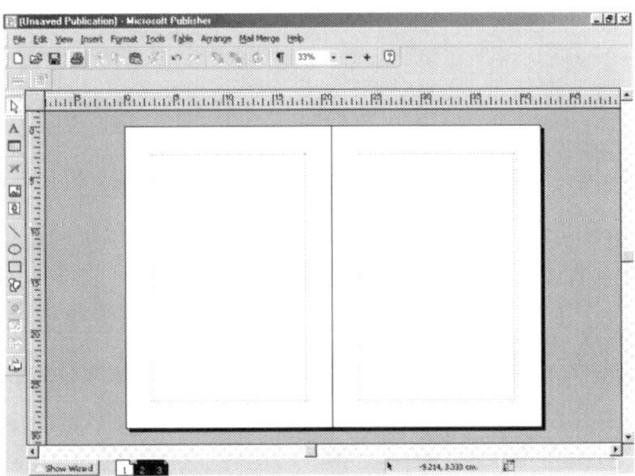

Figure 11.6 You can also view pages as spreads.

To modify the size of a page view, click on the arrow in the Zoom pop-down list and select the display view. You can also click on **View**, **Zoom**.

Frames

In Publisher, you create elements in frames. This applies to all DTP (desktop publishing) applications. Why frames? This is the most practical way to manage elements such as text and pictures, and to place them in the right position, move them, and edit them. To understand this concept better, think of it as a puzzle. When you start a puzzle, you know what you need to achieve as the final outcome. Your page is the final outcome, and every frame that you insert into it is a piece of the puzzle.

Inserting a frame

Each element is inserted from a task-specific frame (text frame, image frame, and so on). To insert a frame:

1. Click on the **Frame Tool** icon on the Objects toolbar.
2. Click on the page, then drag diagonally to draw a frame (Figure 11.7).

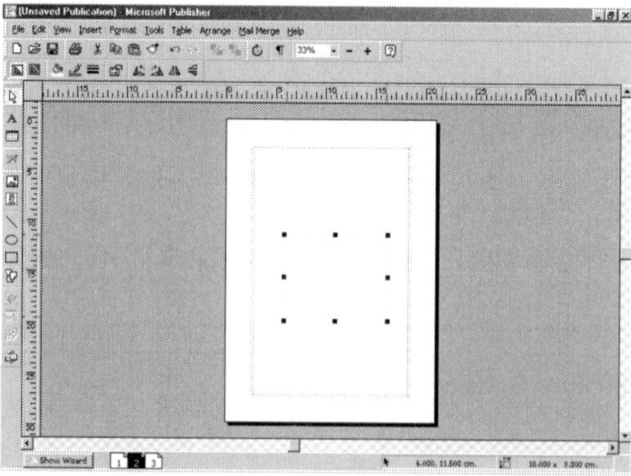

Figure 11.7 Inserting a text frame.

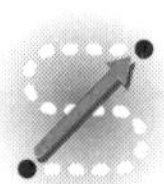

*If, when you click on the page, you do not create a text frame, click on **Tools, Options**. In the **Edit** tab, click on the **Use single-click object creation** option. Click on **OK**.*

To do this even faster, select the Frame tool, then double-click anywhere on the page: the frame is automatically inserted.

Selecting and working on a frame

To be able to work on the text frames you have inserted, you must select them. To select a frame, simply click on it. The frame becomes surrounded by small black squares, known as 'selection handles'. To resize the object, position the mouse pointer over a selection handle and drag. To move the object, drag the border between two selection handles.

According to the handle you are using, you will see an icon with a textual description that indicates the action you can execute. Table 11.1 lists the pointer symbols and their uses.

Table 11.1 Description of pointer symbols

Pointer	Action
MOVE	Moves the selection.
RESIZE	Widens or reduces the selection to the right.
RESIZE	Widens or reduces the selection to the left.
RESIZE	Widens or reduces the selection from top to bottom.
RESIZE	Widens or reduces the selection from the left to the right.
CROP	Clears the selection.

To deselect a frame, simply click outside it.

To delete a frame with nothing inserted, click in the frame to select it, then press the delete key.

To delete a frame that contains an element (text or image), click in the frame to select it, then click on **Edit, Delete Object**.

To resize the frame, position the mouse pointer over a selection handle and drag until you reach the required size. To move the object, drag the border between two selection handles.

Before moving a frame, you must select it. Point to one of the frame borders (but without putting the pointer on a selection handle). The pointer becomes a little cross and displays an icon representing a small van with MOVE written on it. Click on the icon, then drag it to where you want to position the text frame.

To resize a frame retaining its original proportions, press the ***Shift*** *key and keep it pressed while you drag one of the corner handles. Release the* ***Shift*** *key when you have finished resizing the frame.*

Connecting frames

If the text does not fit in the frame, you can widen the frame to make the whole text visible, or create a second frame and then connect the two. In this way, the overflow text will spill automatically into the connected frame.

To connect frames:

1. If the text in a frame is too long, you will see the **Text in Overflow** icon (Figure 11.8). Select the frame and click on **Tools, Connect Text Frames**.

*To unconnect two connected frames, click on the first frame of the connection, then on the **Disconnect Text Frames** icon in the Standard toolbar.*

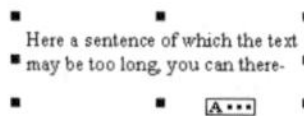

Figure 11.8 Text surrounded by the frame.

2. Click on the **Connect Text Frames** button in the Standard toolbar. The mouse pointer changes to a jug.
3. Click in the text frame in which you want your text to continue (Figure 11.9). The text now flows into the second frame.

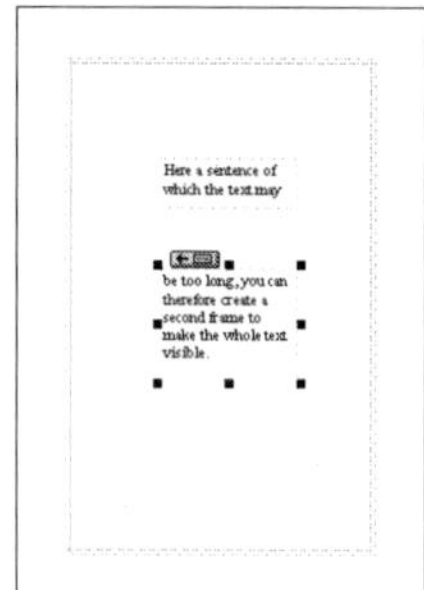

Figure 11.9 Linking text frames allows the text to flow from one frame to another.

Entering text

To enter text, first select the frame that will contain it. The selection activates a flashing cursor, which shows the insertion point for your text. Now type your text.

All text editing, moving and copying functions are exactly as in Word (refer to Chapter 3).

Importing text

You can also insert text that has been saved in another application. Publisher can import several text file types, such as Microsoft Windows Word (2.1, 6.0, 7.0 and 8.0), text only and RTF.

To import text into your publication:

1. Create the text frame, then click on **Insert, Text File**.
2. Select the type of text to be inserted in the **Files of type** box, then display the folder that contains the file you want. Double-click on the file and insert.

Text formatting

Character formatting can be done either before or after entry:

- **Before entry**. Select attributes, styles and options required, then type your text.
- **After entry**. Select the text to be formatted, then choose attributes, styles and options to be applied.

Formatting tools

Publisher offers two tools to format characters: the Format toolbar and the Font formatting command. These tools are exactly the same as those used in Word (see Chapter 3). Here we will look at formatting specific to Publisher.

Scaling means to space characters within the same word. To modify scaling for a word or a text:

1. Click on **Format, Character Spacing** (Figure 11.10).

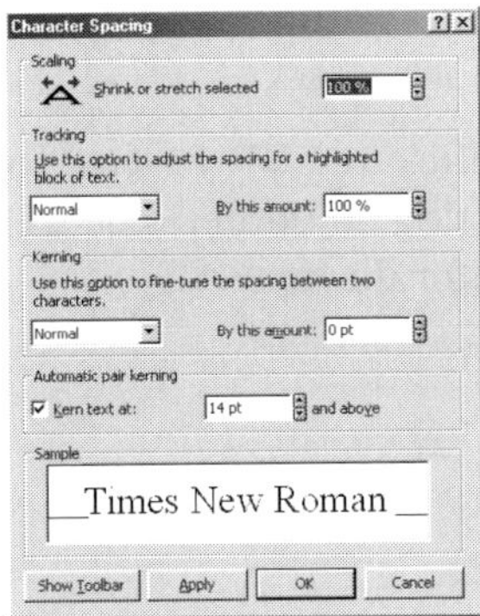

Figure 11.10 Defining the tracking and kerning of text.

2. The **Tracking** area allows you to adjust the spacing in a highlighted block of text. The **Kerning** area allows you to fine tune the spacing between two characters (Expand, Condense or Normal). Define the formatting to be applied. Click on **OK**.

You can create an interesting visual effect by rotating text. Once you have selected your text, use the **Rotation left** icon to rotate it by 45° to the left, or the **Rotation right** icon to rotate it by 45° to the right.

To execute a precise rotation:

1. Select the text, then click on the **Custom Rotate** icon in the Standard toolbar (Figure 11.11).
2. Click on the appropriate rotation button (left or right) to rotate 5° with each click, or type the required rotation value in the **Angle** box. Click on **Apply**, then on **Close**.

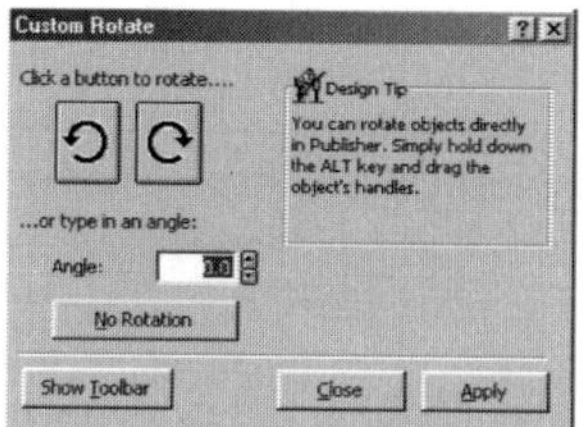

Figure 11.11 Rotating your text.

Page background

To avoid displaying the defined background in one of the publication pages, go to the relevant page and click on ***View, Ignore Background****.*

To understand the background concept, imagine that each page in your publication has two layers: the first layer or level contains the items that make up the page (text frames, image frames, objects, and so on); the second layer – the background – contains all the items required for the whole of the publication (page number, headers, footers, fill colour, and so on).

To display the background of a page, click on **View, Go to Background**: the page you have been working on becomes blank, the Status bar changes and the page navigator disappears.

The Background view allows you to position:

- a rule, frame or line
- a name, reference or logo
- a drawing as a watermark
- a page number
- a header and footer
- a date.

When you insert items into the background, apply ***Fill Color*** *if your background is in colour, otherwise the inserted frame will look empty and will not be displayed in your publication.*

Do not forget that all the insertions executed in the background will appear on all the pages in the active publication. However, you may choose to exclude some background items from certain pages.

To display a coloured background:

1. Click on **Text Frame Tool** in the Object toolbar. Draw a frame all around your page.
2. Once you have selected the background, click on the **Fill Color** icon in the Format toolbar. Select the required colour.

Page numbering, header, footer and date

If you create a single-page publication, you will not need to bother with page numbering. However, publications usually contain several pages, so you will need to know how to paginate them. In order to insert page numbers, you must create a text frame in the background.

To create a text frame in the background, click on **Text Frame Tool**, then insert the frame.

To insert page numbers in a document, click on the text frame that will contain the numbers, then click on **Insert, Page Numbers**. This command inserts only the numbers; you can also enter the word 'Page' before them if you want (Figure 11.12).

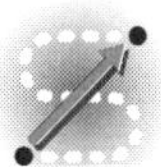

To delete page numbers, click on the frame to select it, then press the delete key.

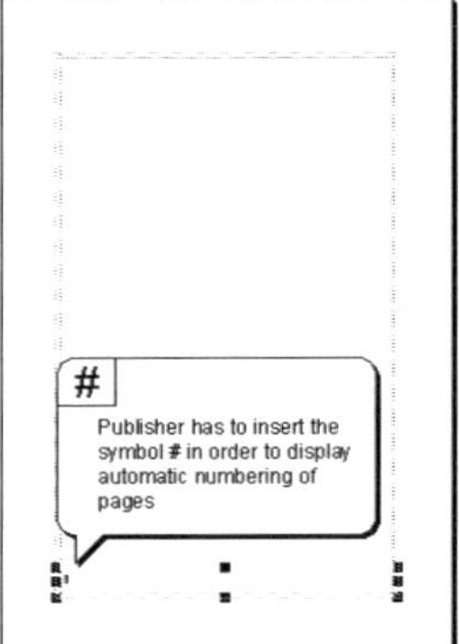

Figure 11.12 Inserting page numbers into your publication.

To create a footer, follow the same procedures as for a header. The only difference is that you place the text frame at the bottom of the background.

Inserting a header and a footer into the background is as simple as inserting a text frame into a page.

To create a header in a background:

1. Create a text frame at the top of the background.
2. Type your text.
3. Apply the various formats (colour, size, font, and so on).

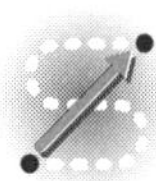

To delete a header in the background, click on the frame to select it, then press the delete key. Follow the same procedure to delete a footer.

To insert a date into a background:

1. Create a text frame at the top or bottom of the background.
2. Click on **Insert, Date and Time**.
3. Select the format in the list.
4. Click on **OK**.

   The system date is inserted into your publication.

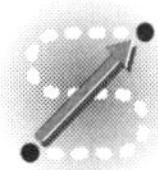

To delete a date in the background, click on the frame to select it, then press the delete key.

Advanced Publisher functions

12

Tables

Text in columns

Mailshots

Pictures

Pictures and text

Design gallery

Drawing

Formatting objects

Managing shapes and frames

In this chapter, we will look at advanced Publisher functions, including inserting tables, creating text in columns, and mailshots.

Tables

A table allows you to set a defined structure for data. Information is often much clearer when presented in a table. In Publisher, the use of tables allows better control when positioning items on the page. The basic building block for a table is the *cell*. A cell is a grid unit that may contain any type of data: text, image, and so on.

Tables have a number of properties that can be defined, including numbers of rows and columns, border thickness and colour, and background colour and texture.

The default choice proposed in the Table format list corresponds to a predefined format, rather than a blank table.

Creating a table

Publisher allows you to create a table with no predefined format.

To do this:

1. Click on the **Table Frame Tool** icon in the Objects toolbar. Click on the page you are working on, then drag to draw a table.

   The Create Table dialog box will be displayed (Figure 12.1).

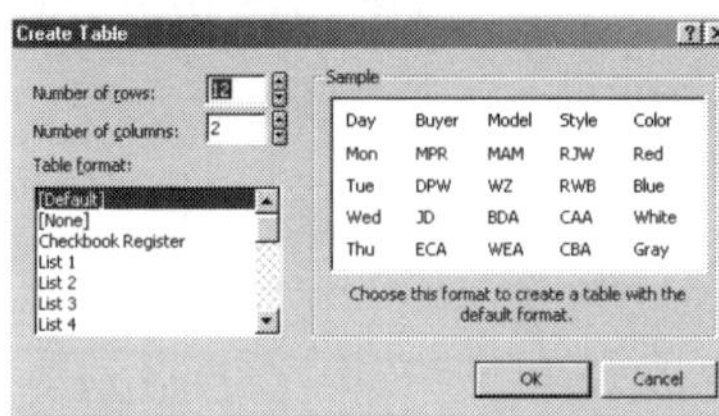

Figure 12.1 The Create Table dialog box lets you choose the number of columns and rows.

*To delete a table, select it, then click on **Edit, Delete Object**.*

2. Specify the options (number of rows, number of columns, and so on), then click on **OK**.

To enter text into a table or navigate within it, refer to the procedures shown in Word (see Chapters 3 and 4).

Text in columns

You can create text frames containing text and distribute them into columns using tabulations. However, this procedure is somewhat risky, because when you need to edit or insert new text, tabulations will move and this will spell disaster! The easiest way is to create columns.

To create columns, set up a text frame, then click on **Format, Text Frame Properties** (Figure 12.2). In the Columns area, specify the number of columns and the spacing between columns. Click on **OK**.

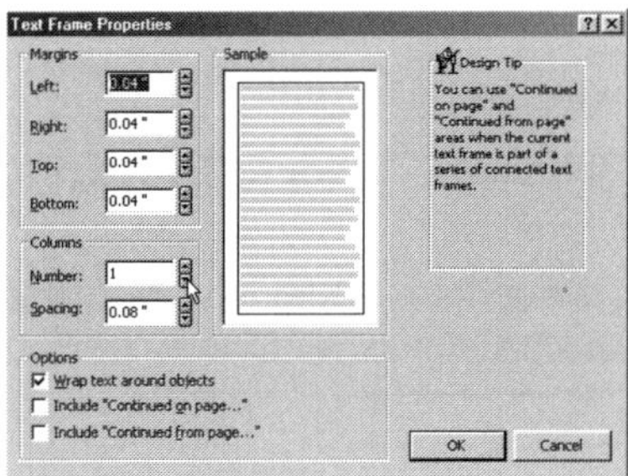

Figure 12.2 Define the number of columns.

To modify the column, use the **Tab** key.

Mailshots

When you execute a mail merge, you must create two types of document:

- **Main document**. A general frame that contains text or the custom publication. This text is common to all addressees, but with reserved places for custom formulas such as name, address, and so on.
- **Database**. Contains all the personal data for your addressees. This document is also known as the *data source*. It is like a table.

Once these two elements have been created, you can start merging and printing the publication. The merge consists of linking these documents by inserting the database fields into the main document for each addressee. The various procedures to execute a mail merge are the same as in Word (see Chapter 4).

Pictures

There are several methods for inserting a picture into a publication (vector image, .bmp image, card, chart, and so on). Just as for text, you must first insert a frame. The picture frame concept is the same as the text frame concept.

ClipArt

The first possibility is to insert a picture from ClipArt. The ClipArt library is much more extensive in the 2000 version, having acquired hundreds of additional pictures. Following the same principle as a book library, pictures are arranged by category. Simply choose the picture you wish to insert into your publication.

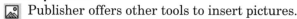

Found in the Object toolbar, this icon allows you to insert a ClipArt picture. Follow the standard procedures for inserting a frame, then select the picture and drag it into the frame.

Other pictures

Publisher offers other tools to insert pictures.

To insert a picture that you have saved in one of your files:

1. Create a picture frame, then click on **Insert, Pictures, From File**.
2. In the Insert Picture dialog box, select the folder you require. Double-click on the file that contains the picture.

Selecting and deleting pictures

To select a picture, simply click on it.

To select several pictures, select the first one, press the **Ctrl** key, then click on the second picture while keeping the key depressed, and so on. This command also allows you to move or copy the set of pictures easily.

To delete a picture, the simplest procedure is to select it, then press the delete key. You can also right-click on the picture, then select **Delete Object**.

Moving and copying pictures

To move a picture within the same page, the procedure is the same as for a text frame:

1. Click on the picture to select it.
2. Point to the picture frame.
3. When the pointer changes to a cross with a little van, drag the van to where you wish to place the picture.

If you wish to move a picture to another page in the publication, select the picture, then drag it to the greyed part outside the page. Display the page in which you wish to insert the picture. The picture is still in the greyed part; now simply place it in the new page.

To copy and paste a picture:

1. Select the picture, then click on **Edit, Copy**.
2. Position the cursor where you want to copy the picture.
3. Click on **Edit, Paste**.

Editing pictures

The options for editing pictures are the same as in PowerPoint (see Chapter 7). Below are the editing procedures specific to Publisher.

To hide images, click on **View, Picture Display**. Select the **Hide pictures** option, then click on **OK** (Figure 12.3).

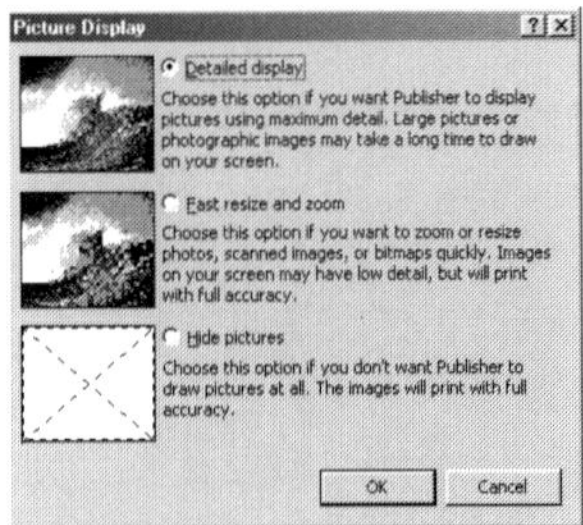

Figure 12.3 Hiding images.

To show the pictures again:

1. Click on **View, Picture Display**.
2. Select the option corresponding to your choice (**Detailed display** or **Fast resize and zoom**). Click on **OK**.

If the picture is too large, but you want to keep the same proportions, just crop a bit out:

1. Select the picture, then click on the **Crop Picture** icon (Figure 12.4).

Figure 12.4 Crop the picture to suit your needs.

*To view the picture as enlarged, click on it, then click with the right mouse button and select **Selected Objects**.*

2. Adjust the various selection handles until the picture shows only the items you need.

You can even apply a different colour to a picture:

1. Select the picture, then click on **Format, Color picture** (Figure 12.5).
2. Select the colour for the item you wish to edit.
3. Click on **Apply and Close**.

Figure 12.5 Changing the colour of a picture.

Pictures and text

When you create a publication, you may wish to insert pictures into the text. Depending on the type of hyphenation you have chosen, the text will either be arranged automatically around the picture, or you will have to fit the picture to the text.

To control text and picture, click on the **Picture Frame Properties** button in the Picture toolbar (Figure 12.6). Specify your choices, then click on **OK**.

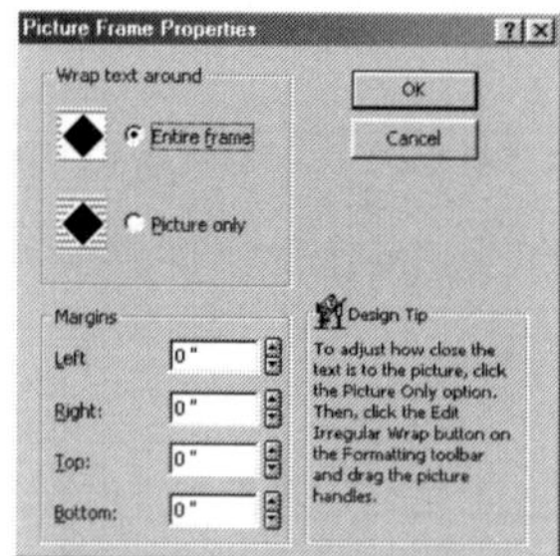

Figure 12.6 The image can be modified to affect the text.

Design gallery

The design gallery contains a number of objects created by Publisher, which you can use for your publication. To open the design gallery, click on the **Design Gallery Object** icon in the Objects bar (Figure 12.7).

There are three tabs:

- **Objects by Category** and **Objects by Design** display a number of objects on which you simply double-click to insert them into your publication. The left pane displays a list of objects sorted by type, and the right pane displays the objects of the selected type.

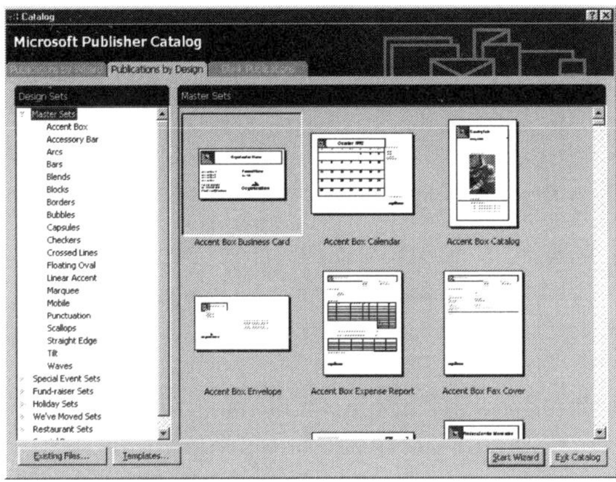

Figure 12.7 Design Gallery.

- **Your Objects** allows you to keep the design elements to create a set of designs for the current publication. When you add objects, they are displayed in this tab and are then available for your publication.

Drawing

Publisher allows you to draw in the design page. It also gives you a number of geometrical shapes that you can insert into the page, then edit at your convenience.

If you are a drawing whiz, you can also draw directly in the design page.

Inserting drawings

If you feel that you are up to drawing directly in the design page, you must first choose one of the drawing programs installed on your PC.

To draw from a drawing program:

1. In the relevant design page, click on **Insert, Object**.
2. If necessary, click on the **Create New** option to activate it. In the drop-down list, select the program to execute your drawing. Click on **OK** to confirm (Figure 12.8).

   The various tools of the selected program are displayed in the active publication in the frame in which you are going to create your drawing.
3. Resize the design frame as you like.
4. Create your design. When you have finished, click outside the frame to go back to the publication.

*In the Insert Object dialog box, the **Create from file** option allows you to find the file that will be used for creating your drawings.*

To go back to the drawing that you have created, simply double-click on the frame that contains it.

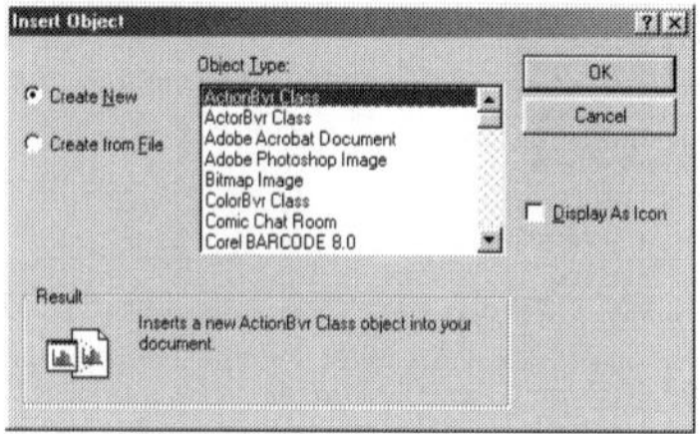

Figure 12.8 Choose one of the graphics applications installed on your PC.

Inserting shapes

Creating a drawing with a drawing application used to be only for click magicians. Recognising this problem, the programmers who created Publisher have generated a number of geometrical shapes that can be inserted and formatted.

When you draw using any of these tools, always remember to click on ***Tool Selector*** *to deselect the tool when your drawing is complete.*

The following shapes are available in the Objects toolbar:

Line Tool. Allows you to trace lines.

Oval Tool. Allows you to insert circles or ellipses.

Rectangle Tool. Allows you to insert squares or rectangles.

To insert a drawing, simply click on the relevant tool, and then on the page, and then drag upwards to achieve the size you want.

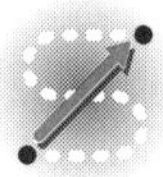

To draw a square, when you click on ***Rectangle Tool****, press on the* ***Shift*** *key, then keep it pressed while drawing the square.*

Inserting custom shapes

As well as traditional shapes, Publisher gives you a number of custom shapes, including arrows, polygons and crescents. These shapes will give your publication a fresh look with a touch of originality. Just as with standard shapes, you can easily format these items.

You can select a shape from the Custom Shapes tool in the Objects toolbar.

To insert a custom shape:

1. Click on the **Custom Shapes** tool in the Objects toolbar.
2. In the menu, click on the required shape (Figure 12.9). Click on the drawing page then, keeping the button pressed, drag the required shape.

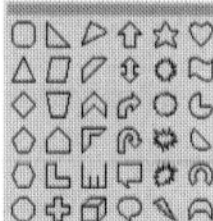

Figure 12.9 Choose the shape to be included.

Deleting shapes

To delete a shape, click on it to select it, then press the delete key.

Formatting objects

Now that you have learned how to insert lines, squares and ellipses, let us have a look at the various formatting possibilities in Publisher. First, however, we need to look at how to move and resize objects.

Selecting, resizing and moving objects

All standard and custom shapes and lines that you insert into your publication are perceived by Publisher as objects. As such, you can move, edit or delete them.

Selecting an object is the same as selecting a frame. Click on the relevant object. Several handles will appear, which you can use to resize and move your object. The number of handles depends on the selected object: a line has two handles, a circle has six.

To move an object quickly, select it, point to the object, then click on it and hold down the mouse button when the pointer icon changes to a cross with a small van. Move it to the right place, then release the mouse button.

To move an object precisely, select it then click on **Format, Size and Position**. In the Position area of the dialog box, specify the exact position for your object, then click on **OK** (Figure 12.10).

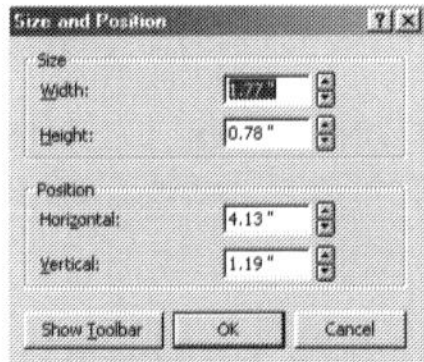

Figure 12.10 The Size and Position dialog box allows you to resize an image and place it precisely on the page.

To resize an object quickly, select it, point to one of the handles, then click on it when the Size icon changes to an arrow pointing in the required direction. Drag to achieve the required size, then release the mouse button.

To resize an object exactly, select it, then click on **Format, Size and Position**. In the Size area of the dialog box, specify the exact size for your object, then click on **OK** to confirm.

Formatting lines

Publisher offers several options for formatting lines.

To modify a line thickness, select the line, then click on the **Line/Border Style** icon. From the menu, select the required thickness (Figure 12.11). The **More Styles** choice allows you to select or specify a precise size, the shape of the line tip, and so on.

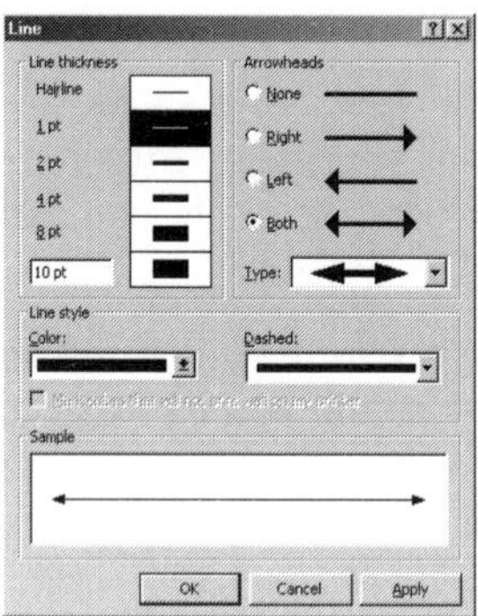

Figure 12.11 You can choose from a variety of line thicknesses and arrowheads.

*The **Line** dialog box allows you to choose other arrowhead options that are not in the Format toolbar.*

To modify the tips of your line, select the line, then click on one of the arrow icons in the Format toolbar.

Formatting shapes

Publisher allows you to modify colour, surface and thickness for both standard and custom shapes.

To modify the outline of an object, select it, then click on the **Line/Border Style** icon in the Format toolbar. Use the same procedures as for modifying text or picture frame borders.

To modify the surface of an object, select it, then click on the **Fill Color** icon in the Format toolbar. Use the same procedure as for modifying text or picture frame colours.

Rotating and flipping objects

Publisher allows you to flip shapes and/or rotate them.

To flip an object, select it, then click on either the **Flip Vertical** or the **Flip Horizontal** icon in the Format toolbar.

To rotate an object, select it, then click on either the **Rotate Right** or the **Rotate Left** icon in the Format toolbar.

Managing shapes and frames

Publisher offers several options for managing and controlling the various objects in your page.

Superimposing frames

When you create a publication, some frames must be superimposed. You can already move frames to superimpose them, but how do you bring to the front frames that are underneath?

To specify the position for a frame, select the relevant frame, and click on the **Bring to Front** icon or the **Send to Back** icon in the Standard toolbar.

Superimposing several objects or frames

The situation gets more complicated when you need to insert more than two objects or frames and they are stacked one on top of the other. Luckily, Publisher has thought it all out.

To modify the position of a frame or an object in a stack, select one of the objects from the top, or any of the frames or objects you can see. Click on **Arrange** and make your choice:

- **Bring to Front**. Positions the selected object or frame at the front.
- **Send to Back**. Positions the selected object or frame at the back.
- **Bring Backward**. Moves the selected object or frame back one place.
- **Bring Forward**. Moves the selected object or frame forward one place.

Aligning objects

Creating a publication is very easy. In fact, tracing lines, creating frames or even inserting pictures can all be done very quickly. However, once you have your creations, the finishing stage is slightly harder: you need to position your items correctly and define their alignment. Publisher offers interesting possibilities.

Let us have a look at the guides. These are horizontal or vertical lines that you place in the publication to control the positions of items.

To display the guides, click on **View, View Boundaries and Guides**.

To choose the type of guide:

1. Click on **Arrange, Ruler Guides**.
2. In the drop-down menu, select **Add Horizontal Ruler Guide** and/or **Add Vertical Ruler Guide**.
3. Click on the guide to place it where you want (Figure 12.12).

You can align objects on the guides by selecting your frames or objects, then clicking on **Tools, Snap to Guides**.

*To delete a guide, click on **Arrange, Ruler Guides**. In the drop-down menu, select **Clear All Ruler Guides**.*

Figure 12.12 Use guides to help you place objects.

A simple guide to

the Internet

Michel Dreyfus & Rob Young

Introduction

It's finally happened – you want to get onto the Internet! Maybe you feel as though you're arriving late at the party, and in some ways perhaps you are. But a few years ago you probably wouldn't have liked the party much: it was hard to get through the door, and there wasn't much happening when you were in.

These days there's *much* more going on. (You probably know a lot of people who are online already, so you don't need us to tell you that.) It's become a lot easier to join in, too. With the ever-increasing popularity of the Internet, the programs you use to sign up for an Internet account and surf the Net are actually designed for ordinary people now!

Like most things in life, the Internet is simple to use *when you know how to use it*. Because we're sure you don't want a lot of technical mumbo-jumbo, we're going to keep it simple: we'll just show you how to get connected and get on with the things you want to do – sending email, browsing websites, and chatting with your friends.

How to use this book

If you're new to the Net, start reading from Chapter 1 to get online and learn the basics in a sensible order. But maybe you already have a connection to the Internet and you just want a bit of help with the next steps? If so, you can skip about the book all you like. You don't have to know *everything* about the Internet to use the part of it you're interested in.

Throughout the book you'll see icons in the margins. These indicate notes that provide extra detail or explain a new idea. The icon used tells you what sort of information the note contains:

This icon introduces handy shortcuts and tips such as keyboard hotkeys, expert options, and quicker ways of getting to the same place.

This icon warns you of any risks associated with a particular action, or any problems you might encounter along the way, and (where possible) shows you how to avoid them.

This icon is used to provide extra information about the topic being covered.

We're not going to try to impress you with jargon, but we can't tell you about a new subject without using a few words you haven't come across before. We'll explain most of them as they crop up, but you'll find them all explained in the Glossary at the end of the book.

What you need to know before using this book

We don't expect you to have a degree in Information Technology, but this book isn't meant to be an introduction to computers either. We're assuming that you already have a computer that runs Windows 95, 98, Millennium Edition or 2000. We're also assuming that you are fairly comfortable with the basic operation of Windows: starting programs, managing folders and files, using the mouse, and so on.

Along with a computer, you must also have a telephone line. There's nothing special about this phone line, but it's the vital link between your computer and the Internet so it's not an optional extra. (We'll look at *how* these things are linked together in Chapter 3.)

Do I need a powerful computer?

Yes and no. It all depends on your patience... and your budget.

Processor and memory

If you get a taste for some of the Internet's multimedia content (movies, animations, virtual reality, video phone calls) a reasonably powerful computer is important – a Pentium II or later with at least 32Mb RAM. If you could still buy such a computer today, of course, it would be at an almost giveaway price, so the Internet doesn't demand a particularly expensive PC. If you're not interested in the multimedia aspects, an old Pentium PC with 16Mb RAM would just about do the job.

Hard disk

You will need to install some new programs to access the Internet, and you will probably collect other files on your travels. At the beginning, like somebody who starts working in a pastry shop, you will want to stuff yourself with everything you see and this information is quickly going to fill up your hard disk. Text doesn't take up much space, but anything to do with multimedia (sounds, pictures, animations, movies) is disk-hungry. Nowadays, a basic hard disk is rarely less than eight gigabytes. You should allow at least 200 megabytes (Mb) for the new software and the other bits and pieces that you will no doubt collect.

Screen

First and foremost, you need a colour monitor. You've almost certainly got one, but if you haven't they can be bought very cheaply. A 15-inch screen is a comfortable size for occasional use, but for any regular computer use (not just the Internet) a 17-inch screen is preferable.

There are two aspects to the way your screen is set up: the number of colours it can display, and the resolution (the number of dots used to make up the whole picture). A minimum setting is 256 colours at a resolution of 800 × 600; a better setting is 65,536 colours (known as High Colour) at 1024 × 768. You can adjust these settings using the **Display** option in the Windows Control Panel.

Modem

The modem is another important piece of equipment, the item which connects your computer to the telephone line. This topic is important enough to warrant more than a passing reference, and we will return to it in Chapter 3.

A last word before you start

Nothing moves as fast as the world of the Internet. It's built by real people like you and me, and whenever they feel like it they can change what they put there, or rename it, or remove it.

We've included screenshots of a lot of Internet sites in this book, and mentioned a lot of site addresses. Although we checked them all at the time of going to print, we can't guarantee that they will still be correct when you use them. That's the Internet for you – it never stands still!

What is the Internet?

1

How does the Internet work?

Internet resources

Internet addresses

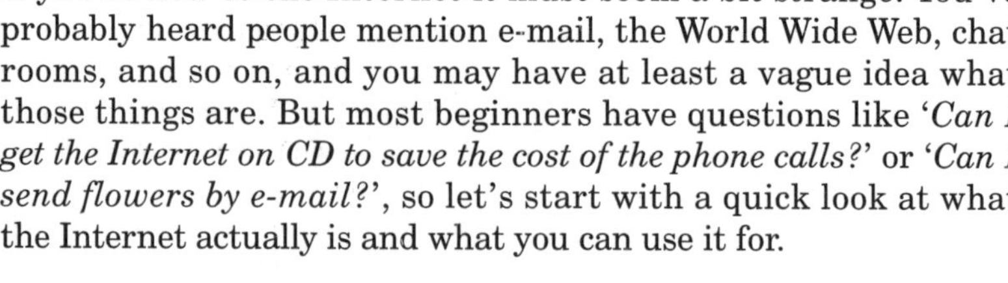

If you're new to the Internet it must seem a bit strange. You've probably heard people mention e-mail, the World Wide Web, chat rooms, and so on, and you may have at least a vague idea what those things are. But most beginners have questions like '*Can I get the Internet on CD to save the cost of the phone calls?*' or '*Can I send flowers by e-mail?*', so let's start with a quick look at what the Internet actually is and what you can use it for.

How does the Internet work?

A network is two or more computers connected together so that information on one machine can be shared/accessed by the other. Users on either machine can also decide for themselves what information is shared and what should remain private. They may also protect information with a password so that only users who know the password can access that information.

The Internet is a vast computer network. Small networks are connected by running cables between the computers, and that's fine for machines that are all in the same office or building, but in a larger network (particularly a worldwide network like the Internet), cabling all those computers together wouldn't be a popular option!

That could have been a major stumbling block in the creation of the Internet, but fortunately all the cables were in place already: they were attached to telephones! We could just pick up a phone in our home or office and those cables could connect us to another telephone on the other side of the world. If it worked for phones, why not let computers talk to each other along the same cables?

And that's how the Internet works. There were a couple of problems to solve, though. First, computers don't talk, of course – when computer information moves around, it does so silently – but telephone cables transfer *sound*. To solve this problem, a new gadget called a **modem** was connected to the computers. This converted the information into sound and sent it down the telephone line; at the other end, another modem attached to the other computer converted the sound back to data.

Routes and routers

The Internet transfers data by passing it along a chain of computers until it reaches its target. This leads to problem number two: what happens if one of the computers in the chain stops working? A computer might be busy, for instance, or it might not be switched on. If that computer were the vital link in the chain between America and Europe, a huge chunk of the Internet would become unreachable.

The solution was to ensure that no single computer in the chain was more important than any other. This could be done with **routers**. Routers are computers that memorise the layout of the whole network. They can then identify the various possible paths for travelling between computers at any time. Since the same computer could be linked to several routers, failure or unavailability of one of these routers wouldn't affect the interconnection. The routers can modify the path followed by the previous pieces of data and select a new one, which may be longer but which would secure delivery. This is called a **dynamic reconfiguration network**.

As an example, Figure 1.1 shows the set of routers used to link to the Netscape Web server from a point in the Sheffield region. If you were to go through the same exercise a few minutes later, there is no guarantee that the list of sites in the path would be the same, but you should always be able to access the Netscape site without problems (as long as the Netscape computer itself is available).

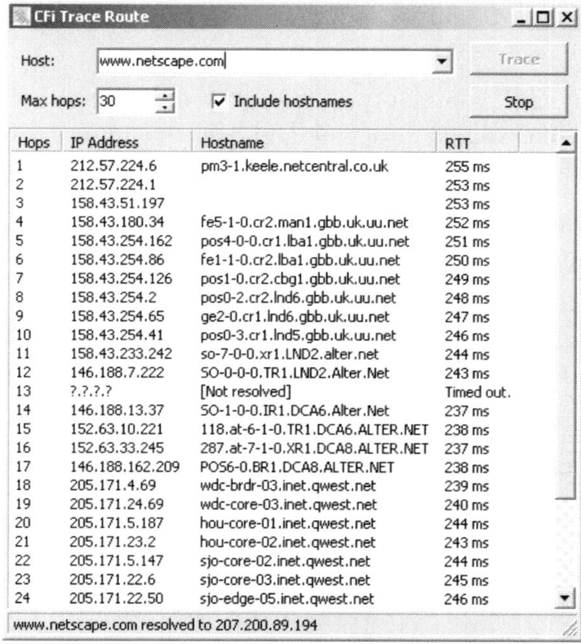

Hops	IP Address	Hostname	RTT
1	212.57.224.6	pm3-1.keele.netcentral.co.uk	255 ms
2	212.57.224.1		253 ms
3	158.43.51.197		253 ms
4	158.43.180.34	fe5-1-0.cr2.man1.gbb.uk.uu.net	252 ms
5	158.43.254.162	pos4-0-0.cr1.lba1.gbb.uk.uu.net	251 ms
6	158.43.254.86	fe1-1-0.cr2.lba1.gbb.uk.uu.net	250 ms
7	158.43.254.126	pos1-0.cr2.cbg1.gbb.uk.uu.net	249 ms
8	158.43.254.2	pos0-2.cr2.lnd6.gbb.uk.uu.net	248 ms
9	158.43.254.65	ge2-0.cr1.lnd6.gbb.uk.uu.net	247 ms
10	158.43.254.41	pos0-3.cr1.lnd5.gbb.uk.uu.net	246 ms
11	158.43.233.242	so-7-0-0.xr1.LND2.alter.net	244 ms
12	146.188.7.222	SO-0-0-0.TR1.LND2.Alter.Net	243 ms
13	?.?.?.?	[Not resolved]	Timed out.
14	146.188.13.37	SO-1-0-0.IR1.DCA6.Alter.Net	237 ms
15	152.63.10.221	118.at-6-1-0.TR1.DCA6.ALTER.NET	238 ms
16	152.63.33.245	287.at-7-1-0.XR1.DCA8.ALTER.NET	237 ms
17	146.188.162.209	POS6-0.BR1.DCA8.ALTER.NET	238 ms
18	205.171.4.69	wdc-brdr-03.inet.qwest.net	239 ms
19	205.171.24.69	wdc-core-03.inet.qwest.net	240 ms
20	205.171.5.187	hou-core-01.inet.qwest.net	244 ms
21	205.171.23.2	hou-core-02.inet.qwest.net	243 ms
22	205.171.5.147	sjo-core-02.inet.qwest.net	244 ms
23	205.171.22.6	sjo-core-03.inet.qwest.net	245 ms
24	205.171.22.50	sjo-edge-05.inet.qwest.net	246 ms

Figure 1.1 The series of routers involved in connecting to the Netscape Web site.

There's a story (which may not be true) that the Internet was originally conceived to allow American intelligence agencies to share sensitive data securely during the Cold War. The system of routers was designed so that if one computer in the chain was taken out by an enemy strike, data could bypass it automatically by taking a different route.

A packet at a time

In a network, data to be exchanged between two users is split into small chunks called **packets**. Before being sent out onto the network, each packet has extra information attached to it containing details of where it came from, where it's going to, and where it belongs in the stream of data being sent. Packets may arrive at their destination via many different routes and in the wrong order (due to the differences in the speed of certain routes), but the extra information ensures that the packets can be reconstructed again on arrival.

Internet resources

So everything you can find on the Internet exists in the form of computer data. (No, you can't send flowers by e-mail!) This data is spread about over hundreds of thousands of computers around the world. These computers perform different *services* – some, for example, deal with handling e-mail messages; others help you chat to friends; more let you look at pages on the World Wide Web. Some Internet-related services are more popular (and more useful) than others, and you'll probably end up using the same two or three most of the time. Here's a quick look at the five most popular Internet services.

E-mail

This is electronic mail, commonly called by its abbreviation *e-mail*. Your credibility will grow no end if, on your business card, under your name and occupation, you can put *yourname@your-company.co.uk*. Using e-mail you can send a message to someone in any part of the world extremely quickly (most messages arrive in a matter of minutes).

E-mail is the most used of the various Internet services: it may not be the most glamorous, but it's quick, easy, and extremely useful. However, the volume of e-mail traffic on the Net represents less than 10% of the total amount of traffic whizzing around. This is because an e-mail message is a tiny amount of data compared with some of the other uses of the Net (Web pages, sound and video, for instance).

Figure 1.2 shows what an e-mail message looks like in a program called Outlook Express. This is the most popular of the many e-mail programs available, chiefly because it's included with the Microsoft Windows operating system.

There are also e-mail-based services known as **mailing lists**. Instead of writing to an individual, you send your message to the list and the message is then sent to all the people on that list.

The World Wide Web

The World Wide Web (often referred to just as 'the Web') is one of the most recent Internet services to appear, and it's the one that really caught the public imagination. So much so, in fact, that many beginners believe the Web *is* the Internet.

Its advantage is that it presents all sorts of information – scientific, technical, political, administrative, humorous, and so on – in a very attractive form (with pictures, sound, and animations for instance). Through a virtual link system called **hypertext**, it allows the surfer to move from one page to another with a single mouse click. The pages may be on different computers, and those computers may be on different continents, but the system hides all that from you. As an example, Figure 1.3 shows the main page (or *home page* as it's known) of a Web site called Castles Unlimited.

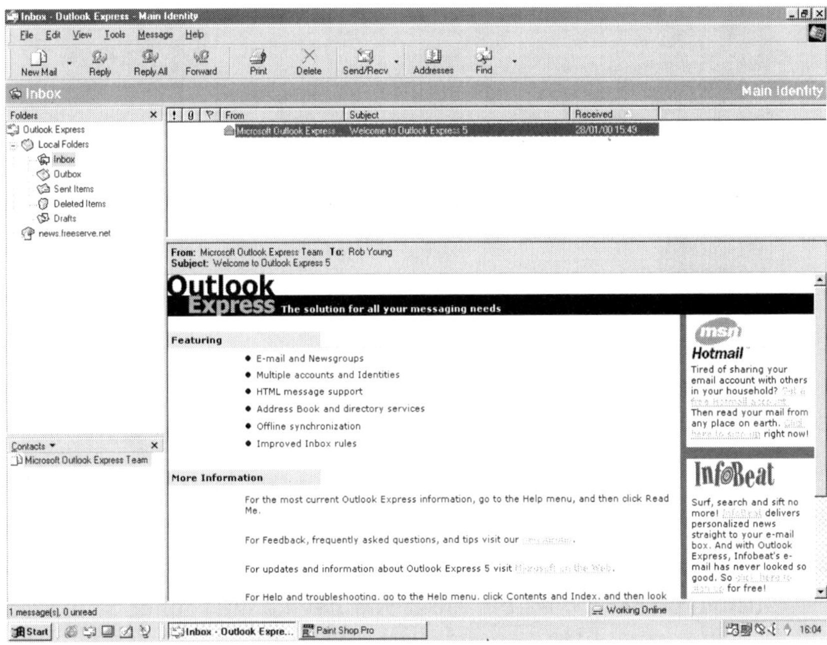

Figure 1.2 Outlook Express, the most popular e-mail program.

*A **Web site** is a term used to describe a set of related pages on the Web: all the pages are related and written by the same person or organisation (in the same way that a set of chapters is known as a book).*

Among the various services offered by the Web, there are two which have quickly become very important: electronic commerce (otherwise known as **e-commerce**, which we'll deal with in Chapter 11 when we discuss Internet security) and search engines (which we'll come to in Chapter 8), which allow you to find information on almost any subject.

Newsgroups

This is an electronic mail system very similar to mailing lists, mentioned above, but with a different structure. There are over 50,000 groups, each of which has its own name and deals with a particular subject. Anyone with an interest in a certain subject can subscribe to one of the groups that deals with it, contribute their own messages and read messages left by others.

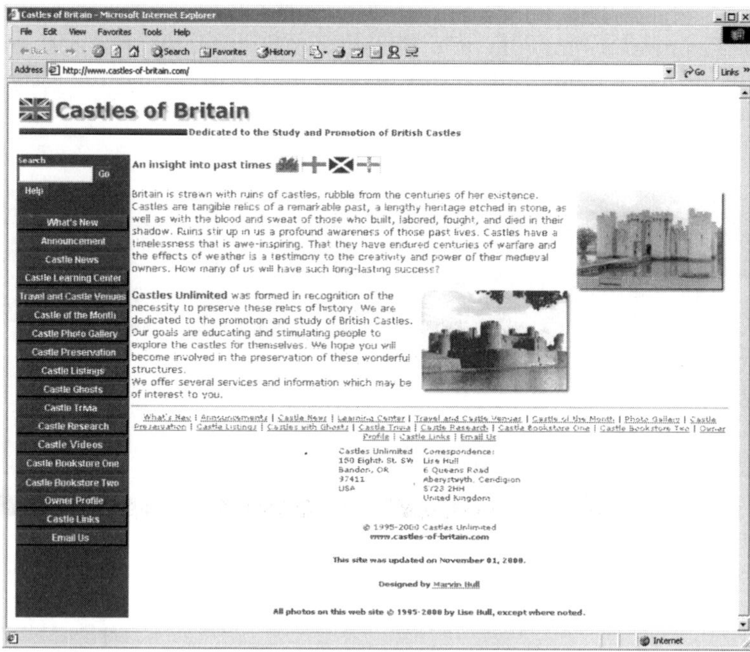

Figure 1.3 The home page of the Castles Unlimited Web site.

Chat

On the Internet, the word 'chatting' doesn't mean verbal chat (although that's possible too if you have a microphone plugged into your computer's soundcard). Instead it means typing messages back and forth to hold a conversation, and those short messages are sent almost instantly to everyone else taking part (perhaps one person or a whole group). Everyone taking part has a small window where the entire conversation is displayed, and a second small window where you type what you want to 'say' and press **Enter** to send it.

Most of the software available on the Internet is offered as shareware which you can 'try before you buy', usually for a period of about a month. If you decide to carry on using it, you are morally obliged to pay the author the (usually fairly small) sum of money he asks for the software.

Chat appears in several different forms including **instant messaging** (which usually involves a conversation between two people) and **IRC** (a chat between any number of people who happen to be in the same virtual 'chat room' at the same time).

File transfer (FTP)

There's some fantastic software available on the Internet, most of it free or almost free. This ranges from pictures, icons and sounds up to complete computer programs. This software is stored on **file servers** which allow Internet users to exchange files. Transfer from the server to the user is known as **downloading**. In the other direction, it is called **uploading**. Although it's a very simple service, it's known by the rather unfriendly name FTP (short for *File Transfer Protocol*).

Finding a file by name when it might exist on only one file server in the whole world is rather a 'needle in a haystack' job for a human being, so another service called **Archie** is used to handle searches of file servers.

Internet addresses

The Internet address system has been much simplified compared with what it was at the beginning. Currently we use IP (*Internet protocol*) addresses, four groups of digits separated by full stops, such as **121.16.295.59**, which allow a computer to be found on the network. An IP address refers to a single computer, but a computer may have several addresses.

Any system that uses numbers rather than words is well suited to computers, but it's not as practical for people, so a second type of address was created using words and dots. The second type of name works as a type of nickname for the first – a name that humans can use and remember – and it's called a **domain name**. The first word of a domain name represents an entity: a company, a public body, a university, and so on. The second indicates the type of professional activity or a country. Examples: ibp.fr, microsoft.com, whitehouse.gov. These *domains* may be subdivided according to the computers or servers that house them, by inserting another word (or a few letters) at the beginning, which produces: ftp.ibp.fr; www.microsoft.com; president.whitehouse.gov; www.almac.co.uk.

Because humans want to use the friendlier domain name format and computers have to use the numeric IP address format, something has to translate between them. This is handled by another Internet service (though not a particularly interesting one), DNS or Domain Name Service. When you want to visit a Web site, for instance, you type the friendly domain name of the site, and the DNS automatically finds the corresponding IP address so that your computer can connect to it.

For the purpose of defining these addresses, the world has been split into two parts: the USA and everywhere else. In the USA, addresses are classified by professional category and end with edu (teaching and research establishments), gov (public administration), mil (military bodies), com (commercial companies), and so on. Other countries have their own two-letter code: the suffix uk is for the UK, fr for France, be for Belgium, ca for Canada, de for Germany, and so on.

E-mail addresses

E-mail addresses work in a similar way. As usual, there's a computer that has the task of collecting e-mail people send to you, and gathering the messages you send and passing them on. This computer has an IP address, of course, and it also has a friendlier domain name (such as **goldcom.co.uk**). Since that computer may also handle the e-mail messages of thousands of other users, it creates a unique mailbox for you and gives it a name (which you'll normally be able to choose yourself). Your e-mail address will then consist of the mailbox name, an @ sign, and the domain name – something like **my.name@ goldcom.co.uk**.

2 Connecting to the Internet

Connection options

What do the connection calls cost?

Free Internet access

How to choose your Internet Service Provider

Internet Service Providers in the UK

Before you can use any of the Internet's services, you need to 'get connected'. The majority of Internet users don't have their computers permanently connected to the Internet: although it's possible, it isn't necessary and it would cost thousands of pounds per year. Instead, most users set up an account with a company that *does* have a permanent connection. These companies are known as **Internet Service Providers** (ISPs). Whenever you want to use the Internet, your computer will connect to your ISP's computer using your telephone line, and will be connected to the Internet through theirs while you surf the Web, send and receive e-mail, and so on. In this chapter we'll look at how to connect, along with what it's going to cost (if anything!).

Connection options

We've already established that you'll connect through an Internet Service Provider, or **ISP**. In the UK, there are several hundred service providers ranging from large companies like Demon Internet, Freeserve, BT Internet and America Online (AOL), all serving many thousands of subscribers, to regional providers with far fewer subscribers.

The simplest and most widespread way to get online is to choose a service provider and connect using a modem and an ordinary telephone line. British Telecom also offers the option of connecting via faster digital lines by purchasing a package it calls **Home Highway**. In this case, instead of a modem you'll use a device called a **terminal adapter**. Most service providers will let you connect using either method, but (as you'd expect) you'll pay a little extra for the faster option. Let's take a look at both.

Standard telephone line

The advantage of normal telephone lines is that they are easily available and they don't cost the earth. Apart from the cost of going online, which we'll look at later in this chapter, what you're mainly concerned with at this stage is how fast the information can reach you from the Internet.

The speed is rather variable: it can depend upon which ISP you set up your account with, how busy the Internet is while you're online, how popular the Web site is that you're visiting, and several other factors. Mostly, though, the speed depends upon your modem. Modern modems have a theoretical maximum speed of 56,000 bps (*bits per second*), although you'll never quite squeeze this much speed out of them. The quality of ordinary telephone lines means that your modem will never manage a speed of more than 50,000 bps.

Using a telephone line to connect to the Internet creates the same problems as using the family TV as a computer screen: only one person can use it at any one time. Be prepared for family upheavals if you're blocking access to the one-and-only telephone line when you surf the Net! There are two possible solutions: one is to get a second telephone line installed especially for Internet use; the second, which we'll look at now, is to upgrade to a Home Highway line.

Home Highway line

This is a British Telecom package aimed at home Internet users, although it's also available to businesses (Figure 2.1). Your normal telephone wall-box is replaced with a larger box, and you'll gain two extra phone numbers. You'll also need to replace your modem with a terminal adapter, mentioned above, or an ISDN card: these are effectively the same thing, but the first is an external unit that plugs into your computer and the second installs inside your computer.

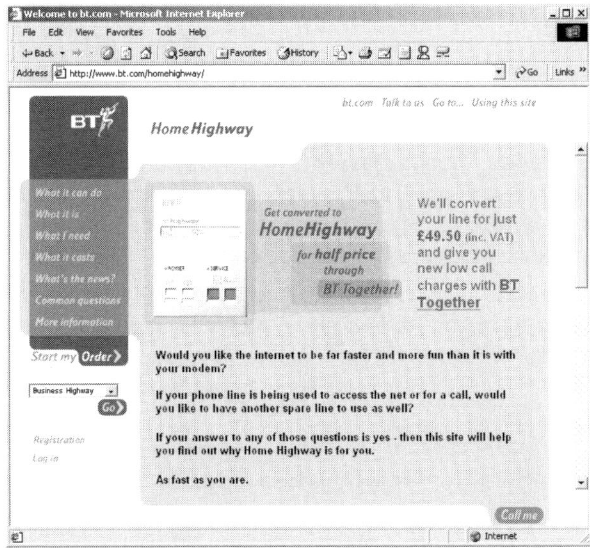

Figure 2.1 If you already have Internet access, you can find out more about Home Highway at BT's Web site (**www.bt.com**).

Along with the convenience of Home Highway, you also get increased speed. Internet connections will be at 64,000 bps and, unlike the humble modem, this is a guaranteed speed. It's also possible to combine the two digital lines to connect to the Net at 128,000 bps, although currently few ISPs allow you to do this.

With these hardware changes made, you can now connect up to two digital devices (such as two computers) and two analogue devices (such as a phone and a fax machine) to the junction box. Best of all, you can use two of these devices at the same time. So you can hold two telephone conversations, or talk to someone while sending someone else a fax, or (as we're concerned with here) surf the Net while making or taking phone calls.

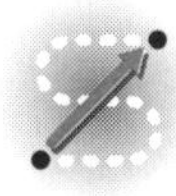

The 'A' in ADSL for 'Asymmetric' is important: it means that information you send doesn't travel at the same speed as information you receive.

When sending information from your computer, the speed drops to 256,000 bps.

ADSL

ADSL (*Asymmetric Digital Subscriber Line*) is another recent arrival on the communications scene, and as of November 2000 it's available in only a few of the UK's major cities. Unlike an ordinary telephone line or Home Highway, with ADSL your computer is permanently connected to the Internet. BT is offering a range of ADSL packages under the brand name **BTopenworld**, and these should also become available (under different names) through service providers such as Virgin Net and AOL during 2001. The speed of an ADSL connection will be at least 512,000 bps (roughly ten times the top speed of a modem connection), with speeds of up to 2 Mbits per second (four times as fast) available at an increased price.

What do the connection calls cost?

If you opt for the ordinary phone line or Home Highway method of connecting to the Internet, the connection is made using your phone line. And although it's not your telephone making the call, the pricing is exactly the same. Once again, there are two variables that affect the cost of the calls: what time you go online, and what number your computer has to dial.

This may soon be academic. Many ISPs are trying to provide what's known as 'unmetered access', meaning that you pay a single fixed annual fee for your Internet calls rather than a per-minute charge, and even the telephone companies are slowly edging towards the holy grail of completely free local calls.

- **Dial-up number:** When you choose your service provider, they should give you a local-rate dial-up number for your computer to call. This may be an 0845 number, or it may be a number with a local STD code. Large national ISPs usually use 0845 numbers. Don't choose a small ISP based in another part of the country unless they also give you a local-rate number or you'll be paying far higher call charges than you need to!
- **Dial-up time:** Telephone charges vary according to time of day. British Telecom's charges at the time of writing are 4p per minute daytime; 1.7p per minute evenings; and 1p per minute at weekends.

Premier Line

In return for a membership fee which can be paid monthly or annually, you receive a 15% discount off direct dialled local, regional, national and international calls if your quarterly phone bill is high enough to qualify for the scheme.

Friends & Family

Free to join, this scheme gives a 10% discount on calls to 10 selected numbers, and a 20% discount on calls to one particular number (your 'BestFriend'). Your selection can include one international and one mobile number.

SurfTime

This BT option can make the Internet more affordable by charging a single monthly rate for your connection calls, no matter how long you spend online (known as *unmetered access*). Direct from BT, the SurfTime option costs around £20 per month for unlimited surfing all day long, or £6 for evenings and weekends only. The same option can be bought through a number of ISPs such as BTclick, Virgin Net and Freeserve.

It's highly recommended that you make your Internet dial-up number your 'BestFriend' in your Friends & Family list. You'll probably spend more time per quarter connected to this-number than talking to one particular friend or family member.

Free Internet access

Before 1999, it was taken for granted that you'd have to pay for your Internet connection; the question was *How much?* Since then, companies have been falling over themselves to give away Internet access for free. The trend started with Freeserve (Figure 2.2), originally part of the Dixons/PC World group and now the largest free ISP in the UK, and was quickly followed by other well-known names including Virgin Net, the Mirror Group with ic24, and Tesco with Tesconet.

Figure 2.2 The home page of Freeserve, the company that began the 'free Internet access' revolution (**www.freeserve.net**).

At the time of writing, 'free' means that you only pay for your connection calls (covered on previous pages). The benefits of signing up with a free ISP are twofold:

- If you're not satisfied with the service you simply stop using it: you're not paying, so you don't need to cancel.
- If you hear of a service that sounds better, you can try it alongside your existing account. With no charges to pay, it's easy to 'audition' a service in this way, and you might even decide to keep using both.

What we'd really like 'free' to mean is that even the cost of the calls is free, and this type of completely free connection is gradually becoming available. Along with the SurfTime package mentioned above, BT is slowly edging towards making local calls entirely free, and the huge Internet service America Online (AOL) is planning to introduce its own form of unmetered access for its subscribers.

There are two catches with free access that you should be aware of. The first (and it's not a major catch) is that you have to pay a massive price for phone calls to the company's support staff if you get into difficulties: most companies charge between 50p and £1 per minute. Fortunately, though, you shouldn't get into difficulties very often, and you'll probably never need to phone that support line.

The second catch is that (at the moment) you get what you pay for. Many users of free services find that they can't connect at certain times of day, or the service is slow, or otherwise unreliable. If you're paying for access, the quality of service is currently much more likely to be high, and the company will make more effort to keep you as a customer.

How to choose your Internet Service Provider

Companies can afford to provide free access to the Internet because instead of taking their money directly from you, they take a percentage of the cost of your connection call from BT and sell advertising on the Web sites.

In choosing an Internet Service Provider, you care about two things: *What do they charge?* and *Are they any good?* If you've decided to go for a free service provider (and that's the recommended place to start for beginners) the first question can be skipped, of course. If you prefer to pay for Internet access, a standard charge is about £10–15 per month plus VAT.

The second question involves rather a lot of different things, so let's go through them one by one. At the end of this chapter, you'll find a list of some of the best-known ISPs in the UK.

User support

You need to know whether the company in question has a support phone line, when it's available, and whether calls to the support line are charged at a premium rate. In general, free services charge for their support line, and pay-for services don't. Needless to say, if support won't be available when you're most likely to be trying to use the Internet, it doesn't matter what it costs!

Points of presence

A Point of Presence (or *PoP*) is a connection point your computer dials into to connect to the Internet. Large service providers have PoPs throughout the country, but smaller providers may have PoPs only in their own county or town. If you live in the same town, that's fine. But if you live miles away you may be paying for a national-rate phone call to connect rather than a local-rate call. Make sure the ISP you choose either has a local PoP or allows you to connect through an 0845 (or equivalent local-rate) phone number.

Number of modems

Some companies are a bit coy about publicising their modem-to-subscriber ratio (and they may not always stick to it) but it's useful information to check if you're planning to pay for your Internet access. The more modems the company has per subscriber, the better your chances of not getting an engaged tone when you try to connect to the Internet. A ratio of about 1:12 is reckoned to be average, meaning that one in twelve subscribers can be online at the same time.

Free Web space allocated

Most ISPs include some **Web space** in their subscriptions. If you decide to build your own Web site, this is where your site will be stored so that the rest of the online world can see it. The amount of space provided varies enormously: some providers still offer only 2Mb Web space while others offer 50Mb! For most non-business sites, 5–10Mb is quite enough space.

Usenet newsgroup access

Does your chosen ISP offer newsgroup access? Usually the answer is 'yes', but a very few don't. How many newsgroups do they offer? There are over 50,000 in existence, and most ISPs won't offer all of them, but you should expect to be able to access at least 50% of them. Does the ISP offer its own groups? These allow subscribers of the same service to communicate with each other, and this could be helpful if you have problems and can't get through to (or afford!) the support line.

Number of mailboxes offered

If somebody else is going to share your Internet access, it's better if your e-mail messages don't get mixed up with theirs. Most service providers offer five or more different names with one subscription, so that you can each have different e-mail addresses.

Choice of username and password

Your **username** is a unique name that identifies you to your chosen service provider. When you sign up, you can usually choose your username (a combination of numbers, letters, dots, hyphens and underscore characters, but no spaces). You will also be assigned a **password**. Keep your username and password secret, and make sure you don't forget them!

Internet Service Providers in the UK

The following is a short list of Internet Service Providers. If you already have Internet access you can find out more about these services by visiting their Web sites or sending them an e-mail message. In some cases you may be able to sign up for a new account at the Web site. If you're new to the Internet, pick up the phone and give the service a call to find out more about them. Many services will be happy to send you everything you need on a CD-ROM; others may direct you to a High Street store to pick up a free sign-up CD.

Company: America Online (AOL)
Telephone: 0800 279 1234
E-mail: queryuk@aol.com
Web site: www.aol.com

Notes: 10Mb Web space, 7 e-mail addresses, single monthly fee with fixed rate 1p per minute connection calls.

Company: BT Internet
Telephone: 0800 800001
E-mail: support@btinternet.com
Web site: www.btinternet.com

Notes: Unlimited Web space and e-mail addresses. Free weekend and evening calls via BT SurfTime.

Company: ClaraNET Ltd
Telephone: 0800 358 2828
E-mail: sales@clara.net
Web site: www.clara.net

Notes: Various account offers, reduced call charges.

Company: CompuServe (CSi)
Telephone: 0870 6000 800
E-mail: UKCSSVC@cs.com
Web site: www.compuserve.co.uk

Notes: 10Mb Web space, 7 e-mail addresses, phone for software or download.

Company: Free-Online
Telephone: 0870 7060504
E-mail: sales@free-online.net
Web site: www.free-online.net

Notes: Unlimited Web space and e-mail addresses, free support.

Company: Freeserve
Telephone: –
E-mail: info@freeserve.com
Web site: www.freeserve.com

Notes: Free disk from Dixons or PC World, or sign up online. 15Mb Web space, unlimited e-mail addresses. Unlimited free evening and weekend access calls via BT SurfTime.

Company: ic24
Telephone: 020 7643 3215
E-mail: ic24@mgn.co.uk
Web site: www.ic24.net

Notes: Phone for software or download. 10Mb Web space, 5 e-mail addresses. Limited free access call time at weekends.

Company: LineOne
Telephone: 0800 111 210
E-mail: support@lineone.net
Web site: www.lineone.net

Notes: 5 e-mail addresses, Web space, sign up online.

Company:	UUNET
Telephone:	0500 474739
E-mail:	sales@uk.uu.net
Web site:	www.uk.uu.net

Notes: 50Mb Web space, 5 e-mail addresses.

Company:	Virgin Net
Telephone:	0500 558800
E-mail:	advice@virgin.net
Web site:	www.virgin.net

Notes: Sign up online. 10Mb Web space, 5 e-mail addresses. Free evening and weekend access calls via BT SurfTime.

Company:	Zetnet Services
Telephone:	01595 696667
E-mail:	info@zetnet.co.uk
Web site:	www.zetnet.co.uk

Notes: 25Mb Web space, unlimited e-mail addresses.

Your first connection

3

Modem installation

Software installation

Using your connection

Some people say that installing an Internet connection on a computer is difficult. A few years ago this would have been true, but these days it's usually as straightforward as installing any other piece of software: you just insert the CD-ROM, follow the on-screen instructions, and Bob's your uncle.

There are two reasons for this. First, most new computers come with a modem already installed, so that's something you won't have to do yourself. Second, recent versions of Windows include complete support for Internet connections, along with most of the software you'll use when you're on the Net.

When you sign up for an account with a service provider, they'll almost certainly give you a CD-ROM and a very short page of instructions, and you'll be online in minutes. You can then skip to the last pages of this chapter, *Using your connection*. It's useful to know how to set up a connection manually, though, in case something goes wrong, and this is what the first part of this chapter is all about.

Modem installation

There are two types of modems: *internal* modems, inserted into a PCI slot inside the computer, and *external* modems, small boxes linked by a cable to the computer's serial port (also known as a COM port, short for 'communications') or USB socket.

Although it costs a little more, the external variety has several benefits:

- You can use it with another computer whose internal connectors may be different.
- Its installation is easier: just plug it in and connect the serial or USB cable.
- It has warning lights which provide information on what's happening during your connection.

The current price of a modem varies between £25 and £100, according to its technical specifications and the gadgets it comes equipped with. Modems usually come with a floppy disk containing a variety of software such as fax programs. The majority of modems are Plug-and-Play-compatible, so installation is extremely easy and all the cables you need will be included with your modem.

Software installation

There are several pieces of software that need installing before you can connect to the Internet:

- The modem driver, which allows your computer to communicate with your modem once the two have been connected. (If you change your modem, you need to uninstall the old driver and install the driver for the new one.) This will be one of the items supplied on the floppy disk accompanying the modem.
- Dial-Up Networking, the software which will manage the TCP/IP connection used by all Internet resources. This is included with Windows 95 and later, and is probably already installed on your computer: if it is, you'll see a folder named **Dial-Up Networking** when you double-click your My Computer icon.
- Connection to the specific Internet Provider with which you have taken up a subscription. You need to create such a connection for each ISP you've signed up with (probably only one so far).
- A **Web browser** to access Web sites.
- An e-mail program to send and receive e-mail messages.

As you'll learn in the next couple of chapters, Windows provides the last two items in the list so you probably have these already. If you don't, they are both freely available on almost any Internet-related magazine cover-disk.

The modem driver

When you installed Windows, if you have an external modem, it is possible that the modem was not switched on. In this case it could not be recognised and you need to install it. Start by checking the modem link to the computer and switch it on. Then restart your computer. When it starts running, Windows will know that there is something new in your computer and will prompt you to proceed with the installation of the software. But you can also follow these instructions, without restarting your computer:

1. Click on Start/Settings/Control Panel.
2. In the Control Panel window, double-click the **Modems** icon.
3. On the General tab, click on **Add**. The Hardware Wizard displays its first page. Don't tick the check box in front of 'Do not detect modem'.
4. Click on **Next** and Windows will search for your modem.
5. If, in the next window, you see that the type of modem recognised is 'Standard Modem', this means that Windows has found your modem but cannot tell which brand of modem it is. In this case, click on the **Modify** button.
6. The next page will display two list-boxes, as you can see in Figure 3.1. In the left one you'll see the names of modem brands: pick the brand that matches your modem. Then, in the right

window, choose your modem type. These indications are usually to be found on its front. Then click on the **Next** button.

If you can't find your modem in these lists, you need to use the drivers on the floppy disk which comes with your modem by clicking on the **Have Disk** button and following the indications provided by the Wizard.

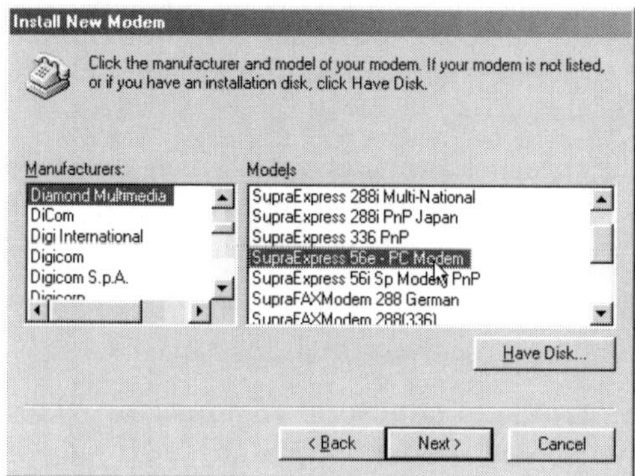

Figure 3.1 Choose your modem from the dual lists in the Install New Modem dialog box.

7. A final window prompts you to click on the **Finish** button.
8. The Modems Properties page is displayed with your modem shown in the list of installed devices (Figure 3.2). To check that Windows can communicate with your modem properly, click on the **Diagnostics** tab and on the port used by the modem (usually COM2), then click on the **More Info** button.

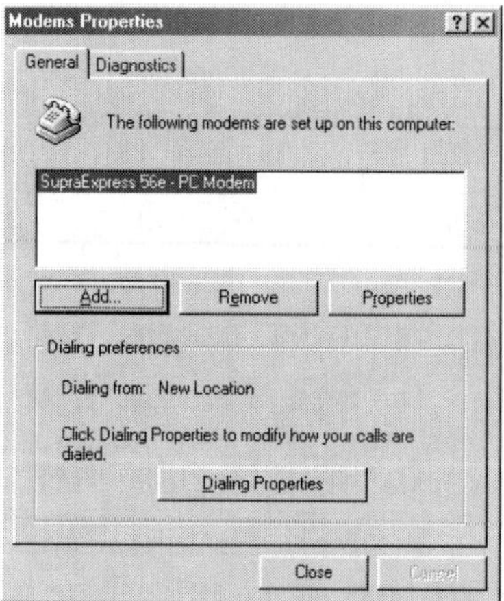

Figure 3.2 After completing the Install New Modem wizard, your modem will appear on the Modems Properties page.

9. Within a few seconds, if everything works as it should, you should see the window filling with mysterious codes. Don't worry about what they mean: for our purposes, they just mean everything works!

Dial-Up Networking

To connect to an ISP through a telephone line, you use a connection protocol known as PPP (*Point to Point Protocol*). For this you will need to use software called a *TCP/IP stack*, because TCP/IP is the connection protocol used on the Internet.

Windows 95, 98, Millennium Edition and 2000 come with all the software you need to connect to a network, as do modern Apple Macs like the iMac. With Windows 95 and later, the first thing to do is to see whether that software is already installed on your computer. To do this, double-click on the My Computer icon and look for the **Dial-Up Networking** icon shown in Figure 3.3. If you can, go straight to the *Creating and configuring a new connection* section below.

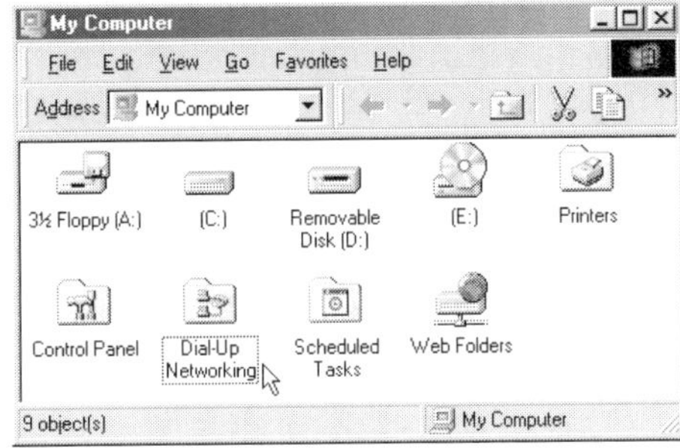

Figure 3.3 The Dial-Up Networking icon shows that Windows' Internet connection software is already installed.

Otherwise, follow these steps:

1. Click on Start/Settings/Control Panel.
2. In the Control Panel window, double-click the **Add/Remove Programs** icon.
3. Click on the **Windows Setup** tab. A dialog box is displayed which tells you to wait while Setup searches for installed components. After a few seconds, the list of components is displayed.
4. Find the **Communications** item in this window and click on it.
5. Click on the **Details** button. In the Communications window which appears (shown in Figure 3.4), tick the box beside **Dial-Up Networking** and click **OK** to close the Communications window.

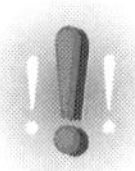

Your password might be chosen by you or may have been assigned to you by your service provider. What matters is that you know it (and can remember it) – without it you can't go online!

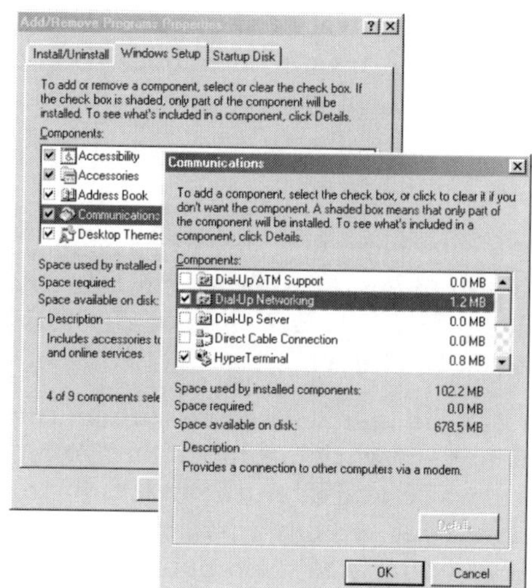

Figure 3.4 Installing Dial-Up Networking from the Windows CD-ROM.

6. Click on **OK** in the main dialog box. If the Windows CD-ROM is not in the appropriate drive, you will be asked to insert it. The required files will be installed on your computer, which takes just a few seconds, and a dialog box will then prompt you to restart your computer.

Creating and configuring a new connection

There are two ways of creating a new connection: either by using a connection CD-ROM which your service provider sends you (or which you find bundled with a computer magazine), or by following the various steps required under Windows if your Internet Provider has simply given you the essential details. Once again, most ISPs will give you a CD-ROM that does everything for you, but here's what to do if you find yourself faced with using the second method.

What you need to know

Before starting to install a new connection, make sure that your Internet Provider has given you the following details:

- The dial-up telephone number to connect to the Internet;
- Your username and password;
- Your ISP's primary DNS address (and, perhaps, a secondary DNS);
- The name of its mail server (usually something like **mail.*serviceprovider.co.uk***);
- The name of its news server (usually ***news.serviceprovider.co.uk***).

Creating a connection

Open My Computer by double-clicking its icon and then double-click on the **Dial-Up Networking** icon. A new window opens, with a single icon labelled **Make New Connection** (Figure 3.5).

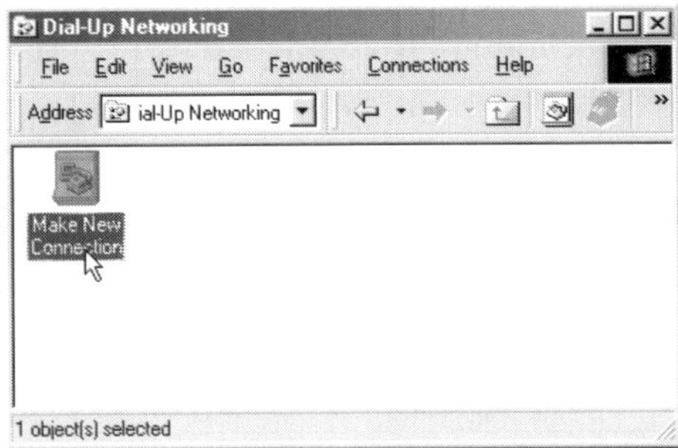

Figure 3.5 Double-click this icon to launch the Make New Connection wizard.

The connection name is entirely for your own use. You can pick any name at all here to give the icon a name you'll recognise in future.

Double-click this icon to launch the Make New Connection wizard which will take you through the following steps:

1. The first window prompts you to name this connection as 'My Connection', which isn't particularly imaginative, so you'll probably want to choose something different. Then click on the **Next** button.
2. In the next window, you will need to enter the Area code in the appropriate box. In the Telephone number box, enter your ISP's dial-up number (with or without spaces – they'll be ignored if you include them) and keep the Country code as it is. Then click on the **Next** button.
3. The third window summarises what you've just done. Click **Finish** to confirm.

When you finish, you'll be returned to the Dial-Up Networking folder where you should see a new icon with the name you chose in Step 1 above. Later you'll be able to double-click this to go online. First, though, there are a few more steps to take care of.

Configuring your connection

To configure the connection you've just created, you need to modify its properties.

1. Right-click the new icon and choose **Properties** from the context menu that appears.
2. Select the Server Types tab, and remove the check marks from most of the boxes on the page so that the only checked items are:

*To make this connection icon more easily accessible when you want to go online, use the right mouse-button to drag it onto the desktop and choose **Create Shortcut(s) Here** when prompted.*

- Enable software compression;
- TCP/IP.

3. If your ISP gave you a primary (and perhaps a secondary) DNS address, click the **TCP/IP Settings** button. Make sure the button beside **Specify name server addresses** is selected, and type your Primary and Secondary DNS addresses into the appropriate boxes (Figure 3.6).

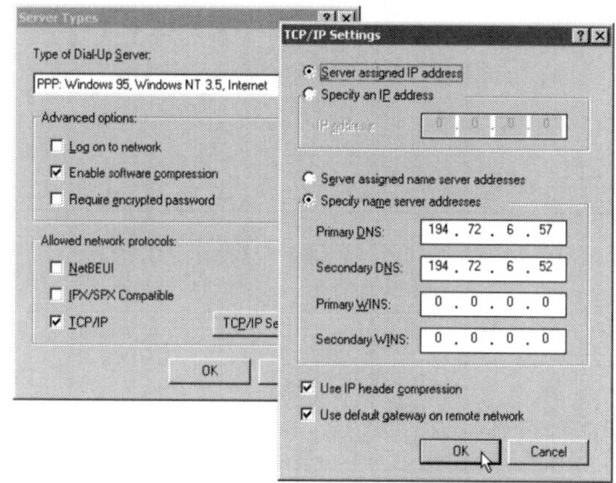

Figure 3.6 The Server Types and TCP/IP Settings pages after modifying them. (Your DNS settings will be different from those shown here.)

4. Click **OK** in all the open dialog boxes to confirm the changes you've made and close them.

Using your connection

That's it! Now you're ready to go online, so you need to grab the two pieces of information we haven't yet used: your username and password. Double-click your connection icon in the Dial-Up Networking folder (or the shortcut to it on your desktop, if you followed the note above) and you'll see a dialog box like the one in the screenshot below. Windows will probably have a guess at your username, but it probably won't get it right; the password field will be blank when the dialog box appears. Type the correct username and the password (which will be automatically masked with asterisks to prevent anyone else in the room reading it from your screen) and click the **Connect** button (Figure 3.7).

You'll hear your modem squeaking and squawking for about 20 seconds (unless you have Home Highway, which is silent) and a dialog should then inform you that you're connected. You'll also see a tiny icon beside the clock at the bottom-right of your screen which flashes to indicate data passing backwards and forwards from the Internet to your computer.

To be absolutely sure that everything is OK, try visiting a Web site. Launch Internet Explorer by clicking on its icon to the right of the Start button, in the Windows taskbar (a blue 'e'). Near the top of the Internet Explorer window you'll see a wide text field labelled **Address**. Click in that field and type **www.yahoo. co.uk**, then press **Enter**. This is the address of the famous Yahoo! Web site, and within a few seconds you should see the home page of this site appear.

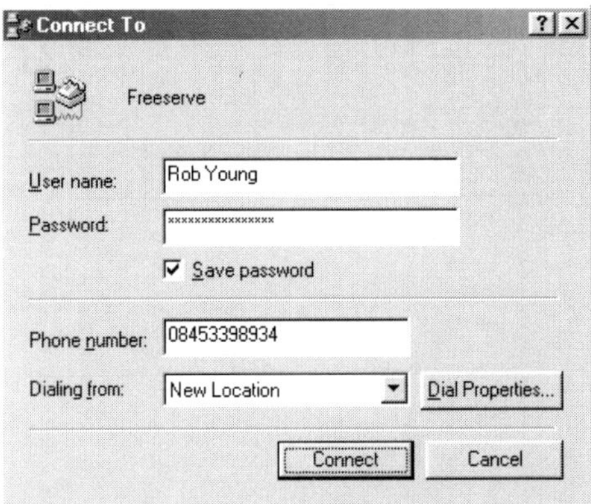

Figure 3.7 Enter your username and password, and you're ready to connect.

So now you're connected, *and* you've visited your first Web site. In Chapter 4 we'll take a closer look at the World Wide Web and the Internet Explorer browser.

In the meantime, though, how do you *disconnect* from the Internet? Just double-click that tiny flashing icon beside the clock. A dialog box will appear giving you some information about how long you've been online and how much data has been sent and received by your computer. You'll also see a button labelled **Disconnect**: click that and your modem will hang up the line (the same as putting the phone down if you'd been making an ordinary telephone call).

Browsing the World Wide Web

4

Web addresses

Installing Internet Explorer

Installing Netscape Navigator

Installing Opera

Getting started on the Web

Customising Internet Explorer

The World Wide Web is so popular that it's often confused with the Internet itself, although in fact it's just one of the Internet's many resources. There are two reasons why the Web has become so widely used. First, it's extremely easy to use (or, more accurately, the software you use to look at Web sites is easy to use); second, it's a true multimedia environment: Web pages can contain text, images, animations, movies, interactive content, small programs, and lots more.

The program you use to access this lot is called a **Web browser** (usually shortened to *browser*). The browser is the most important piece of Internet software you'll have (apart from your e-mail program, perhaps, as we'll see in Chapter 5) since it allows you to do almost everything you need to do on the Net. In this chapter, we'll learn how to surf the Web and how to use your browser.

Web addresses

If you're a Windows user, you'll notice that Internet addresses use forward slashes (/) rather than the backslashes you're more used to (\).

The most important aspect of the Web is that it uses a technology called **hypertext** to let you jump from one page (or *resource*) to another with just one mouse-click. You might have seen similar systems at work in Windows Help files, Apple Hypercard, or multimedia encyclopaedias on CD-ROMs.

Hypertext is a more advanced system than any of these, since it allows that one simple mouse-click to open pages or files on any Internet-connected computer in the world: all the complicated stuff is hidden from view. To make this work, each resource has its own unique address known as a **URL** (Uniform Resource Locator). It's useful to understand how a URL is put together, so let's take an example and pull it apart. Here's a URL which could be a single Web page on a company's Web site:

*The extension for Web pages can also be **.html**. You will come across a few other file extensions which display something that looks a lot like a Web page, such as **.asp** and **.cfm**.*

http://www.city1.co.uk/design/pages/index.htm

This is made up of the following:

- The **http://** prefix, which indicates that this is a resource on the World Wide Web. (Resources on file servers, e-mail servers, etc., will use different prefixes, as Table 4.1 shows.)
- A server address: **www.city1.co.uk/** – most Web servers have a name beginning with www. In this case, the **.co.uk** shows that the server is in the United Kingdom.
- The path **design/pages/** shows which directory on the server's hard disk contains the file we want.
- The file name **index.htm**. The extension **.htm** indicates that the file is a Web page, but files of any type can be placed on a Web server (just as you can place any type of file on your own hard disk).

Table 4.1 Browser actions triggered by the different prefixes

Prefix	Browser action
http://	Display the Web page (or any other file) specified by the address if possible. If the browser can't display this type of file, it will offer to store it on your hard disk so that you can use a different program to open it.
ftp://	Download a file stored on a file server and save it onto your hard disk.
mailto:	This is always followed by someone's e-mail address (such as **mailto:me@myserver.co.uk**). Your browser will start your e-mail program (see Chapter 5) so that you can send that person an e-mail message.
news:	Followed by the name of a newsgroup (such as **news:alt.sport.icehockey**). Your browser will start your newsreader program (see Chapter 7) to let you read and contribute to that group.
file://	Opens a file on your own hard disk rather than the hard disk of some remote computer. (For this, of course, you don't have to be connected to your ISP.)

If a link starts with the **http://** prefix, the browser knows that it has to fetch a Web-based resource. But, as mentioned at the beginning of this chapter, browsers have a few extra talents, so addresses beginning with the prefixes in Table 4.1 can also be used. The table shows what the browser will do when given an address beginning with one of these prefixes.

Installing Internet Explorer

If you use Windows 98, 2000 or Millennium Edition, there is nothing you need to do: Internet Explorer is installed already (Figure 4.1). If you're using Windows 95, you may be able to install Internet Explorer from your Windows CD-ROM, but it's a very old version. (We'd recommend that Windows 98 users upgrade to the latest version too, but the version you currently have isn't as outdated so you may be happy to put this off for a while.)

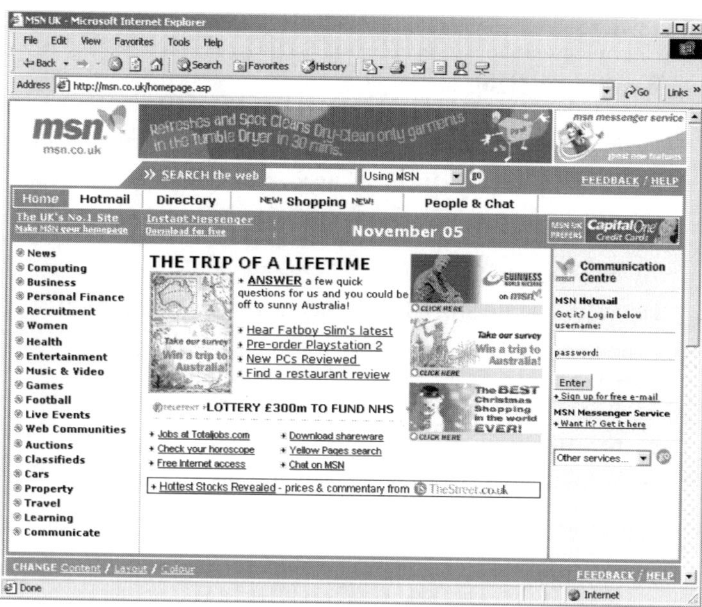

Figure 4.1 The popular Internet Explorer Web browser in action.

Make sure you select Outlook Express from the list of items to install which will be displayed. We will use this program for e-mail (see Chapter 5) and news (see Chapter 6).

You can find the latest version of Internet Explorer (which is free) on the cover CD-ROM of almost any computing or Internet-related magazine. If you have Internet access already, you can download it from Microsoft's Web site at **http://www.microsoft.com**. Start the installation, then answer a few simple questions and the new version will automatically overwrite any older version that was previously installed on your system.

Although you can only have one copy of Internet Explorer installed at any time (and a new copy will always replace the old copy), you can have Netscape and Opera installed alongside Internet Explorer, and you can install any number of different Netscape versions (if you really want to!).

Installing Netscape Navigator

Although we're going to concentrate on Internet Explorer in this book, it certainly isn't the only Web browser available; it's by far the most popular, but you may still like to try something different. The best-known competitor to Internet Explorer is **Netscape** (Figure 4.2). This is unlikely to be already installed on your computer, but it's another piece of free software that you can find on magazine CD-ROMs or download from **http://home.netscape.com**.

At the time of writing, the current version of Netscape is called **Netscape Communicator 4.7**. Along with the browser itself, it includes several other software components including an e-mail program. By the time you read this book, this version may have been replaced with the long-awaited **Netscape 6**, but this should still be free and still offer a similar set of software.

Figure 4.2 The Netscape Web browser.

Installing Opera

A third name in the Web browser market is **Opera** (Figure 4.3). A free version, supported by advertisements, is available. It has some clever features that its competitors don't, and it's widely regarded as being a more reliable piece of software. You may find this on the CD-ROMs of some Internet magazines; alternatively, use one of the other browsers to visit **http://www. operasoftware.com** to find a copy.

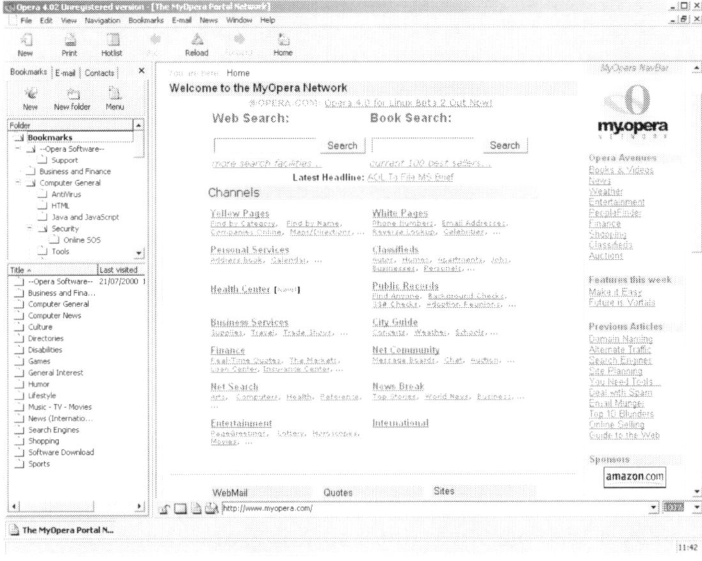

Figure 4.3 The feature-filled and increasingly popular Opera browser.

Getting started on the Web

The best way to get started on the Web is to take a deep breath and just do it. To that end, we'll run through the most important features of Internet Explorer and then get started surfing the Web. Remember that if you make a mistake it won't have any serious consequences: you won't do your computer or the Internet any harm!

If you're using one of the other browsers, you'll find that the buttons and options have different names. However, most of the same options are there somewhere, and they work in a very similar way in every browser.

The Internet Explorer buttons

In Windows 98 and later, click on the Internet Explorer icon in the Taskbar beside the Start button (a blue 'e' icon). You can also find a similar icon on your desktop and inside the Programs folder on the Start menu in a subfolder called Internet (or Internet Tools).

Underneath the Internet Explorer menu bar there is a toolbar, shown in Figure 4.4. Here's a brief explanation of what each button does:

Figure 4.4 The Internet Explorer Toolbar.

Back Switch to the page you visited prior to this one.

Forward After using the Back button, use this to move forward to pages you viewed recently.

Stop If a Web page is taking too long to display, click this button to stop trying to view it.

Refresh Use this to reload the page you're currently viewing.

Home Switch to your home page (see below) with one click.

Search Search the Web for a particular type of site or resource.

Favorites View a list of your favourite Web sites and visit one of them with a single click.

History View a list of the Web sites you've visited recently.

Mail Send e-mail messages or check for new incoming messages.

Print Print out a copy of the Web page you're viewing.

Edit A bit of a misnomer really, but you can click this button to view the code that makes the current Web page display properly in the browser.

Launching Internet Explorer for the first time

Every time you launch it, Internet Explorer tries to connect to its **home page** (Microsoft Network at **http://www.msn.co.uk**) which isn't necessarily what you want. This is because a browser has to display a Web page when it's running, and this is the page set as the default starting page for Internet Explorer. To show this page, your browser must connect to your service provider, so there'll be a pause while your modem dials.

You can change this behaviour, of course. A popular option is to make Internet Explorer display a blank page when it starts. To do this, click on **Internet Options** on the **Tools** menu and you'll see the dialog box shown in Figure 4.5. Click on the **Use Blank** button and confirm your choice by clicking on **OK**.

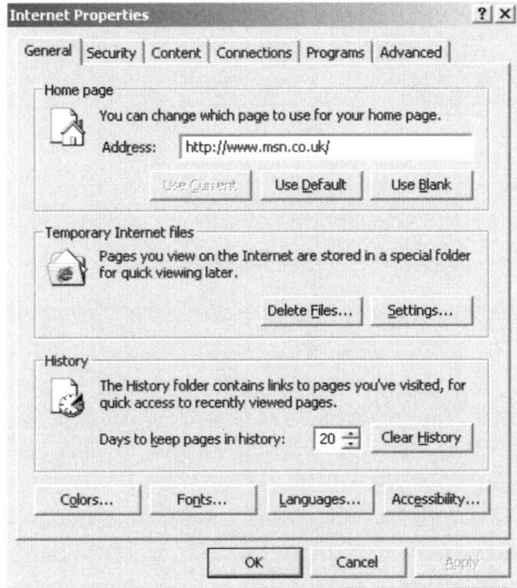

Figure 4.5 Choose your starting page by typing a URL into the box, or clicking the **Use Blank** button.

You may be happy to always start surfing from a particular Web page but would prefer it to be a *different* page. The easiest way to set your home page to something different is to visit the new site first, so let's do it that way. As an example, we'll take the Web site of the National Trust, whose URL is **http://www.nationaltrust.org.uk**. (Remember, a *URL* is just a fancy name for an 'address of a Web site').

At the moment your Internet Explorer window may be too small to see much of the Web page. You can stretch it or maximise it, of course, just like any other window, but a neat alternative is to make it ***Full screen****. To do this, press* ***F11*** *or choose* ***Full Screen*** *from the View menu. To switch out of Full Screen mode, do the same again.*

To visit this URL, click once in the text field labelled **Address** near the top of the Internet Explorer window, and type the URL. Make sure there are no typing mistakes: if there are, you might end up somewhere different, or nowhere at all! After typing the address, press **Enter** to make your browser connect to that address and display the page, and in a few moments your screen should show something similar to the screenshot in Figure 4.6. When the page appears, go back to the Internet Options dialog we were using a minute ago and click the button marked **Use Current**. In future, Internet Explorer will connect to this site every time you launch it.

*To stop a page from loading, click on the **Stop** button. The effect is immediate and this will be displayed as greyed.*

Figure 4.6 The National Trust Web site (as it appears in late 2000 – it may look a little different when you see it!).

Activating links

When you move your mouse pointer on the screen you will see that it changes into a hand with a raised index finger when it hovers over underlined text or some of the pictures. At the same time, a URL will appear in the status bar at the bottom of the window. This shows that there is a **hyperlink** at that point. If you click once on the link, the page you are viewing is replaced by another – the one at the address specified by the URL.

You can go back to your original site at any time by clicking on the **Back** button, the one on the very left of the toolbar, or by pressing the **Backspace** key. If there is no 'previous page', this button is greyed.

If you have stopped loading the page but you wish you hadn't, just click on the **Refresh** button (immediately to the right of the previous one) or press **F5**.

Saving text and pictures

When you find an interesting page, you can save it to your hard disk. To do this, simply click on **File/Save As** (shown in Figure 4.7). In the save-file dialog box displayed, select the folder on your hard disk where you want to save the page and choose a different name for it if you want to.

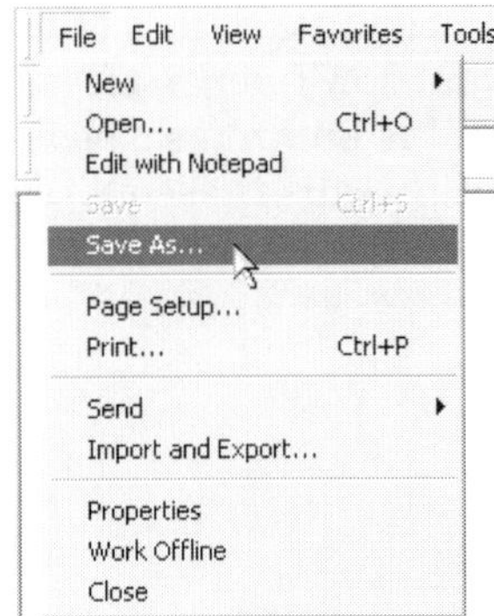

Figure 4.7 Saving a Web page to your hard disk.

To print a page, click on ***File/Print*** *or hold down* ***Ctrl+P****. A fairly faithful reproduction of the whole Web page will be printed on paper. The Print dialog box gives you a few options about exactly what is printed and how.*

In the **Save as type** section of the dialog you can choose whether to save the whole page (including pictures and other items) or just its text. To save the whole page, choose either the **Web Page, Complete** option or the neater **Web Archive** option. To save just the text of the page, choose **Web Page, HTML Only** or **Text file**.

If you just want to save a picture, don't use the File/Save As option. Instead, click on the picture with your right mouse button, then, in the context menu that appears, click on **Save Picture As** (Figure 4.8). (The context menu will contain a few extra options if the picture is also a link.) As before, you will be able to choose a location and name for the saved file.

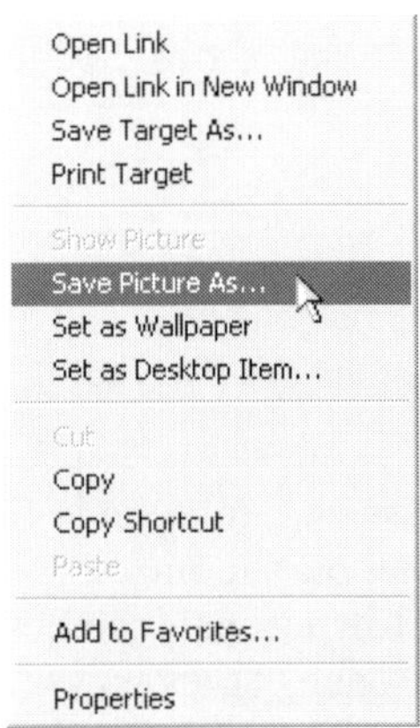

Figure 4.8 Saving a picture from a Web page.

Saving a page address

During your Web surfing activities, you're sure to stumble upon sites that you'd like to visit again in the future. Although you know how to visit a Web page by typing its address into the browser's address bar (that wide text field labelled **Address**), you don't really want to write down and keep track of the URLs of all your favourite Web sites. Fortunately you don't have to: all browsers offer the possibility of creating what is known as a *bookmark*, and Internet Explorer is no different. It calls these stored addresses **Favorites**.

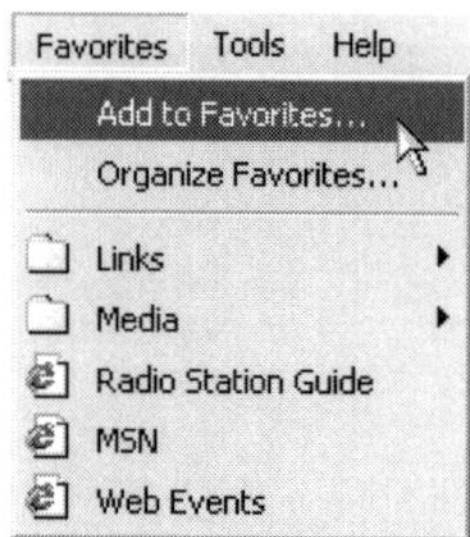

Figure 4.9 The first step in adding the page you're viewing to your list of Favorites.

To add the page you're viewing to your list of Favorites, open the Favorites menu and choose **Add to Favorites** (Figure 4.9). An **Add Favorite** dialog box will appear containing a suggested name for the page (Figure 4.10). If a different name would help you remember what this item is, you can change it to anything you like. Click **OK** to confirm and a new Favorites item will be added.

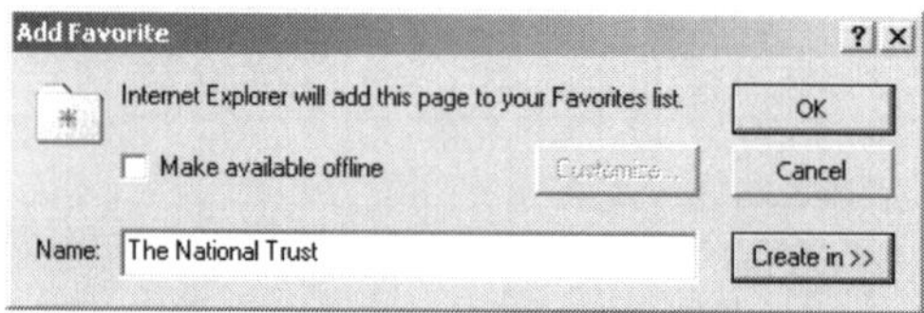

Figure 4.10 Choose a name to help you remember which site this refers to.

There are two ways to use one of these addresses again. One is to click on **Favorites** in the Menu bar again, then on the name you chose for the Favorites item you created. The alternative is to click the **Favorites** icon on the toolbar. In this case, the browser window splits vertically into two parts and, in the left-hand window (shown in Figure 4.11) you will see your Favorites list. Click the name of the site you want to visit.

Organizing your Favorites

Within a short time, your Favorites list may become too long and you'll need to do some housekeeping. To do this, you can reorganise your list by clicking on **Favorites/Organize Favorites**.

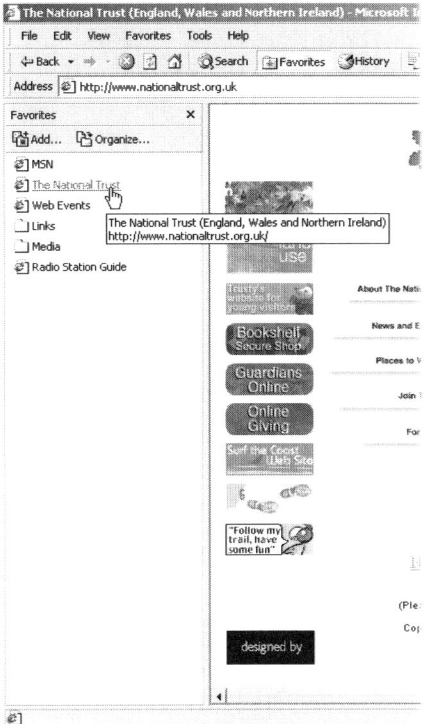

Figure 4.11 The Favorites window can stay open while you surf, making all your favourite sites easy to access.

From the dialog box that appears (shown in Figure 4.12), you can delete Favorites items, rename them, change their order, or divide them into different folders according to their subject. Changing the display order of your Favorites is very easy. Click on the one you want to move and drag it to wherever you want it.

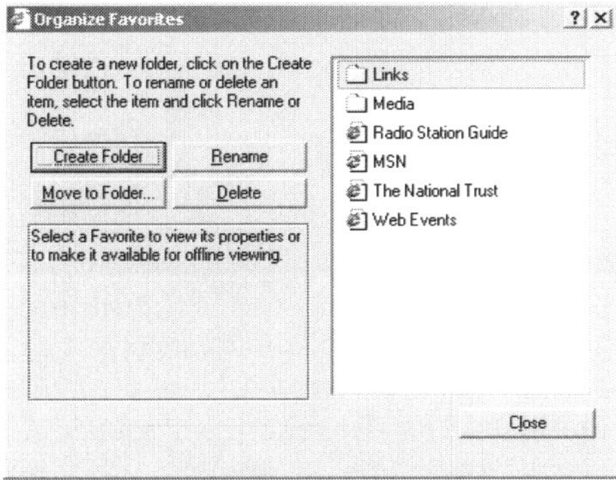

Figure 4.12 Choose Organize Favorites to reorganize your Favorites list.

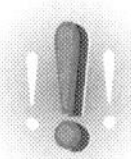

Because you've already visited these sites, Internet Explorer may have stored copies of the pages on your hard disk. If so, you may be able to review the pages without going online. However, not all pages are stored in this way, so this isn't guaranteed.

History

Without you having to do anything, the sites you visit are automatically stored in a history folder whose contents you can explore at any time by clicking on the **History** button on the toolbar. In the left-hand window, you'll see a set of icons corresponding to the previous week and to the days of the week. By clicking on one of these, you will see lists of the sites you visited on particular days. You can then visit one of these sites again simply by clicking on one of these entries.

You can modify the period your pages are kept in the history folder or clear history with the options offered in the Internet Options dialog box that we saw earlier in this chapter.

Downloading files

Most of the links you click on a Web page will fetch a new Web page to display in the browser, but links can point to any type of file at all, including spreadsheets, databases, applications, and other types of file that you can **download** (copy to your own hard disk) for later use.

When you click on the link, a save-file dialog will ask you to choose a folder on your hard disk and, while the transfer is happening, another dialog box will keep you informed on the progress (Figure 4.13). If you find that it is too slow, you can cancel the download without disconnecting from your service provider by clicking on the **Cancel** button, and perhaps try downloading the same file again later.

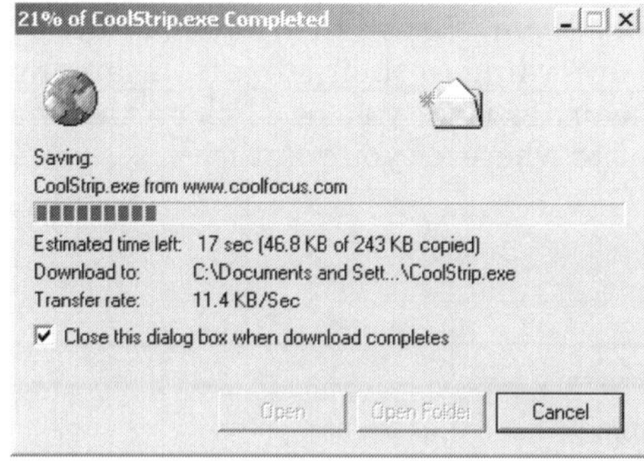

Figure 4.13 Internet Explorer keeps you posted on the progress of the file you're downloading.

During the transfer, there's nothing stopping you from carrying on exploring the Web. Windows is a multi-tasking system and Internet Explorer fully supports this mode. This will cause your download to happen a little more slowly, though, because your modem has to divide its energies between retrieving the file you are downloading *and* the new page you're trying to view.

Closing Internet Explorer

Nothing easier: as with all software running in Windows, click on **File/Close** or on the × icon in the upper-right corner of the window, or press **Alt+F4**. This doesn't interrupt the connection to your ISP, but if you don't have any other Internet-related programs open you may see a dialog box asking if you'd like to disconnect.

Customising Internet Explorer

Internet Explorer has a large number of options you can customise to suit your own needs or tastes.

Removing images

Images add a lot of visual interest to Web pages but, unfortunately, the size of picture files increases the downloading time of a page considerably. If you're in a hurry, or you're more concerned with the text on a page than its appearance, you can prevent the download of images.

To do this, choose **Internet Options** from the Tools menu, and click on the **Advanced** tab. Scroll downwards until you reach the **Multimedia** icon and deselect the check box beside **Show pictures** (shown in Figure 4.14). While you're there, you can also choose to prevent sounds, animations and videos from playing by removing the check marks from the corresponding boxes.

*With the display of pictures turned off (or any time you're waiting for a picture to appear that's taking a bit too long), right-click inside the picture's box and choose **Show Picture** from the context menu.*

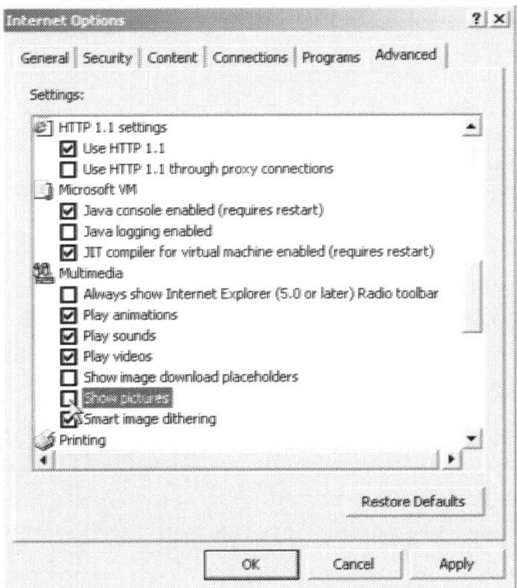

Figure 4.14 You can make Web pages arrive faster by preventing the display of images.

Where the images should be, you'll just see an empty box containing a small coloured icon. If the page's author chose to enter one, you may see a description of the missing image in this box.

Figure 4.15 shows you how a page is displayed when image-display is switched off. As a comparison, Figure 4.16 shows you the same page with normal display of pictures.

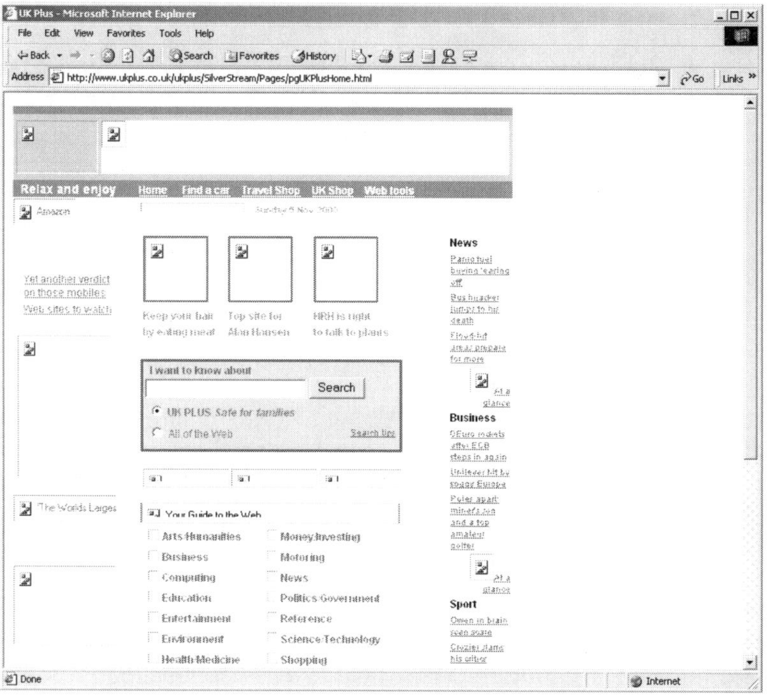

Figure 4.15 A typical Web page displayed after deactivating the display of images.

Cache management

To reduce downloading time for pages, browsers try to keep the contents of visited sites in a section on your hard disk known as the **cache**. You can change the amount of space allocated to the cache in the Internet Options dialog box (which we've already used several times in this chapter) by clicking on the **Settings** button in the Temporary Internet Files section.

Several options are offered, with the default option set to **Automatically**. The default setting isn't too bad, but it's not ideal since you can never be sure when you're seeing the latest edition of a Web page and when you're seeing an old copy stored on your own hard disk. The best setting is **Every time you start Internet Explorer**. This way, every time you start surfing and revisit a site, you can be sure you're seeing any changes that have been made to it since your last visit.

Figure 4.16 The same Web page again, this time with all its images displayed.

Using multiple windows

With a multi-tasking system such as Windows, there is nothing stopping you from launching several Internet Explorer sessions at the same time. There are several reasons why you might have two or more Internet Explorer windows open:

- You can read a page in one window while you're waiting for a page to finish loading in another.
- If you're searching for information, you can search in two or more places at once and perhaps find the treasure a little sooner.
- You can drag-and-drop hyperlinks from one window into another. So if you have a list of interesting links in one window, you can look at each in turn in the second window without moving away from that useful list.

To open a new window, press **Ctrl+N** or choose **File/New/Window**. You can make a link open in a new window by holding the **Shift** key when you click the link, or by right-clicking the link and choosing **Open link in New Window**.

Don't expect to speed up your surfing a lot by using two windows. Ultimately your modem still has to download the same amount of data as if you were using only one window. Using two windows isn't like having two modems!

Multimedia

We've already mentioned that Internet Explorer can display many other types of files apart from the HTML documents and pictures which make up Web pages: video, animation, MIDI, MP3 or WAV audio, and most types of 'multimedia' format are supported. But there are thousands of different types of file, and a browser can't possibly display all of them!

When the program receives a file it doesn't recognise (an application or a compressed Zip file, for example), it displays a dialog box like the one in Figure 4.17 asking you what you wish to do, and prompting you to save the file to disk. When this happens, click **OK** and follow the instructions for downloading which we covered a few pages earlier.

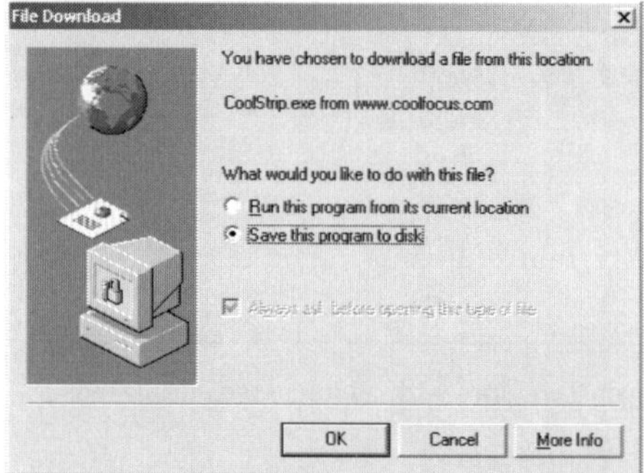

Figure 4.17 If Internet Explorer can't display a particular file, it will offer to download it and save it on your hard disk.

E-mail and mailing lists

5

How e-mail works

How to write messages

Setting up Outlook Express

The Outlook Express window

Mailing lists

It doesn't have quite the same appeal as the World Wide Web, but what e-mail lacks in glitz it more than makes up for in usefulness. That accounts for why e-mail has become the most widely used of all the Internet's services: a message can be typed quickly; one or more computer files can be attached as 'extras' to be sent along with it; and the whole lot can be on the computer of someone on the other side of the world in a matter of minutes. All for much less than the price of a first-class stamp!

How e-mail works

E-mail is a 'real time' system: if you send a message to a friend and you both have permanent Internet connections, your friend will receive this message almost immediately. But what happens if your friend uses an ISP for his connection? He may not be online when you send your message to him, so of course he can't receive it. In his absence, your mail must go somewhere to wait until he *is* online.

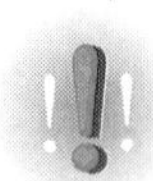

E-mail won't wait in this box forever, but if you go on holiday for a few weeks and can't go online to check your e-mail while you're away, it will still be waiting when you get back. Most ISPs will delete e-mail if the mailbox hasn't been checked for several months.

This is where e-mail servers come in. These applications run on computers permanently linked to the Internet. The protocol used for *sending* messages is known as **SMTP** (**Simple Mail Transfer Protocol**). A second protocol is used for *receiving* messages, known as **POP3** (**Post Office Protocol**, currently in its third version). POP works as though you had a post office box with your username on it. All the messages that arrive for you are placed inside your personal mailbox on your ISP's server, and they'll wait there until you go online and use your e-mail program to connect to the mail server and see what's waiting to be collected (if anything).

How to write messages

A message composed in e-mail is made up of two parts: the **header** and the **body** of the message.

Message header

The header is broken down into the following pieces:

To: The address to which the message is being sent. This would be something like joe.bloggs@freeserve.net, meaning that the message will be sent to the mailbox named joe.bloggs at the Freeserve ISP service.

From: The address from which the message was sent (in other words, your e-mail address).

Reply to: A reply address. Usually this is the same as the e-mail address of the sender, but it's possible to specify a different reply address if, for example, you're sending mail from your business e-mail address but you'd like replies sent to you at home.

Subject: A one-line indication of the topic of the message.

CC: Short for carbon copy. You can type extra e-mail addresses of other people who should receive a copy of the message. (You could alternatively include these extra addresses in the To field, separating each address with a semi-colon.)

BCC: Short for blind carbon copy. This works like the CC field but hides the list of other recipients from view so that the reader won't know who else received a copy.

Attachments: One or more separate computer files that are being sent with the message.

When you start to write a new e-mail message, you'll see text fields for most of these fields and you can fill in the ones you need to.

Message body

This is the main blank section of the message window where you type the message itself. E-mail is an informal method of communication: don't follow the traditions of letter-writing, but keep it short and to the point.

General rules

The relaxed style doesn't give you licence to be careless! Pay attention to your style, especially to your spelling.

NEVER TYPE A MESSAGE IN CAPITAL LETTERS! ON THE INTERNET, WHERE LIVE SPEECH HAS ONLY RECENTLY BECOME POSSIBLE, TYPING IN CAPITALS IS REGARDED AS SHOUTING AND WILL PROMPT SOME ANGRY RESPONSES FROM YOUR RECIPIENTS.

Because e-mail is such an immediate and relaxed form of communication, think twice and re-read what you've written before clicking the ***Send*** *button. If you've written a rude or angry reply to a message, are you sure it's justified? More importantly, are you sure you haven't misunderstood the intention of the writer? Remember that messages you receive may sometimes seem a little brusque simply because they were written quickly.*

Don't include your home address, phone number, or place of work (or school) in a message unless the recipient really needs to know them (and doesn't know them already). This is partly in keeping with the '*It's not letter-writing!*' rule, and partly for basic security reasons. Make sure your children understand and observe this rule, too.

Never, ever, include your credit card details or your username and password in an e-mail message. Anyone who has a valid reason for wanting these details will also be able to offer you a secure way of transmitting them: they wouldn't dream of asking you to send them by e-mail!

Try to resist the temptation to use 'stationery' for e-mail messages (background images, patterns and pictures). They make a normal tiny e-mail message much larger (usually between 10 and 50 times as large). E-mail is supposed to be quick and simple, not a work of art. People who receive a lot of e-mail each day won't want to talk to you if all your messages take 10 times as long to download as everyone else's!

Confidentiality

Never forget that your service provider has the ability to read e-mail messages you send via their computer, as does the administrator of any other server through which the message passes on its way to the intended recipient. Of course, your message is just one of millions, but e-mail is certainly not regarded as a secure or private form of communication – far from it.

As we'll see in Chapter 11, there are measures you can take to encrypt e-mail messages which, although still not foolproof, are a great aid to security. Otherwise, the golden rule is: if you'd be embarrassed to hear it read on the 10 o'clock news, don't write it!

Returned mail

When you sign up with an ISP, you'll automatically be assigned your own mailbox and e-mail account. If you decide to cancel your subscription and switch to a different ISP, that e-mail account will also be cancelled. When someone tries to send e-mail to you at that account, the message will be *bounced back* to them (in other words, it will be returned to them with the error message 'User unknown').

If you switch to a different ISP, you will need to let all your friends, family and colleagues know your new e-mail address. This could take some time, and some may still send you messages that will never reach you. Therefore it's best to hang onto your old account for a while after signing up for your new one, just to be sure you don't miss any important messages. Another option is to sign up for an e-mail forwarding service which will provide you with a fixed e-mail address for life (such as the service provided by Bigfoot at **http://uk.bigfoot.com** – Figure 5.1). Tell your correspondents this permanent address, and all received messages will be automatically forwarded to your current ISP e-mail address. If that changes, just go back to the forwarding service's Web site and modify your account details so that they'll forward e-mail to the new ISP address instead.

How to save on your telephone bill

Those with a permanent connection to the Internet (or those who use it at work) can take their time and read their messages one by one, and reply to each of them carefully and at length. As this is probably not the case for you, it's useful to know how to do as much as possible before actually connecting.

The trick is to go online and retrieve any e-mail messages waiting for you but *don't start reading them yet!* Instead, disconnect from the Net first. Then you can take your time preparing replies without feeling rushed by those expensive minutes ticking by. This is known as **working offline**: most e-mail programs have a folder called an Outbox where messages you want to send are stored if you're not online. When you're ready, reconnect and send all those messages in one batch, quickly and very cheaply, with no wasted online time.

Another option is to sign up for a ***Web-based e-mail account*** *such as Hotmail (****http://www.hotmail.com****) or Yahoo! Mail (****http://uk.mail.yahoo.com****). Because you access this mail account from a Web site it's not dependent upon which ISP you use, and you can access your e-mail from any Net-connected computer in the world.*

Figure 5.1 Sign up for a free permanent e-mail address at Bigfoot.

Setting up Outlook Express

Both Internet Explorer and Netscape, the two most-used browsers, include e-mail programs, but these are by no means the only options. Two of the best-known e-mail programs are Pegasus Mail (for Windows, from **http://www.pmail.com**) and Eudora (for Windows and Macintosh, from **http://www.eudora.com**), which are comparable in their quality.

However, Microsoft offers its own e-mail program, Outlook Express, with Internet Explorer and includes it with Windows, and as a result that's become one of the most popular e-mail programs in use. Since you have Internet Explorer, you already have Outlook Express, so that's what we'll concentrate on for the remainder of this chapter.

Starting Outlook Express

The first time you open Outlook Express, you will have to specify some options so that it can connect to the e-mail and news servers of your service provider and manage your e-mail. Apart from your name and your e-mail address, you must specify the Internet addresses of these servers (which your service provider should have told you).

Adding an e-mail account

When you signed up for your ISP account, the CD-based setup almost certainly created an e-mail account for you in Outlook Express (Figure 5.2). Nevertheless, it's useful to know how to do that in case you ever want to add extra e-mail accounts.

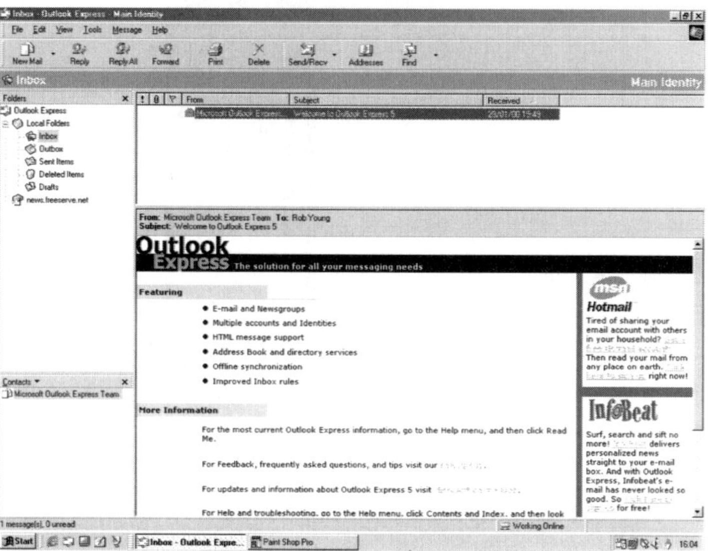

Figure 5.2 The Outlook Express window.

Click on Tools/Accounts to display the Internet Accounts dialog box shown in Figure 5.3. In this dialog you should see the account created by your ISP's setup program, or one you created when prompted after starting Outlook Express for the first time. You can modify its settings (if, for example, you chose one of the wrong ones by mistake) by clicking on the **Properties** button. A dialog box with five tabs will open, allowing you to make the necessary changes.

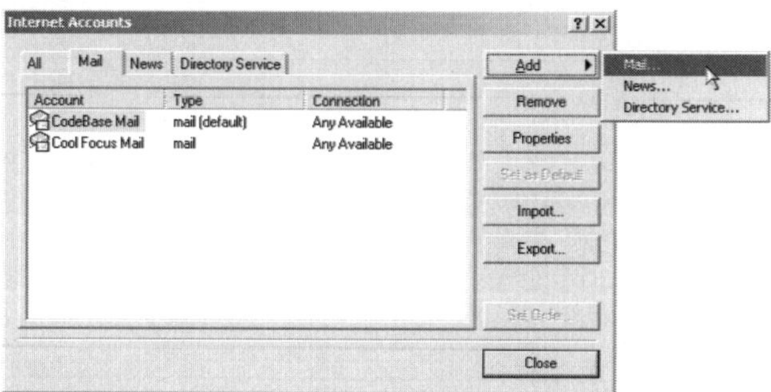

Figure 5.3 The Outlook Express dialog box where you manage your e-mail and news accounts.

To create a new e-mail account, click the **Add** button, then the **Mail** option, which will start the Wizard that helps you create new accounts. In four simple steps you'll enter your name (or the name you want recipients to see when they receive mail from this account); the e-mail address of this account; the names of your ISP's e-mail servers, which your ISP will tell you; and the username and password you use to access your incoming e-mail mailbox. After completing these steps, you'll see an additional account has been added to the list in the **Internet Accounts** dialog box.

Your username and password for your primary (or only) e-mail account will usually be the same as those you use to dial up to the Internet and log on to your service provider.

At the moment your new account has a dull name like **mail.myprovider.com**. To change this to something friendlier, select the account name, click the **Properties** button, and replace that name with something better at the top of the dialog box that appears.

Main e-mail options

By opening the Tools menu and selecting Options, you can customise the behaviour of Outlook Express to suit yourself. Most of the options are set at sensible settings, so you shouldn't need to change much, but we'll show you the main options here and point out the ones that UK users should adjust. Because you'll also use this program for accessing newsgroups in Chapter 6, we'll adjust the settings relating to newsgroups too.

General tab

On this tab, remove the checkmark beside **Send and receive messages at startup** (Figure 5.4). Often you'll want to start Outlook Express to look for a message, or reply to messages, but not actually go online yet, and it would be irritating to have your computer try to dial up.

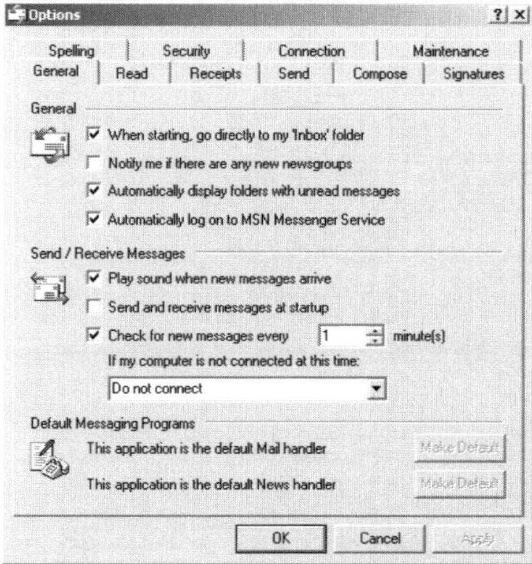

Figure 5.4 The General tab of Outlook Express's Options dialog box.

Send tab

It's a good idea to remove the checkmark beside the option: **Send messages immediately**. This allows you to work offline, as mentioned earlier in the chapter, by putting your outgoing messages into the Outbox folder until you go online. Otherwise, as soon as you finish writing one message your computer goes online to send it, even though you might have five more to write!

In the Mail Sending Format section choose **Plain Text**. Your correspondents will thank you for it, since they will be able to read all of your text much better than if you had chosen HTML. The same should be selected in the News Sending Format section.

Signatures tab

A Signature is a short piece of text automatically added to each outgoing message. It contains your name, and it might also include your e-mail address, Web site URL, company details (but not usually your home address or phone number), and perhaps a short quote that sums up your outlook on life. (Weird? Yes, but it's another common 'e-mail thing'!)

Click on **New** to create a new signature, and you'll see an item named **Signature #1** appear. Click on **Rename** and type a better name for it such as **Business Signature**, or **Personal Signature**. In the text area below, type the text that should appear in the message when you include this signature (Figure 5.5). A signature should be kept fairly short: about 5 lines is the maximum, so the small size of the text box in this dialog should be taken as a hint. Remember, it's a signature, not a CV.

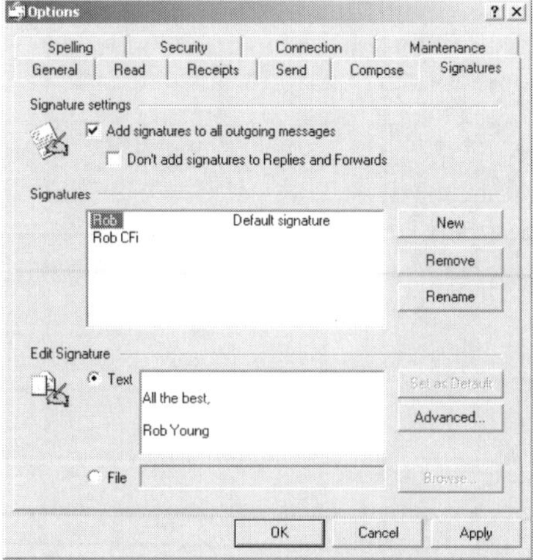

Figure 5.5 A typical example of a simple signature.

Spelling tab
The option to spell-check your e-mail messages will be available only if you've installed Microsoft Office 97 or later (or a part of Office that includes a spell-checking option, such as Microsoft Word). On this tab, you can choose the default spell-checking language to use, and choose related options.

Security tab
This page allows you to sign up for a digital ID (although it forces you to use one supplier of IDs recommended by Microsoft, ignoring many others). This is a type of electronic certificate that confirms your identity, and it can be used to encrypt your message, making it somewhat more secure than ordinary e-mail, or to verify that the message really did come from you. If you like the idea, you can get a free digital ID (for personal use, not business) from Thawte at **http://www.thawte.com**, and installation of this certificate in Outlook Express happens automatically.

The Outlook Express window

The Outlook Express window consists of four separate sections, or 'panes'. You can stretch or shrink each section by moving the mouse over the border between two sections and dragging.

If you go to View/Layout, you can check and uncheck boxes to hide or display various panes in Outlook Express. For example, you can hide the Preview pane, or choose where it should be. (With the Preview pane hidden, you'll have to double-click a message header to read it.)

- The upper-right window displays the list of messages in the currently selected folder. For example, if the Inbox folder is selected, you'll see the list of messages in the Inbox. Messages are shown here as just their header (the To, From, Subject and Date fields).
- The lower-right section is the optional Preview pane: when you click on one of the message headers in the pane above, the body of that message will be shown here.
- The lower-left section is your Contacts list, showing all the people whose addresses you've added to your Address Book (more about that later in the chapter). To send a new message to one of these people, double-click the name.
- The upper-left window is the folders list. Currently it contains five folders (described below), but you can add as many folders as you like and drag messages from the message list on the right into any folder to organise your messages in any way that makes sense to you.

*To move from one field to another, press the **Tab** key. To go through the boxes in reverse order, hold down the **Shift** key while pressing the **Tab** key.*

The first time you start Outlook Express, the folder list contains these five folders:

Inbox. When new e-mail messages arrive, this is where they will be placed.

Outbox. This will contain messages that you've written but haven't sent yet. Once you click on **Send/Receive**, these will be sent and automatically moved into the Sent Items folder.

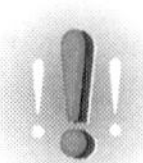

Never attach large files unless the recipient is expecting you to send them. Anything over 100Kb qualifies as 'large', and Outlook Express shows the size of a file in the Attach field to help you avoid mistakes.

Sent Items. This folder holds items that have been successfully sent. This is your confirmation that a message really has been sent.

Deleted Items. Sometimes it's necessary to tidy your e-mail folders and get rid of unwanted mail. When you delete a message, this is where it goes (much like Windows' own Recycle Bin).

Drafts. If you've written a message that you don't want to send straight away (perhaps you haven't finished it), instead of clicking **Send**, choose Save from the File menu, or press **Ctrl+S**. The message will be stored in the Drafts folder. When you want to finish the message, open Drafts and double-click the message header. When you click the **Send** button, the message will be placed in the Outbox and removed from Drafts.

Sending an e-mail message

Click on the **New Message** button, or on File/New/Mail Message, or press **Ctrl-N**. A new message window will open (as shown in Figure 5.6). You'll see the fields we mentioned earlier in the chapter, and the ones you need to complete are the **To** field, where you enter the e-mail address of the recipient, and the **Subject** field (giving a brief description of the topic).

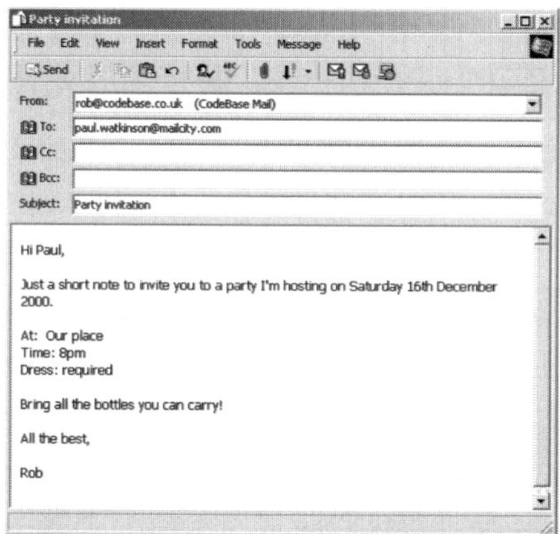

Figure 5.6 An e-mail message ready to be sent.

Depending upon your Signature settings, covered earlier, you may see your default signature in the main part of the window already. If your signature hasn't been added automatically, you can open the Insert menu, move down to Signature, and select which signature you'd like to use. Then, of course, you write the body of the message.

If you wish, you can send copies of any computer files with this message as **attachments** – perhaps a picture, a program, a sound file, anything. To do this, click the paperclip button on the toolbar and you'll be able to choose the file from a standard open-file dialog box. (You can also drag-and-drop a file's icon into this window to attach that file.) The attached file is shown as an icon in the **Attach** field (this field isn't visible unless one or more files have been attached).

Outlook Express displays a number in blue beside folders sometimes. This indicates how many unread messages that folder contains. To find out how many messages are in a particular folder in total, click that folder to open it, then look at Outlook Express's status bar.

Finally, click the **Send** button on the toolbar of the message window. The window will close and the message will be added to the Outbox. If you open the Outbox folder, you'll see the header of the message.

Sending and receiving messages

The only way to find out whether there's any mail waiting to be received is by connecting to your ISP and clicking the **Send/Receive** button on the toolbar. When you do this, any messages waiting in your Outbox will be sent and you'll see a dialog box showing you the progress of messages being sent and then messages being received (if any).

If you look in your Sent Items folder, you should see that all the messages that were waiting in the Outbox are here instead.

Select the Inbox folder, and you'll see the incoming messages arriving in that folder. You'll also see the number beside the word **Inbox** change to indicate how many unread messages that folder now contains. Click the header of any message in the Inbox to read it in the preview pane below.

If you see a paperclip at the right-hand end of the preview window's grey bar, the message you're reading has one or more files attached (Figure 5.7). Click the paperclip to see a list of the files attached and their sizes.

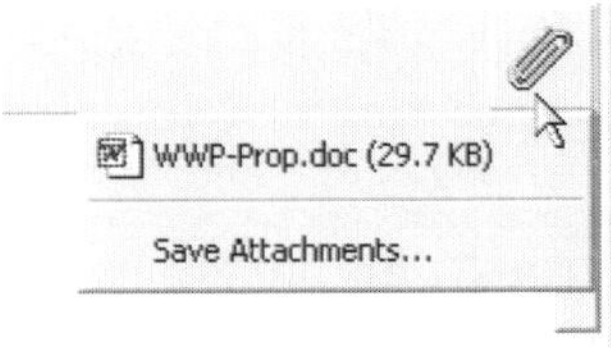

Figure 5.7 The paperclip icon indicates that there's a file attached to the message you're reading.

If you click on one of the files, Outlook Express will ask you whether you want to open it or save it to disk. If the attachment is a picture file (identified by .jpeg or .gif extensions) you can safely open it; for other formats, it's best to save it to disk and check it for viruses before opening (see Chapter 11).

Alternatively, click on the Save Attachments option. This will let you select one or more of the attached files (Figure 5.8) and choose a folder where they should be saved.

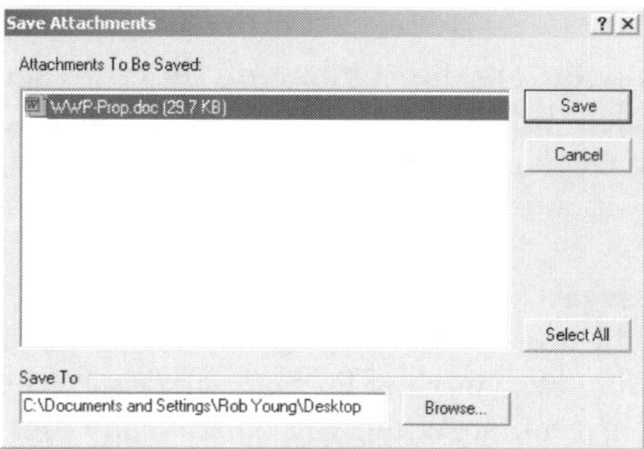

Figure 5.8 Choose **Save Attachments** if you want to choose which to save and where.

Replying to a message

After you've read a message, you're likely to want to send a reply. Click on the **Reply** button on the toolbar. (The **Reply All** button is used only when you wish to reply to many people; for example, when you're replying to a message that was sent to a group of people and you want each to have a copy of your reply.) A window for composing a message (see Figure 5.6) will appear with the headings and the original message text. Note that the letters 'Re:' are added in front of the subject, indicating to the recipient (and yourself) that this is a response to an earlier message.

You'll also notice that the original message is *quoted* in the reply, with a '>' sign inserted before each line. This is a courtesy to help the recipient remember what you're actually replying to, but it shouldn't be necessary to leave the whole message (and you may feel that none of it is needed).

The more text there is in a message, the longer that message takes to send, so trim down any quoted text to the bare memory-jogging essentials. If anything starts with '>>' it's from an old message being quoted a second time, so it can definitely be removed!

Once you've completed your reply, click the **Send** button in the usual way to place this message in the Outbox ready for sending.

Forwarding a message

You can forward a message to another address by clicking the **Forward** button on the toolbar. The message you wish to forward will appear in the message window, and you only have to enter the address it should be forwarded to. There's nothing to stop you from adding to the text or deleting some of it. If it had an attachment, you can remove this.

Returned messages

If you get the address of the message recipient wrong, the message will be sent back to you along with a brief explanation of the reason. That explanation may not always make sense, but it usually means that there's something wrong with the address you sent the message to.

The first thing to do is to check that the address you used is correct: no spelling mistakes, and no spaces. If you're sure the address is correct, there may be a problem with the recipient's mail server, so try to send the message later in the day. If the address was wrong, create a new message (putting in the correct address this time), then copy-and-paste the body of the old message into the new one to save retyping it, and click **Send**.

Your address book

You will almost certainly end up exchanging messages with regular correspondents. In this case, instead of worrying about typing in their e-mail address every time, put them in your address book. It's a useful shortcut for several reasons: first, you don't have to remember anyone's e-mail address (or risk mistyping it!); second, you can refer to people by their real name or an alias; third, you don't have to type anything at all; fourth, you can store extra information such as phone numbers, addresses and Web site URLs in the address book, making it a complete contacts management system.

*If someone sends you a message, you can add them to your address book very easily. Just right-click the message header in the Inbox and choose **Add Sender to Address Book**. To add extra details to someone's address book entry (or change existing details), click the **Address Book** icon on the toolbar, select the required contact and choose **Properties**.*

When an address is added to the address book, the person's name is included. You can also include an easy-to-type nickname; for example, in Figure 5.9, you can see we've assigned the nickname **jb** to our fictitious friend Joe Bloggs. With this contact in the address book, we can send a message to Joe in several ways:

- If the Contacts pane of Outlook Express is visible, just double-click the name **Joe Bloggs**.
- Click the **New Message** button and begin typing **Joe Bloggs** in the **To** field. Before you get far, Outlook Express should recognise this as a name from the address book and complete it for you automatically.
- Type the nickname, **jb** into the **To** field.

Deleting unwanted messages

After a number of weeks or months of using e-mail, your message folders will probably contain a lot of useless and out-of-date information. As a security device, deleting messages is doubly useful. To delete a message, right-click on its header and choose **Delete**, or just select the header and press the **Delete** key. The message is placed in the **Deleted Items** folder, where it will stay until you empty that folder (so you can still open the message if you need to).

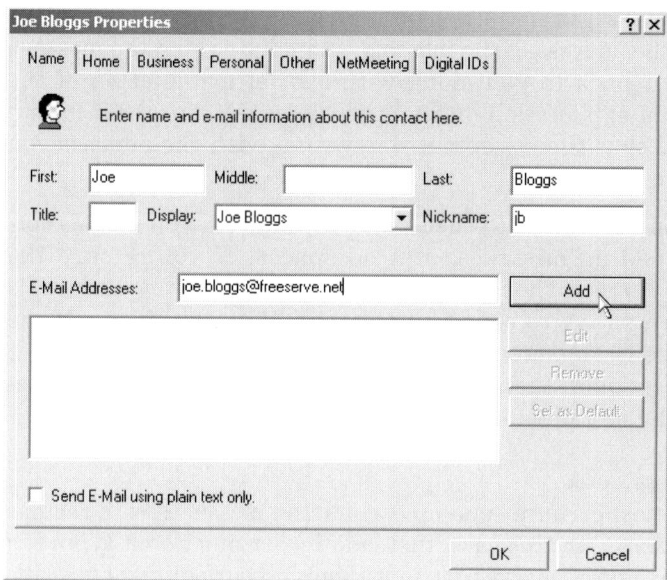

Figure 5.9 The address book can store vast amounts of information about each contact.

Every so often you should empty the Deleted Items folder to recover the space it's using. Right-click on the folder and choose **Empty 'Deleted Items' Folder**.

Sorting your mail

Your original folders will soon fill up and you will have difficulty trying to find your files. To get some order, you need to create your own specialised folders (People, Cooking, Business, Friends, and so on) in which you can store your messages once you've read and replied to them.

To create a new folder, click File/Folder/New. In the Create Folder dialog box (shown in Figure 5.10), enter the name of the new folder in the **Folder name** field, select where to place the folder (usually **Local Folders** unless you'd like the new folder to be inside one of the existing folders), then click **OK**.

Mailing lists

Mailing lists are a special type of electronic mail that are more like Usenet newsgroups, which we'll meet in Chapter 6. Unlike e-mail, instead of mailing someone in particular, you write to an automated list manager which assembles all the messages and sends them to the subscribers.

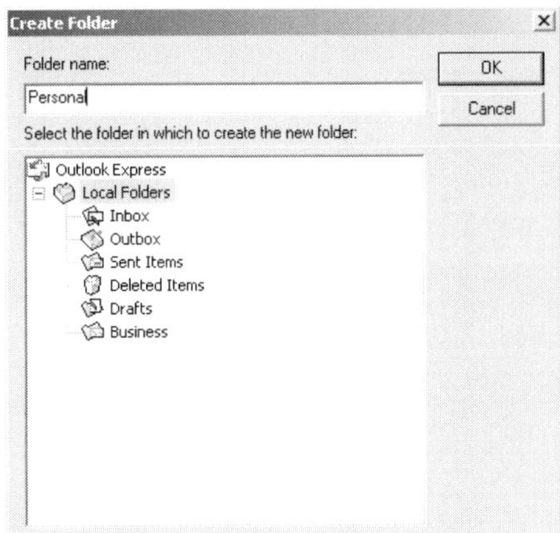

Figure 5.10 Creating additional folders to organise your e-mail messages.

To find mailing lists, use your Web browser to visit ***http://www.liszt.com*** *or* ***http://www.paml.net****.*

Don't sign up for too many lists. After only 12 hours of subscription we were sent 33 messages! You may be able to sign up for a 'digest' version which delivers a single daily or weekly message containing all contributions.

The lists are structured by theme (exotic cuisine, music by Wagner, Microsoft Excel users, and so on) and you can 'subscribe' to any list that interests you. Subscribing means letting the list manager know that you want to receive this list – there are no subscription fees.

Some lists are moderated, meaning that messages won't be distributed until someone has approved them to filter out undesirable or irrelevant contributions. The unmoderated type is more popular, as it provides a completely automatic service.

Operating a mailing list

Mailing lists have two different addresses: one where you send 'command' messages telling the service that you want to subscribe or unsubscribe, or get more information about the list; the other to which you send your contributions to the ongoing discussion. Mixing the two addresses is a common mistake, and a great way to show everybody else that you're new to all this!

The command to subscribe to a list is usually SUBSCRIBE; to remove your subscription, it's UNSUBSCRIBE (but these aren't carved in stone, so always check first!). Each one of these commands needs to specify the name of the list, because the list server may well manage hundreds of different lists.

Get the latest news!

6

What are newsgroups?

Using the Outlook Express newsreader

News on the Web

In the context of the Internet, 'news' doesn't mean the latest headlines from ITN. Newsgroups are more formally known as **Usenet news forums**. Usenet is like a huge notice board divided into lots of different subject-specific areas where anyone can display their questions and offer replies to questions already there (or just put their point of view on a particular topic).

All this is done by writing and sending plain-text messages almost exactly like e-mail. In fact, many e-mail programs work with newsgroups too, including Outlook Express which we used in the previous chapter. The difference is that here you're writing text that may be read by thousands of people, so it's far more important to observe the 'rules'. So important, in fact, that the rules even have their own name: they're referred to as *netiquette* (derived, of course, from Net etiquette).

What are newsgroups?

Usenet consists of over 50,000 different newsgroups (and growing), covering thousands of different subjects. These groups work rather like 50,000 different e-mail mailboxes, all accessible to the public. Anyone can send a message to any of these groups, and anyone can read the messages received by a group. The messages themselves are just like e-mail messages with one exception: instead of sending them to an e-mail address they're sent to a newsgroup address.

There's one other small difference between newsgroup messages and e-mail messages: whereas e-mail messages usually arrive at their destination within seconds or minutes, newsgroup messages may not filter out to the whole Usenet network for 24 hours. The servers that make up this network aren't in constant contact, they usually connect daily to exchange new messages with each other.

Although there are tens of thousands of newsgroups available, you may not necessarily have access to all of them. Newsgroups need vast amounts of disk space: imagine the space needed to store 50,000 groups each containing 2,000 messages, for instance! So your ISP might decide to skip certain less popular groups, and many ISPs refuse to take groups that may offend their users. However, you may still be able to access missing groups through a public news server, as we'll see later in this chapter.

Netiquette

Before you get involved in the groups themselves, it pays to know the 'rules' of Usenet:

Except for in the 'biz' (business) hierarchy of groups, and the 'announce' groups, advertising or sending commercial messages is frowned upon.

If you have a question or comment, make sure it's relevant to the group(s) you're sending it to. You'll probably never have a valid reason to send the same message to more than about five groups; usually you send messages to one group only.

There are specialist 'test' groups such as alt.test, alt.binaries.test and comp.test which you can use to get acquainted with sending messages or finding your way around your newsreader program. Never send test messages to newsgroups that don't have the word 'test' in their names.

AS WITH E-MAIL, DON'T SHOUT! TYPING IN CAPITALS IS REGARDED AS SHOUTING, AND IT'S ONE OF THE WORST OFFENCES POSSIBLE.

Don't send file attachments to newsgroups that don't have the word 'binaries' in their names. This word is a cue that attached files are allowed, and also acts as a warning that messages in that group might be much larger than normal as a result. Users don't want to find huge messages in non-binaries groups.

When you reply to a message in a group, the program you use will *quote* the original message, just as when you reply to e-mail. However, in newsgroups it's far more important to remove anything unnecessary: there are so many messages that it's a courtesy to other users to keep each as short as possible. In fact, since the message you're replying to will still be included in the group, you don't really need to quote *any* of it.

By the same token, keep your signature as short as possible. You'll get some rude comments if you start sending two-line messages that have a 10-line signature!

Newsgroup lingo

Newsgroups have also evolved their own peculiar set of terms and definitions. First, although the whole thing takes place using a form of e-mail, a message to a newsgroup is referred to as an **article**. And you don't *send* an article, you *post* it (so you may see articles termed *postings* as well). Here are a few more oddities:

Spam Spam is an article sent to multiple newsgroups without any thought to whether it's relevant. Most spam is an attempt at cheap advertising (which has a success rate of roughly 0% in newsgroups, but a few people still try it). The word comes from an old Monty Python sketch (ask in the **alt.fan.monty-python** group for a copy!).

Flame A 'flame' is a rude response to an article. You're likely to get flamed if you don't follow the netiquette of newsgroups. In some cases, newsgroups can get so carried away with their internal arguments that the entire group descends into 'flame warfare', with little of interest being said.

FAQ This stands for Frequently Asked Questions, and it's a list of questions with answers. Many newsgroups publish an FAQ regularly, explaining the basics of the topic they're covering so that they can avoid wasting time and effort answering the same simple questions repeatedly. (You'll find FAQs on many Web sites and elsewhere on the Internet – it's become a widespread term.)

Smileys

In spoken English, the speaker's intonation helps to convey the true meaning of what he's saying. For example, you can usually recognise sarcastic humour by the tone of voice or physical gestures, although the words may say something different. In e-mail messages and newsgroup articles you don't have these aids to understanding, so they have been replaced with little symbols designed out of keyboard characters.

These little symbols are called 'emoticons' or 'smileys', and you read them by tilting your head to the left. So when you see this message:

I've just heard that Bill's back :-(

you can tell that the writer regards this as sad news. But if the message read:

I've just heard that Bill's back :-)

it's clear that the writer is pleased about it. You can find lots more smileys at **http://www.cynet.net/smile.html** and **http://www.pop.at/smileys**.

Cross posting

Cross posting means sending the same message to more than one group. As mentioned earlier, you should always keep the number of groups to a bare minimum and be absolutely sure that your message is relevant to the groups you send it to. You can send a message to multiple groups by including each newsgroup name in the **Newsgroups** field of the message, with each separated by a comma or semi-colon.

Public servers

Some service providers do not want to offer newsgroups at all; others only offer a limited number of groups. This leaves you with two problems: how can you tell whether a particular group exists at all, and if it does, where can you access it?

There are two useful websites that can help. The first is **http://www.magma.ca/~leisen/mlnh**. This is a 'master list' of newsgroups that will help you determine whether there's a group dedicated to your favourite subject, and what it's called.

If your ISP doesn't provide the group you want through its own news server, you need a *public access* news server. For a list of public access servers, go to **http://www.newzbot.com** (Figure 6.1). You could also visit **http://www. deja.com**, covered later in this chapter.

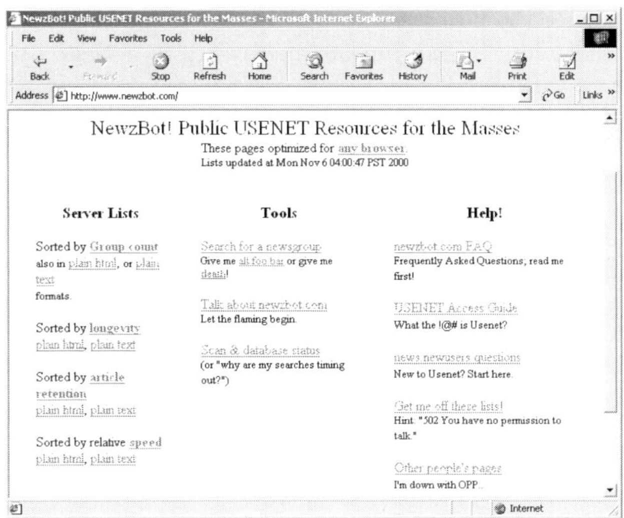

Figure 6.1 Newzbot can help you access a newsgroup that your ISP doesn't provide.

Using the Outlook Express newsreader

As with e-mail in Chapter 5, we're going to use Microsoft's Outlook Express for our examples: after all, you have a copy already, you know how it works, and you've done most of the setting up. However, there are other newsreader programs you can use instead if you'd like to give them a try. Two of the best known are Agent and its free counterpart, Free Agent, both from **http://www.forteinc.com**. Another popular free newsreader is the oddly named TIFNY from **http://www.tifny.com**.

Creating a news account

To work with newsgroups in Outlook Express, go to its **Tools** menu and choose **Newsgroups** (or press **Ctrl+W**).

If you haven't already set up a news account in Outlook Express, the Wizard dialog box will appear to help you create one step by step. You'll be prompted to enter some straightforward information such as your name and e-mail address. You'll also need to know the name of your ISP's news server: this will usually be **news.*serviceprovider.co.uk***, but your ISP can tell you if you're not sure.

At any time, you can create another news account just as easily. Go to Tools/Accounts, click the **Add** button and click **News** to start this Wizard again. You can also modify an existing account by choosing the News tab, selecting your news account and clicking the **Properties** button.

Your news server for the new account will appear at the bottom of Outlook Express's folder list, so you can also switch to newsgroups by simply clicking this item.

The first connection

The first time you use a news account you've created, a message will appear prompting you to download a list of newsgroups available on this news server. Accept by clicking the **Yes** button and then wait while the list of groups is fetched. A dialog box will appear for you to monitor the downloading (Figure 6.2). This can sometimes take five minutes or so, depending on the total number of groups available on the server, but it only has to happen once: the list will be stored on your computer for future use.

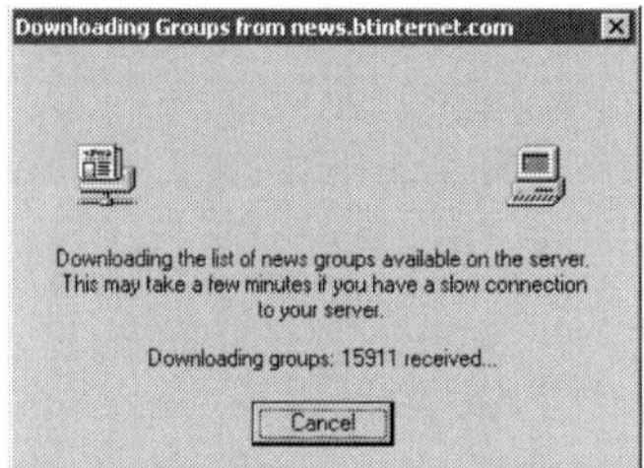

Figure 6.2 The first time you connect to a news server, Outlook Express will download a list of available newsgroups.

Subscribing to newsgroups

Next, you need to *subscribe* to one or more groups. The effect of this operation is to display their names in the folder list so that you can easily retrieve the articles that they contain. Click the Newsgroups button on Outlook Express's toolbar (or choose Tools/Newsgroups) to display the Newsgroup Subscriptions window shown in Figure 6.3.

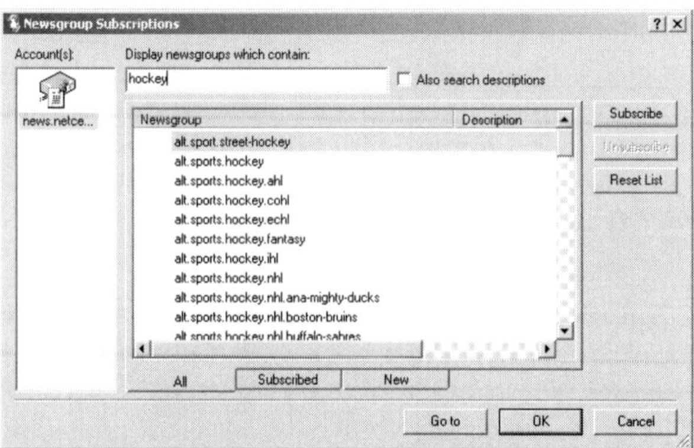

Figure 6.3 Browse through the groups alphabetically, or type a keyword to find matching group names.

This window contains an alphabetical list of all the groups available on the news server. You can see that this tabbed page is labelled **All**. If you subscribe to one or more groups you can click the **Subscribed** tab to see a list of only the groups you're currently subscribed to.

Working through tens of thousands of groups alphabetically isn't very user-friendly: a better option is to type a keyword into the field at the top. Only group names containing this word will be displayed.

To view a newsgroup without subscribing to it, select it and click the **Go To** button. To subscribe to a group, click the **Subscribe** button. You can select any number of groups to subscribe to in the same way (although we recommend you start with just one or two) and click **OK** when you're done. You'll see your subscribed groups in the folder list.

If you chose **Go To**, you'll also see the group name in the folder list. You can subscribe to it by right-clicking it and choosing **Subscribe**.

Cancelling a subscription

Click on Tools/Newsgroups, select the group that you want to cancel your subscription for and click on **Unsubscribe**. Click **OK** when you're done. You can also unsubscribe from a group by right-clicking its name in the folder list and choosing **Unsubscribe**.

Reading the headers of a group

Unlike e-mail, initially only the **headers** of news messages are downloaded. If someone sends you an e-mail message, you'll usually want to read it, so it has to be downloaded, but you won't necessarily be interested in every single article in a newsgroup.

To fetch the headers of a group, you need to be connected to the corresponding news server. By clicking on the small **+** at the left of the name of the server in Outlook Express's folder list, the list of groups you've subscribed to is displayed.

Click once on the name of the group that you want to read and the transfer of the headers will begin. Only the headers posted after your last transfer will be transferred, up to a maximum of 300.

Articles are sorted into **threads**. A thread is a set of articles which all have the same subject line and are part of an ongoing conversation. The first article in a thread will have a little + sign by its name: click that to reveal all the replies (and replies to replies, and so on) that relate to that first article.

Reading an article

The maximum number of 300 headers is because some groups are incredibly popular and generally receive thousands of messages each day. Setting a maximum ensures that you don't have to wait for hours for the latest messages to arrive. You can click the ***Get Next Headers*** *button on the toolbar to get another 300, or change the maximum amount by going to Tools/Options/Read.*

To read the content of an article, you just need to click once on its header. The text of the article is then downloaded from the server (along with any attached files) and displayed in the Preview pane, in the same way as with e-mail (Figure 6.4).

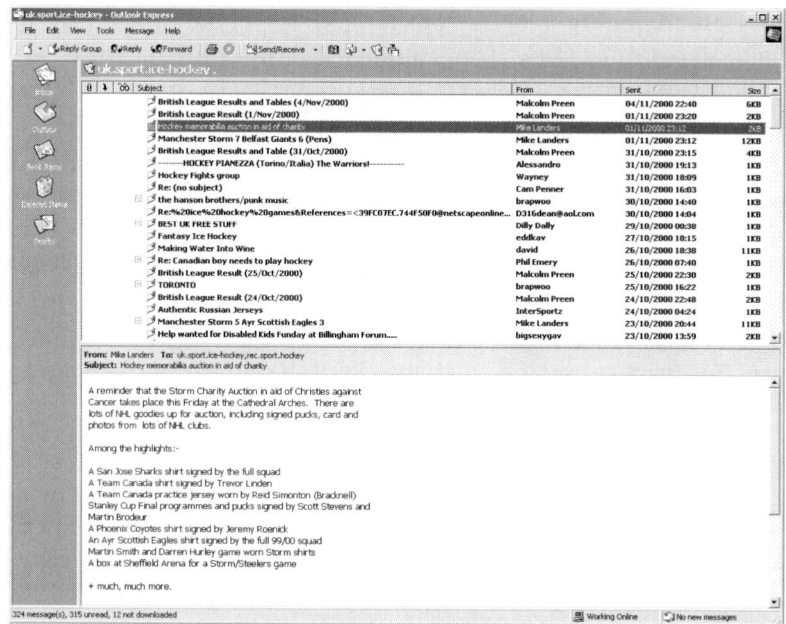

Figure 6.4 Reading an article in the Preview pane.

Although you *can* simply work your way through the articles downloading and reading the ones you're interested in, you might prefer to work with newsgroup articles offline instead, as you do with e-mail. We'll look at how to do this in the section entitled *Reading the news offline*.

Replying to an article

With the news, you have two choices: either reply to the group (where everyone will be able to read the reply), or reply to the author directly by e-mail (the author will be the only one to read it). In general, unless the reply would involve some very personal or irrelevant details, it's best to reply to the group. This way, any other readers can benefit from your reply too.

Unless you're replying only by e-mail, don't forget to remove most (or all!) of the original message from your reply before sending it.

With the message displayed (either in the Preview pane or in a separate message window), click either one of the two **Reply** buttons on the toolbar depending which type of reply you want to send. You can also choose **Reply All** from the Message menu which sends an e-mailed reply to the author as well as posting the reply to the group.

After you've composed your reply, click on the **Send** button in the left-hand corner of the window.

Posting a new article

When you send a reply to an existing article, you are continuing the thread. But if you have a completely new question to ask, or observation to make, you want to create a brand new article and (hopefully) start a new thread. To do this, click the **New Message** button on Outlook Express's toolbar.

In the **Newsgroups** field at the top of the message window you'll see the name of the currently selected newsgroup (Figure 6.5). If this is the name of the group you want to send the message to, you can carry on. If it isn't, click the word **Newsgroups** to its left to select the required groups.

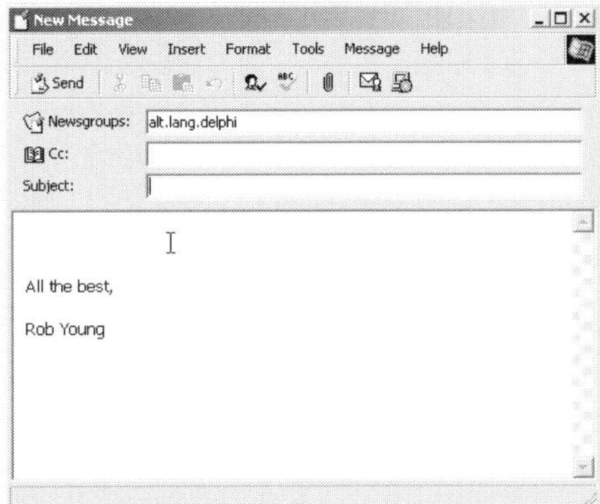

Figure 6.5 The target newsgroup is shown in the top field, but you can click the **Newsgroups** button to select others.

Next, type a subject for the message. Avoid using meaningless subjects like 'Help!' or 'Please read this' – people are unlikely to download your article if they can't tell what it's about! Finally, of course, write the message itself and click the **Send** button.

Attaching a file

You can easily attach a file to a newsgroup message just as you do with e-mail messages: by clicking the paperclip icon on the toolbar of the message window and selecting the required file.

Remember to do this only when the word **binaries** appears in the name of the group. In some cases there are several groups for a particular topic, one of which allows binaries and the rest of which don't. As an example, a graphics application called Lightwave has two newsgroups: **comp.graphics.apps.lightwave** and **alt.binaries.3d.lightwave**. If you have a relevant file to contribute, send it to the second of those. However, it's reasonable to send a message without the attachment to the first group to tell them that you've sent a file to the binaries group that they may find useful.

Reading the news offline

When you download the headers of a group, it's tempting to look down the list of subjects and click on anything interesting to read it straight away. It's similar to surfing the Web, and you can work this way if you want to. A cheaper way, though, is to work offline as much as possible, just as you do with e-mail.

Select each of your subscribed newsgroups in turn to download the latest batches of headers, then disconnect from the Internet and follow these steps:

1. Go to the File menu and click **Work Offline**.
2. Select a group from the folder list on the left to view the headers you downloaded for it.
3. If any subject line seems interesting, right-click it and choose **Download Message Later** (or, if the message is part of an interesting thread, **Download Conversation Later**).
4. A downward arrow will now appear to the left of the header.
5. Repeat the steps above for all messages and all groups until you've marked all the messages and threads that seem worth reading.
6. Open the Tools menu and choose **Synchronize All**. If you're prompted to Connect, say 'yes' to the prompt. Outlook Express will connect to your news server to download all the messages you marked (including their attachments, if they have any).
7. Disconnect from the Internet again and you can read the messages you've downloaded at your leisure.

*If you can't remember which messages you downloaded and which you didn't, go to View/Current View and click **Show Downloaded Messages**. This hides the headers of any messages not downloaded. When you've read the messages, go back and choose the **Show All Messages** option.*

News on the Web

Deja.com is a Web site from which you can search Usenet for either a newsgroup or (even more usefully) text in a news article. In fact, you can even browse through the articles in any newsgroup using your browser instead of your newsreader.

The Deja.com site has grown to offer a lot more than newsgroup searching, but that's what made it famous, and you can reach that section of its site with the URL **http://www.deja.com/usenet** (Figure 6.6). Once you're there, you can pick a news hierarchy from the front page to browse through, look for a newsgroup covering a particular subject by entering a keyword into the text field at the bottom of the window, or look for articles covering the topic you're interested in by using the fields at the top of the page.

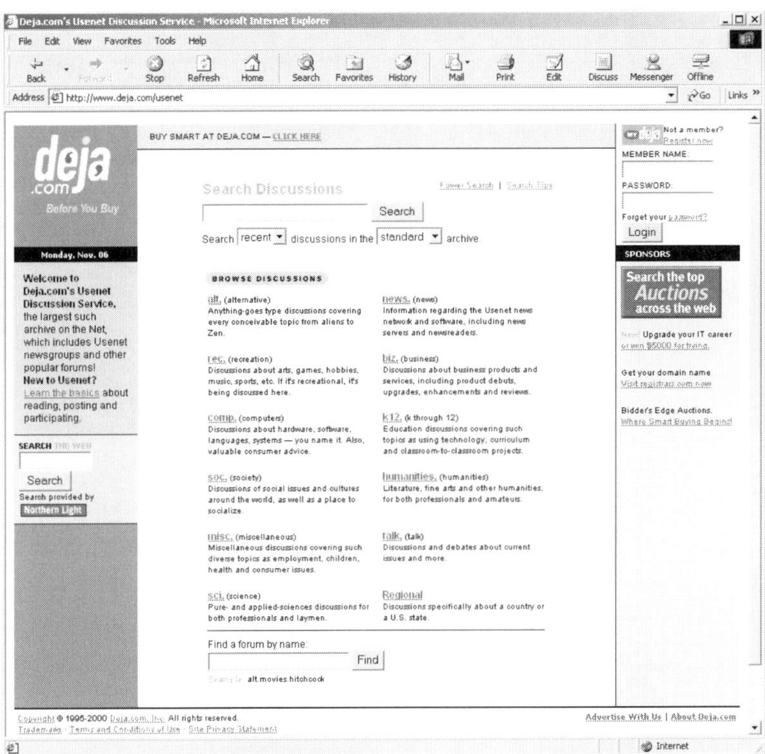

Figure 6.6 Deja.com makes it easy to find a particular newsgroup or search articles for information.

Finding files with FTP

7

File compression

Getting started with FTP

Find that file!

File archives on the Web

On FTP servers, most of the software you'll find will be freeware or shareware programs written by smaller software companies and individuals. You may find previews, demo versions or time-limited copies of some better-known software titles, but don't look for heavyweights like Word, Excel or Lotus SmartSuite – you won't find them!

FTP is short for file transfer protocol, and that probably makes it sound complicated already. It isn't though: it's an Internet service that lets you hunt around the hard disks of other computers looking for files, just as you look around your own computer. If you find something you want, you can copy it to your own computer.

Simply browsing around other computers can be quite enjoyable, but if you're looking for a particular file by name (or even for particular *types* of file, such as screen savers or desktop themes for Windows) it's rather a 'needle in a haystack' proposition. To make it easier, there's an extra tool called Archie which you can use to do the searching for you.

You can also find most types of file on the World Wide Web: there are many shareware archives that have gathered software and popular types of file together (mostly for Windows and Mac users), and we'll look at some of those later in the chapter.

File compression

Before we start looking for files, it's important to know what we're expecting to find. The majority of files placed on the Internet for other users to download are **compressed archives**.

Compression software like this isn't used only on the Internet. The Net has popularised programs like WinZip, so most users have them. This means that you can put compressed files on floppy disks and CD-ROMs, or send them as e-mail attachments, to get the same benefits of smaller and more convenient files, and most users will be able to open them.

An **archive** is a single file that can contain many other files. Most software consists of multiple files: the program itself, a help file, licence details, samples and examples, and so on. Instead of downloading 30 separate files, you just download one big archive file that contains the 30 smaller files.

Most archives are **compressed**. Like Dr Who's Tardis, this means that some technical trickery makes it possible to squeeze perhaps 300Kb of files into a 100Kb archive. For Internet users that's great: you get all the same files, but they download in a third of the time.

The catch, of course, is that you need some method to get the files out of an archive after you've downloaded it (known as **extracting** the files).

On the FTP servers, the majority of the files have the following extensions:

- **.ZIP** The most popular (by far) compression format, mostly used on Windows systems but Apple Mac users can open them too. There are many Zip extraction utilities, but the best is WinZip from **http://www.winzip.com**, shown in Figure 7.1.
- **.HQX** or **.SIT** Popularly used on Apple Macs, these are compressed with StuffIt from **http://www.aladdin.com**. These files can be extracted using StuffIt Expander, from the same Web site.

There's another type of compressed archive: **self-extracting archives**. These are programs which you start like any other program, by double-clicking them. They will then automatically decompress themselves and extract the files inside.

Getting started with FTP

Many of the file servers that you can access using FTP belong to companies, universities and organisations, and they 'mark off' directories as being available for the public to root through. This is known as **anonymous FTP** because you don't have to set up a private username or password to get into this computer. To connect to a computer using anonymous FTP you have to log in, but you use the word **anonymous** as your username, and your e-mail address as your password.

Figure 7.1 The WinZip window displaying the contents of a .ZIP archive.

*The other type of FTP is known as **private FTP**: a company you deal with might give you personal log-in details so that you can access certain files on its computer.*

As you're probably expecting, to get the most out of FTP you need another piece of software. There are dozens of FTP programs available, most of which are either free or very cheap: WS_FTP Professional from **http://www.ipswitch.com**; CuteFTP from **http://www.cuteftp.com**; or the program we'll use in our examples, FTP Explorer from **http://www.ftpx.com**. First, though, if you're not bothered about getting the best from FTP, try using your browser...

Any browser will do

To retrieve files from an FTP server, it isn't absolutely necessary to use a specific type of software. Any browser will do the job, since FTP servers have their own unique URLs just like Web sites. The only difference (as you may remember from Chapter 4) is that addresses for FTP servers start with **ftp://** instead of **http://**.

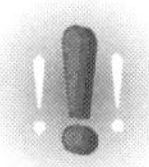

*When using a browser for FTP, you can only download files (copy them to your own computer), you can't **upload** them (copy them from your computer to the remote computer). For that you definitely do need one of the FTP programs mentioned above.*

Type the address into Internet Explorer's address bar in the usual way and press **Enter**. Depending on your settings, Internet Explorer may display the contents of the main directory on the server as a plain list of files and directories, or as folder and file icons as in Figure 7.2. If you don't have this folder view switched on, go to Tools/Internet Options/Advanced and check the box marked **Enable folder view for FTP sites** in the Browsing section near the top of the window.

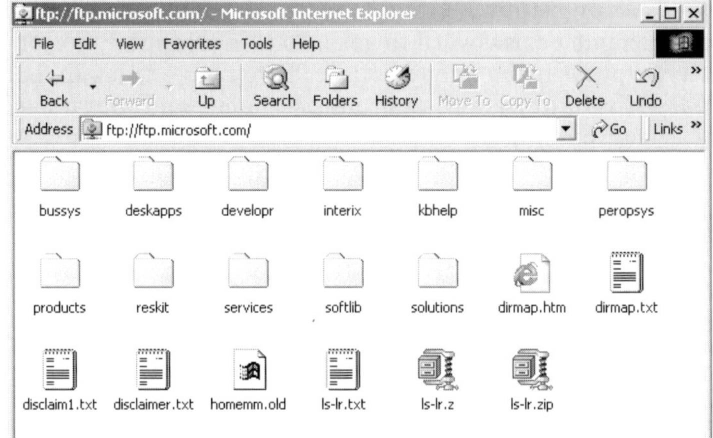

Figure 7.2 Internet Explorer's 'folder view' of an FTP site. Looks familiar!

Once you're in, you can dig around the directories by clicking their name (if you have the plain list of files and directories) or by double-clicking folder icons. In a similar way, you can download any files that look interesting. Look out for files named **index.txt**: these should give a list of files in the current directory, often with a brief description of each.

Using FTP Explorer

FTP Explorer takes its name from the fact that its design is based on that of Windows Explorer, the program you use to browse the files and folders on your own hard disk. Using FTP Explorer is just as easy, as you can see in Figure 7.3: once you're connected to an FTP site, you can open a folder by clicking its icon in the tree to the left, or double-clicking its icon in the main window. To download a file, just double-click it and choose a folder on your hard disk to save it to.

So how do you actually connect to an FTP site? FTP Explorer uses a system it calls 'Profiles'. These are a lot like Internet Explorer's 'Favorites'. When you install FTP Explorer, it will offer to create Profiles for some popular FTP sites and it's a good idea to say yes. Creating a Profile for any other FTP site you want to visit is easy:

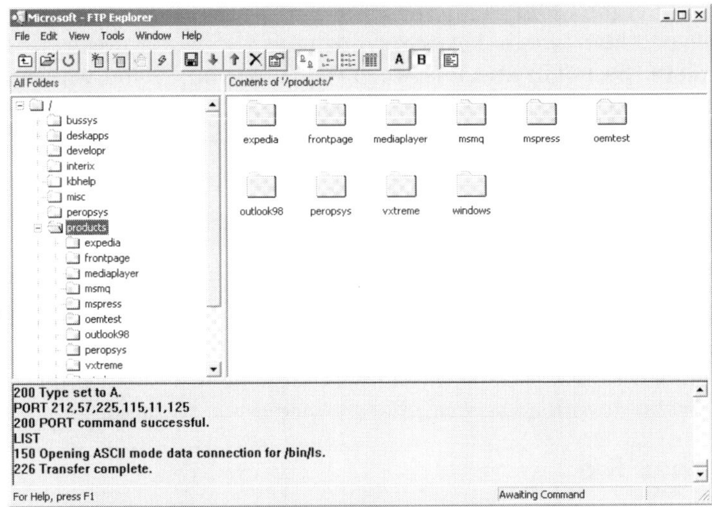

Figure 7.3 The FTP Explorer window.

1. Click the **Connect** button on the toolbar (or choose Connect from the Tools menu) and the dialog shown in Figure 7.4 will appear.

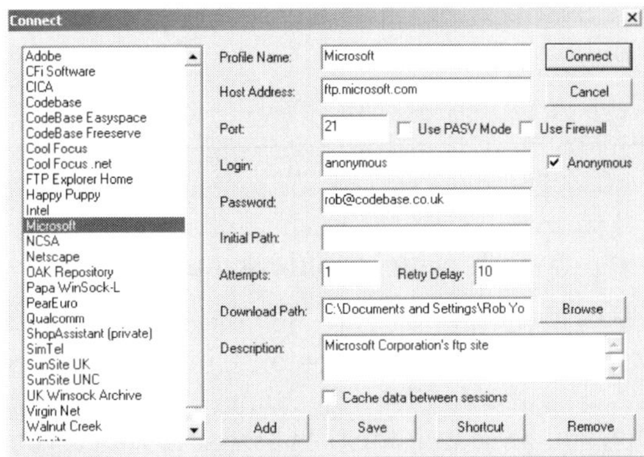

Figure 7.4 FTP Explorer's Connect dialog, where you create and select Profiles of FTP sites to connect to.

2. The last FTP site you connected to will be selected by default – you could click the **Connect** button to visit it again. We want to create a new Profile now though, so click the **Add** button instead.

3. Choose a friendly name for the site in the **Profile Name** field, and type its address in the **Host Address** field. (Don't include the ftp:// prefix – this is used only by Web browsers!)

4. For anonymous FTP, which is what you'll use most often, just check the box labelled **Anonymous** and FTP Explorer will complete the Login and Password fields for you. If you wanted to connect to a private site, you would enter the unique username and password you were assigned by the administrator of that system.
5. You can ignore the remaining options. Click **Save** to store this new Profile and you'll see it added to the list on the left. Finally, click **Connect** to visit the site.

Just like Internet Explorer, when you download files from one of these sites, FTP Explorer will display a dialog that tells you how the download is progressing and how much longer it's expected to take. You can download several files at once if you want to.

Uploading files with FTP Explorer is just as easy. After connecting to the required FTP site, find your way to the directory where you want to place the files, and then just drag them from Windows Explorer or your desktop and drop them into the main FTP Explorer window. (You can even drag whole folders.) As usual, FTP Explorer will show dialogs to keep you informed about the progress of the transfer.

Find that file!

Once you're logged into an anonymous FTP site (using your browser, or using a dedicated FTP program) you can pretty much do whatever you like: read index files to find out what's what; root around in the directories; download files. For computer fans, it's almost like surfing the Web!

But if you're looking for something in particular, this idle wandering about certainly isn't the best way of finding it. There are two far better approaches you can take.

If you're looking for a *type* of file (desktop themes, icons, wallpapers), you may be able to find them by working through the directories on an FTP site. They are usually organised in a structured way from general to specific, so the path to desktop themes may be **pub/computing/pc/windows/win98/desktop/themes**.

If you're looking for a particular file by name (such as **tpd101.zip**) or files with a particular extension (such as all **.ico** files) you need something called **Archie**. Archie is a service that works with FTP: it helps you to search for files by name which you can then download using FTP.

Two of the best places to search for files are **http://ftpsearch.lycos.com** (shown in Figure 7.5) and **http://www.snoopie.com**. Both sites look a little complicated, but don't let that put you off! Just type the name of the file you're looking for into the **Search For** field and click the **Search** button (or press **Enter**).

If you're not sure of the exact filename you can use **wildcards**: an asterisk (*) is used to replace multiple characters; a question mark (?) is used to replace a single character. So to find any files with the extension **.ico** you would search for ***.ico**. To search for a file that's either called tp101.exe or tp102.exe, type **tp10?.exe**.

Figure 7.5 Search for files at Lycos.

There are dedicated Archie programs out there, but there are very few to choose from and they're not easy to find. Increasingly, FTP programs have built-in Archie search options, but most users still use Web-based Archie sites like those mentioned here.

When the search results appear, they will be shown as a list of links to all the matching files found. Because this is a Web page, you can click any of those links to download the file. However, if several instances of a file are found that appear to be identical, there are two things to check before clicking one. First, look at the date to see if one is more recent than another. Second, try to pick a file from a server whose name ends with **.uk** if you can: because this server is closer to home, the file should download more quickly.

Files you download from FTP servers may be infected with viruses. It isn't very likely, but it's certainly possible, and some viruses can trash all your files and make your system unusable. We'll look at viruses in more detail in Chapter 11, but the bottom line is, if you download any programs (including self-extracting archives) you should check them with a virus scanner before using them.

File archives on the Web

As you've already discovered, the Web is extremely easy to use. As a result, anything Internet-related that can be handled on the Web is gradually appearing there, and one popular type of site is the **shareware archive**. This is a lot like the FTP site we've been looking at, with just one difference: on an FTP site all the files in a particular directory are visible as soon as they're put there.

On the Web, someone has to actually write a page containing a link to a file to make it accessible, otherwise we wouldn't know the file was there. Although that takes a lot of work, the benefit is that you can also provide a picture of what the software looks like, a description or review, a rating or score, details of the cost, and so on.

There are a great many software archive sites on the Web, each with its own style, and each offering files and programs that others don't. You can browse through many of these sites just as you browse through the contents of FTP servers, or you can search for something specific, as with an Archie search. Here are the URLs of some of the best software archives on the Web:

- Tucows at **http://tucows.mirror.ac.uk** (Figure 7.6)
- Jumbo at **http://www.jumbo.com**
- Shareware.com at **http://www.shareware.com**
- 32bit.com at **http://www.32bit.com**
- WinSite at **http://www.winsite.com**

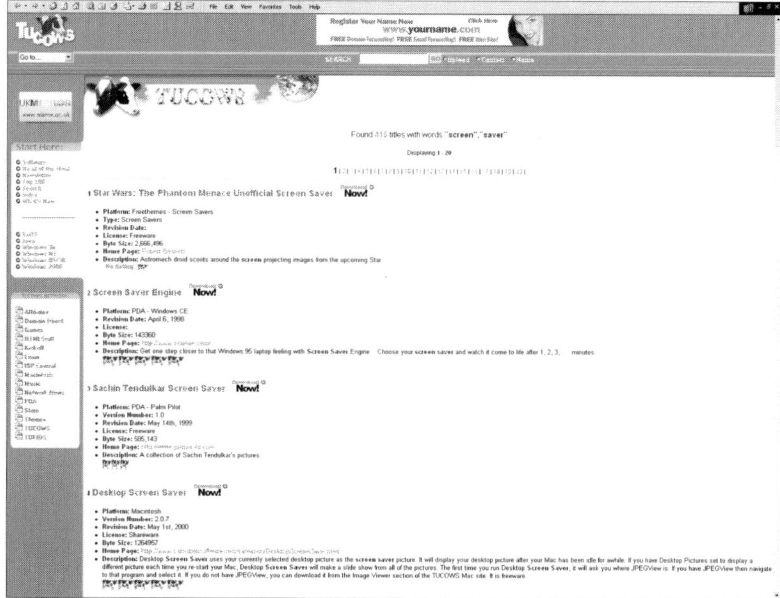

Figure 7.6 The Popular Tucows software archive has files for all operating systems.

Searching, chatting and gaming

8

Search engines and directories

Chatting on the Internet

Instant messaging

Network games

We've dedicated a chapter to each of the four main Internet services: the Web, e-mail, newsgroups and FTP. There are many more Internet services and resources that we could cover, but many of them you'd never use at all. In this chapter we gather together four extra resources you'll find useful (or at least want to try!).

- **Search engines** The quick way to find what you're looking for on the Web.
- **IRC (Internet Relay Chat)** A type of conversation channel where you can hold 'conversations' with one or more people, talking by typing messages back and forth in real time.
- **Instant messaging** Interactive communication on a similar principle to IRC, above, but more flexible.
- **Network games** With a games console, you can only play against the computer. With network games, you can play against other people, each one sitting at their computer anywhere in the world.

Search engines and directories

With the amount of content available on the Internet, it's absolutely guaranteed that whatever information you're looking for, it exists on the Net somewhere. The thing that isn't guaranteed, of course, is that you'll ever find it! There's no central index of Web sites or their content as there is in a library. Fortunately, though, there are many individual Web sites that do their best to catalogue the contents of the Web, and you can use these sites to search for whatever you need. Although many of these indexing sites work in different ways and give different results, they're known by the general term **search engines** (see Figure 8.1 for an example).

What is a search engine?

A search engine is a fairly ordinary-looking Web page containing a text box (there may be a lot more on the page, but it's the text box that matters!). In that text box you type one or more words relating to the subject you're interested in, and then press **Enter**. The words you entered are sent to the server which searches through its database of catalogued sites for anything that matches. After a few seconds, it will send back a list of URLs that may (or may not) be relevant.

The list of search results varies from one search engine to another: since each uses its own methods to create its catalogue, you'll get a different list back from each search engine you visit. But although the Web sites found by the search differ, the way they're presented is universal: there will be a link you can click to visit any promising-sounding Web site and a brief description (or, perhaps, a few lines quoted from the page).

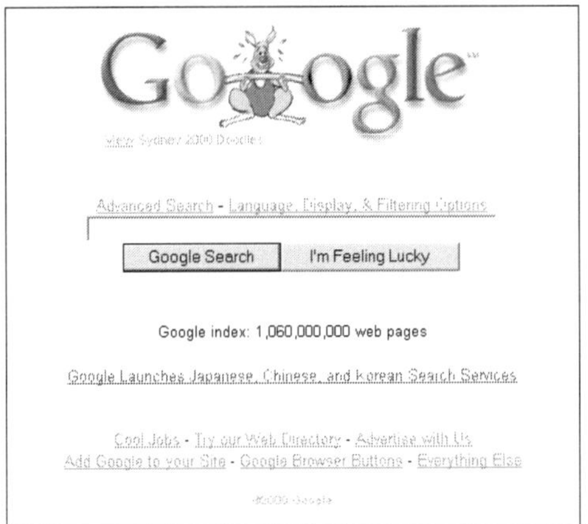

Figure 8.1 Probably the least-cluttered search engine page in existence: **www.google.com**.

Most search engines look for pages containing the word or phrase you typed into the text box. They will usually ensure that pages using the word most often appear at the top of the search-results list, but you can't be sure that one of these pages contains any useful information on the subject without visiting it.

In many cases a search will result in a list containing tens of thousands of Web page URLs (sometimes even hundreds of thousands). Fortunately, only the 10 most relevant pages will be listed, and you'll see buttons or links near the bottom of the page that will take you to the next 10 in the list.

Hit or miss?

As the whole point of searching the Internet is to find what you're looking for as quickly as possible, it's important to phrase your search clearly. For example, if you search for **racing** your search results are likely to number over a quarter of a million Web pages! Most of those pages will be irrelevant, and you may have to look a long way down the list to find pages about the type of racing you wanted. A search for **motor racing** will give far fewer results to trawl through, because links to all those pages about yacht racing, horse racing, greyhound racing (and so on) will now be gone.

There are enough useful tips and options you can use when searching for information on the Internet to fill an entire book. (In fact they *do* fill an entire book: A *Simple Guide to Searching the Internet*, also published by Prentice Hall.) So what follows is just a brief introduction to some of the Web's most popular search engines to get you started. Most of the popular search sites have a Help link that you can click if you have problems using them.

AltaVista
http://uk.altavista.com

This is one of the best-known search engines, and also one of the most flexible (Figure 8.2). When you first arrive at AltaVista you'll see a row of five yellow 'tabs', with the Search tab selected. Here you can search the whole of the World Wide Web or just search for pages from UK sites, and you can search for pages in a particular language. By clicking one of the last three tabs you can search for multimedia files: pictures, video files and sounds.

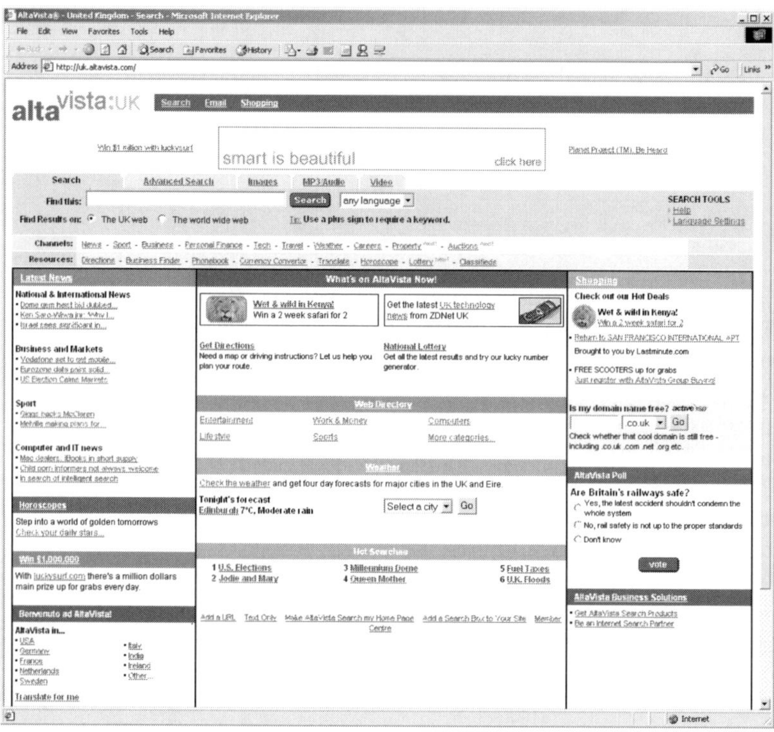

Figure 8.2 The AltaVista search engine.

The Advanced Search tab offers some powerful options to refine your searches: many search engines offer options they refer to as 'Advanced', but at AltaVista they've added a few touches you won't find anywhere else, making this a site worth becoming familiar with. For the moment, however, just type a keyword or phrase into the **Find this** box, decide whether you want to search in the UK or the entire world, and press **Enter**.

Yahoo!
http://www.yahoo.co.uk

Yahoo! is probably the best-known search site in the world, but it's a little different from AltaVista and many other search engines. Although it has the usual text box allowing you to type keywords to search for, you'll also see a number of hypertext 'categories' on its front page such as Arts & Humanities, Entertainment, and Science (Figure 8.3). Instead of running a keyword search, you can just click one of these categories. A new list of sub-categories will appear, and you can burrow your way down through ever more specific category names until you find the type of site you're looking for. This is known as a 'directory structure', and trawling through these categories can be a lot of fun, even if you're not actually searching for anything in particular!

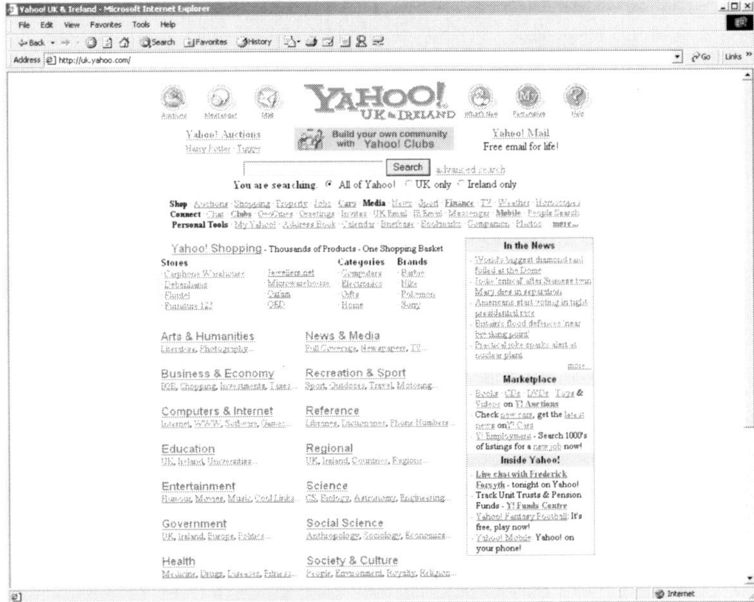

Figure 8.3 Yahoo!, the workhorse of the Web.

If you prefer to use a keyword search, Yahoo! will present its results as two separate lists: the upper list on the page (in bold text) contains links to some of Yahoo!'s own categories which may be relevant; the lower list (in plain text) contains direct links to the Web pages found in the search.

MetaCrawler
http://www.metacrawler.com
Because every search engine uses its own methods to build its indexes, each will obviously provide a different set of results in response to a search. If you think a certain piece of information is going to be elusive, you might consider searching for it at several different search sites to make the most of these differences, but there's an even better option: use a **meta search engine** such as MetaCrawler (Figure 8.4). Although you use this site in exactly the same way as AltaVista, mentioned above, it will simultaneously search over a dozen major search engines for you and return the results from each engine gathered together on a single page.

Sometimes a perfectly innocuous search can lead to search results containing links to 'adult' Web sites which you wouldn't want your children to see. To avoid this, there's a family-friendly search engine at **http://www.mirago.co.uk/zone**, *UK Plus at* **http://www.ukplus.co.uk** *aims to be family-friendly, and the other search engines are starting to provide options to filter out 'adult' links from searches. If you have children, you can point them to* **http://www.yahooligans.com**, *a safe and friendly search site providing links to sites for (or by) children.*

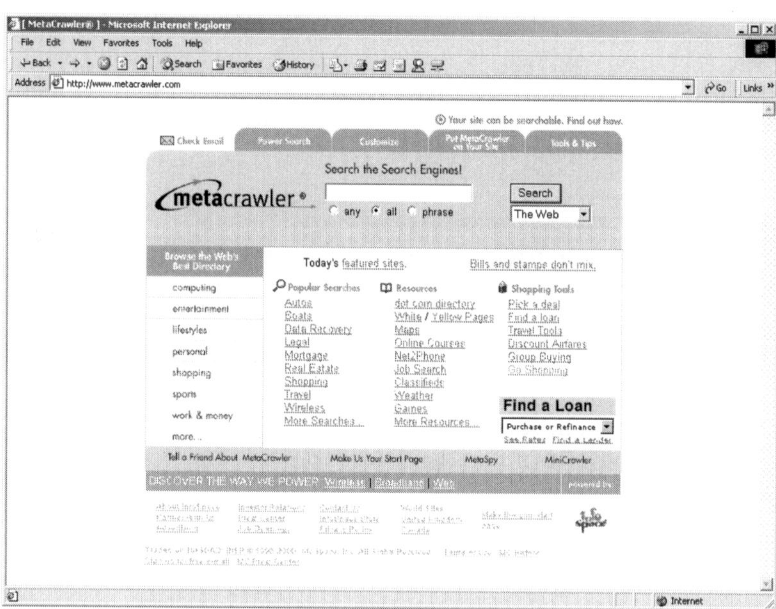

Figure 8.4 Speed up your searching with MetaCrawler!

InfoSpace – Finding people
http://www.infospace.com/info/e-mail1.htm
http://www.infospace.com/info/people.htm

Finding people's e-mail addresses and other details isn't an exact science: just as there's no central repository of Web sites, there isn't the Internet equivalent of a telephone directory either. However, many companies have had a brave stab at creating something similar, and InfoSpace has done the best job (Figure 8.5). The first of the URLs above leads to a page where you can search for someone's e-mail address; at the second URL you can search for phone numbers and addresses. On both pages you'll find several text fields where you'll have to enter the person's full name, and as much of their address as you're able to.

Yell.com – Finding businesses
http://uk.yell.com

Just as there are search engines to help you find Web pages and e-mail addresses, there are others that can lead you to companies. The best of the lot is Yell.com at (not surprisingly) **http://www.yell.com**. When you arrive at the site you can choose between searching for US businesses or for those in the UK; choosing the UK option will lead you to the URL opposite (Figure 8.6).

This site is a lot like our own Yellow Pages phone directory: if you know the name of the business you want to find, type it into the second text box, otherwise just enter the *type* of business into the first box. Type the town or county into the third box and press

Enter. The search results will list all the likely matches, along with contact details and, in many cases, links to the company's Web site and a map of the area.

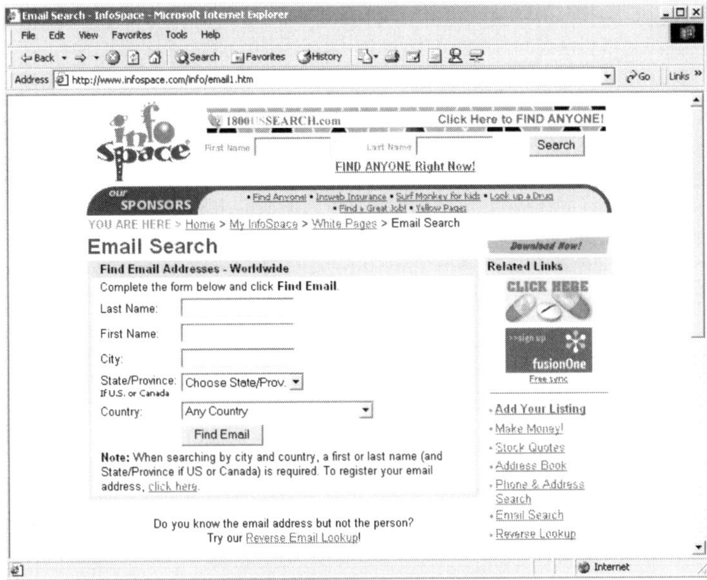

Figure 8.5 InfoSpace is the best choice for finding someone's e-mail address.

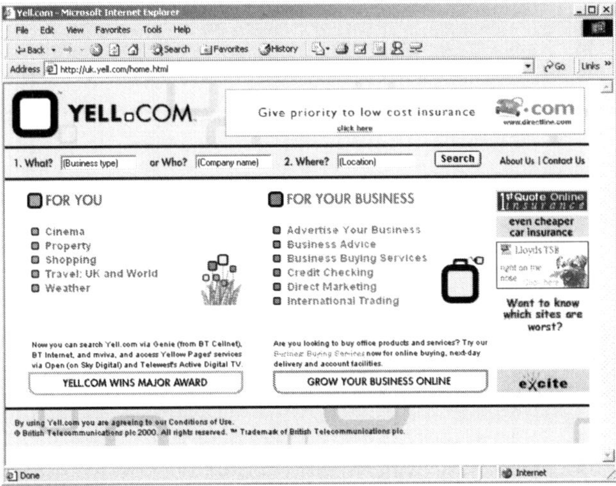

Figure 8.6 Search for British or American businesses at Yell.com.

Chatting on the Internet

Chatting brings you into the closest possible contact with other Internet users, and after talking to them for a while it's easy to forget that you really know nothing about them but what they've told you (which may not be true!). Never, ever, give out personal details such as addresses, phone numbers, passwords, credit card numbers, or school/college location when chatting.

On the Internet, 'chatting' doesn't involve using your voice at all. Instead you hold live conversations with others by typing on your keyboard. You type a line of text into a text field and press **Enter**, and the text is visible almost instantly to everyone else taking part. They can then respond by typing their own messages, and you'll see their responses on your screen.

Chatting usually takes place in a **chat room**, and the room may contain just a couple of people or it may contain several dozen. Fortunately, many of the room's occupants are only 'listening' to the conversation rather than actively taking part. Nevertheless, even with just half a dozen people chatting, things can get rather confused: sometimes nothing happens at all for a minute or so; at other times, everyone is talking at once and it's hard to tell who's talking to who!

The best way to get a taste of chatting is to visit the Freeserve chat site at **http://www.freeserve.com/chat**. When you arrive you'll be able to choose from a list of over a dozen different chat rooms: the name of each room is designed to attract people of different age groups or interests, so you'll have a rough idea what type of conversation to expect in each room by its name. Pick a room and type a nickname that you want to be known by while chatting, and a window like the one shown in Figure 8.7 will open.

Figure 8.7 Typical chat in the Freeserve chat rooms.

If you like the experience of chatting on the Internet, you might want to try some 'real' chat in the form of **IRC** (Internet Relay Chat). IRC is the forerunner to the Web-based chat rooms, and you need a separate program to use it, the best of which is mIRC from **http://www.mirc.co.uk**. The world of IRC is based on CB radio jargon, so chat rooms are known as **channels**. The structure of IRC is more complicated than Web-based chat, so it's worth reading through mIRC's very useful manual before you get started. When you do, make sure you start with a beginners' channel (a channel with 'help', 'mirc', 'newbie' or 'beginner' in its name).

*One of the most common uses for chat is to meet members of the opposite sex, and at some chat sites the conversation may not be suitable for children. AOL has its own **moderated** chat rooms (where a member of the service is keeping an eye on things to keep everything friendly) which are available to AOL members only, and these are a better bet for children.*

Instant messaging

Although various forms of chat have been available on the Net for years, it's always been a bit of a backwater. But a recent arrival on the chat scene has immediately emerged as a firm favourite: the **instant messaging** (or 'IM') service. It all started with a program called ICQ (I Seek You, geddit?) and other well-known companies have since jumped on board offering their own instant messaging software.

Rather than chatting with a group of people in a chat room, instant messaging uses a 'buddy list' to let you chat with another user one-to-one. The idea is simple: download the software (which is free), build a list of all your Net-connected friends, and every time you connect to the Net the software will tell you which of your friends are online. In the same way, your friends will know that you're online. To send an instant message, double-click a name and start typing (Figure 8.8). As well as being either online or offline, you can choose from a variety of other 'online' settings, telling other users that you're on the phone or temporarily away from your computer, for instance.

Figure 8.8 Double-click the name of an online 'buddy' and start chatting one-to-one.

Three of the best-known instant messaging programs are AOL's Instant Messenger (or AIM) from **http://www.aol.com**, Microsoft's MSN Messenger from **http://www.msn.co.uk**, and ICQ from **http://www.icq.com**. The first two are fairly simple to set up and use, making them a good choice for beginners or for personal use. ICQ tries to do far more than the others and may be a bit off-putting, despite giving a choice between Simple and Advanced modes, but it's still the most widely accepted: you'll even see ICQ numbers on people's business cards!

Network games

Games are the most widespread of human passions. From the tiny Gameboys to sophisticated consoles like Sega or Nintendo (not forgetting the traditional computer games), everyone can find a game to suit their tastes and finances. Thanks to the Internet, you can now pit your wits against contestants from all over the world, gamble real money, win real money and (needless to say) lose some very real money.

Games sites

Some games only need a simple browser or to download the correct software beforehand (usually in shareware form, meaning that you'll have to pay a nominal amount for it if you continue using it beyond its trial period), while others like Quake 2 and Total Annihilation require a CD-ROM. Some games must be played by several players, which is why 'virtual games rooms' (which, like chat rooms, are actually Web sites) have been created. Figure 8.9 shows one popular site, The Games Arena. If you like this type of game, try **http://www.gamesdomain.co.uk**, **http://www.ten.net** and **http://www.planetquake.com**.

Role-playing games

Besides the games made popular by specialised software, you can get involved in role-playing games – terrifying medieval sagas, space-based stories or operatic dramas, and so on, among which the famous MUD (Multi User Dungeon) is without doubt the most popular. To try some of these games, go to **http://www.thardferr.com** or **http://www.ssionline.com**, or take a look at the **rec.games.mud** newsgroup.

Chess games

Finally, on a more intellectual note, how about a game of online chess from a specialised chess server? Go to **http://www.chessclub.com** to take part. (It's a good idea to choose a partner of the same ranking as you!)

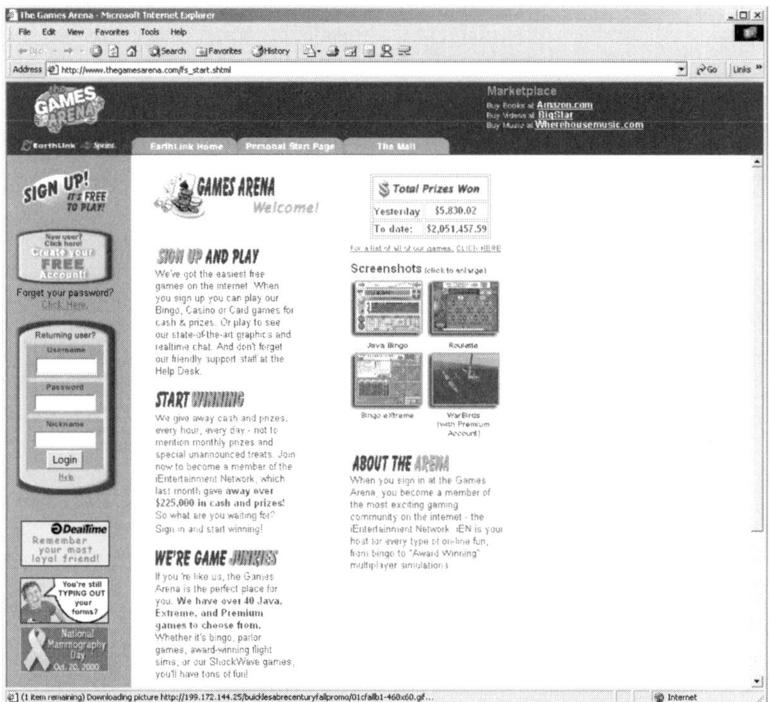

Figure 8.9 **www.gamesarena.com**, one of many online gaming Web sites.

9 HTML and Web site design

The language of the Web

What you need to write Web pages

Getting started with Web design

In earlier chapters you've learnt how to use all the important areas of the Internet, but it's still *everyone else's* Internet you're using! Sooner or later you'll want to grab a little corner of it and make it your own. The mechanics of creating a Web site are simple enough, and in this chapter you'll learn how to do it. Of course, whole books have been written on this subject so this isn't an exhaustive reference, but it should get you off to a flying start. There are many guides and tutorials on the Web itself which can help you improve your skills, and you'll find two of the best at:

- **http://werbach.com/barebones**
- **http://hotwired.lycos.com/webmonkey**

The language of the Web

Pages on the World Wide Web are written in a language called **HTML** (HyperText Markup Language). The hypertext part is straightforward enough, we've met hypertext already – those underlined, clickable links that make the Web so easy to navigate. A *markup language* is a set of codes or signs added to plain text to indicate how it should be presented to the reader, noting bold or italic text, typefaces to be used, paragraph breaks, and so on. When you type any document into your word-processor, it adds these codes for you, but tactfully hides them from view: if you wanted bold text, for example, it *shows* you bold text instead of those codes. In HTML, however, you have to type in the codes yourself along with the text, and your browser puts the whole lot together before displaying it.

These codes are known as **tags**, and they consist of ordinary text placed between less-than and greater-than signs. Let's take an example:

```
<B>Welcome to my home page.</B> Glad you could make it!
```

The first tag, `<B>`, means 'turn on bold type'. Halfway through the line, the same tag is used again, but with a forward-slash inserted straight after the less-than sign: this means 'turn off bold type'. If you displayed a page containing this line in your browser, it would look like this:

Welcome to my home page. Glad you could make it!

Of course, there's more to a Web page than bold text, so clearly there must be many more of these tags. But don't let that worry you – you don't have to learn all of them! There's a small bundle that you'll use a lot, and you'll get to know those very quickly. The rest will begin to sink in once you've used them a few times.

What you need to write Web pages

Believe it or not, creating a Web site is something you can do for free. Because HTML is entirely text-based, you can write your pages in Windows' Notepad, and we'll assume that's what you're doing. But there are other options, so let's quickly run through them.

WYSIWYG editors

In theory, WYSIWYG editors are the perfect way of working: instead of looking at plain text with HTML tags dotted around it, you see your Web page itself gradually taking shape, with images, colours and formatting displayed. There are a couple of drawbacks, though. First, WYSIWYG editors cost serious money compared with most other types of Internet software. Second, they probably won't help you to avoid learning something about HTML. Once in a while the editor won't do what you want it to do, and you'll have to switch to its text-editing mode to juggle the tags yourself.

You might even find that it's far easier to learn the language itself than it is to learn how the WYSIWYG software works, but if you'd like to give the WYSIWYG method a shot, here are three of the most popular programs:

WYSIWYG (pronounced 'wizzywig') is an acronym for 'What you see is what you get'. This is used to describe many different types of software that can show you on the screen exactly what something will look like when you print it on paper or view it in your Web browser.

- **Microsoft FrontPage**. You can find out more about this at **http://www. microsoft.com/frontpage**, but you'll have to take a trip into town to buy a copy. (FrontPage is also included with Microsoft Office Premium edition.)
- **Microsoft FrontPage Express**. A cut-down version of FrontPage included with recent editions of Windows and Internet Explorer.
- **NetObjects Fusion**. A stylish program with a huge number of high-quality page templates, available from **http://www.netobjects.com**.

Markup editors

Using a markup editor is rather like using Notepad – you see all the HTML code on the page in front of you. But instead of having to type in tags yourself, a markup editor will insert them for you at the click of a button or the press of a hotkey, in the same way that you use your word-processor (Figure 9.1). You might still choose to type in some of the simple tags yourself, such as the tag for bold text mentioned earlier, but for more complicated elements such as a table with a lot of cells, this automation is a great time and sanity saver.

Markup editors are also ideal for newcomers to HTML. If you don't know one tag from another, just click the appropriate buttons on the toolbar to insert them: once you've seen them appear on the page a few times, you'll soon start to remember what's what!

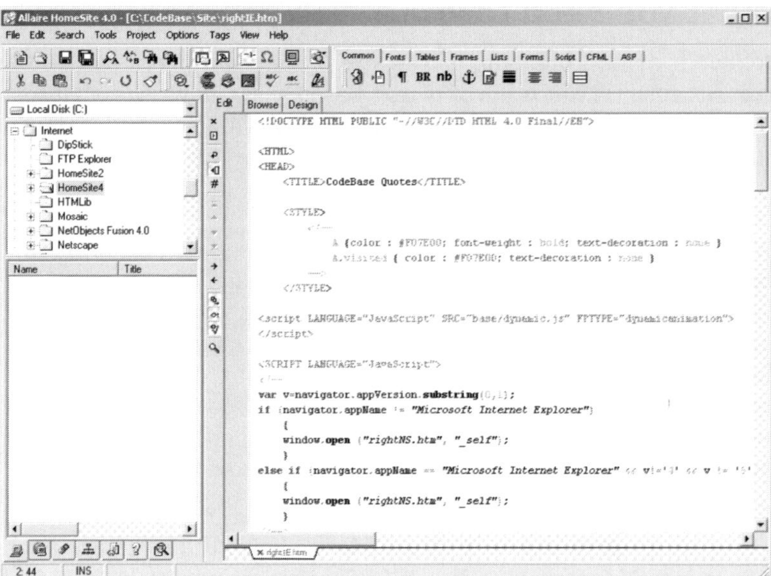

Figure 9.1 Colour-coding and one-click tag insertion in HomeSite.

Here are three of the most popular and feature-packed markup editors. You'll need to register these if you want to use them beyond the trial period.

- **HomeSite** from **http://www.allaire.com**
- **HoTMeTaL Pro** from **http://www.sq.com**
- **HTMLed** from **http://www.ist.ca**

If you use Microsoft Office, the Web authoring features don't stop at Word. Excel allows you to save a worksheet in HTML format, and PowerPoint helps you create multimedia pages by converting slides to Web format. You'll also find a media library of pictures, sounds and animations that you can include in your pages, however you choose to create them.

Text converters

Some modern word-processors like Lotus WordPro and Microsoft Word have begun to include features to turn your documents into Web pages. At their simplest, they'll let you create an ordinary word-processed document and then choose a **Save as HTML** option from the **File** menu to convert it into a Web page. The result won't be as effective as other pages on the Web, but it's an ideal way to convert a long document when the only other option is to add all the tags yourself!

You can also create Web pages from scratch in these programs. For example, Microsoft Word has its own Web Page Wizard that can set you up with a ready-to-edit template. To start it up, go to **File/New...**, then click the **Web Pages** tab and double-click **Web Page Wizard**. You can add and delete elements on the page, and use the standard drawing and editing toolbars to slot in anything else you need.

Getting started with Web design

There are a few bits and pieces that will appear in almost every HTML document you write, so we'll start by making a template file you can use every time you want to create a page. Start Notepad, and type the text below (without worrying about the exact number of spaces or carriage returns). Save this file using any name you like, but make sure you give it the extension **.htm** or **.html**. Every Web page you write must be saved with one of these extensions – it doesn't matter which you choose, but you'll find life a lot easier if you stick to the same one each time!

```
<!DOCTYPE HTML PUBLIC "-//W3C//DTD HTML 4.0//EN">

<HTML>
<HEAD>
      <TITLE>Untitled</TITLE>
</HEAD>

<BODY>



</BODY>
</HTML>
```

None of those tags does anything exciting by itself, but it's worth knowing what they're all for. The first line is a piece of technical nonsense that tells a browser that the document is written in the latest version of the HTML language. The rest of the document is placed between the `<HTML>` and `</HTML>` tags, and falls into two separate chunks: the **head** (the section between `<HEAD>` and `</HEAD>`) and the **body** (between `<BODY>` and `</BODY>`).

The document's head is pretty dull: all it contains is the title of the document, inserted between the `<TITLE>` and `</TITLE>` tags. There are other bits and pieces that can be slotted in here, but the title is the only element that *must* be included.

Although we've used capital letters for the tags in these examples, you don't have to do the same. But typing tags in capitals makes them stand out from the rest of your text, which can be useful for editing.

The body section is the one that matters. Between these two tags you'll type all the text that should appear on your page, and put in the tags you need to display images, set colours, insert hyperlinks to other pages and sites, and anything else you want your page to contain.

Now that you've created a basic template, let's start adding to it to build up a respectable-looking page.

Page title and text

The first thing to do is to replace the word **Untitled** with a sensible title for the document, such as **Links To The Best Multimedia Sites** or **My EastEnders Home Page**. Pick something that describes what the page will be about, but keep it fairly short: the text between the <TITLE> and </TITLE> tags will appear in the title-bar at the very top of most browsers, and if your entry is too long to fit it'll just get chopped off!

Now we'll add some text to the page. Either type the same text as in the example below, or replace the first and second paragraph entries with whole paragraphs if you prefer. When you've done that, save the file as **links.html**, but don't close Notepad yet.

```
<!DOCTYPE HTML PUBLIC "-//W3C//DTD HTML 4.0//EN">

<HTML>
<HEAD>
      <TITLE>Links   To   The   Best   Multimedia
Sites</TITLE>
</HEAD>

<BODY>
<H1>Welcome To My Home page!</H1>
Here's the first paragraph.
<P>And here's the second paragraph.

</BODY>
</HTML>
```

Now take a look at your masterpiece in your browser. There are several ways you can do this: find the file you just saved and double-click it, or open your browser and type the path to the file in the address bar, or choose **File** / **Open** and click on **Browse**. When your browser displays it, it should look just like Figure 9.2.

Figure 9.2 A simple home page.

Another tag, <BR>, will give you a 'line break' to let you start a new line without starting a new paragraph. In other words, the text that follows that tag will start at the beginning of the next line, with no empty line inserted before it.

So what are those new tags all about? Let's take the <P> tag first. This tells your browser to present the following text as a new paragraph, which automatically inserts a blank line before it. And this raises an important point about HTML: you can't insert blank lines just by pressing the **Enter** key. Although *you* can see blank lines in Notepad when you do that, your browser will just ignore them, which is why you need to start a new paragraph by entering <P>. (Notice that you don't have to put in a closing </P> at the end of a paragraph – the act of starting a new paragraph isn't an ongoing effect that has to be turned off again.)

The other pair of tags that cropped up was <H1> and </H1> which formats a line of text as a heading. You can choose from six sizes: H1 is the largest, followed by <H2> and </H2> down to the smallest, <H6> and </H6>. In one nifty little manoeuvre, these tags change the size of the text you place between them *and* make it bold. They also automatically start a new paragraph for the heading (so you don't need to place a <P> tag at the start of the line) and start a new paragraph for whatever follows the heading. Try changing the size of the heading by altering those tags to see the different effects, re-saving the file, and clicking your browser's **Refresh** button to update it.

Using bold and italic text

The tags for bold and italic text are easy to remember: <B> for bold, and <I> for italic. As both of these are ongoing effects, you'll have to enter closing tags (</B> or </I>) when you want the effect to stop. And, just as in your word-processor, you can combine these tags, so if your document contained this:

```
This is <I>italic</I>. This is <B>bold</B>. This
is <B><I>bold & italic</I></B>.
```

the result would look like this in your browser:

This is *italic*. This is **bold**. This is ***bold & italic***.

Lesser-used text formatting tags that might come in handy one day are superscript (^{and}) and subscript (_{and}). If you really feel the urge, you can underline text using another memorable pair of tags, <U> and </U>, but be careful how you use underlining: Web surfers expect underlined text to be a hyperlink, and might find your gratuitous use of these tags confusing.

Linking to other Web sites

It's an unwritten rule of the Internet that a Web site should contain links to *other* Web sites. After all, the entire Web works by being interconnected, and if people surf their way to your site and have to retrace their steps before they can continue surfing, they'll steer clear in future! So let's put in another <P> tag to start a new paragraph, and add that sorely-needed link as shown below:

```
<P>Visit Macromedia's snazzy <AHREF="http://www.
macromedia .com/shockzone">Shockzone</A> site.
```

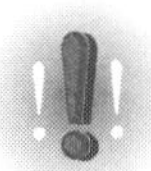

*Just as browsers ignore your use of the **Enter** or **Return** key when you create your Web pages, they have a similar attitude to the spacebar. However many spaces you enter in a row, only the first will be recognised. If you really need more than one space, type in the code ** ** for each space you want (so **   ** would insert three spaces).*

Figure 9.3 Putting links to other sites on your Web site.

This is a more complicated tag, so we'll examine it bit by bit. Although we call these 'links', in HTML they're called **anchors**, and that's where the A comes from after the first < sign. An anchor usually begins with the <A HREF= tag. Following that comes the URL of the page you want to link to, always enclosed in double quotes, and the > sign to finish the opening anchor tag.

Immediately after the opening anchor tag, type the text you want visitors to your page to click on. This might be a single word, a sentence, or even a whole paragraph, but don't forget to put *something* here, or there'll be nothing to click on to reach that site! Finally, type the closing anchor tag, </A>.

You can place elements centrally on the page by placing them between <CENTER> and </CENTER> tags (note the American spelling, though!). This applies to headings, paragraphs of text, images, and almost anything else you might want to include.

Linking to pages on your own site

The link we just added used something called an **absolute URL**. In fact, that's the only type of URL you've seen so far: an absolute URL gives the whole path to the page you want to open, including the http:// prefix and the name of the computer. When you want to create links to other pages on your *own* site you can use a different, simpler method.

Create a new HTML document, and save it to the directory where the other is stored. Let's assume you've called it **morelinks.html**. Now, in your first document, you can create a link to this new page by typing this anchor:

```
<A HREF="morelinks.html">Here's a few more links.</A>
```

Yes, it's just a filename. This is called a **relative URL**. It tells your browser to look for a file called **morelinks.html** and display it. The great thing about relative URLs is that you can test these on your own system to make sure they work: for absolute URLs, your PC would have to connect to your ISP to search for the page. Since the browser hasn't been told where else to look, it searches the directory containing the document it's displaying at that moment. As long as **morelinks.html** really is in that same directory, the browser will find it and open it.

You can make a browser look somewhere different for a file in a similar way. Open the directory containing these two documents, create a subdirectory called **pages**, and move the **morelinks.html** file into it. The link we just added now needs to be changed to the following:

```
<A HREF="pages/morelinks.html">Here's a few more
links.</A>
```

The browser now looks in the current directory for another directory called **pages**, and looks inside that for **morelinks.html**.

Finally, let's open **morelinks.html** and create a link back to our original document (which we called **links.html**) so that you can click your way to and fro between the two. To do this, we need to tell the browser to look in the parent directory of **pages** to find this file: to move up one level in the directory tree, just type two dots:

```
<A HREF="../links.html">Here's my first links page.
</A>
```

So far we've looked at linking to other Web pages, but a hyperlink needn't necessarily point to a .html document. If you have a movie file, a text file, a sound file, or whatever, create the link in exactly the same way, entering the location and name of this file between the double quotes. If the file is particularly large, though, it's good practice to mention its size somewhere nearby so that people can choose whether or not to click that link.

*When you refer to a page or file in your document, the case is vital. If you type in a link to **Index.html** and the file is actually called **index.html** or **Index.HTML**, the page won't be found. Most Web authors save all their files with lower-case names to remove any uncertainty. Similarly, although you can use long filenames, they mustn't include any spaces.*

Colours and backgrounds

So far, in our example Web page, everything looks a bit dull. The background is white, the text is black, the hyperlinks are blue – these are the default colours set up by Internet Explorer, and it's using them because we haven't told it to use anything different. All of this is easily changed, though, by typing our preferences into that opening `<BODY>` tag.

This brings us to a new area of HTML. A tag like `<B>` is self-contained – it simply turns on bold text, with no complications. Other tags need to contain a little more information about what you want to do. A good example is the `<FONT>` tag, which we'll look at more closely later in this chapter. By itself, it isn't saying anything useful: which font? what size? what colour? You provide this information by adding attributes to the tag such as `SIZE=3`, `FACE=Arial`, and so on, so a complete font tag might be: `<FONT SIZE=3 FACE=Arial>`.

The `<BODY>` tag doesn't *have* to contain attributes, but browsers will use their own default settings for anything you haven't specified, and different browsers use different defaults. Most Web authors like to keep as much control as possible over how their pages will be displayed, and make their own settings for the body attributes. There are six attributes you can use in the <BODY> tag:

This attribute...	...has this effect
BGCOLOR=	Sets the background colour of the Web page
TEXT=	Sets the colour of text on the page
LINK=	Sets the colour of the clickable hyperlinks
VLINK=	Sets the colour of a link to a previously visited page
ALINK=	Sets the colour of a link between the time it's clicked and the new page opening
BACKGROUND=	Specifies an image to use as the page's 'wallpaper'

Without further ado, open the original **links.html** document that you created at the start of this chapter, and change the <BODY> tag so that it looks like this:

```
<BODY BGCOLOR=MAROON TEXT=WHITE LINK=YELLOW VLINK=
OLIVE ALINK=LIME>
```

Save the file, and take a look at it in your browser. Okay, the colour scheme may not be to your taste, but it's starting to resemble a 'real' Web page! Try swapping colours around to find a scheme you prefer. There are 140 colours to choose from, and you can find lists of their names at the Web site URLs given at the very start of this chapter.

The other attribute is BACKGROUND=, which places a GIF or JPEG image on the Web page, and tiles it to fill the entire area. Let's assume you want to use an image file called **hoops.gif** which is in the same directory as the current document. Inside the body tag, add: BACKGROUND-"hoops.gif" (not forgetting the double quotes). Your whole <BODY> tag might now look like this:

```
<BODY BACKGROUND="hoops.gif" BGCOLOR=MAROON TEXT=
WHITE LINK=YELLOW VLINK=OLIVE ALINK=LIME>
```

Using different fonts

At the moment your page is still using a single font (probably Times New Roman). Once again, this is set up by your browser by default, and of course, different browsers might use different default fonts. Fortunately, the <FONT> tag leaps to your rescue, allowing you to choose and change the font face, size and colour whenever you need to. Here's an example of a <FONT> tag using all three attributes:

```
<FONT FACE="Verdana,Arial,Helvetica" SIZE=4
COLOR=RED>...</FONT>
```

Let's take these one at a time. The FACE attribute is the name of the font you want to use. Obviously this should be a font you have on your own system, but the same font needs to be on the system of anyone visiting your page too: if it isn't, their browser will revert to the default font. You can keep a bit of extra control by listing more than one font (separated by commas) as in the example above. If the first font isn't available, the browser will try the second, and so on.

Font sizes in HTML work differently than in your word-processor. There are 7 sizes numbered from 1 to 7, where 1 is smallest. The default size for text is 3, so if you want to make your text slightly larger, use SIZE=4. The SIZE attribute doesn't affect the headings we covered earlier, so if you've used one of these somewhere between your <FONT> and </FONT> tags, it will still be formatted as a heading.

Try to pick fonts that most visitors to your site will have on their systems so that they'll see the page as you intended. Most visitors to your site will have Arial and Times New Roman. Microsoft supplies a pack of fonts for the Web which many Web authors now use, including Comic Sans MS, Verdana, Impact and Georgia. You can download any of these you don't already have from ***http://www.microsoft.com/truetype/fontpack/win.htm****.*

The colour of the text has already been set in the <BODY> tag, but you might want to slip in an occasional <FONT COLOR=PURPLE>...</FONT> to change the colour of a certain word, paragraph, or heading. After the closing </FONT> tag, the colour will revert to that set in the <BODY> tag.

With the earlier changes to the <BODY> tag, and the addition of a couple of </FONT> tags, here's what the body of our document might look like now (and see Figure 9.4):

Figure 9.4 A jazzed-up home page.

```
<BODY   BGCOLOR=MAROON   TEXT=WHITE   LINK=YELLOW
VLINK=OLIVE ALINK=LIME>

<FONT FACE="Comic Sans MS" COLOR=YELLOW>
<H1>Welcome To My Home page!</H1>
</FONT>

<FONT FACE="Arial">

Here's the first paragraph.
<P>And here's the second paragraph.
<P>Visit  Macromedia's  snazzy  <AHREF="http://
www.macromedia.
com/shockzone">Shockzone</A> site.

</FONT>
</BODY>
</HTML>
```

Horizontal rules as separators

Horizontal rules are straight lines that divide a page into sections. For the simplest type of rule, the only tag you need is `<HR>`. This automatically puts a horizontal rule across the full width of the page, on a new line, and any text that follows it will form a new paragraph. Because the rule isn't something that needs to be turned off again, there's no closing tag.

If you want to, you can get clever with rules by adding some (or all!) of the following attributes:

Use this attribute...	...for this result
`ALIGN=`	Use `LEFT` or `RIGHT` to place the rule on the left or right of the page. If you leave this out, the rule will be centred
`SIZE=`	Enter any number to set the height of the rule in pixels. The default setting is 2
`WIDTH=`	Enter a number to specify the width of the line in pixels, or as a percentage of the page (such as `WIDTH=70%`)
`NOSHADE`	This removes the 3D effect from the rule. There's no equals sign, and nothing more to add
`COLOR=`	Enter the name of a colour. The default setting depends upon the background colour. Only Internet Explorer supports this attribute – other browsers will ignore it

It's worth playing with the <HR> tag and its attributes to see what unusual effects you can create. For example, the following piece of code places a square bullet in the centre of the page which makes a smart, 'minimalist' divider (see Figure 9.5):

```
<HR SIZE=10 WIDTH=10 COLOR=LIME NOSHADE>
```

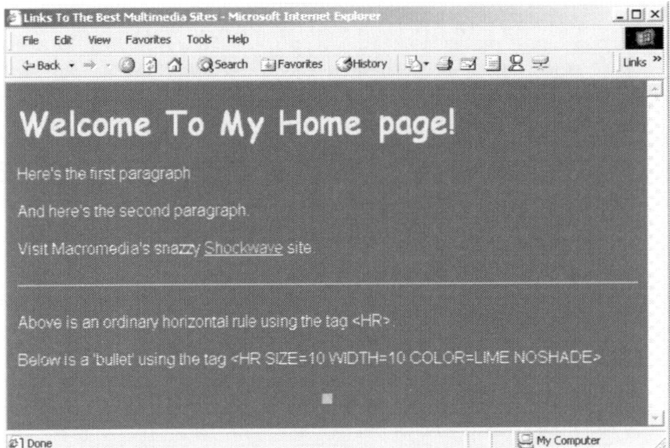

Figure 9.5 Playing around with the <HR> tag.

Adding images

The horizontal rule is the simplest type of graphical content you can include on a page, but it's hardly exciting. To liven up a dull page, you can't go far wrong with a well-chosen image. Images on the Web are usually in one of two formats, GIF or JPEG, which are supported by almost any drawing program.

Once you've chosen the image you want to use, the <IMG> tag will slot it onto the page. This tag works rather like the <FONT> tag – by itself it's meaningless, with all the information being supplied by adding attributes. Let's assume you want to insert an image called **splash.gif**, and the image file is in the same directory as your current HTML document:

```
<IMG SRC="splash.gif">
```

This is the <IMG> tag at its most basic: the SRC attribute (which is short for 'source') tells the browser where to find the image file you want to display, following exactly the same rules as those for relative URLs which we looked at earlier. Unless you preceded this tag with <P> or <BR>, the image will be placed immediately after the last piece of text you entered. If you enclose the entire tag between <CENTER> and </CENTER> tags, the image will be placed below the previous line of text, centred on the page. You do get a little more choice than that about where the image should be, though, by adding the ALIGN attribute:

This attribute...	Does this...
ALIGN=TOP	Aligns the top of the image with the top of the text on the same line
ALIGN=MIDDLE	Aligns the middle of the image with the text on that line
ALIGN=BOTTOM	Aligns the bottom of the image with the bottom of the line of text
ALIGN=LEFT	Places the image on a new line, and against the left margin
ALIGN=RIGHT	Places the image on a new line, and against the right margin

Using these attributes, then, you can place the image roughly where you want it on the page. What's still needed is a bit of fine tuning: after all, if you use ALIGN=MIDDLE, the image will be butted right up against the text on the same line. The answer comes in the form of two more attributes which add some blank space around an image: HSPACE= inserts space either side of the image (*horizontally*), and VSPACE= adds space above and below it (*vertically*). Just enter a number in pixels after the equals sign. There's no need to add a closing attribute. So an image might be inserted with a tag that looks like this:

```
<IMG SRC="splash.gif" ALIGN=MIDDLE HSPACE=30
VSPACE=6>
```

Using images as links

Earlier in this chapter you learnt how to create hypertext links, or *anchors*, to a Web page or file using the tag <A HREF='*URL*'>*clickable text*</A>. But the clickable section that appears on the page doesn't *have* to be text: you can use an image instead, or both image and text. For example, if you slot the whole image tag given above into the anchor tag, the image will appear exactly as it did before, but will now act as a clickable link:

```
<A HREF='morelinks.html'><IMG SRC='splash.gif'
ALIGN=MIDDLE HSPACE=30 VSPACE=6 WIDTH=84 HEIGHT=81
BORDER=0></A>Click this image to open my other
links page.
```

If you want to make both the text *and* the image clickable, add some text before or after the <IMG> tag like this:

```
<A HREF="morelinks.html">Click this image to open
my other
links page.<IMG SRC="splash.gif" ALIGN=MIDDLE
HSPACE=30
VSPACE=6 WIDTH=84 HEIGHT=81 BORDER=0></A>
```

Figure 9.6 shows what those two methods look like when displayed in your browser:

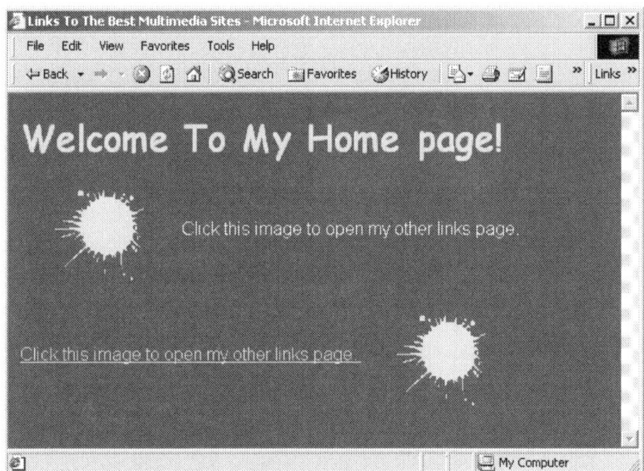

Figure 9.6 Using images as links.

10

The Internet and multimedia

What do you need?

Real Player

MP3 audio

Movies

Shockwave animation

Live cam

One of the most important reasons for the surge in popularity of the Internet when the World Wide Web came along was the fact that the Web made the Internet fun to use. Not only was it possible to find information, it was possible to find entertainment in the form of music, sounds, video, interactivity and animation – a true multimedia experience. In this chapter we'll look at some of the multimedia elements used on the Web, and point you towards Web sites that will give you a taste of what's on offer.

What do you need?

Most of the software you need to enjoy the Web's multimedia offerings is free, and comes in the form of programs called **plug-ins**. A plug-in is a program that attaches itself to your browser (in a metaphorical rather than physical way!) during installation and waits invisibly in the background until you try to play the kind of multimedia file it was designed to handle.

There are hundreds of different plug-ins available, between them handling hundreds of different types of multimedia file. But the good news is that you don't need all those separate plug-ins: some of the best can handle many different types of media, so you probably won't need to install more than two or three extra programs to handle the majority of multimedia files you come across. And if you're using Windows Millennium or Internet Explorer v5.5 (or later versions of either of those) you may not need any new software at all. A Windows Media Player is included with both of these, which is capable of handling almost everything the Web can throw at it. You can download the Windows Media Player as a separate item from **http://www.microsoft.com/ windows/windowsmedia**.

Real Player

You won't travel far on the Web before arriving at a site that uses RealAudio for music, speech, or a mixture of the two. RealAudio is a *streaming* format that plays as the file is being transferred, with none of that tedious waiting around for the sound file to download first. As soon as you click a RealAudio link, your Real Player opens (as shown in Figure 10.1), grabs the first few seconds of the transmission to help it to stay one jump ahead and ensure smooth playback, and then starts to play. You can pause or stop playback by clicking the appropriate buttons, or replay the entire clip from the beginning. If you have Internet Explorer you don't need to do anything more – the RealAudio plug-in is bundled with it. If you're using a different browser, you'll have to visit **http://www.real.com** to download and install the player software.

Once you've installed the Real Player, as with all multimedia plug-ins, your first stop should be the Web site of the people who wrote the program – you'll always find plenty of samples and links to let you play with your new toy once you've installed it. In this case, then, go to **http://www.real.com**. A couple of other good sites are Virgin Radio at **http://www.virginradio.co.uk** and London's Capital Radio at **http://www.capitalfm.com**, where you can hear the live radio broadcasts while you surf.

RealAudio doesn't offer great sound quality – some sacrifices have to be made for the files to transfer this fast. Top-quality sound comes in the form of ***.wav*** *files, which Internet Explorer can play without any extra help, and these weigh in at up to 10Mb for a top-quality one-minute file! Smaller* ***.mid*** *files use the sounds built into your soundcard, so quality of the results depends a lot on the quality of your card.*

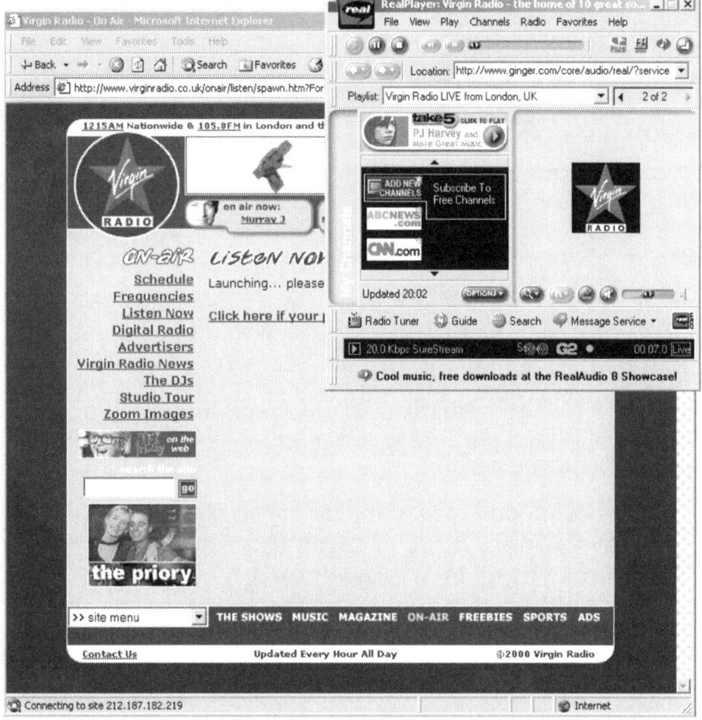

Figure 10.1 A live broadcast from Virgin Radio playing in Real Player.

MP3 audio

The MP3 format is a relatively new innovation that claims to pack near-CD-quality music into comparatively small files (a typical song weighs in at between 1Mb and 2Mb). Whether the quality is near enough to a CD to be listenable for long periods is a matter of taste, but these files have been the 'big thing' on the Net over the last couple of years and hundreds of Web sites have sprung up offering free MP3 music.

One of the most popular MP3 players is Winamp from **http://www.winamp.com** (shown in Figure 10.2) which can also play CDs and other audio formats. Both the Real Player and

Windows Media Player also have MP3 playback capability. To try out the MP3 format for yourself, visit **http://www.mp3.com**, **http://www. mp3now.com** or **http://www.mp3sound.com**.

Figure 10.2 The popular (and very stylish) Winamp MP3 player.

Movies

The first thing to be aware of here is that movie files are *big!* A one-minute movie will be roughly 2.5Mb, and in most cases you'll have to wait for the whole file to download before you can watch it. All the same, as with most multimedia elements, it pays to have the software installed just in case you come across something that really seems worth the wait!

The three most common types of movie file on the Web are MPEG (which will have **.mpeg**, **.mpg** or **.mpe** extensions), QuickTime (**.mov** or **.qt**), and Video For Windows (**.avi**). The Windows Media Player can handle these, but it occasionally has problems with the QuickTime format, so you might want to download the dedicated player from **http://www.apple.com/quicktime**.

Ready to watch some videos? To make the most of your QuickTime Player, head for **http://www.apple.com/quicktime/hotpicks** where you'll find links to movies, music and QuickTime virtual reality. Or visit QuickTime TV at **http://www.apple.com/quicktime/qtv** and pick a channel. To see trailers of the latest cinema releases (shown in Figure 10.3) go to **http://www.apple.com/quicktime/trailers**.

The MPEG format is used mostly for animations nowadays, and you can find a great collection at **http://wwwzenger.informatik.tu-muenchen.de/ persons/paula/mpeg**.

Figure 10.3 Watch movie trailors at QuickTime's Web site.

Shockwave animation

The word *animation* doesn't sound cool, but it's a major multimedia craze on the Internet. Where images and text have always been fixed on the page, they can now move around and react to the mouse passing over them. Part of this popularity lies in the fact that animations are easier for the average user to create than videos, and they take no more time to download than an image.

The most common type of animation is ShockWave, which you can view in Internet Explorer without adding anything else to your software mountain. (If you're not using Internet Explorer, you'll have to visit **http://www. macromedia.com** to download the plug-in.) To find out what all the fuss is about, visit Macromedia's own Shockwave Gallery at **http://www.shockwave. com** (Figure 10.4), or play a few games at **http://clevermedia.com/arcade**.

Live cam

This is an unusual branch of Internet multimedia. With the arrival of cheap video cameras called **Webcams**, users have been able to rig up direct camera-to-Web-site connections that allow anyone in the world to see whatever the camera is pointed at, almost exactly in real time. This might be a street corner, or their desk, or a fishbowl... almost anything that moves, in fact.

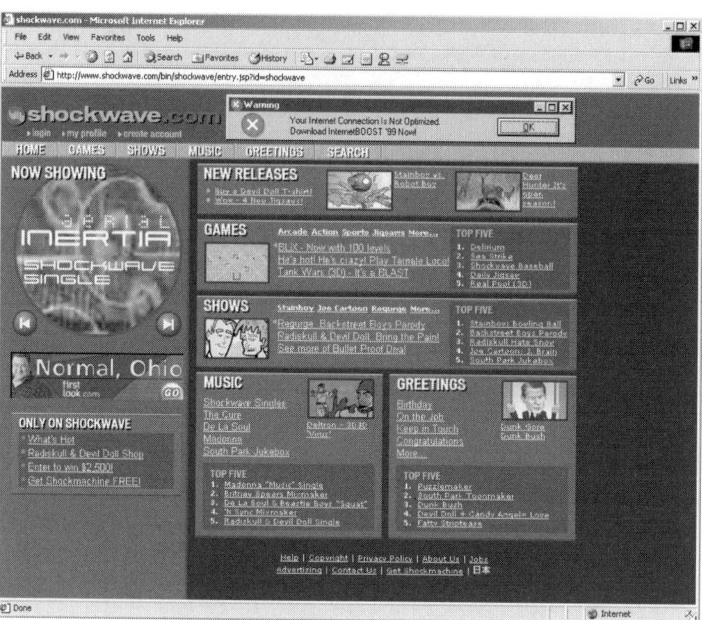

Figure 10.4 Animation really is better than you'd expect: find out at **www.shockwave.com**.

The oddest thing about live cam sites is that many of them really are entertaining! As an example, visit Edinburgh's Cyberia café (**http://www.cybersurf.co.uk/spy**), and click the **Refresh** button on the toolbar every few seconds. You'll see the traffic lights changing, vehicles passing, people walking in and out of shot… and the longer you have to wait for something to actually *move*, the more rewarding it is when it happens. There are thousands of Web cameras running all over the world, some providing pure zany entertainment, others giving more practical information (such as up-to-the-minute pictures of your chosen holiday destination). To round off this chapter, here's a taste of a few more:

- The Almost Amazing Turtle Cam at **http://www.campusware.com/turtles**
- Jason's office at **http://george.lbl.gov/cgi-bin/jason/cavecam**
- The New Jersey Diner Cam at **http://www.nj.com/dinercam/live.html** (Figure 10.5)

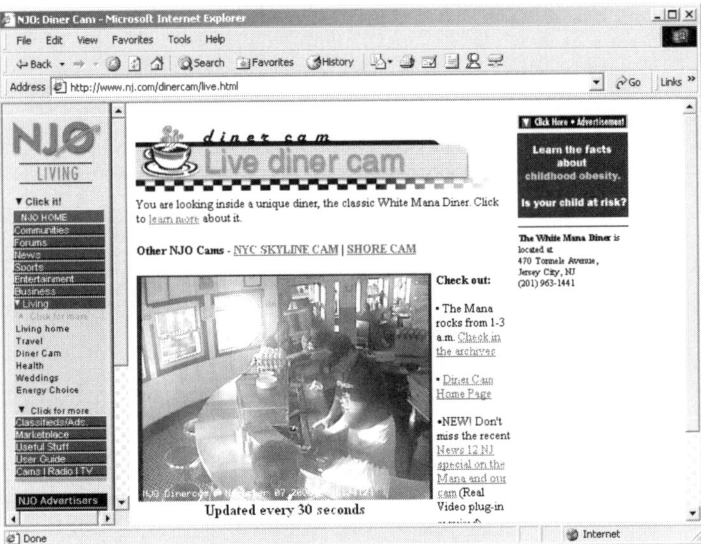

Figure 10.5 Live 'action' from the New Jersey Diner Cam.

11 Security on the Internet

Keeping children safe

Shopping online

Viruses

E-mail privacy

Stolen e-mail indentity

As police lieutenant Frank Drebin says in the film *The Naked Gun*, 'You take a risk crossing the street, getting out of bed, or sticking your face in a fan.' It's funny, but it does actually ring true as far as the Internet goes. There are certainly risks in using the Net that you wouldn't expect, and from time to time people do get caught out by them. But there are other things that most users (if they stopped to think about it for a moment) would realise were stupidly risky.

Unfortunately, the Net can sometimes lull you into a false sense of security: after all, you're comfortable and warm, and sitting safely in front of your computer. What could possibly go wrong? In this chapter we'll point out some of the pitfalls to be aware of when using the Internet.

Keeping children safe

On the Web, the front pages of those private sites are accessible to all, and some contain images and language designed to titillate, and to part you from some cash. The Web's search engines are another risk – enter the wrong keywords (or the right keywords, depending on your viewpoint) and you'll be presented with direct links to explicit sites accompanied by colourful descriptions.

The Internet has its fair share of sex and smut, just as it has motoring, cookery, sports, films, and so on. We won't pretend that your kids *can't* come into contact with explicit images and language, but there are two important points to note. First, you're no more likely to stumble upon pornography while looking for a sports site than you are to stumble upon film reviews or recipes. If you want to find that sort of content, you have to go looking for it. Second, most of the sexually explicit sites on the World Wide Web are *private* – to get inside you need a credit card. Nevertheless, there *are* dangers on the Net, and given unrestricted freedom, your kids may come into contact with unsuitable material.

However, these are not good reasons to deny children access to the Internet. Quite simply, the Internet is a fact of life that isn't going to go away, and will feature more strongly in our children's lives than it does in ours. More and more schools are recognising this, and promoting use of the Internet in homework and class projects. The wealth of Web sites created by and for children is a great indicator of their active participation in the growth of the Net. Rather than depriving children of this incredible resource, agree a few ground rules at the outset: when they can surf, why they should never give out their address, school name or telephone number, what sort of sites they can visit, and what to do if they receive messages that make them uncomfortable. For some excellent practical advice on this subject, all parents should visit Yahooligans at **http://www.yahooligans.com/docs/safety**.

If you're ever concerned about the Web sites your children might be visiting, remember that you can open Internet Explorer's History panel to see a list of recently accessed sites sorted by week and day.

You can also install a 'babysitter' program that can limit the amount of time children spend online, prevent them from accessing certain sites, and monitor the sites they do visit. Two popular programs are Cyber Patrol from **http://www.cyberpatrol.com** (shown in Figure 11.1) and Net Nanny from **http://www.netnanny.com**.

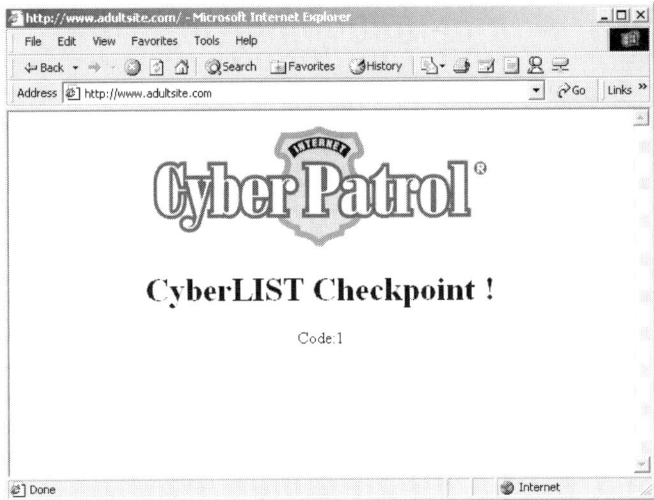

Figure 11.1 Cyber Patrol can prevent access to 'adult' sites.

Shopping online

A popular myth about the Internet is that credit-card transactions are risky because your card number can be stolen. To put this in perspective, consider how you use your credit or debit card in the 'real world'. How many people get to see your card number during a normal week? How much time does your card spend out of your view when you use it? The truth is, card numbers are *easy* to steal. It takes a lot more effort and technical know-how to steal numbers on the Internet.

Making the computer hacker's job more difficult in this department, modern browsers now encrypt the data they send, and most of the Web sites at which you can use your credit card run on **secure servers** that have their own built-in encryption. So when you visit one of these secure sites, enter your card number, and click the button to send it, your number will appear as meaningless gibberish to anyone managing to hack into the system. In fact, credit card companies actually regard online transactions as being the *safest* kind.

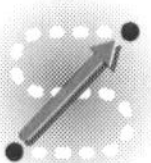

It's easy to recognise a secure site in Internet Explorer: look for a little padlock symbol in the lower right corner of the browser. You'll also notice that the ***http://*** *in the address bar changes to* ***https://*** *(Figure 11.2). More and more shopping sites are becoming secure all the time, and those that aren't usually offer alternative payment methods.*

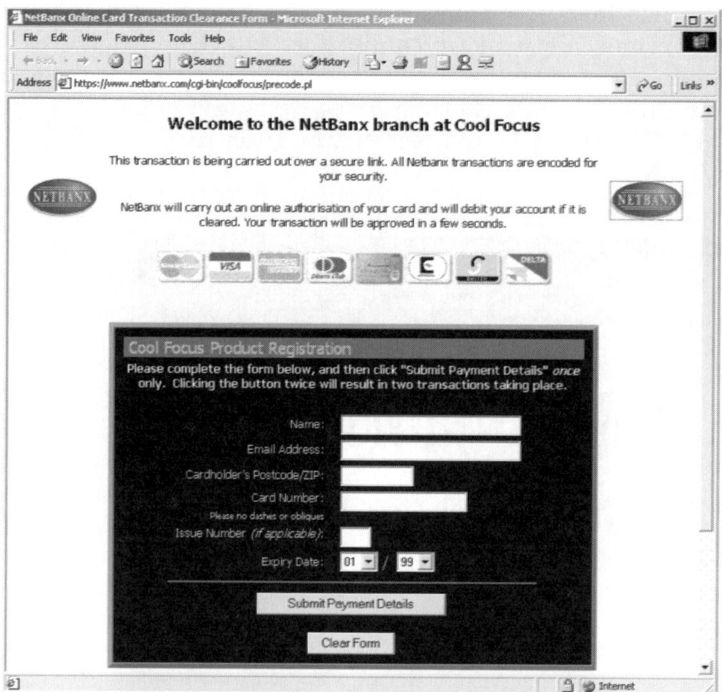

Figure 11.2 Look for **https://** in the address bar and a padlock symbol in the status bar to indicate that a Web site is secure.

One final point about online credit-card use. Many 'adult' sites ask for your credit card details on the pretext that possession of a credit card indicates you're old enough to be allowed in. You'll also see claims that membership of the site is free. Don't be fooled: a credit card number has only one use, and if you can locate the small print on the site you'll find that's the use they've got planned for yours.

Viruses

Viruses can't find their way onto your computer during ordinary Net surfing – you're not taking a greater risk by surfing for two hours a day than only surfing for one. But you might receive a virus-infected program on a floppy disk or CD-ROM, in an e-mail message, or by downloading it from the Internet. In almost all cases, your computer can only become infected by that virus when you run the program, so always use a virus-checker to scan software received by one of these methods before running it. Two of the best-known virus-checker programs can be found at **http://www.mcafee.com** and **http://www.symantec.com**.

An increasingly popular type of virus is the so-called 'e-mail virus'. An ordinary e-mail message is just plain text, making it completely harmless, but you can receive programs as e-mail attachments which definitely *could* be infected with a virus. Always save e-mail attachments and virus-check them before opening them.

Although you should always be suspicious of attachments from people you don't know, remember that viruses can come from friends and colleagues too: they may be unaware that their system is infected when they send you an attachment. Many recent types of virus automatically copy themselves to everyone in your e-mail address book, so nowadays you're actually more likely to receive infected attachments from someone you know than from someone you don't!

A final type of virus risk comes from malicious scripts built into HTML e-mail. Outlook Express supports this type of e-mail, and with so many Outlook Express users out there it's an attractive target for virus writers. To guard against viruses in HTML e-mail, follow these two steps:

1. In Outlook Express, go to **Tools** / **Options** / **Security**, select the option labelled **Restricted sites zone** (as shown in Figure 11.3) and click **OK**.

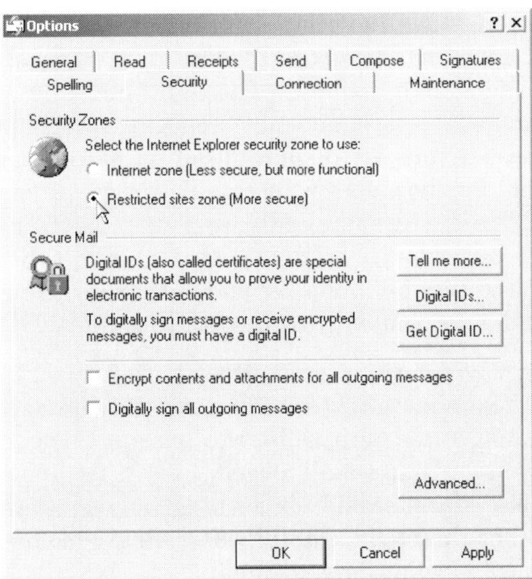

Figure 11.3 Protect yourself from malicious scripts built into e-mail messages.

2. In Control Panel, run the Internet Options applet, and choose the Security tab. Select the **Restricted sites** icon at the top of the page, drag the slider below up to **High** (if it's not there already), and click **OK**.

E-mail privacy

E-mail is certainly not a secure, private way to communicate with someone: it can get you into trouble (and people have got into very hot water from using e-mail where a phone call or a quiet chat would have been wiser). If you're concerned about who could read it, don't write it.

The most obvious problem is that your 'private' messages can be easily forwarded or redirected, or the recipient might simply fail to delete an incriminating message after reading it. But apart from existing on your computer and the recipient's computer, however briefly, the message also spends time on your access provider's mail server and that of the recipient's access provider. Will the message really be deleted from both? And what if the administrator of one of these systems decides to run a backup while your message is waiting to be delivered? If you really must use e-mail to exchange sensitive messages, you might want to consider using **encryption** to scramble messages so that only the intended recipient will be able to *decrypt* them. Even that isn't foolproof, of course: can you really be sure the recipient won't then pass on the decrypted versions?

Stolen e-mail identity

This doesn't happen often, but it does happen: someone can send an e-mail message that appears to have come from you. It's easy to do, too. Every time you send an e-mail message, your name and e-mail address are attached to its header. When the recipient retrieves his e-mail, these details are displayed so that he can see who the message is from. But how does your e-mail program know what details to enter? When you installed your e-mail software and filled in those little boxes on its options page, you told it! So, of course, if you go back to that options page and enter something different, those are the details that will go out with your e-mail.

So it's entirely possible that someone could attach your name and e-mail address to a message they send from their computer, and it would be difficult (although not impossible) to trace it back to them. Actually, it's a wonder that e-mail forgery hasn't become a major pastime on the Net, because there's nothing you can do to prevent it happening other than to be careful what you say in chat rooms and newsgroups, and avoid riling anyone.

Glossary

ActiveX A new multimedia programming system developed by Microsoft for use on the World Wide Web.

alias A nifty short name for something whose real name is much longer. For example, your e-mail software will usually let you refer to yourself as Joe Bloggs instead of j_bloggs@somewhere.co.uk.

animated GIF A type of animation created by loading two or more GIF images into an animation program, setting an order and delay times, and re-saving as a single file.

anonymous FTP A method of getting access to files on an FTP site without needing special permission or a *logon* name. Instead you enter **anonymous** as your logon name, and your e-mail address as your password.

anonymous remailers Services that will forward your e-mail messages or newsgroup articles after stripping out your personal details, so that no one can tell who sent them.

Archie A system that lets you track down files on FTP sites by entering the name of the file (or part of it) into a program that can search through indexes of files on these computers.

archive A single file which usually contains several (or many) other files to make for quicker and easier downloading. Most archives also compress these files into a smaller space than they'd ordinarily take up, speeding up downloads still further.

article For no particularly good reason, the name for a message sent to a newsgroup.

attachments Files included with a message to be sent by e-mail or to a newsgroup. Messages that contain attachments are indicated by a paperclip icon in most software.

attributes In HTML, these are additions to tags that let you specify or change what the tag should do. For example, `<HR>` creates a rule across the page. Adding the `WIDTH=` and `ALIGN=` attributes lets you create a short rule placed on the left side of the page.

bandwidth A general term for the amount of information that can be transferred over an Internet connection. Often used in terms of 'wasting bandwidth' by, for example, sending the same article to 30 different newsgroups when it was only relevant to one.

binaries or binary files The term for a file that contains anything but plain ASCII text (such as a program, movie, or formatted document). Also appears in newsgroup names to indicate that non-text files can be attached to articles in the group.

bookmarks The Netscape Navigator name for Favorites.

bounced e-mail E-mail messages that come back to you instead of being delivered, usually because you typed the e-mail address wrongly.

browser The vital piece of Internet software, ostensibly designed for viewing pages from the World Wide Web, but capable of handling almost all of your Internet activities. The two most popular browsers are Microsoft's Internet Explorer, and Netscape's Navigator.

cache A directory on your own system into which your browser stores all the files it downloads from the World Wide Web in case you want to view those pages another time – it can then load them quickly from this directory instead of downloading them from the Web all over again.

chat A type of conversation that takes place by typing messages back and forth instead of speaking (other than to swear at the chat software). A popular chat system is IRC, but online services have their own chat rooms, and other software allows one-to-one chatting by 'dialling up' an e-mail address rather like using a telephone.

client The name for something (usually a software program) that makes use of a service. For example, your e-mail program is a client that makes use of the e-mail service. The opposite term is server.

compressed files See **archive**.

cookies Small text files that some Web sites store on your computer so that they know who you are next time you visit.

cyberspace A word coined by William Gibson in his novel *Neuromancer*. It's used as a very generalised term for the Internet and everything that comes with it.

Dial-Up Networking The TCP/IP stack built into Microsoft Windows 95, Windows NT 4.0, and later operating systems, that makes setting up an Internet connection a relatively pain-free task.

DNS See Domain Name System.

domain name The name given to a computer on the Internet that's (vaguely) recognisable to human beings, such as www.royalnetwork.com. Every computer on the Net has its own unique name.

Domain Name System (DNS) Also defined as Domain Name Server. This system translates the friendly domain names that we humans like to work with into IP addresses that computers like to work with.

dot address Another name for IP address.

downloading The act of copying files (of any type) to your own computer from some other computer. The opposite term is uploading.

Dynamic HTML (DHTML) The combination of ordinary HTML and script written in languages such as JavaScript which can produce 'dynamic' Web pages – pages in which the content can change according to mouse movement, user input, or time passing.

e-mail Short for 'electronic mail', a system that lets you send text messages over a network from one computer to another.

e-mail address An address consisting of your username and the host name of your service provider's computer, in the form username@host. Because this host name is unique, and you're the only subscriber with that username, the e-mail is as personal to you as your phone number.

emoticons Little pictures (usually faces) made out of typed characters and viewed sideways-on, such as :-) meaning happy.

encryption The term for altering data or text to turn it into meaningless gobbledegook. Only someone with the correct decoding information (or 'key') can read and use it.

FAQ (Frequently Asked Questions) A list of questions and answers on a particular subject. These are frequently placed in newsgroups so that the group doesn't become bogged down with new users asking the same questions all the time. You'll also find FAQs on Web sites, and almost anywhere else in the computing world.

Favorites A menu in Microsoft's Internet Explorer browser (and a corresponding directory on your hard disk) containing shortcuts to sites that you visit regularly. You can revisit a site easily by clicking its name on the menu, and add new sites to the menu with a couple of clicks.

FTP (File Transfer Protocol) One of the many protocols used to copy files from one computer to another on the Internet. Also used in terms like 'an FTP site' (a site that lets you grab files from it using this protocol), and as a verb, as in 'You can ftp to this site'.

flame A negative or abusive response to a newsgroup article or an e-mail message.

follow-up A reply to an e-mail or newsgroup message that contains the same subject line (prefixed with RE) and continues the same thread.

freeware Software that you don't have to pay for.

gateway A program or device that acts as a kind of translator between two networks that wouldn't otherwise be able to communicate with each other.

GIF One of the two major graphics formats used on the Internet (along with JPEG). GIF images can be saved with between 2 and 256 colours, so they contain less information than the 16-million-colour JPEG format, and therefore make smaller files. They're suitable for anything but photographs and the most lifelike art.

Gopher A menu-based system for storing, searching for, and retrieving documents, which was the precursor to the World Wide Web.

history list A list of recently visited sites stored by your browser so that you can see where you've been, get back there easily, or find out what someone else has been using your browser for.

home page Two definitions for this one. 1. The page displayed in your browser when you first run it, or when you click the Home button. 2. The first page (or main contents page) of a Web site.

host A computer connected directly (and usually permanently) to the Internet that allows other computers to connect to it (like your service provider's computer). This also leads to the expression 'host name' which means the same as domain name.

HTML See **Hypertext Markup Language**.

HTTP (HyperText Transfer Protocol) The protocol used to transfer Web pages around the Internet, along with the images and other ingredients that go with them.

hypertext A system of clickable text used on the World Wide Web, as well as in older Windows help files and CD-ROM-based encyclopaedias. A hypertext link can be inserted wherever a cross-reference to another part of the document (or an entirely different document) is needed.

Hypertext Markup Language (HTML) A fairly simple system of textual codes that can be added to an ASCII text file to turn it into a Web page.

Internet Often shortened to just 'the Net'. The Internet is a gigantic network of computers, all linked and able to exchange information. No one owns or controls it, and anyone can connect to it. Without the capital 'I', an internet is a more general term for networks connected to each other.

Internet Protocol (IP) See **TCP/IP**.

IP address (Internet Protocol Address) Every computer on the Internet has its own unique address, which can appear in two forms: the friendlier domain name, or as an IP address that computers themselves use. This consists of four numbers separated by dots, such as 148.159.6.26. Also known as a 'dot address'.

IRC (Internet Relay Chat) An Internet service that provides one of the most popular chat systems which can be accessed using many different IRC programs. Chat rooms in IRC are referred to as 'channels'.

ISDN An abbreviation for Integrated Services Digital Network. An ISDN line allows faster access to the Internet than current modems allow, and can simultaneously handle voice and data.

ISP See **Internet Service Provider**.

Internet Service Provider (ISP) A company that allows anyone to connect to the Internet by dialling into their host computer. All they ask in return is that you give them money.

Java A software-programming language developed by Sun Microsystems Inc. The language is often used to write small programs called 'applets' that can be inserted in a Web page.

JavaScript A similar language to Java, except that it's written in plain text and can be inserted 'as is' into an HTML document to place effects or small programs on a Web page.

JPEG Along with GIF, this is one of the two most used formats for images on the Net. This format saves information for 16.7 million colours, making it ideal for photographs but creating unnecessarily large files for most forms of artwork.

leased line A line leased from the telephone company that provides a permanent, dedicated connection to an Internet Service Provider. Leased lines are lightning fast and cost a small fortune. (Also known as a 'T1 connection'.)

link As a noun, a link is a piece of clickable hypertext, identifiable by being underlined and a different colour from the ordinary text around it. As a verb, to link to a site or page means the same as to open or download it.

log off A synonym for 'disconnect' – logging off means telling the computer you're connected to that you've finished for this session.

log on/logon Either of these can be used as a noun or a verb. When you log on to a service or computer you are identifying yourself, usually by entering a username and password. This act may be referred to as 'a logon', or 'logging on'. Your username may be termed a 'logon name'.

lurking A cute term for observing something without taking an active role. This may refer to visiting chat rooms and just following conversations rather than chatting, or reading newsgroups without posting any articles yourself.

mailing list This can mean two things. 1. A list of e-mail addresses to which you can send the same message without making endless copies of it, all with different addresses inserted. 2. A discussion group similar to newsgroups, but all the messages sent to the group are forwarded to its members by e-mail.

mail server A computer (or program) dedicated to transferring e-mail messages around the Internet. This might be referred to as an SMTP server or a POP3 server.

MIME (Multipurpose Internet Mail Extensions) A method of organising different types of file by assigning each its own 'MIME type'. Most of the Internet software you use can recognise these types and determine what to do with a file it receives (or ask you how you want to treat it). MIME is used to handle attachments in e-mail and newsgroup messages, as well as files found on Web pages.

mirror site An exact copy of a site located on a different computer. Many popular sites have one or more mirrors around the world so that users can connect to the site nearest to them, thus easing the load on the main computer.

modem An acronym formed from the words 'modulator' and 'demodulator'. A modem converts data back and forth between the format recognised by computers and the format needed to send it down telephone lines.

MPEG Along with QuickTime, one of the two most popular formats for movie files on the Internet, requiring an MPEG player and (ideally) special hardware for playback.

MUD (Multi User Dungeon) A type of text-based adventure game that might be played by a single user, or by multiple users adopting characters and 'chatting' by typing messages.

netiquette An amalgamation of the words 'Internet' and 'etiquette' that refers to good behaviour on the Net. Netiquette essentially boils down to two rules: avoid offensive comments and actions, and don't waste Internet resources (or bandwidth).

network Two or more computers that are connected to each other (or can be connected via telephone lines and modems) and can pass information back and forth.

newbie A colloquial name for someone new to the Internet, or to a particular area of it, who is perhaps prone to a bit of fumbling around. Although a slightly derogatory term, it's not meant to be offensive – you might describe yourself as a newbie when appealing for help.

newsgroups A discussion group with a particular topic in which users leave messages for others to read and reply to. There are almost over 50,000 such groups, and many more mailing lists which follow similar methods. Newsgroups are sometimes referred to as Usenet groups.

newsreader The software program you use to access newsgroups, and to read, send, and reply to articles.

news server A computer (or program) dedicated to transferring the contents of newsgroups around the Net, and to and from your computer. This might be referred to as an NNTP server.

NNTP (Network News Transfer Protocol) One of many protocols used on the Net to transfer information around. This particular protocol handles messages from newsgroups.

offline A synonym for 'not connected'. In Net terms, being offline is generally a good thing (unless you're trying and failing to get online): the ability to compose messages offline and send them all in a bunch later, or view downloaded files offline, can save you money in connection charges.

online A synonym for 'connected'. Anything connected to your computer and ready for action can be said to be online. In Internet terms, it means that you've successfully dialled in to your service provider's computer and are now connected to the Net. The opposite term is offline.

online service A members-only service that allows users to join discussion groups (or 'forums'), exchange e-mail messages with other members, download files, and a fair bit more besides. Most popular online services (such as America Online and CompuServe) are now connected to the Internet as well.

packet The name for a unit of data being sent across the Net. A system called 'packet switching' breaks up a file into packets, marks each with the addresses of the sending and receiving computers, and sends each packet off individually. These packets may arrive at your computer via different routes and in the wrong order, but your computer uses the extra information they contain to piece the file back together.

PGP (Pretty Good Privacy) A popular, but complicated, system of encryption.

PING (Packet InterNet Groper) The name of a command (or a program that sends a command) that tests a connection between two computers. It does this by sending a tiny amount of data to a specified computer and noting how long it takes to reply. (The reply, incidentally, is called a PONG.)

plug-in An add-on program for a browser that can play or display a particular type of file in the browser's own window.

PoP (Point of Presence) An unnecessarily technical name for a phone number you can dial to connect to your service provider's computer. Many service providers have PoPs all over the country; others cater just for the major cities or a single small area.

POP3 (Post Office Protocol) One of two protocols (along with SMTP) used to transfer e-mail messages around the Net. POP is used for receiving e-mail, and lets you collect your messages from any computer you happen to be using. The '3' refers to the latest version of the protocol.

posting When you send an e-mail message, the word 'sending' is quite good enough. When you send a message to a newsgroup, it isn't. Instead, for no adequately explained reason, the word 'posting' is used.

PPP (Point to Point Protocol) A protocol used to connect computers to the Internet via a telephone line and a modem. It's similar to SLIP, but more recent and easier to set up.

protocol A type of 'language' that two computers agree to speak when they need to communicate and don't speak each other's native language. In other words, a sort of Esperanto for computers, but networking and Internet connections use a great many different protocols to do different things.

QuickTime Along with MPEG, this is one of the most popular movie file formats on the Net, developed by Apple. To view these files you'll need the QuickTime Viewer. There is also a virtual reality version (QuickTime VR) which is gaining in popularity.

RealAudio The most popular format for streaming audio on the Net, requiring the RealAudio Player (included with Internet Explorer) for playback.

Refresh (or **reload**) Forcing the browser to download a Web page again by clicking a toolbar button labelled **Refresh** (in Internet Explorer) or **Reload** (in Netscape Navigator). You might do this to make sure you're looking at the latest version of a page, or as an attempt to get things moving again if the page began to download and everything ground to a halt.

rot13 (rotated 13) A simple method used to encrypt e-mail and newsgroup messages so that you won't accidentally read something that might offend you.

search engine A Web site that maintains an index of other Web pages and sites, allowing you to search for pages on a particular subject by entering keywords. Because these engines gather their information in different ways, you can get markedly varying results from using different search sites.

server A computer or program that provides a service to a client. For example, your e-mail client (the program that lets you work with e-mail messages) connects to your service provider's mail server when you decide to send or receive your e-mail.

service provider A general term for a company that gives you access to the Internet by letting you dial into its computer. This may be an Internet Service Provider or an online service.

shareware A system for selling software that lets you try before you buy. If you like the program, you pay for it. If you don't, you stop using it and delete it from your system.

signature A short piece of text you can create that is appended to your e-mail and newsgroup messages when you send them. This might give contact information (perhaps your name, e-mail address, company name, etc), a neat little phrase or quote, or perhaps an elaborate piece of ASCII art (rather like an emoticon, but bigger).

SLIP (Serial Line Internet Protocol) A similar protocol to PPP, but older and best avoided (especially if you use Windows 95, Windows NT 4.0, or later).

smiley See **emoticon**.

SMTP (Simple Mail Transfer Protocol) Along with POP3, one of the two protocols that are used to transfer e-mail messages around the Net. SMTP can be used to both send and receive messages, but POP3 has more flexibility for receiving. When POP3 is being used, SMTP simply handles the sending of messages.

Source The name for the HTML document that forms a Web page, containing all the tags that determine what your browser should display, and how. You can look at the source code for a Web page in Internet Explorer by clicking the **View** menu and selecting **Source**.

spamming A Net jargon term for sending the same message to multiple newsgroups or e-mail recipients regardless of their interest (or lack of it). Most spamming consists of unsolicited advertisements. Apart from the personal aggravation it causes, spamming is also a massive waste of bandwidth.

streaming Some of the latest formats for video and audio on the Net allow the file to play while it's being downloaded, rather than forcing you to wait for the entire file to download first.

tags The name for the HTML codes added to a plain ASCII document which turn it into a Web page with full formatting and links to other files and pages.

talk A talk program lets you speak to someone elsewhere in the world using your modem and Internet connection instead of your telephone. You need a soundcard and microphone, and the other person must be using the same program as you. Also known as Voice On the Net (VON). The term 'talk' is also used to describe the kind of typed chat that takes place between two people rather than a group in a chat room.

TCP/IP (Transmission Control Protocol/ Internet Protocol) Two vital protocols that work together to handle communications between your computer and the rest of the Internet.

TCP/IP stack For a computer to connect to the Internet, it must have a TCP/IP stack, which consists of TCP/IP software, packet driver software, and sockets software. Windows 95 and later Windows operating systems come with their own TCP/IP stack called Dial-Up Networking. In Windows 3x, the TCP/IP stack has to be installed separately: one of the best stacks is Trumpet Winsock. (See also Winsock.)

Telnet A program that allows Internet users to connect to a distant computer and control it through their own computer. Nowadays the main use of Telnet is in playing games like MUD.

thread An ongoing topic of conversation in a newsgroup or mailing list. When someone posts a message with a new subject line they're starting a new thread. Any replies to this message (and replies to replies, and so on) will have the same subject line and continue the thread.

TLAs (Three Letter Acronyms) Not necessarily acronyms, and not necessarily three letters either, but TLAs are a type of shorthand for common phrases used in conversation and messages on the Net, such as BTW for 'By the way'.

Transmission Control Protocol (TCP) See **TCP/IP**.

uploading The term for copying files from your own computer to a distant computer, usually by using FTP. The opposite term is downloading.

URL (Uniform Resource Locator) The unique 'address' of a file on the Internet consisting of a protocol (such as http://), a computer name (such as www.computer.co.uk) and a path to the file on that computer (such as /public/files/program.zip).

Usenet A large network that distributes many of the Net's newsgroups.

username A unique name you're assigned by a service that enables you to log on to it and identify yourself, demonstrating that you're entitled to access it. When you set up your Internet access account, your username will usually form part of your e-mail address too.

uuencode/uudecode To send computer files in e-mail or newsgroup messages, they have to be converted to plain ASCII text first. Uuencoding is a system for converting files this way; uudecoding converts the text back into a file at the other end. Special software may be needed to do this, but many e-mail and newsgroup programs have built-in automatic uuencode/uudecode facilities.

VBScript A scripting language developed by Microsoft, similar to JavaScript.

viewer A program used to view, play or display files that you find on the Net. Unlike a plug-in, a viewer will open the file in its own separate window. Because it's a stand-alone program, you can also use it offline to view files already on your own system.

virus A small program created by a warped mind that can use various methods to attach itself to programs. When the program is run, so is the virus. A virus might do no more harm to your system than making it go beep occasionally, or it might trash all your data and even make your computer unusable. The main risk of 'catching' a virus comes from using programs on a floppy disk of unknown origin or downloaded from the Internet without first running them through virus-checker software.

Voice On the Net (VON) See **talk**.

VRML (Virtual Reality Modelling Language) A language used to build 3-dimensional models and 'worlds' that you can view using special software.

WAP (Wirless Application Protocol) Special Web-like pages written in a language called WML (similar to the Web's own HTML) can be downloaded into the new breed of WAP-enabled mobile phones, pagers and PDAs and read while on the move. These devices have 4- or 8-line displays for text and simple graphics.

WEB See **World Wide Web**.

Web page A single document (usually having the extension .htm or .html) forming a tiny part of the World Wide Web, often containing text, images, and links to other pages and files on the Web. To view Web pages you need a browser.

Web server A computer or program dedicated to storing Web pages and transmitting them to your computer to be viewed in your browser.

Web site A collection of related Web pages and files, usually created by or belonging to a single individual or company, and located on the same Web server.

Web space Usually refers to space on a Web server provided to Internet users so that they can create and publish their own Web sites. This space may be provided free, or for a monthly charge.

Winsock An abbreviation of Windows Sockets, the sockets software program for Windows operating systems called Winsock.dll that forms the basis of a TCP/IP stack.

World Wide Web A vast collection of documents and files stored on Web servers. The documents are known as Web pages and are created using a language called HTML. All these pages and files are linked together using a system of hypertext.

A simple guide to

searching the Internet

Gilles Fouchard & Rob Young

Introduction

Imagine you're looking for someone's phone number. You pick up your local phone directory, flick through it, and... it's not in alphabetical order! Still, no problem. You know the number's in there somewhere, so you can just keep looking until you find it.

It probably doesn't sound like much fun. Searching through a few pages isn't too bad, but the entire directory? Fortunately that's not how the phone book works. Unfortunately, though, it is how the Internet works.

The whole of human knowledge and experience is out there somewhere, but where do you find the tiny bit of it you're looking for? It isn't organised into any kind of structure; new pages and Web sites aren't automatically listed in some central directory, and there's no system for cataloguing what particular pages are about or what words they contain. What the Internet does have is hundreds of search tools to help you sort through this jumble of information. Just pick the right tool, ask it the right question, and you'll find what you were looking for quickly and painlessly.

Of course, now you need to know *which* of those hundreds of tools is the best one to use for a particular type of information, and how to phrase the question to be sure of finding the answer. That's the point of this book. Knowing how to search the Internet effectively can save you minutes or even hours. With the Internet continuing to grow at an amazing rate, it could soon mean the difference between finding what you need and *not* finding it!

How to use this book

Like most things in life, searching the Internet is simple *when you know how to do it*. By starting from Chapter 1 and following each chapter you'll progress from the basics to advanced search skills in a structured way. But you don't have to know everything about searching to start improving the results you get: each chapter contains self-contained information, so you can skip about the book all you like.

Throughout the book you'll see icons in the margins. These indicate notes that provide extra detail, introduce a new idea, or explain a technical term that we couldn't avoid using. The icon used tells you what sort of information the note contains:

This icon introduces handy shortcuts and tips such as keyboard hotkeys, expert options, and quicker ways of getting to the same place.

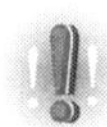

This icon warns you of any risks associated with a particular action, or any problems you might encounter along the way, and (where possible) shows you how to avoid them.

This icon is used to provide additional information about the topic being covered.

Basic skills

1

What is a search engine?

What does a search engine consist of?

Searching the Internet: principles

Getting started with your browser

People usually measure the Internet and its growth in terms of the number of users. With over 300 million surfers throughout the world, and around 1 million new users every month, the Internet is a phenomenon which cannot be ignored. Its content (number of sites, number of Web pages) is also growing at a phenomenal rate. In June 2000 there were 18 million registered Web addresses, compared with 6 million just one year earlier. And the number of domain names is an indication of the number of sites set up on the Web: 13 million in June 2000 compared with 4 million a year earlier. You can imagine the effect of this on the number of Web pages! With such exponential growth, the Web is becoming a veritable labyrinth through which it is difficult to find one's way. Whether a novice or an experienced surfer, you need to use search tools in order to make effective use of the Internet.

In order to achieve what you set out to do, avoiding time wasted surfing aimlessly, it is necessary to use the best tools offered on the Internet in general and the Web in particular. At your service you have search engines, directories, help features, selections, metasearch engines and 'searchbots'. As you will see in this book, there are plenty of good tools. So you will need to make the right choice and then you will need to learn how to use these tools. Among this plethora of tools, the search engine is of unimagined power for the beginner. Experienced surfers will also be able to refine their technique and learn how to select the right tools, optimise searches and interpret results.

Searching the Internet is empirical in nature. You can either work strictly in order to achieve your goal without any detours, or you can proceed by means of trial and error in order to uncover the odd pearl. It is by searching that you learn to search, so don't hesitate to try things out, to overlap requests and to refine your methods and how you express yourself as you progress.

What is a search engine?

For anybody who has already ventured onto the Web, this question does not arise. The search tool on the Internet is as indispensable as a library's catalogue, or the index of an encyclopaedia.

On the Web there are millions of pages and billions of words to be indexed. Like any document, a Web page may be indexed in two different ways:

- using keywords defining the page or document;
- using full text mode indexing.

In the first case, you can, for example, find all the pages relating to 'Tourism' (it is the page author who has indicated the keyword, or a professional surfer who has placed this page in this category).

In the second case, you will have access to all pages containing the word 'tourism'.

A search engine therefore indexes Internet objects (sites, Web pages, images, etc.). This strength is doubled by the updating of these indexes. Hundreds of sites are being created around the world every day and in line with this the content of indexes needs to be updated regularly.

To do this, the larger search engines work automatically and analyse the Internet in order to discover new sites and update their pages.

Here again, several methods of updating are used:

- automatic updating using a Web-trawling program called a 'spider';
- updating of a site by the author who simultaneously registers his pages in a given engine;
- manual updating by professional surfers and cyber-journalists, whose job it is to hunt down new sites and update databases.

Are search engines infallible?

The answer is obviously 'no'. Most engines do not interpret articles such as 'a', 'an' or 'the'. Thus a search relating to the rock group 'The Who' may give surprising results!

It is therefore necessary to make the right choice, supplement your request using Boolean operators (more on these later) or search by category in order to achieve your aims.

Each method has its advantages. Of course, the spider application can do a lot of work. Engines such as Infoseek, Excite or HotBot boast of having indexed millions of pages! But power does not always mean quality, as the more pages the engine has labelled, the more specific your request must be, otherwise you will be overwhelmed by an overabundance of lists of results. Fortunately, engines can also evaluate the results provided and, in this case, can retrieve lists in order of relevance. But how do you evaluate the relevance of each search engine?

Sometimes you may prefer manual selection by professionals. In addition, you may attribute great value to guides provided by cyber-journalists who give their opinion of sites visited and prepare classifications. In this way automated and human methods complement one another.

What does a search engine consist of?

Whether you are a novice on the Web or a pro, search engines constitute your privileged point of entry to the Web. And there is no better way to understand how they work and to demystify the subject than to examine closely how they operate.

Apart from the distinction between UK-specific search engines and the more general search engines that can lead you to Web sites throughout the world, we can loosely group search engines into the following categories:

- those which spend their time indexing Web pages, such as Excite, AltaVista or HotBot;
- those which organise and grade information under headings and subheadings and constitute huge directories (such as Yahoo!, which has both worldwide and UK-specific versions);
- those which also evaluate and comment on the sites visited, such as Magellan, provided by the McKinley company.

As we have stated already, there are many techniques used to build search engines and directories:

- automated location and indexing;
- use of manual recording by Web site designers and editors;
- recording and possibly evaluation of sites by teams of independent surfers.

Indexing Web pages and sites

There are a number of search tools which combine these various possibilities. Search engines that use automatic 'spider' applications can create indexes of millions of pages, e.g. more than 250 million in the case of engines like AltaVista. In fact, current techniques allow around 9 million pages to be indexed each day, allowing the entire index to be refreshed once a month. However, the number of pages indexed is not the essential indicator of an engine's quality.

Furthermore, indexing methods vary greatly from one engine to another. The criteria making it possible to differentiate the techniques used are as follows:

- regularity of updating;
- processing time of pages retrieved for indexing;
- nature of data indexed: text, images, etc.

The components of a search engine

A search engine consists of several components:

The 'spider' or 'crawler' is in charge of connecting with Web servers, visiting sites, reading pages and following the links on these pages within the same site. The 'spider' must go to the site regularly in order to note any changes. A gigantic task!

Everything that the 'spider' finds will be used to compile the index, the second component. Look at the index of this book in order to see the benefits of an index. The most advanced techniques are used to design the indexes of Web sites and pages. The index is regularly updated by adding, deleting or amending entries. But there is still a time lapse between reality, what the spider has been able to detect and this actually being recorded in the index.

The search engine itself is the third component. It is this which analyses the request you enter when you visit the search site, refers to the index to find matching pages and prepares the results. It is also this which has the task of sorting the results in order of relevance before presenting them to you.

Browsing and searching

Bearing in mind the difficult nature of the task (i.e. indexing sites and providing quality results to millions of surfers), no engine can claim to be exhaustive, or to perform the best, or to be infallible in the results transmitted. What is required is speed and reliability. It is easy to see that the operation of a search engine and the techniques used are a matter of compromise.

Performance varies from one system to another and depends on the nature of the search carried out. Each system has its strengths and weaknesses, and at times several engines need to be used in order to overlap and refine searches.

In general, each search engine offers:

- simple searches by keywords;
- complex searches using Boolean operators (AND/OR/NOT) and specific commands;
- searches by subject or site category.

Depending on the performance of the helper application used, the search may be easy or difficult. You must get to know the strengths and weaknesses of each search engine, which sometimes depend on the nature of the search undertaken.

Evaluating results

A search engine's performance lies in its capacity to interpret the request, evaluate the documents found and classify search results (hits). This usually involves allocating a percentage indicating how closely the hit matches your search term, and avoids the lengthy consultation of huge lists of results. The first sites proposed are deemed to best answer the enquiry. Again, this depends on the engine correctly interpreting the request made (the search term used).

You will be able to see that search engines work very fast most of the time, but their results often include sites or pages which are not of interest. It is up to you to sort the good from the bad!

In their defence, it must be acknowledged that search engines are not able to ask you additional questions in order to make their search more specific. It is up to you to take the initiative and if necessary word the request differently. Nor can they become enriched by your questions, although these are experiences which they could record in order to improve with time. We only know that search engines keep track of requests made in order to provide statistics which are of interest to surfers. We also know that search engines interpret the nature of requests in order to return advertising banners relating to them. In short, they are not as stupid as you might think. You can count on the creativity of programmers to constantly include more intelligence in these helper applications.

Again in their defence, search engines are tireless workers and do not draw back from anything. You can tell them 'Tourism' and they will send you thousands of pages of results. Try to ask a librarian the same thing and there is a good chance that you will be asked to be more specific, if not sent packing!

So what do search engines do to establish degrees of relevance in the results sent back to you?

First of all they use the **location/frequency method**. In plain English, they use rules which interpret the position of the words found and their frequency. The word 'Tourism' will have more weight in the title of a page than in the Web page itself. It is the number of times the word appears in the page itself which will eventually decide between two pages where the keyword appears in the title.

The position of a word in the page is also relevant. Thus, the engine can determine whether the word in question appears at the top of the page, in a title or in the first paragraph, all of which will have more weight than its appearance at the bottom of the page.

Most engines use this basic method with their own variations. That is why, among other things, different engines will produce different results for the same request.

As we have said, Internet search engines are far from equal:

- some record more pages than others;
- some update their index faster;
- some are more efficient than others.

Other methods of differentiation are used by search engines. For example, WebCrawler tests the **popularity of links**. It will give preference to a page to which lots of links point rather than to a page which fewer sites have linked to.

We can also assume that directory-based search engines will give better scores to sites that have been reviewed by the search site's own reviewer. A site visited by a professional team will be preferred to sites that are unknown.

Indexing from meta tags

So far we have made no mention of an important ingredient in Web page indexing: **meta tags**. What are these? Meta tags are hidden programming codes which are used by programmers to describe a Web site or page and record the associated keywords.

These commands are used because engines interpret them. So far so good, since meta tags were dreamed up precisely to facilitate indexing and further searches. It is by using these commands skillfully that the programmer will be able to ensure that his page is 'retrieved' by search engines.

While some search engines, such as Excite, ignore the keywords recorded in meta tags, others, such as HotBot, make great use of them. Nowadays, though, few search engines rely on meta tags entirely because they are so open to misuse. A Web author keen to see his site ranked highly may try to 'fool' the engine. Starting from the assumption that there is a great demand for erotic sites, an author might include words like 'nudity' in his meta tags to ensure that his page appears in the results for that type of search — even if the site contains nothing more than pictures of classical Greek statues!

Search engines are wise to this, of course, and they try to filter out this type of abuse. If a word is repeated a hundred or so times one after the other to try to win the 'frequency' competition, the engine may decide to ignore the site completely. Another popular trick, to win points for 'location', is to include lists of keywords in the first paragraph of a page, but to make that paragraph invisible to the reader by making its text colour match the background so that only the search engine will see them.

Since meta tags are absolutely freely defined, it is inevitable that engines will make mistakes in their interpretation. While the Excite solution of ignoring meta tags altogether is protective, it may penalise strict authors. The ideal solution would be to create a description standard accepted at the highest level, a standard on which engines could depend. Doubtless this will come. In the meantime, cyberspace, like the real world, is an imperfect world.

Presenting results

Indexing pages and analysing requests are the basic tasks of the search engine but it still has to display the results as comprehensively as possible for the surfer. Here, too, methods vary from one engine to another. Every kind of site description corresponding to a request may be displayed:

- the descriptions incorporated in meta tags;
- Web page titles;
- the first lines of a Web page;
- the review of the site by the search engine's own team;
- the page address (URL);
- the page size;
- the date of the last update;
- the degree of relevance.

The designers of Web pages and sites have several ways of getting themselves known by indexing applications:

- *site title;*
- *site description: this is a hidden programming code (a tag in HTML) containing the site description given by the editor or author; or*
- *keywords: this is another hidden code which contains a list of keywords attributed to sites.*

Today, everyone is free to describe a site as he chooses, and in the long run this is what can create anomalies in 'hits' (search results).

For the curious, this is how meta tags are coded in HTML language:

```
<META NAME="keywords" CONTENT=" cuisine, gastronomy, soil, wine">

<META NAME="description" CONTENT="A magazine on traditional cooking, good wine and the fruit of the soil.'>
```

And for engines that ignore meta tags there are still comments:

```
<!--A magazine on traditional cooking, good wines and the fruit of the soil.-->
```

Searching the Internet: principles

While some search sites offer you a range of options (drop-down lists, checkboxes, and so on), others leave you to construct your search query yourself and type it into a text-field. Before we look at the different options available, remember that all search engines have Help pages explaining how they work. Although there's no standardised syntax for search queries, many engines offer similar options and follow similar rules: these Help pages will help you find the differences and point out any extra features you can use that may be useful in a particular type of search.

The AltaVista search engine, for example, uniquely allows you to search for images or Java applets on a page, or search in site URLs, amongst other things. Other engines may have (or may add in the future) other options which may not be obvious until you look at their Help pages.

Match any or Match all?

When you type several keywords in the search box, two things may occur:

- The engine searches for pages containing *all* the keywords (the 'Match All' option, used by HotBot, Lycos and Go.com)
- The engine searches for pages containing *at least* one of the words (the 'Match Any' option, used by AltaVista, Excite and WebCrawler)

In the latter case, the number of words found may be one of the relevant criteria. The engine will display at the top the pages where it has found all the words. For the others it will indicate the number of words found, e.g. 2/4.

The site address, or URL (Uniform Resource Locator), is also used in searches. Although it's not the most usual starting point for a search, some engines do offer it as an option. Thus addresses including keywords may be searched for or a search may be restricted to a specific domain.

Bearing in mind these differences in behaviour, this is how each of the families of engine manages to respond to requests:

- to obtain 'Match any' with HotBot, for example, you must use the menu command options or code the request using the OR operator: 'Tourism OR England';
- to obtain 'Match all' with AltaVista, for example, you must use the operators + or AND: 'Tourism + England' or 'Tourism AND England'.

Boolean operators

Boolean operators are used to express logical search conditions. The two basic operators are AND and OR. While the AND operator is unambiguous, OR can take two forms:

The normal OR: in a search for 'A OR B' the page can contain A only, B only, or both A and B to be regarded as a match.

The exclusive OR: in a search for 'A OR B' the page can contain either A or B, but not both, to be regarded as a match.

Only the normal OR is used by default in search engines.

Exclusion

All engines allow you to exclude a word from results. If you are interested in tourism outside the UK, you can exclude the word 'UK'. Nothing complicated, except that the syntax varies from one engine to another.

- the – sign is used with AltaVista or Lycos;
- AND NOT is used with Infoseek, HotBot or AltaVista;
- NOT is used with WebCrawler or Lycos.

You can see from the three subtly different options above that it helps to get to know how your favourite search engines work!

Searching for sentences

The search query **Tourism and UK** does not mean the same as the query '**Tourism in UK**'. In the first case, a search is carried out relating to 3 keywords, probably with non-interpretation of the word 'and' by the search engine. In the second case, pages including the precise sentence 'Tourism in UK' are searched for.

Most engines use double quotes for this, or offer a choice via a menu (Excite or HotBot).

Upper and lower case

Only use capital letters in a search if you expect to *find* capital letters. If you're not concerned whether the word you're searching for is found capitalised or not, use lower case. A search for **egypt** would find instances in a page of **Egypt**, **egypt** or (in a rather unusual page!) **eGyPt**, but if you search for **Egypt** the engine will ignore any other case combinations it finds.

It follows, then, that you may be able to narrow down your search a lot if a word is frequently used in lower case but you expect to find a capital letter in the particular context you're interested in. If, for example, you wanted information about a town called Bucket, you could search for it with a capital 'B' and your search results should contain few links to pages containing general 'bucket information'.

Search engines such as Go.com treat sequences of capitalised words as a phrase so that double quotes are not needed: a search

Remember that a Web site address is structured as follows: http://www.server_name.domain/directory_ name/page_name

- ***http.*** *This is the communication protocol used, in this case HyperText Transfer Protocol; this protocol was designed for transferring Web pages (which are based on 'hypertext') around the Internet.*
- ***www.*** *Short for World Wide Web, the most popular area of the Internet. Developed in 1990, the Web makes use of hypertext technology, i.e. the connection of pages and documents using links. On the Web, one page contains all kinds of links:*
  - ***Links in the same page****. These are also called anchors. They make it possible to move quickly around a large text document (one page).*
  - ***Links with another page of the same site.*** *These links are used to move from one page to another within the same site. They allow the user to navigate the site.*

Continued

- ***Links with a page of another site.*** *These links are offered by the developers of Web sites to reference other useful sites which may, of course, be on other servers (computers storing Web pages). It is possible in this way to move from one site to another, from one Web server to another and often from one country to another by just a few clicks of the mouse. The user navigates without worrying about where data is located, all that matters to him is what he is looking for.*

This natural method of navigating using hyperlinks is commonly known as 'surfing the Internet'.

for **Buckingham Palace** would automatically be regarded as a phrase, for instance, and you can search for multiple phrases like this at once by separating each phrase with a comma (such as **Prince Charles, Buckingham Palace**).

Proximity

Some engines allow you to indicate parameters relating to proximity between the keywords designated. For example, **A NEAR B** indicates that word A must be close to word B (used by AltaVista, Lycos, or WebCrawler).

Note that Go.com offers the command [**A B**]: words between square brackets.

You can even specify the level of proximity: **A NEAR/10 B** indicates that A and B are within 10 words of each other (used by Lycos and WebCrawler).

Wildcards

Wildcards, familiar to DOS users, are probably new to others.

This is how they work in general:

- the * character indicates a string of characters of any length. 'Art*' thus makes it possible to search for art, artist or artisan.
- The $ character indicates a character in a specific position. 'Artist$' carries out a search for artists (in the plural) or artiste.

Searching by field

Some engines offer particular searches by type of field:

- the title of Web pages;
- addresses or URL;
- domain names;
- links.

This is the case with AltaVista, HotBot and Infoseek in particular.

Getting started with your browser

Setting a search engine as your home page

Your Internet browser (Microsoft Internet Explorer or Netscape Communicator, the two most frequently used tools) makes it possible to set a particular Web site to be shown every time you start surfing. As most of your Web sessions could well start with searches for information or sites, you might choose to set your favourite search engine as your browser's starting page.

This is how to proceed with Internet Explorer 5.0:

1. Click on **Tools**.
2. Click on **Internet Options**.
3. Select the General tab, if necessary.
4. In the Home page box, enter the Internet address of the selected engine.
5. Confirm by clicking on the **Apply** button, then on **OK**.

It is very easy to put together a query using a search engine, and the reply arrives quickly. But remember that the engine doesn't know what you're really looking for, it only knows what you've asked for! Make sure you re-read your request before submitting it, and check how the engine works, so that you can be sure that the results really will be relevant.

Search tools integrated in browsers

Netscape (Communicator) and Internet Explorer have a Search button which gives access to specific search resources on the Internet.

This button in fact gives each of them access to a specific Web page which offers links with pre-selected engines.

Searching with Netscape

The Netscape Netcenter page (**http://home.netscape.com**) allows you to choose between a range of popular tools, with the Lycos search engine pushed to the fore.

Four other categories of search tool are also offered:

- search engines in the strict sense, like AltaVista, Excite, HotBot or Google (see Chapter 3);
- Web guides (searching by category): Lycos, Yahoo! (see also Chapter 3);
- yellow or white pages in order to search for companies or people (address, telephone and e-mail): Bigfoot, Infospace (see Chapter 5);
- specialist services: sale by auction, purchase and sale of vehicles.

You will also find access to a subject guide on the home page: Netscape Search at **http://search.netscape.com/**.

Searching with Internet Explorer 5.0

By clicking on the **Search** button on the toolbar of Internet Explorer 5.0, you open a search pane on the left-hand side of the screen. Just choose where you want to search, type your keywords and press Enter (or click the Search button). The available choices are:

Find a Web page: this option is selected by default, and this Web search via UK Plus is probably the one you will use the most

Previous searches: Internet Explorer tracks previous search queries you have used so that you can simply click one to search for it again

Be careful regarding:

- *capitals;*
- *the use of Boolean operators and commands specific to each engine;*
- *the position of brackets in writing complex logical operations;*
- *typing errors!*

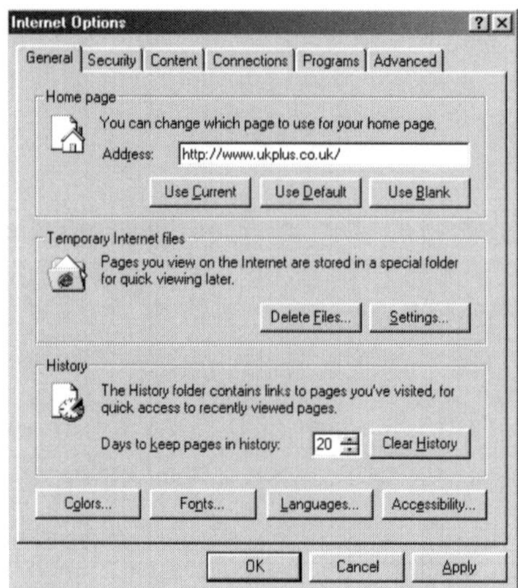

Figure 1.1 Setting the popular UK Plus search engine as start page in Internet Explorer 5.0.

When you have found a search engine which suits you, display the Internet options window as above. Then click on the Use Current button to reference the page of the engine being used.

Find a map: search Microsoft's own Expedia.com site for maps

Find UK entertainment: a search of Virgin Net's guide to find films, gigs and days out

Find in newsgroups: searches for articles posted to newsgroups (covered in Chapter 6).

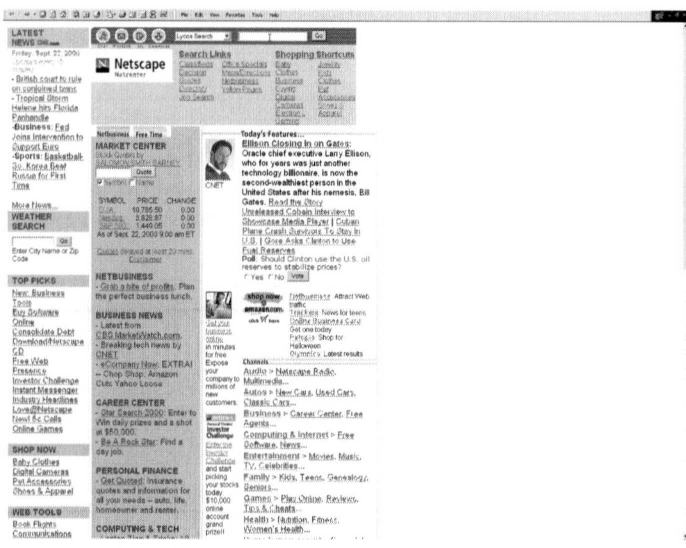

Figure 1.2 The Netscape Netcenter home page.

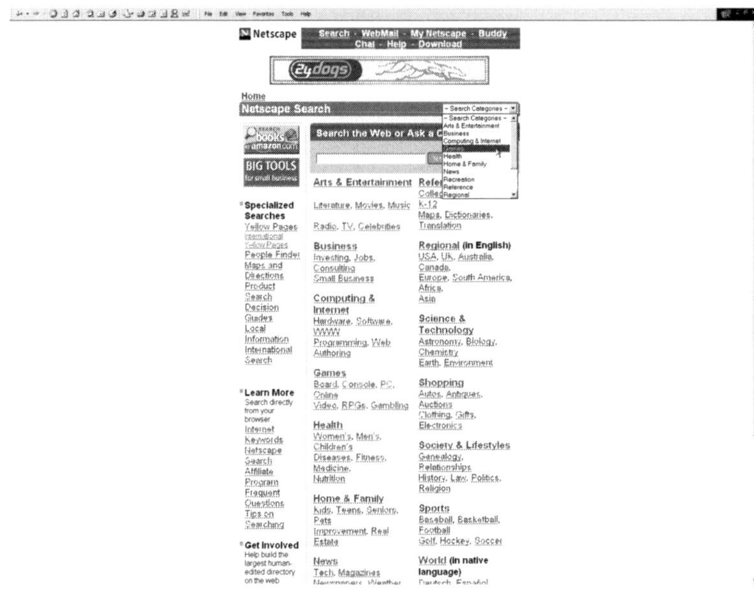

Figure 1.3 The online Netscape Search directory.

The search results open in the same small pane, with the benefit that you can click a link to view the site it refers to in the main part of the window without losing track of the remaining results.

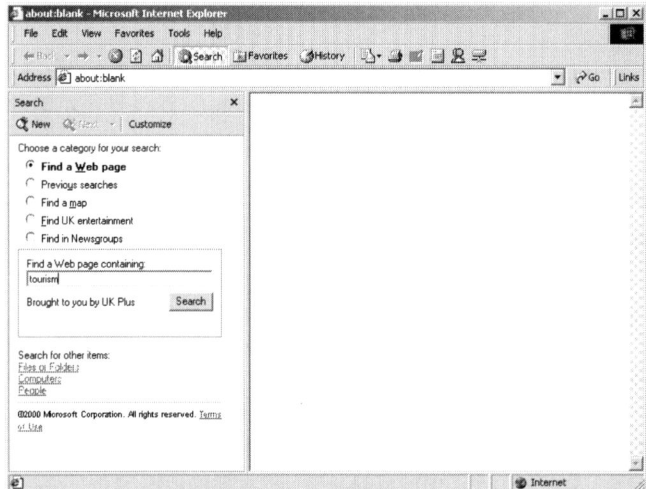

Figure 1.4 Internet Explorer's search pane.

As with any search, you can click the **Next 10** link below the search results to view the next set of results, or click the **Next** button at the top of the search pane to run the same search with a different search engine (for UK users, there is a choice of UK Plus, Voila, Excite and MSN). To start a new search, click the **New** button at the top of the search pane.

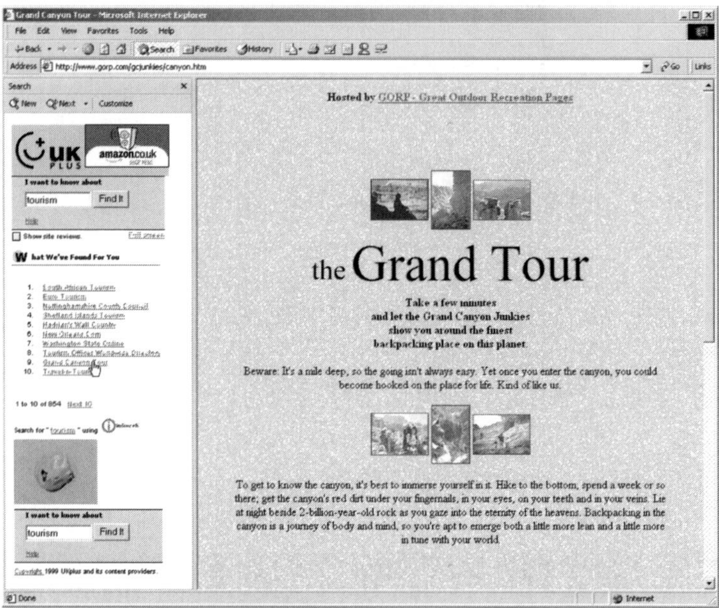

Figure 1.5 Results of a search open in the same left-hand pane. You can click a link to open it in the main window.

You can customise the options presented in the search pane by clicking the **Customize** button, although the options are limited. Essentially, you can switch off options by removing checkmarks from boxes beside them (for instance, you can prevent the **Find a map** option from being offered), or you can change the order in which options are presented so that your favourite search engine or option appears first in the list.

At any time, you can close the search pane by clicking the **Search** button on Internet Explorer's toolbar a second time, or by clicking the **Close** button marked with an 'X' at the top of the search pane.

Microsoft also offers its own search page as part of its Microsoft Network (MSN) site: go to **http://search.msn.com** for this site. If you have Internet Explorer's search pane open, you'll see it change dramatically to offer a choice between five very popular search engines: InfoSeek, Lycos, UK Plus, Yell.com and Yahoo!.

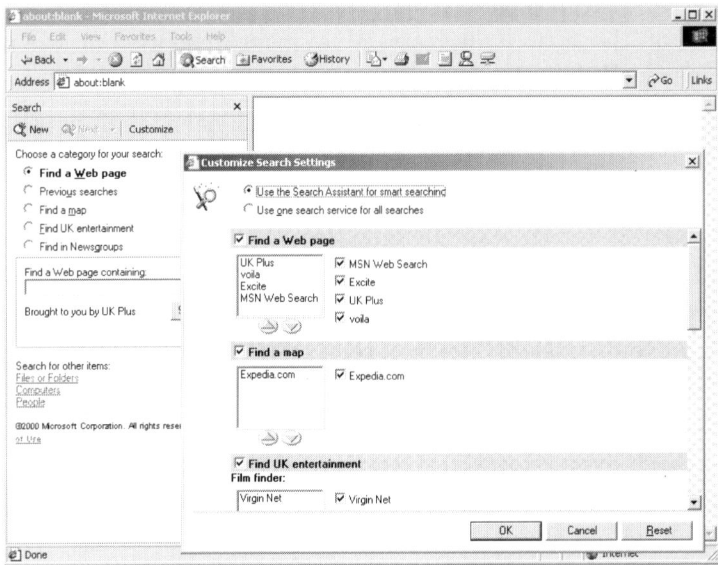

Figure 1.6 Click the Customize button to change the options shown in Internet Explorer's search pane.

By clicking the More Options link at the top of the page you can switch to a page offering advanced search options of the type we discussed earlier in the chapter. By selecting options from menus and checking boxes you can construct a very precise query and choose exactly how you want the results to be displayed.

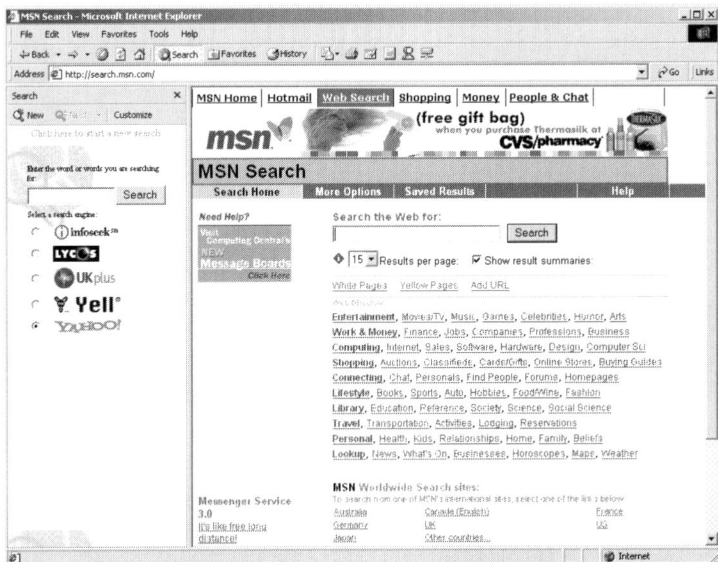

Figure 1.7 Microsoft's MSN Search page, which also makes use of the search pane.

9 tips for successful searches

To round off this chapter, here are nine tips to keep in mind when searching the Web for information:

1. Go from general to specific: use a fast search before refining the request.
2. Select the right tools, according to your requirements.
3. Use the well-known search engines in the first instance.
4. Use UK-specific search engines such as UK plus or Yahoo! UK and Ireland to find UK Web sites.
5. Overlap and possibly enrich results using more than one search engine.
6. Examine carefully the search options offered by the search engine.
7. Use search-by-keywords and search-by-site categories together.
8. If necessary, use advanced search techniques (power searches) and the search engine's help file in order to understand how it works.
9. Use metasearch engines for specific searches, reducing your work time.

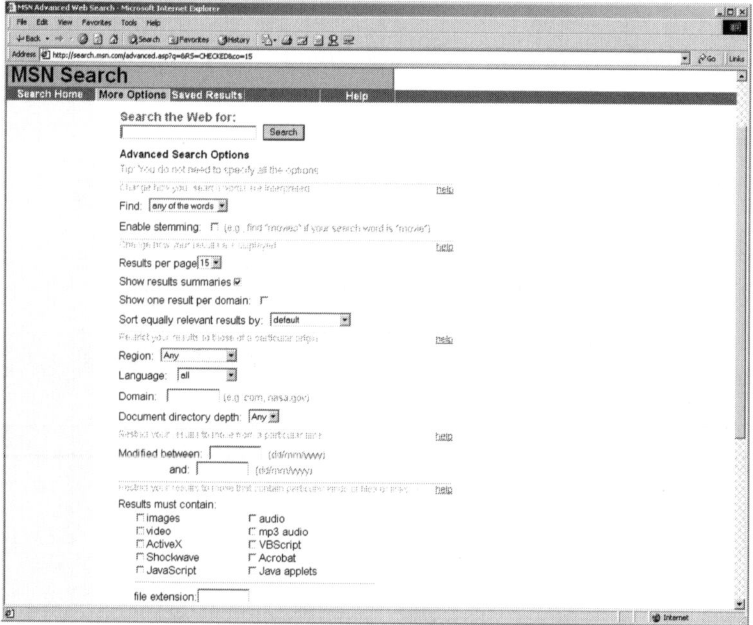

Figure 1.8 MSN Search makes it easy (well, *easier*) to construct very specific searches if you choose to.

UK search engines

2

UK versions of international search engines

UK-specific search engines

For everyday Web surfing and general research, there are large numbers of search engines available that can help you find what you're looking for. But there are times when only a UK site will do. For example, if you need legal or financial advice, want to book theatre or rail tickets, or want to check tonight's TV schedules, international search engines may not be much help. Instead, you want a search engine that's guaranteed to answer your query by providing links to UK web sites.

There is a good choice of UK search engines, falling into two categories:

- UK versions of international search engines (Yahoo! UK and Ireland, for example);
- UK-specific search engines, listing only UK sites and ignoring the rest of the Web.

UK versions of international search engines

'UK version' here means the adaptation of an international search engine (see Chapter 3) to favour UK sites. Popular search engines and directories such as Yahoo!, Lycos, InfoSeek and Excite each offer a UK version. In most cases you can choose whether to search the entire Web or just the UK portion of it, so you may choose to use the UK-specific version in preference to the international version, whatever type of information you want to find.

Yahoo! UK and Ireland
http://www.yahoo.co.uk
More than a search engine, Yahoo! UK and Ireland is a subject directory which offers searching by keywords. It does not provide its own summaries of the sites found, but instead uses (usually very brief) site descriptions submitted by the author of a site.

On the main Yahoo! UK and Ireland page, the search choices are simple:

- **All sites:** searches the entire Yahoo! directory. UK site matches will appear at the top of the list of search results with international sites below;
- **UK & Ireland sites only:** limits the search to sites in the UK and Ireland.

Along with the keywords you want to search for, you can use inverted commas to indicate a sentence or expression, and + or – signs to include or exclude a word.

To gain a little more control over the way the search is conducted, click the **Options** link beside the Search button. From the Options page you can make more detailed selections:

- search Yahoo! (for Web sites), Usenet newsgroups or e-mail addresses;
- search for direct links to Web sites that match your keywords or for matching Yahoo! categories;
- choose to search for the exact phrase you entered, matches on all words, matches on any word, or a person's name.

On this page, you can also choose the number of hits displayed on each page of the search results, and limit the search to include only recently added sites.

Yahoo!'s search results are presented in two sections:

- **Site categories:** this is the subject hierarchy used by Yahoo!. Each category contains a number of Web sites, plus further categories that form a subset of that category (for example, Society & Culture contains a Relationships category, which itself contains a PenPals category).
- **Web sites:** these are direct links to Web sites that match the keywords you entered. UK and Ireland sites are marked with flags to distinguish them from international sites.

Figure 2.1 The Yahoo! UK & Ireland logo.

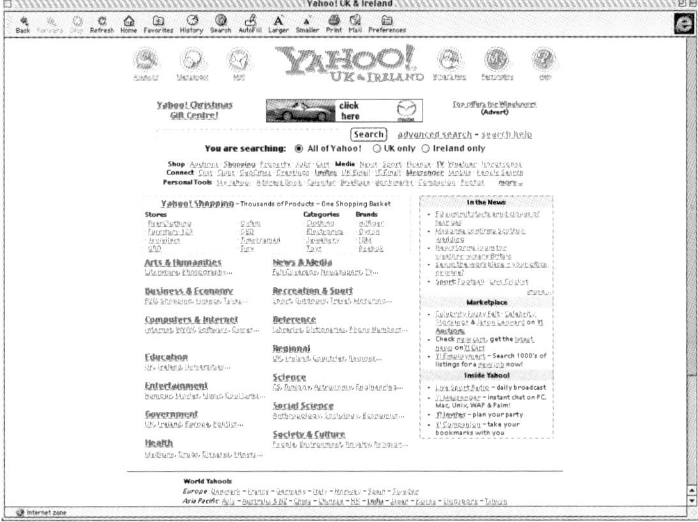

Figure 2.2 The main Yahoo! UK & Ireland search page.

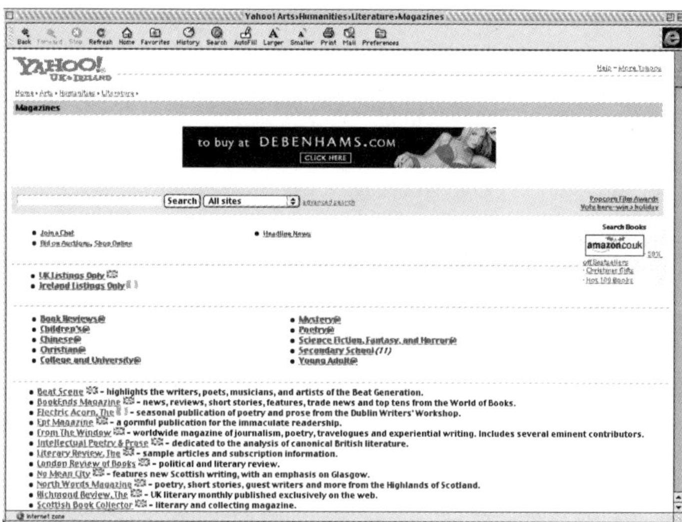

Figure 2.3 Search results from Yahoo! UK & Ireland.

Lycos UK

http://www.lycos.co.uk

Like Yahoo! UK and Ireland, the front page of Lycos UK offers a straightforward choice between searching the entire Web or limiting the search to UK and Ireland sites. The search engine returns a list of hits with a degree of relevance expressed as a percentage.

Lycos offers a range of search services on its Search Options page:

- search the entire Web;
- search for UK and Ireland sites only;
- search for pictures, sounds, books or MP3 audio files.

This page allows you to customise your search in just about any manner you could think of. You can also run searches for UK businesses, jobs and classified advertisements or take advantage of Lycos' translation service.

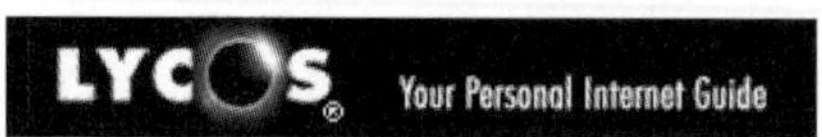

Figure 2.4 The Lycos logo.

For each search made, Lycos keeps track of each word on each Web page listed. Common words such as 'the', 'a' and 'and' have been deleted, allowing the search to be optimised by eliminating words which are not significant. All search engines work in a similar way. However, searching for an expression such as 'To the one' may cause problems.

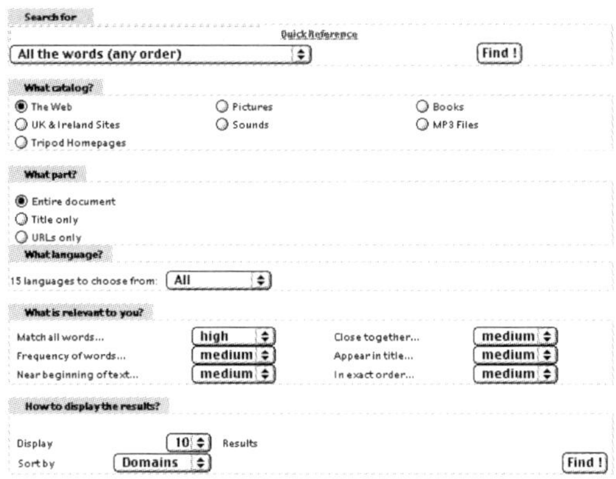

Figure 2.5 Customising your search at Lycos UK.

AltaVista United Kingdom

http://www.altavista.co.uk

AltaVista is another large international search engine with country-specific sites for a number of other countries (Germany, Sweden and India, to name but a few). Along with the usual options to search the entire Web or just the UK portion of it, a drop-down list allows searching in more than a dozen other languages.

Above the search field you'll find a row of three 'tabs'. When you first arrive at AltaVista you're on the **Search** page. By clicking the **Images**, **Audio & Video** tab, you can switch to a similar-looking page to search for multimedia files, and three option-buttons below the search field let you choose which type of multimedia files you want: images, audio or video.

Figure 2.6 The AltaVista UK logo.

The middle tab is labelled **Advanced Search**, and as you might expect, clicking this tab gives you an opportunity to use some of the Boolean search options we covered in Chapter 1. AltaVista supports the terms AND, AND NOT, OR, and NEAR, which must be entered in upper case with spaces before and after them.

Part of the power of all the AltaVista search engines (not only the UK-specific one) is their ability to search more than just the text of pages: AltaVista can search the domain name, the URL, or even the HTML code used to construct the page. These powerful options involve using a single keyword followed by a colon and the text to search for. The following 10 keywords can be used:

anchor:*search text* — Search for pages in which the *search text* appears in a clickable link to another page or site.

applet:*class name* — Search for pages that contain a Java applet named *class name*.

domain:*domain name* — Search for pages within a particular domain (such as **domain:uk** or **domain:com**).

host:*host name* — Search only on a particular server for pages (for example, **host:www.geocities.com** would find pages at www.geocities.com).

image:*file name* — Search for images named *file name* (for example, **image:apple** would find pictures named apple.gif and apple.jpg).

like:*site URL* — Search for more sites that cover similar topics to *site URL*.

link:*site URL* — Search for pages that contain links to *site URL* (you might use this to find out whether anyone is linking to your own site, for example).

text:*search text* — Search for pages that contain *search text* in a readable part of the page (not in its HTML code).

title:*search text* — Search for pages in which the title of the page contains *search text*.

url:*search text* — Search for pages in which *search text* appears somewhere in the URL of the page (which may be the server name, one of the directories in the path, or the page's file name).

To find out more about the AltaVista keywords and their uses, click the **Help** link on the front page of any AltaVista site.

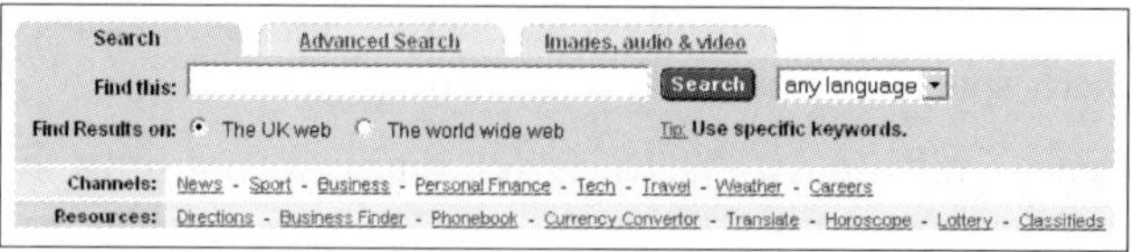

Figure 2.7 A standard search at AltaVista UK.

Excite UK

http://www.excite.co.uk

Excite is an original, powerful search engine which encourages searching by ideas and concepts rather than keywords. It uses the ICE technique (Intelligent Concept Extraction) to determine the correspondence between words and ideas. Hits are sorted according to their relevance, with the pages that best match the search criteria placed at the top of the list.

When the search results appear, a site that corresponds exactly to what you were hoping to find can be used as the basis for a more specific search. To do this, just click the 'More Like This' link beside the URL. The search engine will then use this document as a reference for another search on similar sites.

Excite UK lets you search the entire Web, UK sites only, European sites or Usenet newsgroups. Check the appropriate radio button below the search field. For more precise searching, you can use the + sign to indicate words that must be included in hits and the – sign to exclude a word from the search. You can also use inverted commas to indicate phrases or sentences.

The hits produced by the Excite search engine include the percentage of relevance, the site or page title, the URL and a summary.

Along with its UK version and the international site at **www.excite.com**, Excite offers versions adapted to other languages and countries including Australia, China, Germany, Japan, Italy, France, Sweden and the Netherlands.

Figure 2.8 The Excite UK logo.

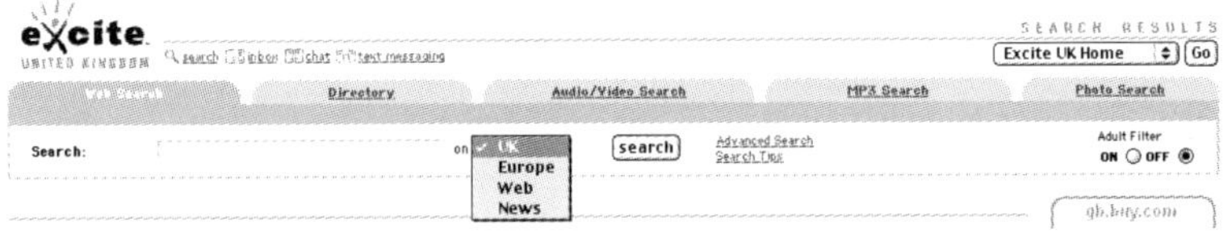

Figure 2.9 Choose whether to search the entire Web, UK sites, European sites or newsgroups.

Using Boolean functions with Excite

Boolean functions override Excite's concept-based searching and allow you to run searches for the exact keywords you specify. The Boolean operators available are AND, AND NOT, OR and brackets. These operators must be entered in upper case, with a space before and after them.

AND: The documents found must contain all the words linked by the AND operator.
OR: The documents found must contain one of the words linked by OR.

AND NOT: The documents found must not contain the word which follows the term AND NOT.

( ): Brackets are used to join together segments of Boolean enquiries to allow even more specific searches. For example, to find documents containing the word 'fruit' and either the word 'banana' or the word 'apple', you would type 'fruit AND (banana OR apple)'.

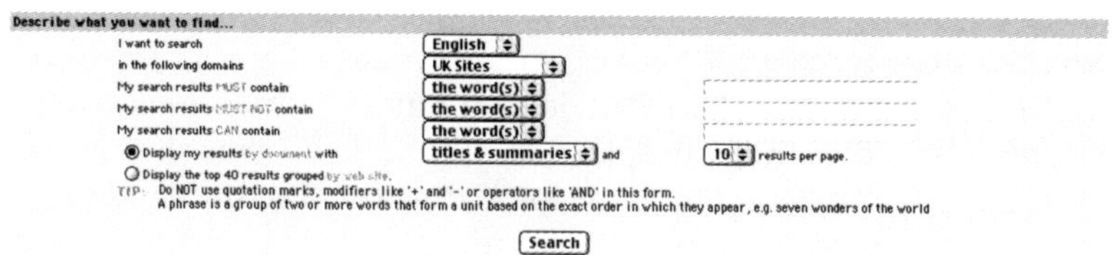

Figure 2.10 Selecting words to add to an Excite search.

LookSmart United Kingdom

http://www.looksmart.co.uk

LookSmart is a directory-based search engine that uses 'categories' in much the same way as Yahoo!. LookSmart comes from the same stable as the popular and powerful international search engine AltaVista, and it's actually this engine which carries out your searches.

The LookSmart search interface is fast and simple: just type in your keywords and click the **Go!** button. Like Yahoo!, LookSmart presents links to matching categories first, followed by links to Web pages that match your search terms. The Web page results give the title of the page or site, a brief description and a link to the LookSmart category in which that site was found, allowing you to browse the category for links to similar sites.

Figure 2.11 The LookSmart logo.

If you prefer browsing by category to running keyword searches, LookSmart offers an 'Explore' mode that makes this easy. Click a major category from the list at the left of the page and a list of subcategories will appear beside it. Click a subcategory to see a third level of categories, and so on. After a few clicks, a page of links to sites related to a specific category will open.

UK-specific search engines

This section takes a look around search engines specifically built to provide links to sites in the UK. If you know that the information you want can only be found on a UK site, these search engines make an excellent starting point.

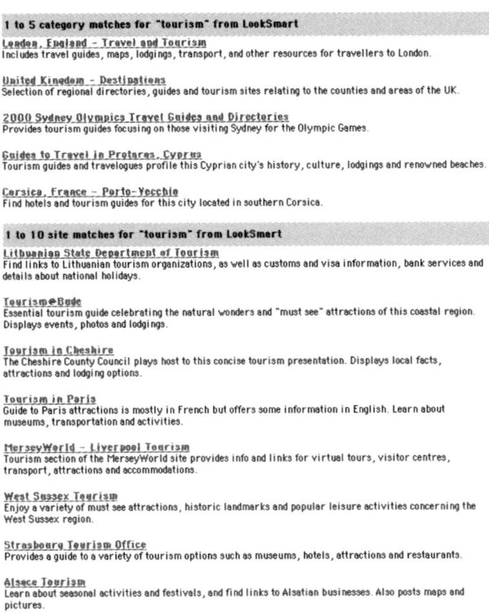

Figure 2.12 Search results from LookSmart.

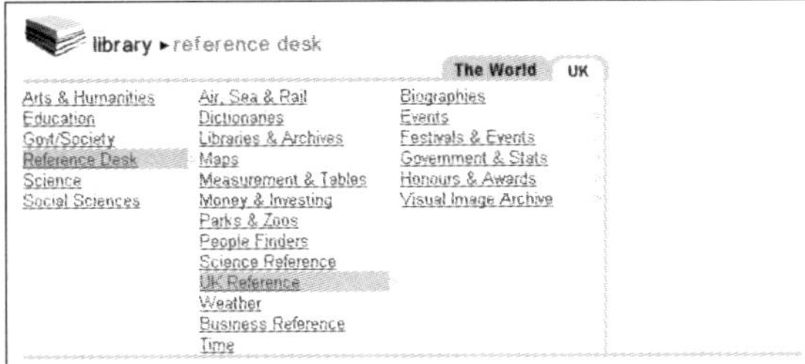

Figure 2.13 Moving through subject categories using LookSmart's 'Explore' mode.

UK Plus

http://www.ukplus.co.uk

UK Plus is a category-based directory site, in a similar vein to Yahoo!. Its great strength is that every site listed has been reviewed by the folk at UK Plus. As this is obviously a time-consuming business, UK Plus is a good deal smaller than traditional robot-built search databases. However, the immediate benefit is that you have a good idea of what a site will contain before you click the link to visit it. Robot-built databases pick up the bad sites with the good, and what you find when you arrive at one of those sites may differ enormously from what the site's description led you to expect!

Figure 2.14 The UK Plus logo.

Figure 2.15 The simple search form and category list at UK Plus.

As with Yahoo! and LookSmart, you can search the directory by selecting a major category from the UK Plus home page and drilling down to more specific subcategories. For a faster automated search, use the text field and buttons at the top of the home page. You can also run an Infoseek-powered search of the entire Web by clicking the radio button marked 'all of the Web'.

There are two extra interesting points to note about UK Plus. First, you can link directly to Scotland Plus, Wales Plus and Ireland Plus by clicking small logos on the front page. These essentially lead to subsets of the main UK Plus site, but if you're looking for information that's specifically Welsh, for instance, this type of option could help you find it a lot faster. Second, UK Plus doesn't restrict itself to UK sites alone. The focus is on the *UK user* and what he or she will find useful, so you will find some American and international sites through UK Plus.

Yell.com

http://www.yell.com

We're not allowed to say that Yell.com is the online incarnation of the Yellow Pages directory, but we can say that it's a powerful search site owned by British Telecom that allows you to find businesses and companies anywhere in the UK from a simple keyword search. You'll find a range of useful services at Yell.com:

Figure 2.16 Searching for business at Yell.com.

- Cinema: pick a region, select one or more towns and/or type in a film title to find out what's showing at your local cinema.
- Property: a variety of property-related services such as estate agents, surveyors and removal firms, along with an invaluable Neighbourhood Information section.
- Travel: for all things travel-related, including airlines, accommodation, ferry services, and a currency converter.
- Weather: five-day weather forecasts for anywhere in the world.
- Shopping: over a dozen categories of online store to choose from, and growing.

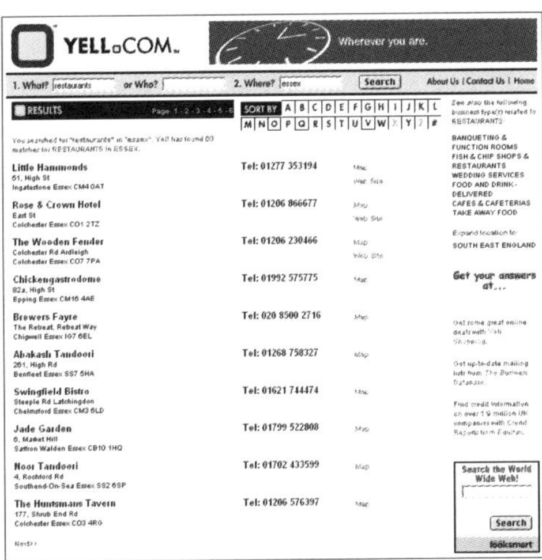

Figure 2.17 A typical set of search results from Yell.com.

Searching for businesses couldn't be easier. At the top of most pages at Yell.com you'll see a yellow strip containing the search fields. Just enter a company name (if you're looking for a particular company) or a type of business, and select the location of the business. If the search engine doesn't recognise your choice of category name, a list of similar names will appear that you can choose from.

The search results list company names, addresses and telephone numbers, along with 'Map' links you can click to find your way on the ground. If the company has a Web site you can visit, you can click a 'Web Site' link to jump straight there.

Rampant Scotland Directory

http://www.rampantscotland.com

What it is that makes Scotland rampant isn't explained, but this comprehensive searchable directory an ideal starting point to find is Scottish sites and information. The large number of categories (and relatively small number of sites) means that a few clicks on the category titles should quickly lead you to what you want. If you prefer, you can run a keyword search of Rampant Scotland, or a metasearch of the entire Web (see Chapter 4) to combine hits from five major international search engines.

UK Index

http://www.ukindex.co.uk

These days many search sites are becoming **portals** – complete Web guides offering links to shopping, finance, news and weather, sport, you name it. The benefit of a portal is that you can start your everyday surfing at your favourite portal and use it as a launchpad to whatever you fancy doing. But if all you want to do is run a quick keyword search (one that isn't going to involve Boolean operators and advanced search options), you'd probably much rather just see a search field and a button! Its simplicity is one area where UK Index wins.

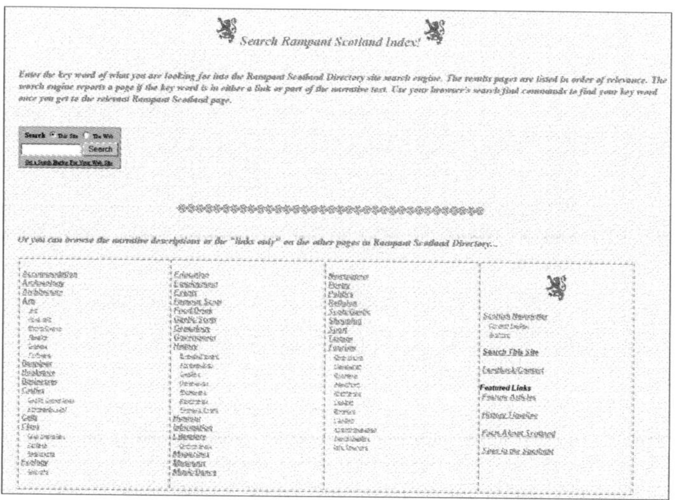

Figure 2.18 The comprehensive category list and simple search form at Rampant Scotland.

Being simple doesn't make UK Index useful by itself, of course. Its unique feature is a set of icons placed beside links in the search results. These icons show the date that the link was last checked by UK Index and what the result of that check was: if a range of sites was found, you can save yourself time by initially ignoring any sites that were noted as 'Not Found', 'Gone', or 'Timed Out' and heading straight for sites with a green tick beside them.

Figure 2.19 Icons in UK Index search results provide extra useful information.

Mirago

http://www.mirago.co.uk

http://www.mirago.co.uk/zone

The Mirago search engine has several features that recommend it, but one in particular stands out: clicking the link marked **Family Friendly** in the upper-left corner will take you to the second of the URLs above – a 'safe' version of the search engine. This option uses a combination of automatic and manual filtering to remove links and site descriptions that you wouldn't want your kids to see (and you might not want to see them yourself, for that matter). While these filters are not entirely infallible, they do give a good reason for adding the 'safe' version of this site to your browser's Favorites or Bookmarks lists.

The search options themselves are equally comprehensive on either version of the site, allowing you to search for UK sites, or sites containing images, sounds, video or multimedia. Simple Boolean operators can be selected from the drop-down 'Look For' box:

- all of the words;
- any of the words;

- a person's name;
- words as a phrase;
- words near each other in the document;
- resources using Boolean operators.

Selecting the last of those options allows you to use advanced syntax to refine your search. The operators AND, OR, NOT and NEAR can be used, and phrases can be specified by enclosing them between double quotes.

You can also enclose expressions in brackets, as with Excite, and add an asterisk wildcard to the end of a word (for example, a search for 'south*' would return hits on 'southern' and 'Southampton').

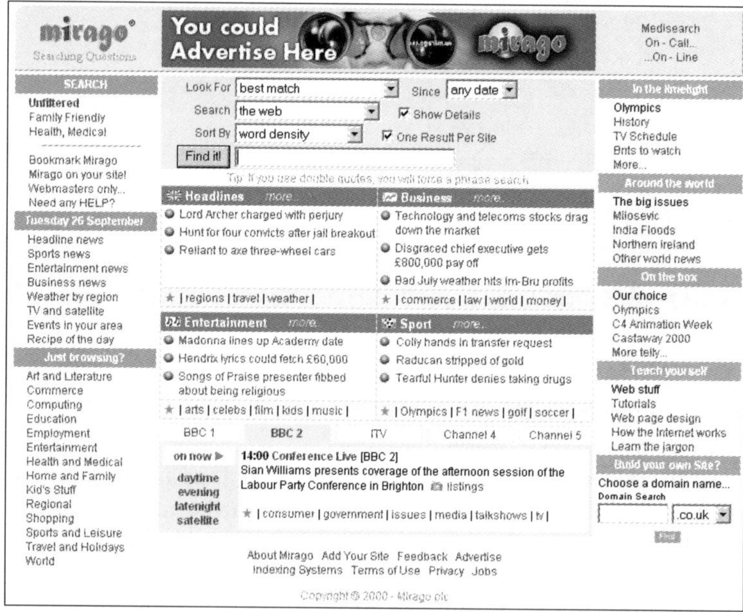

Figure 2.20 Mirago's 'family-friendly' version offers safe but comprehensive searching.

3 Worldwide search engines

Worldwide search engines

Which search engine is best?

Worldwide search engines

These are the giants of the world of search engines, being both the oldest and the largest. Most of them catalogue millions of Web pages. This is what we want, of course, but it can also cause problems: with millions of pages indexed, a search could easily yield several-hundred-thousand hits! Therefore you need to make your request specific using advanced search functions which allow you to combine particular terms and to filter the results.

AltaVista

http://www.altavista.com

The search engine of the computer manufacturer Digital Equipment is one of the leaders on the Internet. A number of search tools, including Yahoo! and Bigfoot, also use AltaVista technology. This was developed in the research laboratories of Digital Equipment at Palo Alto. It was in 1995 that AltaVista first appeared on the Web, with the ambition of cataloguing the entire Internet! A catalogue which represents around 200 Gb in its global version, and which will be polled in less than one second in most cases!

In normal search mode, AltaVista sorts hits by order of relevance. This mechanism is no longer active in Advanced search mode. It is up to you to activate it if necessary, using the Ranking text box, otherwise hits will be shown in random order.

AltaVista offers a global search of the Web or Usenet (newsgroups). It is possible to search in the language of your choice. By default, the search engine is set to Any language. It is possible to indicate your preferences to the search engine, enabling you to save time.

The Advanced search mechanism will be used when, for example, it is necessary to use Boolean expressions or a document validity range (dates).

You can carry out textual searches using inverted commas to quote phrases. You can also run more specific searches using the range of functions mentioned in Chapter 2, such as:

Domain. Search in a particular domain (.com, .org, .fr, etc.).

Image. Search for photographs, for example.

Link. Search for links.

Searching by date

It is possible to filter hits based on the date of documents. To do this you must complete the FROM and TO text boxes. Dates must be completed in the dd/mmm/yy format, where dd and yy represent days and years and mmm represents the first three letters of the month.

AltaVista also allows you to search for images, audio and video files, maps and directions, people, products and companies. Through its BabelFish translator (**http://babel.altavista.com/translate.dyn**) it can also translate free text or entire Web pages. AltaVista offers a 'family-friendly' option which filters descriptions and links relating to adult sites: click the link labelled **Family Filter is Off** to find out more about this option.

Along with its Advanced mode, mentioned earlier, AltaVista offers a Power Search mode which is also available from its front page. Rather than constructing your own advanced search query using

Boolean operators, you can select the options you want from drop-down lists and checkboxes.

Figure 3.1 The main search box of AltaVista.

Since July 1997, AltaVista has offered searching in 25 different languages. It uses a multilingual dictionary to determine the dominant language of each page indexed. It is therefore possible to display the hits corresponding to the language of your choice. This is much more efficient than searching by domain.

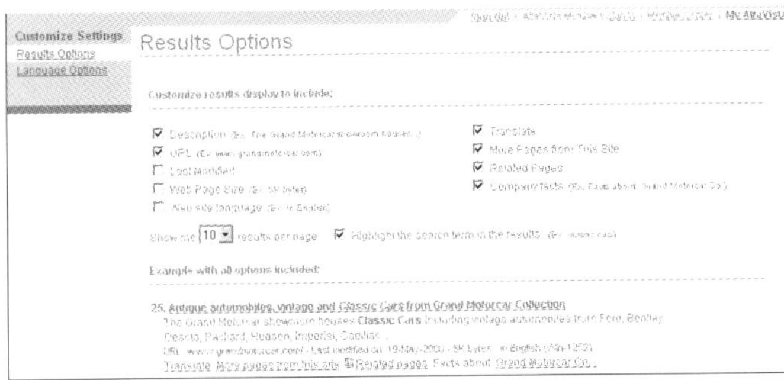

Figure 3.2 Choose how AltaVista's results should be presented.

Excite

http://www.excite.com/

Another giant, since Excite updates an index of 50 million Web addresses (URLs). This search engine is very powerful, offers searching by category and keyword, and produces hits in order of relevance.

Excite is original in more than one way and has a very useful function called *Excite Search Wizard*. At the end of a search, the Wizard suggests a list of words that you can then add to another search. To do this, just check one or more words in the list of suggestions.

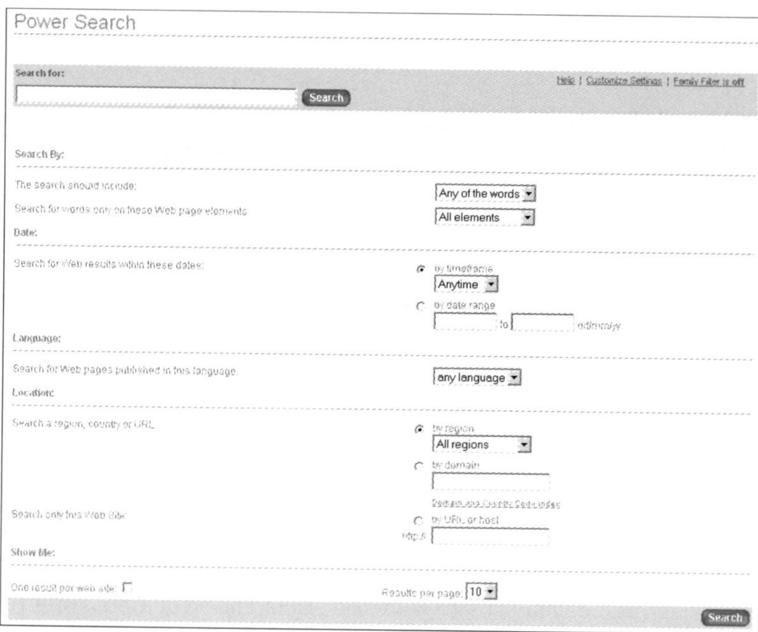

Figure 3.3 Run a 'power search' easily at AltaVista.

The words proposed are derived from words entered in the search text box and sent to the search engine. Excite then makes a list of similar words or concepts to help you to express your requests.

Thus, a search relating to the word 'kennedy' will produce a list of suggestions including 'assassination', 'assassinated', 'jfk' and 'onassis', words which make reference to the life (and death) of the famous US president. The list of suggestions will also include words such as 'shuttle' (space craft), 'launch', 'flight' and 'nasa', which this time relate directly to the *Kennedy Space Center*.

Take note of Excite's suggestions; they can be of real assistance in formulating your requests.

This highly practical mechanism is not yet available in Power Search, but will be in the future. In the meantime, it is quite sufficient to use it in normal search mode.

Excite also offers specialist services such as:

- searching for maps and directions;
- searching for people (People Finder);
- searching for companies in the United States (Yellow Pages).

Figure 3.4 The Excite home page.

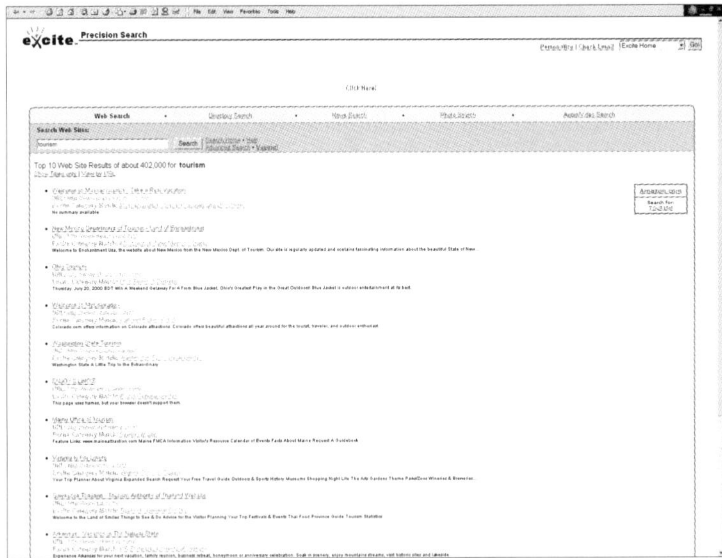

Figure 3.5 The result of searching with Excite.

Yahoo!

http://www.yahoo.com/

Here is another heavyweight search engine. More of a guide-directory than a traditional search engine, Yahoo! operates according to the same general principles for the user. It sends categories and sites corresponding to the request.

Yahoo! also offers a current events search service: News Articles and Net Events.

Yahoo! searches in four directions (or four databases):

- **Yahoo! Categories.** The categories and subcategories constituting the highly detailed classification of the search guide.
- **Yahoo! Web Sites.** Web sites in the strict sense.
- **Yahoo!'s Net Events & Chat.** Live events and chat.
- **Most Recent News Articles.** Current events items.

Yahoo! sends any categories found that match your search query, then a list of matching sites from Yahoo!'s own catalogue. If no matches are found, Yahoo! then runs a full search on the Web using the Google search engine (**http:// www.google.com**) for the job.

Yahoo! evaluates the results of a request according to three main rules:

- documents containing the most keywords are the most relevant;
- documents whose titles contain keywords take priority over those where the words searched for appear only in the body of the Web page or in its address;
- the most general categories (at the top of Yahoo!'s Internet hierarchy) are better ranked than more specific categories (which are therefore at the bottom of the hierarchy).

Yahoo! also offers all sorts of additional services, such as:

- searching for people;
- searching for maps;
- searching for companies.

And also more original services such as:

- Yahoo! Shopping. A search tool for online shopping at **http:// shopping.yahoo.com**.
- Yahooligans! A search engine dedicated to sites for (and by) children, at **http:// www.yahooligans.com**.

Figure 3.6 Searching with Yahoo!

HotBot

http://www.hotbot.com

Created by the famous American magazine *Wired*, and owned by the giant Lycos search network, HotBot also plays in the court of the large search engines.

Figure 3.7 Presentation of results – categories and sites.

With HotBot, you are always running a semi-advanced search. The controls at the left of the page are set at default values, so you can ignore them, type a word or phrase into the text field and click the **Search** button. But you can also easily change options from this panel on the left:

- The language to search for.
- The way the keywords are interpreted (as an exact phrase, separate phrases, a person's name, a Boolean expression, and so on).
- The date the information appeared on the Web.
- Content on the page (images, videos, MP3 audio and JavaScript).

You can also choose how many hits should appear on each page of results, and how detailed the information should be.

If you find yourself setting up the same combination of search options every time you come here, you can save yourself the bother: click the **Personalize These Settings** button, and a long form allows you to set up your search options the way you'd like to see them each time you arrive at HotBot.

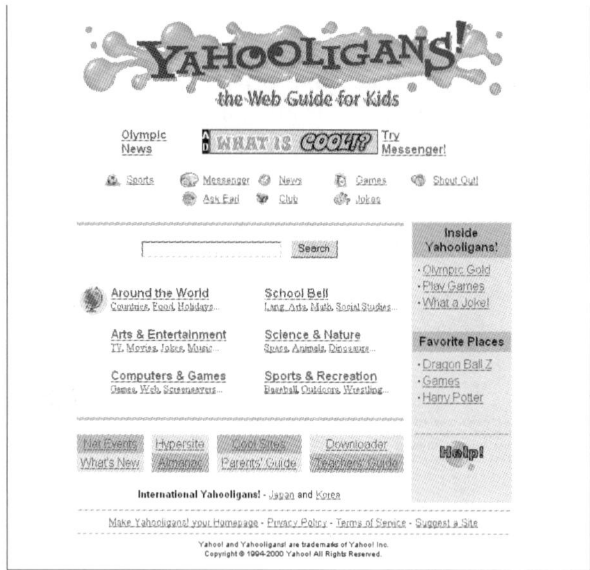

Figure 3.8 A search tool for sites for children.

The HotBot search engine also allows other searches:

- Directories of email addresses
- White Pages (searching for people)
- Yellow Pages (searching for businesses)
- News headlines and stock quotes
- Discussion groups
- FTP search for files (see Chapter 6)
- Music files and sites.

Figure 3.9 Searching with HotBot.

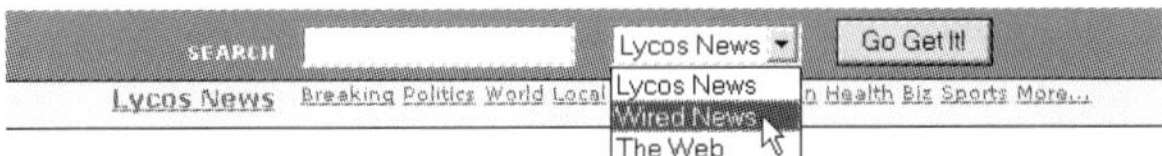

Figure 3.10 Searching for current news headlines at HotBot.

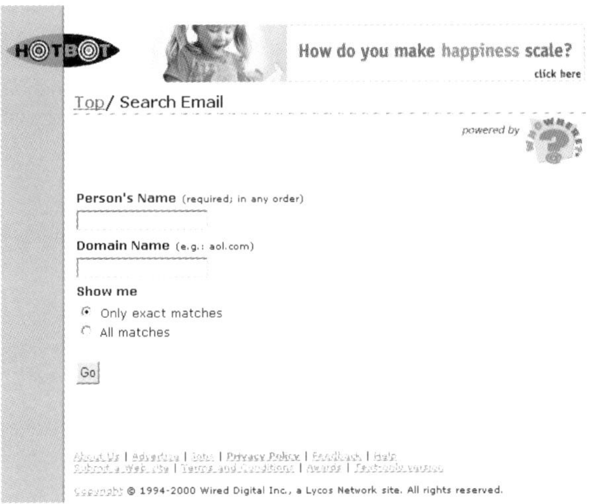

Figure 3.11 Searching for e-mail addresses using HotBot.

HotBot offers a comprehensive set of features when you click the **Advanced Search** link. On the detailed form that appears, you can enter:

- additional words or phrases;
- the date or validity range for pages;
- where to search (a region, continent, Web site, domain or country code);
- how to return the search results;
- the media to be found on pages (images, sounds, animations, etc.). You can even state the type of file searched for by indicating the extension!

Ask Jeeves

http://www.ask.com

Although the precise details can vary from one engine to another, you have probably realised that the majority of search engines offer some method of constructing 'advanced' searches. Here's a search engine that takes things a long way in the opposite direction: you just roll up to the Ask Jeeves Web site and type a question like *When was Beethoven born?* This is known as 'natural language' searching. It isn't as effective as a well-constructed Boolean query at AltaVista, but it isn't trying to be.

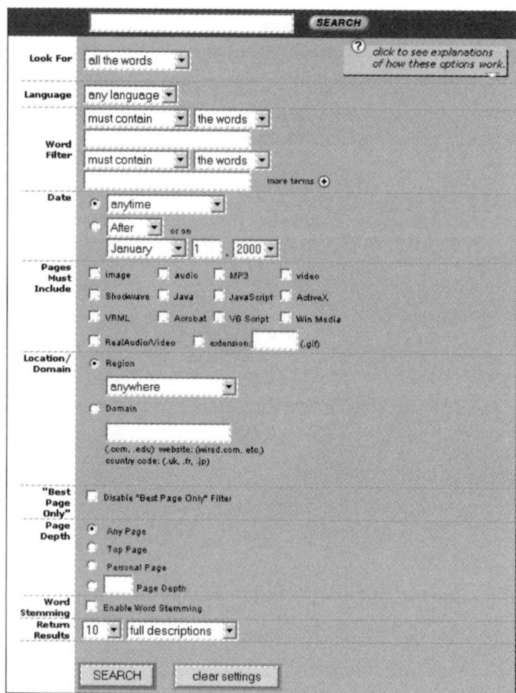

Figure 3.12 Personalising your search options at HotBot.

Ask Jeeves works by identifying the key words in your question, and stripping out the rest. It then consults a list of questions containing the same key words to which it knows the answer and presents those to you to choose from. It's a comfortable feeling to type a 'real' question like the one above, but a little experimentation reveals that simply typing *beethoven* will lead to the same set of responses. The Ask Jeeves method of searching is better suited to children, and if you're a parent a good addition to your Bookmarks or Favorites list would be the Ask Jeeves For Kids site at **http://www.ajkids.com**.

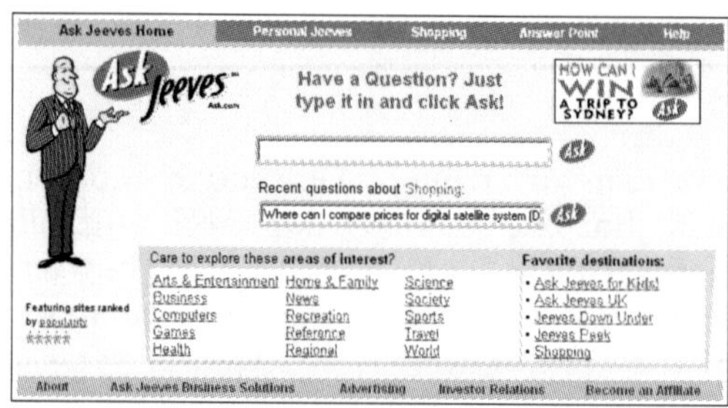

Figure 3.13 Ask Jeeves a question at this refreshingly simple search site.

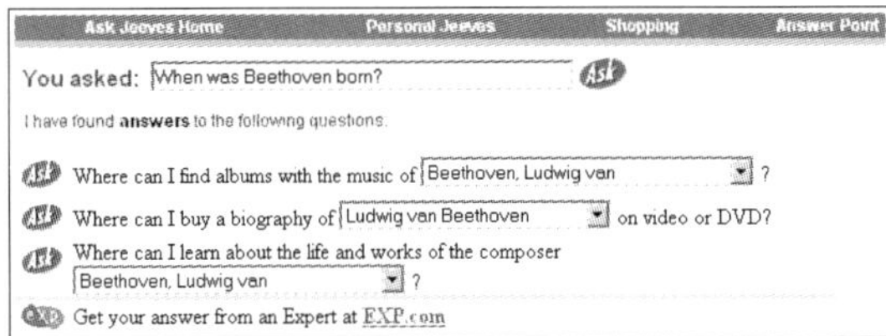

Figure 3.14 Pick the question that most closely matches what you were asking and click the Ask button to find the answer.

One great bonus of Ask Jeeves is its Answer Point section, which you can reach from the main page or directly at **http://answer-point.ask.com**. This is an excellent database of questions asked by Internet users, some with answers and some without. You can search this database, or a particular category of it, submit a question which will (with luck) be answered by another surfer, or browse around and add an answer to any question which hasn't yet been answered (or to which you can add some extra information).

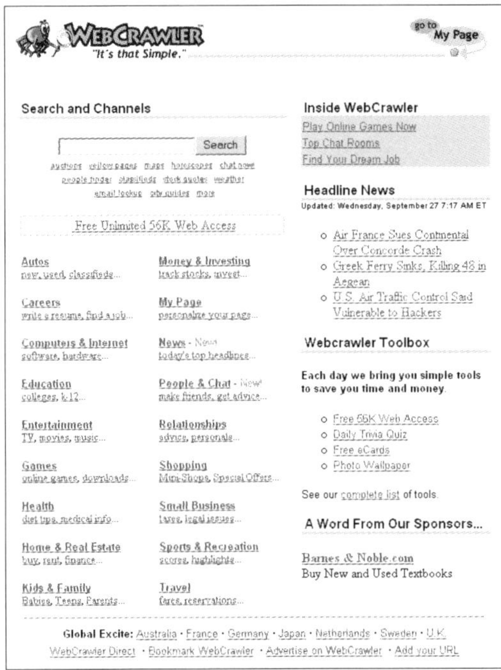

Figure 3.15 The WebCrawler home page.

WebCrawler

http://webcrawler.com/

WebCrawler is a subsidiary trademark of Excite, so may not have a long-term future. However, it exists, and it offers traditional searching by keywords, which gives good results.

WebCrawler also works in natural language. Therefore it allows a request to be expressed simply, without worrying about Boolean operators!

If the search function is not sufficient, you can use the guide part, with more than 5,000 sites per category. The editorial team regularly adds and deletes sites from this catalogue, which therefore records the best of the Web.

In addition, WebCrawler offers the following search services:

- yellow pages;
- newsgroups;
- searching for people (see Chapter 5);
- maps;
- classified ads.

Google

http://www.google.com

Appearing from nowhere, and pitted against giants like Excite, Lycos and AltaVista, the Google search engine has become incredibly popular. The most likely reason for its success is its attractively uncluttered main page: compare this to the front pages of the 'giants', where every inch of screen-space is trying to get your attention, and perhaps you'll feel drawn to Google too.

Not that you can't run an advanced search here, though. Click the **Advanced Search** link above the text field and you'll be moved to a page containing a convenient set of text fields and drop-down lists allowing you to search for:

- Words or a phrases that must be included or excluded
- Domains to include or exclude
- Pages in particular languages
- Pages that link to, or are similar to, a certain page

You can also set up a range of preferences relating to language and the display of search results; these preferences can be saved so that they'll be automatically applied each time you use Google. Best of all, Google offers a SafeSearch feature that aims to filter 'adult' content out of the search results, and this option is also stored with your other preferences.

Figure 3.16 The refreshingly simple Google page.

Go.com

http://www.go.com

This engine was formerly known as InfoSeek, and you can still reach the UK version of the engine at **http://www.infoseek.co.uk**, as mentioned in Chapter 2. Along with the catchier name, Go.com has grown a few new features (although it pays to remember that as an 'international' search engine, the majority of these will be aimed mostly at American users):

- Search for people (white pages)
- Search for maps and driving directions
- Search for businesses (yellow pages)
- Use an online dictionary or translation service

When running a search from the front page of the site, you can choose between searching for Web pages, for images, or for audio and video files. If you prefer, you can delve Yahoo!-style into a comprehensive set of directory categories. Advanced searching happens on a separate page reached by clicking the **Search Options** link below the search field, and you can construct searches using an easy-to-use but powerful set of form controls which allow you to search in page titles, URLs and hyperlinks as well as entire documents. You can opt to show results only from a particular domain, or exclude a domain. Finally, you can choose to confine your search to particular topic categories and/or to certain countries.

While you're on the Search Options page, you can also choose different types of search, such as stocks, newsgroups, shareware and general reference.

As an extra bonus (something that more and more search engines are adding), Go.com offers Goguardian, an option to filter out inappropriate content from search results. This can optionally be password controlled, allowing you to bypass it when you need to.

Figure 3.17 The Go.com home page.

Which search engine is best?

Needless to say, there isn't one search engine that's always better than all the others. The ideal search engine for one purpose may be too simplistic for another and overkill for a third. With experimentation, you'll probably settle on the two or three search engines you like best for regular use, that cover all bases: for example, a directory like Yahoo!, a simple search engine like Google, and a more powerful engine such as AltaVista.

Yahoo! is a directory more than a traditional search engine, but it's been around for years and is a valuable and reliable workhorse. Its range of categories and hierarchical nature makes it easy to understand. It's a good starting point for anyone unfamiliar with the Web. Its 'hand-built' structure also means that you are far less likely to stumble across links to 'adult' sites by accident here. Its children's counterpart, Yahooligans!, provides similar ease of use and safety for kids.

AltaVista is the Web's heavy artillery. Vast and powerful, this search engine is useful for scanning the Web thoroughly, and for tracking down particular types of file (images, audio and video). Its translation tool is sometimes helpful (and often amusing). Its set of keywords to allow searching in page titles, URLs, domain names, and so on, is currently unmatched.

Excite is an intelligent search engine. It tries to interpret your request (by comparing it to past searches by other users) and suggests similar words and concepts to help you refine your search. Excite tends to be less useful when searching for phrases than when searching for single words.

WebCrawler is Excite's directory site. It does things a little differently from Yahoo!, which you may like, and it has a useful Ask An Expert section of question-and-answer sites.

HotBot has a lot in common with AltaVista – to the point, perhaps, that the presence of the Advanced Search controls on HotBot's front page might be the deciding factor on which you prefer. Along with its ability to search a number of resources, HotBot can find pages based on type of content (images, video, scripts, and so on).

Ask Jeeves (and its children's counterpart, **Ask Jeeves For Kids**) are at the simple end of the spectrum. The layout and style is friendly, making this a great search engine for Internet beginners. The AnswerPoint area is useful and unique, and worth remembering whether or not you use the search engine itself.

Google is deceptively simple. Its popularity lies in its uncluttered interface, but advanced options and 'family-friendly' searching are available if you need them.

Go.com is the closest match to Yahoo!, offering a well-constructed directory alongside keyword searching. It's also one of the best sites to search for people (e-mail addresses, phone numbers, and so on).

4 Metasearch engines

Metasearch engines

Collections of search engines and directories

Experienced surfers all have their favourite search engine. Some swear by AltaVista, while others prefer Yahoo! or maybe UK Plus for searching UK sites. To search for information there is another solution: metasearch engines. Their principle is simple: you indicate the keywords corresponding to your request and the metasearch engine sends the request to the various search engines.

Another possibility is to use search engine groupings on the same page. This facilitates intensive searching and allows you to have a list of powerful tools to hand.

Metasearch engines

They use the power of several search engines without you having to worry about it. They differ in terms of the choice of search engine and the evaluation of the results given to you.

CNET Search.com

http://www.search.com

This easy-to-remember URL takes you to a site that was formerly known as Savvy Search, but has now become part of the massive CNET Networks organisation.

A metasearch engine, Search.com gives you the fastest replies in searching Yahoo!, Lycos, GoTo.Com, Inktomi and Direct Hit, along with 700 smaller and specialised search engines.

To start the search, type the keywords and click the search button. You can refine your search using double-quotes to denote phrases, + and – symbols to include or exclude a particular word or phrase, and the Boolean operators **and**, **or** and **not**. Using a standard search, only a small number of search engines are polled. By clicking a category from the directory-structure below, however, you'll be taken to a page from which you can search a collection of engines that specialise in the topic you chose.

Dogpile

http://www.dogpile.com

This powerful metasearch engine can target 10 areas of the Internet for searching. Most usefully, of course, Dogpile searches the Web, presenting search results from 14 popular engines quickly and effectively. By selecting the appropriate radio button you can also search Usenet (newsgroup) archives, FTP servers, world and business news headlines or stock quotes.

Being a US site, the remaining options on Dogpile's main page are not especially useful to the UK user. You'll rarely need to search for businesses, people, maps or weather forecasts in the US. But a click on the International link at the top of the page will take you to a list of similar services covering a number of other countries. The UK is particularly well served here, with search options including Business Finder, People Finder, Local Information and Travel Guide.

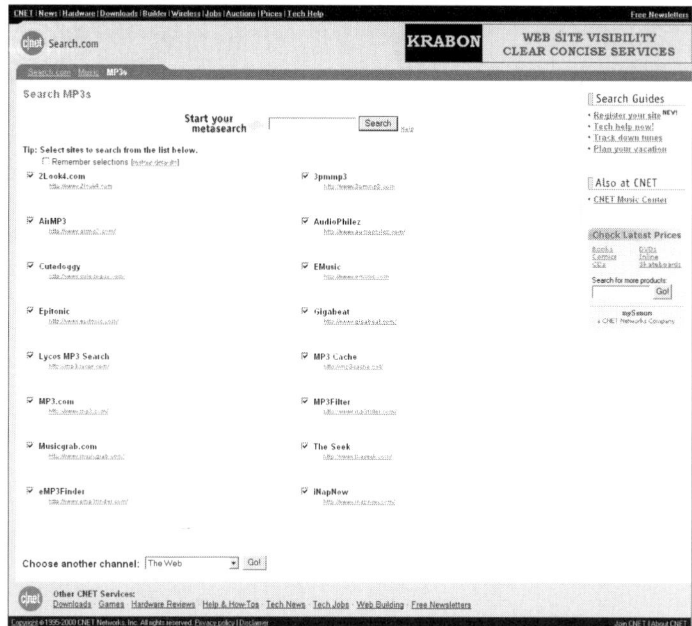

Figure 4.1 A search for MP3 audio at Search.com involves up to 16 different search engines!

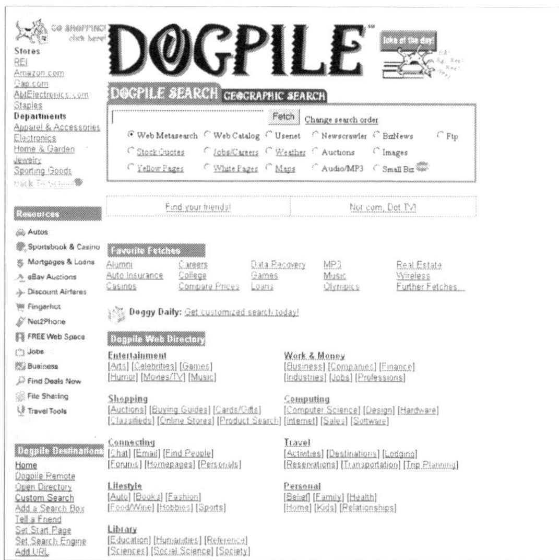

Figure 4.2 The main Dogpile search page.

InFind

http://www.infind.com

InFind is not simply a point of access to the various search engines. It can combine the searches carried out by the different search engines and return a single list to you after deleting redundancies.

InFind polls the best search engines on the Web: Yahoo!, Lycos, AltaVista, Infoseek, Excite and WebCrawler. Each search engine is active in parallel. If one search engine gathers 300 results at once, whereas its neighbour only gathers 10, the latter will be polled 30 more times. With InFind, search engines work flat out! Then all the results from the six sources are analysed. Redundancies and similar documents are eliminated in order to produce the most appropriate list of results.

Figure 4.3 Searching with InFind.

It is impossible to carry out manually what InFind provides automatically, so why go without?

The search time can be limited, which is very often useful. Results are displayed by heading and include a list of titles only, each title giving access to the corresponding site.

Mamma

http://www.mamma.com

Mamma is there to take care of you and will put your request to 10 well-known search engines, including:

- AltaVista;
- Excite;
- Infoseek;
- Lycos;
- WebCrawler;
- Yahoo!.

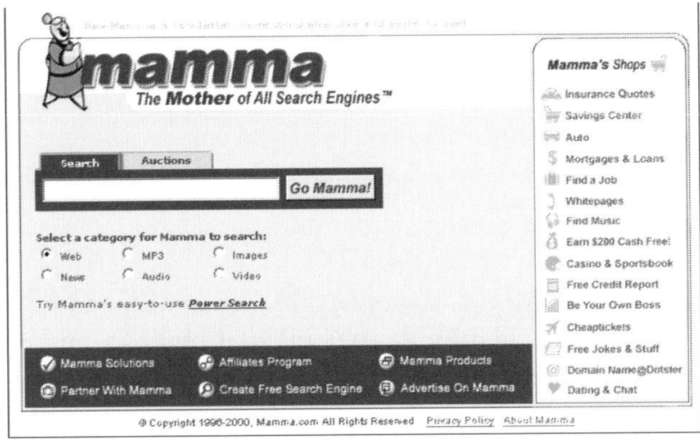

Figure 4.4 Welcome to Mamma!

Not forgetting DejaNews for searching newsgroups (see Chapter 6).

Select the search domain, check the appropriate option boxes (activation of summaries, searches based on a phrase, searches based on page titles) and click on **Search**. Mamma will do the rest for you.

Meta Crawler

http://www.metacrawler.com

This is one of the veteran metasearch engines and uses several search engines to meet your requirements. Created in 1995 at Washington University, Meta Crawler was bought by the go2net company in 1997.

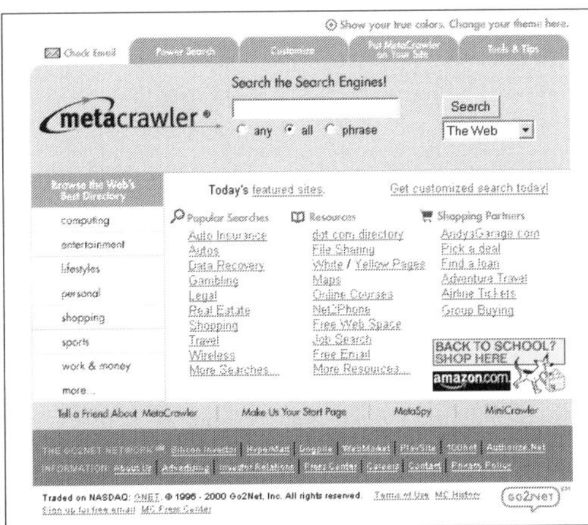

Figure 4.5 Meta Crawler at your service!

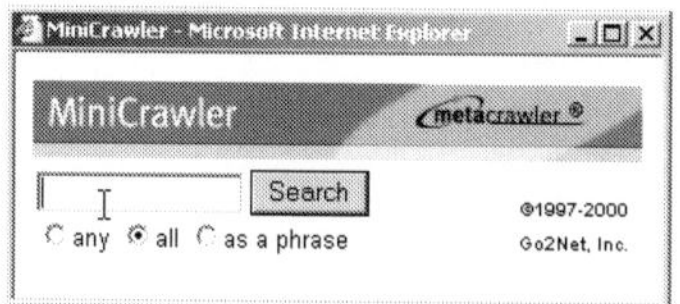

Figure 4.6 The Mini Crawler window.

Also worth discovering is Mini Crawler in which a small window is opened on the screen. This is highly practical as it means that you can have a metasearch engine on standby in a corner of your Windows Office to search the Web at any moment.

Copernic

http://www.copernic.com

Copernic isn't exactly a search engine in the way we've come to think of them – it isn't a Web site, for one thing, it's a software program. Visit the Copernic site to download and install one of the family of search tools available, and you can simply start this program whenever you want to run a metasearch. Over 80 engines can be searched, and you can confine your search to particular categories of engine.

Because Copernic is a program running on your own computer, you can create and save advanced searches for reuse in the future. Just click any of the search results to go to that site in your default browser.

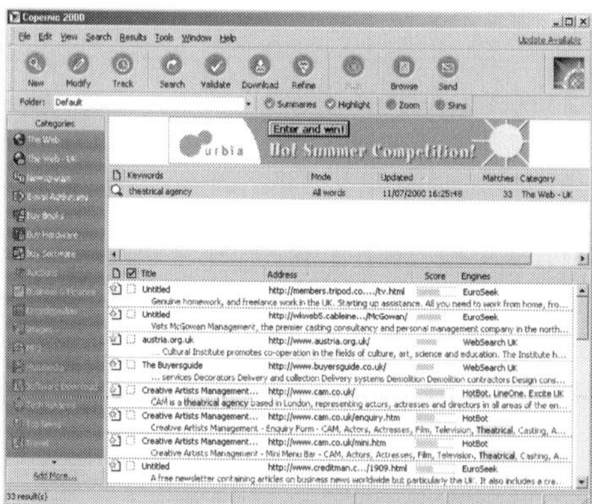

Figure 4.7 The results of metasearching the Web using Copernic

Collections of search engines and directories

These compilations of the best tools are practical for carrying out intensive searches and comparing the results of several search engines.

The Internet Sleuth

http://www.isleuth.com/

This is a fantastic tool which gives access to more than 2,000 databases.

The original feature of the site is that it only catalogues sites having a search text box. The site search mechanism is displayed on Sleuth according to the requests made. Searches are carried out by subject and not by specific request. Do not ask for the recipe for duck à l'orange, since no database is concerned with this. Search for the word 'recipe' instead. You will then have access to databases relating to cooking.

You thus obtain a list of hits, each entry point having its own search text box and that of the database corresponding to the initial search. At this stage you can search for the recipe for duck à l'orange in the databases proposed. Sleuth therefore allows you to search for and find everything worth searching for ... and finding!

Six specific domains are offered:

- search engines;
- directory sites;
- news;
- business and finance;
- software;
- Usenet (newsgroups).

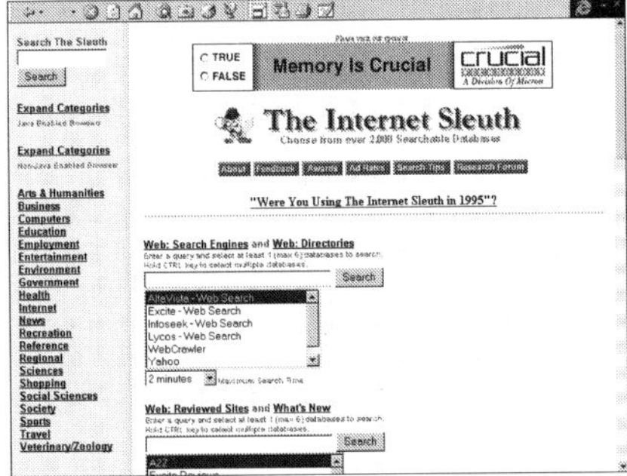

Figure 4.8 The home page of Internet Sleuth.

The method is the same for all six categories. Enter the keywords, select the search engine or site and click on the **Search** button.

On the left of the home page you can select a subject or sub-subject of interest. You can also indicate a maximum search time in order not to tie up your PC unnecessarily. By default, the value is fixed at two minutes.

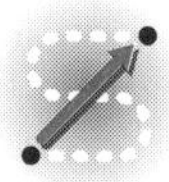

Search engines to search for search engines!

You can use a search engine such as Yahoo! to search for other search engines. Go directly to the following address: ***http://dir.yahoo.com/Computers_and_Internet/Internet/World_WideWeb/Searching_the_Web***

Yahoo! offers the following tools in particular:

- *195 search engines!*
- *109 metasearch engines or search engine grouping pages!*
- *211 Web directories!*

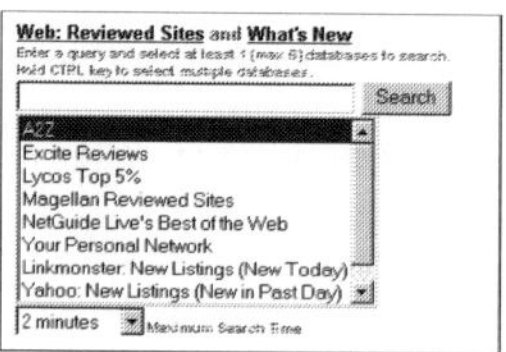

Figure 4.9 Searching in compilations of sites.

Aztech Cyberspace Launch Pad

http://www.aztech-cs.com/aztech/surf_central.html

This site offers a simple list of search engines and the possibility of searching directly from this page.

Directory Guide

http://www.directoryguide.com/

This service is a compilation of search tools, directories and guides – 400 of these have been referenced and are accessible by keywords.

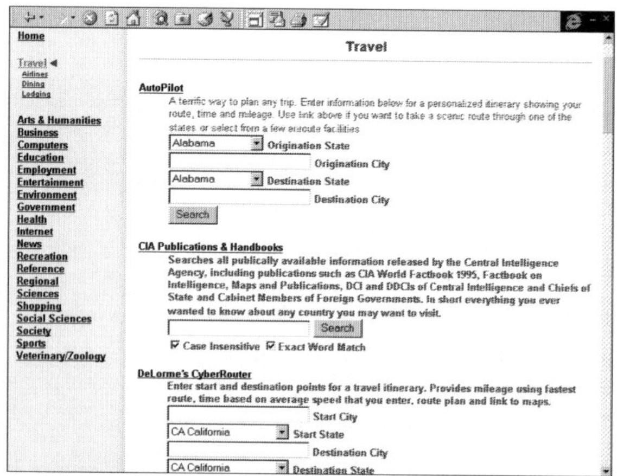

Figure 4.10 An extract from the 'Travel' selection page.

Web Taxi

http://www.webtaxi.com/

Select an international search engine, a regional search engine (by country throughout the world) or a subject, and click on the **Search** button. Web Taxi then displays the tool or tools found at the bottom of the screen. The rest is up to you.

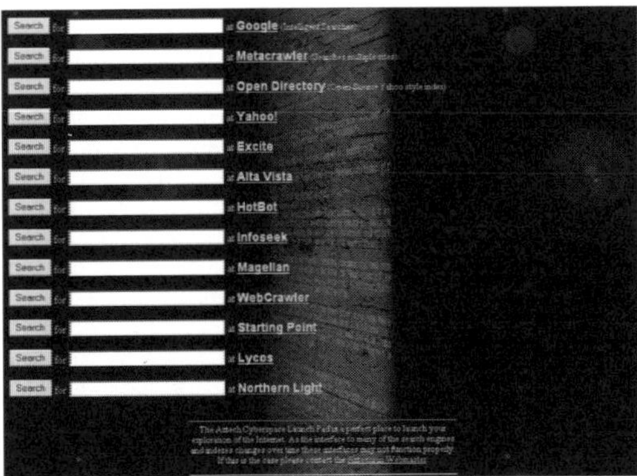

Figure 4.11 The choice of a metasearch engine or one of the large international search engines on the home page.

Directories of people and companies

5

Finding people and e-mail addresses

Trademarks and companies

The Yellow Pages

Apart from the vast source of information and services which the Web constitutes, the Internet is also a means of communication. E-mail is the most frequently used application, just in front of the Web. Contacting others and finding a company are the frequent needs of surfers.

Searches for people may be based on addresses, telephone numbers or e-mail addresses. There are specialist tools and services on the Web for each of these requirements. We have already seen that most large search engines (see Chapters 2 and 3) offer search functions relating to people, e-mail addresses and Yellow Pages services. This chapter gives us the opportunity to introduce some new ones and to look at the most reliable ways of tracking down people and companies.

There are millions of us around the world who use the Internet to communicate. So, if you have lost somebody's details, if you are looking for somebody who has disappeared, if you wish to make contacts abroad, this is your opportunity.

Finding people and e-mail addresses

Some tools specialise in searching individual countries; others search the whole planet unless you choose to restrict searching to a particular country. However, in the UK (as in many other countries), finding people is by no means an exact science – there are no directories relating exclusively to UK residents. We'll begin by looking at the worldwide services most likely to lead you to an Internet user in the UK. Remember that you can actually use these services to find someone anywhere in the world simply by selecting the appropriate country.

In the UK

InfoSpace Email Addresses
http://www.infospace.com/info/email1.htm
By default, the InfoSpace Email Addresses lookup offers a search of 'Any Country', so your first step must be to select 'United Kingdom' from the list of countries. Enter the last and first name of the person you want to find and, optionally, their home town or city. Ignore the State/Province box which relates only to American searches, and click the **Find Email** button.

InfoSpace has various methods of gathering its information, so the details available for each person in the results list will vary. If the person is registered with InfoSpace, you may find their address, phone number and more when you click on their name. InfoSpace doesn't display the e-mail address, but provides a link you can click to send an e-mail message.

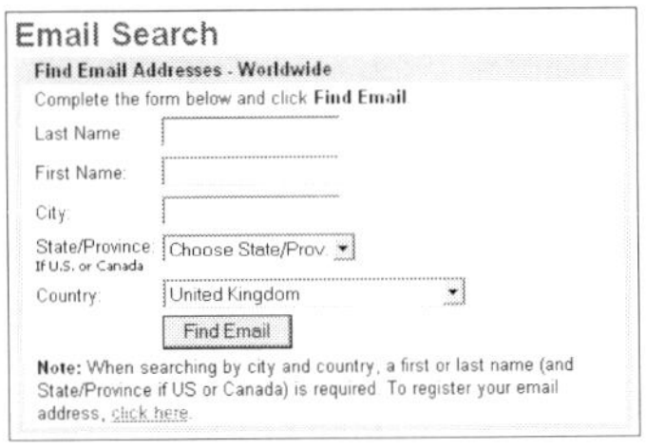

Email Search
Find Email Addresses - Worldwide
Complete the form below and click Find Email
Last Name
First Name
City
State/Province If U.S. or Canada: Choose State/Prov
Country: United Kingdom
Find Email
Note: When searching by city and country, a first or last name (and State/Province if US or Canada) is required. To register your email address, click here.

Figure 5.1 Starting an e-mail address search at InfoSpace.

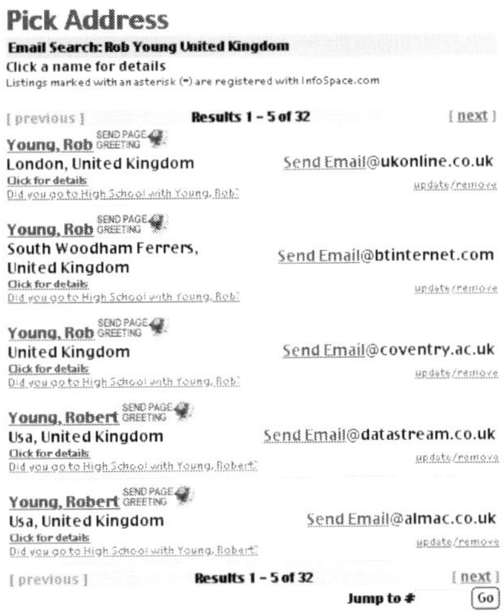

Pick Address
Email Search: Rob Young United Kingdom
Click a name for details
Listings marked with an asterisk (*) are registered with InfoSpace.com

[previous] Results 1 - 5 of 32 [next]

Young, Rob SEND PAGE GREETING
London, United Kingdom — Send Email@ukonline.co.uk
Click for details — update/remove
Did you go to High School with Young, Rob?

Young, Rob SEND PAGE GREETING
South Woodham Ferrers, United Kingdom — Send Email@btinternet.com
Click for details — update/remove
Did you go to High School with Young, Rob?

Young, Rob SEND PAGE GREETING
United Kingdom — Send Email@coventry.ac.uk
Click for details — update/remove
Did you go to High School with Young, Rob?

Young, Robert SEND PAGE GREETING
Usa, United Kingdom — Send Email@datastream.co.uk
Click for details — update/remove
Did you go to High School with Young, Robert?

Young, Robert SEND PAGE GREETING
Usa, United Kingdom — Send Email@almac.co.uk
Click for details — update/remove
Did you go to High School with Young, Robert?

[previous] Results 1 - 5 of 32 [next]
Jump to # Go

Figure 5.2 The result of searching at InfoSpace.

InfoSpace Phone Numbers

http://www.infospace.com/info/people.htm

Along with the e-mail address search mentioned above, InfoSpace also makes a great job of finding someone's postal address and telephone number. The form is almost identical to the e-mail addresses lookup, but there's one difference to note when completing the fields: unless the person you are searching for has an unusual name, try to enter the town or city as well as the country. If you don't, the service may return hundreds of matches!

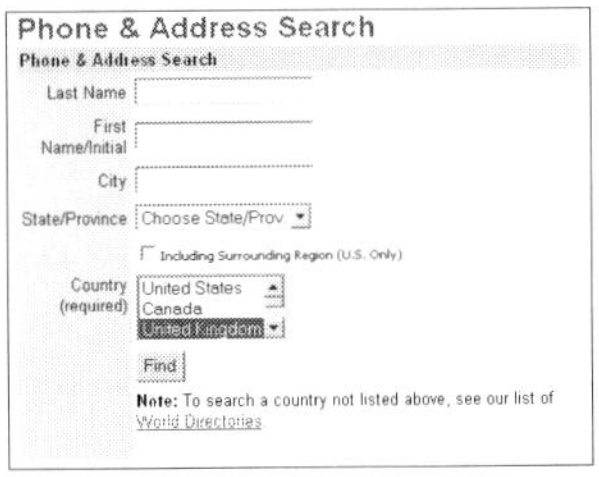

Phone & Address Search
Phone & Address Search
Last Name
First Name/Initial
City
State/Province: Choose State/Prov
Including Surrounding Region (U.S. Only)
Country (required): United States / Canada / United Kingdom
Find
Note: To search a country not listed above, see our list of World Directories

Figure 5.3 InfoSpace is the best place to find a UK resident's address and phone number.

Throughout the world

Yahoo! People Search

http://people.yahoo.com

This site has replaced one of the old stalwarts, Four11 (in fact the URL **www.four11.com** will still get you here), but it's still one of the best places to find an e-mail address. All the same, the fact that your correspondent has an e-mail address does not necessarily mean that you will find it. There is no shortage of addresses! For example, it is not easy to know which is the right Bill Gates from among the 70 found! Is just one of them the boss of Microsoft? By clicking on the headers listed, you obtain more specific information and can then proceed by elimination.

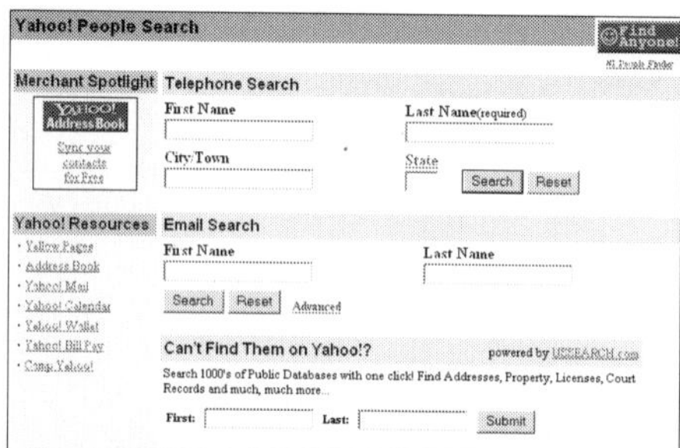

Figure 5.4 The Yahoo! People Search home page.

WhoWhere?

http://www.whowhere.lycos.com/

WhoWhere? is a well-known US search service, part of the Lycos network of search engines. The service delivers highly detailed results which may include the address, phone number and hobbies of people who have registered with the service.

The WhoWhere? search engine works by approximation. The search criterion does not need to correspond to an exact entry in the index. Therefore typing or spelling errors in entering names are not too much of a problem. The search engine will in fact find overlaps of strings of two characters or more. It even allows searches using initials!

The service also offers:

- searching for addresses and telephone numbers;
- searching for companies on the Internet;
- Yellow Pages: all companies (not necessarily present on the Net). Note the Big Book service for finding companies in the United States.

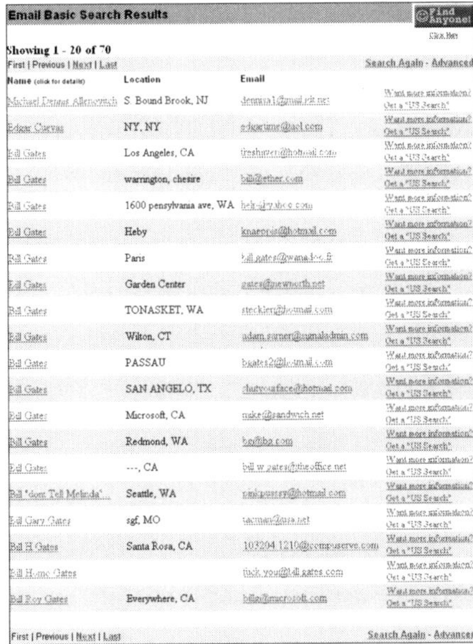

Figure 5.5 Details of contacts found, with e-mail addresses and links to more information.

Bigfoot
http://www.bigfoot.com

The service offers:

- searching for e-mail addresses; or
- the white pages (people's addresses).

In addition to the service, Bigfoot indicates how it has obtained the information. This may be useful in making an unsuccessful search more specific.

At Bigfoot, listed users may remain anonymous if they wish. In simple terms, you can find them, even send them an e-mail, but without knowing their address (this remains hidden).

AOL NetFind
http://www.aol.com/netfind/whitepages.adp

America Online is well-known as an online service offering private content to its members, but AOL also includes a useful range of services at its Web site (**www.aol.com**). The White Pages section of AOL NetFind is actually provided by InfoSpace, mentioned earlier in this chapter, so there are no surprises in its people lookup, but from this page you can jump to international white pages directories or search through AOL's own users.

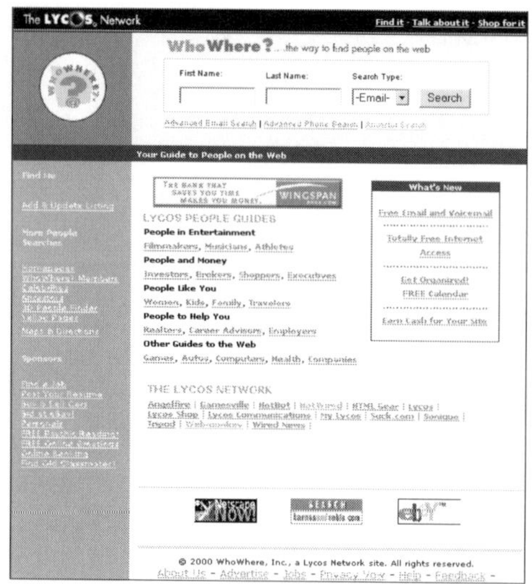

Figure 5.6 The home page of the WhoWhere? service.

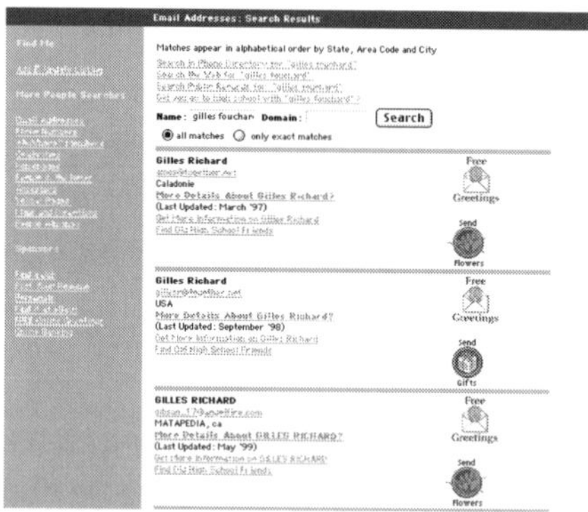

Figure 5.7 Search results are presented in order of relevance (Highly, Probably or Possibly Relevant).

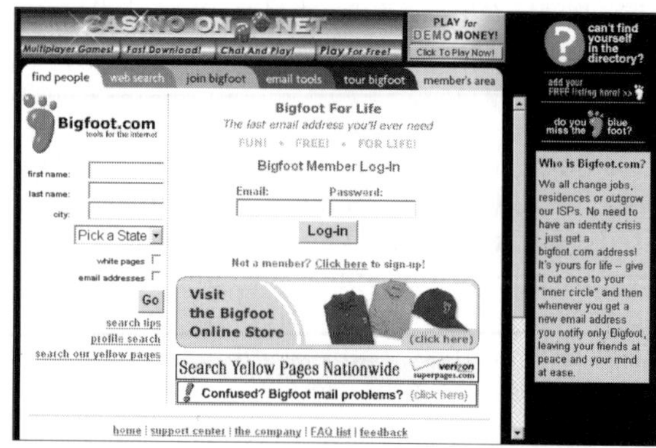

Figure 5.8 The Bigfoot home page.

AOL White Pages

AOL WHITE PAGES HELP

Type in the first and last name of the person you're looking for and click Find. For better results, type in the city, state and the full first name (e.g. William, not Bill).

Last Name (required) James
First Name Scott
City
Metro Search (US Only) Check to search entire metro area for this city.
State/Province Choose a State/Prov.
Country United Kingdom
Find!

Figure 5.9 Searching for a person.

Trademarks and companies

Directories of trademarks and companies are legion on the Net. Here is a useful selection. You will need to distinguish between tools which only list companies present on the Web, and the others, of more general scope.

The Patent Office – Database Search

http://gb.espacenet.com

The Patent Office deals with UK trademark and patent applications. While the main site at **http://www.patent.gov.uk** provides useful background information, the Database Search site allows you to search patent databases in the UK, Europe and worldwide.

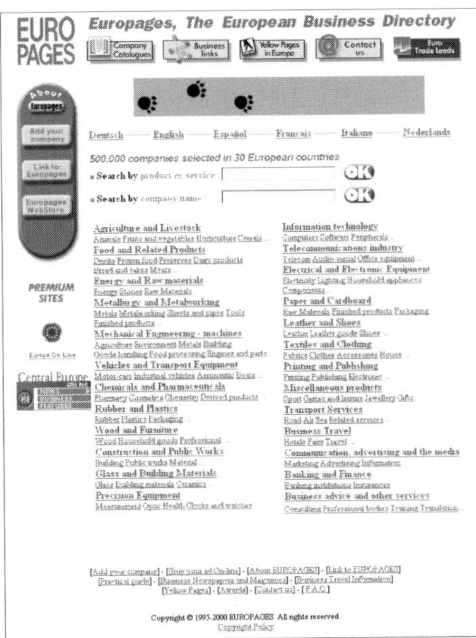

Figure 5.10 Finding companies using Europages.

Collections of search engines

If the search engines mentioned previously are not enough, or if you want to access them from the same page, use one of the All In One services for finding people and e-mail addresses, such as **http://www.allonesearch.com/all1user.html#People**.

Dozens of e-mail address search engines are thus accessible, in alphabetical order, from 411 Locate to Yahoo! People Search.

*The same service is provided on The Front Page (***http://www.thefrontpage.com/search***) where you can select the People & Business options from the home page menu. Are you looking for a telephone or fax number, an address or e-mail address* ***anywhere in the world?*** *Use Telephone Directories on the Web (***http://www.teldir.com/eng***). The directories of 44 countries are easily accessible. The service is quite austere, but highly efficient.*

Europages
http://www.europages.com/
This European directory lists 500,000 companies spread over 30 countries in Europe.

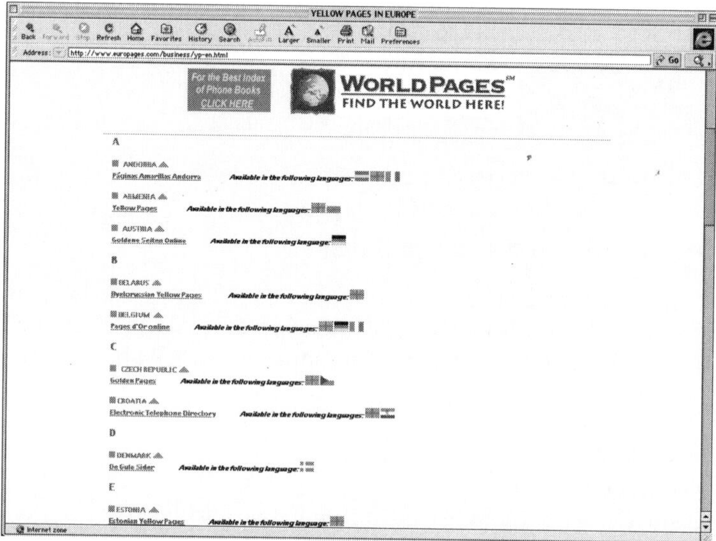

Figure 5.11 Finding directories of companies by country.

You can search in three ways:

- in plain text mode;
- by business; or
- by company name.

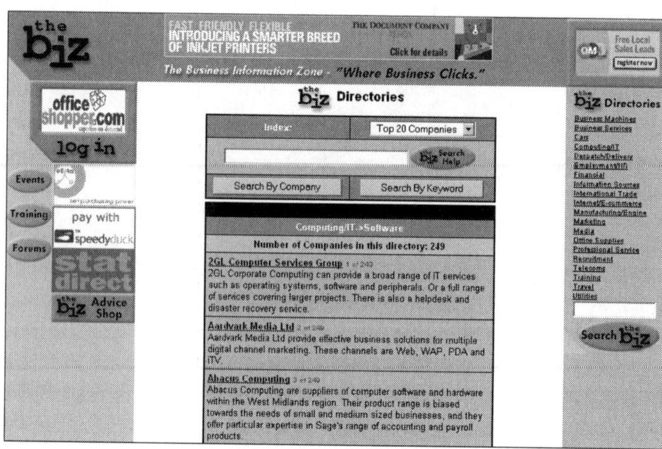

Figure 5.12 Categories, search form and company listings at The Business Information Zone.

Note the Yellow Pages button (**http://www.europages.com/business/yp-en.html**) which allows you to search through 17 European countries. Select the country and one of the languages offered (by clicking on the flag).

You then access a directory of companies for the country selected. Europages thus gives you easy access to the best company directories throughout Europe.

The Business Information Zone (the Biz)

http://www.thebiz.co.uk

This site provides one of the simplest ways to locate a UK company, whether the company you are searching for is present on the Internet or not. Using a directory structure similar to the UK Plus and Yahoo! Web search engines, you work through categories and subcategories until you find the company you are looking for. If that company has a Web site, clicking the link will take you to the company's site. If not, the link will take you to a page giving contact details for the company.

If you're not keen on delving through directory categories to find a company, The Biz also offers the traditional keyword search. From the front page of the site, or from any of the category pages, type keywords and press **Enter**. Your keywords can include the name of the company or organisation you want to find, or words you would expect to find in a description of the company.

Figure 5.13 Search for US companies by name, industry or directory category.

CompaniesOnline

http://www.companiesonline.com

This is yet another service that forms a part of the huge Lycos network, and can provide detailed information about a large number of US companies. Along with contact details this information may include annual turnover, number of employees, the latest stock quote and much more.

Like The Biz, CompaniesOnline lets you choose between running a traditional search or 'drilling down' through category listings.

LookHere Web directory
http://www.lookhere.co.uk
If you know that the UK company you're looking for has a presence on the Web, LookHere may be able to take you to its site. LookHere's categories are organised by initial letter, so clicking 'C' on the home page will lead to a list of categories that includes Cars, Cinema and Construction. Click a category to see a page of links to companies in that category, accompanied by brief descriptions.

The Yellow Pages

The expression 'Yellow Pages' is widely used on the Web. These search sites allow you to find details of businesses and companies on the Internet.

With the formidable development of companies on the Web, there are plenty of Yellow Pages services. The large search engines have them, as we have already seen.

Yell
http://www.yell.com
Yell is the online incarnation of the UK Yellow Pages telephone directory. Its great benefit is that it covers the entire country rather than limiting you to searching in your own telephone area. You can choose between two methods of searching. Either select a business type (such as Painters and Decorators or Airlines) or search for a specific company by name. In the **Where?** Box, type a town, city or country.

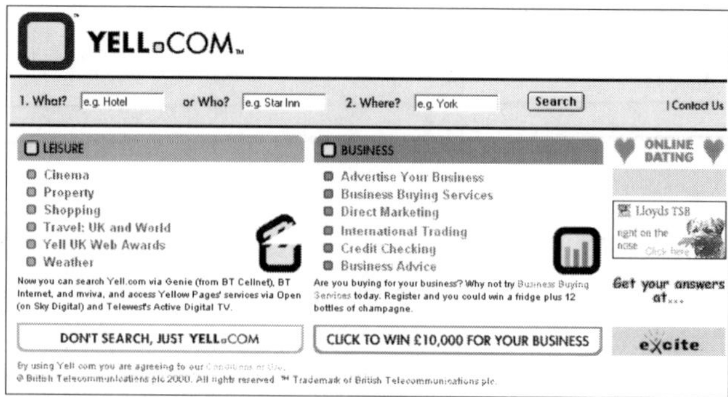

Figure 5.14 Searching for businesses and companies at Yell.

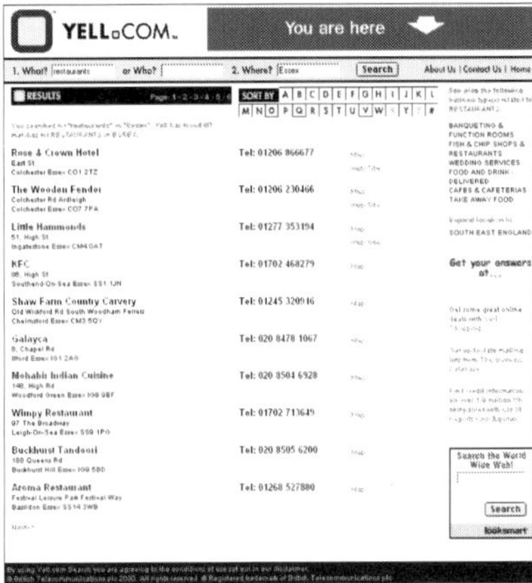

Figure 5.15 Yell's search results include clickable links to extra information.

Along with the name, address and phone number of businesses matching your search criteria, links may be included to indicate that the business has its own Web site, or provide a map or additional information.

Scoot
http://www.scoot.co.uk
Scoot provides a similar set of services to Yell, allowing you to search for a type of business or a company name, selected from links to the right of the search form. A useful extra is the Product Finder page, which can help you find businesses that provide the particular product or service you're looking for.

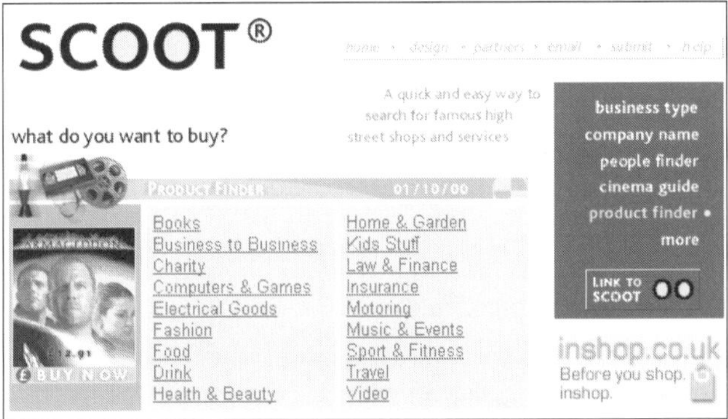

Figure 5.16 Search for a product using Scoot's Product Finder directory.

Kompass
http://www.kompass.com
This is a monster which lists 1.5 million companies throughout the world, spread over 61 countries!

There are two search modes:

- product search; or
- company search.

Instead of a keyword search you can use the Guided Search option, which is actually an unusual name for the directory-structure of categories found on many search sites. One clever addition at Kompass is that if you select a particular country or continent from the listbox above before picking a category, only companies from the selected area will be shown in the categorised lists.

Infospace
http://www.infospace.com
Finding companies is at the heart of this service. But you can also find white pages, and search for online purchasing sites, small ads, maps, etc.

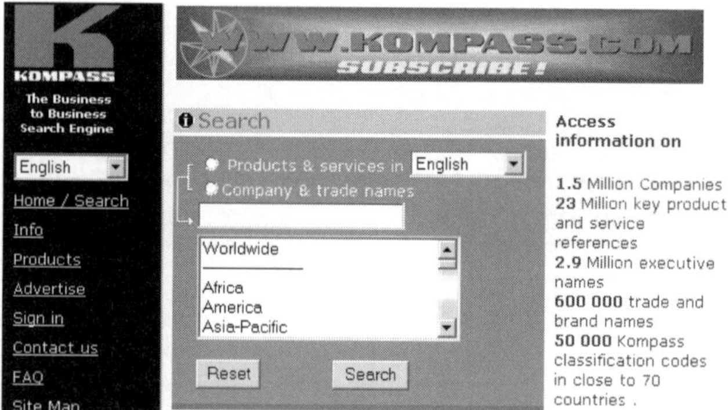

Figure 5.17 Welcome to the search for companies throughout the world.

Infospace offers several modes of operation for finding companies:

- by category;
- by name;
- by address, even if only approximate;
- by telephone or fax number;
- by map (US, Canada and London).

Figure 5.18 All the search tools accessible on Infospace.

6

Searching with Usenet and FTP

Newsgroups

Finding newsgroups on the Web

Finding download sites

Finding shareware

With the huge success of the Web, we have come to confuse the Web and the Internet. In fact, the Internet has a set of older resources such as:

- Usenet: for newsgroups or discussion groups;
- FTP (*File Transfer Protocol*): download sites.

These resources are increasingly accessible on the Web owing to their user-friendliness.

Newsgroups

Newsgroups are discussion groups covering particular subjects: HTML, languages, sciences, politics, humour, ketchup (yes, honestly!), and more. A *lot* more in fact: there are in excess of 50,000 different newsgroups in existence, although you may not be able to access all of them. Much depends upon which newsgroups your Internet service provider has chosen to subscribe to, but you will probably have a few tens of thousands available.

You can access newsgroups using a dedicated *newsreader* program such as Agent or Free Agent (**http://www.forteinc.com**), or TIFNY (**http://www. tifny2.com**), or you may be able to use features built into your e-mail program. For users of Internet Explorer 4 or later, the Outlook Express e-mail program makes it easy to work with newsgroups. Here we'll use Outlook Express, but the principles are the same with any other newsgroup program.

It pays to remember that among all the possible topics for newsgroups, sex and pornography are certainly included, along with other topics you may prefer not to encounter. Fortunately such groups are usually easy to spot by their names: you are less likely to stumble across pornographic newsgroups than Web sites.

Newsgroups are a great way of participating in life in cyberspace, communicating with others, and exchanging information. But, as with the Web, you need to find the right addresses!

Newsgroup addresses take the form *domain.subject.sub-subject*; e.g.: **alt.music.pop**.

Domains are represented by codes: **alt** for alternative, **comp** for newsgroups connected with computers, **rec** for recreational or **talk** for chatting and exchanging ideas.

The All tab in the above figure provides a list of all the newsgroups accessible. The Subscribe tab contains a list of the newsgroups to which you have decided to subscribe.

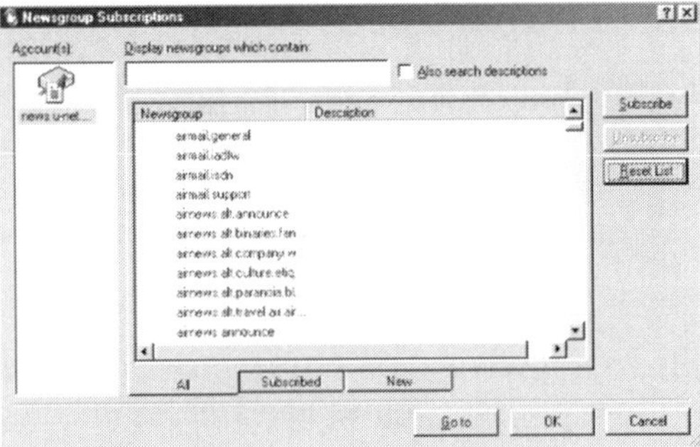

Figure 6.1 Finding newsgroups using Outlook Express.

Among the 50,000 or more newsgroups available, many will be 'worldwide' groups with contributors from anywhere in the world (although the dominant language is English, as elsewhere on the Internet). For some types of information search this wide range of contributors means you should be able to find what you want more quickly.

Don't confuse newsgroups with chat rooms: newsgroup discussions don't take place in 'real time'. You read the messages posted, but you are not in direct communication with their authors. Likewise, when you post a message, this will be read by whoever wants to whenever they want. Interactive, or real time chatting, requires the IRC (or chat) technique, which we will deal with later.

There may be times, however, when only UK-specific information will do: sifting through a worldwide newsgroup for UK legal advice would be a painful process! Fortunately there are a number of UK newsgroups covering a large number of subjects. These are easy to find since their names all begin with 'uk'.

Hundreds of newsgroups, sorted by alphabetical order, are directly accessible using your newsreader software. By typing a few letters in the text box above the list of groups, you access specific newsgroups faster. For example, type **uk** to go to the list of UK-specific newsgroups. Select a newsgroup and connect in order to consult it.

You will then learn:

- how to subscribe to a newsgroup;
- how to read messages off-line;
- how to participate in newsgroups by sending messages;
- how to find, organise and sort messages.

In fact, the enormous number of messages of some newsgroups makes them difficult to consult. However, search functions make it easy to access the information you want. You can carry out searches by indicating:

- the sender's name;
- a keyword or phrase to be matched in newsgroup messages;
- validity dates (posted before, or after).

Finding newsgroups on the Web

Once again, the Web is there to help you to find newsgroups. Some search engines offer this service, such as DejaNews, of which it is a speciality.

DejaNews
http://www.dejanews.com/
The correct URL is actually **http://www.deja.com**, since DejaNews has gone the way of many other search engines and started offering everything but the kitchen sink from its homepage. You then have to look for the option to search Usenet (the 'proper' name for newsgroups). Fortunately the **www.dejanews.com** URL still takes you straight to the part of the site you want.

Figure 6.2 The Deja.com logo, home of DejaNews.

When you arrive, it all looks very straightforward. Using the controls at the top of the page you can type keywords to search for, and choose whether to search only recent discussions, past discussions, or all discussions. From a second drop-down list you can choose to search in the following areas:

- Complete: all newsgroups.
- Standard: all groups except those dealing with adult topics, jobs and small ads.
- Adult: groups and messages dealing with 'adult' (usually pornographic) topics.
- Jobs: groups and messages relating to job vacancies and recruitment.
- For Sale: small ads, goods for sale, and so on.

The 'Standard' option is selected by default, and that's usually the option you would want.

Search results appear as a list of messages, much like e-mail messages in your Inbox. If a message's subject line seems to cover the topic you're interested in, click it to read the message. When the message is displayed, you can do a number of things:

- Switch to the previous or next message listed in the search results.
- Compose a reply to the message.
- Read a profile of the message's author (if a profile exists).

- Click the **Forum** link to switch to the group in which the message was found.
- Click the **Thread** link to read the entire 'conversation' of which this message was a part.

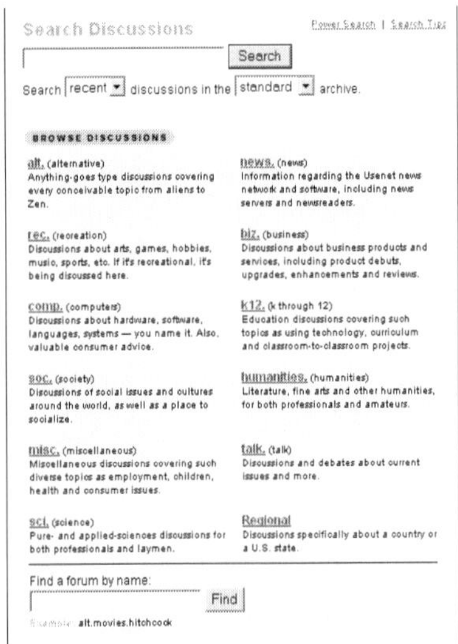

Figure 6.3 Search options at DejaNews.

Date	Subject	Forum	Author
10/14/2000	Re: (old) DZ intro music	alt.fan.dragonball	Malin Schmuck (
10/14/2000	Dragon and the Hawk	rec.music.movies	dcypser
10/14/2000	Re: Dragon and the Hawk	rec.music.movies	Mr Tasslehoff
10/14/2000	Dragon Valor is out...any1	rec.games.video.sony	LNC Shali
10/13/2000	Re: Dragon Subscription at 0	rec.games.frp.dnd	Jason Hatter
10/13/2000	Re: Question #2: What happen	alt.toys.gi-joe	DaWerewolf
10/13/2000	Re: ATTN: The One Who Works	alt.fan.dragons	Nex
10/12/2000	Re: What ever happened to Dr	alt.toys.gi-joe	Jimandlauraw

Figure 6.4 The results of a search at DejaNews.

Also listed on the results page you'll find matches among newsgroup names. By checking boxes beside the appropriate names, you can re-run the search in those groups only to narrow the search. (An alternative is to start by searching for newsgroups by name: at the bottom of the main search page you'll see a second text box where you can search for groups rather than messages.)

Finally, DejaNews offers a comprehensive Power Search option. This has added power in that after setting up the search as you want it, it can be automatically applied to all your future searches. Options on the Power Search page include:

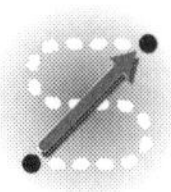

No news?

If you can't find what you want at DejaNews, the chances are you won't find it in the newsgroups at all. DejaNews specialises in newsgroups and maintains a comprehensive database of groups and messages. Choosing the 'Search Usenet' (or equivalent) option at one of the search engines mentioned elsewhere in this book will usually result either in a search that uses DejaNews, or a search of the engine's own less comprehensive database.

- Match: choose whether *all* words or *any* words should be regarded as a match (the equivalent of Boolean AND / OR searches).
- Forum: optionally choose which newsgroup to search in.
- Author: restrict the search to messages from a particular author (by e-mail address).
- Dates: search for messages posted between specific dates.
- Language: search for messages in a particular language.

You can also choose whether search results should be sorted by confidence (how likely they are to be good matches for your search query), subject, author, newsgroup name, or date.

Finding download sites

Download sites are used to import all kinds of things onto your PC:

- programs, utilities and plug-ins (software adding functions to your Internet browser);
- shareware;
- drawings, images, photographs;
- sound files;
- videos;
- text documents.

The advantage of downloading software from a Web site rather than an FTP site is that it is simpler. Instead of going through directories, you let yourself be guided. And that avoids the need to use several different software programs.

FTP Search
http://ftpsearch.lycos.com
This Norwegian site, now operated by the Lycos Network, offers the option of searching FTP servers for files to download. Be warned: this service only works using file and directory names – there is no way to search by keyword (for example, searching for particular *types* of file). You must already know the name of the file you are looking for, or some part of the name. For example, if you want to find Windows screensavers, you might search for ***.scr** (which would find any files with the .scr extension). Or if you are trying to download a file called **newfile102.zip** from an FTP site but you're having trouble, you could find out whether that file exists on any other (perhaps more reliable!) FTP servers.

The search controls might look a bit daunting at first glance, but you can leave most of them at their defaults. Simply type the text you want to search for in the first text box and click **Search**. Other changes you might want to make are:

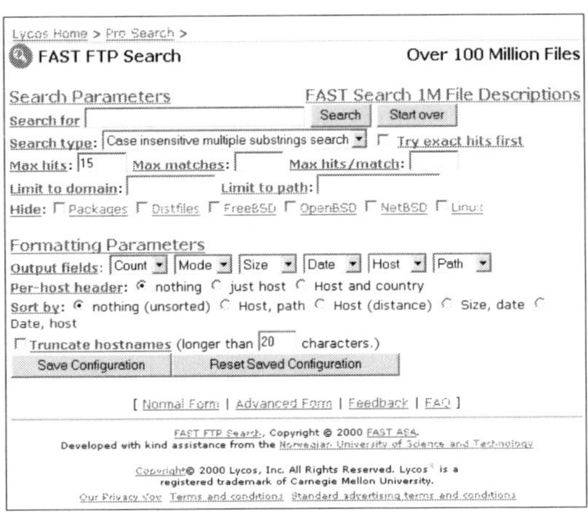

Figure 6.5 The FTP Search page (don't be put off – it really is easy!).

- Increase **Max hits** from 15 to see more matching items per page.
- Check the **Try exact hits first box** if you are searching for a specific filename.
- Change **Search type** to 'Exact Search' if you are sure that non-exact matches will be of no use to you.

Finding shareware

Shareware are programs which offer a free trial. Downloaded from the Web, they meet many requirements. But you still have to know how to find and sort the good, the very good even, from the bad!

Shareware.com
http://www.shareware.com

Shareware constitutes a valuable tool which you can procure directly from the Net. Whatever your need, there is surely software which can satisfy it. And shareware is to be found almost everywhere on the Internet. If only there was a site offering all existing shareware! Where you could get to know all the versions and be sure of downloading the latest. Where you could also find products for Macs, PCs, computers that run under DOS, Windows 3.1 or 95 or even NT. One can dream… There would also need to be a short introduction to each software in order to know what it is used for and what its limits are. But wait, this service exists! It is called shareware.com.

From the homepage you can run a standard search (which involves typing the name or type of software you are looking for, and selecting the operating system you use), or an Advanced search. The Advanced search lets you choose from the following options:

- Search in the file's description.
- Specify words that should not appear in the description.
- Search in the file's name.
- Specify the age of the file.

You can choose whether to search by platform, or to select one or more software archives to search.

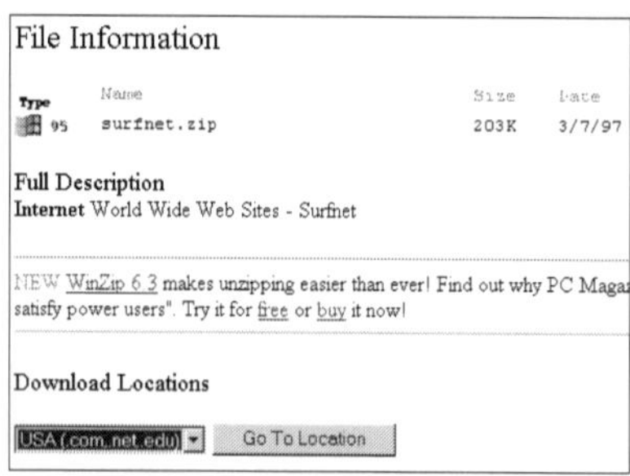

Figure 6.6 Finding software using Shareware.com.

Shareware – how to use it

Shareware is not free software. It is a program which you can try out free of charge. If the program suits you, and you wish to keep it, you must pay the author. The price of the licence and the programmer's details are generally mentioned in a 'readme.txt' file or are accessible when you start the product. Often, it is possible to register and pay for the product online. It is good to pay for the licence, it is one of the rules of the game. Moreover, you will then be able to benefit from upgrades or receive more detailed documentation. On the other hand, if the program does not meet your requirements, just delete it from your hard disk.

The results of a search reveal:

- the name of the file (the software) to be downloaded;
- a brief description of the program;
- the storage directory (category of program);
- the date of the file;
- the file size.

CNET Shareware.com **Search Results for screen saver**

Found: **500** Displaying: **1-25** <Previous 1 2 3 4 5 6 7 8 9 10 11 12 13 14 15 16 17 18 19 20 Next>

Re-sort by Filename	Platform/Type	File Date
0a1image41.exe Display your images as screen savers - play music! **Location:** winsite-win95 archive **Directory:** desktop/ **Size:** 1.8MB	Windows 95	03/29/2000
0acreate1.exe Create and distribute Screen Savers with your images. **Location:** winsite-win95 archive **Directory:** desktop/ **Size:** 4.3MB	Windows 95	11/02/1999
0creata3.exe Create Screen Savers with your photos, images, graphics **Location:** winsite-win95 archive **Directory:** desktop/ **Size:** 1.8MB	Windows 95	03/24/1999
0s_ult56.zip SlideShow ULTRA - Incredible! Screen Saver JPG GIF BMP **Location:** winsite-win95 archive **Directory:** desktop/ **Size:** 3.5MB	Windows 95	10/20/1998
0void01.exe FreeWare Screen Saver featuring beautiful mountains **Location:** winsite-win95 archive **Directory:** desktop/ **Size:** 1MB	Windows 95	06/04/2000
0void02.exe Freeware Screen Saver featuring beautiful Ocean Scenes **Location:** winsite-win95 archive **Directory:** desktop/ **Size:** 825K	Windows 95	06/05/2000

Figure 6.7 The result of a search using the keywords 'screen saver'.

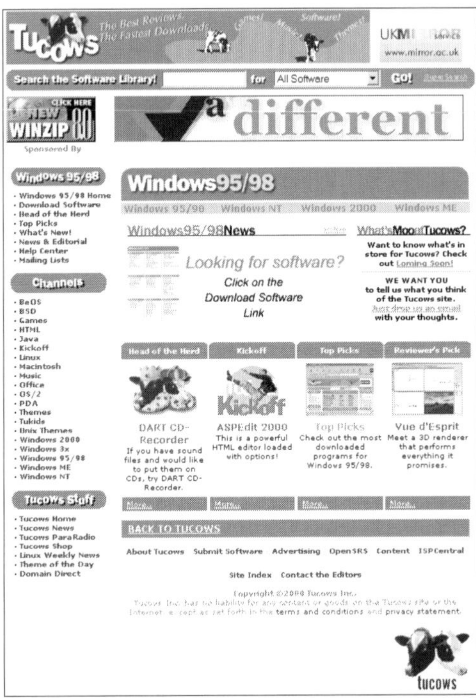

Figure 6.8 The Tucows homepage, with simple search controls at the top.

Tucows
http://tucows.mirror.ac.uk

The oddly-named Tucows has long been a great resource for Internet-related software, although it's been expanding to include other types of software too. Tucows provides a simple search option on its homepage from which you can enter keywords and select the area to search from a drop-down list (a particular operating system, free themes, games, or children's software). This form of search uses the Boolean OR method, finding files whose descriptions contain any of the keywords you enter.

A **Super Search** link takes you to a separate page where your options are almost identical, with the addition of buttons letting you choose whether to search for all words, any word, or the exact phrase. (Like most software archives, you can ignore the search options and simply browse through categories of software if you prefer.)

Every file has a brief description, revision date and version number, download size, and a useful 'cow rating' where 5 cows means that this is 'best-of-breed' software.

Downloading time depends in theory on the size of the file and the speed of your modem. In practice, this time also varies depending on how congested the site and network are.

To download shareware, you must:

1. *Copy the file to a directory on your hard disk.*
2. *Decompress the file.*
3. *Install the program (run the file and follow the on-screen instructions).*

The second step may not actually be necessary: you may be able to just double-click the file you downloaded to begin the installation. If the file is compressed, you will need a decompression program. Most shareware supplied for the PC is in the ZIP format, so you'll need a ZIP program such as WinZip (another shareware program, which you can download from ***http://www.winzip.com****) to decompress it. Macintosh files are often supplied in Stuffit (.sit) archives, and you'll need a program called Stuffit Expander (****http://www.stuffit.com****) to handle these.*

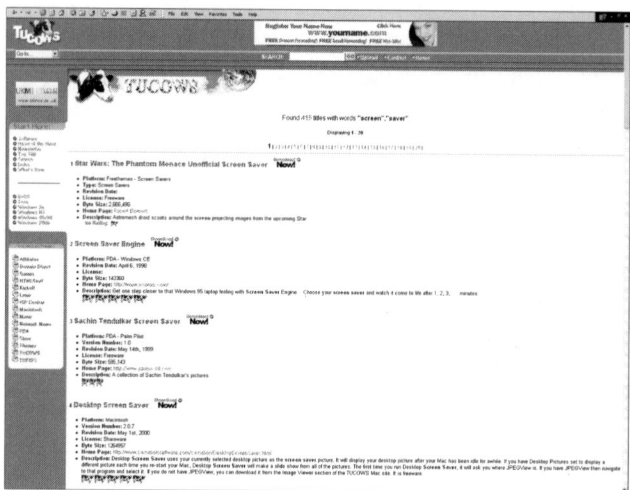

Figure 6.9 Results of a search for 'screen saver' at Tucows.

7 Multimedia searches

Finding images

Finding maps

Finding images

It is not difficult to find images and, more generally, multimedia objects on the Web. Image and multimedia files are easily identified by their extension. It is easy to sort between:

- images in GIF format;
- images in JPEG format;
- sounds (.wav files);
- videos;
- animation.

*Using Windows, you can save an image displayed in your Internet browser by right-clicking on it, then selecting **Save image as**. When saving the image, you can rename it, choose a different format and choose the destination folder.*

GIF and JPEG are in fact the two formats most used on the Web. The GIF format records an image in 256 colours. Developed by Compuserve, it is a highly compact format which is well suited to transfers on slow-speed networks such as our good old switched telephone network. To obtain higher quality, use the compressed JPEG format (*Joint Picture Expert Group*). This format is better suited to transmitting high-quality photographic documents. But, in order not to slow down the loading of pages, images are sometimes presented in the form of small images, called 'thumbnails'. You can open the image on a new Web page in its true size and with the best possible quality just by clicking on it.

Image search engines

Image search engines allow you to scan the Web looking for illustrations, photos or rare documents. Be careful; if the documents retrieved are not free of charge, you will not be able to publish them yourself, unless you pay the author. But for your personal use, you can amuse yourself by collecting everything that interests you.

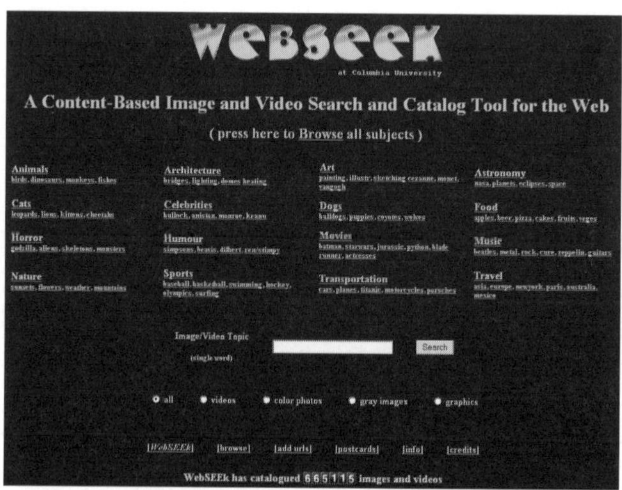

Figure 7.1 The home page with searching by subject.

Figure 7.2 Searching by keyword and media type.

Webseek
http://www.ctr.columbia.edu/webseek/
This is an extraordinary tool from Columbia University in the United States. All image hunters should connect to this site in order to try it out. Webseek offers browsing by menu in addition to searching by criteria. Insofar as images are concerned, the result of your request is presented in the form of a page of thumbnails (see Figure 7.3), and the size of the original images is indicated. You can go to the site where the chosen image is located with just one click and open the image in its original size.

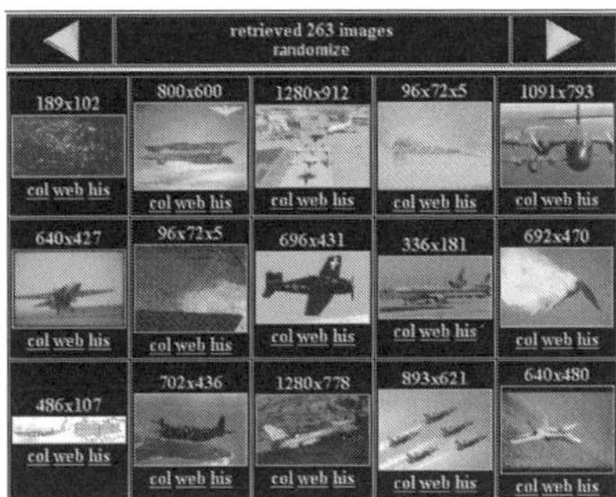

Figure 7.3 The result of a search.

The system allows you to find videos, black and white photos or colour photos. To do this, just check the appropriate box in the keyword text box.

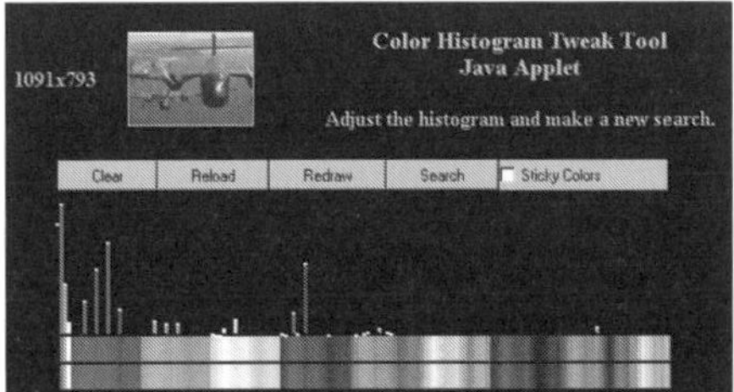

Figure 7.4 The His command (histogram) allows you to search for similar shades.

Figure 7.5 Searching by subject: here, Arts – Painting, then Matisse.

The results are presented in the form of an electronic contact sheet: each corresponding document is displayed in the form of a small image. Then you just click on the image to access a document. The size of the actual image is displayed above the small image.

The service even allows you to find photos with similarities in terms of colours.

Finding sounds on the Web

Lycos also allows you to find sound files. Take care to check the file formats (wav, midi, au or ra) and to ensure that you have the right software to listen to them. A number of sound documents broadcast are coded in ra format (for Real Audio) and can be processed by the Real Player software of the Progressive Networks company. This technique also allows sound to be broadcast live (live radio on the Web). Note that the Real Player program is included in Internet Explorer 4 and 5.

Lycos Image
http://www.lycos.co.uk/search/options.html
You discovered the general purpose search engine Lycos during Chapter 2, but the speciality of Lycos Image is, as its name suggests, that it finds images. To do this it uses a specialised analysis technique which is truly sophisticated. For example, the search engine allows you to find tourist images or photographs of well-known personalities.

Yahoo! Picture Gallery
http://gallery.yahoo.com/
You have already discovered Yahoo! UK and Ireland, then the international version of Yahoo!, and now here is Yahoo! Picture Gallery. This tools allows searching by keywords or from among the 12 categories offered (including arts, leisure, people, games, science and transport).

Once you have selected the category, a panel appears at random. You can specify the object of your search from the text box at the top of the screen.

Here again is a very efficient tool which image hunters should save in their Favorites.

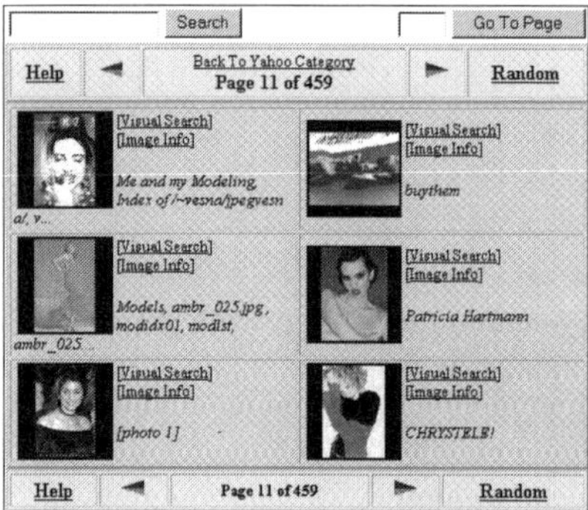

Figure 7.6 Searching by category; here a page on the top models.

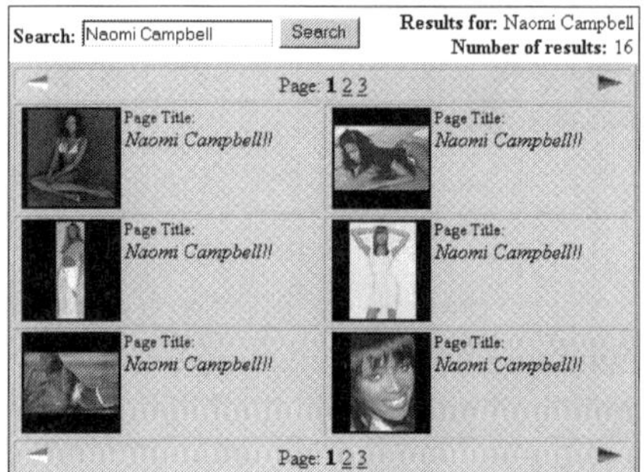

Figure 7.7 The request has been specified with the keyword 'Naomi Campbell'.

Finding erotic sites

We cannot allude to searching for images without mentioning eroticism and pornography. If there is one domain where photographs are used in profusion, it is this one. And there is no shortage of such material on the Internet.

Do we need a search engine for this? Why not? Those who want to get down to the nitty gritty will be able to connect with **http://www.sexhunt.com/**.

Photo agencies

Photo agencies on the Web make a good starting point for browsing through images. These are professional sites offering the best negatives of the best photographers or offering high-quality images for sale. In order to protect themselves against abuse, images are displayed in low resolution and with limited colour palettes. In any case, it is not possible to display photographic- quality images on the Web, as the pass-band of networks is not suited to this. However, these documents may be offered for downloading.

Sygma Agency
http://www.sygma.fr/

The Sygma agency is one of the largest photo agencies in the world. The site presents a stock of over 700,000 images which you can download in high definition for a fee.

The results of a search by keyword are presented in the form of a contact sheet. By clicking on one of the images, you open the document in a separate window, and at the same time you obtain the photo's references.

You can also use online reports (Stories heading). News, People, Magazine and Illustration are the four sections from which you will be able to access recent photos.

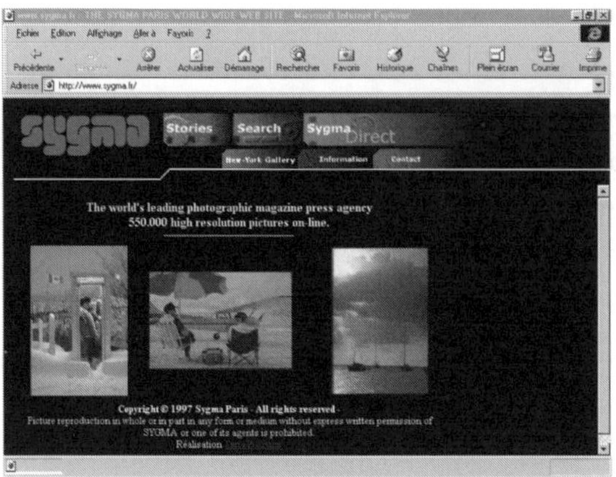

Figure 7.8 Welcome to the Sygma agency.

Figure 7.9 The result of a search on the word 'portrait'.

Giraudon Agency

http://www.giraudon-photo.fr/

The Giraudon photographic agency has a unique base of 200,000 negatives and 70,000 ektachromes combining photographs in various categories including Decorative Arts, Celebrations, Mythology, The East, and Daily Life.

Searches are not carried out automatically on the Web. You must complete a form and indicate what you are looking for. The document base is particularly rich. If you are interested in

Impressionism, more than 1,000 references are in stock. You can find almost 500 documents concerning Napoleon, for example. And if laughter is the subject of your search, almost 100 documents from Gargantua to the Laughing Cow will be offered!

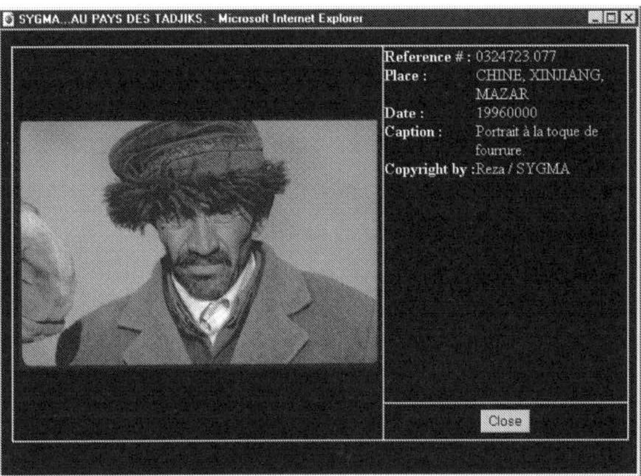

Figure 7.10 A photo is presented on request in a separate window.

Finding sounds or videos

For sound and video you can use the Lycos Multimedia service at **http://multimedia.lycos.com**. *As we also pointed out in Chapter 3, HotBot is an excellent tool for finding sound, video and even Shockwave animations. These animations use a Macromedia technique (***http:/www.macromedia.com***) and you must first download the 'player' from this publisher's site in order to be able to view them on your PC.*

Finding maps

You have been able to see that some general search engines offer map searching. In addition there are sites which specialise in this type of search. If search engines are handy for getting you around cyberspace, maps and plans will be of use to you in getting back to earth!

Maps Database
http:/www.internets.com/smaps.htm
This is a maps search engine which also offers a very full list of sites where maps can be found, with searching by category.

Xerox Map Viewer
http://pubweb.parc.xerox.com/map/color=1/features=alltypes
This software, developed by Xerox in 1993, allows you to discover the world interactively. Set the parameters of the visual representation software, click on the globe and discover the world. Latitude and longitude will no longer hold any secrets for you.

The Perry-Castenada Library Maps Collection
http://www.lib.utexas.edu/Libs/PCL/Map_collection/Map_collection.html
230,000 maps are listed and accessible from this address. There is something of everything here, and the map lover will be in his element. Maps are classified by continent and region. In addition, impressive lists are offered. On the menu are geographical maps, obviously, but also historical, political, economic maps, etc.

Lycos RoadMaps

http://www.proximus.com/lycos/

This is a remarkable service which displays the corresponding map from an address (street and town), with a cross indicating the street number requested. You can also title the map in order to personalise it and send it to a third party. Once the map has been displayed, it is possible to zoom in to obtain greater detail and discover all the surrounding services (hotels, restaurants, banks, etc.).

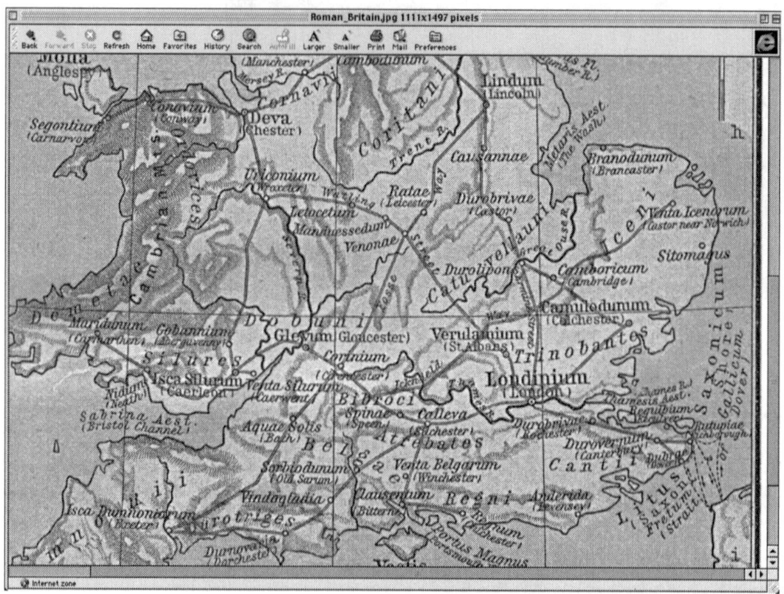

Figure 7.11 As an example, a map of Roman Britain from the historical atlas.

The Zoom In command allows you to obtain greater detail, while Zoom Out gives a more general overview of the place (just click on the graduated scale at the right of the map).

There is just one problem: this service only works in the United States. To make up for this, Lycos offers the City Guide service which you can reach by clicking the 'City Guide' link or by going to **http://cityguide.lycos.com**.

From a map of the world, you click on a continent, then, from the new map, on a country from the list displayed. From the country, you then access the map in question and a list of towns. For example, more than 60 English counties and cities are thus accessible, and there are thousands of towns and cities around the world which you can discover with a few clicks of the mouse. For each town or city, City Guide offers you a summary and a list of links used (culture, recreation, practical, etc.).

New to the neighborhood? Or just going somewhere new? Lycos Road Maps service will create a custom map of your destination. (Don't know the street address? Don't worry. You can even locate a friend by their E-mail address.) Just enter the facts below and see your map appear.

Domain or Email Address:

(Example: mydomain.com)

or

Street Address:

12707 high bluff drive

(House number and street)

City/State/ZIP:

san diego

(US addresses only)

Go Get It

Figure 7.12 Entering an address with Lycos RoadMaps.

Figure 7.13 A personalised map is displayed.

UK Street Map Page

http://www.streetmap.co.uk

This site currently only has street maps for Greater London, but it can also provide road atlas maps for the whole of mainland Britain. A simple search box lets you search by entering a London street, a postcode, a town or city, or (if you prefer to do things the difficult way!) an Ordnance Survey grid reference or latitude and longitude coordinates.

By clicking on an area of the map you can centre the map on that grid square. The Zoom In/Zoom Out links let you view the centre of the current map in greater detail.

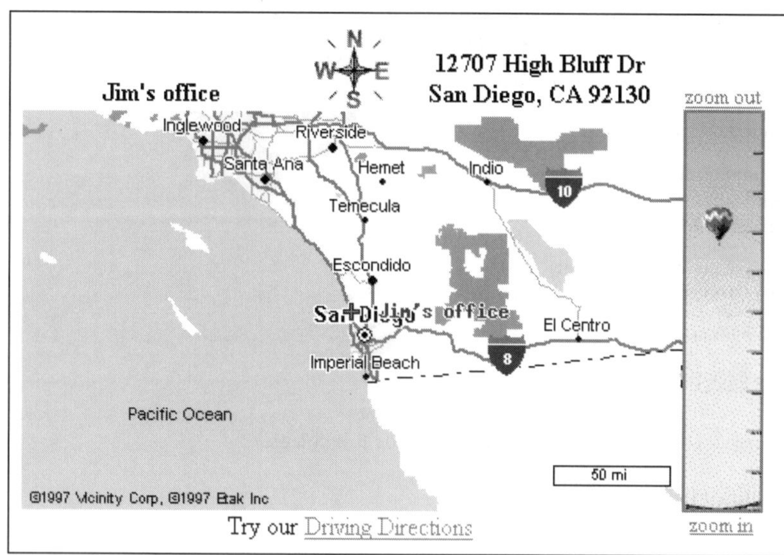

Figure 7.14 A more general view (Zoom Out).

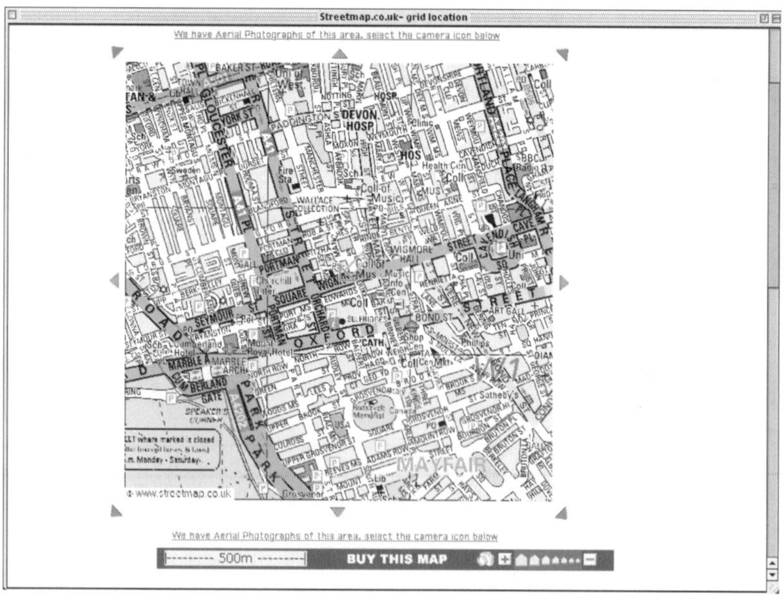

Figure 7.15 The result of a search for a London street.

8 Practical searches

Ferreting in virtual libraries

Window shopping on the Web!

From consulting a document to buying a product on the Web, everything starts with searching. The Web offers you virtual libraries and shops so that you can satisfy your thirst for knowledge or your hunger for consumption. To put it plainly, you can enrich yourself (intellectually) or spend without counting the cost!

Ferreting in virtual libraries

The hypertext technology, which was the main factor in designing the Web, was set up in order to easily exploit any kind of text document and to connect them by means of links. The written word occupies a place of honour on the Web, and you can find different types of document by browsing through the virtual libraries available.

Library of Congress
http://lcweb.loc.gov/
The Library of Congress contains more than 110 million documents in more than 400 languages. Most of the information in the library's catalogue is available online.

From the home page, the first search zone, American Memory, gives access to the following:

- text documents;
- photographic resources;
- the first films;
- sound documents.

From the Exhibition section you access the great exhibitions. Among these you'll be able to read transcriptions of the Gettysburg Address in 29 languages, find out how the American Declaration of Independence was drafted and read the first 'rough draft', or take a detour to the Vatican library with its own range of exhibits. Also discover the revelations of the Russian archives, or even, in another register, the discovery of America by Christopher Colombus in 1492. Or view on your PC the earliest map of California dating from 1562!

The library's services are detailed in Library Services. Here you will be able to access the virtual reading rooms. Twenty rooms await you with research domains as varied as history, science, the arts, rare books or the cinema. For example, connect to the Early Motion Pictures page (1897–1916) to carry out research into early cinema productions.

It is in the Research section that you will find the search tools (Catalogue page/Research and Reference command).

The Catalogue page gives access to all search modes:

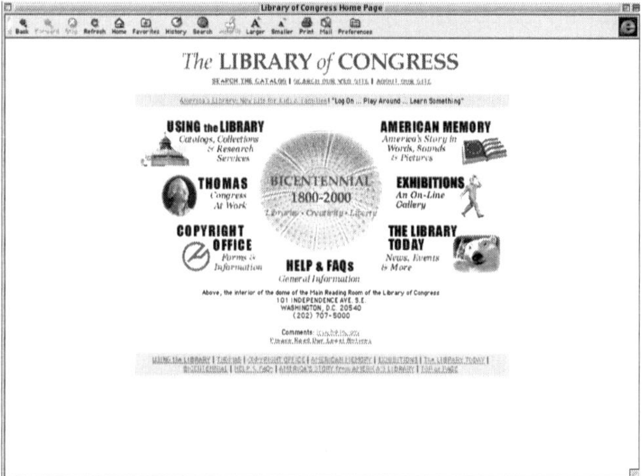

Figure 8.1 The home page of the largest virtual library in the world.

- by word;
- by reference;
- by Boolean expression.

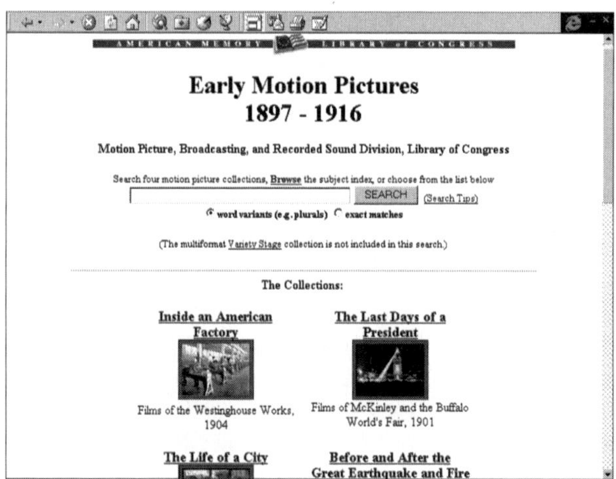

Figure 8.2 Searching for early films.

The search engine of the Library of Congress
Named LOCIS, it contains more than 27 million documents stored in different databases. Equipped with a real turbo, the library's catalogue contains not just its own documents but also other documents found in other libraries or research institutes. Among these documents, for example, you will find books, magazines, maps, music scores, films, posters, photographs or manuscripts. One file allows you to contact more than 13,000 research bodies throughout the world.

About a dozen additional search tools add to the basic mechanisms.

The British Library
http://www.bl.uk
The hub of the British library is Blaise, the British Library Automated Information Service, a collection of searchable databases containing over 19 million records which includes:

- the British Library Catalogue, which offers access to books published all over the world from 1450 to 1975;
- Whitaker, a weekly-updated database of British books published since 1965;
- Eighteenth Century Short Title Catalogue, records of all types of eighteenth-century printed materials;
- the Stationery Office, a database of government and official publications since 1976.

The full Blaise service is available by subscription, and the British Library Web site does little more than give a taste of what's available. However, the main database collections can be searched online without subscription using the OPAC 97 service.

Figure 8.3 Searching the British Library.

Internet Public Library

http://www.ipl.org/ref/

This is a virtual library which offers you hundreds of thousands of works and documents online. Choose a domain or a discipline from the home image, then refine your search until you find the exact subject that interests you. This service will display many online references and as many links with other sites containing information relating to your research.

Also click on the home image desk to ask a specific question. It can be very entertaining to consult the list of questions asked (with the answers). All kinds of things are there – how much is a 1983 Ford Fiesta worth? How much money did Yahoo! earn last year? Why is the sky blue? (Good question!)

This is another address which you should not miss.

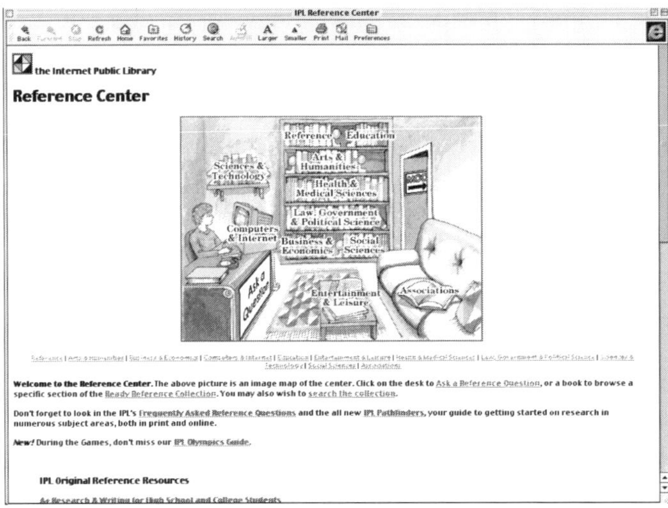

Figure 8.4 Welcome to Internet Public Library.

Athena
http://un2sg1.unige.ch/athena/html/athome.html

This virtual library created in Switzerland is the work of Pierre Perroud, lecturer in philosophy at the Collège Voltaire in Geneva. More than 3,700 literary texts are digitised, with the bonus of links with other consultation or downloading sites (**http://un2sgl.unige.ch/athena/html/booksite.html**).

The Gutenberg Project is the most ambitious project underway on the Internet. Its objective is to digitise works and issue them via the Internet. Therefore the service is developing day by day, with new entries being added all the time. Dante's La Comédie is the 1,000th work thus digitised. It is accessible at the following addresses: **http://www.promo.net/pg, http://www.gutenberg. net** *or* **ftp://ftp.prairienet.org/pub/providers/gutenberg** *(download site).*

ATHENA
Raffaello Sanzio (1483-1520) Scuola di Atene.
Je sème un grain qui pourra un jour produire une moisson.
Voltaire (1694 - 1778), Traité sur la Tolérance (1763).

Figure 8.5 Consult digitised books from Athena.

Window shopping on the Web!

After ferreting through the bookshelves of libraries, you are going to be able to browse through the shelves and racks of the Web's virtual shops. And you will always be able to satisfy your hunger for knowledge by buying books!

While online shopping has been slow to develop in the UK, the United States is literally overflowing with this type of opportunity. And there is no shortage of shopping centres and different kinds of shop. Here too you need to find your feet and select the best services. The polemic surrounding payment guaranteed by bank card was inevitable, but one has to admit that it is no more risky today to buy online than to pay by credit card at a 'real' shop!

Our browsers now integrate the necessary functions for protected payment, so the risk of an ill-willed third party intercepting and using your card number, which is itself encrypted, is very slight.

Therefore you can buy (or rent) just about anything on the Net:

- products: books, clothing, cars;
- services: holiday lets;
- intangible products: electronic magazines, software, stock exchange transactions, etc.

Buying books

Books are some of the products best represented and most sold on the Net (other than computer products: hardware and software). You will have as much fun visiting these sites as ferreting in libraries. And as a bonus, you can order the works of your choice. Setting out to find an author, a forgotten title or a rare edition is a treat!

Waterstone's Online
http://www.waterstones.co.uk

One of the biggest names in High Street book sales is also on the Web, letting you browse titles by subject, read descriptions and buy online. You can carry out a simple search by typing the name of the author, book title or ISBN into the search field that appears on almost every page of the site. If this simple search doesn't turn up trumps, click the **Advanced Search** link. Advanced searches are made using any combination of:

- the author's name;
- the book's title;
- the subject;
- the ISBN;
- words descriptive of the book or subject;
- the publisher.

When you find the book you want, you can order it instantly by clicking the **Add To Basket** link alongside its title.

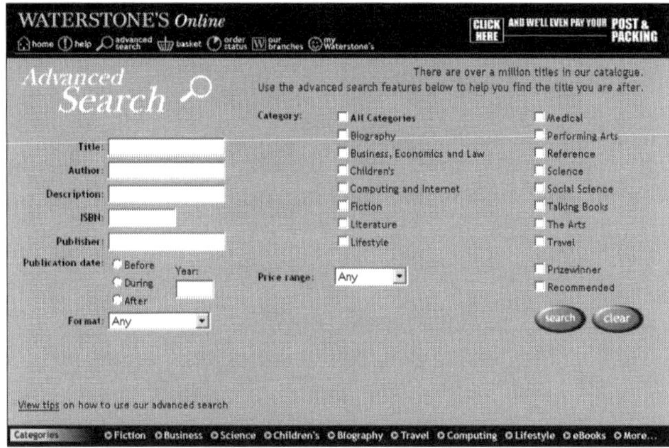

Figure 8.6 An 'Advanced Search' at Waterstone's.

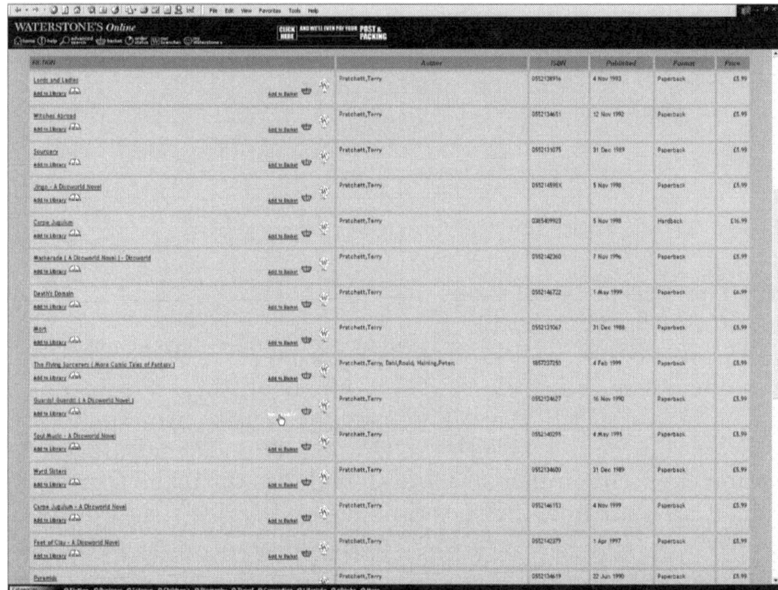

Figure 8.7 The results of a search for fantasy writer Terry Pratchett.

BOL
http://www.uk.bol.com

BOL was originally a US store named Books On-Line. It now has country-specific versions for France, Germany, Sweden and many others as well as this UK store, and has added music, video and DVD to its range of products. You can select the type of product you want from the 'tabs' at the top of the homepage, or browse through BOL's subject categories. Alternatively, run a quick search by book title, author, keywords or ISBN using the drop-down menu and text box at the top of every page.

BOL uses an easy-to-follow shopping basket metaphor for online purchasing. Click the **Add To Basket** icon for any book you want to order. You can then choose to continue browsing or go to the checkout to provide delivery and payment details.

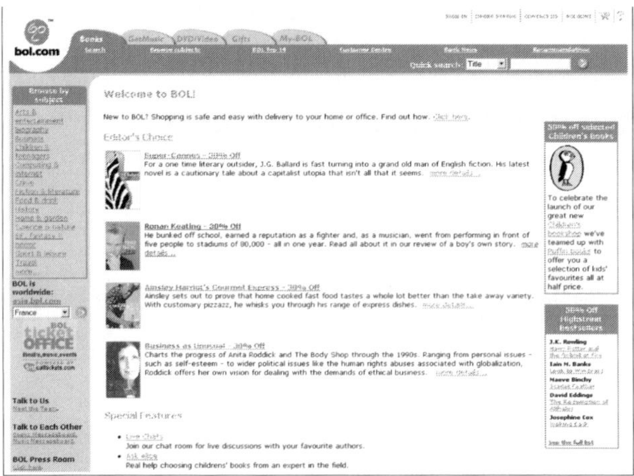

Figure 8.8 Run a quick search or browse by category at BOL.

iBS: The Internet Bookshop

http://www.bookshop.co.uk

iBS is part of the well-known High Street store WH Smith, and has one of the country's largest online bookstores with over 1.4 million UK and US titles. The usual options to browse by category or run a quick search are there, along with a Full Search option. This comprehensive search includes the usual search criteria (title, author, ISBN, publisher and series title), but also allows you to choose how the results should be presented, with options such as:

- Price (cheapest first);
- Alphabetically by Title;
- Publication date (most recent first).

Amazon.com

http://www.amazon.co.uk

With more than 2.5 million books online, Amazon has become the indisputable reference point for anybody wanting to buy a book on the Web. Even the rarest editions or books which are out of print are sold, although the service requires six months to track down a rare work. When the book is found, a price quotation will be sent by e-mail. You can then decide whether or not to buy the work in question.

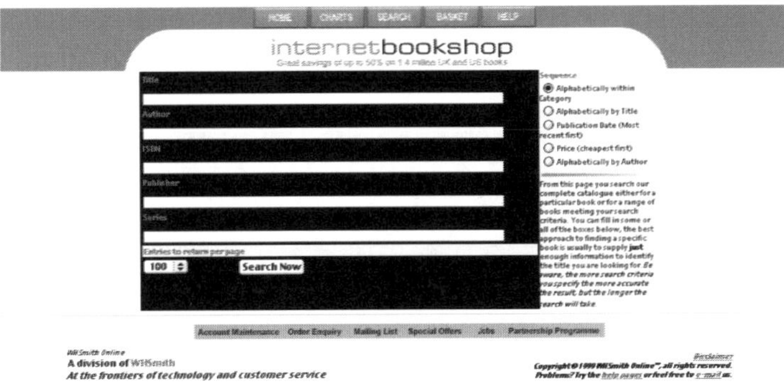

Figure 8.9 The Full Search page at iBS.

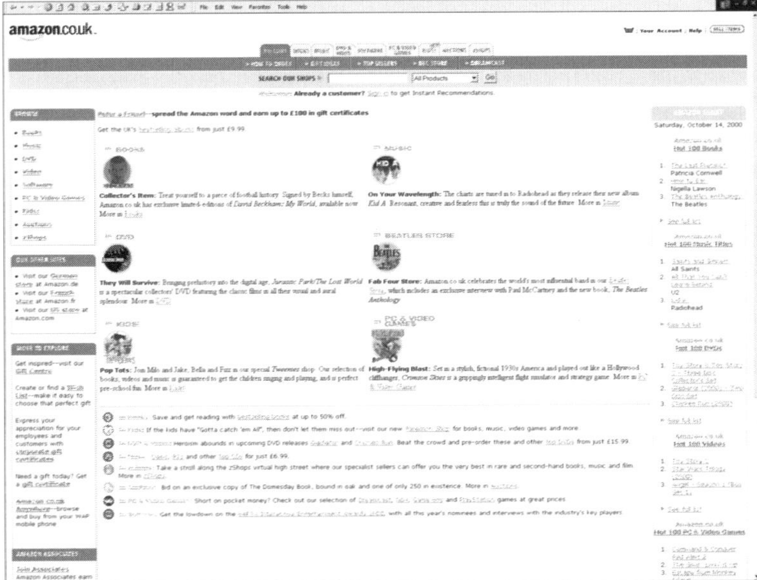

Figure 8.10 Welcome to Amazon, the largest virtual bookshop on the Web.

Research is by keyword or subject. Readers can give their opinion on a work, just like authors and publishers, which is an excellent way of enriching the information base.

Amazon offers numerous services, some of which are as commonplace as choosing the wrapping paper for a gift. But it is these little extras that end up making a site a success.

Barnes and Noble
http://www.barnesandnoble.com/
With more than one million references, the virtual shop window of the famous publisher is highly attractive.

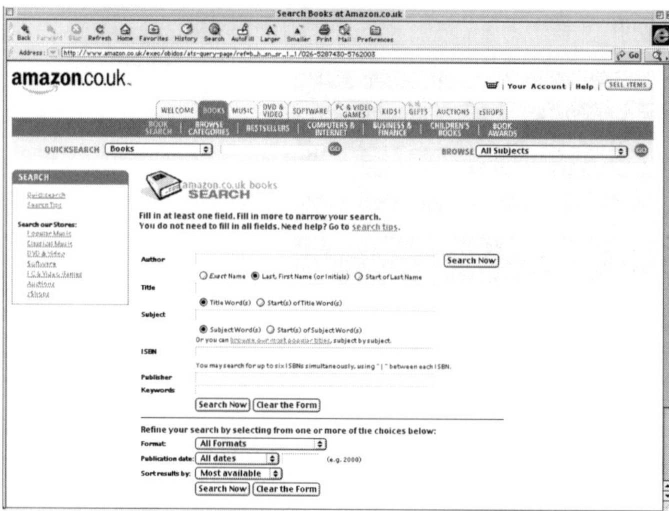

Figure 8.11 The search data entry form using Amazon.co.uk.

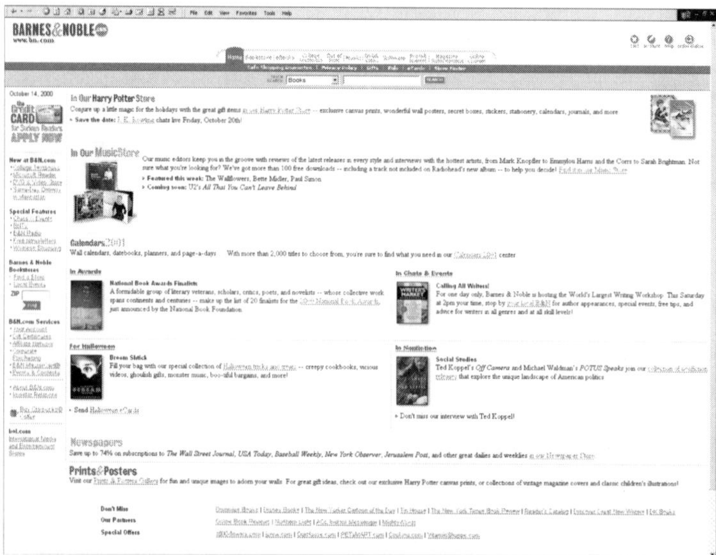

Figure 8.12 The home page of the Barnes and Noble virtual bookshop.

As always, searching is by category, title or author's name, or even by keyword. Just check the box of a work to add it to your virtual trolley before entering ordering mode.

Search: Books

Please select at least one search criteria.
Fill in one or more of the fields below:
Title of Book

Author's Name
Cave, Nick
Keywords

Search | Clear Fields | Search Tips

You can narrow your search by selecting one or more options below:
Price: all prices | Format: all formats
Age: all age ranges | Subjects: all subjects

You can also search by ISBN
ISBN
Search ISBN

Figure 8.13 The Barnes and Noble books search engine.

Book Search Results
We found **9** titles from author **Cave, Nick**.

Below are 1 - 9 of the 9 titles sorted in **bestselling order**.
Re-sort this list in A-Z by Title or Publication Date order.

1. Gray Ghosts and Lefty's Deceiver
Bob Newman (Editor) / Hardcover / Sycamore Island Books / May 1999
Add to Cart

2. King Ink II
Nick Cave / Paperback / Two Thirteen Sixty-one Publications / August 1997
Add to Cart

3. The Gospel According to Mark
Apostle Mark, Barry Hannah (Introduction) / Paperback / Grove/Atlantic, Inc. / March 1999
Add to Cart

Figure 8.14 The result of a search at Barnes and Noble.

Shops On The Net

http://www.shopsonthenet.co.uk

Hundreds of virtual shops at the click of a mouse button. Browse through 34 categories of shops and services, or run a quick keyword search for either a particular shop or a product by clicking the appropriate button beside the search field.

UK Shopping City

http://www.ukshops.co.uk/enter.shtml

The UK Shopping City is a large virtual shopping centre with a number of areas including Retail, Travel and Property. You can browse by selecting an area and touring the different levels of the shopping centre where you'll find some of the biggest High Street names, including Marks and Spencer, Interflora, Argos, Comet and Dixons.

Using the traditional search engines to find shops

*For example, Web Crawler (**http://webcrawler.com/Shopping/**) offers a search of online shopping sites. You thus have hundreds of virtual shops at the click of a mouse, classified by product type. You can find many popular shops: Barnes and Noble for books, Disney Store, CD Now, etc.*

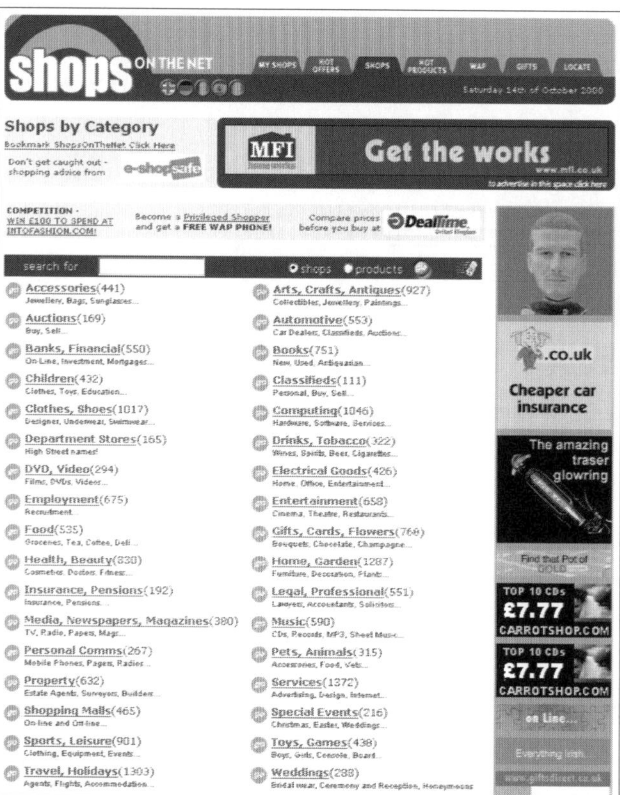

Figure 8.15 The home page of the Shops On The Net shopping directory.

Figure 8.16 Level 1 of the UK Shopping City's Retail area.

9 'Surfing' guides

How to surf

Discovering Web site compilations and guides

Visting top sites

Browsing the whole world

Searching in any language

How to surf

Surfing isn't a search method in the strict sense, of course, but surfing guides make good starting points for finding the best Web sites. This process clearly relies much more on trial and error, or pure luck, but if you find the precision of search queries tiresome, let yourself be guided and ride the wave!

Figure 9.1 The Cool Site of the Day home page.

Cool Site of the Day

http://cool.infi.net/

This selection, made by Glenn Davis of Infinet, is without doubt one of the best starting points on the Web. Each day you can discover a new 'Cool Site'.

Excite Search Voyeur

http://www.excite.com/search/voyeur

Excite's Search Voyeur service displays a list of 10 queries that users are currently searching for at Excite. This list automatically updates every 30 seconds to bring you constant selections of the latest searches. If any search query seems interesting, just click it to run the same search yourself. An ideal way to add a touch of adventure to your surfing!

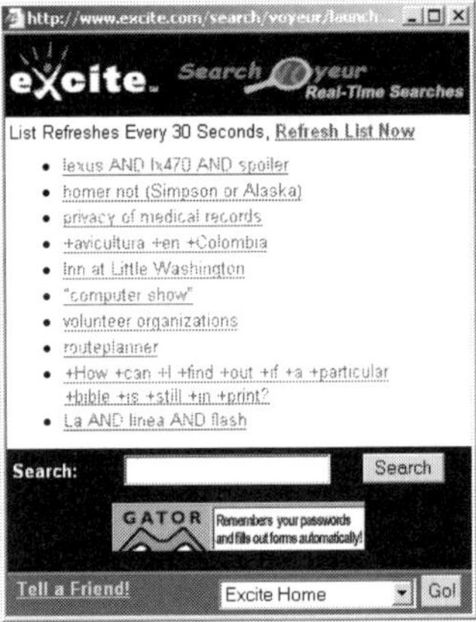

Figure 9.2 Let yourself by guided by Excite Search Voyeur.

Discovering Web site compilations and guides

Guides offer rational surfing. They generally include access by subject and search tools. On the Web, everybody, or nearly everybody, draws up lists of sites to visit and all this may more or less resemble a guide. You will find lists of good addresses on the home pages of other surfers. In the light of this profusion of guides, which we have had the opportunity to present during previous chapters, we have decided to be restrained (for once!) and provide you with just one good address.

Compilations to visit

- *Top 50 UK Web Sites:* **http://www.top50.co.uk**
- *PC Magazine's Top 100:* **http://www.zdnet.com/pcmag/special/web100**
- *The Weekly Hot 100:* **http://www.100hot.com**

MSN Directory

http://search.msn.co.uk

The MSN Directory, published by Microsoft, lists hundreds of top sites for UK surfers in over 50 categories. To browse the directory after arriving at this page, either choose one of the major categories (in bold type) to see the top picks, or select a subcategory (in plain type) to see sites specific to that category.

In many of the categories you'll find not only links to top Web sites but direct links to the top news stories in the national or computing press, reviews of the latest computing products, special offers from UK shopping sites, and many other time-saving links.

Visiting top sites

On the Web you will find all kinds of Web site classification, such as:

- classifications carried out by surfers who choose the best sites;
- classifications prepared by professional teams (cyber-journalists);
- classifications prepared by software based on how often a site is visited, generally known as hits.

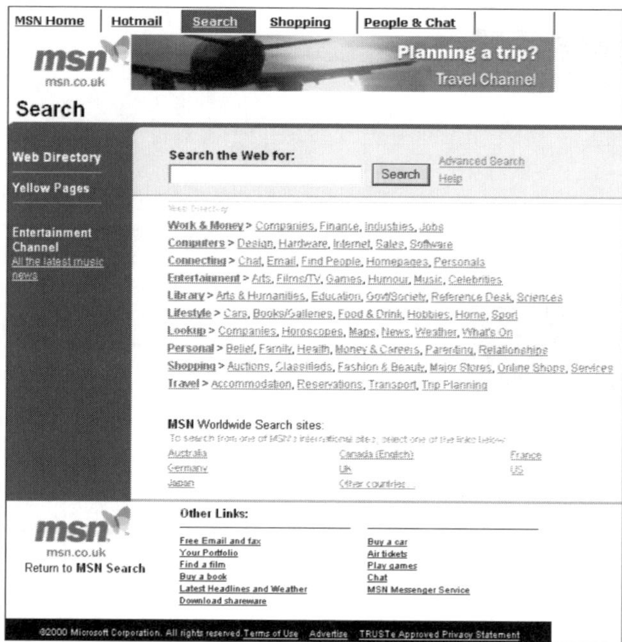

Figure 9.3 Hundreds of ready-sorted links and searches at MSN Directory.

Here are two examples:

Lycos Top 5%
http://www.pointcom.com/
The best of the Web by the Lycos team.

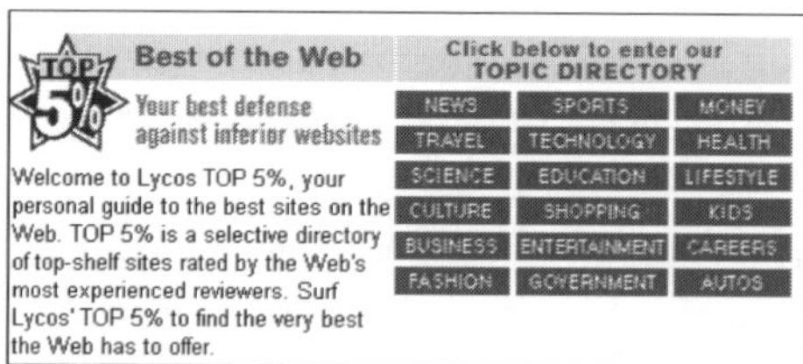

Figure 9.4 Lycos' Top 5%.

Top10Links
http://www.top10links.com
The best sites on the Web in over 1,000 ready-sorted categories.

Figure 9.5 The Top10Links page.

Browsing the whole world

You have had the opportunity to travel the world using the large international search engines. If you want to go further still on your trip into cyberspace, there is an impressive number of specialist tools which will take you from one country to another with ease. A world tour in the space of a few clicks!

Matilda

http://www.aaa.com.au/images/logos/searches/world/

This travelling search engine comes to us from Australia. With more than 200 countries listed and endowed with specific search mechanisms for each of them, Matilda is worth discovering.

You will be astonished to note that lists of hits provide very specific information, including the target audience and even the site's popularity!

Woyaa!

Http://www.woyaa.com

Woyaa! is a specialist search engine for Africa, with subject entries (arts, society, culture, etc.) or keyword searching. A considerable number of sites are listed, and if you want to carry out research into the African continent, this is where to start.

As a bonus, the site offers you Net Radio Earthbeat so you can surf to music!

The Virtual Tourist

http://www.vtourist.com/webmap/

Click on the globe and then on the map of the region of the world selected. You then access specific resources for the country chosen, in English or in the language of the country in question.

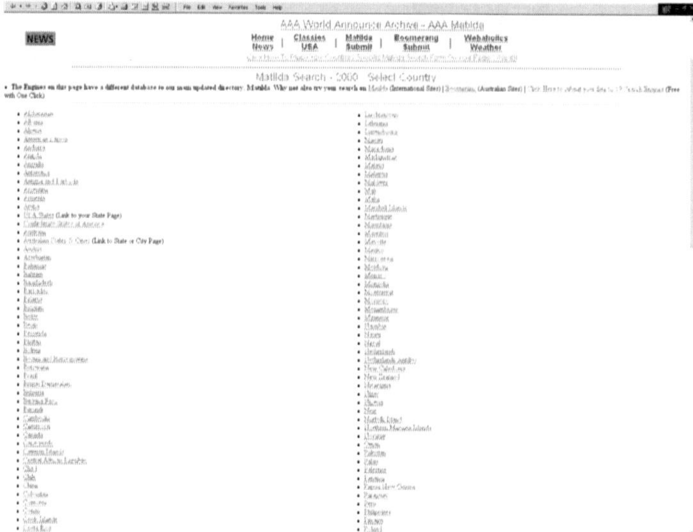

Figure 9.6 The choice of countries offered by Matilda.

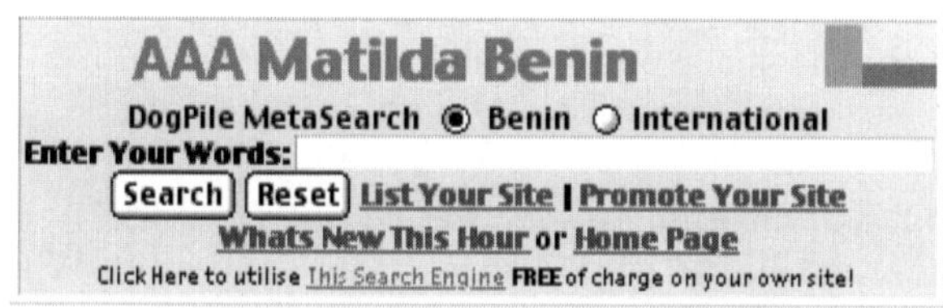

Figure 9.7 Searching by country with Matilda; in this case, Benin.

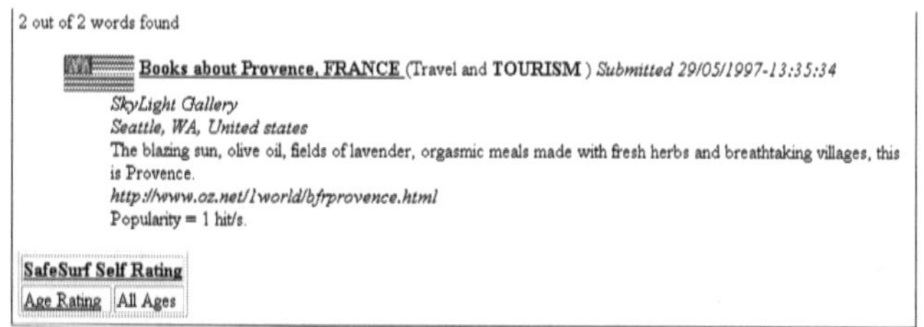

Figure 9.8 An answer from Matilda.

Searching in any language

What we offer here is a selection of languages and sites. A quick tour of the Web to allow you to glimpse its wealth. Also, you must set the parameters of your browser for it to correctly display the characters of the various languages.

Figure 9.9 The home page of the African search engine Woyaa!

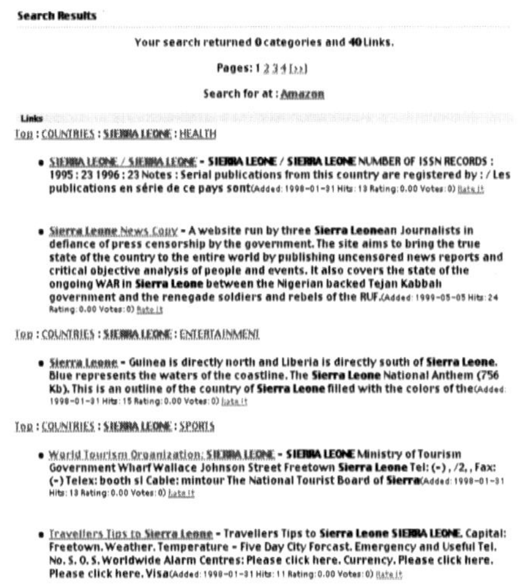

Figure 9.10 The result of a search on the keyword 'Sierra Leone'.

In all languages

EuroSeek

http://www.euroseek.net/page?ifl=uk

This is a remarkable search tool which allows you to target a search on a given country and also to choose the answers (target sites) in the language of your choice. 40 languages are offered, classified in alphabetical order from Bulgarian (Balgarski) to Turkish (Türkçe)!

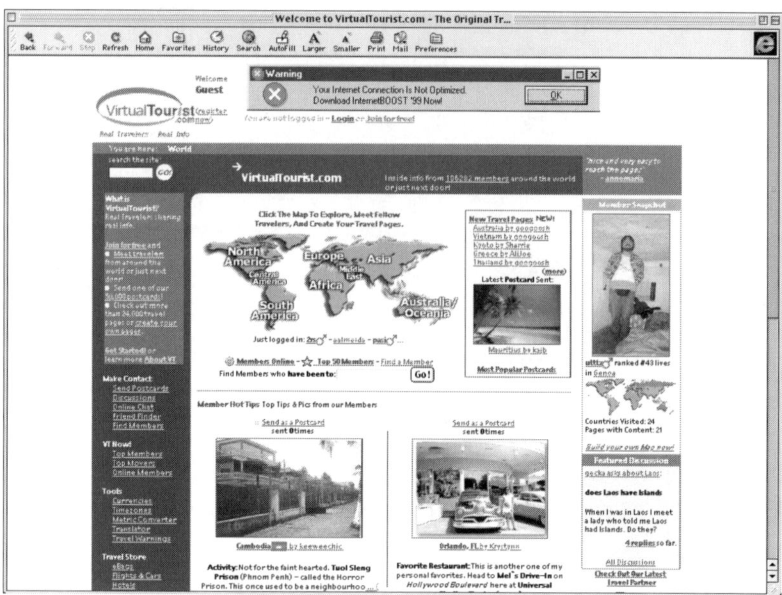

Figure 9.11 Click on the world map to access a continent or a country.

Figure 9.12 Access to Europe.

Figure 9.13 Here, access to the countries of South America.

Figure 9.14 Searching throughout all the countries and in all the languages of Europe.

In English, for non-English speaking countries

Russia on the Net

http://www.ru/

The home page of Russia on the Net is shown in Figure 9.15.

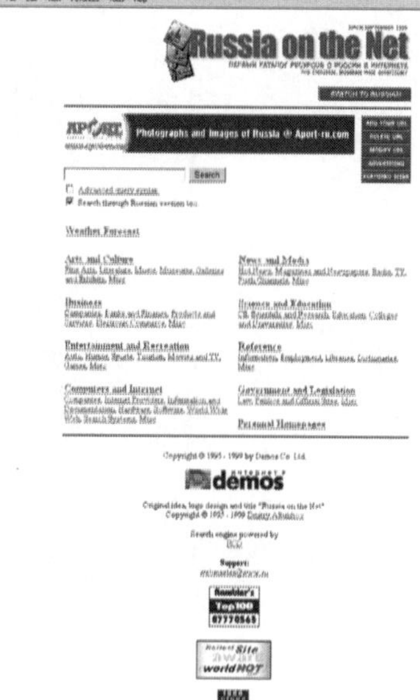

Figure 9.15 Searching sites in Russia.

Jewish Communication Network
http://www.jcn18.com/scripts/jcn18/paper/query.asp

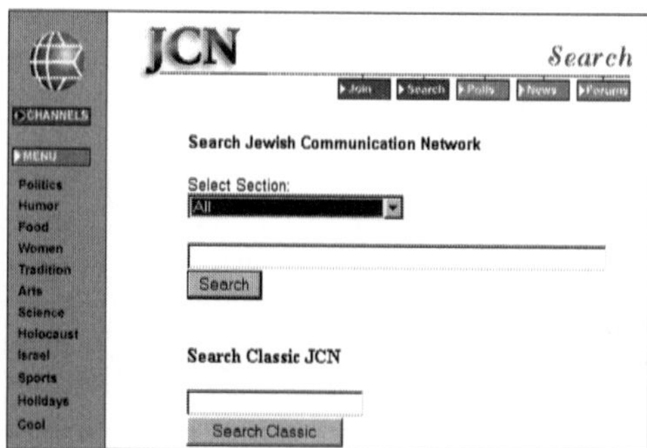

Figure 9.16 A search tool for the Jewish community.

Indonesia Net
http://www.indonesianet.com/search.htm

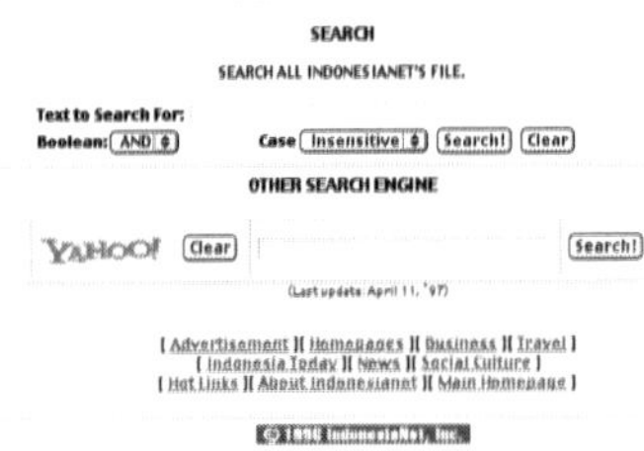

Figure 9.17 Searching in Indonesia.

In Austrian

Austrian Home Page Search Engine

http://www.aco.net/Server-in-AT/

Plain text searching.

Figure 9.18 Searching for Austrian sites.

Austronaut

http://austronaut.at/url.ims

Searching by URL or keyword.

In Danish

Jubii

http://www.jubii.dk

Searching by keyword and by subject.

In Spanish

University of Cordoba

http://www.uco.es/

In Portuguese

University of Aveiro

http://www.ua.pt/

Figure 9.19 Searching in Danish.

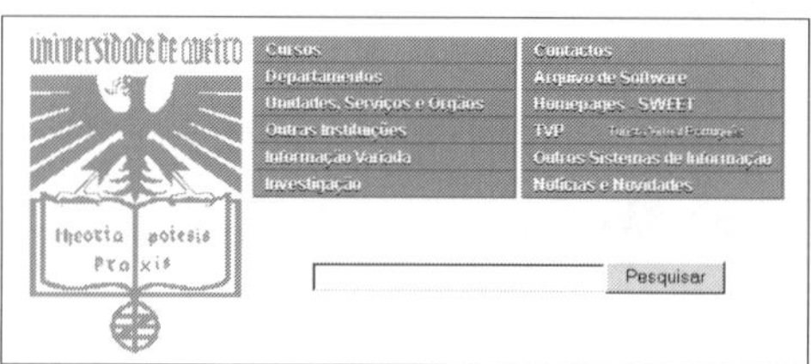

Figure 9.20 Searching in Portuguese.

10 Searching the media

Getting back to the source with press agencies

Rummaging through newspapers and magazines

Searching the international media

Searching in the media is a highly efficient way of finding information on the Web. Here 'media' is taken to mean all the traditional large-scale media (press, radio, television) with Web links, but also cybermedia which have developed on the Web.

Having made this distinction, it must be said that the traditional media have managed to assert themselves on the Web, while many cybermedia have yet to prove themselves.

Online media offer the latest news items and also open up their archives for searching. A new track for finding information!

Getting back to the source with press agencies

If you are interested in current affairs, start here. You can obtain information well before the evening television news. And above all, you can find dispatches from all over the world. On the Internet, you choose what you want to receive, and you are not governed by the choices made by professionals in the world of communications. But beware, some services are, quite legitimately, subject to a fee.

Ananova
http://www.ananova.com
This UK Press Association Web site should be your first port of call to find the latest national, international and business news stories. A 'StoryFinder' service allows you to run a keyword search for news articles, optionally selecting an area of the UK or a particular topic to narrow the search.

Reuters
http://www.reuters.com
This is one of the largest press agencies in the world, and the service offered by the Web is high quality. The options for searching by subject are particularly attractive. For this you use the drop-down list above the Products button.

Computer Wire
http://www.computerwire.com/
Computer Wire is a press agency specialising in information technology (IT). The site even allows you to create your personalised information letter. The Search tool allows you to search using several criteria in the archives of magazines devoted to computers and telecommunications.

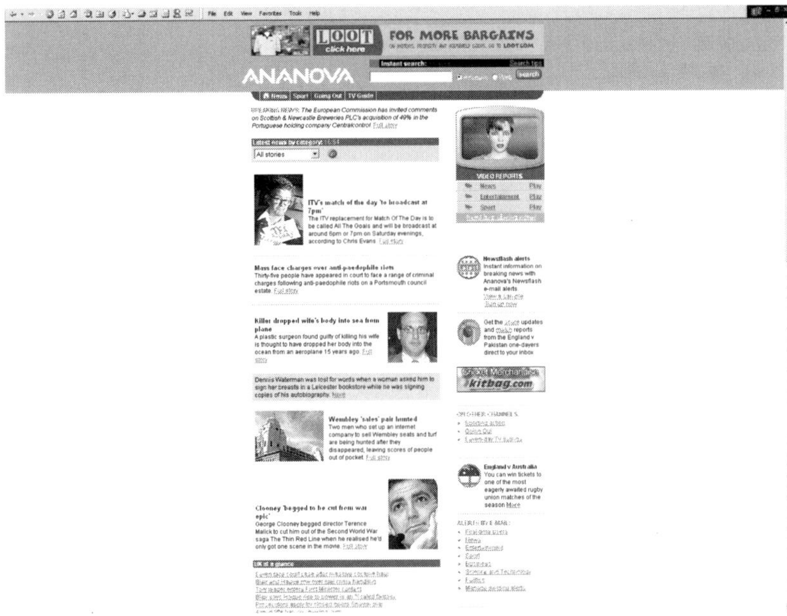

Figure 10.1 Catch the breaking news stories first at Ananova.

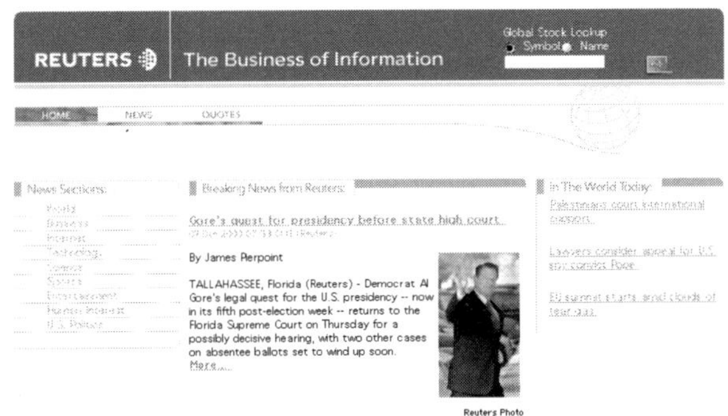

Figure 10.2 The Reuters agency opens its doors to you.

Rummaging through newspapers and magazines

If you want to find a news item or article, then consult the Web sites of the large dailies and explore their archives when they are available online. You can even set up electronic press reviews. You need to identify good sources and learn to rummage around, searching by criteria or in plain text mode (the technique of indexing all significant words contained in an article). Head for the archives!

Finding press agencies with Yahoo!

To go even further, you can use Yahoo! to ask for a list of the world's press agencies. The address is: **http://dir.yahoo.com/Business_and_Economy/Business_to_Business/News_and_Media/News_Service.**

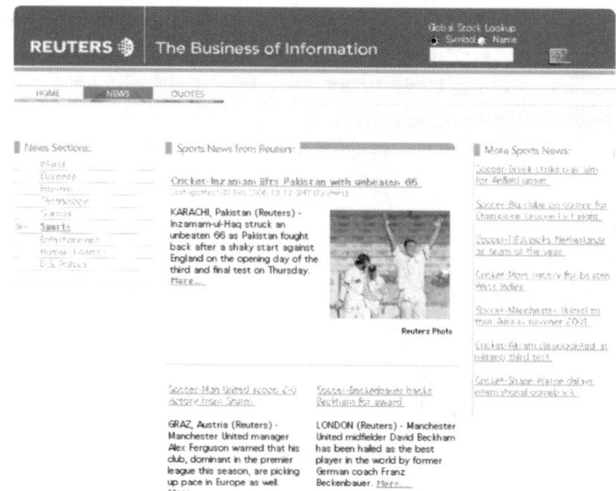

Figure 10.3 Searching for sports news items.

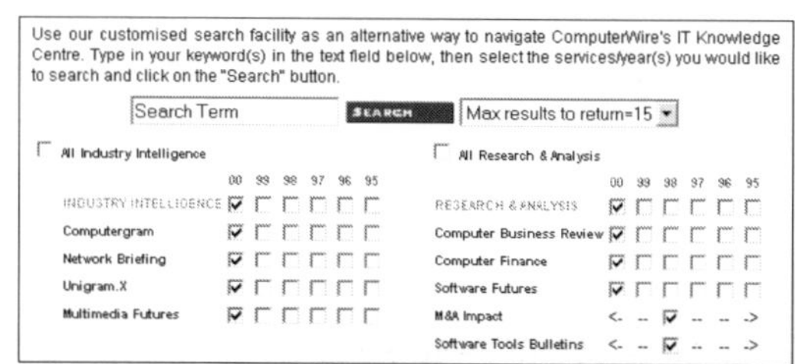

Figure 10.4 Searching through the archives with Computer Wire.

The Electronic Telegraph
http://www.telegraph.co.uk

The online edition of the popular *Daily Telegraph* allows searching of its news archives dating back to 1994, along with separate databases covering travel reports and book reviews. To use this service, you will first need to register with the site. Registration is quick and free, and simply involves providing some personal details. You can then choose a personal user name and password which provide access to the archives.

The search options allow you to:

- search for names (using initial capitals) or keywords;
- specify a particular year, month or date;
- narrow your search to a single section.

When searching by section, you can hold down the **Ctrl** key to select multiple sections for searching.

Results are presented in a list comprising:

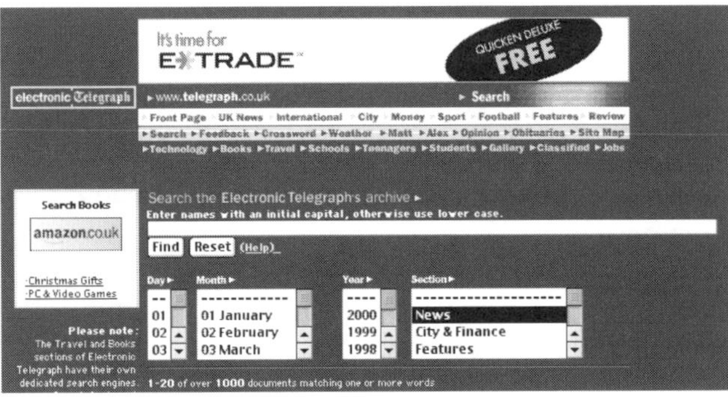

Figure 10.5 Searching for articles in the Electronic Telegraph.

- the date;
- the headline of the article; and
- a relevance score in percent.

Just click on the headline to open the article.

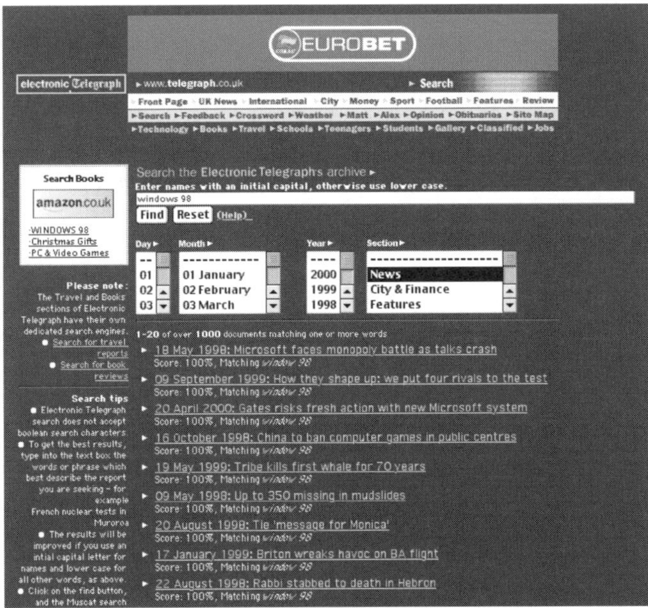

Figure 10.6 The results of an Electronic Telegraph search using the keywords 'Windows 98'.

The Times

http://www.thetimes.co.uk

As the search page itself explains, there are four ways to search The Times. Simple and Advanced searches let you search the current edition of The Times online; an Archive search allows searching for articles in past issues; and a Back Issues search helps you find an entire online edition.

The Guardian/The Observer
http://www.guardian.co.uk
Although its archives date back only to September 1998, The Guardian's search options are more powerful than those of some of its rivals. Searches automatically cover both Guardian and Observer archives in the period you select, and results can be sorted by date or by relevance to your keywords. You can also choose to display only the first paragraph of matching articles, making it easy to see whether you've found what you were looking for.

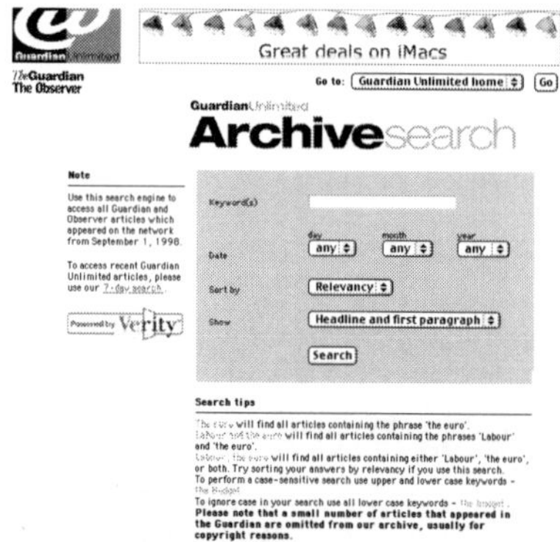

Figure 10.7 Search Guardian and Observer archives using Boolean and case-sensitive keywords.

The Financial Times
http://www.ft.com
Visit the TotalSearch section of the site to search over 10 million articles from a number of business and financial sources dating back to 1996. Among the many search options available, you can:

- choose whether to search in articles' headlines, text or both;
- choose the types of publication to search or pick a single publication (such as the FT itself) from a list of over 3,000;
- search a particular financial sector (such as Banking or Media);
- search by region (such as UK & Ireland or North America).

Searching the international media

There are thousands of titles to discover on the Web. It is not easy to find your way, but information is there somewhere. Here too we will restrict ourselves to a selection of the main titles on the Web (such as *The Washington Post*), or new media (such as MSNBC). While traditional media are sometimes reproached for giving disinformation, one could accuse the Web of over-information. For this reason the search tools and filters which it allows you to use are helpful. That is also why it may be useful to target a few good addresses to serve as a starting point for looking for specific information.

Figure 10.8 The world's financial news at your fingertips, courtesy of the Financial Times.

MSNBC

http://www.msnbc.com/

Born out of collaboration between ABC and MSN (Microsoft Network), as soon as you reach the site MSNBC offers to install a news browser. This plug-in for your browser will be of use to you in looking at international current affairs.

Beware: you will need a fast computer in order to benefit fully from this very multimedia site.

The Washington Post

http://www.washingtonpost.com/

When you have the front page online, you can:

- select a section from the drop-down list;
- activate the paper's index;
- start the search engine.

It is best to search for articles over the last fortnight, but you can restrict this time band.

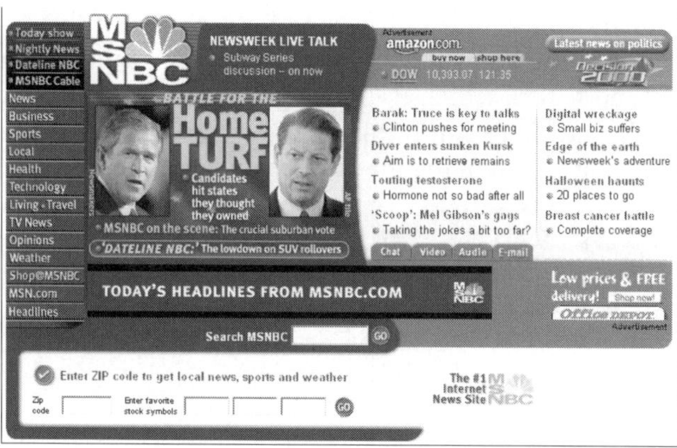

Figure 10.9 Welcome to MSNBC.

The search page also gives access to:

- the news dispatches of the AP (Associated Press) agency;
- a multitude of databases in the business, leisure and entertainment domain.

You can also search for news by country. 220 countries are listed and if you type 'France', for example, you will access a front page relating to France which is particularly rich. You can also travel the entire world!

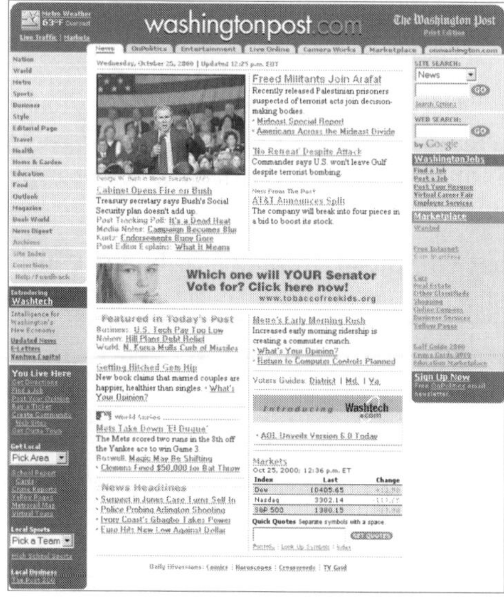

Figure 10.10 The Washington Post home page.

Search Washingtonpost.com
News from The Post | News from the AP | The Post Archives
Entertainment | Shopping | Jobs | Politics | Stocks | Mutual Funds
Yellow Pages | Country News | Weather Forecasts
Enter Keyword(s): Go
News – 14 days of The Washington Post
AP – Breaking news from the Associated Press, updated every minute
Post Archives – Stories back to 1977 (full text available for a fee)
Entertainment – Places and events from our Entertainment Guide
Shopping – Buy the perfect gift for yourself or others
Jobs – Job listings, including classifieds from The Washington Post
Yellow Pages – Business listings from across the Washington Metro area
Search News from The Post
Find articles printed in The Washington Post during the past 14 days. Articles appear in chronological order. This search will soon include stories in The Post's PM Extra and some content produced by washingtonpost.com and its partners.
Any Word(s) in the Article:
Headline:
Author:
Page (i.e. A01): Date Range: 14 Go
Search News from AP
Find articles written by the Associated Press during the past 14 days. The AP frequently sends out multiple versions, and most of these articles were not published in the newspaper. To browse the complete wire, just hit "go." Articles appear in chronological order.
Any Word(s) in the Article:
Headline:
Date Range: 14 Go

Figure 10.11 Searching for articles in The Washington Post.

The Chicago Tribune

http://www.chicago.tribune.com/

The Chicago Tribune is another heavyweight of the media with sophisticated search tools. The online version allows you to search its archives going back to 1985.

You can ask for the following results to be sorted:

- date;
- relevance;
- frequency of appearance of the keyword.

You can search in relation to a specific year, or search through all the archives. It is possible in this way to obtain nearly 3,000 published articles which include the word 'Microsoft'. For each article you get a summary. You will have to click the heading in order to obtain the full version.

An international videotex service on your PC!

*Webdo, a Swiss magazine, offers an impressive list of online media (**http://www.presseweb.ch**). You search by country and have access to thousands of titles!*

*Also take a close look at Chaplin's News (**http://www. geocities. com/Heartland/ 2308/**). The list of subjects is impressive.*

*Use Net Media (**http://www.go-public.com/netmedia/**) if you want to search by country.*

*Or again, with classification by country, The Inkternational News Link (**http://inkpot.com/news/**).*

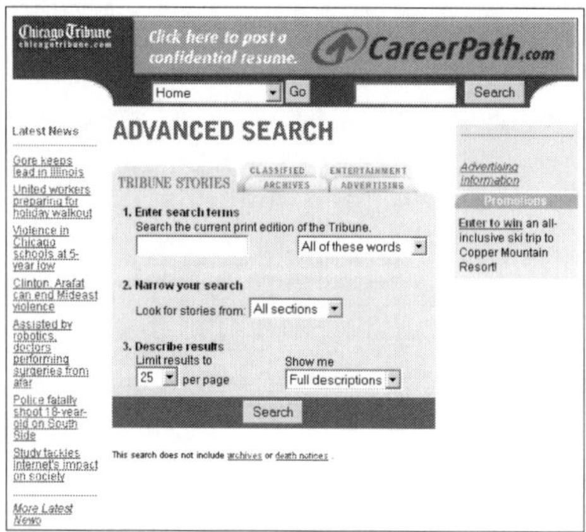

Figure 10.12 Searching for articles in the Chicago Tribune.

11 'Push' technologies

Using personalised newspapers

Receiving information by e-mail

While we have learned to 'pull' information from the Web in the first ten chapters of this book, the final chapter will be devoted to push techniques. This time we do not go to the information, the information comes to us; it is 'pushed' onto our PC.

This method of receiving information adds a few new possibilities to the way you use the Web. You can:

- define your own preferences and receive personalised newspapers and magazines containing only what interests you;
- have information delivered automatically by e-mail;
- use helper applications and other intelligent programs which ferret through the Web for you.

With 'push' technologies, the Web is trying to match the media (which broadcast information), but the major difference between push and pull technology is that with push, the information may be personalised. This is one of the key aspects of service and media on the Internet.

Using personalised newspapers

Consulting a newspaper whose front page and articles are intended for you personally is not just a dream. On the Web there are many services which allow you to define your tastes and preferences. Knowing your profile, these services will then be able to deliver truly personalised information.

Crayon

http://crayon.net/

With Crayon, step by step you can construct your own live daily newspaper free of charge. Choose a password, and then proceed with the choice of a title, formatting, headings, links with information sources, etc.

Two design modes are available:

- standard mode, which scans all information sources in detail;
- quick mode, for the basics (it uses American zip codes to deliver regional information to US users).

By preference use standard mode and select:

- headings (world, tech, science, religion, Web, etc.) by clicking on the colour crayons at the foot of the page;
- information sources included under a heading by checking the media which interest you.

You can also add your suggested information sources. Finally, click on the '**Create my own newspaper now**' button when you are ready!

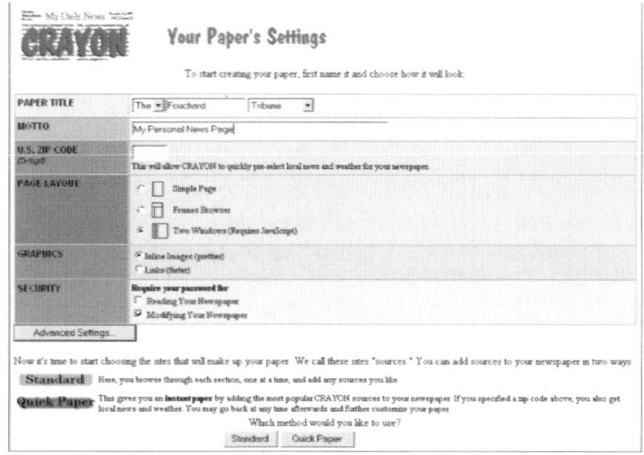

Figure 11.1 Crayon is useful for personalising your newspaper.

Then select the hierarchy of your headings (the different sections about which you have already given information). Click on '**Publish my newspaper**' and it is done. The paper can be consulted immediately. Do not forget to save the page in your Favorites in order to access it easily in future.

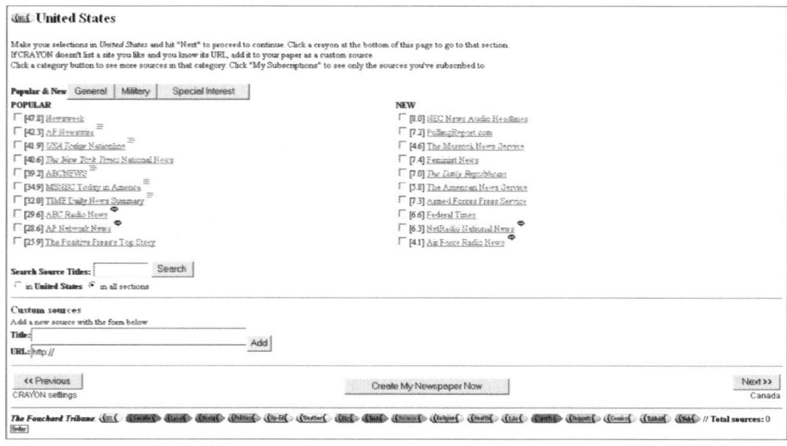

Figure 11.2 The interactive design of a personalised newspaper.

MyYahoo

http://edit.my.yahoo.com/config/login

The famous search engine also offers an *à la carte* information service. Here too you can create your own personalised paper incorporating, for example:

- stock exchange information;
- sports results;
- international current affairs;

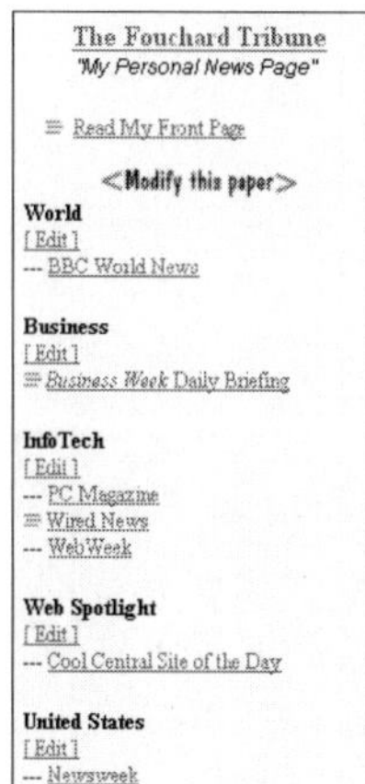

Figure 11.3 The front page of a personal newspaper.

- Web resources;
- and much more!

Follow the step-by-step instructions. From weather reports to computers via sports or television, the list of headings is enormous. Then, MyYahoo takes care of the content and you just have to plug into your daily newspaper. If you are permanently connected to the Internet, you can receive information on your desk in real time. Otherwise, you can download software, News Ticker, which will enable you to access the information with just one click.

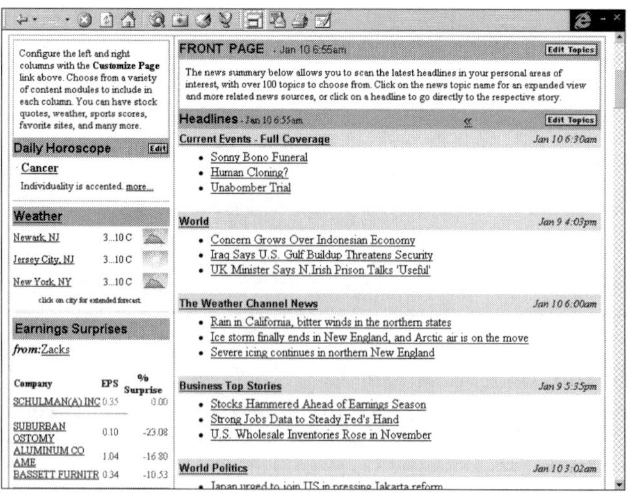

Figure 11.4 An example of a personalised paper using MyYahoo.

Excite

http//www.excite.com/Info/

Yahoo! is not the only search engine that tracks down information for you. Excite offers a similar service with 14 subject channels at your disposal. After identifying yourself, you choose your channels. The Web pages offered can be customised to your requirements.

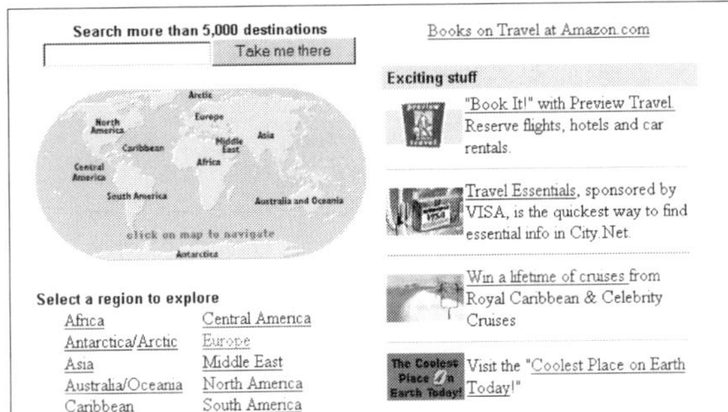

Figure 11.5 Searching Excite's Travel channel – 5,000 possible destinations!

News Tracker

http://nt.excite.com/

This is a new service with the Excite hallmark, which allows you to keep track of current affairs. This gigantic information service compiles more than 300 sources. All current affairs are covered, including computer news. As with a search engine, you can search for information by indicating a few keywords. You can create your 'personalised newspaper' by defining your areas of interest.

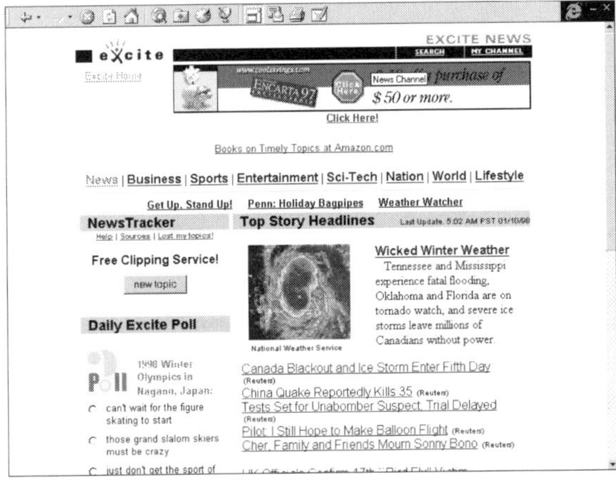

Figure 11.6 An extract from the News Tracker search page.

NewsHub

http://www.newshub.com/tech/

This is not, strictly speaking, a personalised newspaper. NewsHub will track down the titles of the largest information sources in the hi-tech domain every 15 minutes. If you want a lower frequency, you can indicate this under Preferences.

Thus, NewsHub gathers only computer news by scanning information that you can find on sites such as Yahoo!'s Tech, Nando InfoTech, Tec Wire, Gina I-Wire, InfoWorld, PC Week, ZD-net, ComputerWorld or Wired, to name but a few.

Receiving information by e-mail

A very easy way of tracking down information is to subscribe to e-mail delivery services, of which there are many on the Web. Use them, as they are often very helpful. But do not overuse them or your mail box will be snowed under. You can always cancel a subscription by sending a command along the lines of 'unsubscribe' to the server.

Figure 11.7 NewsHub tracks down information for you.

InBox Direct

http://home.netscape.com/ibd

This service offered by Netscape, the publisher of the browser with the same name, allows you to receive information directly to your e-mail in-box. You just have to choose the publications, classified by heading, which interest you. They will then be delivered to you by e-mail in HTML format. Just check that your messaging software accepts this format (the latest generation software does accept this format, e.g. Netscape Communicator and Internet Explorer 4.0 or 5.0).

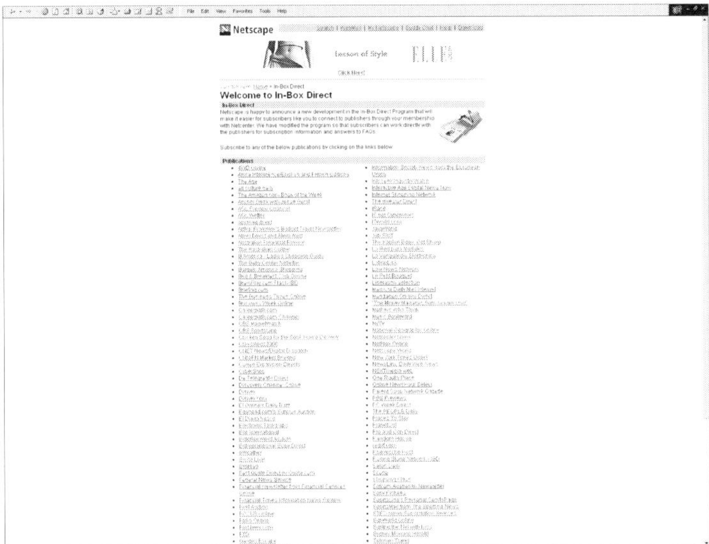

Figure 11.8 The home page of the InBox Direct messaging service.

Slate

http://www.slate.com

This magazine, which belongs to Microsoft, was not designed to relay computer news. It is a general magazine which covers politics as well as culture or leisure.

You can use Slate in three ways:

- just consult the Web site;
- leave your e-mail and you will receive the titles of the articles when they appear. This enables you to go to the site only when you have found interesting articles;
- ask to automatically receive the full edition of Slate in your mail box. You will then receive a file in Word format which you can consult on screen or print.

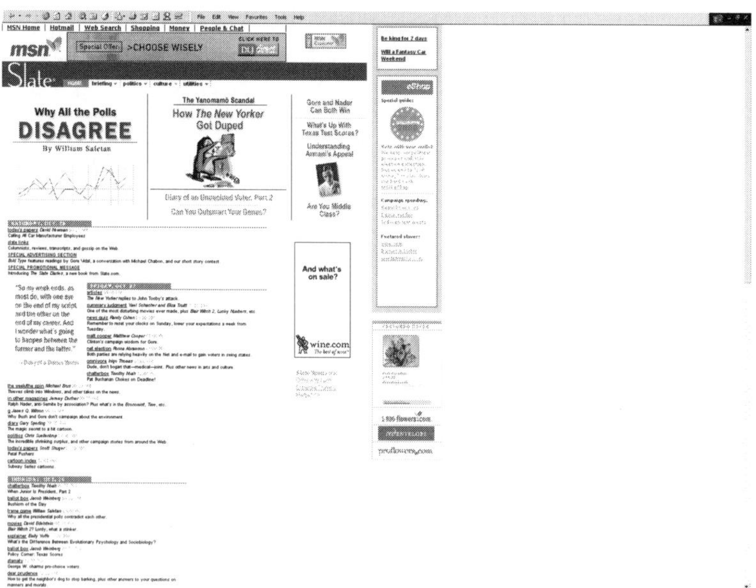

Figure 11.9 Use the Utilities menu to discover the possibilities of the Slate magazine.

International mailing lists

To find international mailing lists, visit the Listz site ***(http://www.liszt.com/)****. It offers more than 80,000 mailing lists. You can search by keyword or by subject. Also worth a visit is the Publicly Availably Mailing Lists site at* ***http://www.paml.net.***

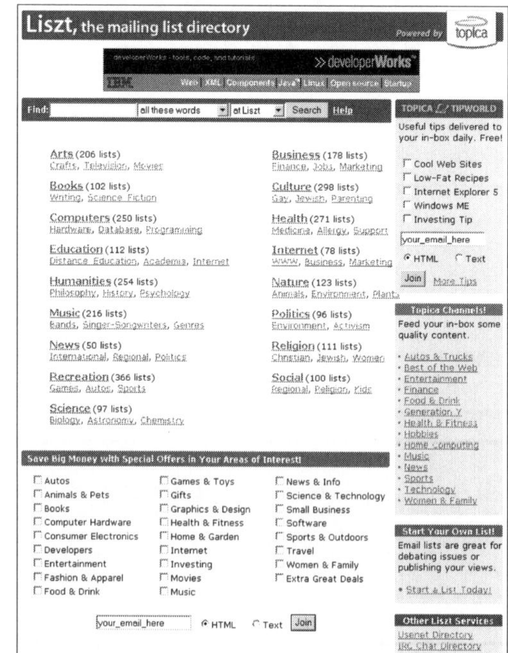

Figure 11.10 Searching for worldwide mailing lists.

A simple guide to

building a website

Rob Young

Acknowledgements

We are grateful to the following for permission to reproduce copyright material:

Figure 1.1 UK Plus (Associated New Media); Figure 1.3 NetObjects, Inc.; Figures 2.2, 5.4, 5.6, 7.1, 7.2, 7.6, 8.3, 8.4, 9.2 and 9.3 Netscape Communications Corporation. Netscape browser window © 1999 Netscape Communications Corporate. Used with permission. Netscape Communications has not authorized, sponsored, endorsed, or approved this publication and is not responsible for its content; Figures 6.1, 6.2 and 6.3 courtesy of JASC Software, Inc.; Figure 10.2 Net Benefit plc (www.domainsnet.com).

While every effort has been made to trace the owners of copyright material, in a few cases this has proved impossible and we take this opportunity to offer our apologies to any copyright holders whose rights we have unwittingly infringed.

Introduction

From the moment you start surfing the World Wide Web, you realise it's unique. After all, where else can you find a never-ending supply of information, entertainment and services, all instantly available from the comfort of your own home? But the Web is unique in other ways too, and those tend to sink in a bit more slowly.

- Most of the pages you find on the Web are written by ordinary people like you and me.
- Anyone can put a site on the Web which could potentially be seen by hundreds of millions of people around the world.
- Pages you publish can cover almost any subject you like, and can include pictures, animations, sounds, and interactive tools like guestbooks and chat rooms.
- A website is *dynamic* – you can change it or add to it at any time you like.
- All this is free! (Okay, there are a few 'extras' that could cost you money if you decide you want them, but if you've got an Internet connection you can get a website up and running without paying a single penny.)

In this book, you'll learn how to design your own website using the two building blocks of Web design – a pair of easy-to-use text languages called HTML and CSS. We'll start off simply, with one basic Web page, and gradually introduce new items and features. Along the way you'll find plenty of copy-and-use examples, and I'll point you towards useful sites where you can find any software you need. Finally I'll show you how to get your site on to the Web for the world to see – and how to tell the world it's there!

In the appendices at the back of the book you'll find handy references to turn to while you're designing your site, along with a list of useful websites offering information, tutorials, free services and extra content to spice up your own site.

Icons

This icon introduces handy shortcuts and tips such as keyboard hotkeys, expert options, and quicker ways of getting to the same place.

This icon warns you of any risks associated with a particular action, or any problems you might encounter along the way, and (where possible) shows you how to avoid them.

This icon is used to provide additional information about the topic being covered.

Throughout the book, I've used different type-styles to make particular meanings clear, as shown below:

Convention	Description
Bold type	Indicates a new term being encountered, or an Internet address.
`SCRIPT/CODE`	Indicates HTML code that you'll type into your own page.
`ITALIC CODE`	In some cases, you'll have to type a particular filename into your HTML code, enter your own email address, or something similar. Italic code-text indicates that you need to replace what I've typed with your choice of text.

Web building basics

1

The Web – you use it, you like it, but what is it?

Learn how URLs work, and how the Web is linked together

Meet HTML, the 'language' used to write Web pages

Find out what software you need to build a website

Are you the curious type? Have you ever wondered how Web pages are written, how entire sites are constructed, or how the whole lot gets onto the World Wide Web for the rest of us to use? If you have, and you've found the answers, it's time to get that smug look ready. If you haven't, it's because up to now you've never really needed to know – one of the great things about the Web is that you can use it without understanding how it works. You need to know a bit more before you can *write* for the Web, of course, and in this chapter we're going to race through the basics.

Throughout this book I'm going to assume that you have a computer with an Internet connection and you've done some Web surfing. That means you already have the two things you need to get started in Web design, a Web browser and a text editor, but we'll also take a quick look at the other options available.

What is the World Wide Web?

Web server

A server is a computer whose main task in life is to send information to another computer connected to it. On the Internet, those connections are made by telephone lines and modems, but a server could sit in the corner of a small office and be connected to other computers in that office by cables. Internet servers usually do one particular job: a Web server stores and sends Web pages, an email server holds your email messages until you're ready to retrieve them, and so on.

There are two vital things to know about the World Wide Web. The first is that it's a **distributed** system, meaning that it's 'spread around'. Let's take a small example of this first: back in 1995, the first edition of Microsoft's Encarta encyclopaedia was small enough to fit on a single CD-ROM; three years later it had grown to the point that two CDs were needed – in other words, the information had to be *distributed* across two CDs. The Web works in a similar way, except that the CDs are replaced with computers called **Web servers**. When you sign up for an account with almost any Internet service provider (ISP) nowadays, they allocate some space for you on the hard disk of their Web server which is where your finished site will be stored. ISPs all over the world have their own Web servers, so the pages that make up the World Wide Web are *distributed* amongst all these computers. The benefits of this are twofold: first, the Web can never become full; and second, the millions of Web users around the world aren't all connecting to the same computer every time they surf!

The second important thing to know about the Web is that it's based on **hypertext**. Hypertext is a system of clickable text links often used in Windows Help files and multimedia encyclopaedias. These let you view information in a non-linear way: rather than working in a 'straight line' from page 1 to page 2 to page 3, you may be able to jump from page 1 to a related note on page 57. The Web takes this system a few stages further:

- These links don't have to take you to another point in the same document, or even to another document on the same computer: you can jump to a page on a computer on the other side of the world.

- A hypertext link in a Web page doesn't have to be a word or phrase: it could be a picture that you click on, or a small part of a larger picture, with different parts linking to different pages (Figure 1.1) (known as an *image map*).
- The link doesn't necessarily open a new Web page: it could play a video or a sound, display a picture, download an application, run a program . . . The list goes on, and gets longer all the time!

How does hypertext work?

Every file on the World Wide Web has its own unique address, in much the same way as every house in the world has its own street address. This is known as its **URL** (short for Uniform Resource Locator). You've probably come across a lot of these already on your Web wanderings: every time you arrive at a new page, its URL is shown in your browser's address bar. As an example, let's take the URL of the Radio 1 website at the BBC and break it up into its component parts. The URL is **http://www.bbc.co.uk/radio1/index.html**.

Figure 1.1 Hypertext links in a typical Web page

http:// This is one of the Internet's many protocols, and it stands for HyperText Transfer Protocol. It's the method Web servers use to transfer Web pages around the Net, so almost all Web page URLs have the http:// prefix.

www.bbc.co.uk/ This is the name of the computer on which the file is stored, identifying one single computer among all the Web servers of the world. Most Web servers' names (though not all) begin with www.

radio1/ This is the directory path to the page we want to open. Just as on your own computer, the path may consist of several directory names

URLs without filenames
Sometimes you'll come across a URL that ends with a directory name, such as ***http://www.bbc.co.uk/radio1/*** *or* ***http://www.bbc.co.uk/radio1*** *(the final slash is optional). When a browser sends this URL to a Web server, the server looks in that directory for a default file, often called* ***index.htm*** *or* ***index.html****. If a file with this name is found, it's sent back to the browser. If not, the server may send back a list of the files in that directory, or (more often these days) it may send a 'file not found' message.*

separated by slashes. Most Web designers structure their sites so that different areas are in different directories with intuitive names: the BBC site also has directories called **radio2** and **radio3**, among many others. Notice that URLs always use forward slashes rather than the back-slashes used for paths in Windows.

index.html This is the name of the file we're opening. The .html (or .htm) extension indicates that it's a Web page, but browsers can handle many different types of file.

Once you know how URLs work, hypertext links are easy to understand. When you write a Web page and want to include a link to another file, you type two things into the page: the first is the URL of the file to link to, and the second is the text that visitors to the page will be able to see and click on. There's a little more to it than that, but not much.

When your browser displays this page, it recognises that what you typed is a link and treats it differently from ordinary text. Initially it displays the text in a different colour and underlines it. If the mouse moves over the text, the usual mouse pointer turns into a hand shape and the URL of the linked page is shown in the status bar at the bottom of the browser window. If you click this text, the browser tries to fetch the appropriate page from the Web server on which it's stored, and (if all goes well) that Web server sends the file back for your browser to display.

HTML – the language of the Web

A moment ago I explained very briefly how a hypertext link was added to a Web page, and said there was a little more to it. Here we are at the 'little more' – a language called **HTML** (HyperText Markup Language).

So what's HTML all about? Well, we've met **hypertext** already – the clickable links that are used to navigate from one Web page to another. A **markup language** is a set of codes or symbols added to plain text to indicate how it should be presented to the reader, noting bold or italic text, typefaces to be used, paragraph breaks, and so on. When you type text into your word processor, it adds those codes for you but tactfully hides them from view: if you wanted bold text, for example, it shows you bold text instead of those codes. In HTML, however, you have to type those codes along with the text, and your browser puts the whole lot together before displaying it.

These codes are known as **tags**, and they consist of ordinary text placed between less-than and greater-than signs. Let's take an example:

```
<B>Welcome to my home page!</B> Thank you for
visiting.
```

The first tag, <B>, means 'turn on bold type'. Halfway through the line the same tag is used again, but with a forward slash inserted straight after the less-than sign: this means 'turn off bold type'. If you displayed a page containing this line in your browser it would look like this:

Welcome to my home page! Thank you for visiting.

Of course, there's more to a Web page than bold text, so clearly there must be many more of these tags. Don't let that put you off – over the coming chapters I'll introduce a few at a time, and you don't have to learn them all! There's a little bundle that you'll use a lot, and you'll get to know those very quickly. Others will begin to sink in once you've used them a few times.

Do I need special software?

Believe it or not, creating a website is something you really can do for free (once you've bought a computer, that is). Because HTML is entirely text-based, you can write your pages in a simple text editor such as Windows' Notepad accessory (Figure 1.2), and throughout this book I'm going to assume that's what you're doing. There are better text editors around that will let you keep several documents open at once and switch between them, and many of those are free to download from shareware sites such as **http://tucows.mirror.ac.uk** and **http://www.shareware.com**. Indeed, you can use any other word processor you want to, but you'll have to remember to save your files as plain text when you've finished. But there are other options, so let's quickly run through them.

uploading

If you've surfed the Web, you already know about downloading *– the act of copying a file from the Web to your own computer. This is what every page has to do before your browser can display it. Uploading is the exact opposite – copying a file from your own computer to some remote computer.*

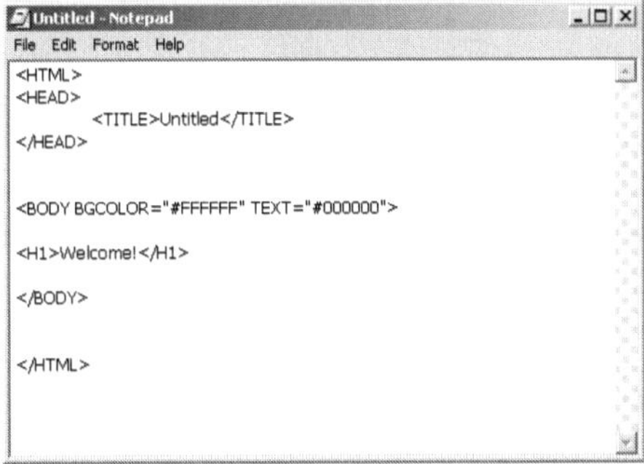

Figure 1.2 A Web page in Notepad – no expensive software needed!

WYSIWYG

A delightful acronym (pronounced 'wizzywig') for 'What you see is what you get'. This is used to describe many different types of software that can show you on the screen exactly what something will look like when you print it on paper or view it in your Web browser.

WYSIWYG editors

In theory, WYSIWYG editors are the perfect tools for designing Web pages and sites: instead of looking at plain text with HTML tags dotted around it, you see your Web page itself gradually taking shape, with images, colours and formatting all displayed. It's a lot like working with desktop publishing (DTP) software, and most DTP applications now offer the option of saving your results as a Web page. Another benefit is that WYSIWYG editors come with a set of preset templates and pre-defined styles or themes: you can sort through the templates to find the right look and feel for your site, and then simply 'fill in the blanks' to add your own content and change the captions on buttons and banner headings.

Maybe now you're thinking: 'Yippee! I don't have to learn all that HTML stuff!' Unfortunately, that's not quite the case. Once in a while, for instance, the editor won't do what you want it to do, so you'll have to switch to its text-editing mode and juggle the HTML tags yourself. And what if you see something clever on someone else's page and want to find out how it was done? If you don't know the language, you might remain envious forever! That said, if you'd like to give the WYSIWYG method a shot, here are some of the most popular applications:

- **Macromedia Dreamweaver** from **http://www.macromedia.com**
- **Adobe GoLive** from **http://www.adobe.com**
- **NetObjects Fusion** from **http://www.netobjects.com** (Figure 1.3).

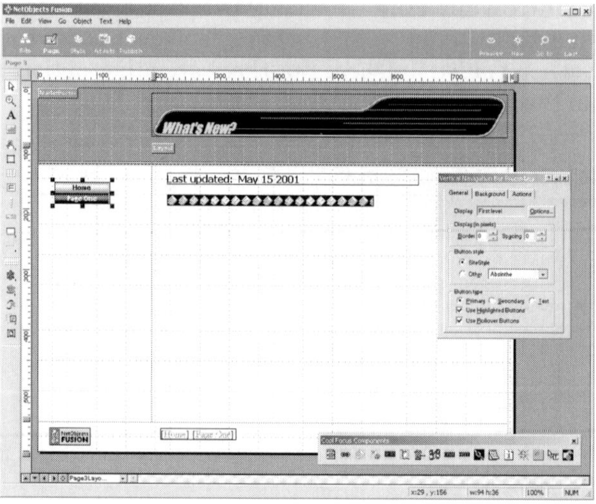

Figure 1.3 Building a page from a template in NetObjects Fusion.

HTML markup editors

Using a markup editor is rather like using Notepad – you see all the HTML code on the page in front of you. But instead of having to type all the tags yourself, a markup editor will insert them for you at the click of a button or the press of a hotkey, in the same way that you use your word processor. For example, if a piece of text should be in bold type, you click the **Bold** button on the toolbar (or press **Ctrl+B**) and then type the text in the usual way. This makes for a speedier way of working, and helps you avoid typing mistakes in the tags.

Markup editors are also ideal for newcomers to HTML. If you don't know one tag from another, just click the appropriate buttons on the toolbar to insert them: once you've seen them appear on the page a few times, you'll soon start to remember what's what! Here are three of the most popular and feature-packed markup editors:

- **HomeSite** from **http://www.allaire.com** (Figure 1.4)
- **HTMLed** from **http://www.ist.ca**
- **HoTMetaL Pro** from **http://www.sq.com**.

Find out how someone else's page was put together

*In Internet Explorer, right-click on the page and choose **View Source** to see the HTML code in Notepad. In Netscape, right-click and choose **View Frame Source**. You can also choose a similar option from either browser's **View** menu.*

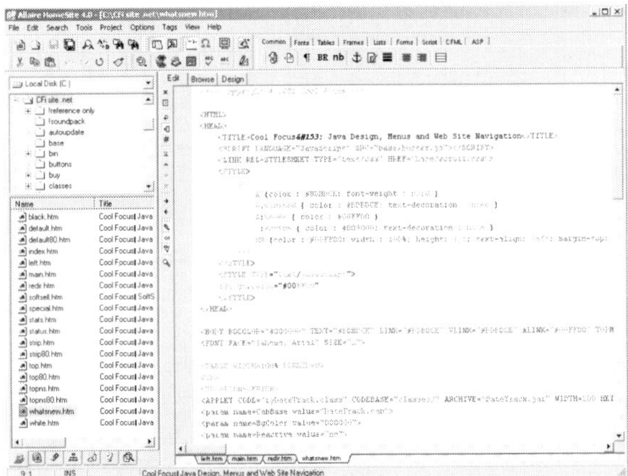

Figure 1.4 Handy colour-coding and one-click tag insertion in HomeSite.

Expanding your browser collection

There are three Web browsers in common use: Microsoft Internet Explorer (the most popular browser by a huge margin), Netscape and Opera. Although all three are very similar, there can be slight differences in the way each displays a particular Web page. More importantly, if you make a mistake in your HTML coding it may make no difference at all in one browser and a huge difference in another!

Ugh, that's horrible!

While you're planning your site, consider what you like (and especially what you dislike) about other sites you've visited and avoid committing the same crimes yourself. It's easy to start adding things simply because you can and forget how irritating they are. Background music that can't be turned off, garish background images that make the text hard to read, links that don't give any clue about what they're linking to – a quick critical look at a few websites from a user's point of view will teach you a lot as a designer.

While you're designing your site, you need at least one browser so that you can look at the result – it doesn't really matter which of those you choose, though I'd recommend Internet Explorer as it's the most widely used of the three. Before you actually publish your site on the Web, though, it's important to check it in all the popular browsers to make sure there are no problems. Fortunately all three are free, so you can just visit their websites to download them:

- Microsoft Internet Explorer from **http://www.microsoft.com/windows/ie** or **http://www.microsoft.com/mac/ie**
- Netscape from **http://home.netscape.com/download**
- Opera from **http://www.operasoftware.com**

A simple Web page

2

Organise your folders and create a basic Web page template

Choose a title, and add a heading and text to the page

Apply bold or italic effects to text

Learn how to align headings and paragraphs

Get to grips with tag attributes

Every great website starts with a single page, and in this chapter we'll get that first page under way. To keep things simple, we will deal first with the text elements of a page, using headings and paragraphs, alignment, and useful text effects such as bold and italic. In later chapters we'll look at ways of making everything more attractive with images, colours and layout options, and we'll link pages together to create a mini website. As you work through these chapters, try creating the same example pages yourself and experimenting with some of the tags to see what happens. Remember, you can't break anything by doing it wrong, so it pays to be adventurous!

Getting organised!

First, you need to decide where all the files that will eventually make up your website are going to be kept: if they're scattered around your hard disk in different places you'll have to remember the names and locations of all those files later on, and that won't be much fun! Make a new folder somewhere on your hard disk, and call it **Site** (or something more imaginative but equally recognisable). Open this new folder, and create another inside it called **Images**. (I do recommend using that name for it: this is where all the image files used on your site will be kept, so the name will be easy to remember and understand in future. We'll return to this in Chapters 4 and 5.)

This leads to two important points about the naming of files and folders (or **directories**, as folders are known on the Internet):

1. Names are case-sensitive, so if your site includes a link to **MyPicture.jpg**, but you actually called the file **mypicture.jpg**, the image won't be displayed. For this reason, it's simplest to name all files and directories using *entirely lower-case names*, removing that potential hazard.
2. The names of files and directories mustn't include spaces. This is a basic rule that applies to any Internet address, including email addresses. The names can be as long as you like, and you can use hyphens, underscores or dots to separate individual words in the names if you really can't bear the idea of having files named **whatsnew.htm** or **productsandservices.htm**.

Throughout the book, I'll refer to your 'Site directory' and your 'Images directory', meaning the two directories you've just created, whatever you've chosen to call them.

Making a template file

There are a few bits and pieces that will appear in almost every Web page you write, so let's begin by making a template file that you can use every time you start work on a new page. Start Notepad, or whichever text editor you're using, and type the text below. Don't worry about the exact number of spaces, tabs or carriage returns you type.

```
<HTML>
<HEAD>
      <TITLE>Untitled</TITLE>
</HEAD>
<BODY>

</BODY>
</HTML>
```

Save this file in your Site directory, giving it the name **template.htm** or **template.html**. When saving from Notepad, make sure you type the .htm or .html extension after the name as well: if you just type **template** as the filename, Notepad will save the file as **template.txt**.

As I mentioned in Chapter 1, the pieces of text between the < and > signs are known as **tags** and they tell the browser how to display the page. None of the tags in this template page does anything exciting by itself, but it's worth knowing what they're for. The entire page is placed between `<HTML>` and `</HTML>` tags, and it's divided into two separate chunks: the **head** (the section between the `<HEAD>` and `</HEAD>` tags) and the **body** (between `<BODY>` and `</BODY>`). You'll notice that these tags are used in pairs. The first instance is the *opening* tag, and the second (which is the same, but has a forward slash after the < symbol) is the *closing* tag. Tags that work in pairs like this could be thought of as on/off switches marking the beginning and end of a section, or the start and finish of an ongoing effect to be applied to their contents. (A good example of this is the tag for bold text I mentioned on page 687.)

The **head** section is pretty dull: all it contains is the title of the page, inserted between the `<TITLE>` and `</TITLE>` tags. There are other bits and pieces that can be slotted in here, but the title is the only element that *must* be there.

The **body** section is the one that matters. Between these two tags you'll type all the text that should appear on the page, and put in the tags needed to display images, set colours, insert hyperlinks to other pages and sites, and anything else you want your page to contain.

Now that we've created and saved a basic template file, let's start adding to it to build up a respectable-looking page. In your Site directory, make a copy of the file (so that you keep this template file unchanged for creating more pages from later). Rename the copy to **index.htm** or **index.html**, and open it in Notepad.

Should I use .htm or .html?

It doesn't matter whether you use .htm or .html as the file extension for your pages; all browsers recognise either of those as being Web pages. However, you'll find life a lot easier if you make a decision now and stick to the same extension for every page you save!

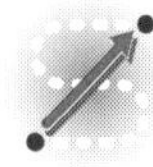

Capital letters

When you type tags, you can use upper-case or lower-case letters. If you prefer `<title>`, or `<Title>`, or even `<tItLe>`, it's all the same to a browser. But typing tags in capitals makes them stand out from the ordinary text on the page, which can be useful when editing a page, and it tends to be simpler to do when you've got to use the Shift key to type the < and > symbols anyway.

Adding a title, heading and text

The first thing to do is to replace the word **Untitled** with a sensible title for the page, such as **A1 Graphic Design Company** or **My EastEnders HomePage**. Pick something that describes what the page will be about, but keep it fairly short: the text between the <TITLE> and </TITLE> tags will appear in the title bar at the top of most browsers, and if your entry is too long to fit, it'll just get chopped off!

Now we'll add some text to the page. To keep things simple, type what is shown below. When you've done that, save the file, but don't close Notepad yet.

```
<HTML>
<HEAD>
      <TITLE>The Computing Site Directory</TITLE>
</HEAD>
<BODY>
<H1>The Computing Site Directory</H1>
Here's an example first paragraph.

<P>And here's a second paragraph.
</BODY>
</HTML>
```

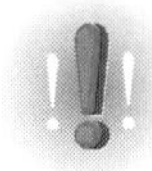

Choose your title carefully!

For a couple of reasons, the title of the page is more important than it might seem. First, most search engines will list the title of your page in their search results (see Chapter 10), so it needs to be interesting so that people will want to visit it. Second, if someone likes your page enough to add it to their Favorites or Bookmarks list, this is the title they'll see in the list when they open it.

Now take a look at your masterpiece in a browser. There are several ways you can do that: one is to go to your Site directory and double-click the **index.htm** file so that your default browser starts and displays it; another is to start your browser and use the **Open** option on its File menu to browse for the file. Simpler still, just drag the file's icon from your Site directory and drop it on to the browser window. When your browser opens the page, it should look like Figure 2.1.

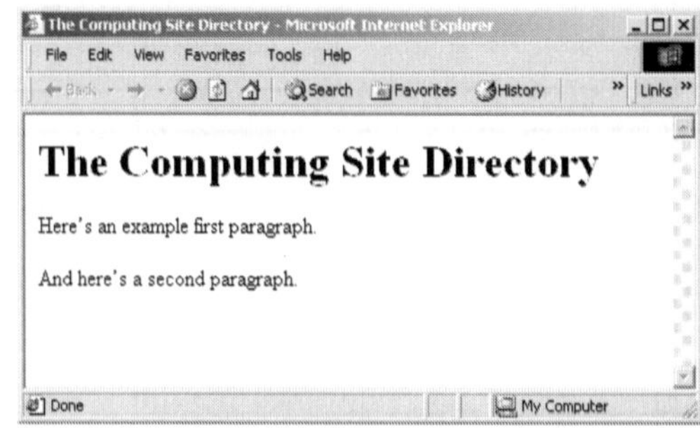

Figure 2.1 That first page when displayed in Internet Explorer.

So what are those new tags all about? Let's take the **<P>** tag first. This tells your browser to present the text that follows as a new paragraph, which automatically inserts a blank line before it. And this raises an important point about HTML: you can't insert blank lines just by pressing **Enter** or **Return** on the keyboard. Although you can see blank lines in Notepad when you do that, a browser will just ignore them, which is why you have to start a new paragraph by entering <P>. So why did I leave a blank line between the two 'paragraphs' in the HTML code above? Simply because it makes the code easier to read: if blank lines in the code are going to be ignored by the browser, you can sprinkle them around liberally to make the code easier to understand at a glance. I could have written the code this way and the result would have been the same in the browser:

```
Here's an example first paragraph.<P>And here's
a second paragraph.
```

Notice that unlike the few other tags we've come across so far, there's no </P> tag needed: the act of starting a new paragraph isn't an ongoing effect that has to be switched off again later.

The other pair of tags that cropped up was <H1> and </H1>, which formats a line of text as a heading. You can choose from six sizes: <H1> is the largest, followed by <H2> and </H2>, and so on down to the smallest, <H6> and </H6>. In one nifty little manoeuvre these tags change the size of the text placed between them and make it bold. They also start a new paragraph for the heading automatically (so you don't need a <P> tag at the start of the line) and start a new paragraph for whatever follows the heading.

Try experimenting with the different heading sizes by altering the <H1> and </H1> tags. After each change, resave the file and click your browser's **Refresh** button to make it load and display the new copy of the page.

Start a new line without starting a new paragraph

Another tag, <BR>, will give you a 'line break'. In other words, the text that follows the <BR> tag will start at the beginning of the next line with no empty line inserted before it. As an example, you could type a list of items with a <BR> tag after each to place it on a separate line (more on that in Chapter 3).

Text formatting

If you've got the idea of the heading tags, you can see that HTML certainly isn't rocket science. Heading tags are easy to use, but not unusually so: there's a large bundle of formatting tags that work in exactly the same way – you type the opening tag, some text, and the closing tag. Let's run through some of those now as a quick and painless way to expand your HTML vocabulary.

The tags for bold and italic text are especially easy to remember: <B> for bold, and <I> for italic, with the appropriate closing tag (</B> or </I>) when you want the effect to stop. And, just as in your word processor, you can combine these tags to produce combined effects, so if your document contained this:

Putting your tags in order

It doesn't really matter in which order the tags appear. As long as you 'switch· off' any ongoing effects before the next piece of text, you'll get the result you wanted. However, it's good coding practice to work on a 'last on, first off' basis, as in `<B><I>Some Text Here</I></B>`

```
This is <I>italic</I>. This is <B>bold</B>. This
is <B><I>bold and italic</I></B>.
```

the result would look like this in a browser:

This is *italic*. This is **bold**. This is ***bold and italic***.

You could also use those tags like this:

```
<B>This is <I>bold and italic</I>. This is bold
but no longer italic.</B>
```

which a browser would display like this:

This is *bold and italic*. This is bold but no longer italic.

If you really feel the urge, you can underline text using another memorable pair of tags, `<U>` and `</U>`, but be careful how you use underlining: most people surfing the Web expect underlined text to be a hyperlink, so they might find your gratuitous use of these tags confusing.

Some more text-formatting tags

Table 2.1 contains a list of similar text-formatting tags. Experiment with these by typing their opening and closing tags into your index.htm page, with a word or two between them, resaving the file and clicking the **Refresh** or **Reload** button in your browser. Figure 2.2 shows the result of using each tag.

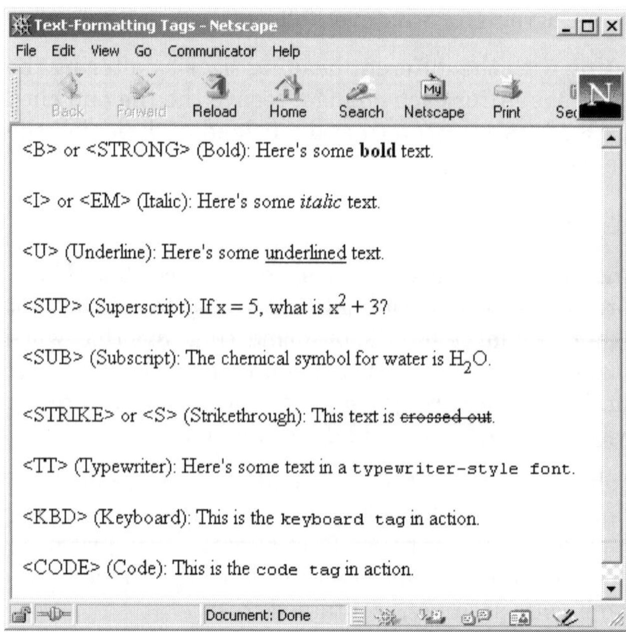

Figure 2.2 The common text-formatting tags, as displayed by Netscape.

You can see from the list above that there are several tags that apparently do the same thing, such as <KBD> and <CODE> or <I> and <EM>. In practice, you can use these interchangeably if your pages are primarily aimed at users of Internet Explorer, Opera and Netscape – the tags really will give the same result whichever you choose. In other browsers there may be subtle differences between <KBD> and <CODE>: in common with any markup language, HTML provides a fairly broad definition for each tag, and it's left to the various software companies to decide precisely how their browser should handle it.

Table 2.1 Text-formatting tags

Tag	Meaning
<SUP>	Formats text as superscript
<SUB>	Formats text as subscript
<STRIKE>	Strikes through (crosses out) the text. An alternative tag that does the same thing is <S>.
<TT>	Displays the text in a typewriter-style font
<EM>	Emphasises the text (usually by making it italic)
<STRONG>	Applies a strong emphasis to the text (usually by making it bold)
<KBD>	Often used to indicate text that should be typed by a user. Browsers usually display this in a monospaced font
<CODE>	Often used to indicate examples of mathematical or programming code. Browsers usually display this using a monospaced font

Adding information with attributes

All the tags we've seen so far are easy to understand and use: they're either self-contained tags, such as <P> and <BR> that you slot in to create paragraph or line breaks, or pairs of tags that work as on/off switches, such as <B> and </B>. However, there are other tags that need to contain a little more information about what you want to do. A good example is the <FONT> tag, which we'll look at more closely in Chapter 4. By itself it isn't saying anything useful: which font? what size? what colour? You provide this extra information by adding **attributes** to the tag such as `SIZE=3`, `FACE=Arial`, and so on, so a complete font tag might look like this:

```
<FONT SIZE=3 FACE=Arial>
```

Attributes are additional pieces of information slotted into a tag. The name of the tag always comes first (the word FONT in the font tag, for example), and the attributes follow the name. Each attribute is separated by a space, and needs an equals sign between the attribute itself and the value you want to set for it. It doesn't matter what order the attributes appear in, and you don't need to include a particular attribute if you don't want to change its value from whatever it was previously set to.

We've already met one tag that has an optional attribute – the heading tags <H1> to <H6>. This can take an **ALIGN** attribute to specify whether the heading is aligned to the left, middle or right of the page, using the values **LEFT**, **CENTER** or **RIGHT**. In our example page we didn't include this attribute for the heading tag, so we got the default result: a left-aligned heading. We'd have got exactly the same result if we'd used this instead:

```
<H1 ALIGN=LEFT>The Computing Site Directory</H1>
```

Watch the spelling! *HTML is an American language, so watch out for those little differences in spelling such as* ***color*** *instead of colour, and* ***center*** *instead of centre. If you spell the name of a tag or attribute wrongly, the browser won't try to make sense of it, it'll just ignore it.*

Clearly there's no point in bloating our Web page with extra code that won't do anything useful, but try replacing that line with either:

```
<H1 ALIGN=CENTER>The Computing Site Directory</H1>
```

or

```
<H1 ALIGN=RIGHT>The Computing Site Directory</H1>
```

As usual, save the edited page and refresh your browser to see the result. In Figure 2.3 the heading is aligned to the centre of the page. Because the window is a little smaller, the browser has wrapped the heading on to a second line: this is handled automatically for all headings and paragraphs. (Of course, if I wanted the heading always to be split over two lines, I could insert a <BR> tag before the word 'Directory'.)

Figure 2.3 Our original page with its heading aligned to the centre (or, er, the 'center').

Aligning whole paragraphs

If you can choose how a heading should be aligned on the page, surely you can do the same thing with a paragraph of ordinary text? Yes you can, and the <P> tag comes to the rescue here in much the same way that the heading tag did earlier: by offering an ALIGN attribute with one of the following values after its = sign (see Table 2.2).

Table 2.2 Paragraph alignment

Value	Meaning
LEFT	Aligns the paragraph to the left of the page
CENTER	Centres the paragraph on the page
RIGHT	Aligns the paragraph to the right of the page
JUSTIFY	Justifies the paragraph (giving a straight edge to the left and right of the page, achieved by adding extra space between words). This is a recent addition to HTML that only the latest browsers understand: older browsers will ignore it and use the default value, LEFT

At the moment our example page just contains a couple of short dummy paragraphs – not enough to do any serious paragraph formatting with – so let's replace those with something more meaningful so that the page looks like this:

```
<HTML>
<HEAD>
      <TITLE>The Computing Site Directory</TITLE>
</HEAD>
<BODY>
<H1 ALIGN=CENTER>The Computing Site Directory</H1>
<P>Welcome to the Computing Site Directory, the
number one resource for all your computing needs:
industry news and comment, freeware and shareware
software, magazines and journals, hardware driver
updates, and much more.

<P>Select a category below to choose from a fre-
quently-updated list of the best sites available.
If any link is broken, please contact the
Webmaster.
</BODY>
</HTML>
```

More white space needed!

If you want to create a block of white space on the page, you can't use several <P> tags in a row to do it. But after a <P> tag (or instead of one) you can type as many <BR> tags as you like. Unlike the <P> tag, <BR> tags are cumulative.

If you were to look at the page in your browser now, you'd see that both paragraphs are aligned to the left: the <P> tags don't include the ALIGN attribute, so we're getting the default alignment. In fact, apart from replacing the text to be displayed, the only change I've made is to add a <P> tag before the *first* paragraph as well as the second. At the moment that first <P> tag is being ignored: the heading automatically created a paragraph break for us, so we've got the equivalent of two <P> tags in a row before the first paragraph. HTML doesn't allow paragraphs to be blank, so one of these is disregarded. (We could type <P><P><P><P><P> and all but one of those would be ignored!)

Now alter those paragraphs again to look like the following (the changes are shown in bold type) and view the result in your browser.

```
<P ALIGN=CENTER>Welcome to the Computing Site Directory, the number one resource for all your computing needs: industry news and comment, freeware and shareware software, magazines and journals, hardware driver updates, and much more.</P>

<P ALIGN=CENTER>Select a category below to choose from a frequently-updated list of the best sites available. If any link is broken, please contact the Webmaster.</P>
```

We've made the same two changes to both paragraphs. First, we've centred the paragraphs by adding the ALIGN=CENTER attribute (Figure 2.4). Second, we've added a closing </P> tag to mark the end of the paragraph. Yes, I know I said earlier that the <P> tag was self-contained. I lied. But although it *does* have a closing tag, that closing tag is only needed when you use the ALIGN attribute: it tells the browser where to stop applying the alignment. If you didn't include the closing </P> tag, you could find that text further down the page was still being centred or right-aligned.

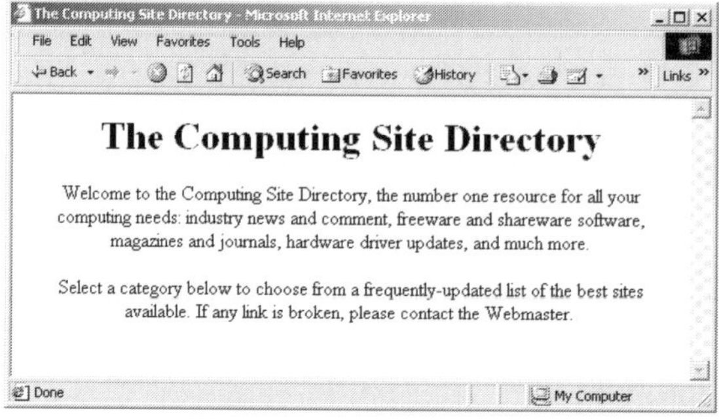

Figure 2.4 Adding <P ALIGN=CENTER> to both paragraphs.

The easy way to centre

Part of the reason I've used the <P> tag to align the paragraphs was to introduce the concept of adding attributes to tags. Most of the time you'll want your paragraphs to be left-aligned, which needs no ALIGN attribute and no closing </P> tag, and you probably won't want to right-align or justify text very often. That just leaves centred text, and there's a better and more memorable way to do that: the **<CENTER>...</CENTER>** tag pair.

The handy thing about the <CENTER> tag is that it can be applied to anything on a page: a heading, a paragraph or an image. Just put the opening tag before the first of the content to be centred and the closing tag where the centring should end. So a less fussy way to centre the heading and the two paragraphs would be this:

```
<HTML>
<HEAD>
      <TITLE>The Computing Site Directory</TITLE>
</HEAD>
<BODY>
<CENTER>
<H1>The Computing Site Directory</H1>

Welcome to the Computing Site Directory, the
number one resource for all your computing needs:
industry news and comment, freeware and shareware
software, magazines and journals, hardware driver
updates, and much more.

<P>Select a category below to choose from a fre-
quently-updated list of the best sites available.
If any link is broken, please contact the
Webmaster.
</CENTER>
</BODY>
</HTML>
```

We're back to one <P> tag, no closing </P> tags, and no ALIGN attributes! It's a lot easier to understand, and it gives the same result as the more complicated version of the page.

DIV – the easy way to align

Apart from the heading and paragraph tags there are other tags that can take an optional ALIGN attribute, such as images and tables (covered in Chapters 5 and 7). If your page contains a number of headings, paragraphs, images and/or tables that have to be aligned the same way, that could add up to a lot of ALIGN attributes. A better option is to use a single tag, **<DIV>** (short for *division*). This also takes an ALIGN attribute, but it works just like the `<CENTER>` tag: everything between the `<DIV>` and `</DIV>` tags will be aligned the same way. In fact, the `<CENTER>` tag is just an abbreviated form of `<DIV ALIGN=CENTER>`. If an element somewhere between the opening and closing `<DIV>` tags needs to be aligned differently, just add the `ALIGN` attribute to its tag: individual tags' own `ALIGN` attributes override the `<DIV>` alignment.

The `<DIV>` tag really comes into its own when used with style sheets. Skip ahead to Chapter 9 to find out more.

Lists, links and special characters

3

Make simple lists using <BR> tags

Create smarter-looking lists with bullets and numbering

Create hypertext links to other Web pages or email addresses

Learn how to link your own site's pages together

Use foreign characters and symbols, and add invisible comments

In Chapter 2 we put together a basic Web page incorporating a heading and a couple of paragraphs of text, and got to grips with some HTML formatting tags and their attributes. In this chapter we'll get down to the nitty-gritty – how one page links to another to create a website of multiple pages. Along the way we'll look at some more aspects of text formatting such as lists, word breaks and spacing, and how you can display symbols and foreign language characters in a Web page. We'll also cover something that's vital in any programming or markup language: how to add comments and notes to the page for your own reference without destroying its appearance.

Making a list

If you've followed Chapter 2 and created the same example Web page I did, your second paragraph refers to a list of categories on the page from which the visitor can choose a section of the site to visit. We'll start by making that list of categories, and later in this chapter we'll convert them to links.

The simplest way to make a list in a Web page is to separate each item by either a `<BR>` or a `<P>` tag (depending on how much space you want between each item). For example, we could insert the following just before the closing `</CENTER>` tag in our Web page, which would give the result shown in Figure 3.1.

Figure 3.1 A simple list of items separated by `<BR>` (line break) tags.

```
<P>Computing News and Reviews
<BR>Free Software
<BR>Shareware Software
<BR>Software Companies
<BR>Hardware Companies
<BR>Magazines and Journals
<BR>Hardware Drivers
```

(Because we've placed this list before the closing </CENTER> tag, every item is centred on the page. For a left-aligned list, place the added code *after* the </CENTER> tag instead.)

The <P> tag is used to place a paragraph break between our second paragraph and the beginning of the list. The <BR> tags then create a line break before the next item of text. Although this is a perfectly valid way to make a list, and I'm going to stick with it for our example page, HTML includes some easy-to-use tags for creating numbered and bulleted lists, so let's run through those.

Bulleted lists

HTML refers to a bulleted list as an *unordered list*, and uses the tags **<UL>** and **</UL>** to mark the beginning and end of the list. Each item in the list is prefixed with an **<LI>** tag (short for List Item). The <LI> tag automatically places each item on a new line, so there's no need to insert line or paragraph breaks. We could make an unordered list of the same items like this (Figure 3.2):

Figure 3.2 A bulleted (or *unordered*) list.

```
<UL>
<LI>Computing News and Reviews
<LI>Free Software
<LI>Shareware Software
<LI>Software Companies
<LI>Hardware Companies
<LI>Magazines and Journals
<LI>Hardware Drivers
</UL>
```

In Internet Explorer, the type of bullet used is decided for you – you have no control over that. Netscape and Opera add a **TYPE** attribute to the <UL> tag which lets you choose the shape of the bullet (Table 3.1).

Table 3.1 Types of bullet

Attribute	Result
TYPE=DISC	The default bullet, a solid circle
TYPE=CIRCLE	A hollow circular bullet
TYPE=SQUARE	A solid square bullet

Using* `TYPE=SQUARE` *in Internet Explorer

If you use the TYPE *attribute and your page is viewed in Internet Explorer, it won't cause any problems. Internet Explorer (and any other browser) will ignore any attributes they don't understand, so your list will still be displayed properly but with the default bullet style.*

Numbered lists

Numbered lists are known as *ordered lists*. They use the tags **<OL>** and **</OL>**, but are constructed in the same way as unordered lists above, using the <LI> tag for each list item:

```
<OL>
<LI>Computing News and Reviews
<LI>Free Software
<LI>Shareware Software
<LI>Software Companies
<LI>Hardware Companies
<LI>Magazines and Journals
<LI>Hardware Drivers
</OL>
```

The code above would create a list that looked like this:

1. Computing News and Reviews
2. Free Software
3. Shareware Software
4. Software Companies
5. Hardware Companies
6. Magazines and Journals
7. Hardware Drivers

In an ordered list, there's another attribute, **TYPE**, that can be added to the <OL> tag, and this is supported by all three popular browsers. The TYPE attribute sets the numbering system to be used (Table 3.2).

Table 3.2 Different numbering formats available

Attribute	Result
TYPE=1	The default numbering system: 1, 2, 3...
TYPE=i	Small roman numerals: i, ii, iii...
TYPE=I	Large roman numerals: I, II, III...
TYPE=A	Upper-case letters: A, B, C...
TYPE=a	Lower-case letters: a, b, c...

Creating links

Linking to other sites

Before we start adding more pages to our example site and linking them together, let's take a quick detour and find out how to create links to *other* websites first. In HTML, links are known as **anchors**, and they use the **<A>...</A>** tag pair. This is a tag that does nothing at all without attributes, and the attribute we need is **HREF** (short for *Hypertext REFerence*) to specify the URL of the site we're linking to. Between the opening and closing anchor tags goes the text that visitors can click on to visit that site. Here's an example that links to Microsoft's website:

```
<A HREF="http://www.microsoft.com">Click here to
visit Microsoft's site.</A>
```

If you added that line of code to the body of a Web page, the result would look like Figure 3.3. As you can see, the text is automatically underlined, a hand-cursor appears when the mouse moves over it, and the URL it links to is shown in the browser's status bar. What's more, it works! If you click it, you'll arrive at the URL you typed into the HREF attribute.

Using quote symbols for attributes

The value of any attribute should really be enclosed between double quotes: ALIGN="LEFT", TYPE="DISC"*, and so on. In practice, though, the only time quotes are actually needed is when the value contains a space or any punctuation that may make it unclear where the value ends (in URLs, for example). The simple rule is: if in doubt, use quotes – it won't do any harm.*

Figure 3.3 A hypertext link to **www.microsoft.com**.

Although we just placed one short line of text between the <A> and </A> tags, we could have used something much longer – several paragraphs, for example. You can use other tags within the linking text as well, perhaps to make the link bold or italic, or format it as a heading, so the code below is perfectly valid (although perhaps not altogether practical!), making everything on the page act as a link to Microsoft's site.

```
<BODY>
<CENTER>
<A HREF="http://www.microsoft.com">
<H1>The Computing Site Directory</H1>
Here's an example first paragraph.

<P>And here's a second paragraph.
</A>
</CENTER>
</BODY>
</HTML>
```

Linking to particular pages or files

The link we used in the examples above was to the URL **http://www. microsoft.com**. We haven't specified a filename, so if this link were clicked Microsoft's server would send back the default Web page from the root directory of this site – in other words, the first page of the Microsoft website. If we'd wanted to link to a particular page on that site, we could have entered the complete URL of that page – perhaps something like **http://www.microsoft. com/uk/preview/default.htm**.

Links don't necessarily have to point to Web pages, though. You can create a link to an image file, a sound or movie file, a zip archive, or any other type of file at all – the anchor tag is constructed in exactly the same way and only the URL has to change. If the user's browser is capable of displaying the file, it will. Otherwise, the user will be offered the choice of downloading and saving the file on their hard disk or choosing a program on the hard disk that is able to display or play the file.

Creating email links

An email link looks like any other link on the page, but when a visitor clicks it their email program will start and they can send a message to the email address included in the anchor tag. That email address is automatically added to the To field of the message, so all they need to do is type the message and click the **Send** button.

Email links use the same `<A>…</A>` tag as other links, with the URL replaced by an email address. The only other difference is that the email address is prefixed with **mailto:**. We can make use of this in our example Web page. At the moment, our second paragraph ends with the words *If any link is broken, please contact the Webmaster*. Let's encourage user feedback by making the last few words an email link: just replace that sentence with the following, replacing my email address with your own:

```
If any link is broken, please <A HREF="mailto:
rob@codebase.co.uk">contact the Webmaster</A>.
```

If you've followed the changes we've made to our example page, it should look something like Figure 3.4.

Linking to pages on your own site

The links we created to Microsoft's website used something called an **absolute URL**. That's probably the only type of URL you've come across so far: an absolute URL gives the whole path to the page or file you want to link to, including the http://prefix and the name of the computer (such as **www.microsoft.com**). When you want to create links to pages on your own site, you can use a simpler method.

Figure 3.4 Our example Web page with an added email link, shown in Opera.

To demonstrate this, of course, we're going to need a second page to link to! Make a copy of the template file you created in Chapter 2 and call it **news.htm**. (Apart from the template file, your Site directory should now contain **index.htm** and **news.htm**.)

Open news.htm in your editor and alter it to look like this:

```
<HTML>
<HEAD>
      <TITLE>Computing News and Reviews</TITLE>
</HEAD>
<BODY>
<CENTER>
<H1>Computing News and Reviews</H1>
</CENTER>
</BODY>
</HTML>
```

Save the changes and reopen **index.htm** in the editor. At the beginning of our list of categories we've got a *Computing News and Reviews* item, so let's make it into a link to the **news.htm** page by enclosing it in an anchor tag (Figure 3.5):

```
<P><A HREF="news.htm">Computing News and Reviews
</A>
```

Yes, it's just a filename. This is called a **relative URL** – it tells the browser to look for a file called **news.htm** and display it. Since the browser doesn't know where else to look, it searches the directory containing the document it's displaying at the moment. As long as **news.htm** is in that same directory, the browser will find and open it when the link is clicked. You can test this by saving the index.htm file and refreshing the browser in the usual way, then clicking this new link. (If a file with that name *isn't* in that directory, the browser will display the all-too-familiar 'not found' message instead.)

Relative URLs

*What's so great about relative URLs? First, there's less typing involved, which also minimises the opportunities to make mistakes. More importantly, though, you can test these links in your browser while you're designing your site to check that they work. If you used an absolute URL such as **http://www.mysite.com/mypage.htm**, your browser would have to connect to the Internet, find **www.mysite.com** and retrieve **mypage.htm** from it. That's time-consuming, and it would only work if you'd actually uploaded mypage.htm to the server.*

Figure 3.5 It's a website! Well almost – the first item in our list of categories is now a working link.

You can also make a browser look somewhere different for a file in a similar way. Go to your Site directory and create a new directory inside it called **pages**. Move the **news.htm** file into this new directory. If you click the link we just created, it will now fail because the browser can't find the file: we need to change the link to the following:

```
<P><A HREF="pages/news.htm">Computing News and
Reviews</A>
```

This tells the browser to look in the current directory for another directory named **pages**, and search inside that for a file named **news.htm**. If you test this in your browser, the **news.htm** page should once again be found and opened. (For another example, you could create a new directory inside 'pages' called 'morepages' and move **news.htm** into that. The link would then need to be: `<A HREF="pages/morepages/news.htm">`. For the purposes of our example site, we'll leave **news.htm** in the 'pages' directory.)

What we're lacking now is a link back to our **index.htm** page from **news.htm**. If **news.htm** were still in the Site directory, we'd use `<A HREF="index.htm">` but it's now in a subdirectory called 'pages', so we need to tell the browser to look in the *parent* directory of 'pages' to find the file. If you're familiar with MS-DOS, you'll recognise this straight away: to move up one level in the directory tree, you just type two dots followed by the usual forward slash. So we can add the following line to the **news.htm** page, after the heading:

```
<A HREF="../index.htm">Home</A>
```

And if **news.htm** were in that 'morepages' directory, the anchor tag to get back to the index page would be `<A HREF="../../index.htm">Home</A>`.

What next?

If you're treating this as a tutorial and building the same site, follow the same steps for the remaining six items in the category list on the index page. Make six copies of **news.htm** inside the 'pages' directory, give the files appropriate names, and edit their `<TITLE>` and `<H1>` tags to correspond to the six categories. You can then add the appropriate anchor tags to those six list items so that the list looks something like this:

```
<P><A  HREF="pages/news.htm">Computing  News  and
Reviews</A>
<BR><A HREF="pages/free.htm">Free Software</A>
<BR><A HREF="pages/shareware.htm">Shareware Software
</A>
<BR><A HREF="pages/softcomp.htm">Software Companies
</A>
<BR><A HREF="pages/hardcomp.htm">Hardware Companies
</A>
<BR><A HREF="pages/mags.htm">Magazines and Journals
</A>
<BR><A HREF="pages/drivers.htm">Hardware Drivers</A>
```

Voilà! You now have a fully linked-together (if rather dull!) website consisting of eight pages.

How to prevent breaks between words

Where the line breaks in your paragraphs will occur depends upon the font being used, the size of the user's browser window, and many other variables that you have no control over. If you have a few words in a paragraph that must appear together on the same line, don't use the ` ` *code between each word: enclose the words between* **<NOBR>...</NOBR>** *(no-break) tags instead.*

Spaces and word breaks

Now that you've worked with HTML for a while, you may have come across this phenomenon: you type two or three spaces into the code, but the browser insists on using just one. Hopefully you didn't spend too much time thumping the keyboard in frustration – that's supposed to happen! Just as browsers ignore your use of the Enter or Return key in your code, they also ignore the Tab key and cut multiple spaces down to one.

You can get around this by using one of a set of special character codes, **` `** (short for *non-breaking space*). This code must be in lower-case letters, and placed between an ampersand and a semi-colon. To insert three spaces in a row, then, you'd enter **`   `**.

Special characters

There are several other characters that browsers can't display when typed into a page in the usual way. These are known as *reserved* characters: they form a part of the HTML language so they have a special meaning to a browser. Like the non-breaking space, there are codes you can use if you need to display these characters in a Web page (Table 3.3).

Table 3.3 Codes for reserved characters

Character	HTML Code	Numeric Code
< (less than)	<	<
> (greater than)	>	>
" (quote)	"	"
& (ampersand)	&	&
© (copyright)	©	©
™ (trademark)	™	™
¼ (quarter)	¼	¼
½ (half)	½	½
¾ (three-quarters)	¾	¾
£ (pound)	£	£
° (degrees)	°	°
× (multiply)	×	×
÷ (divide)	÷	÷

You can use either the HTML code or the numeric code, so to display the text "**Give & Take**" you'd type either of the following:

```
&#34;Give &#38; Take&#34;
```

```
&quot;Give &amp; Take&quot;
```

Yes, it looks a mess, but browsers understand it!

Commenting HTML code

Whatever language you're programming or coding in, it's useful to be able to add your own notes or **comments** to the code that will be ignored when the code is compiled, run, or (in the case of Web pages) displayed in a browser. You may want to mark particular sections of code to make them easier to find during editing, add reminders about what a section of code does, or make a note of items you want to add later. HTML has its own comment tag pair, **<!--** and **-->**, just for this purpose. Anything enclosed between these tags will be ignored by the browser when the page is displayed.

Another handy use for these tags is to *comment out* sections of HTML code: you can effectively remove chunks of text or HTML code from the page by enclosing them between comment tags rather than deleting them. In the code below, for example, only the first two items in the list would be displayed on the page. The remaining five are enclosed between comment tags, making them invisible to the browser.

```
<P><A HREF="pages/news.htm">Computing News and
Reviews</A>
<BR><A HREF="pages/free.htm">Free Software</A>
<!--<BR><A HREF="pages/shareware.htm">Shareware
Software</A>
<BR><A HREF="pages/softcomp.htm">Software Companies
</A>
<BR><A HREF="pages/hardcomp.htm">Hardware Companies
</A>
<BR><A HREF="pages/mags.htm">Magazines and Journals
</A>
<BR><A HREF="pages/drivers.htm">Hardware Drivers
</A>-->
```

Colours, fonts and rules

4

Choose colours for the background, text and links

Add a tiled background image to the page

Pick fonts, and change the font type or colour for particular items of text

Use horizontal rules to divide up a Web page

At this stage you're the proud owner of a basic website consisting of several pages (although only the index page contains anything useful so far). As it stands, it won't win any awards, but what matters is that you've worked with a bundle of HTML tags and their attributes and seen the effect they have on plain text when the result is viewed in a browser. Armed with this experience, let's improve the look of the site by adding colours, choosing fonts, and applying a few more design touches.

You too can have a <BODY> like mine!

Even in our most impressive page, **index.htm**, everything still looks a bit dull. The background is white, the text is black, the hyperlinks are either blue or purple (depending upon whether you've clicked them or not) – these are the default colours set up by most browsers, and they use those colours because we haven't told them to use anything different. All this is easily changed, though, by adding attributes to the `<BODY>` tag.

I mentioned at the beginning of Chapter 2 that the `<BODY>` tag and its closing `</BODY>` tag must be included in every page: they tell the browser where the displayable part of the page begins and ends. The `<BODY>` tag's attributes are all optional, but for any attribute that's missing a browser will use its own default setting, and different browsers may have different defaults. Since most Web authors like to keep as much control as possible over how their pages will be displayed, they add these attributes. Table 4.1 shows the possible colour attributes.

Table 4.1 Colour attributes

This attribute...	...has this effect
BGCOLOR	sets the background colour of the page
TEXT	sets the colour of ordinary text on the page
LINK	sets the colour of a hyperlink
VLINK	sets the colour of a link to a previously visited page
ALINK	sets the colour of an 'active' link (the time between the link being clicked and the new page opening)

Open **index.htm** in your editor and change its `<BODY>` tag so that it looks like this:

```
<BODY BGCOLOR=MAROON TEXT=WHITE LINK=YELLOW
VLINK=OLIVE ALINK=LIME>
```

Save the page and view the result in your browser (Figure 4.1). The colour scheme may not be to your taste (in fact, I hope it isn't!), but you can clearly see the difference made by adding colour attributes to the <BODY> tag. Try swapping colours around to find a scheme you like. There are 140 **named colours** to choose from like those above, and you'll find them listed in Appendix B at the back of the book. If you'd like each page of your site to use a similar scheme, copy and paste the new <BODY> tag into your other pages to replace their empty <BODY> tags.

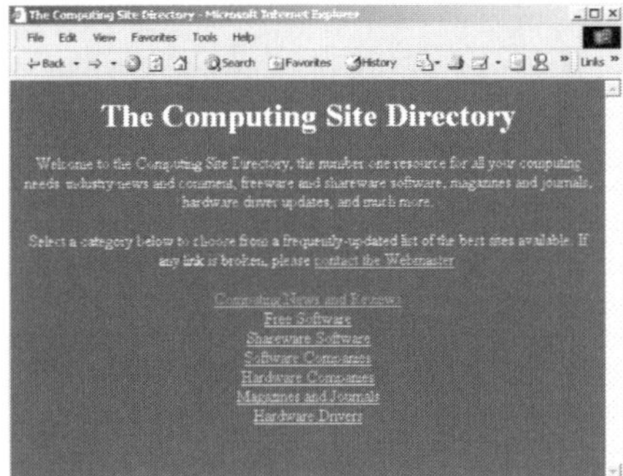

Figure 4.1 A little added colour (maybe too much!)

Rather than copying and pasting identical <BODY> tags into all your pages to change their colours, you could create a single style sheet to be applied to every page, so that a simple change to the sheet would be reflected throughout your site. Skip ahead to Chapter 9 to learn about style sheets.

Adding a background image

Another attribute you can add to the <BODY> tag is **BACKGROUND**. This specifies a GIF or JPEG image file to be used as a background to the Web page, and the image is automatically **tiled** to fill the user's browser window. Because this is a file that the browser has to find, it's entered as a URL just like the HREF attribute of the anchor tag (see Chapter 3). And, as with the anchor tag, although you could enter an absolute URL, you'd have to go online to see the result, so a *relative* URL is preferable.

Tiled image

When an image is tiled, multiple copies of the image are placed side by side in rows and columns to fill a specified area. You'd usually choose or create an image that can be tiled seamlessly so that the joins between each individual tile are invisible.

At the beginning of Chapter 2 you created a directory named **images** in your Site directory, and here's your chance to use it. Find any GIF or JPEG image on your hard disk, or download one from the Web, and copy it into your 'images' directory. You can then add the following attribute to the <BODY> tag of **index.htm**, changing 'space.jpg' to your own image file's name:

```
BACKGROUND="images/space.jpg"
```

Figure 4.2 shows the result of using the background image I chose. If I published a page that looked like this, I'd deserve to have my computer taken away: the size of the image is distracting, its repetition is too obvious, and it involves so many colours that the text of the page would be hard to read whatever text colour was used. In Figure 4.3 I've used something far more subtle: it has a much smaller pattern involving several shades of one colour, and it isn't as eye-catchingly repetitive. A smaller pattern (although it wouldn't reproduce well on the page of this book) would be a better choice still.

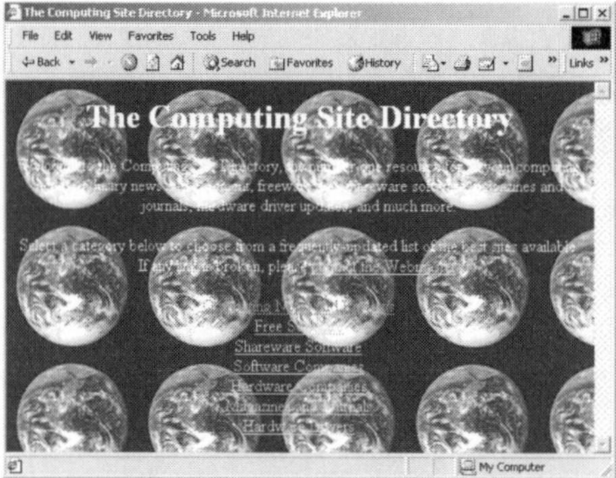

Figure 4.2 **Bad:** an appalling choice of background image. Just shoot me.

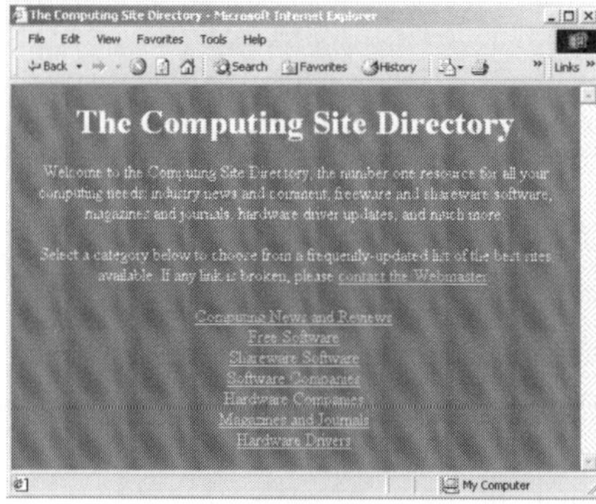

Figure 4.3 **Good:** the less aware you are of the image, the better.

Setting up your font options

At the moment you're stuck with a single font throughout your site (probably Times New Roman in Windows, and Geneva on a Mac). Like the colour options mentioned at the beginning of this chapter, your browser sets a default font, and different browsers may use different defaults. Fortunately the **<FONT>...</FONT>** tag pair leaps to your rescue, allowing you to choose and change the font type, size and colour whenever you need to. Here's an example of a <FONT> tag using all three possible attributes:

```
<FONT FACE="Tahoma,Verdana,Arial", SIZE=4
COLOR=red>
```

Let's take these attributes one at a time. The **FACE** attribute sets the name of the font you want to use, and to prevent errors it's best to always enclose its value in double quotes. Obviously you'd want to choose a font that's available on your own system so that you can see what it looks like, but the same font needs to be on the system of anyone visiting your site too; if it isn't, their browser will revert to its default font. You can't control which fonts your users have available, of course, and adding suggestions on your site that visitors should install a particular font will be treated with deserved indifference. You can keep a bit of extra control by listing more than one font name (separated by commas) as in the example above. If the first font isn't available, the browser will try for the second, and so on. This way, you can start by specifying the font you'd want used in a perfect world, and work through to something that's at least bearable and likely to be available.

Big text, small text

If you find it hard to keep track of the font size you're currently using, don't bother trying! Instead you can use <BIG> and </BIG> to make the text one step larger than its current setting, or <SMALL> and </SMALL> to make it one step smaller.

Font sizes in HTML work differently than in your word processor. There are seven sizes numbered (unsurprisingly) from 1 to 7, where 1 is smallest. The default size for text is 3, so if you wanted to make your text slightly larger, you'd use SIZE=4. The SIZE attribute doesn't affect the headings we covered in Chapter 2, so if there's a heading tag somewhere between your <FONT> and </FONT> tags it will still be formatted in its usual way.

The colour of the text has already been set in the TEXT attribute of the <BODY> tag, covered at the start of this chapter, but you might want to slip in an occasional <FONT COLOR=ivory>... </FONT> to change the colour of a certain word, paragraph or heading. After the closing </FONT> tag, the text colour will revert to the one set in the <BODY> tag.

Choosing fonts

The ability to specify several fonts gives you a lot of flexibility, but you should include at least one font that the majority of users are likely to have. The increased use of Internet Explorer has been useful in that department: recent versions have included a 'font pack' known as Web Core Fonts which contains Arial, Times New Roman, Georgia, Verdana, Comic Sans MS, Trebuchet MS and Impact, so these fonts will be available on the majority of users' systems (including Macs). The same font pack is included with recent Windows versions, and can be downloaded from **http://www.microsoft.com/truetype**.

Adding fonts to the index page

Having discovered the <FONT> tag, let's improve the look of our **index.htm** page by setting a few fonts for it. Alter the code of the page to match the code below (I've marked the changes in bold type) and the result should look similar to Figure 4.4 when viewed in your browser:

```
<HTML>
<HEAD>
      <TITLE>The Computing Site Directory</TITLE>
</HEAD>
<BODY BGCOLOR=white TEXT=black LINK=blue VLINK=navy
ALINK=red>
<CENTER>
<FONT FACE="Georgia,Times New Roman" SIZE=3>
<FONT FACE="Verdana,Arial"><H1>The Computing Site
Directory</H1></FONT>

Welcome to the <FONT COLOR=maroon>Computing Site
Directory</FONT>, the number one resource for all
your computing needs: industry news and comment,
freeware and shareware software, magazines and
journals, hardware driver updates, and much more.

<P>Select a category below to choose from a fre-
quently-updated list of the best sites available. If
any link is broken, please <A HREF="mailto:rob@code-
base.co.uk?subject=Broken link">contact the
Webmaster</A>.

<P>
<FONT FACE="Verdana,Arial" SIZE=4>
<A HREF="news.htm">Computing News and Reviews</A>
<BR><A HREF="free.htm">Free Software</A>
<BR><A HREF="shareware.htm">Shareware Software</A>
<BR><A HREF="softcomp.htm">Software Companies</A>
<BR><A HREF="hardcomp.htm">Hardware Companies</A>
<BR><A HREF="mags.htm">Magazines and Journals</A>
<BR><A HREF="drivers.htm">Hardware Drivers</A>
</FONT>
</CENTER>

</FONT>
</BODY>
</HTML>
```

Figure 4.4 The **index.htm** page, with improved colours and the addition of a few <FONT> tags.

The first <FONT> tag sets the default font to use for the page; its corresponding </FONT> tag is just above the closing </BODY> tag. This means that everything on the page will be displayed in that font and size unless we specify something different for particular sections. And we've done just that in three places:

- The heading has <FONT> tags enclosing it that specify a different font face. Its size is set by the <H1> tags (we could make it smaller using <H2> or <H3>) and its colour is set in the body tag's TEXT attribute.
- The words 'Computing Site Directory' in the first paragraph have been set to a different colour. Because we haven't included FACE or SIZE attributes, these remain the same as the other text in that paragraph, set in the very first <FONT> tag.
- The list of links has been set a different font and size in a similar way. Adding a COLOR attribute here would be ignored: the link colours are set by the LINK/ALINK/VLINK attributes of the body tag and can only be changed through the use of style sheets (see Chapter 9).

Page divisions with horizontal rules

Horizontal rules are straight lines with an engraved 3D look that divide a page into sections. For the simplest type of rule, the only tag you need is **<HR>**. This automatically puts a horizontal rule across the full width of the page, placing a paragraph break before and after it. Because the rule isn't an effect that needs to be 'switched off', there's no closing tag.

If you want to, you can get clever with the <HR> tag by adding some (or all!) of its available attributes, shown in Table 4.2.

Table 4.2 Horizontal rules

Use this attribute...	...for this result
ALIGN=	Use LEFT or RIGHT to place the rule on one side of the page. Without this attribute the rule will be centred
SIZE=	Enter any number to set the height of the rule in pixels. The default size is two pixels high
WIDTH=	You could enter a number to specify the width of the rule (in pixels), but as you don't know how wide the user's browser window is, this is usually to be avoided. Instead, specify a percentage of the window's width, such as WIDTH="70%"
COLOR=	Enter a colour name or hex number to set the colour of the rule. Only Internet Explorer supports this; other browsers will ignore it. The default colour varies according to the page's background colour (<BODY BGCOLOR>)
NOSHADE	This removes the 3D shading from the rule, leaving a solid line. There's no equals sign and no value to add

It's worth experimenting with the <HR> tag to find out what you can do with it. For example, the following piece of code places a square bullet in the centre of the page which makes a smart, 'minimalist' divider (Figure 4.5):

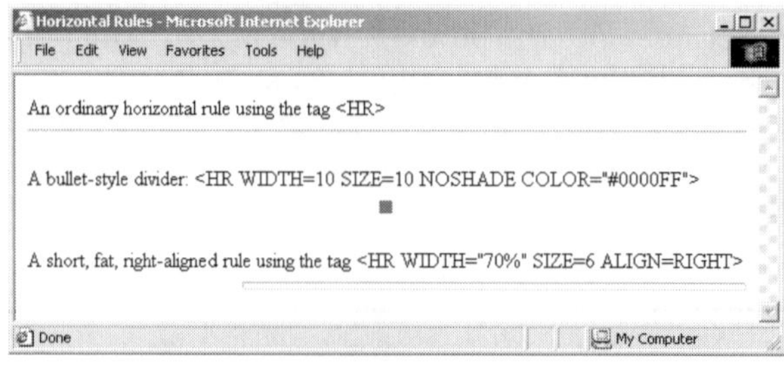

Figure 4.5 The <HR> tag in action.

```
<HR WIDTH=10 SIZE=10 NOSHADE COLOR=blue>
```

Getting graphic – adding images and buttons

5

What you need to create your own Web graphics

Find out how to add images to the page

Place images exactly where you want them

Set the size and spacing of images

Use images as links instead of text

So far the example site we're building is 'text only' – there is not a single image in sight. From the point of view of speed, that's not a bad thing: we could work through the seven empty 'category' pages we created, adding links and descriptions for hundreds of great computing sites, and our entire site would probably still weigh in at less than 30 Kb! There won't be much that's attractive or fun about the site, but maybe the content is good enough to make up for that? The odds are that you want a more stylish site, though, and a well-chosen image or two can make a lot of difference to visual impact and layout.

Creating your own images

To create and edit images for use on the Web, you'll need a graphics program capable of working with GIF and JPEG formats (which I'll explain in a moment). These are very common formats, so you may find that the software bundled with your operating system (such as Windows Paint) or your scanner or printer (Adobe PhotoDeluxe, perhaps) will do the job.

Graphics is one area where the quality of the tool can make a lot of difference to the quality of the result, so here are two of the tools used by most professional designers. Although they're both commercial programs, they can be downloaded for a free 30-day trial, so I'd recommend picking one of these and giving it a try.

- **Macromedia Fireworks** from **http://www.macromedia.com**. This is an easy-to-use but comprehensive program aimed at Web graphics creation, with many useful features.
- **Paint Shop Pro** from **http://www.digitalworkshop.co.uk**. (Figure 5.1). This is one of the most popular graphics tools among Web designers, and includes an animation program.

Figure 5.1 Paint Shop Pro, one of the most popular tools for creating Web graphics.

The images you use on the Web must be in either **JPEG** or **GIF** format. Unlike some of the other computer graphics formats you can choose from when you save an image, these are *compressed* formats – they save the picture into a much smaller file, and size matters a lot on the Web!

- **JPEG** (pronounced *jay-peg*) stands for Joint Photographic Experts Group and, as the name suggests, it was designed for working with photographs (or more generally, images containing lifelike colouring and shading). JPEG images can contain up to 16.7 million colours.
- **GIF** (pronounced with a hard or a soft 'g' according to taste) is an acronym for Graphics Interchange Format, and again the clue is in the name: GIF was designed as a format for computer-created images – pictures that typically contain blocks of a single colour. GIF images can contain up to 256 different colours, which is usually fine for graphics you design yourself, but often gives poor results with photographs.

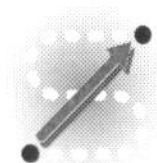

Deciding between JPEG and GIF

If you're unsure which is the best format for your image, create it with your graphics program set to use 16.7 million colours and save it in JPEG format. Next, reduce the number of colours to 256 and save again in GIF format. You can then compare the file sizes and picture qualities to decide which you want to stick with.

In most graphics programs, saving an image in one of these formats is simple: choose **Save As** from the File menu, and select the format to use from the **Save As Type** list before you click the **Save** button. GIF images will be given the extension .gif, and JPEG images will have either .jpg or .jpeg.

Help! I'm artistically challenged!

We can't all be good artists, but modern graphics programs contain many features to help the graphically inept produce amazing results. All you need is the ability to recognise an effective graphic when you see one, and to spend some time getting to know your chosen software.

If you really can't be tempted into experimenting, though, there are plenty of ways to get your hands on free artwork for the Web. One of those is the Web itself, of course, and I've included a list of sites offering free graphics in Appendix C at the back of the book. If you have one of the WYSIWYG site creation programs I mentioned in Chapter 1, you may be able to use the graphics provided with the software's templates. If you have an Office suite such as Microsoft Office, Microsoft Works or Lotus SmartSuite, you may be able to use images from their clip-art galleries. You can also buy CD-ROMs containing thousands of examples of free-use graphics, although the quality of these can vary enormously.

Finally, if you have a scanner you can scan photographs or graphics you've created on paper. Most good graphics programs have an **Acquire** option among their menus: clicking that will start the scanning process and load the finished result into the graphics software for touching up and saving in the correct format for the Web.

Adding images to the page

In Chapter 4 we looked at out how to add a tiled background image to a Web page by adding the BACKGROUND attribute to the page's <BODY> tag. To do that, we used a relative URL giving the location of the image file relative to the location of the current Web page. Adding an **inline image** to the page works in just the same way, but there's a particular tag we use to do the job: the **<IMG>** tag.

Returning to our **index.htm** page, I've created an image to replace the heading at the top of the page and called it **banner.gif**. At the moment we're using the code below to put the heading on the page and set a font for it:

```
<FONT FACE="Verdana,Arial"><H1>The Computing
Site Directory</H1></FONT>
```

Inline image
This really just means 'an image on a Web page'. The word inline *is often used to differentiate between an image displayed among the text of the page itself and an image used as a background or shown only if a link to the image is clicked.*

To replace that heading with the image, replace that code with this:

```
<IMG SRC="images/banner.gif"><P>
```

As usual, it's sensible to put the image file in the 'images' directory so that we'll know where to find it if we want to reuse it on future pages. I've also added a <P> tag: the <H1> tag we were using before gave us a paragraph break after the heading which the <IMG> tag doesn't, so we need to add it ourselves. The result should look like Figure 5.2.

Figure 5.2 The **index.htm** page with an image replacing the text heading.

The code above shows the <IMG> tag at its most basic. The **SRC** attribute (short for 'source') tells the browser where to find the image file you want to display, following the same rules as those for relative URLs covered in Chapter 3. The only thing the <IMG> tag does is to put an image on the page, so of all the possible attributes that could be added to this tag, the SRC attribute is the only one that *must* be included.

Aligning images

Like most of the HTML tags that add something new to the page (a paragraph, a heading, a horizontal rule, etc.), the <IMG> tag can have an ALIGN attribute to give you some control over where the image should be placed in relation to the items around it. In fact, you have a *lot* of control! The <IMG> tag's ALIGN attribute (Table 5.1) has more values available than any we've seen so far.

Table 5.1 Aligning images

This attribute...	...does this
ALIGN=TOP	Aligns the top of the image with the top of the tallest item on the same line
ALIGN=TEXTTOP	Aligns the top of the image with the top of the tallest text on the same line. This is similar to ALIGN=TOP, but ignores anything on the line that isn't text
ALIGN=MIDDLE	Aligns the baseline of the text on the same line with the middle of the image
ALIGN=ABSMIDDLE	Aligns the middle of the line of text with the middle of the image
ALIGN=BOTTOM	Aligns the baseline of the text on the same line with the bottom of the image (ALIGN=BASELINE does the same thing)
ALIGN=ABSBOTTOM	Aligns the bottom of the text with the bottom of the image. This is subtly different from ALIGN=BOTTOM: the *baseline* of the text is the line that characters such as 'm', 'b' and 'r' sit on; characters such as 'g' and 'y' drop below that line, and *bottom* is the lowest point that those characters reach
ALIGN=LEFT	Places the image on a new line against the left margin, with any text that follows the image wrapped to its right
ALIGN=RIGHT	Places the image against the right margin, with text wrapped to its left

Figure 5.3 shows the result of using those ALIGN values in an image tag and placing a short line of text immediately after the image, such as <IMG SRC="images/box.gif" ALIGN=TOP>Align=TOP. I've put a <P> tag after the text in each case to create a reasonable gap between each image for clarity.

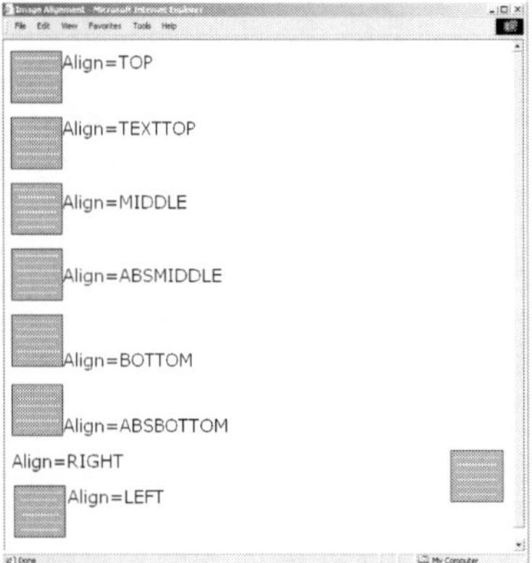

Figure 5.3 Fine-tuning the alignment of an image with a line of text.

Creating space around images

Using the ALIGN attribute, then, you can place the image roughly where you want it in relation to text or other images around it. What's needed is a bit more fine-tuning: after all, if you use ALIGN=ABSMIDDLE, the image will be butted right up against any text on the same line, and any text on the line preceding or following it.

The answer comes in the form of two more attributes which add some blank space around the image: **HSPACE** inserts space either side of the image (*horizontally*), and **VSPACE** adds space above and below it (*vertically*). Just enter a number in pixels after the equals sign. As usual with attributes, if you only need to use one of these, there's no need to enter the other. In Figure 5.4, the top image is inserted using <IMG SRC="images/box.gif" ALIGN=LEFT>; the bottom one uses <IMG SRC="images/box.gif" ALIGN=LEFT VSPACE=10 HSPACE=15>.

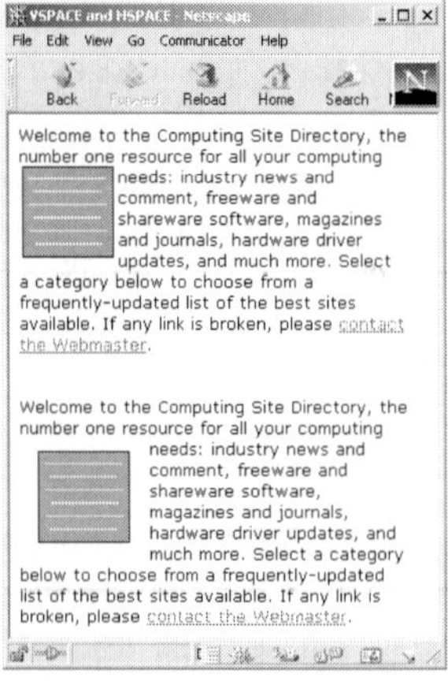

Figure 5.4 Adding HSPACE and VSPACE attributes to the image tag in the second example adds blank space around the image.

Getting the size right!

Two of the most important <IMG> attributes are **WIDTH** and **HEIGHT**, with which you specify the dimensions of the image. If you've experimented with the image tag, you'll have noticed that your browser displays the image properly without these attributes, so you're probably wondering why you would need to find and enter the image's dimensions.

At the moment you're looking at pages and images that are already on your computer – there's no downloading involved yet, so your browser loads the page and shows the images in the blink of an eye. When your page is on the Web and someone visits it, things work a bit differently. When the browser arrives at an <IMG> tag with no WIDTH or HEIGHT attributes, it has to download the image, work out its dimensions and display it before it can decide how to lay out anything below the image. However, if the browser already knows how much space to reserve for the image, it can display an empty box until the image has downloaded, with the text correctly positioned around it.

You can find an image's dimensions easily by loading it into almost any good graphics program. In Paint Shop Pro, for example, you'll see them displayed in the bottom-right corner of the window. Make a mental note of the figures and add them to your tag like this:

```
<IMG SRC="images/banner.gif" WIDTH=503 HEIGHT=58>
```

Bear in mind that when you enter the dimensions of an image, the browser will take your word for it! In other words, the browser will resize the image to these dimensions regardless of what the original image was supposed to look like. This can be useful to increase or decrease the size of an image without creating a new version of it (or to create weird effects), but it's also a prime opportunity to screw things up!

Size matters!

If you need another good reason to add WIDTH and HEIGHT attributes, here it is: most browsers have an option to surf the Web without displaying images, and some people use it – pages load faster that way. Where images should appear on the page, the browser draws a 'placeholder' box containing a small icon. If you don't enter the dimensions of your images, those users will see a tiny box just large enough to contain the icon, which might upset your carefully-planned page layout. With the image dimensions entered, the placeholder box will be the size you wanted it to be.

Using alternative text

Another useful attribute of the image tag is **ALT**, which specifies alternative text to display in place of the image. This is shown in the placeholder box on the page while the image is downloading, and in Internet Explorer and Netscape it's also displayed in a tooltip when the mouse moves over the image. For any visitors surfing without images displayed, this alternative text is the only clue to what that image would be if they could see it. So let's change the <IMG> tag in the **index.htm** page to add the correct dimensions and some alternative text. For visitors who've turned off image display, the page will look something like Figure 5.5.

```
<IMG SRC="images/banner.gif" WIDTH=503 HEIGHT=58
ALT="The Computing Site Directory">
```

Figure 5.5 With dimensions and alternative text added, the result is still meaningful when images are switched off.

Button it! Images as links

In Chapter 3 you learnt how to create hypertext links to a Web page or file using the tag `<A HREF="URL">clickable text</A>`. But the clickable section that appears on the page doesn't have to be text: you can use an image instead. (In fact, you can use an image *and* text if you want to – just place it all between the opening and closing anchor tags as you want it to appear on the page.)

Let's replace the seven category-links on the **index.htm** page with button images to demonstrate this. I've created seven images, all with the same dimensions but with different text on each. In the section of the page containing the seven links, remove the <FONT> tags surrounding this block of code (we won't be displaying text there any longer, so they're redundant), and replace the text between each anchor tag with the appropriate image tag like this:

```
<P><A HREF="pages/news.htm"><IMG
SRC="images/news.jpg" WIDTH=185
HEIGHT=27></A><BR>

<A HREF="pages/free.htm"><IMG
SRC="images/free.jpg" WIDTH=185
HEIGHT=27></A><BR>

<A HREF="pages/shareware.htm"><IMG
SRC="images/shareware. jpg" WIDTH=185
HEIGHT=27></A><BR>

<A HREF="pages/softcomp.htm"><IMG
SRC="images/softcomp. jpg" WIDTH=185
HEIGHT=27></A><BR>

<A HREF="pages/hardcomp.htm"><IMG SRC="images/
hardcomp. jpg" WIDTH=185 HEIGHT=27></A><BR>
```

```
<A    HREF="pages/mags.htm"><IMG    SRC="images/
mags.jpg" WIDTH= 185 HEIGHT=27></A><BR>

<A  HREF="pages/drivers.htm"><IMG  SRC="images/
drivers.jpg" WIDTH=185 HEIGHT=27></A>
```

If you look at the page in your browser, you'll see that there's a problem: because we're using these images as links, the browser puts a border around each one in the same colour as hyperlinked text. The intention, of course, is to make it clear that these *are* links, but on this page that should be pretty obvious to anyone visiting; those borders just make the page look messy. Fortunately the <IMG> tag has another attribute, **BORDER**, that can help us out. We can add any number after the equals sign to set the thickness of the border, and zero is as valid as any other figure, so add a BORDER=0 attribute to each of the <IMG> tags. The result should look like Figure 5.6.

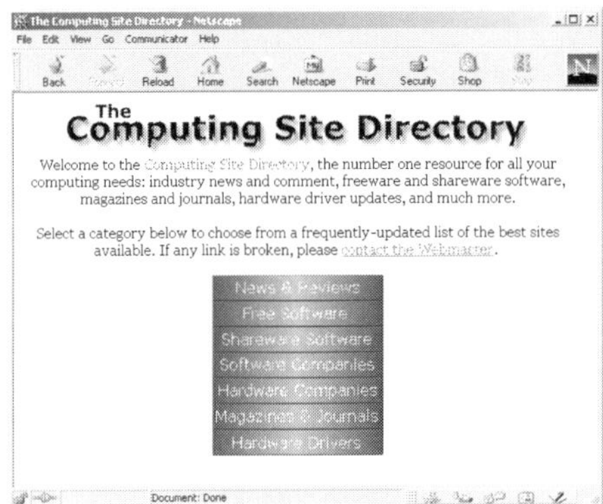

Figure 5.6 The **index.htm** page, after replacing the text links with images.

Border or no border?

The BORDER attribute can be added to any <IMG> tag, whether the image is a link or not. Non-linking images don't have a border by default, but you can create one by adding BORDER=1 to the tag (change the number according to the thickness you want).

Looking around the Web, you'll notice that most site designers remove the border from linking images. What matters most is that visitors can tell that an image is a link by looking at it, and the design of the image itself can usually get that across. Images containing text, for example, are generally expected to be links, as are any similarly-styled collections of images placed close together. If a page doesn't contain much in the way of hyperlinked text, most visitors will pass the mouse over images to see if they're links. In these situations, hypertext-coloured borders are unnecessary and probably spoil the appearance of the page.

One of the few situations in which you might want to consider leaving the border intact is if you have a single image on the page some way away from other images. For example, you may have an envelope icon at the bottom of the page acting as an email link (see Chapter 3). A border will help to draw attention to it as well as make it clear that it's a link.

Web multimedia

6

It sounds cool, but what's it all about?

Build GIF animations from a sequence of still images

Add music and video to your website

Keep it live with automatic webcam feeds

Add style, animation and interactivity with Java

Yes, it's showtime! Up to this point in the book, we've only dealt with text and images which, although they obviously fall into the *multimedia* definition, don't really have the glitz conjured up by that magic word. In this chapter we'll take a look at some of the other forms of media you can add to your pages, from the obvious (animation, audio and video) to the less obvious (live camera feeds and small interactive programs).

Using GIF animation

Animation is one of the first ingredients you think of when you set out to design an all-singing, all-dancing multimedia website. Something that moves, after all, catches the eye far more quickly than something that doesn't, which is why most advertising banners are animated. But there's a balance to be struck here, as usual: a site that sings or dances *too much* is just annoying! Animated images can be used to good effect to draw the eye towards your logo or to create small animated bullets beside your links, but animations shouldn't be scattered over a wide area of the page.

The most-used type of animation is the **animated GIF**, and it's very easy to add to a Web page: it just slots into an `<IMG>` tag's `SRC` attribute as if it were an ordinary, non-animated image. Animated GIFs are easy to make, too – you just create a series of separate images with small differences between each (the way cartoons are created) and then load them into your animation program to assemble them into a single file. *What* animation program? Here are a few to choose from:

- **Animation Shop** (Figure 6.1), an animation program included with Paint Shop Pro from **http://www.digitalworkshop.co.uk**.

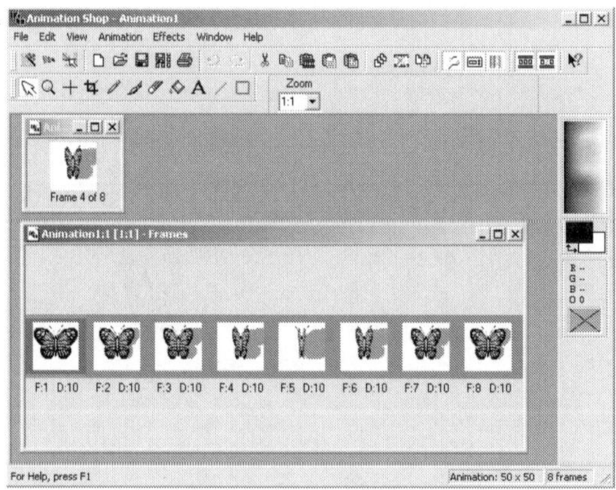

Figure 6.1 Animation Shop displaying one of its sample animations and the eight separate images from which it was formed.

- **Ulead GIF Animator** from **http://www.ulead.com**.
- **Macromedia Fireworks**, one of the graphics programs I mentioned in Chapter 5, has built-in animation options. Visit **http://www.macromedia.com** for this one.

I'm going to plump for Animation Shop, but the methods and options will be very similar whatever program you decide to use yourself.

Animation, or a very fast slideshow?

It's not easy to judge how smooth the animated result will be while you're creating a set of still images. To keep the file size down, the number of frames (separate images) should be kept to a minimum, and the differences between each frame should be small enough to give smooth transitions from one to the next. After creating three or four images, load them into your animator and check the result before going any further – if the animation looks too jerky after adjusting the delay times of each frame, you'll have fewer images to edit!

Creating an animated GIF

The first job, of course, is to create the sequence of separate images that will form the frames of the animation. Animation Shop can use images in most formats, but since the final movie file will be in GIF format, it's sensible to save each image as a GIF too. To save headaches later, make sure the dimensions of each image are identical.

Fire up Animation Shop and choose **Animation Wizard** from the File menu. Follow the six steps to set the amount of time that most (if not all) the images should be displayed, and choose a background colour. At step 5, click the **Add Image** button to select all the separate images you created, and use the two **Move** buttons to assemble them into the correct order.

When you've completed the Wizard, the strip of frames will be shown, as in Figure 6.2, and you can make changes to any single frame. For example, if a frame should be displayed for a different amount of time from that set in the Wizard, right-click it, choose **Properties** and type a new delay time. You can preview the result at any time by choosing **Animation** from the View menu.

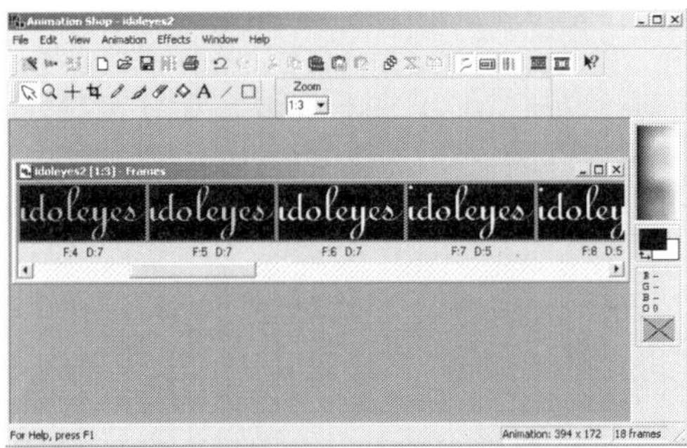

Figure 6.2 Animation Shop displays each frame along with its index number in the sequence and its delay time.

Animation Shop includes a set of effects and transitions on its **Effects** menu that you can apply to an animation – in fact, you can create an entire animation by combining just a single image with one or more effects. Pick carefully though: these effects create extra frames in your animation and may make a huge difference to its size. The effect I used took my simple 25 Kb animation up to an unusable 636 Kb! Use the options in the **Define effect** section (Figure 6.3) to choose how long the effect should last and how many frames it should cover.

Easy animation editing

Another benefit of animated GIFs is that they're easy to edit. You don't have to keep the original sequence of files; you can simply load the animated file into any GIF animator to view, edit or export individual frames, adjust timings and transparency, and so on.

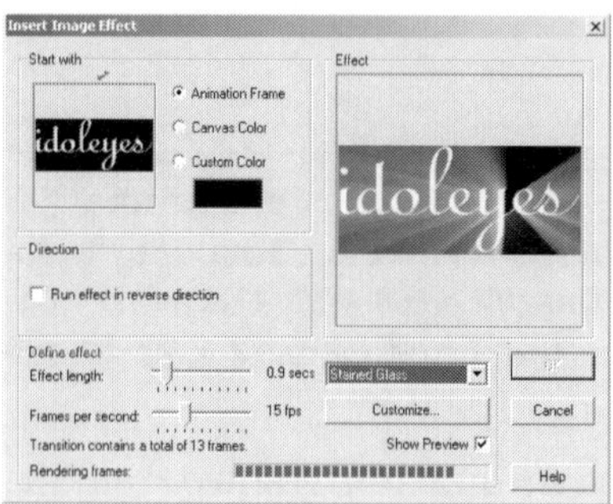

Figure 6.3 Select a frame and choose a transition or effect to be inserted after it.

When you're happy with the result of previewing the animation, choose **Save As** from the File menu and save the result. Next, start the **Optimization Wizard** (also on the File menu) to experiment with reducing the size of the file. If you decide you've over-optimised and lost too much quality, you can reload the original animation and try again.

Viewers and plug-ins

A viewer is an entirely separate program that you could run by itself if you wanted to. Most plug-ins can also be used as viewers, so if you were to install a plug-in that would handle a particular type of movie format found on a Web page, it could probably be used to play any movies of the same type that you'd saved to your hard disk. A plug-in is a program that embeds itself into the Web page, rather like an image.

How does Web-based multimedia work?

By itself, the Web browser has built-in support for a very small range of media types – essentially just text and a few image formats. For other types of media it relies on extra software in the form of a **plug-in** or **viewer**, and uses a system called **MIME** (Multipurpose Internet Mail Extensions) to determine which of the user's installed plug-ins to use for a particular type of content.

Whenever content is sent from the Web server to the user's browser, that content is accompanied by a **MIME type** such as **text/html**, **text/css**, **image/gif**, or **video/mpeg**. If the browser recognises the type as something it can handle unaided (as with the first three types) it gets on with it. If not, it looks at the user's system to see if any installed software has been set to handle the type. If it has, the software will appear on the page as a plug-in, or in its own window as a viewer, and take over the management of that particular piece of content from the browser.

So what happens if there's *no* compatible software installed? In some cases, the browser will offer to download the file containing the anonymous content so that the user can save it and play it later (after installing some suitable software). In other cases, the browser may simply ignore the content and place a little 'broken multimedia' icon on the page to indicate that the content can't be displayed, or it may offer to install the required plug-in.

Linked versus embedded media

When you decide to add multimedia content to a page, you have to make a choice: do you want to embed it into the page, or link it?

- **Embedded** media appears on the page like an image, and therefore has to be downloaded along with all the other items on the page.
- Using **Linked** media means adding a link to the file on your page, letting visitors choose whether to click-and-play or ignore it. The URL in the link may point directly at the media file, or it may point to a different page in which you've *embedded* the media.

As a general rule, if the media file is particularly large or the user is unlikely to have a compatible plug-in installed, use a link. That way, you can add a note to tell users the size of the file and where to download the plug-in before they continue (Figure 6.4).

Figure 6.4 An embedded audio file, with visible controls giving visitors a chance to turn it off!

Background sounds (if you must!)

It seems to me that however much you dislike the people that visit your site, forcing them to endure background music is inhumane. At best, they'll be forced to mute their computer's audio output; at worst, they'll be gone so fast they leave skid-marks. Will anyone actually *enjoy* it? Perhaps, but only the first time they visit, and only if the music doesn't loop endlessly.

If I haven't deterred you with that (and I hope I have!), here's the HTML code to embed a background audio file into the page:

```
<EMBED SRC="island.mid" LOOP=FALSE HIDDEN=FALSE>
```

The `SRC` attribute does the same job here that it does with the `<IMG>` tag, giving the URL of the audio file to be used. You can specify any type of sampled sound or MIDI file, but it's best to stick with common formats such as .wav, .mp3, .mid and .au.

The `LOOP` attribute can be `true` or `false`, but I strongly recommend using `false`, meaning that the file plays just once. The `HIDDEN` attribute offers the same two values to determine whether the control interface for the player plug-in will be visible (shown in Figure 6.4). This gives your visitors a chance to turn off the music, but the interface is rarely attractive. Fortunately it doesn't matter where you place the `<EMBED>` tag, so you can put it at the bottom of your page to avoid detracting from your other visible content.

Play-on-demand audio

Remember that your audio options aren't limited to embedded background sounds – you can create links to sound files and let visitors choose which files to listen to (Figure 6.5). (The same applies to videos, animations, and any other type of media you want to include, of course.)

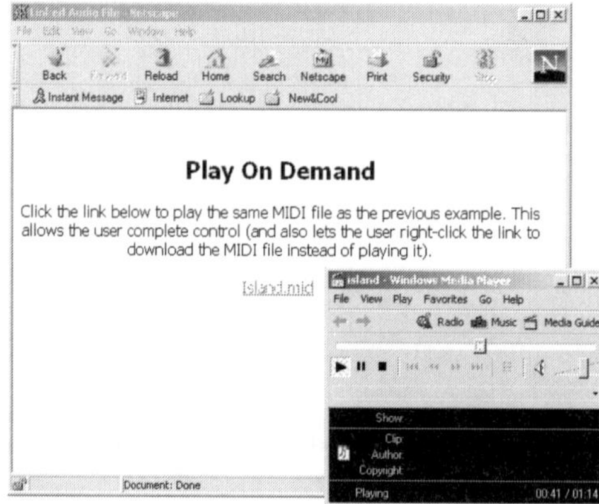

Figure 6.5 Using links to media files (or to pages containing embedded media files) hands control back to the visitor.

If you want to create your own audio files, there's plenty of software around to help you do it. In fact, your operating system may already offer everything you need: most versions of Windows include the Sound Recorder utility, for instance, to create digital audio recordings. If you have musical talents, you can create your own MIDI files using software such as Cubase (**http://www.us. steinberg.net**), Cakewalk (**http://www.cakewalk.com**) or the simpler Band-In-A-Box (**http://www.pgmusic.com**). Or you can convert existing CD tracks and wave audio files to the popular MP3 format using Xing's AudioCatalyst or MP3 Encoder (**http://www.xingtech.com**). Most Web users will have plug-ins that can handle the types of audio file I've mentioned so far. However, the MP3 format is a comparatively recent arrival, so you may want to point visitors in the direction of the free Winamp plug-in (**http://www.winamp.com**) if your site is going to include MP3s.

Movie time: adding video

Video files are pretty rare things on the Web, chiefly used to show clips from feature films and home movies. They're also *big* files: 20 seconds of video can easily amount to over 1 Mb, meaning that it takes a lot longer to download the movie than it does to watch it!

There are three video formats in use:

1. **AVI** is the Windows video format, and it's best avoided for movies unless you also offer one of the following formats as an alternative.
2. **QuickTime** is a movie format from Apple (**http://www.apple .com/quicktime**) which requires the QuickTime Viewer plug-in. An interesting alternative to the video file is QuickTime VR, an interactive virtual reality format. Click the **Developer** link on this site's button-bar to learn more about the QuickTime Pro content-creation program.
3. **MPEG** (pronounced *emm-peg*) is the best-known video format. To create MPEG video files or convert from existing image and movie formats you need an MPEG encoder such as the Xing MPEG Video Encoder (**http://www.xingtech.com**).

As with the popular audio formats, most of your visitors will have an MPEG-compatible movie viewer (particularly since Windows 98 and later versions all include Microsoft's ActiveMovie or Media Player), but it won't necessarily be able to handle QuickTime videos. If you plump for the QuickTime video or VR formats, include the attribute `PLUGINSPAGE="http://www.apple.com/quicktime/download"` in your `<EMBED>` tag. The browser will then offer unequipped visitors the option of installing the QuickTime Viewer (Figure 6.6).

Here's the tag you'll use to embed a video into your Web page. Remember not to include the `HIDDEN` attribute for video embedding, or the movie won't be visible!

```
<EMBED SRC="mymovie.mpg" LOOP=FALSE>
```

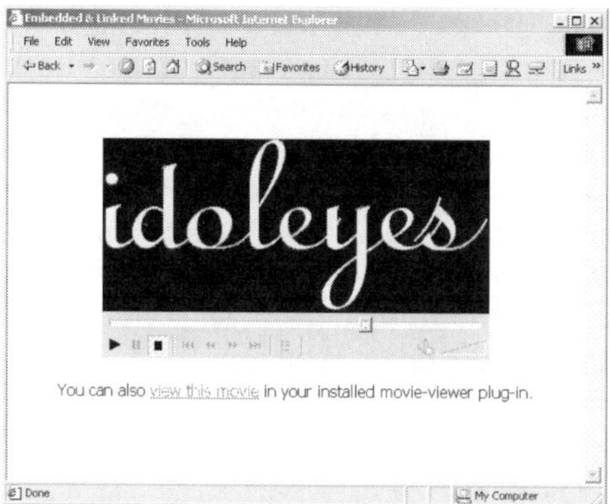

Figure 6.6 An embedded movie file, shown using the Windows Media Player plug-in.

The live cam experience!

If you haven't come across live cam sites, the whole idea will probably seem a bit weird. You buy a little webcam for around £50, connect it to your computer, and set a few options in the software that accompanies it – how often it should take a picture, how to upload the result to your website, and so on – then point it at something interesting. If you'd like a sample, try the New Jersey Diner Cam at **http://www.nj.com/dinercam/live.html** (Figure 6.7).

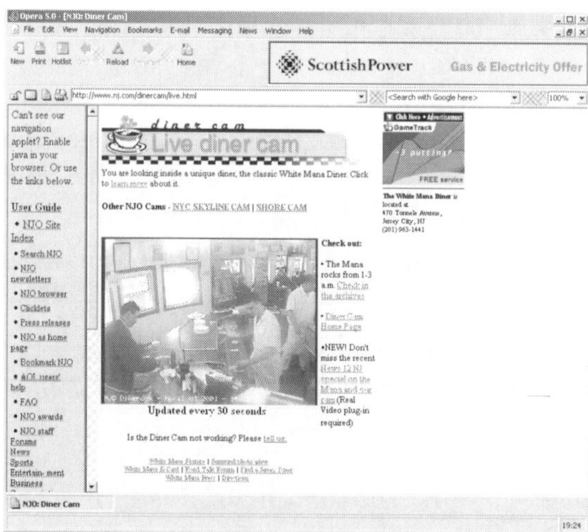

Figure 6.7 The wonders of live cam at the New Jersey Diner Cam website.

The whole live cam thing is a gimmick, of course, but it does have practical value. Live cam sites are popular, and good sites (where the camera is actually switched on and something moves once in a while) are few and far between, so this really can attract visitors. You may be able to think of something useful to point the camera at, too; for instance, there are live cams showing up-to-the-minute snow conditions in ski resorts, and traffic conditions on busy roads in major cities.

The catch with live cam is that a new picture has to be uploaded to your Web server every minute or so at most: if there's too much waiting around involved, visitors won't bother. The software bundled with your camera can do all this for you, but if you have to pay call charges for your Internet connection it'll cost a small fortune! It's an option best suited to those with DSL, cable, or some other form of 'always on' connection.

Java applets: action and interactivity

In computer terms, an **applet** is a small application or utility that forms part of a bigger piece of software. On the Web, it's a small program written in a programming language called **Java** and slotted into the page like an image. Being a program rather than a single type of content, a Java applet can do quite a lot: it can be animated; it can display GIF or JPEG images; it can play sounds; it can provide hyperlinks; it can react to mouse movement and clicks in any way you wish, and a lot more (Figure 6.8).

Vested interest alert!
I won't ramble on about the life-enhancing qualities of Java applets. My own company designs Java applets, so of course I think they're pretty great. Nevertheless, they're just another option to consider, and you may feel they're not suitable for your own site.

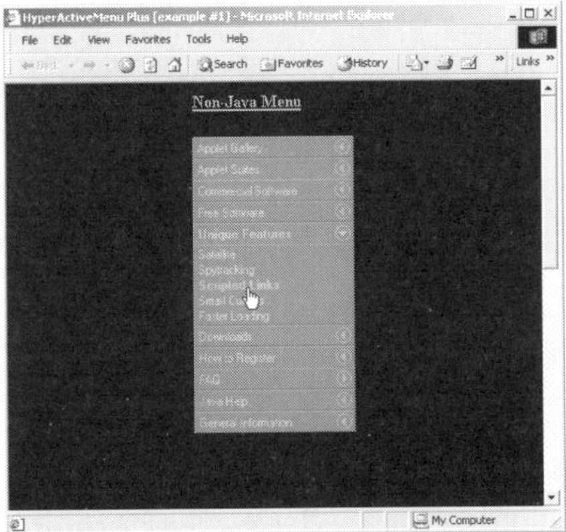

Figure 6.8 An animated, interactive Java menu system in action, with an HTML link to an alternative non-Java page.

Although Java programming is more complicated than HTML, there are many free applets available on the Web, and for this section I'll assume that you've got your hands on one of those and just need to slot it into your page. Here are a few places to find free Java applets online. Whatever applet you use, make sure it comes with documentation or an example Web page.

- **Cool Focus** at **http://www.coolfocus.com**, freeware and shareware applets from my own company (you knew I'd get that in somewhere, didn't you?)
- **JavaSoft** at **http://www.javasoft.com/applets**, free applets from Sun, the creators of Java.
- **JavaFile.com** at **http://www.javafile.com**, a collection of applets from a variety of companies and programmers.

A Java applet consists of one or more files with a **.class** extension, which together form the program itself. Along with the .class files, there may be image and sound files. You might have a file with a .jar extension: this is a zip-like compressed archive file that contains the .class files (and perhaps copies of those images and sounds). Modern browsers can find all the necessary files in the .jar archive, making the applet download and start running more quickly.

Java applets have their own tag for placement on a page, the **<APPLET>** tag. A very simple Java applet could be placed on the page like this:

```
<APPLET CODE="myapplet.class" WIDTH=100 HEIGHT
=100>
</APPLET>
```

The three attributes, CODE, WIDTH and HEIGHT are all required. The CODE attribute is the important one: it gives the name of the .class file that the browser should load. (If your applet uses several .class files, check the documentation to find out which one should be used here.) Note that this isn't a URL, it must be just the *name* of the file.

To these attributes, you can add ALIGN, HSPACE and VSPACE, using the same alignment and spacing options as the <IMG> tag (see Chapter 5). If the applet came with a .jar file, add the attribute ARCHIVE="myapplet.jar", once again using just the name of the file, not its URL.

The CODEBASE attribute: find those files!

As yet, then, we haven't included any URLs at all in the <APPLET> tag, so the browser is going to assume that the applet files are in the same directory as the current Web page. If you prefer to put all the files somewhere else, such as your 'images' directory or a new 'applets' directory, you need to tell the browser to look in the right place. Another attribute, **CODEBASE**, is used for the job.

The CODEBASE attribute is a URL, but it's the URL of a directory, not a file. The way to work it out is to take the URL of one of the applet files, strip the filename from the end, and put the remainder into the CODEBASE attribute. So if your Web pages were in the root directory of your site (your 'site' directory) and the applet files are all in a subfolder called 'applets', the attribute would be **CODEBASE="applets/"**. (The slash at the end is optional.)

Choosing options with parameters

Most Java applets have a range of options you can choose from to customise its appearance or behaviour, and these are specified using the <PARAM> tag. You can include as many <PARAM> tags as you need to, placed in any order between the <APPLET> and </APPLET> tags.

The <PARAM> tag has two compulsory attributes, NAME and VALUE, and this is where it's vital to have some documentation for the applet or an example Web page – you need to know which parameter names you can use, and what the available values are for each. (Guesswork is no good here: applet designers make up their own names, and can choose anything they like!) Here's an example of a complete <APPLET> tag that includes three parameters:

```
<APPLET CODE="myapplet.class" WIDTH=100
HEIGHT=100 CODEBASE="../classes">
<PARAM NAME="BackgroundColour" VALUE="800000">
<PARAM NAME="Text" VALUE="Home Page">
<PARAM NAME="URL" VALUE="../index.htm">
</APPLET>
```

Help – Class not found!

If you load a page containing an applet and see a blank box on the page, with the words 'Class ... not found' shown in the browser's status bar, the browser can't find your .class file(s). Make sure you've got the correct name in the CODE attribute, and the path to the correct directory in CODEBASE. Also make sure that all the files are in the same directory, and that you have been given every file you need!

What else?

In this chapter we've covered all the major types of Web multimedia, but there are other less important types – an example would be virtual reality (VRML), which was much hyped as the future of Web design a couple of years ago, and has since pretty much vanished. The catch with VRML, as with many other forms of media, is that companies created their own extensions to the VRML language to add irresistible new features, all of which required the user to download a huge proprietary plug-in. A diehard VRML fan could arm himself with 20 Mb of plug-ins and *still* find virtual reality scenes he couldn't view!

If you stick with the common types of sound and movie format we've talked about, you can be sure that a large part of your audience will have the necessary software to enjoy them. If you're tempted towards a less common type of media, bear these final tips in mind:

- Include a clear link to the site from which the plug-in can be downloaded (don't just include it in the <EMBED> tag).

- If the plug-in is more than a few hundred kilobytes in size, you'll have to do a good selling job to explain why visitors should install it! Try to include links to other sites that use it.
- Avoid embedding unusual media types into pages and catching visitors by surprise. Let them read about the format, install the plug-in, and follow links to the media pages.

7

Tables – the number one layout tool

Tables? Surely they're just lists in boxes?

The three tags that make a table

Add style and colour to visible tables

Use tables for simple data display or advanced page design

If the word *tables* has got you thinking of rows and columns of dull-looking data, you're on the right lines: that's what HTML tables were originally planned for. But what makes them especially valuable to Web designers is that a cell in a table can contain anything at all – text, images or another table – and its contents can be aligned separately from anything else on the page. This gives a similar kind of design freedom to that found in desktop publishing. Even without getting to grips with style sheets (as we will in Chapter 9), tables can be used to put things almost exactly where you want them on the page.

The obvious table

The easiest way to get started with tables is to create an 'obvious' table – a structured list of items grouped into rows and columns. This introduces the three tags that matter most in table creation: **<TABLE>**, **<TR>** and **<TD>**. The <TABLE> tag is used as a <TABLE>...</TABLE> pair to mark the beginning and end of a table; <TR> is used to mark the start and end of a row of cells in a table; and <TD> is used to mark the start and end of a single cell in a row.

```
You can contact some imaginary people at the
email addresses below:

<TABLE BORDER=1>
<TR><TD>AnthonyTurnip</TD><TD>anthony@turnipfam-
ily.com</TD></TR>
<TR><TD>DuanePipe</TD><TD>dp@gutter.org</TD></TR>
<TR> <TD>Bill Stickers</TD><TD>1045878@parkhurst
.co.uk</TD> </TR>
</TABLE>
```

The code above creates the simple table shown in Figure 7.1. The entire table is contained between <TABLE> and </TABLE> tags, and consists of three rows and two columns – in other words, each of the three rows contains two cells. I've placed the HTML code for each row on a separate line for clarity.

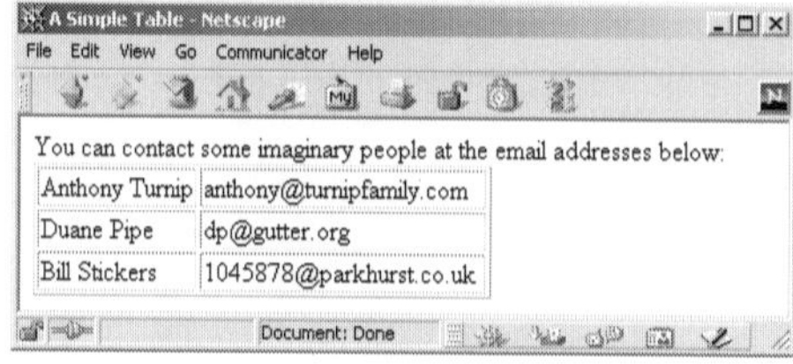

Figure 7.1 A simple three-row two-column table with visible borders.

You'll notice that I've added an attribute to the <TABLE> tag, **BORDER="1"**. By default, an empty <TABLE> tag won't show a border around the table or any of its cells, and I wanted to make it obvious in the figure what effect those <TR> and <TD> tags were having. But it's the option of having those borders hidden that makes tables such a great page-layout tool: to hide the table borders, either remove the BORDER="1" attribute or set its value to "0" instead.

Borders are useful!

I usually add a BORDER="0" attribute to table tags anyway. Once in a while you get a bit lost about which row or column you're working in, or the table doesn't display as expected, so you can just change the 0 to a 1, refresh the browser to see where all the cells are, then fix the problem and switch back to 0 again. (Incidentally, adding the word BORDER to the tag with no equals sign or value will also give a single-pixel border.)

Customizing the table tag

The BORDER attribute mentioned above is just one of the <TABLE> tag's attributes, and it's simple enough to work with: set it to zero to hide the borders or to any positive number to create tables with thicker visible borders. It's worth noting that if you remove the BORDER attribute, although no borders will be shown, the table will be laid out as if the border were still there: setting it to 0 regains the space that would have been used for the border.

Table 7.1 lists the other attributes you can add to the <TABLE> tag to affect the appearance of the table.

Table 7.1 Table attributes

This attribute...	...does this
ALIGN	Sets the alignment of the table on the page, using LEFT, CENTER or RIGHT. The default alignment is LEFT (you can also do this by enclosing the table in <CENTER> or <DIV ALIGN=?> tags)
BGCOLOR	Sets the background colour for the entire table (although individual rows and cells can override this using their own BGCOLOR attributes, as we'll see later)
WIDTH	Sets the width of the table either using an exact number of pixels (not usually a good idea) or as a percentage of the browser's width, such as WIDTH="80%"
HEIGHT	Sets the height of the table. You wouldn't usually use this, since the browser will automatically create a table tall enough to display whatever data it contains
CELLPADDING	Sets the amount of space between a cell's four edges and its contents. The default is 1, so you can create extra space around a cell's contents using something like CELLPADDING="5"
CELLSPACING	Sets the amount of space between each cell in the table. The default spacing is two pixels

Here are two modified examples of the table used in the earlier example. The first adds space around the table contents using cellpadding and cellspacing along with a thicker border; the second goes all out for compactness (see Figure 7.2):

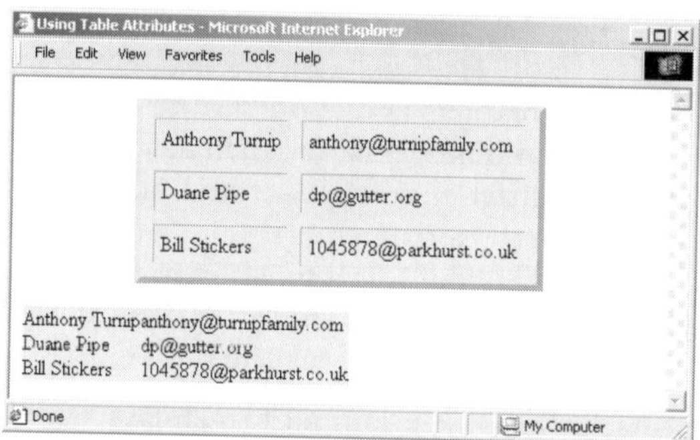

Figure 7.2 Two very different ways of displaying the same information in a table.

```
<TABLE BORDER=5 CELLPADDING=5 CELLSPACING=10
ALIGN=CENTER BGCOLOR=ivory>
<TR><TD>AnthonyTurnip</TD><TD>anthony@turnipfamily
.com</TD></TR>
<TR><TD>Duane
Pipe</TD><TD>dp@gutter.org</TD></TR>
<TR><TD>BillStickers</TD><TD>1045878@parkhurst.co
.uk</TD></TR>
</TABLE>
<P>
<TABLE BORDER=0 CELLPADDING=0 CELLSPACING=0
BGCOLOR=ivory>
<TR><TD>AnthonyTurnip</TD><TD>anthony@turnipfamily
.com</TD></TR>
<TR><TD>Duane
Pipe</TD><TD>dp@gutter.org</TD></TR>
<TR><TD>BillStickers</TD><TD>1045878@parkhurst.co
.uk</TD></TR>
</TABLE>
```

Table design with Internet Explorer

Internet Explorer versions 2 and upwards offer a few extra tricks with the <TABLE> tag. Most other browsers won't know what to do with these, so (as with all unsupported attributes) they'll ignore them gracefully.

BACKGROUND works like the same attribute in the <BODY> tag (see Chapter 4), letting you add a tiled image behind the content of all the table's cells.

BORDERCOLOR lets you set a colour to be used to draw the borders of the table and its cells. This will give a two-dimensional (flat) look to the table.

With **BORDERCOLORLIGHT** and **BORDERCOLORDARK** you can choose two separate colours to achieve your own style of three-dimensional table design: the first attribute sets the colour of the two lighter edges of the table or cell, the second sets the colour of the two darker edges (see Figure 7.3).

Figure 7.3 A 2D result using BORDERCOLOR (top), compared to a 3D result using BORDERCOLORLIGHT and BORDERCOLORDARK (bottom).

And back to borders...

The <TABLE> tag has two more attributes that determine where and how borders are displayed: **FRAME** and **RULES**. FRAME determines how the outside edges of a table are displayed, and RULES sets the internal borders. The BORDER attribute must be included for either of these to have any effect. Unlike the Internet Explorer additions mentioned above, these *are* included in the HTML specification. Unfortunately, Netscape 4 and Opera don't support them, and Netscape 6 just leaves out a few borders that have little bearing on what your code specifies, so the end result is still that they're Internet Explorer-only effects.

- The values for FRAME can be ABOVE, BELOW, RHS or LHS (borders at the top, bottom, right or left sides respectively), HSIDES (top and bottom borders), VSIDES (left and right borders), VOID (no borders), or BOX (all four borders).
- RULES can be ROWS (horizontal borders between each row), COLS (vertical borders between each column), NONE (no internal borders) or ALL (all internal borders).

Rows: just containers for cells

Compared to the <TABLE> tag, the **<TR>** tag that starts a new row in a table is pretty dull, so we can quickly skip through its possible attributes (Table 7.2). Because a row is just a container for cells, the attributes for a row can provide a quick way of making settings that apply to every cell in that row. As we'll see later in this chapter, individual cells can still override these settings.

Table 7.2 Table attributes

This attribute...	...does this
ALIGN	Sets how contents of cells in the row should be aligned, using LEFT, CENTER, RIGHT, or JUSTIFY, which are all self-explanatory, or CHAR, explained below
CHAR	If you use ALIGN=CHAR, the contents of each cell will be aligned to the first instance of a particular character in a cell's contents. Use CHAR="*character*" to specify the character used, such as CHAR="." to align numbers to a decimal point
VALIGN	Sets the vertical alignment of the content in all this row's cells, which can be TOP, MIDDLE, BOTTOM or BASELINE
BGCOLOR	Sets the background colour of all the cells in this row. This overrides any BGCOLOR attribute used in the <TABLE> tag

Fonts in tables

If you display tables in Internet Explorer, you'll find that the contents of the cells use whatever font was set at that point in the page, as if you'd added another paragraph of text. Netscape and Opera, on the other hand, don't pick up the current font settings: every table cell uses the browser's default font unless specifically told otherwise. If you particularly want a certain font, colour or size in your table cells, you have to include a <FONT> tag in each cell. (You can get around this much more neatly by using style sheets, which we'll come to in Chapter 9.)

Along with the four attributes above, you can also use Internet Explorer's BORDERCOLOR, BORDERCOLORLIGHT and BORDERCOLORDARK attributes mentioned on page 749, which will override the colours set in the <TABLE> tag.

Cells: what tables are all about

As you've seen in the examples earlier in this chapter, all the displayable content of a table appears in a cell – in other words, it comes between **<TD>** and **</TD>** tags. The <TD> tag has a range of attributes to set the appearance of the cell and its content: WIDTH, HEIGHT, ALIGN, BGCOLOR, CHAR and VALIGN, all of which we've come across already, and the Internet Explorer-specific BACKGROUND, BORDERCOLOR, BORDERCOLORLIGHT and BORDERCOLORDARK. If any of these attributes is included in a <TD> tag, its value will take precedence over the same attribute used in the <TABLE> or <TR> tag. Along with those old favourites, the <TD> tag has two extra attributes of its own:

COLSPAN lets you join several cells together horizontally to create a single wide cell that spans several columns. For example, COLSPAN=3 creates a single cell of three columns.

ROWSPAN joins cells vertically to create a single cell spanning two or more rows, such as ROWSPAN=2.

Here's some code that shows how the COLSPAN and ROWSPAN attributes work, with the result shown in Figure 7.4. The table contains four rows. The first row uses four <TD> tags to create four ordinary cells. In the second row there's a single <TD> tag with a COLSPAN=4 attribute making this cell span four columns (the entire width of this table). The third row contains four cells again, but the first <TD> tag includes a ROWSPAN=2 attribute: as long as there's another row below this one, this first cell will take the height of that row as well. Finally, the fourth row contains just three cells because the ROWSPAN attribute in the previous row has used one cell's worth of space (Figure 7.4).

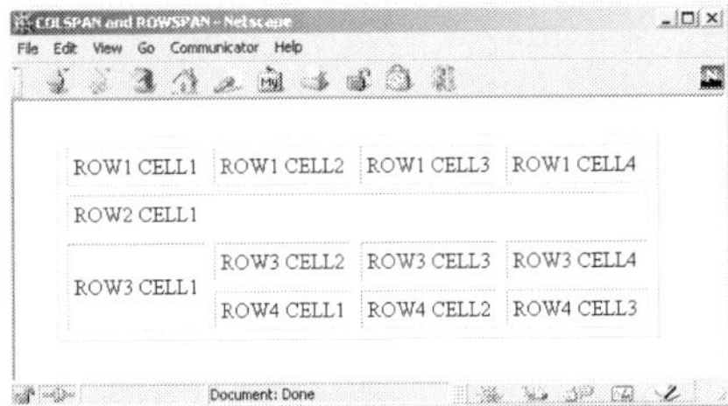

Figure 7.4 A table using ROWSPAN and COLSPAN to create cells that span multiple columns or rows.

```
<TABLE BORDER CELLPADDING=4 CELLSPACING=7
ALIGN=CENTER>

<TR><TD>ROW1 CELL1</TD><TD>ROW1
CELL2</TD><TD>ROW1 CELL3</TD><TD>ROW1
CELL4</TD></TR>

<TR><TD COLSPAN=4>ROW2 CELL1</TD></TR>

<TR><TD ROWSPAN=2>ROW3 CELL1</TD><TD>ROW3
CELL2</TD><TD>ROW3 CELL3</TD><TD>ROW3
CELL4</TD></TR>

<TR><TD>ROW4 CELL1</TD><TD>ROW4
CELL2</TD><TD>ROW4 CELL3</TD></TR>

</TABLE>
```

Tables in the real world

The examples we've used so far look a bit dull – they have the typical 'spreadsheet look' that the word *table* conjures up. Although tables obviously can be used to present tabular data in a Web page (and the first example below does just that, with some added style), their greatest value is in helping you to fine-tune your page layout.

A typical data table

The code below creates a table displaying a typical kind of tabular data, pictured in Figure 7.5. The data itself is pretty dull, but there are a few points of interest about the table:

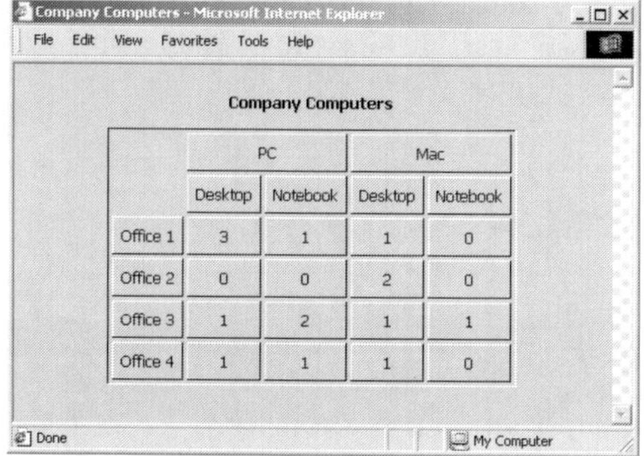

Company Computers

	PC		Mac	
	Desktop	Notebook	Desktop	Notebook
Office 1	3	1	1	0
Office 2	0	0	2	0
Office 3	1	2	1	1
Office 4	1	1	1	0

Figure 7.5 A typical table that uses column-spanning, empty cells, and a <CAPTION> tag.

- In the first two rows I've used empty cells (<TD></TD>). There was nothing to be displayed in these cells and by leaving them blank no borders are shown around them. To show the borders, just include a non-breaking space ( ) between the opening and closing tags.
- The <CAPTION> tag makes an appearance. If used, this must immediately follow the <TABLE> tag (although there are any number of other ways to place a text caption above a table, of course). The caption will be aligned to the top-centre by default, but you can choose from TOP, BOTTOM, LEFT and RIGHT for its ALIGN attribute.
- For effect in Internet Explorer, I've used the BORDERCOLORLIGHT and BORDERCOLORDARK attributes to swap the usual highlight and shadow colours, giving a raised-3D appearance. (I've cheated slightly by using a style sheet to set a few extra options. Find out more about styles and style sheets in Chapter 9.)

```
<TABLE BORDER=1 BGCOLOR=lightgray BORDERCOL-
ORLIGHT=black BORDERCOLORDARK=white CELLSPACING=3
CELLPADDING=6 ALIGN=CENTER>
<CAPTION ALIGN=LEFT><B>Company Computers</B></CAP-
TION>
<TR>
      <TD></TD><TD COLSPAN=2
ALIGN=CENTER>PC</TD><TD COLSPAN=2
ALIGN=CENTER>Mac</TD>
</TR>
<TR>
<TD></TD><TD>Desktop</TD><TD>Notebook</TD><TD>Deskt
op</TD> <TD>Notebook</TD>
</TR>
<TR ALIGN=CENTER>
 <TD>Office1</TD><TD>3</TD><TD>1</TD><TD>1</TD><TD>
 0</TD>
</TR>
<TR ALIGN=CENTER>
 <TD>Office2</TD><TD>0</TD><TD>0</TD><TD>2</TD><TD>
 0</TD>
</TR>
<TR ALIGN=CENTER>
 <TD>Office3</TD><TD>1</TD><TD>2</TD><TD>1</TD><TD>
 1</TD>
</TR>
<TR ALIGN=CENTER>
 <TD>Office4</TD><TD>1</TD><TD>1</TD><TD>1</TD><TD>
 0</TD>
</TR>
</TABLE>
```

Page layout using tables

The next example uses a table for layout only. It consists of two rows, each with three cells. In the first row the middle cell is empty, and in the second row the two outer cells are empty. The three cells that do contain something useful are all identical: their content is aligned to the centre and vertically aligned to the top (Figure 7.6).

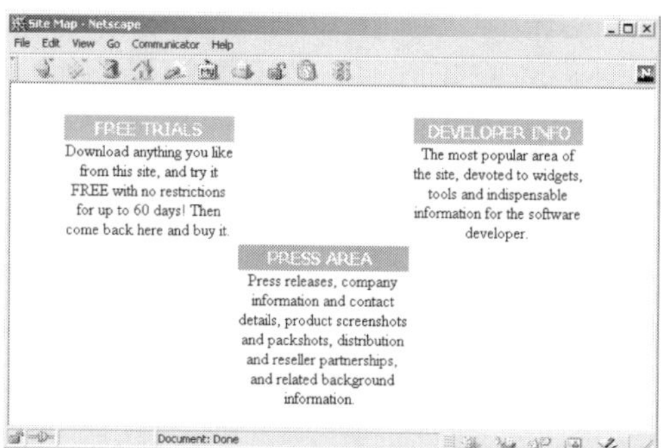

Figure 7.6 Without tables, it wouldn't be possible to create even simple-looking layouts like this.

```
<TABLE WIDTH="80%" ALIGN=CENTER BORDER="0">

<TR>
<TD VALIGN=TOP ALIGN=CENTER><IMG SRC="trials.
gif" WIDTH= 169 HEIGHT=25><BR> Download anything
you like from this site, and try it FREE with no
restrictions for up to 60 days! Then come back
here and buy it.</TD>
<TD></TD>
<TD VALIGN=TOP ALIGN=CENTER><IMG SRC="dev.gif"
WIDTH=169 HEIGHT=25><BR>The most popular area of
the site, devoted to widgets, tools and indis-
pensable information for the software developer.
</TD>
</TR>

<TR>
<TD></TD>
<TD VALIGN=TOP ALIGN=CENTER><IMG SRC="press.gif"
WIDTH=169 HEIGHT=25><BR>Press releases, company
information and contact details, product screen-
shots and packshots, distribution and reseller
partnerships, and related background information.
<TD></TD>
</TR>

</TABLE>
```

The table itself is centred and limited to 80% of the window width. This means that each column could be about a quarter as wide as the browser, making the paragraphs of text wider and with fewer lines. If you wanted to keep each column to the same width as the image, just remove the `WIDTH=80%` attribute from the `<TABLE>` tag, and add a `WIDTH=169` attribute to the three `<TD>` tags containing text. The result will be a table of about 507 pixels wide containing three columns of unchanging widths.

Setting *fixed* widths for tables or cells (widths in pixels rather than as percentages) is something to avoid, except where you know that the number of pixels you're specifying is small enough to fit into a reasonably-sized window. If you set particular widths for cells, remember that the width of a cell also sets the width for the whole column of cells it's contained in! If you try to give the top-left cell a width of 50 and the cell below it a width of 75, one or both will be ignored by the browser.

Nested tables

A 'nested' table simply means one table created inside the cell of another. You'll come across 'nested framesets' in the next chapter, which means a new set of frames created inside another frame.

A more advanced page layout

In Figures 7.7 and 7.8, the table has been used partly for effect as well as for layout: I've used the BGCOLOR attribute of the <TD> tag to create a stripe of colour, and the WIDTH and HEIGHT attributes to make sure the stripe is always 20 pixels wide. I've also made use of the <TD> tag's WIDTH attribute in the first row: every cell but one has a fixed width, so when the browser's size is changed, the downward-pointing stripe at the right remains the same distance from the edge of the window.

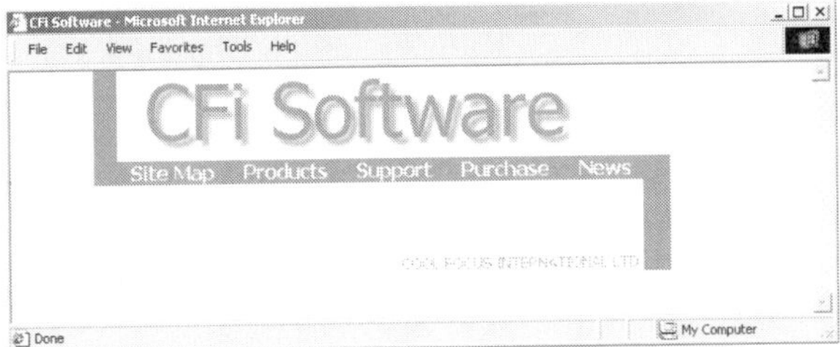

Figure 7.7 Three rows, six columns, and a little judicious use of the BGCOLOR attribute.

Figure 7.8 The same page with a visible table border to show how the rows and columns are arranged.

```
<TABLE  WIDTH="100%"  BORDER=0  CELLPADDING=0
CELLSPACING=0>
<TR>
<TD WIDTH=70> </TD>
<TD WIDTH=20 BGCOLOR=RoyalBlue HEIGHT=20>  
</TD>
```

Planning complex table layouts

The golden rule is to work out the maximum number of cells you're going to need in a row before you start writing. In this example, the maximum was six cells (used in the first row). You can then make sure that every row contains that number of cells, remembering to include COLSPAN *figures too. The third row, for instance, has one cell that spans four columns, plus two single cells.*

```
<TD WIDTH=20> </TD>
<TD HEIGHT=75 VALIGN=MIDDLE><IMG SRC="cfisoft-
ware.jpg" WIDTH=366 HEIGHT=59></TD>
<TD WIDTH=20> </TD>
<TD WIDTH=120> </TD>
</TR>

<TR>
<TD WIDTH=70> </TD>
<TD BGCOLOR=RoyalBlue HEIGHT=20> </TD>
<TD  COLSPAN=3  BGCOLOR=  RoyalBlue  HEIGHT=20
ALIGN=CENTER>
<!-- … LINKS INSERTED HERE… -->
</TD>
</TR>

<TR>
<TD  COLSPAN=4  HEIGHT=7  ALIGN=RIGHT  VALIGN
=BOTTOM>
<FONT  FACE="Tahoma,Arial,Sans-Serif"  SIZE=2
COLOR=Royal Blue>
COOL FOCUS INTERNATIONAL LTD </FONT></TD>
<TD BGCOLOR=RoyalBlue HEIGHT=20> </TD>
<TD> </TD>
</TR>
</TABLE>
```

Frames and windows

8

Make links open new browser windows

Pick sensible names for your windows and frames

Meet the all-important <FRAMESET>, <FRAME> *and* <BASE> *tags*

Frames give you a different way of structuring your site (or a part of it) by splitting the browser window into two or more 'panes', with each pane displaying a different document. In some ways these frames function like separate windows – for example, a frame can be scrolled if it contains a long document, or resized by dragging its border, and opening a document in one frame doesn't affect the documents displayed in any others.

Whether to use frames or not is one of those big decisions you'll have to make about your site. Either way, you're not restricted to using a single browser window – any time it makes sense to do so, you can force a link to open in a new window. In this chapter we'll look at how frames are created, what you can do to change their appearance and behaviour and, most importantly, how you can make documents open into particular frames or windows.

Working with multiple windows

Before we delve into the (slightly more complicated) world of frames, let's deal with windows. This gives us an easy way to get to grips with a new attribute of the <A> tag introduced in Chapter 3: the **TARGET** attribute. So far the only attribute we've used in the <A> tag is HREF, which gives the URL of the page to open. Because we haven't specified anything different, the new page replaces the old one in the browser when the link is clicked. The TARGET attribute lets you choose a different window (or, as you'll learn later, a particular frame) where the page should be opened, like this:

```
<A HREF="mypage.htm" TARGET=MyNewWindow>
```

When you click a link that includes the TARGET attribute in its anchor tag, the browser checks to see if a frame or window with the given name exists. If it does, the page is retrieved and opened into it; if it *doesn't* exist, the browser opens a new window and assigns the given name to it. The name isn't actually displayed anywhere in the window itself, so the name you choose can be as simple or as silly as you want it to be.

Let's take a simple example: make a new Web page containing the code below and call it **001.htm**. Next create three pages named **001a.htm**, **001b.htm** and **001c.htm**, each containing some dummy text so that you can tell which page has opened where.

```
<HTML>
<HEAD>
      <TITLE>Main Window</TITLE>
</HEAD>
<BODY>
<H1>Main Window</H1>
```

```
<A HREF="001a.htm" TARGET=WindowOne>Open a window
called &quot;WindowOne&quot;</A><P>
<A HREF="001b.htm" TARGET=WindowTwo>Open a window
called &quot;WindowTwo&quot;</A><P>
<A HREF="001c.htm" TARGET=WindowOne>Load a
different page into &quot;WindowOne&quot;</A><P>
</BODY>
</HTML>
```

Open **001.htm** into your browser (it should look like the top window in Figure 8.1) then follow these steps:

Figure 8.1 You can make a link open into a different window using the `TARGET` attribute in the anchor tag.

1. Click the first link. A new window will open containing the page you called **001a.htm**. This is because the browser couldn't find an existing window called WindowOne, so it had to create one.
2. Click the second link. As in step 1, you should have another new window containing **001b.htm**, for exactly the same reason.
3. Click the last link. Because you *do* now have a window called WindowOne the browser doesn't need to open a new one. The page named **001c.htm** opens into the window called WindowOne that was created in step 1.

While we're on the subject, opening new windows is a great way to annoy people! Most users know that they can shift-click a link to open it in a new window, and prefer to choose for themselves. You might want to open links to other websites in a new window, especially if your site uses frames – it's not good manners to load someone else's site into one frame of your own site. Otherwise, good reasons for new windows are few and far between.

Naming frames and windows

Choosing names for frames and windows isn't complicated – the rules are minimal, and basically just say that names mustn't start with an underscore (the underscore character is used by internal HTML names which we'll meet in a moment). Frame names are also case-sensitive, so **windowone** isn't the same thing as **WindowOne**. (This is well worth remembering: if you're working with frames and your pages persist in opening new windows rather than loading into your carefully-constructed set of frames, it's almost always a simple mistake like a missing capital letter in the name that's causing the problem!)

You can also refer to frames or windows using the five names supplied by HTML explained in Table 8.1. Notice that these all start with an underscore and they're always lower-case.

Table 8.1 Names for frames or windows

This name...	...refers to
`_self`	The same frame or window as the one containing the link being clicked. If you don't use a `TARGET` attribute in the anchor tag, this is the frame or window used by default
`_top`	The window containing the link being clicked. If the window is split into frames, the frames will all be closed and the new document will replace them (if the current window isn't split into frames, this means the same as `_self`)
`_parent`	The frame or window containing the *parent document* of the current frame; in other words, the document that created the frame being clicked. If the current frame doesn't have a parent, this defaults to `_self`. Rather than using `_parent`, it's simpler to refer to the required frame by whatever name you assigned it
`_blank`	A new window without a name. This will always result in a new window being opened: if you have three links with `TARGET="blank"`, the result will be three extra windows open after all have been clicked
`_new`	A new window, but one that's reused by the browser. If you have three links with `TARGET="_new"`, a new window will open when the first is clicked, and the second and third will open into that same window

Setting a default target with <BASE>

Imagine you've got one frame or window containing a long list of links, and another frame or window you've called 'main' where those linked pages should open. Your page of links might look something like this:

```
<HTML>
<HEAD>
      <TITLE>Links</TITLE>
</HEAD>
<BODY>
<A HREF="page1.htm" TARGET="main">Page 1</A><BR>
<A HREF="page2.htm" TARGET="main">Page 2</A><BR>
<A HREF="page3.htm" TARGET="main">Page 3</A><BR>
<A HREF="page4.htm" TARGET="main">Page 4</A><BR>
</BODY>
</HTML>
```

Every link has to open into the 'main' frame, so every link needs an identical TARGET attribute. Surely there's a better way?

Yes there is, and it comes in the form of the **<BASE>** tag. This takes exactly the same TARGET attribute and sets the frame or window name to be used by default for any link that doesn't have its own TARGET attribute. The <BASE> tag goes into the head of the page rather than its body, so that link page can be changed to this:

***The right place for* <BASE>**

It doesn't matter where in the page's head section you put the <BASE> tag. The section between <HEAD> and </HEAD> is very free and easy: the entire section is read and acted upon before the body of the page is dealt with, so wherever you place a particular tag the result will be the same.

```
<HTML>
<HEAD>
      <TITLE>Links</TITLE>
      <BASE TARGET="main">
</HEAD>
<BODY>
<A HREF="page1.htm">Page 1</A><BR>
<A HREF="page2.htm">Page 2</A><BR>
<A HREF="page3.htm">Page 3</A><BR>
<A HREF="page4.htm">Page 4</A><BR>
</BODY>
</HTML
```

Frame basics

A common use of frames is to split the window into two: the smaller frame contains the site navigation, and the larger frame displays the pages opened when the links are clicked. Perhaps you can find a good reason to use a third frame – a fixed copyright notice, advertising banner display, company logo or secondary navigation – but you probably won't find good reasons to use any more than that. Remember that for each frame you create there's a document to be downloaded when someone visits your site!

Frames don't suit every site, of course. If the content of more than one frame needs to change when links are clicked, the result might be more confusing for the user than sticking to a 'single-page view'. Instead of using frames, you could create a template file containing your logos, links, and anything else that should appear on every page, then create each page from that template, ensuring that the whole site has a consistent style and feel.

Getting started with frames

In Figure 8.2 you can see a fairly typical use of frames, with the borders between the three frames clearly visible. The left and bottom frames contain links to other pages on the site, and the larger 'main' frame is where those pages will be displayed.

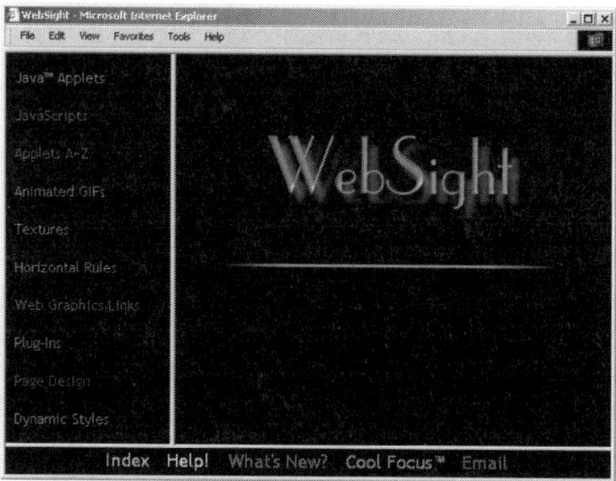

Figure 8.2 A typical framed site: two permanent navigation frames and a 'main' frame for the changing content.

To build a site like this takes four web pages. Three of those you can see in the three frames, and they're no different from any other Web page. The fourth page is the one that defines the **frameset** – it creates the frames and opens the required pages into them when the site is first shown. Appropriately enough, this is done using the **<FRAMESET>** tag.

Dividing the window: the <FRAMESET> tag

The framesetting page contains no displayable content at all. As a result, it has no <BODY>...</BODY> section either: the body of the page is replaced by the framesetting code, so a template for a framesetting page would look like this:

```
<HTML>
<HEAD>
      <TITLE>Untitled</TITLE>
</HEAD>
```

```
<FRAMESET>
</FRAMESET>
</HTML>
```

The <FRAMESET> tag tells the browser that the window is to be split into frames, but currently it isn't doing any more than that. To define how many frames we want and what size they should be, we have to add either of two attributes to the <FRAMESET> tag: **COLS** or **ROWS**. Which of these attributes you use depends on whether you want to split the window into columns or rows, but both are used in exactly the same way:

```
<FRAMESET COLS="width1, width2, width3">
```

or

```
<FRAMESET ROWS="height1, height2, height3">
```

In both code samples above, the window is split into three frames. In the first it's split into three columns of the specified widths; in the second it's split into three rows of the specified heights.

There are three different ways of specifying the width or height for a frame: as a fixed value in pixels, as a percentage of the entire width or height of the browser, or with an asterisk (*). The asterisk tells the browser to devote whatever space is left to this frame after creating the others. Each value is separated by a comma (and a space if you like to keep things tidy!). Here's an example <FRAMESET> tag that creates a window split like the one in Figure 8.3. (Don't try typing this into your own page to test it just yet: you won't get the result I'm showing here, for reasons we'll come to in a moment.)

```
<FRAMESET COLS="25%, 80, *">
```

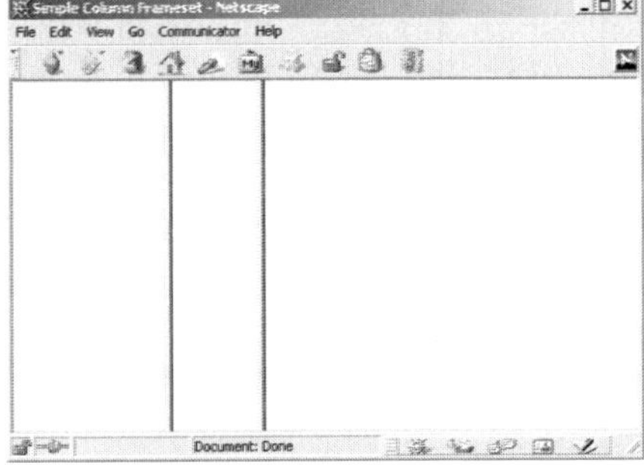

Figure 8.3 A simple three-column frameset using COLS="25%,80,*"

That line of code has split the window into three columns. The left-hand column occupies 25% of the size of the window; the middle column is fixed at 80 pixels wide; and the column on the right takes

Avoid fixed frame sizes!
There's only one instance when you might consider specifying a frame's width or height in pixels: when you know the maximum size of the content it will display (for example, an image of a particular size) and if the size is a lot smaller than the user's browser window would ever reasonably be. Otherwise stick to percentage values and always use at least one asterisk in each <FRAMESET> *tag.*

Using more than one asterisk
Using multiple asterisks is valid. After the percentage values and pixel values have been determined, the remaining space is split equally between the asterisk values. For instance, the code <FRAMESET ROWS="25%, *, 25%, *"> *would split the browser into four identically-sized rows. The code* <FRAMESET ROWS="*, *, *, *"> *would do exactly the same: as there are no numbers to work with, the browser splits its remaining 100% into four equal portions.*

whatever space is left. If you resize the window, the width of the left-hand frame will change slightly, the right-hand frame will change more, and the middle frame will remain at 80 pixels wide.

Let's take another example, this time using the ROWS attribute: the complete tag is <FRAMESET ROWS="25%, *, 25%">, giving the result shown in Figure 8.4. The first thing you'll notice is that the asterisk doesn't have to be the last value defined: the browser has split the window into three frames where the outer frames occupy 25% of the window's size and the centre frame takes the rest. That leads to another point: why not just put 50% where the asterisk is? In the example above we could certainly do that and the result would be the same. However, it's good practice to get into the habit of always including an asterisk: that way there's never any risk of creating a frameset adding up to more or less than 100%.

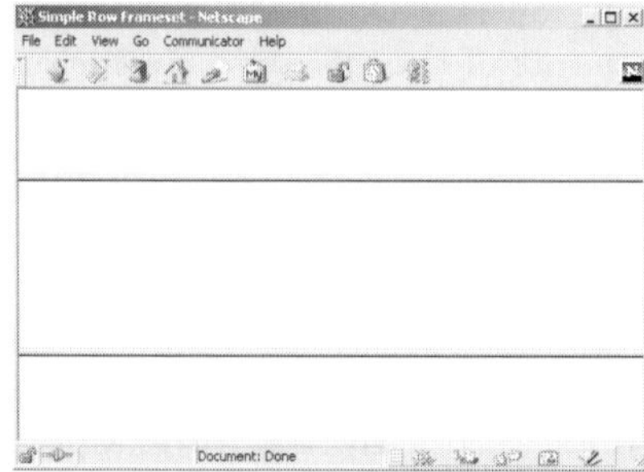

Figure 8.4 A three-row frameset using ROWS="25%,*,25%"

Filling and naming: the <FRAME> tag

I've been cheating a bit in the examples from the previous section. Although the <FRAMESET> tag and its ROWS or COLS attribute is required, alone it won't produce the examples shown in the figures. A frame can't be empty – it has to contain a document – and there's nothing in the code we've seen so far to load any documents. For this step we need to add a **<FRAME>** tag for each frame we created in the <FRAMESET> tag, like this:

```
<HTML>
<HEAD>
      <TITLE>My Frameset</TITLE>
</HEAD>
<FRAMESET COLS="25%, *">
      <FRAME SRC="leftframepage.htm">
      <FRAME SRC="mainframepage.htm">
</FRAMESET>
</HTML>
```

Two frames are defined in the <FRAMESET> tag, so two <FRAME> tags are needed to load documents into each. The first <FRAME> tag corresponds to the first value in the COLS or ROWS attribute ('25%' in this example), the second <FRAME> tag to the second value, and so on. The **SRC** attribute of the <FRAME> tag is short for 'source': it works in the same way as the SRC attribute of the <IMG> tag (covered in Chapter 5), specifying the URL of the page to be loaded into the frame.

The page in the example code above is complete: you can load this page into a browser and the two frames will be shown. Provided the pages specified in the <FRAME> tags really do exist, they'll be loaded into the frames, otherwise the frames will contain 'page not found' messages.

We're off to a good start, then, but we're missing out on something important: the frames don't have names, so if one of the pages contains links, we can't target the links to the other frame. That's easily fixed using another attribute of the <FRAME> tag, **NAME**, like this:

```
<HTML>
<HEAD>
      <TITLE>My Frameset</TITLE>
</HEAD>
<FRAMESET COLS="25%, *">
      <FRAME SRC="leftframepage.htm" NAME="left">
      <FRAME SRC="mainframepage.htm" NAME="main">
</FRAMESET>
</HTML>
```

Now we can add some links to the page named leftframepage.htm, making sure we also include a <BASE TARGET="main"> tag in the head of the page. When one of those links is clicked, the page it refers to will open in the larger frame we called *main* (Figure 8.5).

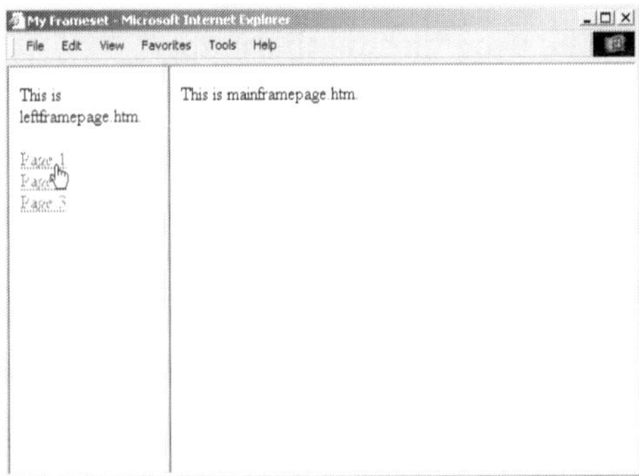

Figure 8.5 A working frameset: links in the left frame target the main frame.

Title fight

With several Web pages open, each of which has its own title, you might expect things to get a bit hit-or-miss in the <TITLE> tag department. In fact, when pages are displayed in a framed environment, their <TITLE> tag is ignored completely and the title of the framesetting page is used exclusively. This makes your choice of title for that page all the more important since it remains permanently on show.

Customising your frames

The SRC attribute of the <FRAME> tag is *required* and must specify the URL of the document to load into the frame when it's created. The NAME attribute is optional, but you'll need to include it for any frame that you need to target from a link. Apart from those, Table 8.2 lists a few extra attributes that you can add to the <FRAME> tag to customise its behaviour or appearance.

Table 8.2 Frame attributes

This attribute...	**...does this**
MARGINWIDTH	Takes a value in pixels to set the width of the left and right margins of a frame
MARGINHEIGHT	Takes a value in pixels to set the height of the top and bottom margins of a frame
SCROLLING	Takes a setting of **auto**, **yes** or **no** to whether the user should be able to scroll the frame. The default setting is **auto**, meaning that scrollbars will be added to the frame if the content is too wide or long to fit the frame; **yes** means that scrollbars will always be visible; **no** means that the frame can never be scrolled. Avoid using **no** unless you're absolutely sure that the content of a frame will always be fully visible without the need to scroll through it
NORESIZE	By default all frames can be resized by dragging them. To prevent a frame from being resized by the user, include this empty attribute in its <FRAME> tag
FRAMESPACING	In Internet Explorer only, this attribute can be used to create blank space around a frame by entering a value in pixels

A complex frameset

So far all our frameset examples have been simple: we've split the browser into columns or rows, but we haven't tried to combine the two. A good candidate for a more complex frameset is our long-running 'Computing Site Directory' site, last seen at the end of

Chapter 5. Figure 8.6 shows the result we want to achieve; for complex framesets, as with complex tables, it's a good idea to scribble a rough diagram of what you're trying to create before you start.

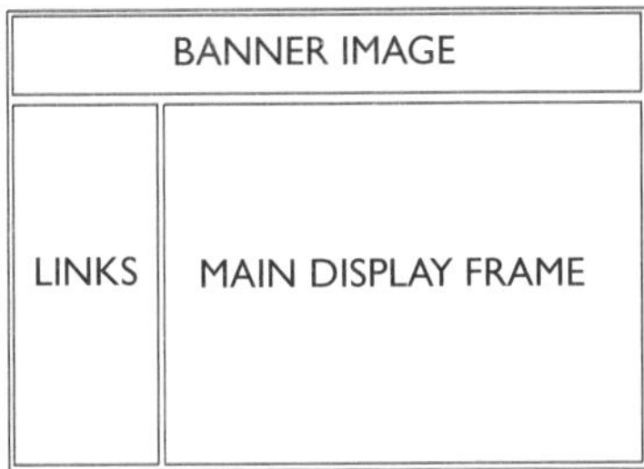

Figure 8.6 A rough mock-up of the frameset we want to create.

Now we hit the first complication: do we use the `ROWS` or `COLS` attribute in the `<FRAMESET>` tag? The window is clearly split into two rows, the lower row containing the two larger frames, but there's also a column split between the two large frames. The answer is to see whether any frames stretch from the extreme left to the extreme right of the window: if they do, use `ROWS`; if they don't, use `COLS`. In this case, the top frame fills the entire width of the browser, so we'll use `ROWS`.

The top frame is just going to contain the banner image: it's a fixed size (58 pixels high), so we can set a pixel value for the height of that frame, allowing a few extra pixels for frame and page margins (and testing carefully in all browsers to make sure the frame really is tall enough for the image!). The remainder of the window is left for the frames below. So far, then, we can enter the following code into the page:

```
<FRAMESET ROWS="80, *">
      <FRAME NAME="top" SRC="banner.htm" SCROLLING
      =NO NORESIZE>
      <!-- more code here -->
</FRAMESET>
```

Now we've got a line missing from the code. Normally we'd put a second `<FRAME>` tag there to create the frame that forms the second row, but in our mock-up we've got *two* frames in that row. That means we need another `<FRAMESET>` tag instead. Putting one frameset inside another in this way is known as a **nested frameset**. We don't have to do anything differently though: we just treat the remaining space as if it were the entire browser window. We want to split the space into two columns, so we'll use the `COLS` attribute in this frameset tag:

```
<FRAMESET ROWS="80, *">
      <FRAME NAME="top" SRC="banner.htm" SCROLLING
      =NO NORESIZE>
      <FRAMESET COLS="220, *">
            <FRAME NAME="left" SRC="links.htm">
            <FRAME NAME="main" SRC="home.htm">
      </FRAMESET>
</FRAMESET>
```

The left frame is going to contain our linking images which, like the banner, are a fixed size. That means we can set a fixed width of 220 pixels for the left frame, with the remainder of the window devoted to the main display frame. The resulting code goes in our **index.htm** page, straight after the closing </HEAD> tag.

Having created the frameset in **index.htm**, we need to create the three pages to be loaded into the frames. We're basically pulling chunks of code out of the original index page and dropping them almost unaltered into new pages, so this is fairly straightforward. Here are the steps to be taken:

1. Make a page called **banner.htm** which contains just the <IMG> tag for the banner image between <CENTER> tags. You can also copy the <BODY> tag from the original index page to this one.
2. Make a page called **links.htm**. Into that, copy the block of code that put the linking button-images on the page, once again between <CENTER> tags and using the same <BODY> tag. In the head of the page, add <BASE TARGET="main"> so that all the links open into the frame called *main*.
3. Make a page called **home.htm** that uses the same <BODY> and <FONT> tags as the original index, and move the two introductory paragraphs into it (Figure 8.7).

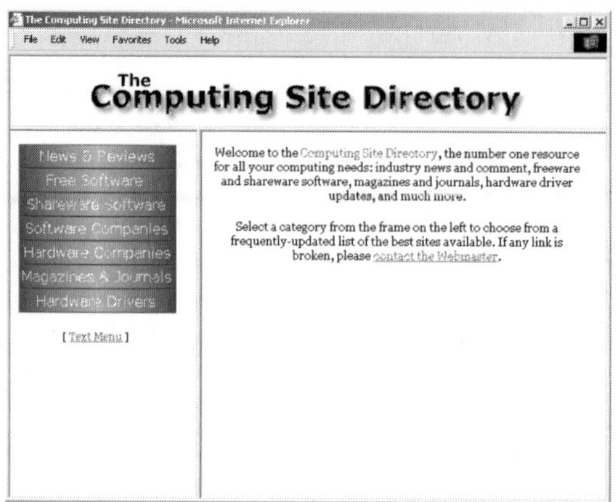

Figure 8.7 Combining rows and columns to create a more complex frameset.

Style sheets

9

What are style sheets, and are they worth bothering with?

How to create simple but useful style sheets

CSS property names and measurements

How to customise and create your own style classes

How to move styles into separate files for complete flexibility

By now you've probably realised that HTML isn't much like desktop publishing in Serif PagePlus or presentation graphics in Microsoft PowerPoint: you can't determine precisely where items will be placed on the page, and if you can get everything the way you want it in one browser, there's little chance of it looking exactly the same in another.

That's not a limitation of HTML though: the whole point of a *markup language* such as HTML is that content is king and stylistic options are only needed to make the meaning of the content clearer. A heading doesn't need to be 30-point extra-bold Arial in green and indented by 26 pixels to be recognised as a heading, it just needs to be bigger.

The trouble is, you want your heading to be 30-point extra-bold Arial in green, and you don't care a jot how a markup language is meant to be used! If that means wrapping every heading on your site in `<FONT>` tags, you'll do it. And if redesigning your site means editing 500 identical font tags, you'll do that too. But wouldn't it be nice if there were a quicker, easier and more reliable way to exert some control over appearance? Looks like you've come to the right chapter...

What are style sheets?

The 'quicker, easier and more reliable way' comes in the form of **Cascading Style Sheets** or CSS (often just referred to as *style sheets*). Style sheets let you specify just once that a heading should be 30-point Arial in green, and apply that style to a whole page or, better still, an entire site. The result is a faster and more economical way to give a set of Web pages a consistent appearance, and gives you as little as one line of code to edit if you decide that all the headings on your site would actually look better in blue. Not only that, style sheets give vastly more control over the positioning and styling of any element on the page than HTML alone can offer, as you can see from Figure 9.1.

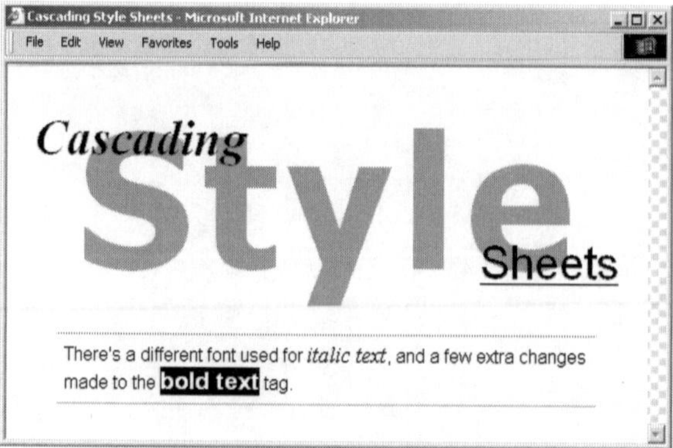

Figure 9.1 Style sheets at work: try doing this with ordinary HTML!

A 'style sheet' itself is pretty much what it sounds like: a list of named styles known as **rules** that you define yourself and can then apply by name to elements on the page. Styles can be created in three ways:

- An **external style sheet** is a separate document containing the defined style rules. This document can be used by any Web page that should share those styles by **linking** the style sheet to the document.
- An **embedded style sheet** is a list of style rules included in the head section of the Web page itself. Those styles are accessible to that page only.
- **Inline styles** are styles added as attributes to ordinary HTML tags using a `<P STYLE="style info">` or `<H1 STYLE="style info">` tag.

Creating a simple style sheet

To start with we'll stick with *embedded* styles, style sheets included in a Web page rather than in a separate document. To define style rules in a Web page we use the **<STYLE>...</STYLE>** tag pair somewhere in the head of the page like this:

```
<HTML>
<HEAD>
      <TITLE>Untitled</TITLE>
      <STYLE TYPE="text/css">
      <!--
      style rules here
      -->
      </STYLE>
</HEAD>
```

One of the first things you'll notice about the added code is that everything between the opening and closing <STYLE> tags is commented out by being enclosed between <!-- and --> tags (see the section on commenting HTML code in Chapter 3). This prevents errors in older browsers that don't recognise the <STYLE> tags. You might expect new browsers to ignore the text we put between those comments too, but they don't. Code within the <STYLE> tags is written in the 'language' of CSS, which is different from HTML. Browsers that understand CSS switch into that mode when they see the <STYLE> tag, and the <!-- tag is meaningless in CSS so the browser ignores it and skips straight to what follows.

Now let's define a style rule for headings. If you wanted every heading in your page to use the Verdana font, the HTML way of doing that would be:

The age-old compatibility question

By now you'll probably be expecting this: style sheets don't have universal support among browsers. The most reliable support comes from versions 4 and later of Internet Explorer and Netscape, and Opera 3 or later. Internet Explorer 3 had some support, but not enough to be relied on. Even now, some style properties are supported by one browser and not by another. The answer, as always, is to test in the browsers that matter before publishing, and (if you choose to) include the minimum amount of stylistic HTML to make your pages look okay in older browsers such as Netscape 3.

```
<FONT NAME="Verdana,Arial,sans-serif"><H1>My
First Heading</H1></FONT>
```

```
etc…
```

```
<FONT NAME="Verdana,Arial,sans-serif"><H1>My
Second Heading</H1></FONT>
```

```
etc…
```

Let's create a style rule for that instead:

```
<HTML>
<HEAD>
      <TITLE>Untitled</TITLE>
      <STYLE TYPE="text/css">
      <!--
      H1 {font-family: Verdana,Arial,sans-serif}
      -->
      </STYLE>
</HEAD>
<BODY>
<H1>My First Heading</H1>
etc…
<H1>My Second Heading</H1>
etc…
</BODY>
</HTML>
```

The added line (shown in bold type) creates a style rule for the <H1> tag. The rule specifies that the <H1> tag should use the Verdana font if possible, so all <H1> tags on the page will do so without the need for font tags or repetition.

The format of a style rule always follows the same simple format:

```
tag-name { property1: value1; property2: value2;
property 3: value3 }
```

The tag-name (minus its < and > signs) starts the rule, and is followed by property-names and their values all enclosed in curly brackets. There's a colon between the property-name and its value, and there's a semi-colon between each name-and-value pair (the semi-colon is optional after the last value). The use of spaces and carriage returns is ignored, as in HTML, and the property names aren't case-sensitive.

If you copy the code above into a new page and open it in your browser, you'll see that everything else about the headings remains unchanged: they have the same colour, alignment and size as they would if we'd specified the font-face using a <FONT>

tag. When you specify a value for a particular property, you're effectively overriding its default value; any properties you leave out will remain at their defaults.

Let's test that by adding another property to our H1 rule. At the moment the headings in your browser are probably black, so change the style rule to this (not forgetting the semi-colon after the `font-family` property):

```
H1   {font-family:   Verdana,Arial,sans-serif;
color: navy}
```

Look at the result in your browser now, and you'll find that the headings are navy blue.

A few CSS property names

You can probably see that creating a style rule for a tag isn't difficult: all you're lacking at this stage is the property names to use. Table 9.1 lists some of the most useful ones.

Table 9.1 CSS property names

This property...	...does this
`font-family`	Specifies the names of the font-faces to be used, in order of preference, such as **`font-family: Arial,Helvetica, sans-serif`**
`font-style`	Sets the style of the font, with a choice of **`normal`** or **`italic`**
`font-weight`	Sets the weight of the font, with a choice of **`normal`** or **`bold`**, or a fixed weight of 100, 200, 300, 400, 500, 600, 700, 800 or 900 (normal is 400, Bold is 700. Others may be ignored in some browsers)
`font-size`	Sets the size of font. There are named sizes (**`large`**, **`medium`**, **`small`**, **`x-large`**, **`x-small`**, **`xx-large`** and **`xx-small`**) or sizes can be given using one of the CSS units of measurement covered below
`text-decoration`	A choice of **`none`**, **`underline`**, **`overline`** or **`line-through`**.
`text-align`	Aligns text with a choice of **`left`**, **`center`**, **`right`**, or **`justify`**

`letter-spacing`	Sets the amount of space between each letter
`color`	Sets the foreground colour of text contained in the element. A hex colour (**`color: #00FF00`**), a colour name (**`color: lime`**) or an RGB colour (**`color:RGB(0,255,0)`**)
`background-color`	Sets the background colour of an element using the same syntax as the `color` property (you can also use the shorter property-name, **`background`**)
`left`	Sets the position of the left edge of the element
`top`	Sets the position of the top edge of the element
`border-style`	Sets the style of border shown, with a choice of **`solid`**, **`double`**, **`groove`**, **`ridge`**, **`inset`**, **`outset`**, **`dotted`** and **`dashed`**
`border-width`	Sets the width of borders, with a choice of **`thin`**, **`medium`**, **`thick`**, a percentage value, or a CSS unit of measurement

Using unsupported property names
As with HTML tag attributes, if a browser doesn't recognise a property name you enter it will just ignore it. That may be because you've experimented with an inappropriate property in an element (such as `text-decoration` for `IMG` elements), or because you've made a spelling mistake.

That's not an exhaustive list of properties by any means, but it should give you plenty to go on with. Not every property can be used with every HTML tag (or *element*), of course: the `font-style` and `text-align` properties clearly have no place in an image tag, for instance, because an image doesn't have associated text, but they could be used in a style rule for a paragraph or a table.

CSS measurement units: even *more* flexibility!

Quite a number of properties cover widths, positions, indents and sizes – properties that need a numerical value – and style sheets let you specify these as precisely as you want to by giving you a choice of units of measurement that you can use interchangeably. The two you'll probably want to use most are pixels (notated as **px**) and points (**pt**), but any unit can be used in any numerical property.

Table 9.2 Units of measurement

Unit name	Unit notation	Meaning
Pixels	`px`	A pixel is a single dot on the screen
Points	`pt`	A point is $\frac{1}{72}$ inch, the unit used to measure the height of fonts
Picas	`pc`	12 points
Ems	`em`	The width of the current font's letter *m*

Exes	ex	The height of the current font's letter *x*
Millimetres	mm	A figure in millimetres
Centimetres	cm	A figure in centimetres (10 mm)
Inches	in	A figure in inches (2.54 cm)

Building a complete style sheet

A complete style sheet is simply a list of the rules you want to apply to particular HTML elements. As is usual for anything appearing in the head of a page, the order in which you define them doesn't matter. The code below shows an example of a style sheet containing five style rules. Let's look at each rule individually to see what it's doing, then view the result in a Web page:

```
<STYLE TYPE="text/css">
<!--
BODY {font-family: Georgia, serif; font-size:
11pt; background-color: ivory; color: navy;
margin: 2pc}
A {font-weight: 900; text-decoration: none}
I {background-color: navy; color: ivory}
TD {font-family: Georgia, serif; font-size:
11pt; text-align: center}
H1, H2 {font-family: Tahoma, sans-serif; color:
maroon}
-->
</STYLE>
```

- The **BODY** rule is setting a default font face and size for the whole page (the equivalent of enclosing the body of the page between `<FONT>…</FONT>` tags in HTML). It also sets the page's background colour to pale yellow (equivalent to `<BODY BGCOLOR="ivory">`) and the text colour to navy blue (equivalent to `<BODY TEXT="navy">`). Finally we've used **margin: 2pc**: we can use this instead of using the separate `margin-left/right/top/bottom` properties to set the same two-pica margin around all four edges at once.
- The **A** rule specifies that any links should have a font-weight of 900 (the 'heaviest' available weight of bold text). It also sets text decoration to 'none', which, for ordinary text, would be redundant. For links, which are automatically underlined, it removes the underlining.
- The **I** rule specifies that any italic text in the page (text enclosed between `<I>…</I>` tags) should have a navy background and pale yellow text – the opposite of other text on the page.

- The **TD** (table data) rule doesn't appear to do anything very useful: apart from setting the text alignment it just repeats the same font-family and size properties we've already set in the BODY rule. However, you may remember from Chapter 7 that table cells in Netscape and Opera don't inherit the font set for the rest of the page, so you had to include an identical <FONT> tag in every cell. Netscape 4 has the same problem even when the font is set in a CSS BODY style, but this time we can get around it far more economically: we just add a rule specifying the font to use in any TD tag.
- Finally there's a rule marked for **H1**, **H2**. This is a valid way of creating a rule that will be applied to two different tags. In this case, any **H1** or **H2** heading we use in the page will be shown using the specified font type and colour.

To see the result of using this style sheet, open your template file to make a new Web page, and copy the code above into its head section. Then copy this code into its body section and look at the result in your browser (see Figure 9.2).

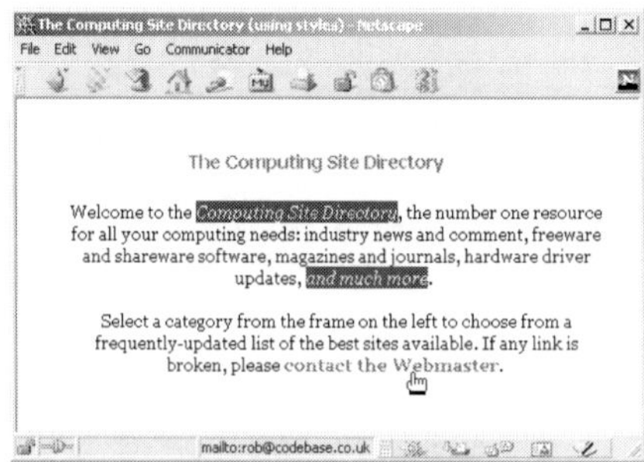

Figure 9.2 Combining a complete style sheet with a complete Web page.

```
<BODY>
<H1>The Computing Site Directory</H1>
<TABLE BORDER=0><TR><TD>
Welcome to the <I>Computing Site Directory</I>,
the number one resource for all your computing
needs: industry news and comment, freeware and
shareware software, magazines and journals,
hardware driver updates, <I>and much more</I>.
<P>Select a category from the frame on the left to
choose from a frequently-updated list of the best
sites available. If any link is broken, please <A
HREF="mailto:rob@codebase.co.uk">contact the
Webmaster</A>.
</TD></TR></TABLE>
</BODY>
```

Creating your own style classes

The examples we've used so far allow a fair bit of flexibility, but we're still a bit restricted. We can set a style rule for `<P>` tags that determine what a paragraph of text should look like, but what if we want an occasional paragraph of text to look different?

The solution is actually very easy: we can *extend* the existing tags by creating our own named variations on them. Imagine we'd already defined a fairly plain-looking paragraph style like this:

```
P {font-family: Arial; font-size: 11pt; color:
navy}
```

We'd also like our document to contain a couple of paragraphs that have a border around them. We can do it like this:

```
P.boxed {border: 1px solid; padding: 5px}
```

We've created a new **style class** based on `P` and named 'boxed'. All we had to do was put a dot after the basic tag name, followed by the name we wanted to use for the new style.

To use the class we've defined, we add a **`CLASS`** attribute to the basic tag in the form **`CLASS="classname"`**. The `CLASS` attribute is a generic attribute that can be added to any tag that places something on the page or marks out a page section – `<A>`, `<IMG>`, `<P>`, `<TD>`, and so on.

In Figure 9.3, the text is split into three paragraphs, each enclosed between `<P>` and `</P>` tags. The second paragraph differs from the other two in just one respect: its opening `<P>` tag is **`<P CLASS="boxed">`**. As a result, this paragraph inherits all the properties of an ordinary HTML paragraph, and the font family, size and colour set in the first rule for the `P` tag. It also has the border and padding we've defined for any paragraph using the 'boxed' class.

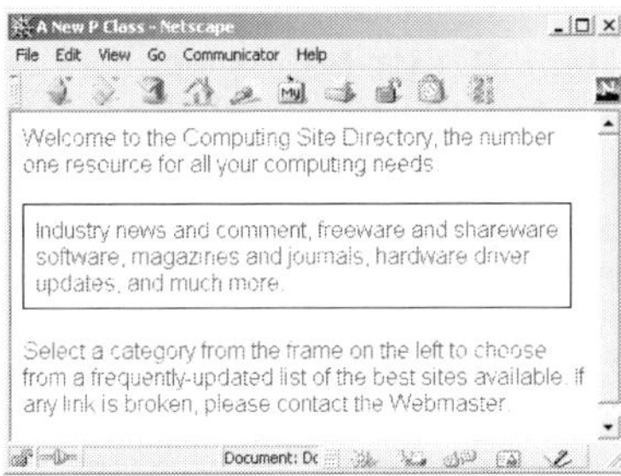

Figure 9.3 You can define any number of classes based on existing tags and refer to them by name in the `CLASS` attribute when you want to use them.

In a similar way we could define a class of bold text that's always green by creating a new bold-text class called 'green' (or something much less appropriate if you prefer – the choice of name is up to you!).

```
B.green {color: lime}
...
Here is some <B CLASS="green">green bold
text</B>.
```

Using and reusing external style sheets

So far we've only worked with one way of getting style information into a Web page, the **embedded** style sheet. The problem with putting style information in the head of a web page like this is that the style rules you create are only accessible to that page – if the rest of your pages should look the same, you'll need the same set of style rules in those pages too. And, needless to say, if you want to restyle your entire site, you've got to edit the style rules in every page.

A far more efficient way of working is to create *external* style sheets which can be used by any Web page on your site. And it's easier than falling off a log: just move all the rules into a separate text file, leaving out the `<STYLE>` and `</STYLE>` tags and the comment tags, and give the resulting file a **.css** extension. You now have an external style sheet!

The second step is to *link* that style sheet to a Web page. That just takes a single line of code in the head of the page:

```
<HTML>
<HEAD>
      <TITLE>Untitled</TITLE>
      <LINK REL=STYLESHEET TYPE="text/css"
      HREF="mystyle.css">
</HEAD>
```

The **`<LINK>`** tag tells the browser that an external file is to be read in conjunction with this page; the `REL` attribute specifies the *relationship* of the Web page to the external file; and the `TYPE` attribute specifies its MIME type as `"text/css"` (just as in the `<STYLE>` tag). The only part of the tag you need to change is the **`HREF`** attribute which gives the absolute or relative URL of the style sheet to be read.

Apart from the fact that the style rules only need to be downloaded once when the visitor arrives at your site, using an external file will greatly improve your life as a Web designer. You can link this style sheet to every Web page on your site, refer to style classes named in the file, and restyle the entire site just by making a few changes to this one file.

Using inline styles

Once in a while you'll want to do something special in just one Web page, something that needs CSS to accomplish, such as making text overlap an image. You could create a named class (something like **.overlap**) in your external style sheet, or add it as an embedded style in the head of the page, but if you really do need it only once it would be simplest just to type it into the tag it applies to.

This is known as an **inline style**: it applies CSS properties and values to the current tag using a **STYLE** attribute. As with the CLASS attribute, mentioned earlier, the STYLE attribute can be used with any tag that places content on the page or marks out a section. So to move some text upwards so that it overlaps an image placed above it, you might place it between <DIV> tags containing an inline style, like this:

```
<IMG SRC="fan.jpg" WIDTH=248 HEIGHT=338>

<DIV STYLE="margin-left: 165px; margin-top: -210px; font-size: 24pt"><B><I>Everybody needs fans!</I></B></DIV>
```

The STYLE attribute is followed by an equals sign and the list of **property: value** pairs you want to apply, separated by semicolons in the usual way with the whole lot enclosed in quotes. Because you're itching to know whether such a tasty effect really can be done that easily, Figure 9.4 shows that it can. Better still, it looks identical in each of the major browsers!

The 'cascading' effect
What is it about cascading style sheets that cascades anyway? In fact, although it's a rather odd word to use for it, cascading refers to the different priority levels of the various types of style rule. External style sheets have the lowest priority, followed by embedded style sheets, followed by inline styles. So if an external style sheet contains a rule setting all H1 heading text to green, but an embedded style rule sets H1 text to red, headings would be red in that document. And if a particular <H1> tag includes an inline style setting the text colour to blue, that particular heading would be blue.

Figure 9.4 Using an inline style to force text to overlap an image.

Fun with <DIV> and <SPAN>

Two tags that are more or less purpose-built to use inline styles are the **<DIV>** and **<SPAN>** tags. The <SPAN> tag is used to apply a style to some ordinary text within a paragraph, like this:

```
Here's some normal text. <SPAN STYLE="background:
blue">Here some text with a blue background.
</SPAN> And more normal text.
```

Using the <SPAN> tag here simply applies a blue background to the text it encloses. It doesn't alter the layout of the paragraph at all. (You can use <SPAN CLASS="..."> to apply a named style class instead if you need to.) There's really only one situation in which <SPAN> is useful: when you want to apply an effect that isn't available in HTML, as in the example above.

The <DIV> tag is a lot more useful. If you wanted to apply an inline style that indented a large chunk of content by 50 pixels, and that 'chunk' included images, paragraphs and headings, you'd have to apply the same inline STYLE attribute to all of them, or define a style class and apply it to each tag using CLASS attributes. In other words, you're repeating yourself, and in any form of programming you should avoid doing that if possible: it makes the code larger and increases the risk of mistakes.

<DIV> works a lot like the <BODY> tag, in that any amount of content and other tags can be placed between its opening and closing tags. So you can use this tag, with a STYLE attribute to define an inline style, to enclose that chunk of content. The <DIV> tag automatically starts a new line for the chunk of content and whatever follows the closing </DIV> tag – in other words, it makes a *division* between this block and its surroundings. (It also supports an optional ALIGN attribute, as I mentioned at the end of Chapter 2.) So a simple solution to our 'chunk indentation' problem would be something like this:

```
<DIV STYLE="margin-left: 50px; color: blue">
<IMG SRC="blah.gif">
<P>Blah blah blah...
<H1 STYLE="color: red">Big Blah</H1>
<P>More blah
</DIV>
```

There are two extra points of interest to the code above. First, although I've included a color property in the style, the <IMG> tag clearly doesn't support it. No problem — it's gracefully ignored for that tag and applied only to the textual content. Second, I've added a color property to the heading tag. This has greater priority than the same property in the division tag, so the heading will indeed be red.

From hard disk to Web

10

How to find and choose a Web hosting company

Register your own snappy domain name

Get your site online using FTP

Testing times – checking and troubleshooting your new site

Promotion and fellback: search engines, banners and guestbooks

Now that you know something about HTML, it's time to put on your hard hat and start building. But what happens when you've finished? How does your site get onto the Web? What will its URL be? And how will anyone else know it's there? In this chapter, we'll find the answers to all those questions and more.

The perfect host

Once your site is finished, you're ready to **publish** it on the Web. Publishing your site means copying all the files in the 'Site' directory on your hard disk to a similar directory on a Web server. That directory will have its own URL, formed from the name of the server and the directory's name, and that's the URL you'll give out to anyone who'll listen when you promote the site. It may not be a very good URL (too long, hard to remember, difficult to type, and so on), so you might want to pick your own snappy *domain name* – we'll look into that later in the chapter.

First, you need someone to **host** your site – in other words, you need to find a company willing to provide space on their Web servers for it. As you already have an Internet connection, your service provider probably includes free Web space, so you've got that question answered already. If your ISP doesn't give you space for free, don't pay yet – believe it or not, there are companies out there that provide Web space completely free of charge. Here are a few to try:

- **GeoCities** at **http://uk.geocities.yahoo.com**
- **EasySpace** at **http://www.easyspace.com**
- **Tripod** at **http://www.tripod.com**
- **FortuneCity** at **http://www.fortunecity.com** (Figure 10.1).

Figure 10.1 Free Web space and a stack of useful site-building tools at FortuneCity.

There are a few negative aspects to these free hosting companies. First, if the company deletes all your files, or their computers go down for six months and your site becomes unavailable, you're not in a strong position to complain. Second, you may find that your pages and graphics are unusually slow to load. Third, you might be required to display the hosting company's choice of banner ads or logo on your pages (or the company may insert these automatically at the server); in some cases, a popup advertising window will open whenever a link is clicked. Be sure to look at few sites belonging to other users of the service before committing yourself!

It's not your space!
Whether you opt for free or pay-for hosting, remember that the space isn't actually yours. The hosting company shares legal responsibility for its content with you, and they decide the terms and conditions. Some free hosts will not allow certain types of file, or delete them from your site, and most hosts will remove content they regard as illegal or immoral.

The name game

Whether you buy Web space, use Web space provided by your ISP, or go to one of the free space providers, you'll be given a username for the account and a directory with the same name on their server (perhaps prefixed with a ~ symbol) such as **www.mywebhost .com/~myname**, and that will be the URL of your website. It's long, it isn't easy to remember (particularly if it contains numbers as well as letters), and it gives a poor first impression of your site. Fortunately you have a couple of options available to replace this with something shorter and snappier.

The first and most popular option is to register your own domain name, such as **myname.co.uk**. There are dozens of companies in the UK selling domain names on the Web, and you can simply choose the name you want, pay for it, and then decide how you want to use it. The price you pay gives you ownership of the domain name for two years, with an option to renew it annually when the two-year period is up. There are some variations in pricing depending upon the **top-level domain** you choose (a .co.uk domain can be bought for under £10 if you shop around, whereas a .com or .net domain will usually cost £30 or more).

top-level domain
A domain name comes in two parts: the unique name ('dodgygoods') and a suffix (.com, .net, .org, .co.uk, and so on). This suffix is called the top-level domain *(TLD). The four I just mentioned are the well-established TLDs for UK users, but from June 2001 it should be possible to register domains for seven more TLDs: .aero, .biz, .coop, .info, .museum, .name and .pro. The .eu TLD should also be available soon. Bear in mind that some TLDs are restricted to limited companies, governments, and so on.*

It's important to buy your domain name from a reputable company, partly so that you can be sure you really have got the rights to it, and partly because if the company goes out of business it's just possible that you won't get a renewal reminder and your domain name could go back into the pool to be bought by someone else. Here are some well-established companies to consider:

- **NetNames** at **http://www.netnames.co.uk**
- **DomainsNet** at **http://www.domainsnet.com** (Figure 10.2)
- **UK Reg** at **http://www.ukreg.com**

Each of these sites gives plenty of straightforward information about the process and the services available. In a nutshell, you start by choosing a name (such as 'dodgygoods'), then pick one or more top-level domains (such as .com), and then check to see whether the chosen combination is available. (Don't include a 'www.' prefix: that's only used in the address of your website, it's not a part of the domain name.) If your chosen combination hasn't been snapped up by someone else, you can slap your money on the table and register it.

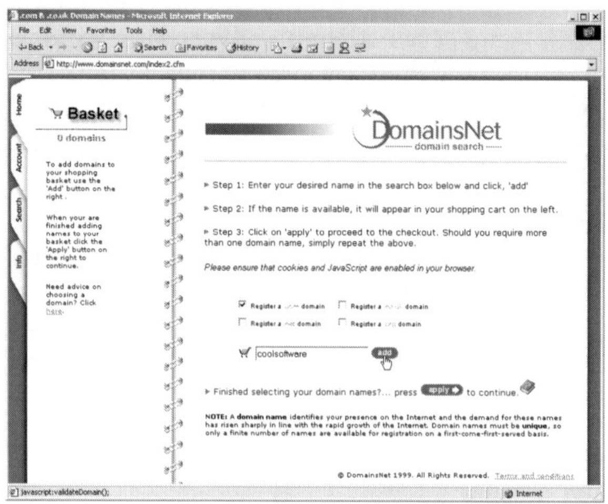

Figure 10.2 At DomainsNet, just type a name, pick a TLD, and click **Add** to add it to the shopping basket. If it's not available, a message will tell you.

Domain name transfer and forwarding

Once you've registered your domain name, you can do either of two things. One is to ask your ISP or hosting company to **transfer** the name to your Web space. You won't usually be able to do this if you're getting Web space for free, and some pay-for hosting companies will charge for the service. The other option is to use the registration company's **forwarding** service. Most registration companies offer this service, and few charge for it.

The way forwarding works is that after registering the name, you fill in a form that gives your current Web URL and your preferred email address. You tell everyone your snappy new URL (**www.dodgygoods.com**) and email address (**me@dodgygoods.com**), and the registration company's servers automatically *forward* visitors to your website and redirect email messages to the email address you gave.

The benefits of using Web forwarding services are twofold. First, it's quick and easy, and it saves you money if your host charges for domain transfers. Second, if you decide to switch to a different ISP or hosting company later on, you can simply visit the registration company's site and change the forwarding details.

Getting a free redirect URL

If you don't fancy spending money on a domain name, there's another option that works in a similar way to Web forwarding, but it's completely free. If you visit **http://www.v3.com** (Figure 10.3), you can choose a URL along the lines of come.to/dodgygoods or surf.to/dodgygoods, and enter the real URL of your website. Give out the new, snappy URL to everyone you know, and visitors will automatically be redirected to your site.

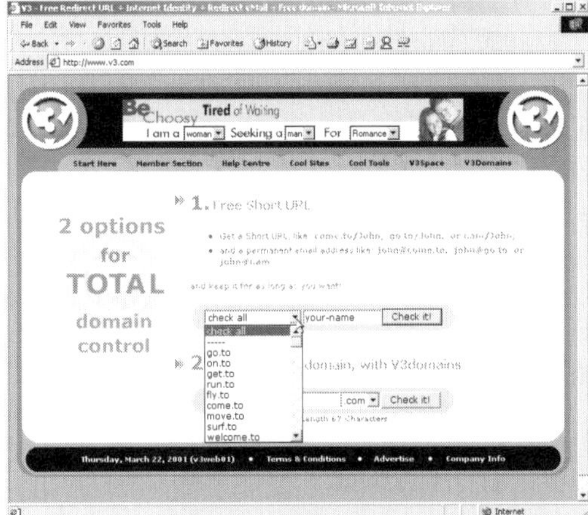

Figure 10.3 Surf to V3 and choose a free short URL like surf.to/mysite.

Uploading your site

When you're ready to put your site on the Web, you'll use a system called **FTP** (File Transfer Protocol). FTP is one of the two major systems used to transfer files around the Internet, along with HTTP. The HTTP system is used for the Web, but it can only be used for *downloading* files (sending Web pages to your browser, for instance, which is why Web URLs begin http://). FTP can be used to download files, but it can also *upload* them – send them to a remote server – which is what you need to do.

This is one of the few tricks your browser can't easily do, so you need to get your hands on an FTP program. Here are a few of the best:

- **FTP Explorer** from **http://www.ftpx.com**
- **CuteFTP** from **http://www.cuteftp.com**
- **WS_FTP Professional** from **http://www.ipswitch.com**.

I'm going to assume you're using FTP Explorer, but most FTP programs look and work in much the same way. When you install FTP Explorer, it will offer to create a set of *Profiles* for you. These are links to FTP sites you can visit, a lot like browsers' Favorites and Bookmarks lists, so it's worth saying yes to this offer. You'll be prompted to enter your email address the first time you use the program, but you shouldn't need to change anything else.

Creating a profile

Your hosting company or ISP should have given you all the details you need to log into your Web space – a username, a password, and an FTP host address. The first job is to create a 'profile' for the site so that you can log in with a couple of clicks any time you want to make changes, so follow these steps:

1. Start FTP Explorer and, if you don't see the Connect dialog (shown in Figure 10.4), choose **Connect** from the Tools menu. Click the **Add** button to create a new blank profile.
2. In the **Profile Name** box, type any friendly name that you'll recognise as being your own site.
3. Type the FTP host address you were given into the **Host Address** box. If the address includes a path (forward slashes and directory names) only use the host name itself – the part before the first forward slash.
4. As this isn't a public FTP site that you log into anonymously, remove the checkmark from the **Anonymous** box, then type your username and password in the **Login** and **Password** boxes.
5. If you had to leave out path details from the address in step 3, type that path into the **Initial Path** box, starting with the first forward slash. This is the directory that FTP Explorer should open when it connects to the host.
6. Click the **Save** button, and you'll see the new profile appear in the list to the left.

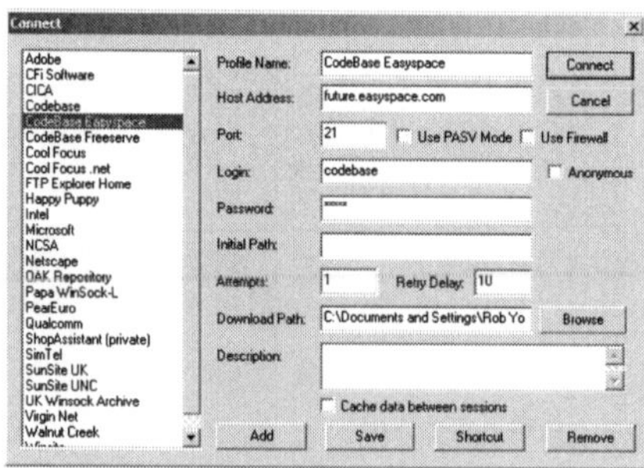

Figure 10.4 Creating a new profile for your Web space in FTP Explorer.

You're ready to upload!

With your FTP profile created (or the equivalent in your chosen FTP program), you're ready to publish your site to the Web. Select this profile in the Connect dialog's list and click the **Connect** button. In a few seconds you should be logged into your Web space and you'll see a two-pane view that will be familiar to Windows users: directories are shown in the left pane, with the contents of the current directory shown on the right. At the moment, of course, you won't see much there at all!

Find the 'Site' directory on your hard disk containing all the files belonging to your website and open it so that you can see the files and directories it contains. Select its entire contents and drag-and-drop them into FTP Explorer's window. This is the simplest way to upload – it saves you having to remember which files you've uploaded and which you haven't. FTP Explorer will copy all the files to your Web space one by one, creating new directories as needed, and you can just sit back and watch (Figure 10.5). (Some FTP programs don't allow drag-and-drop, or won't let you drop directories, so you might have to click a button to create a directory with the same name as one in your 'Site' directory, and then upload the files it contains.)

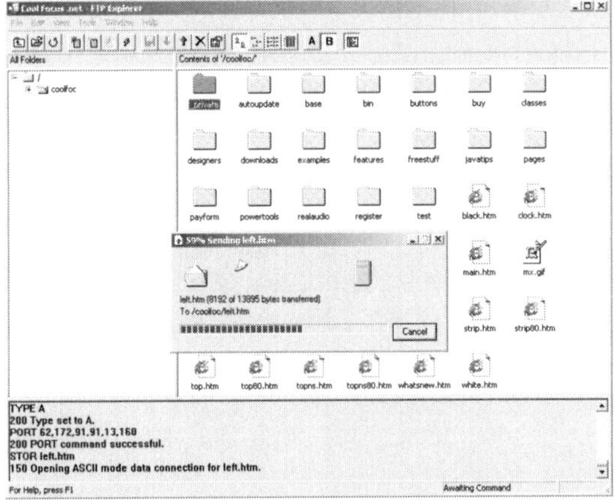

Figure 10.5 Drop your site's files and directories into FTP Explorer, then make coffee while it all happens for you!

FTP transfer modes

*Most FTP programs give you a choice between two transfer modes, **ASCII** and **Binary** (FTP Explorer has buttons labelled A and B on its toolbar for this). ASCII mode can only be used to transfer plain text files, and will do so a tiny bit faster than Binary mode, which has to be used for any other type of file (zip files, images, programs, and so on). Since text files tend to be small anyway, the time saved by using ASCII mode is negligible, and you'd probably spend more time choosing and switching modes than you could ever save! It's simplest to stick with Binary mode for everything.*

If you need to create a new folder manually in FTP Explorer, just right-click on a blank area in the main window, choose **New** and **Folder**, and type a name. You can then just double-click this new folder to open it and start copying files into it.

And now...test!

This is the big one! Fire up your browser, type the URL of your Website into its address bar and press Enter, and you should see its index page. If you don't, take a look at the troubleshooting tips below. If you do, congratulations!

Now you need to calm down, get a grip, and do a thorough test of every page, every link, and every item of content. It's not unusual to find that odd things have 'broken' in the transfer from hard disk to web, and you may need to do some fixing. Along with testing all your internal links (and 'hidden' links such as external style sheets), remember to check links to other sites. At long last you'll be able to judge the speed of your site too.

Testing a site is a vital step, not only when you first upload it, but whenever you add or alter pages – you can make a whole page of content disappear just by missing out a closing script, style or comment tag, forgetting a closing quote, or deleting a > symbol!

Troubleshooting

If everything goes right first time, your site will work just as well online as it worked on your hard disk. Just in case you hit a snag, though, here are a few troubleshooting tips to help you sort it out. If you need to make changes to a page, remember to change the copy on your hard disk. You can then upload that to the same online directory to replace the original version. Similarly, if you rename an online file using your FTP program, rename the copy on your hard disk too – keeping both copies of the site identical will help your future maintenance no end!

'I can't see my site!'

First, make sure you've typed your URL correctly and you really are online. Next, check that the HTML file that should form the front page of your site can be found – try including it in the URL like this: **http://www.mysite. com/index.htm**. If the page loads, that means that your Web server uses a different default filename, such as default.htm, which your hosting company can tell you. If so, rename the file on your hard disk and use your FTP program to rename the online copy.

'My links don't work!'

Make sure none of the files you're linking to has a space in its name. If you find a space, rename the local and online copies of the files to remove the space, and edit any pages linking to it. Next, check that you haven't used any upper-case letters in links that don't appear in the filenames (or vice versa). On the majority of Web servers, filenames are case-sensitive. Finally, of course, make sure you really have uploaded the files you're linking to, and that they're in the same relative location online as they are on your hard disk.

'Everything takes ages to download!'

That may be a problem of page-weight: using the hard-disk copy of your site, look at the size of the HTML file and any images, applets, scripts and other content that it links to, and add up the sizes. If the page loads a frameset, remember that it's actually loading two or more pages and all their content. Try experimenting with the images to see if you can reduce their size, or cut down the amount of content by splitting a large single page into two smaller linked pages. Of course, the problem may be that your host's server is slow (either temporarily or chronically); a common problem, especially with free hosting.

'Part of the page has disappeared!'

This usually has an easy answer: a closing tag has gone missing! Check the offending page for <SCRIPT>, <STYLE>, <APPLET> and other content-related tags and make sure that each has a matching closing tag (such as </STYLE>). If the page uses tables, make sure you have a closing </TABLE> tag and that every <TD> and <TR> tag is closed before the next cell or row begins.

'The links open in a new window instead of a frame!'

This means that the TARGET attribute of the <A> or <BASE> tag is set to a frame name that doesn't exist. Compare the name in that attribute with the names in the <FRAME> tags of your frame-setting page: you've probably spelt the name wrongly in one or the other, or used an upper-case letter that should be lower-case.

Hitting the publicity trail

So you have a website, and it works. Now you want people to come and visit it, so you need to let them know it exists. One method is to contact the authors of sites covering similar subjects and ask if they'd like to exchange links – you add links to their sites in return for links to yours.

Another method is to use banner advertising. A handy free service called Banner Exchange operates in a similar way to the link exchange suggestion above: in return for displaying other members' advertising banners on your own site, your ads will be displayed on theirs. The more pages you're willing to include a banner on, the more your own banners will be shown. If you fancy using this method, visit one of the sites below, fill in the online forms, add the HTML code generated by the service to your pages, and then upload your own banners.

- **Banner Exchange** at **http://bannerexchange.mycomputer.com**
- **UK Banners** at **http://www.ukbanners.com**

- **Link Exchange** at **http://store.bcentral.com/le/index.html**

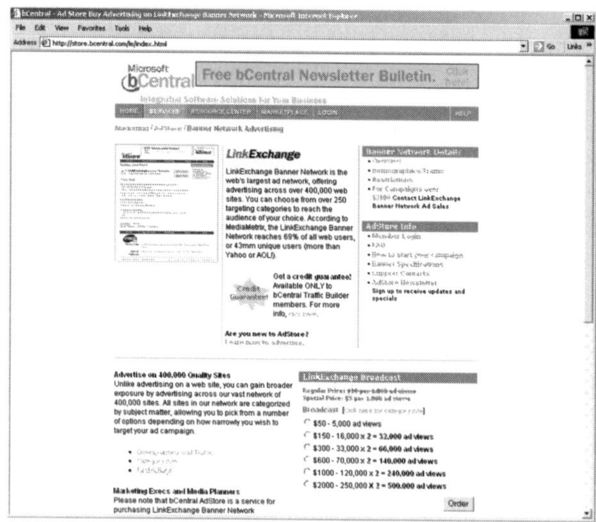

Figure 10.6 Visit MicrosoftbCentral to trade advertising space with other members.

Another vital step in promoting a website is to try to get it listed with the major search engines. Because search engines work in different ways, this is a two-step process. Some search engines use a software 'robot' that scours the Web for new sites and indexes them by reading their pages, so the first step is to make some changes to your site to make it 'search engine-friendly'. Other engines only index a site when you ask to have it included, so the second step is to manually submit your site to as many search engines as you can.

For the first of those steps, begin by making a list of the important keywords and short phrases that describe your site – the words that you think people will type into a search engine when looking for a site like yours. Aim for between 10 and 20 keywords, putting the most important words first. Next, write a description of your site (using up to about 100 words), trying to include your most important keywords in the description. Finally, add the keywords and description to the head section of your site's index page using **<META>** tags like this:

```
<META NAME="keywords" CONTENT="keyword1, keyword2, keyword3, keyword4">

<META NAME="description" CONTENT="A description of my page, including a few keywords, that could be shown in the search results.">
```

Make sure that the titles of your pages (between the <TITLE> and </TITLE> tags) are as meaningful as possible and try to include at least one of your keywords. It also helps if the first paragraph of text on your index page is reasonably descriptive and appetising.

After you've made your site more search engine-friendly and uploaded the edited pages to your site, it's time to embark on the second step – the manual submissions. As there are literally hundreds of search engines on the Web, this is a job that could take forever, but fortunately you don't need to visit every single one personally. The vast majority of search engine-introduced hits come from the five big players, Yahoo!, Google, Excite, AltaVista, and Lycos, and they give preference to sites that have been submitted manually, so visit those first and take your time filling in the details. At each site, look for a link marked **Submit URL**, **Add Your Site** or something similar (usually a small link at the foot of the page), and then follow the instructions.

When you've taken care of the major search engines, you may not have the time or patience to visit dozens of smaller engines, read their rules and fill in their forms. If not, there are services available that can do the legwork for you. You just fill in a single form, then follow a step-by-step process to submit to a bundle of sites. Along the way you'll be prompted for any extra information needed by a particular site (such as picking a subject category) without repeatedly entering the same information. Here are three free services to start you off:

- **AddMe** at **http://www.addme.com** submits your site to 25 search engines
- **CNET Search.com** at **http://www.search.com** submits to up to 15 engines (Figure 10.7)
- **Submit Express** at **http://www.submitexpress.com** will submit to 40 search sites.

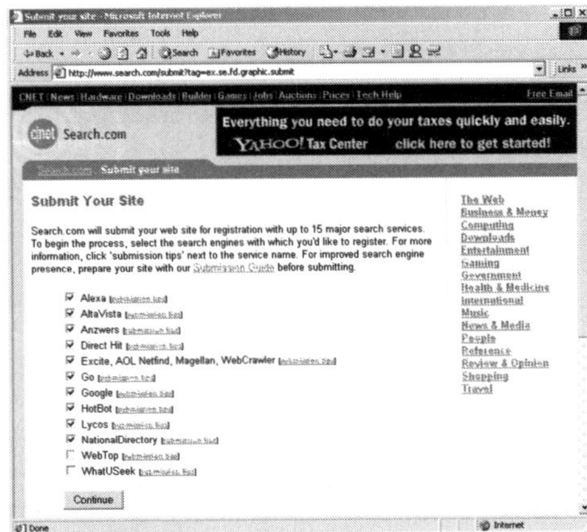

Figure 10.7 CNET Search.com can submit your site to 15 search engines quickly and painlessly.

So... has it worked?

With your promotion under way you obviously need some way of knowing how many people are actually visiting your site – at the very least you need a hit counter. But why settle for a simple tally of the number of visitors to a particular page when you can get a complete statistical analysis? As you've probably come to expect, this is something you can get your hands on for free.

Two of the best site-stats services are at **http://www.webstat.com** (Figure 10.8) and **http://www.thecounter.com**. At either of these, sign up for a free account, entering your site's URL and your email address, and you'll receive a small chunk of HTML code in return. Place this code at the bottom of your site's index page, and every visitor's details will be logged by the service. At any time you can log into your account and check how many hits you're getting, where they're coming from, which browsers they're using, and lots more. Even if it's not all actually *useful*, you'll find it fascinating.

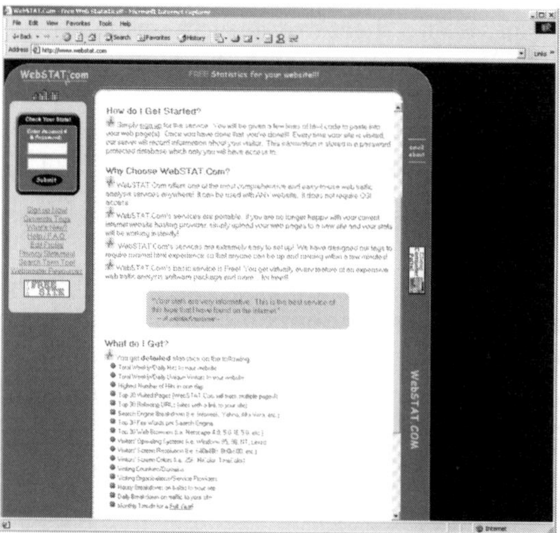

Figure 10.8 WebSTAT.com can tell you everything you want to know about who's visiting your site, when, and how.

What do *you* think?

As a Webmaster, your number one resource is your audience – if they like what you've got, you're on to a winner; if they don't, you lose. So an important part of running a website is to encourage visitors to give you feedback, and there are two good ways to do this. The first is to make sure you've made email links easily accessible (see Chapter 3), either by placing them on every page or by adding a Contact Us link to your site's main navigation.

The second method is to add a **guestbook** to the site. Visitors can visit the guestbook page to read the comments left by others and add their own at the click of a link. As with so much in Web life, guestbooks are something you can find for free. Two services worth a look are Guestbook4free.com at **http://www.guestbook4free.com** (Figure 10.9) and TheGuestbook at **http://www.theguestbook.com**, but a search for 'guestbook +free' at any search engine should turn up a mass of links to others.

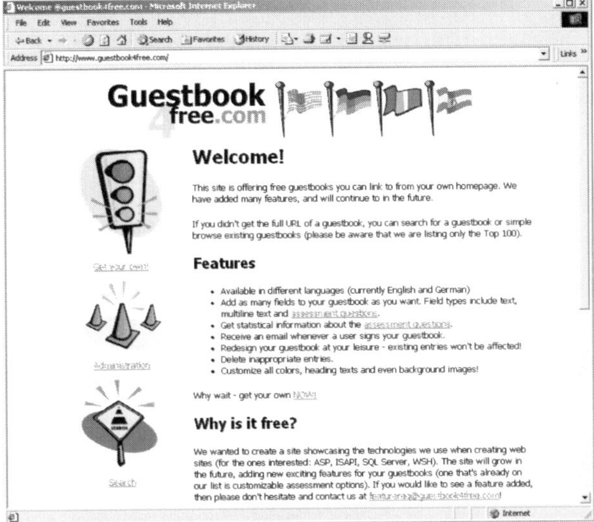

Figure 10.9 Sign up for a free, flexible guestbook at **guestbook4free.com**.

Appendices

Appendix A – HTML tag reference

Appendix B – HTML colour names

Appendix C – Useful Websites

Appendix A: HTML tag reference

The following is an alphabetical quick reference guide to the most useful HTML tags and their attributes. The emphasis is very much on *useful* here: I haven't included every tag and attribute available in the HTML specification, or majored on any particular browser. Instead I've stuck to the tags and attributes you're most likely to want to use. The list is set out as follows:

- For HTML elements that must have a closing tag, both the opening and closing tags are included, separated with an ellipsis (...) which is where your own text or other HTML will go.
- Italic text indicates that you'll enter your own value here, such as a frame name, URL or style definition. The word *string* means that you'll enter a text string; n indicates a number.
- Where a choice of attribute values is available, these have been separated with a pipe symbol, such as **left|right|center**, indicating that you can choose any of those values.

<!-- ... -->

Specifies that the enclosed text or code is a comment that shouldn't be displayed by the Web browser.

<A> ... </A>

Creates a hypertext link using the `HREF` attribute, or a named anchor in a document using the `NAME` attribute.

<table>
<tr><td>ACCESSKEY=character</td><td>A shortcut key accessed by pressing ALT+character.</td></tr>
<tr><td>CLASS=classname</td><td>Applies a style sheet class.</td></tr>
<tr><td>HREF=url|#name</td><td>A hypertext link to the URL or a link to the anchor named name (or a combination of the two)</td></tr>
<tr><td>ID=string</td><td>Assigns a name, enabling the tag to be accessed through scripting.</td></tr>
<tr><td>NAME=string</td><td>Defines a named anchor in a document.</td></tr>
<tr><td>STYLE=string</td><td>Applies inline style settings.</td></tr>
<tr><td>TARGET=window|_self|_top|</td><td>Specifies the frame or window to open _new|_parent|_blank the link into.</td></tr>
<tr><td>TITLE=string</td><td>Informational tooltip text.</td></tr>
</table>

<ACRONYM> ... </ACRONYM>

Specifies that the enclosed text is an acronym, such as 'JPEG'.

CLASS=*classname*	Applies a style sheet class.
ID=*string*	Assigns a name, enabling the tag to be accessed through scripting.
STYLE=*string*	Applies inline style settings.
TITLE=*string*	Informational tooltip text.

<ADDRESS> ... </ADDRESS>

Specifies that the enclosed text is an address, usually shown as a separate paragraph formatted in italics.

CLASS=*classname*	Applies a style sheet class.
ID=*string*	Assigns a name, enabling the tag to be accessed through scripting.
STYLE=*string*	Applies inline style settings.
TITLE=*string*	Informational tooltip text.

<APPLET> ... </APPLET>

Places a Java applet on the page. The CODE, WIDTH and HEIGHT attributes are required. Often used in conjunction with the <PARAM> tag.

ALIGN=TEXTTOP|TOP|MIDDLE| BOTTOM|BASELINE|LEFT| RIGHT|ABSMIDDLE|ABSBOTTOM	Sets the alignment of the applet.
ALT=*string*	Alternative text for browsers with Java support switched off.
ARCHIVE=*jarname*	Name of a compressed .zip or .jar file containing the applet classes.
CLASS=*classname*	Applies a style sheet class.
CODE=*classname*	The name of the applet .class file.
CODEBASE=*URL*	The URL of the directory containing the applet's class and/or .jar files.

ID=*string*	Assigns a name, enabling the tag to be accessed through scripting.
HEIGHT=*n*	Height of the applet in pixels.
HSPACE=*n*	Horizontal spacing in pixels.
MAYSCRIPT	Allows applet/JavaScript communication if included.
NAME=*string*	Applies a unique name to this instance of an applet on the page.
STYLE=string	Applies inline style settings.
VSPACE=*n*	Vertical spacing in pixels.
WIDTH=*n*	Width of the applet in pixels.

<AREA>

Defines the shape and coordinates of a hotspot in an image-map, in conjunction with the `<MAP>` tag. The `COORDS` attribute is required.

CLASS=*classname*	Applies a style sheet class.
COORDS=*coordinates*	Sets the coordinates of the hotspot.
HREF=*url*	The URL to which the hotspot links.
ID=*string*	Assigns a name, enabling the tag to be accessed through scripting.
SHAPE=RECT|CIRCLE|POLY	Defines the shape of the hotspot.
STYLE=*string*	Applies inline style settings.
TARGET=*window*|_self|_top|	Specifies the frame or window to open _new|_parent|_blank the link into.
TITLE=*string*	Informational tooltip text.

<B> ... </B>

Displays the enclosed text using a bold typeface.

CLASS=*classname*	Applies a style sheet class.
ID=*string*	Assigns a name, enabling the tag to be accessed through scripting.
STYLE=*string*	Applies inline style settings.
TITLE=*string*	Informational tooltip text.

<BASE>

Sets the base URL from which all relative links should be resolved, and/or the frame or window name to target for all <A> tags in the page that have no TARGET attribute.

HREF=*url*	The URL to use as the base.
TARGET=*window*|_self|_top|_new|_parent|_blank	The frame or window to use by default.

<BASEFONT>

Sets the default font face, size and colour for the page (although only the SIZE attribute is supported by Netscape 4).

CLASS=*classname*	Applies a style sheet class.
COLOR=*colour*	The default text colour.
FACE=*font1, font2, font3...*	The default font for the document.
ID=*string*	Assigns a name, enabling the tag to be accessed through scripting.
SIZE=*n*	The default size of body text in the document.

<BGSOUND>

Plays a background sound (in IE only). Use <EMBED> for cross-browser support. The SRC attribute is required.

BALANCE=*n*	Sets stereo balance using a value between –10000 and 10000 (where 0 is centre).
CLASS=*classname*	Applies a style sheet class.

ID=*string*	Assigns a name, enabling the tag to be accessed through scripting.
LOOP=*n*|INFINITE	Sets the number of times the clip will play, or allows 'infinite' looping.
SRC=*url*	The URL of the audio file to play.
TITLE=*string*	Informational tooltip text.
VOLUME=*n*	Sets the volume of the clip using a value between –10000 and 0, where 0 is equal to the user's current volume setting. (The clip can't be played louder than the user's own setting.)

<BIG> ... </BIG>

Displays the enclosed text at a slightly larger font size.

CLASS=*classname*	Applies a style sheet class.
ID=*string*	Assigns a name, enabling the tag to be accessed through scripting.
STYLE=*string*	Applies inline style settings.
TITLE=*string*	Informational tooltip text.

<BLOCKQUOTE> ... </BLOCKQUOTE>

Signifies that the enclosed text is a quotation, usually by placing it in a new paragraph evenly indented at the left and right.

CLASS=*classname*	Applies a style sheet class.
ID=*string*	Assigns a name, enabling the tag to be accessed through scripting.
STYLE=*string*	Applies inline style settings.
TITLE=*string*	Informational tooltip text.

`<BODY> ... </BODY>`

Specifies the beginning and end of the body of the page, containing all content to be displayed.

`ALINK=`*`colour`*	The colour of an active link.
`BACKGROUND=`*`url`*	The URL of an image to use as the page's background.
`BGCOLOR=`*`colour`*	The colour of the page background.
`BGPROPERTIES=FIXED`	In IE only, prevents a back ground image from scrolling with the page content.
`BOTTOMMARGIN=`*`n`*	In IE, the height of the bottom page margin.
`CLASS=`*`classname`*	Applies a style sheet class.
`ID=`*`string`*	Assigns a name, enabling the tag to be accessed through scripting.
`LEFTMARGIN=`*`n`*	In IE, the width of the left page margin.
`LINK=`*`colour`*	The colour of hypertext links.
`MARGINHEIGHT=`*`n`*	In Netscape, the height of top and bottom page margins.
`MARGINWIDTH=`*`n`*	In Netscape, the width of left and right page margins.
`RIGHTMARGIN=`*`n`*	In IE, the width of the right page margin.
`STYLE=`*`string`*	Applies inline style settings.
`TEXT=`*`colour`*	The default colour of the page's body text.
`TITLE=`*`string`*	Informational tooltip text.
`TOPMARGIN=`*`n`*	In IE, the height of the top page margin.
`VLINK=`*`colour`*	The colour of visited links.

**
**

Inserts a line break, with text that follows appearing on a new line.

CLASS=*classname*	Applies a style sheet class.
CLEAR=ALL|LEFT|RIGHT	Forces the next line to begin at the first point on the page where there is a clear margin at the left, right, or both.
ID=*string*	Assigns a name, enabling the tag to be accessed through scripting.
STYLE=*string*	Applies inline style settings.
TITLE=*string*	Informational tooltip text.

<CAPTION> … </CAPTION>

Creates a caption to be displayed beside or above a table, used in conjunction with the <TABLE> tag.

ALIGN=TOP|RIGHT|BOTTOM|LEFT	Sets the alignment of the caption.
CLASS=*classname*	Applies a style sheet class.
ID=*string*	Assigns a name, enabling the tag to be accessed through scripting.
STYLE=*string*	Applies inline style settings.
TITLE=*string*	Informational tooltip text.
VALIGN=TOP|BOTTOM	Sets the vertical alignment of the caption.

<CENTER> … </CENTER>

Centres all content enclosed between these tags on the page (or within a table cell, etc.).

CLASS=*classname*	Applies a style sheet class.
ID=*string*	Assigns a name, enabling the tag to be accessed through scripting.
STYLE=*string*	Applies inline style settings.
TITLE=*string*	Informational tooltip text.

<CODE> … </CODE>

Specifies that the enclosed text is code (such as a programming or scripting language), usually by displaying it using a fixed-width font.

`CLASS=`*`classname`*	Applies a style sheet class.
`ID=`*`string`*	Assigns a name, enabling the tag to be accessed through scripting.
`STYLE=`*`string`*	Applies inline style settings.
`TITLE=`*`string`*	Informational tooltip text.

<DD>

Specifies that the following text is the definition of a term in a definition list, used in conjunction with `<DL>` and `<DT>`.

`CLASS=`*`classname`*	Applies a style sheet class.
`ID=`*`string`*	Assigns a name, enabling the tag to be accessed through scripting.
`STYLE=`*`string`*	Applies inline style settings.
`TITLE=`*`string`*	Informational tooltip text.

<DIV> … </DIV>

Defines a 'division', a section of a Web page that can contain other content.

`ALIGN=CENTER│LEFT│RIGHT`	Sets the alignment of the division's content.
`CLASS=`*`classname`*	Applies a style sheet class.
`ID=`*`string`*	Assigns a name, enabling the tag to be accessed through scripting.
`STYLE=`*`string`*	Applies inline style settings.
`TITLE=`*`string`*	Informational tooltip text.

<DL> ... </DL>

Creates a definition list by the inclusion of <DT> and <DL> tags to specify the terms and their definitions.

CLASS=*classname*	Applies a style sheet class.
COMPACT	Formats the list in a more compact style if included.
ID=*string*	Assigns a name, enabling the tag to be accessed through scripting.
STYLE=*string*	Applies inline style settings.
TITLE=*string*	Informational tooltip text.

<DT>

Specifies that the following text is a term in a definition list, used in conjunction with <DL> and <DD>.

CLASS=*classname*	Applies a style sheet class.
ID=*string*	Assigns a name, enabling the tag to be accessed through scripting.
STYLE=*string*	Applies inline style settings.
TITLE=*string*	Informational tooltip text.

<EMBED> ... </EMBED>

Embeds media objects such as sounds and animations into the page to be played or displayed using a plug-in. The SRC attribute is required.

ALIGN=TEXTTOP|TOP|MIDDLE|BOTTOM|BASELINE|LEFT|RIGHT|ABSMIDDLE|ABSBOTTOM	Sets the alignment of the embedded content.
ALT=*string*	Alternative text for display by browser unable to display the embedded content.
BORDER=*n*	Creates a border around the content.
CLASS=*classname*	Applies a style sheet class.

HEIGHT=*n*	The height of the content.
HIDDEN=TRUE|FALSE	Specifies whether the plug-in's user interface should be shown.
HSPACE=*n*	The horizontal space around the content.
ID=*string*	Assigns a name, enabling the tag to be accessed through scripting.
NAME=*string*	Assigns a name to the tag, as with the ID attribute.
PLUGINSPACE=*url*	Directs the user to a URL where the required plug-in can be downloaded if it isn't installed.
SRC=*url*	The URL of the content to be embedded.
STYLE=*string*	Applies inline style settings.
TITLE=*string*	Informational tooltip text.
TYPE=*mime-type*	Describes the MIME type of the embedded content, enabling the browser to determine which plug-in to use.
VSPACE=*n*	The vertical space around the content.
WIDTH=*n*	The width of the content.

<FONT> ... </FONT>

Applies a particular font face, size and/or colour to the textual content enclosed by the tag-pair.

CLASS=*classname*	Applies a style sheet class.
COLOR=*colour*	Sets the colour of the font.
FACE=*font1,font2, font3...*	Specifies the name or family of the font to use. The first available font listed will be applied.
ID=*string*	Assigns a name, enabling the tag to be accessed through scripting.

SIZE=1|2|3|4|5|6|7	Sets the size of the font.
STYLE=*string*	Applies inline style settings.
TITLE=*string*	Informational tooltip text.

<FORM> ... </FORM>

Specifies that the enclosed content is a Web form. Controls are added using <INPUT>, <TEXTAREA>, <SELECT> and <OPTION> tags.

ACTION=*url*	The URL to which the name/value data of the completed form are to be sent when the form is submitted.
CLASS=*classname*	Applies a style sheet class.
ENCTYPE=*mime-type*	The MIME type that should be used to encode the form data for submission.
ID=*string*	Assigns a name, enabling the tag to be accessed through scripting.
METHOD=POST|GET	Specifies the method used by the browser to access the URL given in the ACTION attribute.
NAME=*string*	As with ID, assigns a name to the form for access by scripting.
STYLE=*string*	Applies inline style settings.
TARGET=*window*|_self|_top|	Specifies the frame or window to use _new|_parent|_blank when displaying the results of the form submission (if any).
TITLE=*string*	Informational tooltip text.

<FRAME>

Used within <FRAMESET> tags to define a single frame in a browser and load a Web page into it.

BORDERCOLOR=*colour*	Sets the colour of the frame's borders.
CLASS=*classname*	Applies a style sheet class.
FRAMEBORDER=0|1	In IE, specifies whether the frame will have a visible border ('1') or not ('0').
FRAMESPACING=*n*	In IE, creates space around frames to give an effect similar to the <IFRAME> tag.
ID=*string*	Assigns a name, enabling the tag to be accessed through scripting.
MARGINHEIGHT=*n*	Sets the height of the frame's top and bottom margins.
MARGINWIDTH=*n*	Sets the width of the frame's left and right margins.
NAME=*string*	Assigns a name to the frame to allow it to be targeted using the TARGET attribute of <A>, <FORM> and other tags.
NORESIZE	Prevents a frame from being resized if included.
SCROLLING=AUTO|YES|NO	Specifies whether scrollbars should be visible to allow the user to scroll through the frame's content. The default is AUTO.
SRC=*url*	The URL of a document to be loaded into the frame.
STYLE=*string*	Applies inline style settings.
TITLE=*string*	Informational tooltip text.

<FRAMESET> ... </FRAMESET>

A container for frames (defined using the <FRAME> tag) and optionally for more framesets within those frames.

BORDER=*n*	In Netscape, the width of the borders of frames within the frameset.
BORDERCOLOR=*colour*	Sets the colour of the frameset's borders.
CLASS=*classname*	Applies a style sheet class.
COLS=*string*	A comma-separated list of column widths corresponding to the number of frames required in the frameset.
FRAMEBORDER=0|1	In IE, specifies whether the frame will have a visible border ('1') or not ('0').
FRAMESPACING=*n*	In IE, creates space around frames to give an effect similar to the <IFRAME> tag.
ID=*string*	Assigns a name, enabling the tag to be accessed through scripting.
ROWS=*string*	A comma-separated list of row-heights corresponding to the number of frames required in the frameset.
STYLE=*string*	Applies inline style settings.
TITLE=*string*	Informational tooltip text.

<HEAD> ... </HEAD>

A collection of tags containing information (in any order) about the document and how it's to be displayed. Common tags used within the <HEAD> section are <TITLE>, <META>, <SCRIPT> and <STYLE>.

CLASS=*classname*	Applies a style sheet class.
ID=*string*	Assigns a name, enabling the tag to be accessed through scripting.

`STYLE=`*`string`*	Applies inline style settings.
`TITLE=`*`string`*	Informational tooltip text.

<H*n*> … </H*n*>

A set of six tag-pairs that format the enclosed text as a heading, where *n* is a figure from 1 to 6.

`ALIGN=LEFT|RIGHT|CENTER`	Sets the alignment of the heading.
`CLASS=`*`classname`*	Applies a style sheet class.
`ID=`*`string`*	Assigns a name, enabling the tag to be accessed through scripting.
`STYLE=`*`string`*	Applies inline style settings.
`TITLE=`*`string`*	Informational tooltip text.

<HR>

Places a 'horizontal rule' on the page – a dividing line to break up the page's content.

`ALIGN=LEFT|RIGHT|CENTER`	Sets the alignment of the rule.
`CLASS=`*`classname`*	Applies a style sheet class.
`COLOR=`*`colour`*	In IE, sets the colour of the rule.
`ID=`*`string`*	Assigns a name, enabling the tag to be accessed through scripting.
`NOSHADE`	Turns off shading to create a solid rather than a three-dimensional rule.
`SIZE=`*`n`*	Sets the height of the rule.
`SRC=`*`url`*	In IE, allows an image to be used as a rule by specifying its URL. (This is more reliably done using the `<IMG>` tag.)
`STYLE=`*`string`*	Applies inline style settings.
`TITLE=`*`string`*	Informational tooltip text.

WIDTH=*n*	Sets the width of the rule, either in pixels or as a percentage of the page width.

<HTML> ... </HTML>

Identifies the document as an HTML page. This pair of tags encloses the entire document, making them the first and last tags on the page.

TITLE=*string*	Informational tooltip text.

<I> ... </I>

Displays the enclosed text using an italic typeface.

CLASS=*classname*	Applies a style sheet class.
ID=*string*	Assigns a name, enabling the tag to be accessed through scripting.
STYLE=*string*	Applies inline style settings.
TITLE=*string*	Informational tooltip text.

<IFRAME> ... </IFRAME>

Creates an inline (or 'floating') frame within a page that can contain other pages and can be targeted by <A> links. Supported by IE only.

ALIGN=TEXTTOP|TOP|MIDDLE|BOTTOM|BASELINE|LEFT|RIGHT|ABSMIDDLE|ABSBOTTOM	Sets the alignment of the frame.
BORDER=*n*	Sets the width of the frame's border.
BORDERCOLOR=*colour*	Sets the colour of the frame's border.
CLASS=*classname*	Applies a style sheet class.
FRAMEBORDER=0|1	In IE, specifies whether the frame will have a visible border ('1') or not ('0').
FRAMESPACING=*n*	In IE, creates space around frames to give an effect similar to the <IFRAME> tag.

HEIGHT=*n*	The height of the frame.
HSPACE=*n*	The horizontal space around the frame.
ID=*string*	Assigns a name, enabling the tag to be accessed through scripting.
MARGINHEIGHT=*n*	Sets the height of the frame's top and bottom margins.
MARGINWIDTH=*n*	Sets the width of the frame's left and right margins.
NAME=*string*	Assigns a name to the frame to allow it to be targeted using the TARGET attribute of <A>, <FORM> and other tags.
NORESIZE	Prevents a frame from being resized if included.
SCROLLING=AUTO|YES|NO	Specifies whether scrollbars should be visible to allow the user to scroll through the frame's content. The default is AUTO.
SRC=*url*	The URL of a document to be loaded into the frame.
STYLE=*string*	Applies inline style settings.
TITLE=*string*	Informational tooltip text.
VSPACE=*n*	The vertical space around the frame.
WIDTH=*n*	The width of the frame.

<IMG>

Places an inline GIF or JPEG image on the page. The SRC attribute is required.

ALIGN=TEXTTOP|TOP|MIDDLE|BOTTOM|BASELINE|LEFT|RIGHT|ABSMIDDLE|ABSBOTTOM	Sets the alignment of the image.
ALT=*string*	Alternative text to display if image display options have been switched off.

`BORDER=`*n*	The width of the border displayed around the image.
`CLASS=`*classname*	Applies a style sheet class.
`CONTROLS`	In conjunction with `DYNSRC`, specifies that movie-player controls are visible, if included.
`DYNSRC=`*url*	In IE, the URL of an AVI video clip to display in place of the image.
`HEIGHT=`*n*	The height of the image.
`HSPACE=`*n*	The horizontal space around the image.
`ID=`*string*	Assigns a name, enabling the tag to be accessed through scripting.
`LOOP=`*n*`|INFINITE`	In conjunction with `DYNSRC`, sets how many times the movie is repeated.
`LOWSRC=`*url*	The URL of a lower-quality (but faster-loading) image to display while the remaining page contents are loading.
`NAME=`*string*	Assigns a name to the image, as with `ID`, allowing it to be accessed in scripts.
`SRC=`*url*	The URL of the image to display.
`START=MOUSEOVER`	In conjunction with `DYNSRC`, specifies that the movie plays only when the mouse moves over the static image.
`STYLE=`*string*	Applies inline style settings.
`TITLE=`*string*	Informational tooltip text.
`USEMAP=`*url#mapname*	The URL (if necessary) and name of a coordinate-map created with the `<MAP>` tag, used when the current image is an image-map.

VSPACE=*n*	The vertical space around the image.
WIDTH=*n*	The width of the image.

<INPUT>

Places a form-input field such as a checkbox, text field or button on the page. Used in conjunction with the <FORM> tag.

CHECKED	If included, specifies that the checkbox or radio button control is marked as 'selected'.
CLASS=*classname*	Applies a style sheet class.
DISABLED	If included, prevents the input field from being selected or its contents changed by the user.
ID=*string*	Assigns a name, enabling the tag to be accessed through scripting.
MAXLENGTH=*n*	When the input type is 'text', specifies the maximum number of characters that may be entered.
NAME=*string*	The name of the field, to be returned (along with its value) when the form is submitted.
READONLY	If included, the user can select this field but can't modify its contents.
SIZE=*n*	Specifies the width of a text field (the number of characters that may be seen at once, rather than the number that can be entered).
SRC=*url*	When the input type is an image, specifies the URL of the image to display.
STYLE=*string*	Applies inline style settings.

TITLE=*string*	Informational tooltip text.
TYPE=BUTTON|CHECKBOX|HIDDEN|IMAGE|PASSWORD|RADIO|RESET|SUBMIT|TEXT	The type of input field to create.
VALUE=*string*	Specifies the initial value of the input field (such as the text shown in a text field), or the button label if the input type is a button, or the value to be returned from a checkbox or radio button if selected.

<LABEL> … </LABEL>

Creates a text label for a form input control such as a checkbox or radio button, allowing the control to be checked or unchecked by clicking the label. The FOR attribute is required. Supported by IE only.

CLASS=*classname*	Applies a style sheet class.
FOR=*input-ID*	Specifies which form control on the page this label will activate, using the name given in the control's ID attribute.
ID=*string*	Assigns a name, enabling the tag to be accessed through scripting.
STYLE=*string*	Applies inline style settings.
TITLE=*string*	Informational tooltip text.

<LI>

Creates a list item in an ordered or unordered list, in conjunction with the <OL> or <UL> tags.

CLASS=*classname*	Applies a style sheet class.
ID=*string*	Assigns a name, enabling the tag to be accessed through scripting.
STYLE=*string*	Applies inline style settings.

TITLE=*string*	Informational tooltip text.
TYPE=1|a|A|i|I|DISC|CIRCLE|SQUARE	Resets the type of bullet or numbering system used for this and subsequent items.
VALUE=*n*	In an ordered list, resets the number-count to the chosen value from this item onwards.

<LINK>

Used to define relationships between documents, although few browsers now support this concept. The primary use is in linking an external style sheet to a document.

CLASS=*classname*	Applies a style sheet class.
DISABLED	If included, indicates that the link is to be ignored in this document (for instance, the style sheet's rules won't be applied).
HREF=*url*	The URL of the related document.
ID=*string*	Assigns a name, enabling the tag to be accessed through scripting.
REL=*relationship*	The relationship being defined, such as STYLESHEET.
STYLE=*string*	Applies inline style settings.
TITLE=*string*	Informational tooltip text.

<MAP> … </MAP>

Defines the shapes and coordinates of the hotspots used in a client-side image map, in conjunction with the <AREA> tag. The NAME attribute is required.

CLASS=*classname*	Applies a style sheet class.
ID=*string*	Assigns a name, enabling the tag to be accessed through scripting.
NAME=*string*	Assigns a name to the map, allowing it to be linked to an image via the <IMG> tag's USEMAP attribute.

`STYLE=`*string*	Applies inline style settings.
`TITLE=`*string*	Informational tooltip text.

<MARQUEE> ... </MARQUEE>

In Internet Explorer only, scrolls the enclosed text in an animated fashion across the screen.

`ALIGN=LEFT|RIGHT|TOP|MIDDLE|BOTTOM`	Sets the alignment of the marquee.
`BEHAVIOR=SCROLL|SLIDE|ALTERNATE`	The animation behaviour of the marquee.
`BGCOLOR=`*colour*	The background colour of the marquee.
`CLASS=`*classname*	Applies a style sheet class.
`DIRECTION=LEFT|RIGHT`	Sets the direction in which the marquee should move.
`HEIGHT=`*n*	The height of the marquee in pixels, or as a percentage of page height.
`HSPACE=`*n*	The horizontal space around the marquee.
`ID=`*string*	Assigns a name, enabling the tag to be accessed through scripting.
`LOOP=`*n*`|INFINITE`	How many times the animation should be looped, or 'infinite' looping.
`SCROLLAMOUNT=`*n*	Sets the number of pixels the text should move between each repaint.
`SCROLLDELAY=`*n*	Sets the number of mil liseconds to pause between each repaint of the scrolled text.
`STYLE=`*string*	Applies inline style settings.
`TITLE=`*string*	Informational tooltip text.
`VSPACE=`*n*	The vertical space around the marquee.

WIDTH=*n*	The width of the marquee in pixels, or as a percentage of page width.

<META>

Used in the head of the page to include document-specific information. The CONTENT attribute is required, along with one or both of the other attributes.

CONTENT=*string*	The value, setting or information to be associated with the given meta-name or HTTP response header.
NAME=*string*	The name of the meta-information to be created.
HTTP-EQUIV=*response-header*	Specifies an HTTP response header (read by the server when providing the document) to which the information relates.

<NOBR> … </NOBR>

Prevents the enclosed text from wrapping to a new line. If the window size would normally cause a line break to occur somewhere between these tags, the enclosed text will be moved to the next line intact. Can be used in conjunction with <WBR>.

CLASS=*classname*	Applies a style sheet class.
ID=*string*	Assigns a name, enabling the tag to be accessed through scripting.
STYLE=*string*	Applies inline style settings.
TITLE=*string*	Informational tooltip text.

<NOFRAMES> … </NOFRAMES>

Used in a document that defines a frameset and frames (using the <FRAMESET> and <FRAME> tags) to provide alternative HTML content for browsers without frame support.

CLASS=*classname*	Applies a style sheet class.
ID=*string*	Assigns a name, enabling the tag to be accessed through scripting.

STYLE=*string*	Applies inline style settings.
TITLE=*string*	Informational tooltip text.

<OBJECT> ... </OBJECT>

Allows media objects such as ActiveX controls to be inserted into a Web page. Often used in conjunction with the <PARAM> tag. Currently supported by IE only.

ALIGN=TEXTTOP|TOP|MIDDLE|BOTTOM|BASELINE|LEFT|RIGHT|ABSMIDDLE|ABSBOTTOM	Sets the alignment of the image.
BORDER=*n*	The width of the border displayed around the object.
CLASS=*classname*	Applies a style sheet class.
CLASSID=*string*	A unique identifier specifying a particular installed object.
CODEBASE=*url*	Directs the user to a URL where the required object can be downloaded if it isn't installed.
HEIGHT=*n*	The height of the object in pixels, or as a percentage of page height.
HSPACE=*n*	The horizontal space around the object.
ID=*string*	Assigns a name, enabling the tag to be accessed through scripting.
NAME=*string*	Assigns a name to the object, as with ID, allowing it to be accessed in scripts.
STANDBY=*string*	Like the ALT attribute in other tags, displays alternative text while the object is being downloaded.
STYLE=*string*	Applies inline style settings.
TITLE=*string*	Informational tooltip text.

VSPACE=*n*	The vertical space around the object.
WIDTH=*n*	The width of the object in pixels, or as a percentage of page width.

<OL> ... </OL>

Creates an ordered (numbered) list, using the <LI> tag to create list items.

CLASS=*classname*	Applies a style sheet class.
COMPACT	Formats the list in a more compact style if included.
ID=*string*	Assigns a name, enabling the tag to be accessed through scripting.
START=*n*	Allows the list to begin at a number other than 1.
STYLE=*string*	Applies inline style settings.
TITLE=*string*	Informational tooltip text.
TYPE=1|a|A|i|I	The type of numbering system to be used.

<OPTION>

Adds an item to a <SELECT> form field.

CLASS=*classname*	Applies a style sheet class.
ID=*string*	Assigns a name, enabling the tag to be accessed through scripting.
SELECTED	Sets this option as selected when the control appears.
STYLE=*string*	Applies inline style settings.
TITLE=*string*	Informational tooltip text.
VALUE=*string*	The value to be returned if this option is selected when the form is submitted.

<P> [… </P>]

Specifies a new paragraph of text. The closing tag is required only when one or more attributes are added to the opening tag.

ALIGN=LEFT|RIGHT|CENTER	Sets the alignment of the paragraph.
CLASS=*classname*	Applies a style sheet class.
ID=*string*	Assigns a name, enabling the tag to be accessed through scripting.
STYLE=*string*	Applies inline style settings.
TITLE=*string*	Informational tooltip text.

<PARAM>

Provides optional settings for an embedded object or Java applet, and used in conjunction with the <APPLET> or <OBJECT> tags. The NAME and VALUE attributes are required.

ID=*string*	Assigns a name, enabling the tag to be accessed through scripting.
NAME=*string*	The name of the parameter to which the value should be applied.
VALUE=*string*	The value to apply to the named parameter.

<PRE> … </PRE>

Treats the enclosed text as 'pre-formatted' and displays it as is, using a fixed-width font and observing use of spaces and carriage returns.

CLASS=*classname*	Applies a style sheet class.
ID=*string*	Assigns a name, enabling the tag to be accessed through scripting.
STYLE=*string*	Applies inline style settings.
TITLE=*string*	Informational tooltip text.

<SCRIPT> ... </SCRIPT>

Embeds a block of script into a Web page.

ARCHIVE=*url*	The URL of a .zip or .jar file containing one or more external script files.
CLASS=*classname*	Applies a style sheet class.
EVENT=*event-name*	In conjunction with the FOR attribute, specifies an event for the element which would cause this script to be executed. IE only.
FOR=*id*	Specifies the ID of an element on the page to which the script should apply. IE only.
ID=*string*	Assigns a name, enabling the tag to be accessed through scripting.
LANGUAGE=JAVASCRIPT|	The language in which the script is JSCRIPT|VBSCRIPT written.
SRC=*url*	The URL of an external file containing a script to be used with the current document.
STYLE=*string*	Applies inline style settings.
TITLE=*string*	Informational tooltip text.

<SELECT> ... </SELECT>

Adds a selection list to a form, in either box or drop-down style, in conjunction with the <OPTION> tag.

ALIGN=TOP|MIDDLE|BOTTOM|LEFT|RIGHT|TEXTTOP|BASELINE|ABSBOTTOM|ABSMIDDLE	The alignment of the list.
CLASS=*classname*	Applies a style sheet class.
DISABLED	If included, specifies that the user cannot select or alter the control.
ID=*string*	Assigns a name, enabling the tag to be accessed through scripting.

MULTIPLE	If included, specifies that more than one item can be selected in the list.
NAME=*string*	The name to be associated with this control's value when the form is submitted.
SIZE=*n*	The number of items visible at one time. Use '1' for a drop-down list, or any higher number for a box.
STYLE=*string*	Applies inline style settings.
TITLE=*string*	Informational tooltip text.

<SMALL> ... </SMALL>

Displays the enclosed text at a slightly smaller font size.

CLASS=*classname*	Applies a style sheet class.
ID=*string*	Assigns a name, enabling the tag to be accessed through scripting.
STYLE=*string*	Applies inline style settings.
TITLE=*string*	Informational tooltip text.

<SPAN> ... </SPAN>

Specifies inline CSS styles for the enclosed text when no other tag (such as <B>, <P> or <IMG>) is available or wanted.

CLASS=*classname*	Applies a style sheet class.
ID=*string*	Assigns a name, enabling the tag to be accessed through scripting.
STYLE=*string*	Applies inline style settings.
TITLE=*string*	Informational tooltip text.

<STRIKE> ... </STRIKE>

Displays the enclosed text as strikethrough ('crossed out') type.

CLASS=*classname*	Applies a style sheet class.
ID=*string*	Assigns a name, enabling the tag to be accessed through scripting.
STYLE=*string*	Applies inline style settings.
TITLE=*string*	Informational tooltip text.

<STYLE> ... </STYLE>

Defines a style sheet (a set of CSS style rules) that will be available for the current document.

DISABLED	If included, indicates that the style rules are to be ignored. IE only.
ID=*string*	Assigns a name, enabling the tag to be accessed through scripting.
SRC=*url*	The URL of an external file containing style information to be imported. Netscape 4 only.
TITLE=*string*	Informational tooltip text.

_{...}

Displays the enclosed text as subscript, using a smaller font.

CLASS=*classname*	Applies a style sheet class.
ID=*string*	Assigns a name, enabling the tag to be accessed through scripting.
STYLE=*string*	Applies inline style settings.
TITLE=*string*	Informational tooltip text.

^{...}

Displays the enclosed text as superscript, using a smaller font.

CLASS=*classname*	Applies a style sheet class.
ID=*string*	Assigns a name, enabling the tag to be accessed through scripting.

STYLE=*string*	Applies inline style settings.
TITLE=*string*	Informational tooltip text.

<TABLE> … </TABLE>

Creates a table on the page in conjunction with the <TR> and <TD> tags.

ALIGN=LEFT|RIGHT|CENTER	Sets the alignment of the table.
BACKGROUND=*url*	The URL of a background image to be tiled behind the table's cells.
BGCOLOR=*colour*	The background colour of the table.
BORDER=*n*	The thickness of the table border, or 0 to remove the border and the space held in reserve for it.
BORDERCOLOR=*colour*	The colour of the table's border.
BORDERCOLORDARK=*colour*	The colour of the two darker edges of a three-dimensional border.
BORDERCOLORLIGHT=*colour*	The colour of the two lighter edges of a three-dimensional border.
CELLPADDING=*n*	The number of blank pixels between the inner edge of a table cell and the cell's content.
CELLSPACING=*n*	The number of blank pixels placed between each of the table's cells.
CLASS=*classname*	Applies a style sheet class.
FRAME=VOID|ABOVE|BELOW|HSIDES|VSIDES|LHS|RSH|BOX	In conjunction with the BORDER attribute, specifies which external borders of the table are to be shown.
HEIGHT=*n*	The height of the table in pixels or as a percentage of page height.

ID=*string*	Assigns a name, enabling the tag to be accessed through scripting.
RULES=NONE|BASIC|ROWS|COLUMNS|ALL	In conjunction with the BORDER attribute, specifies which internal borders of the table are to be shown.
STYLE=*string*	Applies inline style settings.
TITLE=*string*	Informational tooltip text.
VALIGN=TOP|MIDDLE|BOTTOM	The vertical alignment of text in a table's cells.
WIDTH=*n*	The width of the table in pixels or as a percentage of page width.

<TD> … </TD>

Adds a cell to a row in a table, in conjunction with the <TABLE> and <TR> tags.

ALIGN=LEFT|RIGHT|CENTER|JUSTIFY	Sets the alignment of the cell's content.
BACKGROUND=*url*	The URL of a background image to be tiled behind this cell.
BGCOLOR=*colour*	The background colour of the cell.
BORDERCOLOR=*colour*	The colour of the cell's border.
BORDERCOLORDARK=*colour*	The colour of the two darker edges of a three-dimensional border.
BORDERCOLORLIGHT=*colour*	The colour of the two lighter edges of a three-dimensional border.
CLASS=*classname*	Applies a style sheet class.
COLSPAN=*n*	The number of table-columns this cell should span.
HEIGHT=*n*	The height of the cell in pixels or as a percentage of table height.

`ID=`*`string`*	Assigns a name, enabling the tag to be accessed through scripting.
`NOWRAP`	If included, prevents lines of text in the cell from being wrapped.
`ROWSPAN=`*`n`*	The number of table rows that this cell should span.
`STYLE=`*`string`*	Applies inline style settings.
`TITLE=`*`string`*	Informational tooltip text.
`VALIGN=TOP|MIDDLE|BASELINE|BOTTOM`	The vertical alignment of the cell's content.
`WIDTH=`*`n`*	The width of the cell in pixels or as a percentage of table width.

<TEXTAREA> … </TEXTAREA>

Adds a multi-line text control to a form. Default text can be shown in the control by enclosing it between the opening and closing tags.

`ALIGN=TOP|MIDDLE|BOTTOM|LEFT|RIGHT|TEXTTOP|BASELINE|ABSBOTTOM|ABSMIDDLE`	The alignment of the list.
`CLASS=`*`classname`*	Applies a style sheet class.
`COLS=`*`n`*	The width of the control, as a number of fixed-width characters.
`DISABLED`	If included, specifies that the user cannot select the control or change its content.
`ID=`*`string`*	Assigns a name, enabling the tag to be accessed through scripting.
`NAME=`*`string`*	The name to be associated with this control's value when the form is submitted.
`READONLY`	If included, the text in the control can be read and selected by the user, but not altered.

ROWS=*n*	The number of lines of text that the control should be able to display at one time.
STYLE=*string*	Applies inline style settings.
TITLE=*string*	Informational tooltip text.
WRAP=VIRTUAL|PHYSICAL|OFF	Determines whether and how multiple lines of text are wrapped within the control, and how they're formatted for form submission.

<TITLE> … </TITLE>

Specifies the title of the current document, usually displayed in a browser's title bar.

ID=*string*	Assigns a name, enabling the tag to be accessed through scripting.
TITLE=*string*	Informational tooltip text.

<TR> … </TR>

Adds a row to a table, in conjunction with the <TABLE> tag.

ALIGN=LEFT|RIGHT|CENTER|JUSTIFY	Sets the alignment of the cell's content.
BACKGROUND=*url*	The URL of a background image to be tiled behind this row.
BGCOLOR=*colour*	The background colour of the cells in this row.
BORDERCOLOR=*colour*	The colour of this row's cell borders.
BORDERCOLORDARK=*colour*	The colour of the two darker edges of a three-dimensional border.
BORDERCOLORLIGHT=*colour*	The colour of the two lighter edges of a three-dimensional border.
CLASS=*classname*	Applies a style sheet class.
ID=*string*	Assigns a name, enabling the tag to be accessed through scripting.

NOWRAP	If included, prevents lines of text in the cells from being wrapped.
STYLE=*string*	Applies inline style settings.
TITLE=*string*	Informational tooltip text.
VALIGN=TOP|MIDDLE|BASELINE|BOTTOM	The vertical alignment of this row's cell content.

<TT> … </TT>

Displays the enclosed text in a fixed-width typewriter-style font.

CLASS=*classname*	Applies a style sheet class.
ID=*string*	Assigns a name, enabling the tag to be accessed through scripting.
STYLE=*string*	Applies inline style settings.
TITLE=*string*	Informational tooltip text.

<U> … </U>

Displays the enclosed text as underlined.

CLASS=*classname*	Applies a style sheet class.
ID=*string*	Assigns a name, enabling the tag to be accessed through scripting.
STYLE=*string*	Applies inline style settings.
TITLE=*string*	Informational tooltip text.

<UL> … </UL>

Creates an unordered (bulleted) list, using the <LI> tag to create list items.

CLASS=*classname*	Applies a style sheet class.
COMPACT	Formats the list in a more compact style if included.
ID=*string*	Assigns a name, enabling the tag to be accessed through scripting.

STYLE=*string*	Applies inline style settings.
TITLE=*string*	Informational tooltip text.
TYPE=DISC|CIRCLE|SQUARE	The style of bullet to be used.

<WBR>

When a line of text is enclosed between <NOBR> ... </NOBR> tags to prevent line breaks occurring, the <WBR> tag can be used to insert a 'soft' break that tells the browser where the text can be broken if necessary.

CLASS=*classname*	Applies a style sheet class.
ID=*string*	Assigns a name, enabling the tag to be accessed through scripting.
STYLE=*string*	Applies inline style settings.
TITLE=*string*	Informational tooltip text.

Appendix B: HTML colour names

AliceBlue
AntiqueWhite
Aqua
Aquamarine
Azure
Beige
Bisque
Black
BlanchedAlmond
Blue
BlueViolet
Brown
Burlywood
CadetBlue
Chartreuse
Chocolate
Coral
CornflowerBlue
Cornsilk
Crimson
Cyan
DarkBlue
DarkCyan
DarkGoldenrod
DarkGray
DarkGreen
DarkKhaki
DarkMagenta
DarkOliveGreen
DarkOrange
DarkOrchid
DarkRed
DarkSalmon
DarkSeaGreen
DarkSlateBlue
DarkSlateGray
DarkTurquoise
DarkViolet
DeepPink
DeepSkyBlue
DimGray
DodgerBlue
Firebrick
FloralWhite
ForestGreen
Fuchsia
Gainsboro
GhostWhite
Gold
Goldenrod
Gray
Green
GreenYellow
Honeydew
HotPink
IndianRed
Indigo
Ivory
Khaki
Lavender
LavenderBlush
LawnGreen
LemonChiffon
LightBlue
LightCoral
LightCyan
LightGoldenrodYellow
LightGreen
LightGray
LightPink
LightSalmon
LightSeaGreen
LightSkyBlue
LightSlateGray
LightSteelBlue
LightYellow
Lime
LimeGreen
Linen
Magenta
Maroon
MediumAquamarine
MediumBlue
MediumOrchid
MediumPurple
MediumSeaGreen
MediumSlateBlue
MediumSpringGreen

MediumTurquoise
MediumVioletRed
MidnightBlue
MintCream
MistyRose
Moccasin
NavajoWhite
Navy
OldLace
Olive
OliveDrab
Orange
OrangeRed
Orchid
PaleGoldenrod
PaleGreen
PaleTurquoise
PaleVioletRed
PapayaWhip
PeachPuff
Peru
Pink
Plum
PowderBlue
Purple
Red
RosyBrown
RoyalBlue
SaddleBrown
Salmon
SandyBrown
SeaGreen
Seashell
Sienna
Silver
SkyBlue
SlateBlue
SlateGray
Snow
SpringGreen
SteelBlue
Tan
Teal
Thistle
Tomato
Turquoise
Violet
Wheat
White
WhiteSmoke
Yellow
YellowGreen

Appendix C – Useful Websites

HTML and general reference

Website	URL
Bare Bones Guide to HTML	**webach.com/barebones**
BrowserWatch	**browserwatch.internet.com**
Cnet.com – Web Building	**www.cnet.com/webbuilding**
Facts & Stats	**www.dotcom.com/facts/quickstats.html**
Freesite UK	**www.freesiteuk.com**
HTML Code Help	**www.netmechanic.com**
HTML Goodies	**www.htmlgoodies.com**
The HTML Writers Guild	**www.hwg.org**
ISP Review	**www.ispreview.co.uk**
Searchterms.com – The Top 10	**www.searchterms.com**
SiteExperts.com	**www.siteexperts.com**
StatMarket	**www.statmarket.com**
W3C – World Wide Web Consortium	**www.w3.org**
WebDeveloper.com	**www.webdeveloper.com**
Web Developer's Virtual Library	**www.wdvl.com**
WebMonkey	**hotwired.lycos.com/webmonkey**
WebReference	**www.webreference.com**
webresource.net: HTML Center	**www.webresource.net/html**
WebSiteGoodies	**www.websitegoodies.com**
Web Site Garage	**www.websitegarage.com**
yesWebmaster.com	**www.yeswebmaster.com**

Graphics

Website	URL
Absolutely Free Backgrounds	**www.free-backgrounds.com**
Abstract Dimensions PSP Filters	**psptips.com/filters**
Andrew's GraphXKingdom	**www.graphxkingdom.com**
ArtToday.com	**www.arttoday.com**
bannerblast.com	**www.bannerblast.com**
Clipart.com	**www.clipart.com**
ClipArtConnection.com	**www.clipartconnection.com**
CoolText.com	**www.cooltext.com**
Corbis	**www.corbis.com**
Filter Factory Plug-ins	**showcase.netins.net/web/wolf359/plugins.htm**
Free Graphics	**www.freegraphics.com**
Free Images	**www.freeimages.co.uk**
HitBox Image Search	**hitbox.gograph.com**
IconBazaar	**www.iconbazaar.com**

Jeffrey Zeldman Presents	**www.zeldman.com**
MediaBuilder	**www.mediabuilder.com**
PhotoDisc	**www.photodisc.com**
ScreamDesign	**www.screamdesign.com**
Textureland	**www.textureland.com**
webresource.net: Graphics Center	**www.webresource.net/graphics**
yesWebMaster.com Graphics	**www.yeswebmaster.com/graphics**

Flash

Website	URL
ExtremeFlash	**www.extremeflash.com**
Flahoo	**www.flahoo.com**
Flash Kit	**www.flashkit.com**
Flash Planet	**www.flashplanet.com**
Macromedia	**www.macromedia.com**
ShockFusion	**www.shockfusion.com**
shockwave.com	**www.shockwave.com**

Javascript

Website	URL
Cut-N-Paste JavaScript	**www.infohiway.com/javascript/ indexf.htm**
Dynamic Drive	**www.dynamicdrive.com**
JavaScript.com	**www.javascript.com**
JavaScript City	**www.javascriptcity.com**
JavaScript Search	**www.javascriptsearch.com**
JavaScript Source	**javascript.internet.com**
JavaScript Tip of the Week	**www.webreference.com/javascript**
JavaScript World	**www.jsworld.com**
WebCoder.com	**www.webcoder.com**
webresource.net: JavaScript Center	**www.webresource.net/javascript**

Dynamic HTML

Website	URL
Comet Cursor	**www.cometcursors.com**
DHTML Lab	**www.webreference.com/dhtml**
Dynamic HTML Developer Zone	**www.projectcool.com/developer/dynamic**
Dynamic Drive	**www.dynamicdrive.com**

Dynamic HTML Resource	**www.htmlguru.com**
Dynamic HTML Zone	**www.dhtmlzone.com**
Experience DHTML!	**www.bratta.com/dhtml**
MSDN Online Voices	**msdn.microsoft.com/voices/dude.asp**
WebCoder.com	**www.webcoder.com**

Java

Website	**URL**
Cool Focus	**www.coolfocus.com**
Gamelan	**softwaredev.earthweb.com/java**
JARS	**www.jars.com**
JavaSoft (Sun)	**www.javasoft.com**
The Java Boutique	**javaboutique.internet.com**
webresource.net: Java Center	**www.webresource.net/java**

Guestbooks, counters and statistics

Website	**URL**
1-2-3 WebTools	**www.freeguestbooks.com**
Beseen Free Web Tools	**www.beseen.com**
Guestbook4free.com	**www.guestbook4free.com**
GuestBooks.net	**www.glacierweb.com/home**
HitBox.com	**www.hitbox.com**
I-Count	**www.icount.com**
MyComputer.com	**guestbook.mycomputer.com**
RealTracker Free	**www.showstat.com**
theCounter.com	**www.thecounter.com**
theGuestBook.com	**www.theguestbook.com**
WebTracker	**www.fxweb.holowww.com/tracker**
XOOMCounter	**www2.pagecount.com**
ZapZone	**www.zzn.com**

Forums, chat and other content

Website	**URL**
Ballot-Box.net	**www.ballot-box.net**
BeSeen Bulletin Board	**www.beseen.com/board**
BeSeen Enhance: Quizlet	**www.beseen.com/quiz**
BeSeen Chat	**www.beseen.com/chat**
BoardHost	**www.boardhost.com**
EZBoard	**www.ezboard.com**
EZPolls	**ezpolls.mycomputer.com**
Free Forums	**www.freeforums.com**

Free Site Search Engine	**www.freefind.com**
Free Tools	**www.freetools.com**
liveuniverse.com	**liveuniverse.com**
Mister Poll	**www.misterpoll.com**
Multicity.com	**www.multicity.com**
NetVotes	**www.netvotes.com**
ParaChat	**www.parachat.com**
PollIt	**www.pollit.com**
QuickChat	**www.quickchat.org**
Web BBS	**awsd.com/scripts/webbbs**
ZapZone	**www.zzn.com**

Domain name registration

Website	**URL**
DomainBook.com	**www.domainbook.com**
Domains365	**www.domains365.co.uk**
DomainsNet	**www.domainsnet.co.uk**
interNIC	**www.internic.net**
NetNames	**www.netnames.co.uk**
Simply Names	**www.simplynames.co.uk**
UK Reg	**www.ukreg.com**

Website promotion, marketing and advertising

Website	**URL**
AddMe	**www.addme.com**
AdValue	**www.advalue.co.uk**
BannerExchange	**bannerexchange. mycomputer.com**
Bpath	**www.bpath.com**
DoubleClick	**www.doubleclick.com**
GoTo Search Suggestions	**inventory.goto.com/ inventory/ Search_ Suggestion.jhtml**
EReleases	**www.ereleases.com**
Internet Advertising Bureau	**www.iab.net**
Internet PR Guide	**www.internetprguide.com**
JimTools	**www.jimtools.com**
Microsoft bCentral	**www.bcentral.com**
Refer-It.com	**www.refer-it.com**
SearchAbility	**www.searchability.com**
Search Engine Watch	**www.searchengine watch.com**
Submit Corner	**www.submitcorner.com**
Submit Express	**www.submitexpress.com**
Submit It!	**www.submit-it.com**
SubmitWizard	**submitwizard.my computer.com**

TopWebSite	**www.topwebsite.co.uk**
ukaffiliates.com	**www.ukaffiliates.com**
UK Banners	**www.ukbanners.com**
ValueClick	**www.valueclick.com/uk**
WebPromote	**www.webpromote.com**
WEBpromotion.co.uk	**www.webpromotion.co.uk**
Web Site Garage	**register-it.netscape.com**

Cool site collections and awards

Website	**URL**
Cool Central	**www.coolcentral.com**
Cybersmith's Hot Site of the Day	**www.cybersmith.com/hotsites**
Dr Webster's Site of the Day	**www.drwebster.com**
Family Site of the Day	**www.worldvillage.com/famsite.htm**
Hot 100 Websites	**www.web21.com**
Too Cool!	**www.toocool.com**
Webby Awards	**www.webbyawards.com**
Web Pages That Suck	**www.webpagesthatsuck.com**
World Best Websites	**www.worldbestwebsites.com**
Xplore's Site of the Day	**www.xplore.com**

Shareware directories

Website	**URL**
32bit.com	**www.32bit.com/software**
DaveCentral	**www.davecentral.com**
Jumbo	**www.jumbo.com**
KeyScreen	**www.keyscreen.com**
MacShare.com	**www.macshare.com**
NoNags	**www.nonags.com**
Shareware.com	**www.shareware.com**
Thingamabobs	**www.thingamabobs.com**
Tucows	**tucows.mirror.ac.uk**
WinSite	**www.winsite.com**
ZDNet Downloads	**www.zdnet.com/downloads**

Search engines

Website	**URL**
All The Web	**www.alltheweb.com**
AltaVista	**www.altavista.com**
AOL Search	**search.aol.com**
Ask Jeeves	**www.ask.com**

Canada.com	**www.canada.com**
CNET Search.com	**www.search.com**
Direct Hit	**www.directhit.com**
Dogpile	**www.dogpile.com**
Excite	**www.excite.com**
Galaxy	**www.galaxy.com**
GO.com	**www.go.com**
Go2Net	**www.gotonet.com**
Google	**www.google.com**
GoTo.com	**www.goto.com**
HotBot	**www.hotbot.com**
ICQ Search	**www.icqit.com**
InfoSpace	**www.infospace.com**
LookSmart	**www.looksmart.com**
Lycos	**www.lycos.com**
Mamma.com	**www.mamma.com**
MetaCrawler	**www.metacrawler.com**
Mirago	**www.mirago.co.uk**
MSN	**search.msn.com**
NationalDirectory	**www.nationaldirectory .com**
NBCi	**www.nbci.com**
Netscape Search	**search.netscape.com**
Northern Light	**www.northernlight.com**
OneSeek	**www.oneseek.com**
Open Directory Project	**www.dmoz.org**
ProFusion	**www.profusion.com**
Scrub The Web	**www.scrubtheweb.com**
Search Engine Colossus	**www.searchenginecolossus .com**
Search UK	**uk.searchengine.com**
Starting Point	**www.stpt.com**
UK Plus	**www.ukplus.co.uk**
WebCrawler	**www.webcrawler.com**
WebTop.com	**www.webtop.com**
WebZone	**www.infohiway.com**
whatUseek	**www.whatuseek.com**
Yahoo!	**www.yahoo.com**

Index

Q